THE LATIN AMERICAN REPUBLICS

The

Latin American

Republics

A HISTORY

By DANA GARDNER MUNRO

William Stewart Tod
Professor of History
Princeton University

 THIRD EDITION

New York

APPLETON-CENTURY-CROFTS, Inc.

PREFACE

MANY HISTORIANS AND TEACHERS have wished that it were possible to deal with the history of Latin America in broad outline, without confusing the student with details about twenty different countries. It is impossible, however, to get away from the fact that the countries are different—in their geography, in the makeup of their populations, and in other factors that have shaped their development. Each of them must receive consideration if we are to have a faithful picture of the American community as a whole. Each republic, furthermore, is of interest to North Americans as a neighbor and an ally, and the peculiar problems of some of the smaller states are at least as important, from the standpoint of our foreign policy, as those of the larger ones.

In this new edition, I have endeavored to give the reader some idea of the great changes that are taking place in Latin America at the present time. It is clear that new forces are at work that will radically alter the existing social and economic organization, especially in some of the larger countries. It is hardly possible today, however, to reach conclusions about their significance or their ultimate effects.

The story of each country and the story of inter-American relations have been brought down to date. It would be inappropriate, in a general history, to discuss current political problems in detail, but the most important recent events in each country are at least noted.

To avoid the accumulation of footnotes, sources of information are not generally cited in the text. I wish, however, to acknowledge my indebtedness to the numerous American historians who have given us authoritative studies of the various aspects of Latin American history and civilization. Most of the more important books in English are mentioned in the Reading List at the end of this volume. I have also relied heavily on some of the Latin American historians: Levene, Galdames, Henao and Arrubla, Zavala, Acevedo, Amunátegui Solar, Arguedas, Bellegarde, Basadre, Varnhagen, Gonzales Guinán, Reyes, and many others.

D.G.M.

CONTENTS

MAPS

ACKNOWLEDGMENT

The map of Indian tribes on pages 8 and 9 is a modification of a similar map in W. S. Robertson, *History of the Latin-American Nations* which in turn is adapted from maps by J. W. Powell, C. Thomas, J. R. Swanton, and A. E. Chamberlain. The maps on pages 129 ("Latin America in 1800") and 233 ("Territory under Dispute in the War of the Pacific") have also been adapted from similar maps in the Robertson book.

PART I

BEFORE
INDEPENDENCE

CHAPTER 1

Pre-Conquest
Indian Civilizations

THE TWENTY INDEPENDENT REPUBLICS below the Rio Grande are called "Latin American" because of their historic relationship to three of the Latin nations of Europe. Eighteen of them were colonies of Spain. Brazil was Portuguese; Haiti was French. All owe their official language, the culture of their upper classes, and much of their political and social tradition to the European mother countries. In most of them the better educated and more influential families are largely of European descent.

The population as a whole, however, is not of European origin. There are only a few countries—Argentina, Uruguay, Costa Rica, and perhaps Chile—where people of European descent are greatly in the majority. In Brazil and the Caribbean, a substantial part of the laboring classes are the descendants of Negro slaves. Elsewhere they are Indian or part-Indian; and in the highlands of Mexico and the Central Andes, where populous civilized communities existed long before the Spaniards came, there are still millions of people who retain the languages and to some extent the customs and social organization of the period before the Conquest. It is impossible to understand the history of the Latin American nations or their political and social problems today without knowing something of the Indian heritage.

The ancestors of the American Indians were probably Mongoloid tribes that crossed the Bering Strait from Asia, at least 10 to 12 thousand years ago and perhaps much earlier—at any rate before the beginnings of the first known higher cultures in the Old World. Coming presumably in several waves of immigration, they spread throughout the continent from Hudson Bay to Tierra del Fuego. They were a primitive people, living by hunting and fishing, with no domestic animals except the dog. They never learned the use of iron or the use of the wheel, which played

3

so large a part in the development of Old-World civilizations. At the time of the Conquest they still depended chiefly on stone weapons and instruments, though some of them made a limited use of copper, gold, and silver. On the other hand, they had developed several native food crops like corn and beans which made possible the rise of several higher civilizations that astonished the Spanish invaders.

Differences in physical environment probably encouraged the development of higher cultures in some regions while the people of others made less progress. In any study of Latin America, geography is a factor that must constantly be borne in mind. In the tropics, where most of the Indians settled, and where a majority of the people of Latin America live today, variations in altitude and rainfall have an even greater effect on the conditions of human life than in the temperate zones. Regions like the hot plains of the Amazon with their excessive rainfall offered little encouragement for the evolution of a higher civilization, but in the highlands of Mexico and the Central Andes a cooler climate and more moderate precipitation favored the establishment of settled agricultural communities. It was in these regions that the first advances toward civilization seem to have taken place.

We know little of the long period when the predecessors of the Maya and the Incas were developing the indigenous food plants on which their civilization rested and were gradually changing from nomadic hunters to settled farmers. At least 2,000 years ago they were already living in permanent villages; cultivating corn, beans, and cotton; and making pottery. It was from this early culture, which extended through most of the highland region from Mexico to Peru, that the later, more advanced, cultures evolved. The evolution seems to have taken place independently in two great centers, one in the Middle American region and the other in the Central Andean highlands and the nearby valleys of the Pacific coast. There was some contact between the two regions, through migrations or trade, but at the time of the Conquest the people of each knew little of the other, for the mountains and jungles of the Isthmus of Panama and northwestern South America were then as now a formidable barrier to communication.

MIDDLE AMERICA: THE MAYA

In Mexico and Central America there are many groups of ancient pyramids and ruined temples that could only have been erected by well-organized civilized communities. Many of the more impressive ones seem to date from a period between the fourth and the ninth centuries of the Christian era, when Teotihuacán and Monte Albán in Mexico and a great number of places in the Maya region farther south were apparently im-

portant ceremonial centers to which the people of the surrounding country came for religious observances. The archeological remains indicate
that there were several different advanced cultures but that there had
been much interchange of ideas and techniques between them.

The most notable was that of the Maya, who still occupied the Guatemalan highlands and the Yucatán Peninsula at the time of the Spanish
Conquest. The great center of the ancient Maya civilization was in a hot,
humid belt between these two regions, extending from northwestern
Honduras across Guatemala into southern Yucatán. Why a great civilization should have flourished in this area, where few people would wish
to live today, is a mystery. It is clear, however, that the country once
supported a large population, for at site after site, buried in the tropical
jungle, we find the ruins of massive, skillfully built stone temples and
beautifully sculptured monuments. Among the monuments are the series
of *stelae* which were erected in many of the centers at the end of each
period of five or ten years. Sometimes as much as 30 or 40 feet in height,
these monoliths bear row after row of intricate glyphs which show that
the Maya had a system of writing superior to that of any other American
people. Some of the word signs, and especially those standing for dates
and numbers, can be deciphered because they were still in use in Yucatán
at the time of the Conquest, and it has thus been possible to read parts
of the inscriptions. They indicate that the Maya had a remarkably accurate calendar and an astonishing skill in astronomical calculation. In
mathematics, in fact, they were ahead of their contemporaries in Europe,
for they had learned to use the quantity of zero and a system of enumeration by position before these concepts had come into use in that part of
the world.

We know little of the ancient Maya beyond what we can learn from
the monuments. The dates on the *stelae* tell us something, though arche-
ologists differ as to the correlation of the dates with our own chronology.
Their culture apparently developed early in the Christian era, if not before that time. The similarity of the architecture and the glyphs at the
various sites indicates that there was constant intercourse and probably
a close political and religious connection between the communities. The
absence of pictures of weapons and warlike subjects suggests that they
were peaceful groups, little troubled by civil strife or foreign invasion.
The sculptures show clearly that religion was the subject most important
to the people who made them and bear out the tradition of the later
Maya that their ancestors were ruled by priests. They tell us little of
customs or social organization or historical events. It seems clear, however, that there had been less advance in matters of daily life than in
art and astronomy. The ceremonial centers were not cities, and the masses
of the people probably lived in simple huts scattered through the coun-

try, supporting themselves by growing corn on little patches of land carved out of the jungle just as the people in the more backward parts of Central America do today.

The ancient Maya civilization seems to have collapsed rather suddenly between 800 and 900 A.D. The people of the central region stopped erecting dated monuments and seem to have abandoned the use of the ceremonial centers. Then or later the region was deserted by most of its inhabitants. We know nothing of the reasons. The other advanced cultures in Mexico declined about the same time, but in their case invasions by savages from the north seem to offer an explanation. There is no evidence of foreign attack in the central Maya area.

The culture of the central Maya area had extended into the Guatemalan highlands and into Yucatán, and its decline was also evident in these regions. In Yucatán, however, the eleventh and twelfth centuries saw a revival of temple building, typified by the magnificent remains at Chichén Itzá. The later Yucatán Maya were much influenced by the Toltec culture which was dominant at the time in central Mexico, and Chichén Itzá and other cities were for some time ruled by Mexican invaders. Their architecture was impressive, but the sculpture never attained the perfection of the monuments in the older cities. The ancient system of writing was still used, not only for carving records on stone but also for keeping histories and genealogies in books of maguey fiber. Only a very few of these have survived, and only a part of their contents can be deciphered. We know something of the history of the later Maya, however, not only from the archeological remains but from traditions still extant at the time of the Conquest. Chichén Itzá seems to have been the most important city until the end of the twelfth century when the dominance passed to Mayapán. Another period of cultural decline seems to have set in about this time.

The Maya were nevertheless among the more advanced of the American peoples at the time of the Conquest. They still made fine pottery and textiles, and continued to use their elaborate calendar and system of writing. Their agricultural methods were primitive, as they probably always had been, for land was plentiful and they were able to supplement their food supply by hunting. In Yucatán, the great majority of the people lived in simple wooden huts, well adapted to the needs of a population that frequently moved from place to place in search of new lands. In the highlands of southern Guatemala and Chiapas, on the other hand, there were populous nations of Maya stock which had stone-built cities and well-organized governments. All of the later Maya peoples were ruled by hereditary chiefs who seem to have had more power than the priests.

THE AZTECS

In the sixteenth century, the most important Indian civilization of Middle America was not in the Maya area but in the region around what is now Mexico City. Mexico, north of the Isthmus of Tehuantepec, is a great triangular plateau, flanked by mountain ranges that fall off sharply to a narrow coastal plain on either side. The most fertile portion is the southern apex of the triangle, in the Valley of Mexico and the nearby highlands. This region, with its high altitude and an invigorating climate, had long been the home of populous communities whose culture was similar in many respects to that of the Maya. The civilizations that produced the great ceremonial centers at Teotihuacán and Monte Albán seem to have flourished and declined at about the same time as the ancient Maya, to be succeeded after a century or two by the Toltec culture which dominated central Mexico and influenced the later Maya in Yucatán. Traditions about the Toltecs survived in Mexico at the time of the Conquest; but when the Spaniards came, most of the people of central Mexico were by their own account descendants of nomadic hunters who had come into the region from the north. These newcomers had retained their own language, called *Nahua*, but they had absorbed much of the civilization of the older inhabitants and had gradually built up a new culture of their own.

The Aztecs, the most powerful of the Nahua tribes at the time of the Conquest, probably entered the Valley of Mexico in the thirteenth century. Finding the best lands already occupied by stronger peoples, they settled in a small area surrounded by marshes and water in the lake region in the center of the Valley. Here they built their city of Tenochtitlán, or Mexico. At first they maintained a precarious existence by fishing, hunting, and growing such scanty crops as their limited territory permitted, but it was not long before their warlike qualities made them welcome allies of their stronger neighbors in the continual struggles between the cities of the lake region. The inaccessibility of Tenochtitlán gave them an advantage over the people of the more exposed cities on the mainland, and this was increased by the construction of a causeway that penned up the waters flowing through the nearby marshes, so that the city came to be entirely surrounded by a large lake. About the beginning of the fifteenth century, the Aztecs defeated the people of Azcapotzalco, who through their aid had acquired a temporary supremacy over the other tribes of the Valley. Soon afterward Tenochtitlán joined with Tezcoco and Tlacopán in a confederacy that extended its conquests into other parts of the plateau and into the lowlands of the coasts. When the Spaniards reached Mexico, the Aztecs and their allies were dominant from the Pánuco River and Lake Chapala to the Isthmus of Tehuantepec.

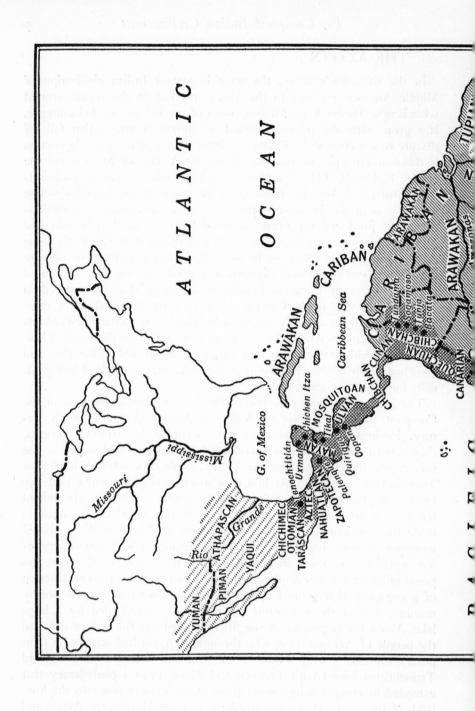

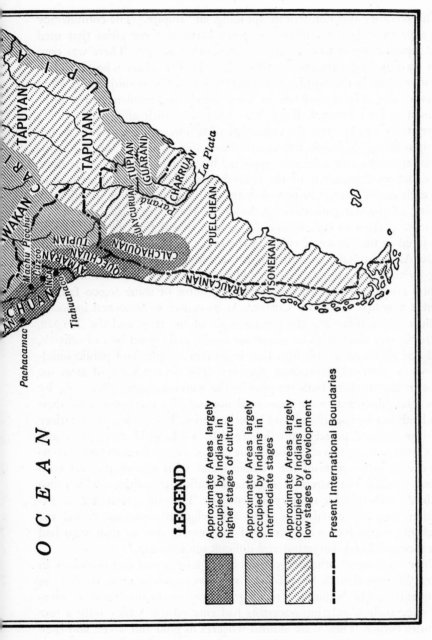

INDIAN TRIBES

LEGEND

Approximate Areas largely
occupied by Indians in
higher stages of culture

Approximate Areas largely
occupied by Indians in
intermediate stages

Approximate Areas largely
occupied by Indians in
low stages of development

Present International Boundaries

OCEAN

TAPUYAN

TAPUYAN

WAKAN CAR

TUPIAN

GUARANI

CURUAN

GUAYCURUAN

CHARRUAN

La Plata

Paraná

Paraná

PUELCHEAN

CALCHAQUIAN

QUICHUAN

AIMARAN

ANCHUAN

Machu Picchu

Cuzco

Inca

Tiahuanaco

Pachacamac

ARAUCANIAN

TSONEKAN

This territory was not, strictly speaking, an "empire." The confederacy was a partnership for military purposes between three cities that used their superior power to exact tribute from other peoples. There was constant warfare, and some nearby tribes, like the Tlascalans, who played an important part in the Spanish Conquest, had never been subjugated. Even the cities that paid regular tribute were largely independent in the management of their internal affairs. The Aztecs and their allies sent officials among them to supervise the collection of tribute and possibly to watch for signs of revolt, but in most cases these officials had no other governmental authority and were not supported by resident garrisons. The three cities that were members of the confederacy had separate governments, and each might engage in private wars on its own account. By the beginning of the sixteenth century, however, the Aztecs had become the dominant partner in the alliance, to such an extent that they frequently interfered in the choice of rulers in the other cities.

The Aztec capital Tenochtitlán, in the midst of the lake and accessible only by three long causeways, excited the wonder and admiration of the Spanish conquerors. It was apparently the home of some 60,000 families when it was first visited by Cortez.[1] At its center were several imposing public edifices, including the great temple of the tribe and the *Tecpán*, where the war chief, with his numerous family and a great host of officials, lived and dispensed hospitality. Less important temples and public buildings were scattered throughout the city. The houses were of stone or adobe, many of them built on piles in the water and accessible only by boat. The inhabitants were supported not only by the product of their own lands but by the tribute paid by other cities. This took a great variety of forms—slaves, pottery, textiles, feather work, gold ornaments, and other works of art, as well as food. The city also carried on an active commerce with other parts of the "empire" and with regions not yet conquered, sending out carefully organized trading expeditions which also obtained much valuable military information. The safe return of these expeditions was celebrated with feasts and religious observances, and the merchants themselves were accorded the respect due to men who had been successful in a dangerous and difficult undertaking.

There were many other large cities in the lake region and elsewhere in central Mexico, though few of them were so populous or so wealthy as Tenochtitlán. The Nahua had made great progress in the arts of civilization since their wandering ancestors had entered the Valley only a few centuries before. They were skillful workers in gold and silver, and they made weapons and other articles out of copper and copper alloys, although the limited supply of metals forced them to rely mainly on stone as material for weapons and utensils. They showed much skill also in their

---

[1] Merriman, *The Rise of the Spanish Empire*, Vol. III, p. 470. Vaillant, *Aztecs of Mexico*, pp. 122, 234.

architecture, their stone carving, their painting, and their pottery. They wove textiles from maguey fiber and cotton and made paper from maguey fiber. There were artisans especially trained in each craft, and those following certain callings, such as the goldsmiths and silversmiths, were highly honored.

The people of central Mexico were of several racial stocks and spoke many different languages, but there seems to have been a general similarity in their social organization and religion. We know something about their institutions, and especially about those of the Aztecs, from the reports of Spanish chroniclers and from the very small number of Indian manuscripts preserved after the Conquest.

Among the Aztecs, the most important governmental units were the *calpulli* or clans, of which there were 20 in Tenochtitlán, and these clans owned most of the land. A part of each clan's holdings was apportioned among the heads of families, and other portions were cultivated, either co-operatively or by hired labor or slaves, for the support of the officials and the priesthood. Each clan had its own temples and its own gods, though all joined in the worship of the great tribal gods. Each received its share of the war prisoners for sacrifice and of the tribute from subject cities. Within the clan, a council of old men, probably the heads of families or of households, exercised supreme authority, except on the rare occasions when all of the members met to consider an especially weighty question. The council elected two chief officials: the *Teachcauhtli*, who led the troops of the clan in time of war and was responsible for the maintenance of order and the military education of the young men, and the *Calpollec*, the principal civil official. The latter collected the taxes and distributed the land and the clan's share of the tributes, keeping written records with colored plats to show the lots held by each family. Both officials administered justice in minor cases, but more serious matters were reserved for action by the council.

For the government of the city as a whole there were also a council, composed of representatives of the clans, and two principal executive officers: the *Tlaca-tecuhtli*, or war chief, and the *Cihua-cohuatl*, who was in general charged with the administration of civil affairs, though he was also a war leader. The *Tlaca-tecuhtli*, at the time of the Conquest, wielded much authority, not only in the city but throughout the region that the Aztecs dominated. He was chosen by election, but usually from among the members of one powerful family. He was assisted by a great number of lesser officials who were supported by the tribute from conquered cities or by produce of the lands that each clan set aside for the benefit of the central government.

Nearly all of the activities of the Aztecs, and of the Nahua communities in general, were closely connected with religion. There were a multitude of gods. Some of them, like the war god Huitzilopochtli, were apparently tribal deities whom the Aztecs had worshiped before their arrival in Mexico. Others had been taken over from the more civilized earlier inhabitants of the valley. Of these, the most interesting was Quetzalcoatl, the god of the arts, who was also worshiped by the Maya under the name of Kukulkán. The priests, of whom there were said to be 5,000 in Tenochtitlán alone, were educated in special schools in the temples where they were subjected to rigorous discipline and trained to an austere life. One of their principal occupations was the study of astronomy and the calculation of the dates of the numerous religious festivals, for the Aztecs had an intricate calendar which bore a marked resemblance to that of the ancient Maya. The priests also prepared the religious and historical manuscripts, but in a system of writing far inferior to that of the Maya. They had a few conventional symbols, but in general they recorded events and ideas pictorially, much as the North American Indians did.

The religious festivals were celebrated in a way that horrified the Spanish conquerors. Human sacrifices were practiced to some extent by many of the American peoples, but nowhere did they assume such gruesome form as at Tenochtitlán. Nearly all of the Aztec festivals were celebrated by the immolation of numbers of war prisoners or women or children, whose bodies were usually eaten after the sacrifice by the priests and the populace. Wherever the first Spanish invaders went they found the temples noisome with the smell of blood. One of the chief purposes of the frequent wars that the Aztecs waged against neighboring peoples was to obtain victims for sacrifice.

The Aztecs were continually engaged in war, either with unconquered tribes or with cities which rebelled against the payment of tribute. Boys began their military education at the age of six or seven, and a youth had to capture a prisoner before he could attain full standing as a warrior. Prowess on the battlefield brought much honor and substantial material awards. Successful soldiers, in fact, were often given land and slaves in conquered territory so that a hereditary, landowning nobility seemed to be growing up in the years before the Conquest.

THE INCAS

Another great Indian civilization, on the west coast of South America, had developed along somewhat different lines. In Middle America, as one authority puts it, nearly all of the great cultural achievements took the form of "material religious expression." [2] The Maya and their contemporaries and successors used their art and architecture, their calendars and mathematical knowledge, and even their systems of writing, chiefly in the worship of the gods. They made less progress in the organization of society or in improving the conditions of daily life for the masses of the

[2] Vaillant, in *The Maya and Their Neighbors: A Symposium*, p. 296.

people. In Peru, architectural and engineering skills were devoted not only to temple building but to useful public works, and the Incas also developed a remarkably efficient political and economic organization.

The Inca empire, at the time of the Spanish Conquest, may have had some 6,000,000 inhabitants. The Andes, in Peru and Ecuador, form two or three generally parallel chains, snow-covered at their summits but enclosing fertile valleys where every foot of arable land was under cultivation when the Spaniards came. There were also many inhabitants on the bleak, higher slopes and on the great Bolivian plateau, 12 to 14 thousand feet above sea level, where the altitude and the cold make life uncomfortable for persons accustomed to other climates. Much of the plateau was too arid for agriculture, but it afforded pasture for the great herds of llamas and alpacas that provided the empire with meat and wool. A third center of population was in the valleys of the rivers that flow from the Andes across the rainless desert of the Peruvian coast.

As in Middle America, we are dependent on still incomplete archeological investigation for the earlier history of the Andean region. It is clear that civilized peoples lived in the region from a remote time. The domestication of the llama and the alpaca and the development of the potato and other useful plants from very different ancestral varieties were probably the work of many generations of people who had already emerged from a state of savagery. There seems to have been a primitive farming population in some of the coastal valleys as early as 2500 B.C.; and later, several advanced cultures rose and declined, much as they did in Mexico.

The earliest of these, so far as we know at present, was the Chavín culture, which seems to have been brought in by immigrants around 1000–800 B.C. The newcomers brought with them the cultivation of corn, on which all of the archaic cultures of America depended. They also made pottery and wove textiles, and they built relatively large stone temples adorned with carvings of a feline god whose worship was widespread through the northern highlands of Peru and the nearby coast. The most notable of these were at Chavín de Huantar in the northern highlands. After the Chavín period there were several different cultures in the coastal valleys, characterized by improving agricultural methods and the spreading use of irrigation. The magnificent textiles found in graves on the Paracas Peninsula seem to date from this time.

In the first centuries of the Christian era, possibly a little before the time of the ancient Maya, a number of different groups attained a civilization that was hardly surpassed by any of the later Peruvian Indians. The Mochica people, who had a powerful state on the northern coast, built impressive temples and irrigation works and used copper for weapons and tools. We know something of their daily life from realistic and beautifully executed pictures on their pottery. Another high culture centered in the Nazca Valley farther south, and it is thought that the famous ruins at Tiahuanaco also date from this period. Tiahuanaco, on the high plateau south of Lake Titicaca, was probably a ceremonial center rather than a city, for the rather bleak surrounding country could hardly have supported a very dense population. Though much of the stonework was demolished to provide building material for the Spanish city of La Paz, one can still see the remains of many impressive temples or palaces, built of great blocks of stone cut and fitted together with marvelous accuracy, and especially the remarkable monolithic doorway, carved with the figure of the god who was evidently the principal object of worship.

The religion, and perhaps the political control, of Tiahuanaco was later spread through much of Peru, probably by military force, for images of the god of the monolithic doorway appear on textiles and pottery in other places. Later still there was a general decline of culture, and then a revival, at least on the coast. By this time the population had greatly increased, and most of the coastal people lived in large, planned cities. The most important group were the Chimu, whose empire dominated many of the same valleys that the Mochica had ruled. The Chimu were still perhaps the most civilized people in Peru when they were conquered by the Incas in the fifteenth century.

The Incas were originally the rulers of the fertile valley of Cuzco in the mountains north of Lake Titicaca. According to their traditions, their ancestors, claiming to be children of the Sun, had come into the valley some four centuries before the Spanish Conquest and had persuaded the people there to accept their rule. They gradually expanded their domain, first in the basin of Lake Titicaca, and then in the valleys north and west of Cuzco. At the beginning of the fifteenth century their empire was still a relatively small state, but in the hundred years before the arrival of the Spaniards three great rulers had extended its frontiers until it included present-day Ecuador and much of Chile and northwestern Argentina as well as most of modern Peru and Bolivia.

The conquered territories were not merely tributary states, like those dominated by the Aztecs, but integral parts of a centralized kingdom. The Incas seem from the beginning to have shown an astonishing statesmanship in consolidating their conquests. Their dominance was effectively secured by building fortresses and roads, and the loyalty of each group of new subjects was obtained by skillfully harmonizing their political and social system with that of the empire. In most cases the former rulers were allowed to remain in power, under the supervision of the Incas' representative, and local customs were interfered with as little as possible. The inhabitants were required, however, to learn *Quechua*, the language of Cuzco, in order to simplify the problem of administration, and this is the prevalent tongue in the Andean highlands today. The process of assimilation was doubtless made easier by the fact that the more important parts of the Andean region were occupied by tribes of a similar culture and closely related languages, and also by the great prestige which the Incas acquired as their power grew.

The *Sapa Inca*, the ruler of the empire, was an absolute monarch whose claim to descent from the Sun invested him in the eyes of his subjects with a divine character which strengthened his temporal power. When he was not leading the army or engaged in long tours of inspection in outlying parts of his domains, he lived in great state at Cuzco, surrounded by a numerous court and a large harem. Among the later Incas, at least, the heir to the throne must be the son of the monarch by his own sister—a custom evidently adopted to enhance the sacredness of the royal family in the eyes of the people. The other princes of the royal blood, including all legitimate descendants of former rulers, formed the high nobility from whose ranks were selected the principal military and civil officials and the chief priests. They, with the other descendants of the original inhabitants of Cuzco, were entitled to call themselves Incas and to wear the large ornaments in the lobes of their ears which led the Spaniards to call them *orejones*. Many of the special privileges that they enjoyed were also enjoyed by the *curacas*, the hereditary chiefs of conquered provinces, whose children were usually educated at Cuzco to imbue them with a spirit of loyalty. Below these were a host of minor officials, charged with the supervision and control of the political and economic life of the people of the empire.

The social and economic organization was perhaps the most remarkable feature of the Inca regime. Its basis was the communal ownership of land which had doubtless existed among the Andean peoples for centuries. The land belonged to the *ayllu*, usually a kinship group, and each family, as in Mexico, was allotted a portion for its own use. Other portions were tilled for the benefit of the government and the priesthood, and their product was used if necessary to relieve famine in any part of the empire. The well-filled storehouses of the Incas afforded a security against want which might be envied by the people of many modern countries.

Agriculture was the principal occupation, and a great variety of fruits and vegetables were grown in the various climatic zones from the hot valleys east of the mountains to the cold *páramos* near their summits. Potatoes, in the highlands, and maize, at altitudes of less than 11,000 feet, were the chief crops. In the mountains the scanty area of arable land was increased by well-built terraces following the contours of the hillsides. Agricultural implements were crude, but the use of fertilizers, including guano in the coast regions, was understood and practiced. In the higher and less fertile parts of the mountain regions the people were herdsmen rather than farmers. The llamas and alpacas provided wool and meat so that *charqui*, or dried flesh, was a staple article of diet. Wild game was captured in great officially organized annual hunts.

The Incas attempted to control the most minute details of the lives of their subjects. Theoretically, there were officials charged with the supervision of each group of 10 families, over whom were others ruling groups of 50, 100, and 1,000. The people were divided into 10 classes, according to age, and the character of the work to be done by individuals of each class was fixed by law. Certain inhabitants of each community were selected in turn to serve the state as soldiers, shepherds, miners, artisans, messengers, or laborers on public works, and this service was credited to the community as a part of its tribute. Marriage, travel, and costumes were officially regulated. Violations of the laws were severely punished because even trivial offenses were looked upon as a sacrilegious disobedience of the *Sapa Inca's* commands, but crime is said to have been rare.

The imperial government frequently transplanted whole groups of its subjects from one region to another. The inhabitants of a newly conquered district whose loyalty was doubtful were often compelled to exchange homes with people from an older section of the empire. At other times, pioneers were sent from overpopulated provinces to newly conquered and undeveloped frontier regions. In either case the colonists, or *mitimaes*, were given special privileges and material assistance to mitigate the hardships of the transfer.

Among the most notable of the Incas' achievements were their public works. The irrigation systems that already existed in the coastal valleys were improved and extended. Water was brought in some cases for many miles, through tunnels or channels cut in the mountains or over aqueducts supported by masonry walls, and reservoirs were built to assure a continuous supply. The country thus supported a far larger population than it did after the Spaniards, in their ignorance and improvidence, allowed these works to fall into disrepair. The roads, which connected Cuzco with all parts of the empire, were scarcely less remarkable. They were frequently surfaced either with slabs of stone or a mixture of stone and clay, beaten hard, and the steeper slopes were ascended by steps cut in the rock. The gorges in the mountains, which would otherwise have been almost impassable, were crossed by suspension bridges of osier or maguey fiber. At intervals there were storehouses of grain and other supplies for the use of the army, and at more frequent intervals huts for the accommodation of travelers. Messengers, stationed at posts so near together that it was possible to run from one to another at top speed, enabled the ruler to send orders to any part of his domains and to be informed within a few days of all important happenings in the outlying provinces.

So elaborate an administrative organization could hardly function without some means for recording and conveying information. The Incas had no system of writing, but they had developed a substitute in the form of the *quipus* which served to show the quantities of articles of various kinds on hand in the storehouses, the population of each district in the empire, and the amount of tribute rendered by their people.

These quipus were cords on which were made knots of almost infinite multiplicity. For the purposes of reckoning, each form of knot represented a different number, and each string a different subject; to some of the strings, subordinate strings were attached, serving as footnotes, and the strings forming one set of accounts were arranged as a fringe along a master-string. An indication of the nature of the objects enumerated was furnished by the colour of each string, and the combinations of colours and types of knots gave an almost endless variety to the uses to which this method of recording could be put.[3]

A specially trained force of *quipucamoyac* or accountants was entrusted with the keeping of these records. The *quipus* seem to have served even to keep alive the memory of historical events, though their usefulness in this connection was obviously limited.

The cities, and especially the Capital, were adorned with public buildings of stone laid in regular tiers and cut and fitted with marvelous exactness. Today, the visitor to Cuzco walks through streets where the Inca masonry still serves as the outside walls of the houses. There were many great palaces, for each ruler built a new residence for himself, leaving that of his predecessor as a sort of shrine, and many buildings were erected for religious purposes. The most impressive of these was the *Coricancha*, the great temple. Here, in the sanctuary of the Sun, the mummies of former monarchs sat before the great altar, in a room lavishly decorated with plates of gold. The same building had chapels dedicated to the Moon, the planet Venus, the Lightning, and the Rainbow, besides many apartments for the use of the priests. In the temple precincts, according to Garcilaso de la Vega, a descendant of the Incas who wrote their history after the Spanish Conquest,[4]

[There was] a garden of gold and silver. . . . It contained many herbs and flowers of different kinds, many small plants, many large trees, many large and small animals both wild and domestic, and creeping things, such as serpents, lizards, and toads, as well as shells, butterflies, and birds. Each of these things was placed in its natural position. There was also a large field of maize, the grain they call *quinua*, pulses, and fruit trees with their fruit; all made of gold and silver.

Religion, as among the other civilized peoples of America, played an important part in the life of the community and was closely identified with the civil authority. Both the peoples of the sierra and the peoples of the coast worshiped a multitude of local gods, or *huacas*, such as rocks,

[3] Joyce, *South American Archaeology*, pp. 102–103.
[4] *The Royal Commentaries of the Incas*, Pt. I, Bk. III, Ch. 24, Markham's translation, Vol. I, pp. 282–283.

rivers, natural forces, and animals which the various tribes regarded as
their ancestors. Homage was also universally paid to the dead. The Sun,
the special *huaca* of the Incas, was the great deity of Cuzco, and its worship was imposed upon the conquered peoples as the empire expanded.
The already existing local cults, however, were not in most cases suppressed, and even among the Incas the Sun was by no means the sole
deity. Each locality, and even each family, had its *huacas*, and all of the
people, from the *Sapa Inca* down, had personal fetishes that were supposed to influence the fortunes of the owner during his life and to be
buried with him at death. A higher religious conception was represented
by the creator god, Huiracocha or Pachacamac, who was worshiped by
the Incas and also by some of the coast people, and whose worship, at
least among the Inca nobility, was abstract and spiritual rather than material.

There was a numerous priesthood, headed by the *Villac Umu* who
was always a brother or close relative of the ruling Inca. Under him were
other religious functionaries of high rank, for the most part of royal or
noble blood, but the minor positions were filled by persons serving only
for short periods and thereafter returning to their usual occupations. An
important function of the priesthood was to ascertain the will of the deity
by omens of various sorts, or by consulting oracles. Sacrificial offerings of
llamas, precious metals, and food were made to the Sun and also to other
huacas and to the spirits of ancestors. Human sacrifices, common in earlier
times among the Andean tribes, were to a great extent suppressed by the
Incas though it is probable that they were practiced on rare and important
occasions.

Among the most famous institutions of the empire were the convents
of the Virgins of the Sun. In these buildings, hundreds of maidens, selected
for their noble birth or their beauty, wove the garments used by the
royal family and the priests and made bread, *chicha*, and other articles for
religious purposes. They were rigorously secluded from contact with the
outside world, under the guardianship of older women, but the more
beautiful often left the convents to enter the harem of the ruler or to become the wives of lesser chiefs.

In practical statesmanship and in their genius for organization and administration, the Incas far surpassed any other group of American Indians about whom we have definite knowledge. If their culture was in
some other respects inferior to that which the Aztecs and their neighbors
had inherited from the earlier inhabitants of the Mexican Valley—for the
Mexicans surpassed the Peruvians in architecture and sculpture, in their
astronomical knowledge, and in possessing a system of writing—it was
nevertheless of a high order. Such fragments of their poems and prayers
as have come down to us show a well-developed capacity for self-expres-
sion and a depth of real spiritual feeling. Intellectual progress, however,

seems to have been confined almost entirely to the ruling class. The masses of the people, living in rude and comfortless stone huts, were doubtless better fed and better cared for than they had been before the time of the Incas, or than they have been since the Spanish Conquest, but they were kept in a state of ignorance, and the system under which they lived must have precluded the growth of any spirit of initiative or self-reliance. The tradition of unquestioning obedience to despotic authority made it relatively easy for the Spaniards to conquer and hold Peru after they had once obtained control of the person of the monarch.

THE CHIBCHAS

In the highlands north of the Inca empire, in what is now the Republic of Colombia, there were a number of other relatively advanced Indian groups. The most important were the Chibchas, or Muiscas, of the plateau of Bogotá where there were five independent states ruled by priest-kings. The Chibchas worshiped several deities, including the Sun, the Moon, and Bochica, the legendary teacher of the arts of civilization. Their culture was much like that of the other Andean peoples, but they did not have the llama or the alpaca, which played so important a part in the economy of the Indians farther south. They spun and wove cotton, made good pottery, and were especially skillful in working with gold. They lived in towns, but their buildings were of wood rather than stone.

One of the customs of the Chibchas gave rise to the famous myth of *El Dorado*, the gilded man. Certain lakes in their territory, and especially those of Guatavita and Ubaque, were places of pilgrimage at which all the tribes gathered from time to time, laying aside hostilities to engage in foot-races and drinking bouts. There were especially elaborate ceremonies when a new chief of the principality of Guatavita was to be consecrated. While his subjects gathered on the shore, lighting bonfires and making prayers, the prince, with several priests, embarked on a raft. He was stripped of his clothing, covered with adhesive earth, and sprinkled with powdered gold, while the raft itself was laden with gold and emeralds to be thrown into the sacred waters. Reports of this ceremony were carried into distant lands, so that Belalcázar, the conqueror of Ecuador, heard reports at Quito of a country so rich in gold that the prince was covered from head to foot with the precious metal for his coronation. The legend grew, and many Spanish expeditions braved terrific hardships in search of the mythical *El Dorado* long after Guatavita itself had been conquered.

OTHER INDIANS

Most of the other tribes in Spanish and Portuguese America were less civilized. Those who were practically exterminated after the Spanish Conquest, like the inhabitants of the Antilles, or who merely survived as primitive savages in regions never effectively occupied by Europeans, need not be described here. There were other tribes, however, that played an important rôle in the history of the European settlements.

Among these were the peoples of the Tupi-Guaraní linguistic stock living in the subtropical region east of the Paraná-Paraguay River system, which includes modern Paraguay, much of south-central Brazil, and nearby portions of Argentina. The Tupis, in the eastern part of this area, were a savage race given to cannibalism and constantly at war among themselves, and they and the numerous other native tribes of the Brazilian coast fought savagely against the Portuguese, who reduced great numbers of them to slavery. Though relatively few of them survived, because they were unaccustomed to hard labor and susceptible, like other Indians, to the white man's diseases, their blood is still noticeable among the people of several regions in modern Brazil.

More important were the Guaranís, a somewhat more civilized race who lived in semipermanent communities with large houses of latticework and straw accommodating 20 or 30 families. They were fairly skilled in making pottery and polished stone implements, and they cultivated the usual Indian crops—corn, beans, and tobacco. At the same time they depended for much of their food on hunting and fishing. Less warlike than their Brazilian relatives, they were easily brought under control by the early Spanish settlers and later by the Jesuit fathers, who established among them the famous Paraguay missions. They were the only Indians east of the Andes who survived to become a considerable element in the population of modern South America. Their descendants, with an admixture of white blood, form the bulk of the inhabitants of Paraguay today, and their language is still generally spoken there.

On the grassy *pampas* of the River Plate region and in the temperate valleys of central Chile there were Indians of a very different type. Nomads, living by hunting and practicing agriculture in a primitive way, they were a warlike people, incorrigibly attached to their personal and tribal independence. Like the Indians of North America, they were pushed back but not conquered by the earlier European settlers. In Argentina they continued to make trouble until they were virtually exterminated by the army in the last quarter of the nineteenth century. In Chile, the tribes north of the Bío-Bío River, who had been conquered by the Incas and had adopted a relatively settled way of life, were subdued by the Spaniards after some hard fighting and formed the bulk of the laboring class during the colonial period. The Indians south of the Bío-Bío savagely resisted the invaders for more than 300 years. Like the pampas tribes, they were finally defeated late in the nineteenth century, and those who survive are living peaceably on reservations today.

SURVIVAL OF THE INDIAN RACE

Much of the culture of the great Indian empires was destroyed by the Conquest, but the majority of the inhabitants of Mexico, Guatemala, Peru, Bolivia, and Ecuador today are either full-blooded Indians who still retain much of their ancient way of life, or people of mixed blood who owe almost as much to their Indian as to their Spanish heritage. Relationships between these three groups, whites, mestizos, and Indians, present many of the most difficult political and social problems that confront these five countries today.

Indians still form an important part of the population of several other American countries. The survival of the Guaraní stock in Paraguay has been mentioned. Many of the people of Colombia are wholly or partly of Indian descent, though most of them now speak Spanish and do not form an important separate community. Somewhat the same situation exists in parts of Venezuela and of Central America, where settled agricultural tribes were also converted into a subject laboring class under Spanish rule. There was a very different situation in regions like the River Plate and southern Chile, where there were only wild nomads. The history of a European community in such a region was certain to be very different from that of a colony in Mexico or Peru. In the one case, it would be almost entirely European in blood. In the other, the white element would be a small ruling class, living on the labor of the conquered race. The striking contrasts that impress the traveler as he goes from one Latin American republic to another today arise largely from differences in the character of the aboriginal population.

CHAPTER 2

Discovery
and Conquest

THE SPANISH PENINSULA BEFORE 1492

THE SPANISH PENINSULA is peopled by the descendants of several dissimilar races. It became a part of the civilized world when the primitive Celtic and Iberian inhabitants were conquered by Rome late in the third century B.C. and was soon one of the richest parts of the empire. Roman political and social institutions were not entirely destroyed when the peninsula was overrun by Germanic tribes in the fifth century, and the Catholic religion was soon adopted by the Visigothic kings who ruled the greater part of Spain during the next 300 years.

Early in the eighth century the country was again conquered, this time by the Saracens from North Africa. The invaders brought with them an advanced culture that made Spain the most civilized portion of medieval Europe and profoundly influenced its later history. The original inhabitants, on the whole, were well governed and fairly treated. There was little attempt to convert them by force to Islam, though many of them embraced that faith to escape the taxes imposed on nonbelievers or, in the case of slaves, to obtain freedom from their Christian masters. The tolerant policy of the Moorish rulers also embraced the Jews, and large numbers of these came to Spain to add yet another to the many racial stocks in the peninsula.

The Moslems had hardly consolidated their power before the long wars of the reconquest began. After the Saracen advance into France was turned back, the Frankish kings helped to preserve Christian rule in Aragon and Catalonia at the base of the Pyrenees. Farther west, in the mountains of Asturias, there were other independent Christian communities that later grew into the kingdoms of Leon and Castile. All of these little states gradually extended their domains. The Moors early abandoned much of the plateau of northern Spain, and their hold on the more attractive regions in the south was often made precarious by factional strife between the Arabs and the North African Berbers or between ambitious local potentates. The Christians also fought among themselves as often as against the infidels; but they were occasionally able to combine their forces, and in 1212 they decisively defeated the Moors in the battle of Las Navas de Tolosa. During the next half-century all of southern Spain was reconquered except the little kingdom of Granada which remained under Moorish rule until 1492.

For 200 years after the breakup of the Moorish empire there were five separate kingdoms in the peninsula. Castile and Leon, united under one crown after 1230, was the largest and most populous. The realms of the kings of Aragon, who had conquered Catalonia in the twelfth century and the Moorish kingdom of Valencia in the thirteenth, lay east of Castile along the Mediterranean coast. To the west was Portugal, which had become independent in the twelfth century; to the south Granada; and in the northeast the little kingdom of Navarre. These states were constantly at war with one another or torn by internal struggles. In Castile especially there were few intervals of peace in the strife between rival claimants to the throne and between the Crown and the great nobles—a state of affairs that left little opportunity for intellectual or economic advance. Aragon, with more stable political institutions, fared better, and Catalan merchants developed an important commerce throughout the Mediterranean region.

The marriage of Ferdinand of Aragon and Isabella of Castile and Leon in 1469 made it possible for Spain to become a great nation. The union of the heirs to the thrones of the two principal Spanish states came at a time when much of the peninsula was in a state of anarchy. Isabella obtained recognition as Queen of Castile and Leon only after a long struggle, but once established on her throne she showed an ability and statesmanship that her predecessors had lacked. The unruly nobles were brought under control and compelled to cease their private wars, while brigandage and disorder were checked by the organization of an effective police force. When Ferdinand succeeded his father as King of Aragon in 1479, the two realms were united under one effective government, though they retained their separate constitutions. The new monarchs' first great enterprise, after the establishment of order at home, was the conquest of Granada, which was accomplished in 1492 after ten years of warfare. The end of the war made it possible for the two sovereigns to consider the venture that Christopher Columbus proposed to them a few months later.

THE PORTUGUESE DISCOVERIES

The Portuguese had already initiated the great era of exploration in which the discovery of America was but one event. The development of the art of navigation, which made Columbus' voyages possible, was largely the work of a Portuguese prince, Henry the Navigator (1394–1460), who devoted his life to the improvement of seamanship and the extension of geographical knowledge. The expeditions he sponsored explored much of the African coast and paved the way for his countrymen's later efforts to open a new trade route to the Orient by way of the Cape of Good Hope, which attained success when Vasco da Gama made his voyage to India in 1497–1499. The Portuguese posts on the African west coast barred other nations from the route around the Cape and for a long time gave the Portuguese control of the African slave trade, which was to be an important factor in the development of America.

THE DISCOVERY OF AMERICA

Columbus' idea was to reach the Orient by sailing westward across the Atlantic. The Genoese sailor had himself been in the service of the King of Portugal and had married a near relative of one of Prince Henry's captains. He had attempted to interest the Portuguese court in his project, and it was after his failure at Lisbon that he began his long struggle to obtain support from the Spanish monarchs. The story of his efforts is a familiar one and need not be retold here. He finally signed an agreement with Ferdinand and Isabella which assured the needed financial support and granted him the position of Viceroy and the hereditary rank of Admiral in any new lands that he might obtain for the Crown.

Columbus' three little ships sailed from Palos on August 3, 1492, and from the Canary Islands on September 6. On October 12 the expedition reached one of the smaller islands of the Bahamas, probably that now called San Salvador, and the Admiral took formal possession of it in the name of the King and Queen. Understanding from the gestures of the natives that a larger island, rich in gold, lay farther south, he went on to the coast of Cuba, and then eastward to an island which he named Española because its mountains reminded him of Spain. Here the Indians were friendly and had considerable quantities of gold, which came, they said, from mines farther east. He was sailing along the coast in this direction when his flagship, the Santa María, ran aground and was wrecked. This compelled him to leave 40 of his men on shore in a fort which he named La Navidad.

The Admiral returned to Spain, where his exaggerated description of the riches that he had found created a sensation. Ferdinand and Isabella at once took steps to obtain recognition of their sovereignty in the new lands. A papal bull issued in 1455 had confirmed Portugal's exclusive dominion "through all Guinea and beyond toward that Southern shore," [1] and it was feared that this vague grant, which had been formally recognized by Spain, might be interpreted to include the islands that Columbus had reached. The Pope, therefore, was persuaded to lay down a line 100 leagues west of the Azores and the Cape Verde Islands, beyond which lands not already in the possession of any Christian prince were to belong to the Crown of Castile. This was unsatisfactory to the King of Portugal, and the Treaty of Tordesillas, signed in 1494, finally provided that the "line of demarcation" should run from pole to pole 370 leagues west of the Cape Verdes. Not until six years later was it discovered that a part of South America lay east of this new line—a fact that gave Portugal her claim to Brazil.

The Spanish monarchs meanwhile made hurried preparations to establish a permanent colony in the New World. On September 25, 1493, Columbus sailed from Cádiz with 17 ships and a large company of artisans, farmers, and missionaries, as well as seamen and soldiers. No women were taken along, but the fleet carried everything else necessary for a permanent settlement: domestic animals, seeds, fruit trees, and tools. When the expedition reached La Navidad, Columbus was horrified to find only the ruins of his fort. The Indians, at first so friendly, had been enraged at the abusive conduct of the Spaniards and had murdered them to a man.

A new settlement, called Isabela, was established on the coast farther to the east, but things went badly from the start. The Admiral, as a foreigner, was unpopular with his followers, and the Spanish soldiers resented his insistence that they as well as the paid laborers should take part in the work of building the town. Disease and the effects of unaccustomed exertion in a hot climate thinned the colonists' ranks. The Indians were soon driven into open hostility by the settlers' demands for food and the abuse of their women and were only defeated after several months of hard fighting. Notwithstanding these difficulties, Columbus found time to explore the south coast of Cuba and to discover Jamaica, but in 1496 he was compelled to return to Spain to defend himself against charges brought against him by discontented colonists. He was so far successful that he was again permitted to set sail for his colony in 1498.

On this third voyage the Admiral followed a new route in the hope of finding richer lands to the south of those already discovered. He reached the Island of Trinidad and soon afterward the nearby mainland where he found natives more civilized than those of Española, wearing golden ornaments and strings of pearls. Impressed by the Indians' appearance, by the pleasant climate, and by the beauty of the landscape, Columbus concluded that he had reached the very border of the terrestrial para-

[1] Davenport, *European Treaties Bearing on the History of the United States and Its Dependencies to 1648*, p. 24.

dise itself, for this was reported to be in Asia, beyond the realm of Cathay. After exploring the coast for some distance to the west, he turned north to Española. There he found that his brother Bartholomew, left in charge in his absence, had moved with most of the colonists to the south shore of the island and had established the city of Santo Domingo, the first permanent settlement in America. The troubles with the Indians had continued, and some of the Spaniards, under one Roldán, had revolted and established a separate camp in the interior. Columbus succeeded in making an agreement with the malcontents, but not in allaying the bitter feeling caused by the severity with which his brother had attempted to rule the colony—a bitterness which was aggravated by the colonists' sufferings from want and disease.

Reports of these occurrences made a painful impression on the King and Queen. Isabella also questioned the propriety of Columbus' conduct when he sent a cargo of Indians to Spain for sale as slaves. The slave trade had long been the chief factor in the development of Portugal's profitable African commerce, and it was not unnatural that Columbus should turn to this source of potential wealth when he was disappointed in his hopes of finding substantial amounts of gold or other valuable products in the lands he had discovered. But Isabella from the outset adopted a more enlightened view of her obligations toward the inhabitants of her new possessions. Her disapproval of Columbus' venture was the first of a long series of efforts by the Spanish Crown—efforts which as we shall see were not very successful—to protect the Indians from the rapacity of the Spanish conquerors.

The monarchs were finally convinced that Columbus was unfit to act as Governor of the new colony, and in 1500 Francisco de Bobadilla was sent to Española to take his place. The Admiral and his brother Bartholomew were shipped back to Spain in irons after a one-sided investigation. They were soon released, but Columbus was never restored to the authority which had been promised to him for life. During his fourth and last voyage to America, upon which he embarked in 1502, he was not even permitted to land at Santo Domingo. He explored a long section of the Central American coast, suffering much from storms and other disasters, and returned to Spain, broken in health, to die at Valladolid on May 20, 1506.

Since access to the rich markets of the Orient seemed more important than the possession of lands occupied only by primitive savages, exploration of the American coast during the first quarter-century after the discovery was directed chiefly toward the search for a route past the new continent to Asia. Several other mariners made important voyages before Columbus' death. In 1497 and 1498 John Cabot, an Italian sailing under a patent from the King of England, visited the North American coast. In

Spain, Columbus' claim to a monopoly of the right of exploration in the Indies was respected until 1499, when both Alonso Niño and Alonso de Ojeda made voyages to the north coast of South America. Niño returned with a cargo of pearls and dyewood; and Ojeda, who gave Venezuela its name because an Indian village built on piles in the Gulf of Maracaibo reminded him of Venice, also seems to have been fairly successful. In 1500 Vicente Yáñez Pinzón reached the Brazilian coast, discovered the mouth of the Amazon, and followed the shore north and west for some 2,000 miles. Only three months after Pinzón, the Portuguese navigator Pedralvares Cabral also landed in Brazil while on a voyage from Lisbon to India. There were other expeditions of less note, and in 1504, when Columbus returned from his fourth voyage, it was possible for geographers to draw a fairly accurate map of the coast line from Cape Gracias a Dios in Central America to the easternmost point of Brazil.

It is one of the injustices of history that the American continents were named not for their discoverer but for another Italian mariner who achieved fame more by accident than by desert. Amerigo Vespucci had taken part in some of the early voyages to the New World, and letters that he wrote describing them had been printed and widely read throughout Europe. In 1507, a German professor of geography reprinted one of these and proposed that the land that had been discovered in the South Atlantic should be named "America." This suggestion was gradually accepted in other European countries, but in Spain the new possessions continued to be called "The Indies."

EXPLORATION AND SETTLEMENT, 1504–1522

For some years after 1504 the search for a strait lagged, and Spanish activity in the New World centered in the Caribbean. Santo Domingo was still the chief settlement. The colony's white population numbered only 300 when Columbus' none-too-successful management of its affairs ended, but Governor Ovando, who came to the island in 1502, brought with him 2,500 new settlers. Although many of these died of hardship and disease, further immigration increased the number of Spanish inhabitants to 12,000 by 1506. After 1508 the colonists gradually spread into the neighboring islands of Cuba, Jamaica, and Puerto Rico. Gold, hides, and sugar were exported to Spain in increasing quantities, and somewhat later, when expeditions to the mainland were undertaken, the breeding of horses became profitable. The settlements in the islands nevertheless failed to attain any great prosperity. Within a remarkably short time, their native Indian population was exterminated by disease and cruel treatment, and extensive slave raids on other parts of the Caribbean litoral failed to maintain the supply of labor. Many of the Spanish inhabitants abandoned

Santo Domingo and Cuba after the discovery of Mexico and Peru. In the meantime, however, they had been the starting points for the expeditions that conquered a great empire on the mainland.

The story of the Spanish occupation of Middle and South America is strikingly different from that of the British colonization in North America. The great majority of the people who went out from Spain were not settlers but restless adventurers, avid to seek their fortune in the discovery and conquest of new territory. For centuries, the typical Spaniard had been a fighting man. The end of the war against Granada and the suppression of internal strife in the Spanish kingdoms, under the firm rule of Ferdinand and Isabella, had left thousands of soldiers with little occupation, and many of them found an outlet for their energy and ambition in the New World.

The *conquistadores* were inspired not only by a craving for adventure and an avidity for wealth and power, but also by an intolerant crusading spirit. The conversion of the Indians was one of the prime objectives of the Conquest, both for the Crown and for the individual soldier, even though the Christian spirit was little evident in the *conquistadores'* treatment of the Indians or in their conduct toward one another. The story of the Conquest is replete with incidents of treachery and outrageous brutality, but it is also an amazing story of fearless audacity and persistence in the face of terrific hardships. The physical obstacles which the *conquistadores* surmounted—the all-but-impassable, disease-infested jungles of the lowlands, the rugged slopes of the *cordilleras*, and the waterless deserts of the South American west coast—were even more formidable than the resistance of the overwhelmingly more numerous armies of the Indians.

The hardships experienced by the first Spaniards who attempted permanent settlements on the mainland were an example of what lay ahead. In 1509, Alonso de Ojeda was given permission to colonize and govern the region between Cape de la Vela and the Gulf of Urabá, and Diego de Nicuesa got a similar grant covering what is now the Isthmus of Panama and the east coast of Nicaragua. Ojeda met with savage resistance from the Indians and finally left 60 survivors of his original force of 300 in a fort near the Gulf of Urabá and returned to Santo Domingo for reinforcements and supplies. He was shipwrecked on the voyage and died soon afterward. Nicuesa, meanwhile, had established a settlement which he called Nombre de Dios, near what is now the Caribbean end of the Panama Canal, but hunger and disease reduced the number of his followers from 700 to 60 or 70. When he learned that the survivors of Ojeda's expedition had moved across the Gulf of Urabá into his territory, he attempted to assert his authority over them. This was a mistake, for the colonists compelled him to put to sea in a worm-eaten vessel which never was heard from again.

The transfer of Ojeda's colony to Santa María la Antigua de Darién, as the new settlement was called, had been the work of Vasco Núñez de Balboa, an adventurer who had escaped from his creditors at Santo Domingo by having himself nailed in a cask and loaded on one of Ojeda's ships. Balboa's energy and natural gift for leadership had led the discouraged colonists to follow him rather than the lawyer Enciso, whom Ojeda had left as his representative. The result showed the wisdom of their choice, for by their new leader's diplomacy the Spaniards were able to obtain food and a small amount of gold from the nearby Indian tribes. They also learned of a great sea, lying beyond the mountains, on the shores of which there were said to be kingdoms far richer in the precious metals than any they had yet seen. On September 25, 1513, after an arduous journey of 24 days through the tropical jungle, Balboa saw the Pacific from the top of a hill, and four days later he walked into the waters of the Gulf of San Miguel and took possession of the ocean in the name of the King of Spain.

Balboa's exploit caused the King to excuse his usurpation of leadership and to grant him the title of "Adelantado of the South Sea," but before the report of the expedition reached Spain, the King had already appointed Pedrarias Dávila Governor of the Darién colony. Pedrarias was a narrow-minded and vindictive but energetic official, already past his seventy-second birthday but destined to play an important part in the history of Central America until his death 18 years later. He was jealous from the start of Balboa's popularity and independent spirit, and in 1519 he had his rival beheaded, on apparently trumped-up charges of plotting a revolt. In the same year he moved the seat of government from Santa María across the Isthmus to Panama, so as to carry on more effectively the exploration of the coast on that side.

The discovery of the South Sea led to new efforts to find a way past the continent to Asia. The veteran explorer Juan Díaz de Solís, carrying the search for a strait farther south, reached the River Plate in 1516, but was killed by Indians when he attempted to land. In 1520 Ferdinand Magellan, a Portuguese in the service of the King of Spain, sailed down the coast of Patagonia and succeeded with much difficulty in passing through the strait which still bears his name. He found the ocean on the other side unusually calm, and it was he who christened it the Pacific. After exploring part of the Chilean coast, he struck out boldly westward and finally reached the Philippines. There Magellan himself was killed in a battle with the natives, but some of his followers continued their journey and in 1522 completed the first circumnavigation of the world. The route to the Orient had been found, but it did Spain little good, for neither the Strait of Magellan nor the later discovered route around Cape Horn was easily navigated by the clumsy sailing vessels of the sixteenth century.

THE CONQUEST OF MEXICO

The net result of the first quarter-century of Spanish enterprise in America had been disappointing. Little profit was to be hoped for from lands occupied by the primitive Indians along the coast from Central America to the River Plate. It was not until the Spaniards came into contact with the richer and more civilized people of Mexico that the real value of Columbus' discovery began to be appreciated.

The first explorers to visit Mexican territory were the members of a slave-catching expedition from Cuba led by Francisco Hernández de Córdoba, who was badly defeated by the Maya when he attempted to land in Yucatán in 1517. The next year, another expedition under Juan de Grijalba explored the coast as far north as Vera Cruz and returned with a small quantity of gold. The reports of these two Captains encouraged Diego Velásquez, the Governor of Cuba, to send out a larger force, which he placed under the command of Hernando Cortez.

Cortez had come to Española in 1504, when he was only nineteen, and had played a distinguished part under Velásquez in the Conquest of Cuba. He had later quarreled with the Governor and had at one time been imprisoned. Relations between the two men had evidently improved, but when Cortez was about to sail the Governor became suspicious of him and ordered him to surrender his command. Cortez refused and proceeded to recruit men and obtain supplies at the smaller settlements along the Cuban coast in spite of Velásquez' effort to stop him. He was thus practically an outlaw when he finally set out for Yucatán in February, 1519. His defiance of the King's representative was to affect the whole course of his expedition.

Cortez set sail with 11 ships and about 600 men. He had 10 bronze cannon and a few smaller firearms, as well as a number of crossbows, but his most important military assets, as events later proved, were 16 horses. The terror caused by these strange and apparently supernatural beasts, more perhaps than that inspired by the artillery, repeatedly gave the Spaniards the victory over far larger native armies in the months to come.

At Cozumel Island, where Cortez first landed, he was well received by the natives and was so fortunate as to find a Spaniard named Jerónimo de Aguilar who had been shipwrecked there eight years before and had learned the Maya language. From Cozumel he went on to Tabasco where the Indians opposed him but were defeated with much slaughter. As a peace offering they gave the Spaniards 20 women, and one of these was able to speak both Maya and Nahua. This was the famous Marina who later became Cortez' mistress. Through her and through Aguilar the Spanish leader was now able to communicate with the inhabitants of the territories that he was about to invade.

On April 22, 1519, the Spaniards landed near the site of modern Vera

Cruz. Two days later they were greeted by emissaries from Montezuma, the *tlacatecuhtli* of Tenochtitlán. Reports of Grijalba's arrival on the coast in the preceding year, with pictures of the Spaniards and their ships, had already reached the Aztec capital, and they had aroused superstitious fear as well as interest. The Nahua had a legend that Quetzalcoatl, the fair god who was often portrayed with a long beard, would one day return from the East across the sea, and they were by no means sure that the light-skinned, heavily bearded foreigners were merely human beings. They were thus disposed to accord them a respectful if not enthusiastic welcome.

The Spaniards could see that they had to deal with a state far wealthier and more powerful than any thus far discovered in America, and there were many who felt that its conquest would be too difficult and dangerous a task for a few hundred men to undertake. Cortez, however, could not turn back, for his only hope of escaping punishment as a rebel was to win the King's forgiveness by some sensational achievement. His immediate problems were to give an appearance of legality to his actions and to make sure that none of his force could desert him, and he proceeded at once to attain both objectives. First, after giving secret instructions to his own loyal supporters, he announced that the expedition was about to return to Cuba because it had already gone as far as Velásquez' instructions authorized. The men whom he had taken into his confidence at once objected, asserting that they had been promised an opportunity to found a new colony. Cortez ostensibly yielded to their demands and permitted them by formal vote to create the municipality of Villa Rica de la Vera Cruz. After he himself had been elected Captain General he sent messengers to Spain to explain and attempt to justify what had been done. He then cut off all possibility of retreat by secretly ordering that all of his remaining ships be sunk. The most discontented and faint-hearted had now no alternative but to follow him.

In the meantime Cortez had been gathering much useful information about conditions in Mexico. He learned that the Totonacs along the coast were restive under the domination of the Aztec confederacy, and he encouraged them to revolt. At the same time he endeavored to assure the Aztec leaders of his good intentions. When the people of a nearby town at his suggestion seized the confederacy's tribute collectors, he saved the prisoners from death and secretly sent two of them back to Montezuma with friendly messages. He had already sent gifts to the Aztec war lord and announced his intention to visit Tenochtitlán, but Montezuma, though he sent magnificent presents in return, urgently begged him not to undertake so difficult and dangerous a journey.

After four months on the coast the Spaniards started into the interior, leaving a strong garrison at Vera Cruz. They met with no resistance as they ascended into the highlands, and after two weeks of marching they entered the territory of the Tlascalans, one of the few peoples of central Mexico whom the Aztecs had never been able to conquer. Here they were attacked by tremendous forces of natives, but the horses and the artillery gave them decisive victories in two hard-fought battles. The Tlascalans then decided to make peace and to join the Spaniards in their march against the tribe's traditional enemies at Tenochtitlán. Their help from that time on was of the greatest importance, and the remembrance of it gave the Tlascalans a privileged position among the Indians of Mexico throughout the colonial period.

With some thousands of his new allies, Cortez now proceeded to Cholula which was one of the chief cities of the Aztec realm. The Tlascalans had warned him that Montezuma planned to have the Spaniards entrapped and murdered in this city; but he refused to show any evidence of fear, and the Cholulans welcomed him with protestations of friendship. He soon learned through Marina, however, that the Tlascalans had been well informed, and he promptly forestalled his hosts' treacherous plans by massacring all of the chiefs and some thousands of the other inhabitants. This exhibition of cruelty, following so closely upon the apparently miraculous defeat of the overwhelmingly superior Tlascalan armies, doubtless did much to dissuade the Aztecs from offering further resistance to their unwelcome visitors.

Early in November, 1519, the invaders reached Tenochtitlán, where Montezuma came out in great state to welcome them and to assure them of his friendship. The Spaniards, with their horses and their native allies, took up their residence in one of the buildings on the public square. The Indians brought them gifts and entertained them royally, but the Spanish situation, in an island city surrounded by hundreds of thousands of potential enemies, was clearly precarious. As usual, Cortez decided on a bold stroke. Taking as a pretext a reported plot against the garrison at Vera Cruz, he visited Montezuma with a strong guard and compelled him to come to live with the Spaniards in their quarters. Cortez rightly conjectured that the inhabitants of the city would be reluctant to attack while he held their ruler as a hostage, and he was able in fact to give orders to the Indians through his unwilling but thoroughly frightened guest. One of his first acts was to have Montezuma send for large quantities of gold and silver which were promptly divided among the officers and soldiers. The Emperor was treated at times with respect, at times with a brutality calculated to impress on him the danger of resistance. His princely bearing and noble character soon won the sympathy and admiration of his captors.

For a time all went well, though the extreme danger of the invaders' position was always evident. The temper of the Indians grew more and more ugly, especially after Cortez decided that he could no longer postpone an attack on the native religion. The crusading spirit was always a powerful motive with the Spanish expeditions to the New World, second only to the desire for wealth and power, and it was impossible for the *conquistadores* to imagine the toleration of pagan cults among Indians who came under their control. Cortez had already compelled the Indians near Vera Cruz to accept Christianity, and he had attempted to convert his Tlascalan allies. Here, however, he had met strong opposition and had compromised by permitting the Tlascalans to combine the Christian religion with their own. At Tenochtitlán, closer acquaintance with the horrible character of the native rites made a compromise impossible, and when all efforts at persuasion failed, Cortez proceeded to destroy the Indians' chief idols himself. For the moment the natives did not openly resist, but it was evident that they were horrified and infuriated.

When Cortez had been at Tenochtitlán about six months, a new threat suddenly loomed up. Pánfilo de Narváez, sent by Governor Velásquez, appeared on the coast with a force that outnumbered Cortez' by more than two to one. Between the Aztecs on the one side and this new enemy on the other, resistance seemed hopeless; but Cortez left Pedro de Alvarado at Tenochtitlán with part of his men and boldly went to meet Narváez with the rest. For some days the two Spanish forces camped a short distance from one another. Cortez took advantage of the interval to bribe or cajole many of his opponent's lieutenants, and when the overconfident and careless Narváez was surprised by a night attack and badly defeated, the greater part of his followers returned with Cortez to Tenochtitlán.

There the situation had grown worse. Alvarado, aroused by the Aztecs' continued refusal to abandon their idols, had attacked the participants in one of their religious festivals with great slaughter. The Indians had taken up arms in earnest; and when Cortez arrived, the Spanish garrison was besieged in its quarters. Cortez entered the city without resistance, but on the following day the Indians made a savage general onslaught. They had elected Montezuma's brother Cuitlahua as *tlacatecuhtli*, and when the former ruler appeared on the roof of the barracks in an effort to pacify them he was mortally wounded by a shower of stones. The Spaniards, short of provisions, realized that their only salvation lay in getting out of the city.

On the night of June 30, 1520, famous as the *noche triste*, the sad night, they made their retreat. They had to cross one of the long causeways, hard pressed from their rear and attacked by fleets of war canoes on their flanks. Crowded in a narrow space and loaded down with spoils which they refused to abandon, they could make little use of their superior weapons. Hundreds of Spaniards and thousands of Tlascalans were cut down. Scores were captured, to be sacrificed later to the Aztec gods. The heaviest losses occurred at the openings in the causeway where the Indians had raised the drawbridges. Less than half of those who started reached the mainland, and all of the cannon and most of the precious horses were gone. The survivors were again attacked by the Aztecs a few days later, but this time, after a hard fight, they won a sanguinary victory. They then marched to Tlascala where their faithful allies received them with undiminished friendship.

Cortez still refused to abandon his purpose. After a short rest he proceeded to restore Spanish prestige and the morale of his forces by a series of successful raids against allies of the Aztec confederacy. He also received much-needed reinforcements and supplies, for a number of men whom Velásquez had sent to join Narváez were persuaded to join him, and other adventurers, attracted by reports of the wealth of Mexico, were beginning to arrive. One of these was a Negro ill with smallpox. This disease, hitherto unknown among the Indians, soon spread throughout Mexico, carrying off vast numbers of people and undermining the Aztecs' power of resistance. Cuitlahua was among those who died, and his nephew Guatemoc took his place.

By the end of 1520 Cortez was again ready to attack Tenochtitlán. He defeated, or won over by diplomacy, several of the tribes hitherto allied with the Aztecs and occupied the points where the causeways reached the mainland. More important still, he launched on the lake a fleet of small vessels that had been built at Tlascala and brought in pieces from that city by 8,000 Indian carriers. An incipient revolt in his own forces, inspired by friends of Velásquez, was discovered and suppressed. In May, 1521, he began active operations against the Aztec Capital. The causeways and the aqueduct that supplied the city with fresh water were seized, and a part of the city itself was occupied. The Indians fought so savagely that progress was slow. On one occasion some 50 Spaniards were captured and sacrificed in plain view of their horrified comrades. The invaders were not to be turned back, however, and the terrific losses inflicted by their firearms and pikes combined with suffering from lack of food and water to bring about the collapse of all resistance on August 13. Hardly more than desolate ruins were left. The Spaniards found disappointingly little treasure, although they cruelly tortured Guatemoc in an effort to compel him to reveal where more was hidden.

Cortez' persistent effort to obtain the approval of the Crown now met with success. He had so far had the worst of the contest between his emissaries and those of Diego Velásquez at the court in Spain. Bishop Fonseca, the official most concerned with affairs in the Indies, had in fact sent an official to Mexico in 1521 to investigate his conduct, but Cortez had refused on specious pretexts to recognize the Commissioner's authority and had bribed him to return to Spain. With the fall of Tenochtitlán, the conqueror of Mexico had become so powerful that prudence as well as gratitude counseled a recognition of his services. In

1522, therefore, the Emperor formally appointed him Governor, Captain General, and Chief Justice of the new colony. Cortez was thus free to turn his restless energy to the work of reconstruction and the completion of the Conquest. The new city of Mexico rose on the ruins of Tenochtitlán, and the tribes in the neighborhood were rapidly reduced to submission.

In 1523–1524, Cortez sent two expeditions into Central America. The first, under Pedro de Alvarado, overcame the Maya tribes in the highlands of Guatemala after some hard fighting. Alvarado later became Governor of the colony that he established there. The other, led by Cristóbal de Olid, was less successful. Olid repudiated his allegiance to Cortez and imprisoned Francisco de las Casas who had been sent by Cortez to reduce Olid to obedience. He then captured Gil González Dávila who had landed on the north coast of Honduras with an expedition from Santo Domingo. Las Casas and González, however, escaped and killed Olid; and soon afterward Cortez himself arrived in Honduras, after a long and difficult overland journey, and was cordially welcomed by all factions.

Cortez was soon compelled to return to Mexico, where things were going badly in his absence. His enemies had again persuaded the Emperor to send an officer to investigate his conduct. Though this investigation produced no result, because both the Commissioner and his successor opportunely died, Cortez decided to go to Spain in an attempt to clear himself. There he obtained a title and the grant of great estates in Mexico, but the Emperor had already decided to reduce his authority in the government. An *audiencia*, a commission of five judges, was created in 1527 to take charge of civil affairs, and in 1529 the Emperor appointed Antonio de Mendoza Viceroy of Mexico. Mendoza proved to be one of the ablest administrators in Spanish colonial history, and after his arrival in 1535 Cortez had little influence in the colony's affairs. He busied himself for some years in attempts to explore the coast northwest of Mexico; but his luck seemed to have deserted him, and he finally returned to Spain, where he died in 1547.

Meanwhile, the Conquest of Central America had been completed, chiefly by expeditions from Panama. Gil González Dávila had explored Nicaragua in 1522, and two years later Pedrarias, the Governor at Panama, sent Francisco Hernández de Córdoba to conquer the country. Hernández de Córdoba defeated the Indians and founded the towns of León and Granada, but when he attempted to claim the province for himself the aged Pedrarias suddenly appeared on the scene and beheaded him. Pedrarias was then appointed Governor of Nicaragua, having been supplanted in his post at Panama. His effort to extend his control to Honduras brought him into conflict with Cortez' representatives, and the situation became more confused when a new Governor appeared with a commission from the royal authorities at Santo Domingo. For some years intermittent armed strife between the various factions made the history of Central America a gloomy one.

THE CONQUEST OF PERU

Spaniards exploring the Pacific coast below Panama soon heard vague stories of a great and rich empire far to the south, and in 1524 Francisco Pizarro, an illiterate adventurer who had been prominent in the affairs of the colony on the Isthmus since its first establishment, was given command of an expedition to investigate them. To obtain resources for the enterprise, Pizarro formed a partnership with Diego de Almagro, another adventurer of the same type, and a priest at Panama named Hernando de Luque. Almagro was to help in the work of exploration, whereas Luque, who did not live to see his partners' final triumph, was helpful in raising funds.

Two small ships were obtained, and Pizarro set out in one of them in November, 1524. The weather at that season was especially unfavorable, and he struggled for 10 weeks against head winds and currents without reaching any well-settled region where he could replenish his provisions. He finally had to send the ship back to Panama while he and the greater part of his men waited on the shore, almost starving on a diet of seaweed and palm nuts. When the ship returned, he went on down the coast; but a hard fight with savage Indians convinced him that he could accomplish nothing without a larger force, and he turned back to Panama. Almagro, who followed with the other ship, also had bad luck, and of 180 men who sailed with the two leaders only some 50 survived.

The partners were nevertheless able, with some difficulty, to raise money and enlist men for a new expedition which left Panama in 1526. This time they reached the more populous districts along the Ecuadorean coast and were so encouraged by what they saw that Pizarro decided to remain on the small island of Gallo, in the Bay of Tumaco, while Almagro returned for reinforcements. When Almagro reached Panama, however, Pedro de los Rios, the new Governor, not only refused to permit the recruiting of additional men but sent a ship to bring back those who had remained with Pizarro. There was a dramatic scene at Gallo when the ship arrived. Pizarro refused to obey the Governor's order to return, and 16 of his companions responded to his eloquent appeal not to abandon the undertaking in which they had already suffered so much. The little group were to suffer still more in the months that ensued, but their associates at Panama finally obtained permission to send a ship to relieve them and to continue, though only for six months, the exploration of the coast.

In the time that the Governor allowed him, Pizarro reached northern

Peru and saw unmistakable evidence of the wealth and the high civilization of the Inca empire. The natives seemed fairly friendly, and the explorers were able to obtain gold and silver and fine textiles, and even llamas, to convince the incredulous at home of the truth of their story. They also carried off two Peruvians, who were valuable later as interpreters. There could no longer be any question of the importance of their discoveries; but the partners had exhausted their resources and their credit, and the governor was still unfriendly. Pizarro consequently decided to go to Spain to seek the support of the Crown, and on July 26, 1529, he obtained authorization to conquer and settle the coast for a distance of 200 leagues south from the Gulf of Guayaquil and the promise of a life appointment as Governor and Captain General of this territory. The Crown provided a substantial sum toward the expenses of a new expedition and freed those settling in Peru from certain taxes for a period of years.

After enlisting several followers in Spain, including his brothers, Hernando, Gonzalo, and Juan, Pizarro returned to Panama. In January, 1531, he sailed from that port with 180 men and 27 horses, in three ships. Landing in northern Ecuador, he proceeded along the coast, finding much gold and silver and meeting with little resistance. The ships meanwhile were sent back for reinforcements, which arrived in small groups as the march continued. At the populous Island of Puna, in the Gulf of Guayaquil, the Spaniards remained for some time, resting and gathering information about what lay before them. The Indians of the Island were at first friendly; but later they began to show signs of hostility, and Pizarro defeated them with much slaughter. He then crossed to the mainland of what is now Peru and founded the city of San Miguel to serve as a base for further operations. Fifty-five soldiers became the city's first citizens.

Pizarro could hardly have proceeded so far without encountering serious resistance had it not been for events that had recently occurred in Peru. The Inca empire reached the height of its power shortly before they arrived. Huayna Capac, who lived to receive reports of Pizarro's first expeditions along the coast, completed the conquest of what is now Ecuador and devoted much of his life to the consolidation of his authority there. He was much troubled by rebellions in the recently acquired territories, and it was perhaps a feeling that the empire had grown too large to be controlled from Cuzco which led him to arrange for the division of his possessions after his death. Atahualpa, his son by a princess of the royal family of Quito, was given the territory that his mother's ancestors had ruled, and Huascar, the legitimate heir, succeeded to the throne at Cuzco. It was not long before the two brothers quarreled and war began. Huascar was defeated and made prisoner, and many Incas of the blood royal were massacred. When Pizarro arrived, Atahualpa, who had assumed the crimson fringe of the *Sapa Inca*, was not yet firmly established on the throne, and the imperial government's control in outlying, recently conquered districts, like those through which the Spaniards first marched, was doubtless relaxed.

The Spaniards had already heard much of the civil war and had learned that Atahualpa was at Cajamarca, 10 or 12 days' journey from San Miguel, with a large army. Pizarro therefore resumed his southward march, proceeding slowly from one valley to another along the coast and then over the mountains to meet the Emperor. On the way, he received envoys with gifts and a friendly message from Atahualpa. The storehouses along the Inca road provided ample food and lodging, but the Spaniards suffered much from cold and altitude when they crossed the coastal range and were not a little alarmed lest the troops of the Indians should attack them in the narrow defiles. They finally reached Cajamarca on November 15, 1532, and took up their quarters in stone buildings surrounding the plaza in the center of the town. With his little force of 62 horsemen and 102 foot soldiers, Pizarro calmly laid his plans for the defeat of an army that numbered, according to his Indian guides, 50,000 men. The Inca's encampment, two or three miles away, was clearly visible.

Hernando Pizarro and Hernando de Soto, the future discoverer of the Mississippi, were sent to speak with Atahualpa and returned with a promise that the Inca would visit the newcomers on the following day. It was evening before he came, accompanied by a vast force of soldiers. What followed is best told in the words of Pizarro's secretary, Francisco de Xerés: [2]

The Governor ordered all the Spaniards to arm themselves secretly in their lodgings, and to keep the horses saddled and bridled, and under the orders of three captains, but none were to show themselves in the open space. The Captain of the artillery was ordered to have his guns pointed towards the enemy on the plain, and, when the time came, to fire. Men were stationed in the streets leading to the open space, and, taking twenty men with him, the Governor went to his lodging. These had the duty entrusted to them of seizing the person of Atabaliba [Atahualpa], if he should come cautiously with so large a force as was coming; but the Governor ordered that he should be taken alive. All the troops had orders not to leave their quarters, even if the enemy should enter the open space, until they should hear the guns fired off. The sentries were to be on the alert, and, if they saw that the enemy intended treachery, they were to give the signal; and all were to sally out of the lodgings, the cavalry mounted, when they heard the cry of *Santiago*.

· · · · · · · · · · · ·

[2] The quotations are from Sir Clements Markham's translation of Francisco de Xerés' *Narrative of the Conquest of Peru*, Publications of the Hakluyt Society, Vol. 47 (London, 1872), pp. 51 ff.

Soon the van of the enemy began to enter the open space. First came a squadron of Indians dressed in a livery of different colors, like a chess board. They advanced, removing the straws from the ground, and sweeping the road. Next came three squadrons in different dresses, dancing and singing. Then came a number of men with armour, large metal plates, and crowns of gold and silver. Among them was Atabaliba in a litter lined with plumes of macaws' feathers, of many colours, and adorned with plates of gold and silver. Many Indians carried it on their shoulders on high. Next came two other litters and two hammocks, in which were some principal chiefs; and lastly, several squadrons of Indians with crowns of gold and silver.

Father Valverde, the chaplain of the expedition, went forward and spoke briefly to the Inca about the Christian religion, handing him a copy of the Bible. This Atahualpa threw to the ground, with a scornful demand that the Christians return at once the cloths which they had taken from the storehouses along the road. When Valverde reported the incident to Pizarro,

. . . the Governor put on a jacket of cotton, took his sword and dagger, and, with the Spaniards who were with him, entered among the Indians most valiantly; and, with only four men who were able to follow him, he came to the litter where Atabaliba was, and fearlessly seized him by the arm, crying out *Santiago*. Then the guns were fired off, the trumpets were sounded, and the troops, both horse and foot, sallied forth.

Within a few minutes Atahualpa had been captured and some thousands of his followers had been killed.

During the whole time no Indian raised his arms against a Spaniard. So great was the terror of the Indians at seeing the Governor force his way through them, at hearing the fire of the artillery, and beholding the charging of the horses, a thing never before heard of, that they thought more of flying to save their lives than of fighting.

The captive Inca was treated with consideration, eating at Pizarro's table and sleeping in the Governor's own room. He soon learned some Spanish and told his captors much about the affairs of Peru. His authority among his subjects seemed little diminished, and the safe conducts that he gave enabled small groups of Spaniards to visit Cuzco and other parts of the empire without molestation. Atahualpa's first thought was naturally to regain his liberty. To this end he offered as a ransom gold sufficient to fill a room 22 feet long and 17 feet wide, up to a line 8 or 9 feet from the floor, and enough silver to fill another smaller room twice over. Pizarro agreed to this proposal, and the Indians during the next few weeks brought great quantities of precious vessels and ornaments from palaces and temples. The full amount was not perhaps completed, but Pizarro accepted it; and a treasure worth, at the lowest estimate, some millions of dollars was divided among the members of the expedition according to their rank and services. The King's share of one-fifth was set aside as the law required, and another portion was given to Almagro and his followers, who had just arrived from Panama.

The Inca, however, was not released. His faithless captors had decided that his death would be expedient, and he was placed on trial for a long series of offenses ranging from adultery and idolatry to murder and rebellion. Of murder, he was probably guilty, for his brother the ex-Inca Huascar had been drowned, presumably by order of Atahualpa, soon after the latter had fallen into Pizarro's hands. The trial was a mere formality, and the Inca was publicly executed in the plaza of Cajamarca on August 29, 1533.

With his force augmented by the men whom Almagro had brought, Pizarro now undertook the long and difficult march through the mountains to Cuzco. The Spaniards encountered some opposition along the way, but none at the Capital itself. There they obtained more treasure and set up a city government in the name of the King. They also installed as Inca a brother of Huascar named Manco, for a younger brother of Atahualpa, who had been invested with the royal fringe after the latter's execution, had died on the road to Cuzco.

By this time reports of the riches of Peru were reaching the outside world and arousing the interest of the hordes of adventurers in the older settlements of the Indies who were always on the lookout for an opportunity to improve their lot. The forces of Pizarro and Almagro were constantly augmented by new arrivals, and their hold on the conquered territory became gradually stronger. They had been at Cuzco only a few months, however, when they received alarming news. Pedro de Alvarado, the conqueror of Guatemala, had conceived the idea of obtaining for himself the region of Quito and had landed at the Bay of Caráquez in March, 1534, with 500 Spaniards and 2,000 Indians—an army stronger than any which Pizarro could well hope to send against him. Almagro at once left Cuzco for the north to deal with this invasion of the partners' rights. He found that Quito had already been occupied by Sebastián de Belalcázar, the Commander of the garrison at San Miguel. The combined forces of the two leaders were still smaller than Alvarado's, but the latter's men were worn down by hunger and the exposure that they had suffered while crossing the mountains. They showed little wish to fight, especially when they learned how small a quantity of treasure had been found at Quito, and realized how much more attractive their prospects would be if they joined Almagro and Pizarro in the south. Alvarado was rather easily induced to sell out his whole expedition for 100,000 *pesos de oro* and to return to his own domain in Guatemala.

Meanwhile, Hernando Pizarro had reached Spain with the royal share of Atahualpa's ransom and had persuaded the King to extend the limits of his brother's territory to a point 70 leagues farther south. At the same time Almagro was given a domain of his own extending 200 leagues down the coast beyond Pizarro's grant. The jealousy that had long existed between the two partners was revived by this arrangement, for Cuzco lay near the border line and was claimed by both. Each was hotly supported by his own followers, and actual fighting occurred before an agreement reached in June, 1535, averted further conflict for the time being but left the main question undecided. Soon afterward, Almagro left Cuzco with a strong force to undertake the Conquest of Chile, which was indisputably his. Pizarro returned to the coast, where he had been engaged since the first of the year in building the new City of the Kings, now called Lima, which was soon to become the chief center of Spanish power in South America.

The dissensions among the *conquistadores* and the weakness of the force that remained after Almagro's departure encouraged the Inca Manco to make a last desperate effort to drive the Spaniards from Peru. The Indians of the whole highland area suddenly rose in arms, and Hernando Pizarro was besieged at Cuzco for several months in 1536. Four relief expeditions which Francisco Pizarro sent from Lima were defeated with heavy losses, but with the approach of the planting season Manco could no longer hold his forces together. He retired to Ollantaytambo, and in 1537 he was defeated by the force which Almagro had just brought back from Chile. This ended the revolt, though Manco escaped into the fastnesses of the eastern slope of the Andes and continued for some years to commit depredations against the Spaniards.

Almagro had returned to begin the first of a series of civil wars in which many of the conquerors of Peru were to lose their lives. He had found nothing in Chile to console him for the loss of his rights in Peru. The journey through the desolate and sparsely inhabited Andean highlands had been a trying one even for men inured to hardships, and the fertile soil and delightful climate of central Chile offered little attraction to adventurers whose appetites had been whetted by the gold and silver of the Incas. Almagro was easily persuaded by his followers to return to reassert his claim to Cuzco. The trip back, through the waterless deserts of the coast, was even more difficult than that through the mountains, but his forces were nonetheless ready to fight when they reached southern Peru. After defeating Manco they occupied Cuzco, in violation of a truce arranged a short time before, and imprisoned Hernando and Gonzalo Pizarro. Gonzalo soon escaped, but Hernando was not released until his brother Francisco had agreed that Almagro should hold Cuzco until the King decided to whom it belonged. Such agreements meant nothing to men like the conquerors of Peru, and Francisco Pizarro renewed the war as soon as his brother was free. Almagro's forces were defeated in the battle of Las Salinas, near Cuzco, on April 6, 1538, and Almagro himself was captured and put to death.

A year later, Gonzalo Pizarro, who had been sent to Quito as Governor, decided to explore a region east of that city which was said to be rich in cinnamon and other precious spices. The party met with terrific obstacles in crossing the Andes and descending into the jungles at their base, and they were in desperate straits when they reached one of the larger tributaries of the Amazon. A boat that had been built to carry the sick and the baggage was finally sent ahead down the river in search of food. Pizarro entrusted the command to Francisco de Orellana, who seized the opportunity to win fame for himself by an act of treachery. Leaving the men with Gonzalo Pizarro to shift for themselves, Orellana and his companions went on down the river and then down the much larger stream which they soon reached. Among the Indians with whom they had encounters along the way there were some whose women fought as fiercely as the men, and it was from these that the Amazon received its name. With great good luck, Orellana and his companions finally reached the sea in 1541 and made their way to Spain by way of the West Indies to receive credit for their exploit. Gonzalo Pizarro, with the remnants of his party, did not get back to Quito until 1542.

By that time civil war had again broken out in Peru. Francisco Pizarro's harsh treatment of the defeated followers of Almagro had kept alive the bitter feeling between the two factions, and the "men of Chile," as they were derisively called, became desperate when they heard an untrue report that a royal official who was on his way to Peru to look into the recent occurrences had perished in a shipwreck. On June 26, 1541, a group of them killed Francisco Pizarro in his own house and forced the *cabildo* of Lima to recognize Almagro's young son, Diego, as Governor of Peru.

Vaca de Castro, the King's representative, had indeed been shipwrecked, but he reached shore and continued his journey overland. He had been authorized by the King to assume the governorship in case of Pizarro's death, and the Pizarro faction at once recognized his authority. Almagro retired to Cuzco, asserting that the city belonged to him under the Crown's grant to his father, but his forces were defeated in a bloody battle near that city on September 16, 1542, and the young leader and many of his advisers were executed as rebels.

There were further disorders when the Spanish government promulgated the "New Laws of the Indies" a few months later.[3] These laws, which restricted the *conquistadores'* exploitation of the conquered Indians, aroused a storm of protest in all the American colonies. In Mexico, the royal officials wisely suspended their operation, but in Peru, a new Viceroy, Blasco Núñez Vela, attempted to enforce them. The turbulent and greedy adventurers who had flocked to the country in the hope of sharing the spoils of conquest were little disposed to sub-

[3] See below, p. 57.

mit to anything that interfered with the gratification of their ambitions, and the Viceroy's ill-judged and tactless actions soon produced a revolt. In October, 1544, Gonzalo Pizarro occupied Lima at the head of a rebel army and forced the *audiencia*, or high court, to recognize him as Governor. The Viceroy continued the war in northern Peru, but he was killed in January, 1546, in a battle near Quito.

Before Núñez Vela's death, the King ordered a priest named Pedro de la Gasca to go to Lima as President of the *audiencia* to reassert the royal authority. La Gasca had no forces at his disposal, but at Panama he succeeded in winning over the Commander of Gonzalo Pizarro's fleet. He then sent messages promising a free pardon to those who returned to their allegiance and announcing the suspension of the most objectionable provisions of the New Laws, and when he reached Peru the rebel army gradually melted away. Gonzalo Pizarro was captured and executed in April, 1548, and La Gasca remained at the head of the government until he returned to Spain in 1550.

The Viceroy of Mexico, Antonio de Mendoza, was appointed to the same office in Peru in 1551, but he died ten months after his arrival and left the government in the hands of the *audiencia*, which was too weak to control the unruly Spanish settlers. There were further disturbances, and a rebellion under Francisco Hernández Girón in 1553–1554 was not put down until after the royal forces, led by the Archbishop and the senior judge of the *audiencia*, had suffered humiliating defeats. The disorder and bloodshed that had characterized Peru since the beginning of the Conquest was finally brought to an end by Andrés Hurtado de Mendoza, the Marquis of Cañete, who took office as Viceroy in 1556.

VALDIVIA IN CHILE

In the meantime, Chile had been conquered by Pizarro's lieutenant Pedro de Valdivia, who left Cuzco early in 1540 with a small force of Spaniards and 1,000 Indian auxiliaries. Since Valdivia planned to establish a permanent settlement, he took with him seeds, domestic animals, and agricultural implements. The journey across the deserts of the coast was long and arduous, but the party finally reached the first irrigated valley, where Copiapó now stands, and formally took possession of the country. The Indians were sullen and refused to furnish food, but they offered little resistance, and Valdivia pushed on until he reached the northern end of the great central valley, then as now the most populous and fertile part of Chile. Here, on February 12, 1541, he founded a city which he called Santiago de la Nueva Estremadura—a vain attempt to cause the colony's earlier name, associated as it was with poverty and failure, to be forgotten.

At first the colony did not prosper. A few gold and silver mines were discovered, and an effort was made to raise crops; but the natives were unwilling and intractable laborers. A few months after the colonists established themselves at Santiago the Indians revolted and burned most of the new city before they were overcome. It was clear that more men and greater resources would be needed to hold the colony and to conquer the fertile regions south of Santiago, and Valdivia determined to return to Peru to obtain recruits and supplies. Since he could not succeed in such a mission without money, he offered to permit those of his followers who had accumulated a little more gold and silver than their comrades to return to Peru with their wealth, and then, when the treasure had been placed on board his ship, he quietly slipped away without its owners. He reached Lima just in time to help La Gasca suppress Gonzalo Pizarro's rebellion and thus not only won the Viceroy's favor but gained a prestige which was helpful in obtaining recruits for his own enterprise.

Returning to Chile, Valdivia led a force southward from Santiago as far as the Bío-Bío River where he founded the city of Concepción in 1550. Here he came into contact with the savage Araucanians, a rude nation of hunters with little organized government outside of the temporary confederacies that they formed for war. These Indians had defied the Incas, and it was to be more than 300 years before they were finally conquered by the Spaniards. Valdivia at first defeated them, after severe fighting, and established several forts and towns, including that which still bears his name, in and near their territory. In 1553, however, the Indians rose in rebellion under a young chief named Lautaro, who had for a time been employed by Valdivia as a stable boy. They had learned to seek cover against firearms and to dispose their forces so that the Spanish cavalry was of little use, and when Valdivia marched against them he was captured and killed.

During the next four years, Lautaro destroyed most of the new Spanish settlements. At one time he penetrated almost to Santiago, but it was difficult for him to persuade his unorganized troops to leave their own homes and their scanty crops for a long campaign, and an epidemic of disease reduced the fighting population. Fortunately for the Spaniards, moreover, the Indians in the northern part of the central valley showed no inclination to join the Araucanians. Lautaro was finally defeated and killed, and his followers withdrew beyond the Bío-Bío, which was the frontier between the Indian and the Spanish settlements throughout the colonial period.

THE CONQUEST OF NEW GRANADA

The most important region that remained to be conquered after the occupation of Peru was the highlands of what is now Colombia, the home of the Chibchas and several other settled Indian tribes. This was one of the most inaccessible parts of South America, cut off from the Pacific by several high, heavily forested mountain ranges and from the Caribbean by hundreds of miles of swamp and jungle in the Magdalena Valley.

What is now the north coast of Venezuela and Colombia had been explored at an early date and had been much frequented by pearl fishers and hunters of Indian slaves. The deadly climate and the implacable hostility of the natives made it unattractive to colonists, but a few settlements had nevertheless been established. In Venezuela, Cubagua Island, the center of the pearl fisheries, was the scene of much activity until the oyster beds began to give out about 1535. In 1528, the Emperor Charles, who ruled over much of Germany as well as Spain, granted a large section of the Venezuelan coast to the Welsers of Augsburg, and this banking firm sent out a mixed company of German, Spanish, and Portuguese adventurers to take possession of the territory. These explored much of the hinterland, and one party, as we shall see, reached the Chibcha country in the interior. The colony nevertheless did not thrive. The German leaders' cruel treatment of the Indians aroused much criticism, and the company's grant was rescinded in 1546.

Farther west, Santa Marta was founded in 1525 and Cartagena in 1533. In 1535, Pedro Fernández de Lugo, a member of a powerful Spanish family, was made Governor of these settlements and came out to the colony with a large following. He at once began to explore the surrounding country, and in April, 1536, the colony's Chief Magistrate, Gonzalo Jiménez de Quesada, set out to investigate reports of a nation of civilized Indians far in the interior.

Quesada went overland from Santa Marta to the Magdalena River while boats carrying supplies were sent around by sea. From the point where the two groups met, he marched southward through the jungle along the river bank, suffering from heavy rains and the attacks of insects, and often from hunger. Eight months after the expedition left Santa Marta, a large part of his force had perished from starvation, disease, and the attacks of the Indians, and no sign of human habitation had been seen for a month. Quesada's companions wished to return, but he insisted upon pushing on. The boats were sent back down the river with the sick and wounded, and the leader, with 200 picked men and 60 horses, began the tedious and dangerous ascent from the river valley into the mountains, now confronted by the new enemies of cold and exposure. It was not long before the party came out upon the broad plateau of Bogotá, where cultivated fields and human habitations told them that they were near their goal.

They had reached the country of the Chibchas, and they were soon attacked by a large army under the *Zipa,* the ruler of Bogotá. Quesada won an easy victory, for the Indians were terrified by the Spanish cavalry, and then proceeded to Tunja where the other great Chibcha chief, the *Zaque*, was likewise defeated and captured. Here the invaders found a great treasure in gold and emeralds. Soon afterward the Indians ceased their resistance and begged for help in repelling an attack by the Panches, their savage neighbors whom they feared more than the Spaniards. A successful campaign against the Panches made Quesada master of the plateau region, but he was not satisfied with the treasure which he had obtained, and the *Zipa*, who had joined the Spaniards as an ally, was tortured to death in a vain effort to force him to disclose where his wealth was hidden.

In 1538, Quesada founded the city of Santa Fé de Bogotá, where he proposed to leave a part of his forces while he returned to Spain to give an account of his conquest. He was preparing for the journey when he was astonished to learn that another group of white men had appeared on the plateau. This was an expedition from the Welsers' colony in Venezuela, led by Nikolaus Federmann, which had reached the highlands by way of the upper tributaries of the Orinoco—an exploit hardly less remarkable than that of Quesada himself. At almost the same time Sebastián de Belalcázar, coming from Quito, appeared on the banks of the upper Magdalena. He had already conquered the important tribes of western Colombia, and he now laid claim to the Chibcha territory as a part of the King's grant to Pizarro. Ordinarily such an encounter between rival explorers would have resulted in bloodshed, but the three leaders reached a friendly agreement to lay their case before the King in Spain. They departed for the coast together, leaving a strong force to hold the newly conquered territory.

All of them were disappointed, for the Crown decided to place Bogotá under the jurisdiction of Alonso Luís de Lugo who had just inherited the governorship of Santa Marta from his father. The younger Lugo had some time before absconded to Spain with a large sum of money stolen from his father and from the royal treasury, but he enjoyed so much influence at court, through his marriage to a relative of the Emperor's secretary, that he was able not only to escape punishment but to deprive Quesada and his companions of the fruits of their toil. Belalcázar was somewhat consoled by an appointment as Governor of Popayán, but Quesada and Federmann got nothing. Later, however, Quesada was permitted to return to Bogotá in an honorable official position, and he died there in 1579. New Granada, the region that he had conquered, became one of the more important portions of Spain's American empire.

EARLY SETTLEMENTS IN THE
RIVER PLATE REGION

The River Plate, discovered by Juan Díaz de Solís in 1516, was further explored by Sebastian Cabot between 1527 and 1530. A country inhabited by primitive and warlike Indians had little attraction for Spanish settlers, and no real effort at permanent occupation was made until Pedro de Mendoza went out with a large expedition in 1535 to endeavor to open up a new route to Peru by way of the Paraná River. Mendoza founded a settlement which he named Nuestra Senora de Buen Ayre in 1536, and an expedition up the Paraná and Paraguay Rivers, under Juan de Ayolas, was said to have reached Peru and to have been returning laden with treasure when it was wiped out by the Indians in the wilderness. This was but one of many misfortunes that beset the new colony. Other expeditions into the interior accomplished little, and Mendoza himself fell ill and died in 1537 while on his way back to Spain. The Spaniards could not conquer the nomadic *pampa* tribes, whose raids soon compelled the abandonment of the settlement.

A part of Ayolas' expedition had stayed in what is now Paraguay, and had fared somewhat better. Partly by diplomacy and partly by force, the Spaniards were able to dominate the peaceable Guaranís, and most of them married native women. Domingo Martínez de Irala, the founder of Asunción, had taken as wives the seven daughters of one of the principal Indian chiefs. Far in the interior of the continent, the colony had little contact with Spain, and the colonists claimed the right, under a royal order sent them after Mendoza's death, to choose their own Governor in the absence of the King's appointee. Irala was the first person so chosen. The great explorer Alvar Núñez Cabeza de Vaca came out from Spain as Governor in 1542; but the colonists deposed him two years later, and Irala was re-elected, to serve until his death in 1556.

The settlement at Asunción gradually expanded. Juan de Garay founded Santa Fe in 1573 and resettled Buenos Aires in 1580, giving the colony a seaport that soon had a larger population than Asunción itself. Even Buenos Aires, however, was a relatively unimportant town until late in the colonial period because few immigrants would go to a region that had neither precious metals nor useful Indians. The one source of wealth was the great herds of wild and half-wild horses and cattle. A number of horses left behind by Mendoza's followers when they abandoned the first settlement at Buenos Aires had multiplied amazingly in the grassy *pampas*, and the horned cattle imported a little later had been hardly less prolific.

The northwestern and western parts of modern Argentina were settled not from Buenos Aires and Asunción but from Peru and Chile. The northwest, with its relatively advanced Indian population, had been a part of the Inca empire, and its chief cities, including the important town of Córdoba, were founded by expeditions from Peru. Mendoza and the nearby towns in the west, on the other hand, were settled from Chile, and long formed a part of that province.

OTHER SPANISH EXPLORERS

The reports of Cortez and Pizarro not only drew great numbers of fortune seekers to the territories that they had conquered but encouraged many others to seek for new Mexicos and Perus in regions still unexplored. In South America there were several expeditions into the lowlying, sparsely inhabited region east of the Andes. *El Dorado* was long believed to lie somewhere in the upper part of the Orinoco Valley, and many lives were lost in fruitless exploration of the inhospitable *llanos*, where heavy rains made travel difficult during several months of each year. In North America there were several equally unprofitable efforts to explore what is now the southern part of the United States.

One of the most notable was the journey of Alvar Núñez Cabeza de Vaca whose later experience in Paraguay was mentioned above. Cabeza de Vaca accompanied Cortez' former rival Pánfilo de Narváez on an expedition to Florida in 1528. Most of the party perished when they lost touch with their ships and attempted to return to Mexico in boats that they built themselves, but Cabeza de Vaca and a few other survivors made their way overland to the coast of Texas. There they were captured and held for some years as slaves by the Indians. Cabeza de Vaca and three companions finally escaped. During their captivity they had acquired a great reputation as healers and sorcerers, and great hordes of Indians followed them as they made their way westward on foot across the continent to the Pacific, a 10-months' journey. They finally reached Mexico City in 1536. A few years later, when he was appointed Governor of Paraguay, Cabeza de Vaca made almost equally notable journeys from the Brazilian coast to Asunción and from Asunción to the borders of Peru.

In Mexico, Cabeza de Vaca's story revived interest in rumors already current about great cities to the north of the country through which he had passed, and in 1540–1542 Francisco de Coronado made a long and unprofitable journey through the southwestern part of the United States as far as Kansas in search of them. About the same time, between 1539 and 1542, Pizarro's former lieutenant Hernando de Soto was exploring a great area from South Carolina to Arkansas and discovering the Mississippi River. De Soto died of fever, after three years in the wilderness. The principal result of these two expeditions, perhaps, was to show that there was nothing to attract Spanish settlers in what is now the southern part of the United States.

THE SETTLEMENT OF BRAZIL

The Treaty of Tordesillas in 1494 gave Portugal all of South America east of the line of demarcation, and her claim to the area was reinforced when Cabral visited the coast of Brazil in 1500. For some years, however, the government at Lisbon made no effort to occupy the territory which it had acquired more by accident than by design. A coast inhabited by primitive savages had little attraction for a people whose scanty resources were fully occupied in the exploitation of their new trading empire in India and the Spice Islands.

The region did offer one valuable commodity: the brazilwood from which the country soon took its name. This dyewood was in great demand in Europe, and Portuguese and other mariners frequently visited the coast to obtain it from the Indians who were taught to cut it and to barter it for tools and trinkets. By 1530 a number of Europeans were living among the natives. Some were shipwrecked or marooned sailors; others were convicts or daring adventurers who had been put ashore in the hope that those not eaten by the Indians would learn their languages and thus become useful as interpreters. There had been a small Portuguese agricultural settlement in Pernambuco as early as 1516, but this was destroyed by a French raid in 1530.

French shipmasters, half trader and half pirate, were at least as active in the brazilwood trade as were the Portuguese, and their intrusions finally compelled the government at Lisbon to send Martim Affonso de Souza to establish a permanent colony in the territory in 1530. Souza's original destination was the River Plate, which was thought or at least alleged to be east of the line of demarcation; but bad weather turned his ships back, and he finally landed near the site of modern Santos. There a Portuguese named João Ramalho, who had been shipwrecked on the coast 20 years earlier, helped him to found São Vicente, the first permanent European settlement in Brazil. Ramalho himself had been living at Piratininga in the nearby highlands, and another small group of colonists joined him there, forming a half-Portuguese, half-Indian community from which the great city of São Paulo later developed.

Meanwhile, King João III decided to attempt to colonize the whole coast. Brazil was divided into 12 "captaincies," extending in most cases 50 leagues along the shore and indefinitely into the interior, and each was granted to a "donatory" who was to settle and exploit it for his own account. These "donatories" were feudal lords, empowered to charter cities, to apportion land among the colonists, and to administer justice, though they might not inflict the death penalty on persons of

gentle blood. Their privileges, both economic and political, were hereditary. For itself the Crown reserved little more than the right to receive
the greater part of the customs duties, the royal fifth on minerals, and
the tithes, leaving the proceeds of other taxes to the proprietor.

Only a few of the grantees had the enterprise or the resources needed
for the establishment of successful colonies. Some of them did not seriously attempt to exercise their rights. Others tried but failed. Of the
six settlements which endured, three, at Victoria, Porto Seguro, and
Ilheos, barely managed to survive the internal dissensions and the constant Indian attacks of their early years. On the other hand, São Vicente,
which was granted to Martim Affonso de Souza, gradually increased in
population, and the nearby colony of Santo Amaro, founded by Martim Affonso's brother Pero Lopes, shared its modest prosperity. A
new settlement in Pernambuco was more successful, chiefly because
Duarte Coelho, the energetic proprietor, himself assumed the direction
of affairs instead of leaving them, as most of the other donatories did,
in the hands of unscrupulous or incompetent agents. Within a few years
the mills of this colony were furnishing an important part of the world's
sugar supply, and Olinda, its capital, was the chief city in Brazil. A
strong hand like Duarte Coelho's was needed in the new colonies. A
large proportion of the first inhabitants were convicts, banished to
America as a punishment, and the task of governing them would have
been difficult even if the small and widely scattered Portuguese settlements had not constantly been exposed to hostile attacks.

The chief danger came from the Indians. The tribes of Brazil were
far less civilized than those whom the Spaniards had encountered in
Mexico and the Andean countries, though somewhat more advanced
than those of the pampas. The coast and much of the interior were occupied by peoples of the Tupi stock, related to the Guaranís of Paraguay, living in small, seminomadic groups, and constantly at war with
one another. Nearly all of them were cannibals. Many of the native
chiefs allied themselves with the French, who were still active along the
coast and who furnished the savages with firearms and other weapons.
Others were glad to accept the help of the Portuguese against their
enemies and in return to assist the colonists in establishing their homes
and plantations; but these, too, frequently became hostile as the colonists encroached more and more on their lands. Furthermore, the colonists had already begun to rely on the labor of Indian slaves captured
in war or purchased from other natives, and even the friendly Indians
were frequently reduced to servitude on one pretext or another.

When it became evident that the scattered, badly administered settlements faced destruction unless the Crown could come to their aid,
the King decided to appoint a governor general who would take over
the political and military authority that the donatories had hitherto ex-

ercised. Thomé de Souza, an illegitimate scion of a noble family who had distinguished himself as a soldier and administrator in other Portuguese colonies, was consequently sent to Brazil in 1549 with 600 soldiers, 400 convicts, and a number of married couples. There were also six Jesuits, whose work was to have consequences of the utmost importance. The sparsely settled region of the Bay of Todos os Santos was purchased from the heirs of the original donatory as the site of a new capital, and the city of São Salvador, better known in English as Bahia, was founded there. Like Martim Affonso, the new Governor General was greatly aided by a Portuguese who had already been living among the Indians for many years—the famous Diogo Álvares, or Caramurú. Within a short time Bahia was a flourishing village of 100 houses, surrounded by gardens and new sugar plantations. Meanwhile, Souza had sent representatives to establish his authority and to improve the administration of justice and the collection of the royal revenues in the other captaincies.

The Jesuits, under the leadership of Manoel da Nobrega, lost no time in starting their work both among the Portuguese and among the Indians. They were shocked by the low state of religion in the settlements. Most of the colonists were a godless lot, and the clergy were few in number and in many cases were living in a way that reflected no credit on their calling. The Jesuits endeavored to improve matters, and on their recommendation a bishopric was created in Brazil in 1551. Nobrega and his followers also established several schools, not only for Portuguese children but for the increasingly numerous *mamelucos*, or persons of mixed blood. One of these institutions was founded on the plains near Piratininga by José de Anchieta, who was not yet twenty when he arrived in 1553 to begin the career which made him one of the most famous members of the order. This "College of São Paulo" soon became the center of a community that took the same name, for the settlers in the neighborhood were persuaded by the fathers to move from João Ramalho's original village to the lands around the new institution.

It was as missionaries that the Jesuits did their greatest work. Visiting the Indians of all the colonies along the coast, they learned their languages and gradually won their affection. The task of conversion grew easier as the savages began to realize that they could rely on their new friends to protect them against abuse by the other Portuguese. By a combination of persuasion and force many of them were gathered in villages where they were taught better methods of agriculture and otherwise encouraged to lead a more civilized life. The Jesuits' activities made it more difficult to obtain Indian slaves and consequently aroused much opposition among the Portuguese colonists, but they were effectively supported during these first years both by the Crown and by Thomé de Souza. Nobrega and Anchieta, in fact, soon enjoyed an authority hardly inferior to that of the Governor himself.

Duarte da Costa succeeded Thomé de Souza as Governor in 1553. He at once began to quarrel with the other authorities at Bahia and especially with the bishop, and when the latter sailed for Lisbon to defend himself at court he was shipwrecked and eaten by the Indians. This sacrilege, which horrified even the none-too-devout Brazilians, was followed by worse disasters. Encouraged by the spectacle of the settlers fighting among themselves, the natives revolted all along the coast. Even Pernambuco, which had a weaker government after Duarte Coelho's death in 1554, was seriously menaced. The Indian attacks were fomented by French and other foreign interlopers, and while they were at their height it was learned that French enterprise had taken a still more dangerous form with the establishment of a strong colony in the hitherto unoccupied bay of Rio de Janeiro.

The leader in this was Nicolas Durand de Villegagnon, a distinguished naval officer who had the support of the King of France and also of the powerful Admiral Coligny. Coligny hoped that the settlement would serve as a refuge for Huguenots, many of whom had joined the expedition, but he lost interest when Villegagnon quarreled with his Protestant followers and sent home the two ministers whom Calvin himself had appointed to accompany the expedition. The colony nevertheless maintained itself for several years, cultivating friendly relations and trade with the Indians. In 1560, Mem de Sá, the third Governor of Brazil, finally attacked it. Father Nobrega, who accompanied the expedition, raised a force of Indians friendly to the Portuguese, and the French were easily dislodged from the fort that they had built on an island at the mouth of the bay. Many of them were captured, but others took refuge among their native allies on the mainland.

Hostile Indians, meanwhile, continued their raids on the Portuguese settlements all along the coast from Bahia to São Vicente. Communication between the colonies was interrupted, and many of the weaker settlements were all but destroyed. São Paulo was attacked by a great force but was successfully defended by the converted Indians under the Jesuits' leadership. When the situation seemed desperate, Nobrega and Anchieta undertook to visit the principal hostile chiefs in an effort to make peace, and Anchieta remained for five months as a hostage among the natives, repeatedly facing what seemed almost certain death. The two Jesuits' heroism and persistence finally made possible a treaty which ended the immediate danger to the colonies. The French were driven out of the district around Rio de Janeiro in 1567, a year after the Governor's nephew, Eustacio de Sá, had founded there the city which was later to become the capital of Brazil.

Though both Indians and interlopers continued to cause trouble, the

Brazilian settlements advanced rapidly during the latter part of the sixteenth century, and particularly under the able rule of Mem de Sá. In 1549 there were only some 5,000 colonists, including both white immigrants and Negro slaves. Forty years later there were perhaps eight times that number. Bahia and Pernambuco were by far the most important of the captaincies, with many sugar plantations and a flourishing trade in cotton and brazilwood. Their capitals were little more than villages, but many of the planters who lived in them were quite wealthy. Elsewhere along the coast the Portuguese communities were less prosperous, and the life of many of the settlers was hardly less primitive than that of their Indian neighbors. The great majority, in fact, were living with Indian women, giving rise to a population of mixed blood to which a strong Negro strain was soon to be added.

CHAPTER 3

The Early Colonial Period

THE SPANISH SETTLERS AND THE INDIANS

IN THE QUARTER-CENTURY after Cortez landed in Mexico, most of the vast area that is now Spanish America was conquered or at least explored. There were European settlements throughout the highlands from Mexico to Chile. Most of them had only a few score or at most a few hundred white inhabitants, and many of these were foot-loose soldiers who were constantly moving from place to place in the hope of improving their lot; but the towns grew larger and more stable as the settlers raised families and new immigrants arrived from Spain. They were the centers from which large numbers of Indians in the surrounding country were governed and exploited.

Unlike the British colonists in North America, the Spaniards came to America as conquerors, a ruling class that expected to appropriate the wealth and exploit the labor of the natives. Most of them came from the formerly turbulent realms of the Crown of Castile, where generations of warfare had perhaps developed the qualities that made the Conquest of America possible but had also brought out other traits of character less desirable for settlers of a new country. Among these was a deep-seated aversion to manual labor, arising not so much from laziness as from a belief that a member of the upper class, to which all Spaniards in America aspired to belong, would degrade himself by working with his hands. With this prejudice, the settlers were little interested in fertile, temperate regions like the River Plate or what is now the United States, where the savage Indians were of no use as laborers. Mexico, Guatemala, Peru, and New Granada offered far greater attractions, and it was these countries that became the most important Spanish colonies.

In these territories the Indians were effectively subjugated, and most of them were persuaded before the end of the sixteenth century to accept at least the outward forms of Christianity. The native ruling classes were either destroyed or won over to the new order. There were occasional local revolts, but the Indians never showed themselves capable of any concerted resistance to Spanish rule. The native population seems to have decreased greatly during and after the Conquest, for it was particularly susceptible to some of the diseases that the Spaniards brought, and there must have been much suffering from the dislocation of the old economic and social organization. Some millions of Indians nevertheless remained, and they were an all-important factor in the colonies' economic life. The establishment of a workable relationship between them and the European settlers was one of the most difficult problems that confronted the Spanish government. The Crown was genuinely interested in preserving them and converting them, but its efforts to protect them against cruelty and exploitation at the hands of the colonists were often made less effective by its own desire to make the colonies profitable.

The problem first presented itself in the early days of the colony in Santo Domingo where the colonists came close to starvation when the Indians were no longer able or willing to provide them with food. If the settlement was to continue, the Indians had to be made to cultivate the soil and to work in the gold placer mines which provided the only important export. Columbus, after the native revolt of 1495, sought to solve the problem by exacting an annual tribute, payable either in gold or in labor, but this did little to improve the situation. Four years later, therefore, he did what Spanish kings had often done after the conquest of territory from the Moors and granted many of his followers tracts of land with the right to use the labor of the Indians who were already cultivating them. Thenceforth the Indians were exploited more and more ruthlessly. Reports of the cruelties to which they were subjected soon reached Spain.

Queen Isabella wished to protect the Indians, but she realized that the colony could not prosper without their labor. It did not seem unreasonable to ask them to work, like other people, in return for wages, and their reluctance to give up their own simple way of life seemed only an evidence of indolence. Their conversion to Christianity, in which the Queen was genuinely interested, would be impossible if the colony were abandoned, and would be difficult if they were permitted to flee from contact with the Spaniards, as many of them were doing. Governor Obando, who had at first been instructed to leave the Indians free to go where they wished, was therefore authorized in 1503 to gather them in villages near the white settlements. Each village was to be placed under the protection of a Spanish colonist who was to see that the Indians were instructed in the Christian faith and who was to be recompensed by the tribute that they were required to pay. The Indians might also be compelled to work for their protector, though as free men and for fair wages. Thus originated the *encomienda* which was to become an important institution throughout the Spanish colonies.

Among the primitive people of the Greater Antilles, the *encomienda* lent itself to shocking abuses. The *encomenderos* exploited their charges to the utmost but paid little attention to their obligations. Overwork and mistreatment, combined with the new diseases brought by the white men, practically wiped out the Indians of Santo Domingo and Cuba within a generation. As the local labor supply diminished, it was replenished by raids in other parts of the West Indies and on the mainland. The victims of these did not even enjoy the doubtful benefits of the *encomienda*, for the Crown had been persuaded to authorize the reduction to slavery of Indians guilty of rebellion or cannibalism, and this afforded a pretext for the capture of thousands of inoffensive savages in regions not yet occupied. People torn from their homes in this way died off even faster than the local Indians, and it was not long before hardly a trace of native blood remained in many of the smaller islands.

A Dominican friar named Montesinos, who went to Santo Domingo in 1510, was so shocked by what he saw there that he returned to Spain to urge the King to order reforms. This was the beginning of a long struggle at court between those who wished to help the Indians and the groups that profited by their exploitation, a struggle in which Bartolomé de las Casas was the most famous leader on the humanitarian side. Las Casas was himself an *encomendero* in Española and Cuba until the sufferings of the natives touched his conscience and inspired him to start a lifelong campaign for their relief. He went to Spain in 1515 and persuaded the government to send him back to Santo Domingo as Protector of the Indians, but he accomplished little because of the hostility of the colonists. He then tried to establish a settlement in Venezuela to demonstrate that a colony could prosper without enslaving Indians, but the hostility of the local natives made the venture a disastrous failure. For some years after this disappointment he secluded himself in a Dominican convent in Española, writing one of the notable histories of the Spanish Conquest, but he later resumed his crusade and continued for many years to work for the welfare of the Indians in Spain and various parts of the Indies.

The humanitarian group was powerful at court because there were several prominent churchmen, some of them more influential than Las Casas, who were concerned about the moral aspects of Indian slavery and the *encomienda*. On the other hand, many powerful officials, including members of the clergy, held *encomiendas* as absentee proprietors, and the colonists in America vigorously opposed any changes. Under pressure from the two groups, the Crown's policy vacillated. The laws of Burgos, in 1512, authorized *encomiendas* and forced labor but attempted to check some of the worst abuses. The abuses nevertheless continued, and in 1520 the Emperor Charles ordered that the *encomienda* be done away with. If this order had been enforced, it might have changed the whole history of Mexico and Peru. Cortez, in the early days of the Conquest, advised against the granting of *encomiendas* in Mexico, in the hope of saving the Mexicans from the fate of the Indians of the Antilles. But he changed his mind when he realized that he had no other means of rewarding his followers and persuading them to remain in the colony, and he strongly recommended that the *encomiendas* that he had granted be allowed to stand. The Emperor finally gave in, though he made another unsuccessful attempt to wipe out the system after Cortez was supplanted by the *audiencia*. When Pizarro went to Peru, he was authorized to grant *encomiendas* there. The system was thus firmly implanted in the mainland colonies immediately after the Conquest.

The Crown's attitude toward Indian slavery, as distinguished from the forced labor of persons who were theoretically free, was equally ambiguous. Slavery was, of course, an accepted institution in the case of people who were legally in bondage, but the Spanish monarchs early took the position that the Indians were free men who could not legally be enslaved. As we have seen, however, an exception was made in the case of cannibals and rebels. Settlers also bought slaves from the Indians, a method of acquisition that was known as the *rescate*. Both the taking of war prisoners, as rebels, and the *rescate* led to scandalous abuses, and the Crown from time to time tried to stop the taking of slaves on any pretext, only to reverse itself when less humane considerations prevailed.

The humanitarian group won what seemed a decisive victory when the Crown promulgated the "New Laws" of 1542 which made provision for the more effective government of the American colonies and especially for the protection of the Indians. The New Laws did not abolish the *encomiendas*, but they provided that no new ones should be granted and that those already in existence should terminate with the death of the holders. All officials, priests, and religious institutions were to give up their *encomiendas* at once—an important provision because many of those whose duty it was to protect the Indians had been personally interested in perpetuating the abuses of the system. Furthermore *encomenderos* were prohibited from exacting personal service from the Indians under their charge. All they could demand of them in the future was the fixed tribute that the Indians owed to the Crown. The enslavement of the natives was to cease altogether, and the officials were ordered to release all slaves held without a clear legal title.

There was consternation in the colonies when the provisions of the New Laws became known. The *encomiendas* were the principal form of wealth, and the holders had in most cases been granted the right to pass them on at least to their children and in many cases to subsequent generations. The former companions of Cortez and Pizarro were little disposed to give up what they had won at the cost of many perils and hardships. Feeling ran so high in Mexico that both the Viceroy Mendoza and a special representative sent to put the reforms in operation recommended that they not be enforced. In Peru, as we have seen, the colonists revolted under the leadership of Gonzalo Pizarro, and the Crown's control was not re-established for some years. As the result of these events, the government repealed some of the most important parts of the new code, including the clause prohibiting the granting of new *encomiendas* and the provisions against inheritance. On the other hand, the prohibition against the exaction of personal service by the *encomenderos* was generally enforced—though it did not save the Indians from forced labor under other guises—and many thousands of Indian slaves were released. The enslavement of war prisoners did not entirely cease as the Crown permitted the continuance of the practice in the case of persistently hostile groups like the savages on the northern frontier of New Spain and the Auracanians in Chile.

A majority of the Indians near the principal Spanish settlements continued under the *encomienda* system, at least through the sixteenth century. It was estimated that 4,000 out of 32,000 Spanish families in the colonies held *encomiendas* in 1574.[1] The proportion of Indians paying tribute to individuals gradually decreased, but the institution did not disappear until the eighteenth century. It was far less oppressive in the great mainland colonies than it had been in the Antilles because it conferred only the right to collect the fixed tribute which the Indian would otherwise have paid to the Crown. There were many places where the prohibitions against personal service and other forms of exploitation were not enforced, but in general the Indians suffered less at the hands of the *encomenderos* than from mistreatment by other persons who had less interest in their welfare.

The *encomendero* had obligations as well as privileges. According to the Laws of the Indies, "the motive and origin of the *encomiendas* was the spiritual and worldly welfare of the Indians, and their indoctrination and instruction in the articles and precepts of our holy Catholic faith, and that the *encomenderos* should have charge of them and defend their persons and properties, endeavoring to see that they receive no injury."[2] The *encomendero* had to take oath to treat his Indians well and was to be deprived of his position if he did not do so. One of his chief obligations was to maintain horses and weapons, since grants of Indians were made not only to reward the conquerors but to provide them with means to

[1] Zavala, *New Viewpoints on the Spanish Colonization of America*, p. 90.
[2] *Recopilación de leyes de los reinos de las Indias, Libro VI, Título IX, Ley I.*

defend the colony. He had to live in the province, and he could not sell or transfer his privileges. The man to whom the *encomienda* was granted might pass it on to his immediate heir, or in some cases, especially in Mexico, to the third or fourth generation; but thereafter it lapsed and might be incorporated in the Crown or given to someone else.

The tribute which the *encomenderos* received was an annual head tax on all male Indians of working age. Its amount varied from time to time and from place to place, and was theoretically based on ability to pay and on the amount customarily paid to native rulers before the Conquest. In parts of New Spain, it seems to have been a dollar or less at the beginning of the colonial period and somewhat more than four dollars at the end. In South America it was higher and reached as much as ten dollars in certain regions. It might mean a week's wages or several months'. The law forbade its being commuted into labor and required that it be paid in money or produce. Indians who were not in *encomiendas* paid their tribute to the *corregidores de indios,* who were representatives of the King.

The *encomiendas* conferred no rights to the Indians' land. The Spanish government always endeavored to protect the native communities in the possession of the land that they were tilling for their own use. It considered, however, that the tracts formerly set aside to be cultivated for the support of the tribal officials and the priesthood had been public property, which had reverted to the Crown at the time of the Conquest, and it also felt free to dispose of tracts that had not been effectively occupied or that had been abandoned. When a Spanish town was founded, each householder was given a piece of land near the settlement which he was expected to farm, though not, of course, with his own hands. In the first years of the colonies, there was a special effort to encourage the production of wheat, which was a necessary part of the Europeans' diet.

Indian labor was indispensable for wheat farming and also for the silver mines which the Spaniards started to work at any early date both in Mexico and in Peru. The need to supply workers for these enterprises was in fact probably one of the considerations that led the Crown to forbid the exaction of personal service by the *encomenderos*. It was hoped that the Indians would give their labor voluntarily, in return for fair wages, but they showed little willingness to do so. The idea of wages was foreign to their experience, and money meant little to them because they could satisfy their simple wants by cultivating their own land.

The Spanish government consequently authorized *repartimientos,*[3] or

---

[3] *Repartimiento* means a "distribution." There has been much confusion in the use of this term because it was also used to describe the distribution of Indians among the first settlers in *encomiendas* and was later used in connection with forced sales of goods to the Indians by the *corregidores*.

drafts of labor, in places where workers were needed to cultivate the fields, to raise cattle, or to operate mines of gold, silver, mercury, or emeralds. Forced labor by the Indians was permitted in these occupations because the work was necessary for the maintenance of the colonies. It was not to be used in other undertakings of a private character. *Repartimientos* were also used for public works, like the building of roads or towns or churches, and for such necessary purposes as service in inns or with wagon and mule trains. Frequently a certain proportion of the Indians in each town were required to present themselves in the market place each Monday morning to be hired for the coming week by nearby Spanish landowners and other employers. Wages and conditions of work were regulated by the authorities, and an effort was made to see that all Indians except those in privileged positions took their turn. In Peru, the system of *repartimientos* was called the *mita*, a Quechua word applied to a similar institution used by the Incas. In Mexico it was known as the *cuatequil*.

The law forbade the use of forced labor in the cultivation of coca, grapes, or olives. In certain other occupations, like the grinding of sugar cane, the preparation of indigo, and the extraction of pearls, Indians could not be employed even of their free will. The purpose of these restrictions was to protect the Indians from work that was considered too heavy for them and to prevent the sending of people from the highlands into the hot country where they would soon die. In some cases, as in the attempt to prohibit Indian labor in textile factories, there was likewise a desire to prevent competition with producers in Spain. The restrictions were not always enforced, because Negro slaves, the only alternative source of labor, were scarce and expensive. Late in the eighteenth century, for example, Indians were still being compelled to work under shocking conditions in textile factories in Peru.

The work which bore most cruelly upon the Indians, and which, especially in South America, gave the *mita* a fearsome reputation, was that in the mines. Not only was this harder and more unhealthful, but it involved taking a large number of Indians far from their homes and forcing them to live under miserable conditions for months at a time. This caused an appalling loss of life, especially in Upper Peru, where many of the mines were in desolate and sparsely populated regions. Where the production of silver and gold was involved, the Crown's avarice seemed stronger than its desire to protect the Indians. It did, however, adopt regulations intended to prevent the complete destruction of the labor supply for the mines. In Peru, for example, only one-seventh of the Indians in a given area might be drafted for mining at one time, and in Mexico only one twenty-fifth. Unfortunately, such limitations were hard to enforce when labor was needed.

EFFORTS TO PROTECT THE INDIANS

Though the Spanish government refused to permit what was repeatedly referred to as the Indians' "natural indolence" to stand in the way of its exploitation of the colonies, it made a real effort to promote their welfare and to protect them against the greed of the colonists and of its own officials. The Indians continued to live in separate communities, speaking their own languages and retaining much of their ancient culture. In local matters they were governed by native officials who were in many cases their hereditary *caciques* or chiefs. These were a privileged class who represented the community in dealings with the Spaniards and collected the tribute due to the *encomendero* or the King. The Indians were exempted from most of the taxes paid by other classes in the community. The Crown attempted to make sure that each village had enough land for its support, and this was often administered by the local community much as it had been in Mexico and Peru before the Conquest. The royal government was particularly interested in the spiritual welfare of the natives, and priests were maintained in each village.

Legally, the Indians had the right to move freely from place to place, and even to leave villages that had been granted in *encomiendas,* provided they paid their share of the tribute up to the time of their departure and did not try to evade payment of tribute or the fulfilment of their religious duties in their new homes.[4] In practice, this right was restricted in many ways, and especially by the Crown's policy of compelling those who lived in scattered groups to come together to found new towns where it would be easier to collect the tribute and to provide for religious instruction. The law provided that these *congregaciones* should be brought about by persuasion rather than force and that every effort should be made to assure the prosperity of the new settlements. Force was nevertheless used, and the arbitrary movement of people from one place to another caused great hardship.

The viceroys and other officials were commanded to treat the Indians with special favor and to punish offenses against them more severely than if they had been committed against Spaniards. A special court was created in Mexico for their protection, and elsewhere the *audiencias* were required to give special consideration to cases where Indians were involved. To prevent their being unfairly exploited, the law provided that they could make contracts and sell property only under judicial supervision. No Spaniard, Negro, or mulatto could live in their villages, and no *encomendero* might stay among his Indians more than one night or maintain workshops or farms on their lands.

[4] See Silvio Zavala, *La Libertad de Movimiento de los Indios de la Nueva España,* Mexico, 1948.

A whole series of laws prohibited specific abuses. Neither *encomen-deros* nor officials might compel Indians to work for them as household servants or interfere with them in the selling of their produce. Since Indians under the legal age paid tribute if they were the heads of families, it was found necessary to legislate against the *encomenderos'* practice of compelling children to marry. Indians were not to be kept away from their homes and shut up in workshops, even for debt or crime. Travelers were not to carry off native women or take food and other articles by force. The use of men as carriers was an especially troublesome question. This had been almost the only means of transport before the Conquest, and it was the only means the Spaniards had before pack animals were introduced and roads were built for them; but it was the occasion of much cruelty and abuse. Laws forbidding the practice could not be enforced, and it was finally necessary for the Crown to content itself with limiting loads and the length of journeys and with restricting the classes of people by whom carriers might be used.

The mere enumeration of the prohibitions against mistreatment of the natives and, still more, the frequent official admissions that these prohibitions were not effective indicate that the treatment the Indians received was often different from that which the Crown desired. As a matter of fact, no other class suffered so much from the corruptness and irresponsible selfishness which characterized the whole Spanish regime. For every case where they obtained redress for injuries or relief from oppression, there were probably many others where they were helpless against the officials and landowners who joined forces to exploit them. Their own *caciques* and other village officials seem to have been among their worst oppressors, and they suffered even more at the hands of the *corregidores de indios*, the royal officials who had charge of Indians not granted to settlers in *encomiendas*. They also contributed heavily to the support of the Church, paying fees for baptisms, marriages, and burials, as well as numerous "voluntary" offerings. The provisions of the Laws of the Indies, as well as the reports of travelers, indicate that the parish priests sometimes joined with other members of the ruling class in exploiting their charges. Nevertheless, the clergy were often the Indians' most active advocates and protectors. Without the influence of the Church, the natives' lot would have been far worse.

THE WHITE SETTLERS

Living apart from the Indians was the Spanish-speaking community, made up of the white upper class, the *mestizos* or people of mixed Spanish and Indian descent, and the Negro slaves. The white upper class was increased by new immigrants who arrived from Spain at the rate of a few thousand each year throughout the colonial period. Theoretically, emigration to America was carefully controlled. Unlike other powers, Spain did not use her overseas possessions as a dumping place for persons who were not wanted at home; permits to go to America were granted only to those who were considered desirable as settlers. Since nothing could be permitted to endanger the colonists' loyalty or the purity of their religious beliefs, all foreigners were legally excluded, as were persons of doubtful orthodoxy, such as the sons and grandsons of Spanish Jews and Moors who had been compelled to accept Christianity as an alternative to exile or death. The laws, it is true, were not always enforced, and many foreigners and "new Christians" found their way first and last to Spanish America. The Portuguese were the most numerous, especially between 1580 and 1640 when Spain and Portugal were united under one crown. Nevertheless, the influence of the non-Spanish element was always relatively small.

Though most of the Spanish settlers got their incomes from farms or mines, few of them lived on their estates. The wars with the Moors, which forced people to gather inside walls for mutual protection, had made the Castilians a race of city dwellers, and in the colonies there was the same need for keeping together for defense against possible Indian revolts. Usually, although there were exceptions like Cuzco and Mexico City, the Spaniards built new towns, apart from those of the Indians. These were laid out on one uniform plan, with streets running at right angles and blocks of equal size, insofar as possible. Most of them presented much the same external appearance. In the center was the plaza, or open park, about which were grouped the church, the *cabildo* or town hall, and the houses of the principal inhabitants. Less wealthy white families lived in the adjoining streets, the *mestizos*, and the poorer people generally, in the outskirts. In a town of any size there were other churches in the various wards, as well as a number of monasteries and convents. The house of a wealthy man often covered a large area. Because of earthquakes, such houses usually had only one or at most two stories, but there were many rooms, grouped about several courtyards and accommodating not only the family with its numerous servants and hangers-on but the horses and other domestic animals. Poorer families lived in less comfort, often crowded into one or two windowless, dirt-floored rooms, though even they usually had a small *patio* which gave access to light and air.

The white population early divided into two distinct groups: the *criollos*, or creoles, who had been born in America, and the *peninsulares*, or immigrants from Spain. Between these groups there grew up a feeling of hostility which was not much mitigated by the fact that the children of peninsular Spaniards, if they were born in the colonies, became creoles themselves. The creoles were, of course, far more numerous. Some of them were *encomenderos* or merchants or miners; but the majority had farms or cattle ranches. These estates were often very large, and they were frequently entailed to assure the succession of the oldest son in each generation. Some of the wealthier landowners and miners had titles of nobility, which were sold by the Crown as a means of raising money.

Most of the higher officials in the government and the Church, and most of the great merchants, were *peninsulares*. The ranks of the Spanish-born were constantly augmented by adventurers who came to America to seek their fortunes. In the first part of the colonial period, most of the bakers, carpenters, shoemakers, and other artisans seem to have been Spaniards, and the members of these trades were organized into guilds like those in Europe. This situation soon changed, apparently because the members of the dominant race disliked even skilled labor in a community where work was the function of Indians and slaves. The skilled trades thus fell more and more into the hands of *mestizos* and mulattoes.

MESTIZOS AND MULATTOES

Below the whites in the social scale were the people of mixed race who were eventually to be the most numerous group of all. Since few women had come to America with the earlier expeditions, intermarriage with the Indians was frequent and was encouraged by the authorities. Less regular unions were still more common. Some of the *mestizos*, as people of part-white, part-Indian blood were called, inherited property and the privilege of citizenship in the towns from their white fathers and became members of the upper class. Others simply remained with their mothers in the Indian communities. The majority formed a group apart, not accepted as equals by the Spaniards but feeling themselves superior to the Indians. The mulattoes, who began to appear with the introduction of Negro slaves, and the part-African, part-Indian *zambos* had a still lower social position.

NEGRO SLAVES

From the beginning, many of the colonists had Negro slaves. These were brought in chiefly as laborers in regions where the supply of Indians was inadequate or in industries where Indians could not profitably be employed. Many were also used as household servants or workmen in the larger cities. They were better workers than the Indians, though more expensive. Since they were legally slaves, even the humanitarians saw little objection to employing them and had in fact advocated their use as a means of saving the Indians. Contracts for supplying them to the American settlements were granted from time to time, usually to Portuguese or other foreigners, and it was not long before they formed a large part of the population of the West Indian Islands, the Caribbean coast of Central and South America, and a few other districts where sugar and other plantation crops were raised.

In contrast with the callous contempt that marked the creoles' attitude toward the Indians, the treatment of the Negroes was relatively humane. They were regarded as human beings and as Christians rather than as mere chattels, and the Church took an active interest in their spiritual welfare, which helped to make their situation easier. One of the most attractive figures in the colonies' history is San Pedro Claver, a Jesuit father who befriended and baptized many thousands of newly arrived Africans at Cartagena in the seventeenth century. Both the Church and the law encouraged manumission, so that there were soon a considerable number of freedmen. Slavery was of course at best a cruel and degrading institution, but it seems to have been less cruel in the Spanish colonies than in those of France and England, partly because there were relatively fewer Negroes and consequently less fear of slave revolts.

THE GOVERNMENT IN THE SPANISH COLONIES

Columbus' first voyage was financed by Queen Isabella, but nearly all of the subsequent expeditions in the period of the Conquest were private ventures, financed by the leaders and their friends or by moneylenders. Many of the members of the expeditions took part in them at their own expense. In most cases—Cortez was a notable exception—the Crown made formal contracts with the leaders, promising them valuable economic privileges and the right to govern any territory that they might occupy. It was easy to make promises of this kind when the lands to which they applied were unknown and unconquered, but it was not easy to honor them when these lands turned out to be an extensive and valuable possession, with millions of aboriginal inhabitants for whose welfare the Crown felt a responsibility. The reckless audacity and ruthlessness that made the Conquest possible were hardly qualities to recommend the *conquistadores* to the Crown when it faced the problem of setting up orderly and efficient governments in the American colonies.

Many of the great *conquistadores* were murdered or killed in battle before the problem arose. The others, in almost every case, were deprived of many of the privileges and especially of the governmental authority that they had hoped to enjoy. Columbus was the first example. Columbus' hereditary rights in the Indies were indeed partly recognized when his son Diego was made Governor of Santo Domingo in 1508, but Diego's authority was restricted in 1511 when an *audiencia*, or court of appeals, was set up in the islands. Another *audiencia*, as we have seen, supplanted Cortez in the government of Mexico in 1527, but it proved so corrupt and inefficient that the Crown decided to place a viceroy at the head of the colonial administration, while continuing the *audiencia* as a check on the viceroy's authority. A second viceroyalty was created in Peru in 1542, but there the civil wars prevented the establishment of orderly government until some years later.

From the beginning, the settlers in America had little or no voice in the colonial government. This was not surprising at a time when the royal authority was so great in Spain itself. The *cortes*, or parliaments, of the Spanish kingdoms had formerly been important institutions, but in the fifteenth century they lost much of their independence because the selection of the *procuradores* or representatives fell more and more under the control of the Crown. In the sixteenth century they ceased to have any real power. The cities likewise had been deprived of much of the autonomy that they once enjoyed, and this was especially true of Castile where Isabella's centralizing policy had been welcomed after the disorder and misgovernment prevalent before her accession. The Catholic Queen and her successors ruled that kingdom practically as absolute monarchs, though the consent of the *cortes* was theoretically required for levying new taxes and the forms of municipal self-government were partially observed. It is important to note that the Indies were regarded as belonging to Castile rather than to Aragon where the people had retained more of their ancient liberties.

The people of the colonies could not claim even such traditional political privileges as might still exist in Castile, for the Indies were the property not of the nation but of the Crown. No one could go there without the royal permission, and no one could acquire rights there except by grant from the king. The *conquistadores* had been partners of the king in what were essentially business enterprises, and they and their successors in the government were responsible only to the king. Sometimes, it is true, they were unable to assert their authority, and the settlers temporarily took matters in their own hands; but such irregular proceedings never resulted in the colonists' obtaining any recognized right of self-government.

The governmental institutions that took form in the first years after the Conquest continued with very little change for 200 years. From the beginning, the king ruled the Indies through an administrative system quite separate from that of Spain. Juan Rodríguez de Fonseca, a priest who later became Bishop of Burgos, was appointed to make arrangements for Columbus' second voyage in 1493. Except for brief intervals, he continued to handle American affairs at court until his death in 1524. In that year the organization that he built up was converted into the Council of the Indies. This body thenceforth had full authority, under the king, in all matters relating to the overseas possessions. It drew up laws and gave advice on appointments and questions of major policy. As the organ through which the royal commands were transmitted to the colonies it exercised a close and continuous supervision over the conduct of all officials there, both civil and ecclesiastical. It acted as a court of appeals in cases decided by the colonial judges and had general supervision over the *Casa de Contratación* which controlled commerce with the Indies. Similar in its organization and functions to the great councils through which the king governed Spain itself, it had in the sixteenth century a president, a chancellor, eight councilors, and a number of secretaries and other officials. Decisions were taken by vote of the councilors, among whom some at least were usually qualified for their work by previous experience in important official posts in America. The Council was a hard-working body, in session several hours each day, but it was not free from the corruption and favoritism that characterized other branches of the Spanish administration.

In the colonies the viceroys were the most important officials. They were usually great nobles, whose loyalty to the Crown could be trusted, and in the sixteenth century many of them were men of outstanding ability. Under the supervision of the Council of the Indies it was their duty to enforce the laws and to see that the revenues were collected, that justice was properly administered, and that the Christian faith was preached among the Indians. As captains general, they had command of the military forces. Since they were expected to maintain a court which by its pomp and ceremony would keep alive among the colonists a sense of the greatness of the Spanish monarch, they were paid princely salaries.

The viceroy, as representative of the king, had great prestige and theoretically the power to do everything that the king himself could do if he were present in the colonies. In practice, however, his authority was diminished by the fact that his subordinates also held their appointments from the king and were permitted to correspond directly with the Council of the Indies. Furthermore, his freedom of action was limited by a great mass of detailed instructions and regulations. The king and the Council of the Indies attempted to dictate policy even in matters of minor importance, especially where any expenditure of funds was involved. They also endeavored to make sure that the viceroy did not become too friendly with the people of the community where he served and that he did not use his position to benefit himself and his family. He was not permitted to invite residents of the colony to dine at his table, and he might not bring his married sons and daughters to America with him, or himself engage in any commercial enterprise. These provisions, and many others of similar character, suggest that the temptations against which they were aimed were not always resisted.

Second in importance only to the viceroys were the *audiencias*, which continued to exist at Mexico and Lima and were later established at several other capitals. The *audiencias* were primarily courts of justice, but they also had political duties. At Mexico and Lima they acted as advisory councils to the viceroy and had the very important right to hear the complaints of persons who considered themselves injured by that official's acts and to inform the king in cases where they considered that the viceroy had exceeded his authority. At these two capitals they usually assumed control of the government in the viceroy's absence. In other provinces they had a similar relationship to the captain general or governor. At Quito, and at Charcas in Upper Peru (which is now Bolivia), it was the president of the *audiencia* who administered political and even military affairs. As courts, the *audiencias* decided civil and criminal cases though the parties might appeal to the Council of the Indies in suits where large sums were involved. The individual *oidores*, or judges, were also sent out regularly on inspection trips to watch over the conduct of lesser officials. The viceroys and captains general were the presidents of the *audiencias* in their capitals, but they had no authority to interfere with certain phases of the work of the *audiencias*. The viceroy, for example, did not have a vote in legal cases unless he were himself trained in the law.

The captains general were officials who exercised practically the same functions as the viceroys in less important areas, and especially in regions where the danger of foreign aggression or Indian depredations made the problem of defense important. These officers were nominally subordinate to the viceroys, but in practice they received their instructions directly from Spain because the great distances from one colonial capital to another and the obstacles to intercommunication made decentralization inevitable.

The principal administrative units might thus be under the direct control of a viceroy or a captain general or an *audiencia*, the president of the *audiencia* being in this last case the nominal head of the government. The boundaries and the status of each unit varied from time to time. Until the eighteenth century, when new viceroyalties were set up at Bogotá and Buenos Aires, the viceroy of Peru usually had at least nominal jurisdiction over all of Spanish South America except Venezuela, and the viceroy of New Spain over Mexico, Central America, and Venezuela.

The collection of revenues and the custody of funds were entrusted to the *oficiales reales*, the "royal officials," who were in some respects independent of the viceroys and directly responsible to the king. Three of these—a factor, an accountant, and a treasurer—were stationed in each important town. The actual collection of taxes was usually farmed out to contractors, but the royal officials received the proceeds, paid salaries and other expenses authorized by law, and remitted any balance to their superiors for shipment to Spain. Funds in their possession were kept in a chest which had three separate locks and could thus be opened only when all of the officials were present. Except in an emergency, even the viceroy could not draw money from the treasury without an order from the king, and it was the duty of the *oficiales reales* to prevent or report unauthorized disbursements. The home government's avid interest in its income from the colonies made the financial administration very important. Among the chief sources of revenue were the Crown's royalty on gold and silver, which was usually a fifth of the amount produced, and the tribute, or head tax, collected from the Indians. There was also the much disliked *alcabala*, or tax on sales, which at times reached 6 per cent of the value of merchandise that had already paid a still higher tax before exportation from Spain. Customs duties and other charges on commerce were also collected.

For purposes of local government, the colonies were divided into smaller districts, usually called provinces, where the representative of the Crown might be a governor, or a *corregidor*, or an *alcalde mayor*. These local officials dealt with financial, military, and ecclesiastical matters and also acted as judges, for there was no clear division between administrative and judicial functions. Their decisions were usually subject to review by the *audiencia* or the viceroy.

In practice, though the law did not so provide, the higher offices under the Crown were nearly always filled by peninsular Spaniards. Three creole nobles were viceroys of Mexico between 1696 and 1741, but such exceptions to the general rule were rare. Natives of the colonies occasionally served as governors or *corregidores*, but never in their home districts. The officials were thus a class apart, forbidden to form ties that might create any bond of sympathy with the local community. This had unfortunate results. On the one hand it did much to intensify the antagonism between *peninsulares* and creoles. On the other, the creoles' lack of administrative experience had disastrous effects when they attempted to set up independent national governments.

THE CITY GOVERNMENTS

City government was the only branch of the administration in which the colonists themselves customarily participated. The forms and traditions of municipal autonomy had survived in Spain even though the reality had disappeared; and when the *conquistadores* came to America, city governments based on these forms and traditions were the first political institutions they set up. The principal officers of the *ayuntamiento*, or *cabildo*, as the municipal corporation was called, were the council of *regidores* and one or more *alcaldes*, or magistrates, elected by this council. The first *regidores* were usually appointed by the leader who founded the city, or they were sometimes elected by the *vecinos*, or householders. Their successors were in most cases named by the royal governor or by the Crown, which frequently gave or sold life appointments or even hereditary seats in the councils of the larger cities. Toward the end of the sixteenth century, in fact, it became customary to sell the positions for the benefit of the royal treasury, and more and more of them became hereditary in certain families. In some places, especially in poorer towns where the municipal offices seemed less attractive, the outgoing council elected some or all of its successors, acting to a greater or less extent under the influence of the royal governor.

It should be noted, however, that the members of the *ayuntamientos* were usually persons born in the colonies or at least immigrants from Spain who had made their homes there. The city government thus represented local interests and was in some measure responsive to local sentiment. The *ayuntamiento* was nominally responsible for nearly all governmental activities of a purely local nature, such as the enforcement of police and sanitary regulations, the cleaning and repairing of the streets, and the maintenance of markets. It regulated wages and the prices of foodstuffs and other necessities and took action to procure adequate supplies when a scarcity threatened. It often had to administer a considerable amount of property, for besides the areas used in common by the inhabitants for pasture and cutting firewood, it was customary for a newly founded city to be given a tract of land which was rented to private individuals as a means of increasing the municipal revenue. Its jurisdiction extended not only to the city proper but to all of the territory to the borders of the next municipality—a natural arrangement when the landowners lived for the most part in the towns rather than upon their estates. In some cases the area was a large one. Buenos Aires, to take an extreme example, at one time reached 300 miles westward toward Córdoba, 170 miles northward toward Santa Fe, an indefinite distance southward into the wild Indian territory, and eastward across the River Plate into what is now Uruguay.[5] The municipality was thus a subdivision of a province rather than a city government in the modern sense.

The power actually exercised by the city officials varied. In the larger capitals they were treated with great respect, and membership in the *ayuntamiento* was a distinction for which wealthy citizens were willing to pay a high price; but their authority was completely overshadowed by that of the viceroy or the captain general. In outlying provinces, as in Buenos Aires before the establishment of a viceroyalty, they had more real autonomy. Even in such places, however, they could not effectively resist the centralizing policy of the Crown, though they were constantly involved in conflicts with other civil and ecclesiastical officials over questions of authority and prerogatives. The control of the sale of offices in most of the *ayuntamientos* by the royal treasury officials was enough in itself to assure their subservience.

[5] Kirkpatrick, *The Argentine Republic*, p. 19.

VISITAS AND RESIDENCIAS

The Spanish government sought to control the conduct of its representatives in America through two practices called the *visita* and the *residencia*. *Visitas* were inspections carried out by an official sent from Spain, if the actions of a viceroy or of other high officials were to be investigated, or by an *oidor* or another person designated by the viceroy where local officials were involved. They were undertaken at irregular intervals, usually in response to especially serious complaints, and were of doubtful value as a means of preventing misconduct. The *residencia* was a formal, public investigation to which every official, from the viceroy down, had to submit after he relinquished his authority and before he left the country. It was undertaken by the official's successor or by a judge appointed for the purpose. All who had complaints were invited to submit them, and the offending official might be compelled to make reparation for any injustices proved against him. The *residencia* often produced much scandal, and the prospect of it perhaps prevented some abuses, but the impartiality of such an investigation was always open to question, especially in the case of persons so influential at court as most of the viceroys. The principal effect of the system, with the viceroy and with other functionaries, was to discourage individual initiative in cases where action might have been desirable. An official who did only what his specific instructions authorized could not be found guilty of exceeding his power or making mistakes of judgment.

THE CHURCH

The civil and military administration was one of the two branches of the governmental system through which Spain ruled her American colonies. The other, no less important, was the hierarchy of the Catholic Church which was controlled by the Crown to an extent unusual in other parts of the world. In a bull of 1493 the Pope gave Ferdinand and Isabella the same right to make ecclesiastical appointments in the Indies which he had earlier conferred on Prince Henry the Navigator in Africa, and this right was confirmed and extended in later grants. The Catholic Monarchs were likewise given permission to receive all tithes in the colonies in return for their promise to support the Church there. Taken together, these and other privileges obtained from the Holy See constituted the *patronato*, the right of patronage, which was one of the Spanish kings' most valued and jealously guarded prerogatives.

All members of the clergy were thus dependent upon and responsible to the Crown. Bishops and other high ecclesiastical officials were named directly by the king, whereas less important appointments, such as those of parish priests and curates, were made by the viceroy or his subordinates acting as vice-patrons, though usually from among candidates presented by the bishops after an examination conducted by the church authorities. No priest could go to America without a license from the Council of the Indies, and none could return without express permission from the Crown or the viceroy. The movements of the clergy in the colonies were directed by the authorities, and an order from the king was necessary to build a church or a convent or to establish a mission among the Indians. The Crown's collection of the tithes gave it control of the Church's most important revenue. Under such conditions, the Church became an integral part of the government. Many clerics, in fact, held high positions in the civil administration itself, and in Mexico the archbishop frequently served for a short time as viceroy when the office accidentally became vacant.

Among the white colonists, the overwhelming majority accepted without question the spiritual authority of the Church and the control that it exercised in many matters of conduct and personal relations which are not now considered purely spiritual. The confessional alone gave the priesthood an immense power, and a threat of excommunication inspired fear in the most influential officials. The cemeteries were under Church control, as were the parish registers which were the official record of births, marriages, and deaths. Offenses against religion could be punished by fine or imprisonment and often by more severe penalties. The Church's influence was increased by the very real services that it rendered the community. It provided nearly all the schools, maintained the hospitals and asylums, and took care of the poor. Persons who wished to give or bequeath money for charity invariably entrusted it to a priest or to one of the religious orders.

The Indians near the larger Spanish settlements were at least outwardly converted at the time of the Conquest, though we may suspect that it was some time before they grasped the meaning of the mass baptism to which they had been subjected. To see that they were instructed in the faith was an important duty of the viceroys, and ostensibly the main purpose of the *encomienda* system; and the law required that all Indians, Negroes, and mulattoes in each community should be assembled daily for religious instruction. Even where the old pagan worship secretly survived, the new gods, whom the Conquest had proved so much more powerful, were accepted also. The Indians were the more inclined to accord respect and obedience to the Church because they found it their most effective protector. The Church thus acquired an immense authority over the natives which was reinforced by the support of the government. It was the principal channel through which the Indians absorbed a little of the civilization of the conquering race. The influence of the priests and friars probably did more than any other factor to keep the masses of the Indian population submissive to the Spanish regime.

Although all of its activities were controlled and directed by the Crown, the Church in the colonies was not a unified, centralized organization. The numerous religious orders worked independently of each other and of the bishops, and there was much rivalry between different groups. A long conflict occurred because the friars, after converting the Indians, clung to their positions as parish priests in the native communities despite the efforts of the secular clergy to displace them. There were also jealousies and quarrels between the various religious orders, several of which usually had establishments in each important town.

The various branches of the Church amassed a great amount of wealth. The tithes, a 10 per cent tax on products of the soil, were collected by the Crown, but the greater part of the proceeds was turned over to the ecclesiastical authorities. There were also other fruitful sources of revenue. Especially important were pious gifts and bequests, for few wealthy persons died without seeking to assure the welfare of their souls by leaving something to the Church. Since many of the bequests were in the form of liens on undivided landed estates, and since the monasteries invested a large part of their other funds in mortgages, religious foundations gradually acquired an interest in a large proportion of the agricultural properties and city real estate and came to own great amounts of land themselves. The Crown made repeated efforts to check this process, but with little result. After independence, the Church's wealth became an explosive political issue and a source of danger to the Church itself in several of the Latin American republics.

This wealth was very unevenly divided. Some charitable foundations like hospitals and orphanages were heavily endowed, and some of the monasteries had large investments and much land which they farmed themselves or rented to other persons. The incomes of several of the bishops and other important church officials were likewise very great, occasionally exceeding those of the viceroys or of any but the wealthiest members of the creole aristocracy. The parish priests, on the other hand, often had little income beyond the fees and contributions paid by the poverty-stricken Indians and *mestizos* of the rural villages.

One of the most powerful branches of the Church was the Inquisition, which had tribunals at Mexico and Lima after 1569 and at Cartagena, in New Granada, after 1610. The Inquisition attempted to punish any departure from orthodoxy, not only in religion but also in the field of political ideas. Fortunately, it was not given jurisdiction over the Indians, who were regarded as children in the faith and whose frequent backslidings into heathen practices were punished by the ordinary clergy. In general, the Inquisition in the colonies was a less horrifying institution than in Spain. Serious offenses against religion were not common among the white and *mestizo* colonists because immigration was carefully sifted to prevent spiritual contamination and contact with the outside world was slight. It is said that only a hundred heretics were burned at the stake in Mexico and Peru during the whole colonial period,[6] and many of these were captured foreign pirates. The Inquisition nevertheless found much to do with minor heresies and sacrileges and accumulated much wealth. It was especially dreaded because of the secrecy surrounding its procedure. The fines that it collected belonged legally to the king, but few royal officials had the courage to ask an accounting of an organization which could imprison and ruin persons of any rank without answering to any other authority for its conduct, and whose officials and employees were immune from prosecution except in their own courts.

The power and wealth of the Church inevitably attracted many persons who were unworthy to be priests. We find severe criticism of the conduct of some of the clergy both in travelers' accounts and in the official reports of the viceroys. It was charged that parish priests frequently exploited or mistreated the Indians and that their moral conduct left much to be desired. The ecclesiastical courts were accused of lenience and partiality in dealing with clerical offenders. There were also unedifying quarrels within the Church or between church and civil officials, and these sometimes led to noisy scandals and even riots.

On the other hand, the Church rendered great services to the colonial community through its schools and charitable work and through its vast influence for social stability. It gave the colonies their men of letters and many of their ablest government officials. Its financial resources, and the enterprise and organizing ability of some of the religious orders, especially in their missions among the Indians, were important factors in the colonies' economic development. It was the great prestige and influence of the Church, rather than its shortcomings, that made its position a major political issue after independence.

ECONOMIC LIFE:
AGRICULTURE, STOCK RAISING, AND MINING

Most of the people of the colonies were farmers. The Indians, when they were not working for the white settlers, grew corn and other native products on their own lands, for themselves or for the payment of their tribute. Many of the white settlers had *haciendas,* where they produced food and draft animals for sale in the cities and mining camps, or great, carelessly managed cattle ranches which furnished hides and tallow for export as well as meat for local consumption. In warmer regions, like the West Indies and the lower valleys of the mainland, there were plantations of sugar, indigo, cacao, and other tropical products, and these commodities were exported in considerable quantities, though they never achieved so much importance as in the British and French West Indies.

[6] Bourne, *Spain in America,* p. 313.

The planters were handicapped both by the lack of adequate labor, for the Indians were of little use in the hot country and Negro slaves were scarce and expensive, and by the commercial system, which failed to provide adequate transport for perishable tropical products.

The Spanish government's interest in the economy of the colonies centered chiefly in their production of silver and gold. Most economists of the time believed that the acquisition of the precious metals for their own sake was the principal benefit that a nation could obtain from trade. The *conquistadores* eagerly sought for mines and placer deposits in each country that they invaded, and they worked thousands of Indians to death in the West Indies to obtain rather small quantities of treasure. On the mainland they had better luck. Rich deposits of silver were found in Mexico within a few years after the Conquest, and the fabulously profitable mines of Potosí, in the viceroyalty of Peru, were discovered about 1545. The city of Potosí, on the bleak plateau of what is now Bolivia, was for a period the largest in the New World, with all the turbulence and reckless extravagance characteristic of the center of a mining boom. Other provinces also produced much mineral wealth, though none of them compared in this respect with Upper Peru and Mexico. The output of silver was far more important than the output of gold.

By law, all mineral deposits belonged to the Crown, even though the surface of the land had been granted to another owner. The government usually permitted the discoverer or some other private individual to operate the mines, and reserved for itself a royalty which varied from one-tenth to one-fifth of the gross product. It assured the collection of the royalty by making the supply of quicksilver a government monopoly. The amount that the miners paid was based on their consumption of this metal, which was used in extracting silver and gold from the ore, rather than on the production that they themselves reported.[7] The great Huancavelica mine in Peru provided quicksilver for that viceroyalty, while Mexico was usually supplied from Spain.

COLONIAL TRADE:
THE *CASA DE CONTRATACIÓN*

Partly because it wished to maintain a close control over the shipment of precious metals from the colonies, the government endeavored to confine the colonies' trade to a few narrow channels. In Spain, the regulation of all phases of commercial intercourse with the Indies was entrusted to the *Casa de Contratación* at Seville. This institution was set up in 1503 when the needs of the little settlements in Española were doubtless best served by one central bureau; and its power was perpetuated by the conservatism that always characterized Spanish policy, combined with

[7] Whitaker, *The Huancavelica Mercury Mine*, p. 6.

the influence of the powerful vested interests that grew up around it. It continued for almost three centuries to examine cargo going to or coming from America and to arrange for the sailing of the fleets.[8]

> Nothing might be sent to the Indies without the consent of the Casa, nothing might be brought back and landed, either on the account of merchants or of the king himself, without its authorization. Bullion from the colonies consigned to Spanish merchants belonged to them only when the Casa permitted its release. It controlled and regulated the character of ships, crews, and passengers. In short, it saw to the execution of all the laws and ordinances relating to trade and navigation with America.

Sitting as a court, the *Casa* had jurisdiction over crimes committed on the voyages and in certain classes of civil suits arising in connection with American trade. It also conducted a school of navigation and devoted much attention to map-making and the improvement of nautical instruments, under the general direction of the pilot major. The first occupant of this post was Amerigo Vespucci, and the second, Juan Díaz de Solís, the discoverer of the River Plate.

At first, all ships trading with the Indies had to clear from and return to Seville, but this caused much inconvenience because the city was many miles from the sea on the narrow and shallow Guadalquivir River. In 1508, therefore, permission was granted for outgoing vessels to load at San Lucar, at the mouth of the river, or in the nearby harbor of Cádiz; and in 1535 the *Juzgado de Indias*, an agency of the *Casa de Contratación*, was established at Cádiz. Vessels coming from the Indies were still usually required to go to Seville, or at least to send their cargoes and documents to the *Casa* for examination. There was much jealousy between Seville and Cádiz, and the regulations governing their trade were changed from time to time in favor sometimes of one, sometimes of the other. The merchants at Cádiz usually enjoyed some share in the trade of the colonies, even when the fleet sailed from the Guadalquivir.

Except for occasional special dispensations, Seville and Cádiz were the only ports through which trade between Spain and America could legally be carried on. The Emperor Charles V granted permission in 1529 for ships to sail directly to the Indies from several other Spanish ports, provided they put in at Seville on the return voyage, but this privilege seems to have been little used and was discontinued in 1573. Later efforts of other cities in the kingdom to obtain a share in the American trade were defeated by the influence of the powerful vested interests which grew up at Seville, or were discouraged because the authorities believed they could cope with smuggling more effectively if shipments were confined to a single channel. As the commerce of the colonies increased, such centralization became more and more harmful to the mother country and

[8] Haring, *Trade and Navigation between Spain and the Indies*, pp. 33–34. The description of the Spanish commercial system in the present chapter is based largely on this book.

to the overseas possessions, especially as internal customs barriers in Spain made it unprofitable for other regions of the peninsula to send goods to or buy goods from the Indies.

For a time, Charles V permitted all subjects of the Hapsburg empire to engage in commerce with America, and the great German banking houses, the Fuggers and the Welsers, helped finance several of the expeditions to the Indies and had properties there. The Welsers were given permission in 1528 to establish a colony in Venezuela, but their outrageous mistreatment of the Indians and their quarrels with the officials in Santo Domingo led the Emperor to rescind the grant in 1546. After Charles' reign, the law excluded all non-Spaniards from the colonial trade.

THE FLEET SYSTEM

In America trade was restricted to a few ports. This was partly because of the convoy system which the depredations of foreign enemies compelled the government to adopt. French privateers and pirates began to cause trouble early in the sixteenth century, during the wars between the Emperor Charles and Francis I, and in 1522–1523 they captured the ships despatched by Cortez with the King's share of the spoils from the capture of Mexico City. The seas became increasingly unsafe as marauders of other nationalities followed their example. It soon became necessary to have merchant vessels sail in groups protected by warships, and after 1550 practically all trade was carried on in this way. Ordinances adopted in 1564 established the fleet system in the form which it was to retain until well into the eighteenth century.

Normally, two fleets sailed for America each year: the "galleons," with cargo for South America, and the Plate Fleet which served New Spain and the Antilles. There were usually from 30 to 90 ships in each in the sixteenth century, but the number decreased later, partly because ships grew larger and partly because the growth of smuggling caused legitimate commerce to decline. The merchantmen were accompanied by several warships which themselves frequently carried goods for trade. Great convoys of this sort were awkward to handle, and losses by shipwreck were heavy.

Trade with the west coast of South America, which was the wealthiest and most populous part of the Spanish empire in the earlier part of the colonial period, was carried on by way of the Isthmus of Panama. The galleons made their first stop at Cartagena. There goods were unloaded for New Granada and messengers were sent overland to Lima to give the signal for the departure of the vessels that would carry the products of Peru, Chile, and Quito to Panama. After some weeks of trading the fleet proceeded to the Isthmus of Panama. Nombre de Dios was at first the chief port on the Caribbean side of the Isthmus, but it was superseded at the end of the sixteenth century by Porto Bello. We have contemporary accounts of the fair that took place at Porto Bello when the fleet arrived. Hundreds of officials, merchants, mule-drivers, and hangers-on were crowded into the hot little jungle village for 40 or 50 days until the textiles and other European goods brought by the galleons had been exchanged for the gold, silver, cacao, and other products of the colonies. With insufficient accommodations and appalling sanitary conditions, a large proportion of those attending the fair always succumbed to the diseases which made the Isthmus dreaded by travelers until the twentieth century. Only the expectation of great profits, which increased the burden already imposed upon the consumer by heavy taxation and by the greed of the Seville monopolists, could have induced merchants to engage in a commerce so dangerous to life and health.

From Porto Bello goods had to be transported overland to Panama for reshipment to the west coast ports. While the distance across the Isthmus was short, the difficulty and risk were great, for the roads were mere trails through a tropical jungle where impassable mudholes and swollen rivers took a heavy toll of mules and cargo. In the rainy season, goods were sent by sea from Porto Bello to the mouth of the Chagres, a journey often made dangerous by pirates lurking along the shore, and from there poled up the Chagres River in boats to Venta Cruz, which was but five leagues from Panama. In the dry season the safer overland trail was used. The Panama–Porto Bello and Panama–Venta Cruz trails were not paved with stone until the eighteenth century, and even then they were impassable for anything but pack animals.

Commerce with the Antilles and with New Spain was less difficult. The settlements in the islands, as well as those in Honduras and Yucatán, were supplied by small ships which left the Plate Fleet after its arrival in American waters. The main part of the convoy proceeded to Vera Cruz. The Mexican fair was held in the interior at Jalapa, where accommodations were better and the climate more healthful than on the coast, and the transportation of goods from Vera Cruz to Mexico City was far less costly than from Porto Bello to Lima. It is not surprising that the commerce of New Spain became more important than that of Peru in the latter part of the colonial period.

The main purpose of the fleet system was to assure the safe and regular shipment of silver and gold from Peru and Mexico to Spain. Every effort was made to close all avenues through which bullion might be illegally exported. Although the mines were operated by private individuals, all gold and silver had to be presented at the royal assay office for the deduction of the "royal fifth" before it might be sold or used in any way. From there it was shipped under close supervision to the *Casa de Contratación*, where the owner could obtain it "only after long and minute formalities." [9] Despite the most elaborate precautions, there was

[9] *Ibid.*, p. 168.

much smuggling. Aside from the desire to evade the payment of the royalty, there was a powerful temptation to resort to clandestine shipments because the government repeatedly seized properly manifested shipments as forced loans.

THE SEVILLE MONOPOLY

The most powerful of the vested interests that opposed changes in the fleet system was the *Consulado* of Seville, a close corporation of merchants dealing with the colonies which was set up in 1543. Through this organization the bigger exporting houses combined to exploit the American consumer and to treat with the royal government for special privileges. The *Consulado* was able to obtain many important concessions by payments of money or by its influence with the *Casa de Contratación*, and outside firms found it difficult to trade with the colonies in competition with its members. The regulations of the *Casa*, in fact, tended to prevent smaller merchants from loading goods on the fleet at all. The Seville houses worked in close co-operation with their correspondents at Mexico and Lima where the chief importers were also organized in *consulados*. In the South American trade, for example, the exporters at Seville refrained from sending goods on their own account to points beyond Porto Bello, and the Peruvian importers agreed in return not to make purchases in Spain but to supply their needs by purchases at the fair on the Isthmus. There all prices were determined before trading began by an agreement between representatives of the Spanish merchants on the one hand and the American merchants on the other.[10] Such co-operation made possible great profits for the firms participating in the system, and efforts to change the legislation upon which their virtual monopoly rested met with strong opposition.

The effort to prevent trade outside of the fleet system led to the imposition of intolerable and unenforceable restrictions upon commerce by other routes. The chief sufferers in this respect were perhaps the settlers in the River Plate region. Although Buenos Aires was 1,000 miles from Upper Peru, the Spanish government feared to open the port for trade lest it become an outlet for illegal shipments of bullion from the mining region and a point of entry for smuggled goods. The settlers were permitted to engage in a limited commerce with Brazil and the Guinea Coast of Africa where their grain and jerked beef were in great demand, but after 1618 the two small ships that were allowed to go to Brazil each year were required to continue to Seville and return directly to Buenos Aires, so as to prevent direct imports from Brazil.[11]

[10] Juan and Ulloa, *Relación histórica del viaje a la América Meridional*, Vol. I (1748 ed.), pp. 140–141.
[11] Haring, *The Spanish Empire in America*, p. 330.

Trade between New Spain and Peru, the two great centers of Spanish enterprise in America, was also restricted within narrow limits and at times altogether prohibited. In this case the purpose was to prevent goods imported into New Spain from the Philippines from competing with Spanish manufactures in Peru. All intercourse between Spain and the Philippines was carried on through the Mexican port of Acapulco, and though only one or two vessels sailed each year this was an important part of the colonies' commerce. The Manila galleons brought great quantities of silks and other prized oriental products to Mexico, and these found their way through irregular channels to other centers where the settlers were rich enough to buy them. At the same time great quantities of Mexican silver dollars reached the Orient and became the principal form of money there as they did eventually in the British North American colonies.

One result of the Spanish commercial system was that few residents of the colonies could afford to buy imported goods. The fleet system and the restrictions that went with it aggravated the effect of the already formidable natural obstacles to commerce—the long ocean voyage, the difficult transhipment at the Isthmus, and the lack of roads in the interior—and the trade of the colonies was still further burdened by high taxes. Besides the *almojarifazgo,* or customs duties, collected both when the goods left Spain and when they arrived in the colonies, there were the *avería,* a contribution toward the cost of providing the fleets with military protection, the *alcabala,* or sales tax, and a number of lesser imposts. Moreover, the merchants at Seville combined to force prices even higher than they might normally have gone by deliberately undersupplying the colonial markets in order to make larger profits on each shipment. The price of goods in Chile, for example, was often ten times their value in Cádiz.[12]

BRAZIL IN THE SIXTEENTH CENTURY

Though the institutions and the culture that the Portuguese took with them to Brazil were in many ways not unlike those of Castile, the early history of their settlements was quite unlike that of the Spanish colonies. Portugal was a smaller and weaker nation than Spain, and while Spain was conquering the rest of South America, Portugal's scanty resources were occupied in developing her trading empire in the Far East. Brazil, with no rich native communities like Mexico and Peru, seemed relatively unimportant. The home government's interest increased as time went on, but it never established a centralized paternalistic regime like that of Spain, and the development and expansion of the colony were left largely to local enterprise. At the end of the sixteenth century, the little

[12] Galdámes, *Jeografía Económica de Chile,* p. 215.

Brazilian settlements were scattered along 1,500 miles of coast between Pernambuco and São Paulo, on the edge of a vast stretch of little-known country occupied by wild Indians.

The Indians at first furnished the labor for the sugar plantations which were the colonists' chief source of wealth. Since they were less civilized and for the most part seminomadic, they could not be exploited under systems like the *encomienda* and the *repartimiento* of the Spanish colonies, and those who fell into the hands of the Portuguese were usually simply enslaved. Slave-hunting was carried on even when it endangered the very existence of the new settlements, for the first thought of the immigrant was to obtain possession of a few Indians to hunt and till the ground for him. The larger numbers needed for the sugar plantations were procured in various ways. Many Indians were simply kidnaped or induced to sell themselves or their children into servitude for a term of years, often probably without realizing what they were doing. Others were purchased from tribes which had captured them in war, or taken by the Portuguese themselves in suppressing "rebellions." In their endeavor to increase the supply of captives, the settlers often sought pretexts to attack the natives and systematically encouraged feuds between them. Constant fighting, combined with pestilences brought by the white men, rapidly destroyed the natives on the coast, and within a century after the Portuguese arrived it was necessary to go farther and farther into the interior to obtain slaves.

The Jesuits exerted all of their influence to put a stop to these abuses, and their efforts to protect the natives led to a long and bitter conflict. Under pressure from both sides, the Portuguese government, like that of Spain, followed a vacillating policy. It attempted to confine the taking of slaves to officially authorized wars and to prevent frauds by requiring that all slaves be registered. The *rezgate*, or purchase of Indians from other Indians, was at one time forbidden but later permitted under restrictions. A law was even issued in 1609, while Portugal was subject to the king of Spain, declaring all Indian slaves free, but protests from the colonists prevented its enforcement.

The enslavement of Indians continued until after the middle of the eighteenth century, but on the larger sugar plantations Negroes soon began to replace them as field hands and workers in the mills. Negroes were far more expensive, but they were better able to endure regular sustained labor. Their importation was encouraged by the Portuguese government which controlled the chief depots of the slave trade on the African coast. Their number increased in the latter part of the sixteenth century, and as time went on they practically supplanted the Indians as a laboring class in the older settlements. Though the death rate among new arrivals was exceedingly high, they were on the whole well treated compared with the Indians. As in Spain's colonies, both the law and local custom encouraged emancipation, so that free Negroes, as well as mulattoes, soon became numerous. Many slaves escaped into the wild country back from the coast and established free communities, called *quilombos,* which occasionally gave the colonists some trouble. The most famous of these was Palmares, in Alagoas, which was estimated to have 20,000 inhabitants after the wars with the Dutch, and which was finally destroyed in 1697 after ten years of fighting.

The government of colonial Brazil, as compared with the elaborate if not always-efficient political machinery in Spain's possessions, was a somewhat haphazard affair. In Portugal, the king was an absolute monarch. He was assisted by various boards such as the privy council, the inspectors of finance, and the *Mesa da Consciencia e Ordens,* in charge of ecclesiastical matters; but there was little plan or co-ordination in the governmental structure. Confusion inevitably resulted when the authority of each board in its own sphere was simply extended to colonial matters. There was no central organization responsible for affairs in Brazil. The governor at Bahia was nominally the head of the colonial administration; but poor means of communication made it hard for him to exercise authority in the other settlements, and the local governors in these usually received their orders directly from Lisbon. In the absence of any effective control, the officials were often corrupt and oppressive, but their authority was frequently defied by the lawless colonists or by the local clergy. The Crown never supported its representatives in Brazil with any adequate force of regular troops, and the undisciplined local militia might take either side when dissensions arose.

Thomé de Souza, when he went to Brazil in 1549, took with him a *provedor mór,* or superintendent of finances, and an *ouvidor geral,* or chief judge. The departments headed by these two officers continued to be the most important branches of the civil administration. The principal revenues of the Crown were the customs duties, the product of royal monopolies like the trade in brazilwood, the royal fifth on metals and precious stones, and the tithes, which were paid to the civil authorities as they were in the Spanish colonies, although the proceeds were supposedly destined for the support of the Church. Though the actual collection of the taxes was usually farmed out to contractors, a practice that always led to abuses, neither the burden of taxation nor the dues which the heirs of the original donatories were entitled to receive, even after they had been deprived of their political authority, seem to have been particularly onerous. The donatories' privileges were gradually extinguished by purchase or confiscation in the eighteenth century.

One of the weakest points in the colonial government was the administration of justice. Only minor offenses and disputes could be dealt with by the municipal judges named by the local authorities or by *ouvidores*, sent out from Lisbon. Even the *ouvidor geral*, for a long time the highest judicial authority in the colony, did not have final jurisdiction in civil suits when the amount involved exceeded about $300, and he could not inflict the death penalty or other severe punishment except on persons of the lowest rank. All important cases therefore had to go to Lisbon for trial, an arrangement which involved intolerable inconvenience and caused many crimes to go unpunished. In 1588 the Crown tried to establish a court of more ample jurisdiction, but the galleon carrying the judges failed to reach Bahia, apparently simply because of poor seamanship, and returned to Lisbon more than a year later. A *Relação*, or high court of justice, was finally set up in Bahia in 1609, but it was abolished in 1626 to save money for the war against the Dutch and was not re-established until 1652. It seems to have been a doubtful blessing even to the people of Bahia, for many lawyers came to Brazil with it and litigation greatly increased. The inhabitants of some of the other captaincies found it less convenient to have important cases tried in Bahia than in Portugal where many of the richer colonists had agents and business connections.

Official corruption and inefficiency were at least as prevalent as in the Spanish possessions. The governors and other officials were in fact apparently permitted to augment their salary by private business ventures until 1673 when a royal order forbade them to engage in trade, to establish monopolies for their own profit, or to bid for tax collection contracts. There were many frauds in connection with the royal revenue, and the judges were notoriously venal. Many officials were also ignorant and incompetent, for the general level of education among the upper classes and the standards in the public service in Portugal were inferior to those in Spain. The very weakness of the governmental organization, however, was perhaps a benefit, for local initiative was given freer play than in most of the Spanish colonies.

Theoretically, natives of the colony were eligible to any office, and a royal order issued late in the seventeenth century, which was perhaps not much observed in practice, provided that they be given preference in making appointments to positions in Brazil. The more lucrative and important posts, however, usually went to Portuguese who had influence at court, and others, especially in the courts of justice, required a training at the University of Coimbra which few Brazilians could obtain. Offices were filled by royal appointment rather than by sale, and it was sometimes difficult, at least during the first century of the colonial period, to persuade or compel Portuguese officials to accept posts in Brazil.

Local initiative had some chance to express itself in the municipal governments. In each city there was a *Senado da Camara*, or municipal council. In most cases *vereadores*, or aldermen, were chosen theoretically either by the principal inhabitants or by their own predecessors. In practice, the elections were frequently controlled by the governors, and after 1696 the members of the council were simply appointed in some of the most important cities. Nevertheless, the *Senado da Camara*, usually composed of influential native landowners, was a very important branch of the government, especially during the first two centuries of the colonial period. From motives of economy, the Crown entrusted to these bodies many functions which might more appropriately have been performed by royal officials, and in the absence of any institution like the *audiencia* of the Spanish colonies they alone provided continuity in the administrative organization. Their influence was increased by the fact that the governors and other representatives of the Crown usually served only three years and were consequently dependent upon the councilors for advice and information. When there was a vacancy in the governor's office, the *Senado da Camara* often chose a temporary incumbent or itself assumed control. In many cases it defied the governor's authority to the point of open rebellion, and *procuradores*, or representatives of the towns, were frequently sent to Lisbon to petition the king for legislation desired by the colonists or to complain of the conduct of obnoxious officials.

When Philip II of Spain successfully asserted his claim to the throne of Portugal in 1580, he became the sovereign of Brazil also. The Spanish monarchs governed the colony through Portuguese officials and under Portuguese laws, without attempting to make it an integral part of their existing empire in America, so that the effect on Brazilian institutions was not very great. But the union did expose the Brazilian settlements, as we shall see, to attack by Spain's enemies.

THE CHURCH

The Church was less influential in Brazil than in Spanish America. It was equally subject to the royal authority, for the king, in his capacity as Grand Master of the Order of Christ, had full control of the patronage, but the Portuguese monarchs showed less concern for the spiritual welfare of their colonies. Many suspected heretics were sent to Brazil as settlers, and even non-Catholic foreigners were not completely excluded from residence and trade. Backsliding "new Christians" or other heretics were occasionally sent to Portugal for trial, but no council of the Inquisition was established in the colony.

The Jesuits were the richest and most powerful of the religious orders. Their most important work was the conversion and protection of the Indians of whom there were thousands in the mission villages, and the fathers sometimes took the lead in making war on heathen tribes to increase the number of their neophytes. Unlike the principal missions in the Spanish colonies, many of these villages were founded near the Portuguese settlements, and their inhabitants traded with the Europeans or worked for them under the supervision of the priests. The Jesuits were supported by the Crown, and sometimes by the officials in Brazil; but they were constantly in conflict with the settlers and the municipal councils over the Indian question, and they consequently had less influence with the people of European descent than in the Spanish colonies.

Some of the other religious orders had large plantations and other property, but the Church as a whole was poor. Even the principal bishops had revenues that seem insignificant compared with those of prelates in the Spanish colonies. The salaries of the parish priests were too small to be attractive to men of ability or high social position. Nevertheless, religious observances and the celebration of church festivals occupied much of the colonists' time, and such education as their children received was obtained from the Jesuits or other members of the clergy. There were already 62 churches and 3 monasteries in the Bahia district in 1581.[13]

COMMERCIAL POLICY

Portugal's commercial policy, like Spain's, was directed chiefly toward increasing the royal revenues and benefiting privileged interests in the mother country. Royal monopolies controlled the trade in brazilwood and, less completely, the trade in tobacco. All sugar had to be sent to Portugal to be refined, and the cultivation of grapes, olives, and mulberries, which might have competed with industries in Portugal, was forbidden. Even some of the regulations intended to encourage production often did more harm than good. Fortunately for the Brazilians, perhaps, such legislation was frequently not enforced.

In some ways, trade was at first less restricted than in the Spanish colonies. Foreigners were permitted to engage in commerce and agriculture in Brazil until after the union with Spain in 1580, though they were subject to taxes and regulations from which Portuguese were exempt. Dutch firms carried on much trade and had factories and plantations in Brazil before 1580, and they refused, as we shall see in the next chapter, to give up their interest in the colony when the less liberal policy of the Spanish kings attempted to exclude them. Any Portuguese ship was free to go to Brazilian ports until 1649 when the Dutch war led to the adoption of a convoy system.

[13] Southey, *History of Brazil*, Vol. I, p. 318.

CHAPTER 4

Foreign Aggression and Internal Expansion 1600-1700

REPORTS OF THE FABULOUS RICHES of America inevitably aroused envy elsewhere in Europe, and the claims of Spain and Portugal to exclusive dominion in the Western Hemisphere were soon challenged by several other powers. The most important Spanish settlements, on the Mexican plateau and in the western part of South America, were well protected by their geography, but the colonies in the Caribbean and the Portuguese colonies along the Brazilian coast were more exposed.

In the sixteenth and seventeenth centuries, conditions in the Spanish colonies reflected the growing weakness of the mother country where the stirring days of the Conquest were followed by a long period of stagnation and decline. The Emperor Charles V (1516–1556) had been the most powerful ruler in Europe, with extensive territories in the Netherlands, Germany, and Italy. His son Philip II (1556–1598) inherited most of these, though without the imperial title, and annexed Portugal by force when the royal line in that country died out. It was evident even before Philip's death, however, that Spain's greatness rested on insecure foundations. Constant wars had drained her wealth and her manpower, and her population had begun to decrease. The seventeenth century was a period of brilliant achievement in literature and art but one of retrogression in other respects. Commerce, industry, and agriculture had been hurt by the expulsion of Jews and Moors who refused to accept Christianity, and even the treasure pouring in from the Indies could not check the country's economic decline. The kingdom's military strength was likewise affected, and a series of disasters, beginning with the defeat of the great armada sent against England in 1588, all but destroyed its naval power. Other nations were not slow to take advantage of this state of affairs. In the seventeenth century the Dutch and Portuguese obtained their independence, and the Dutch and English and French attacked the Spanish possessions in America and set up colonies in defiance of Spain's opposition. Many of these attained a prosperity that was in conspicuous contrast with the backwardness of the older Spanish settlements.

FOREIGN INTERLOPERS

Under the incompetent monarchs who followed Philip II, Spain was too weak to prevent foreign interlopers from settling in places that she herself had not occupied or to check effectively the buccaneers who preyed on her ships and looted her coastal towns. She could not even prevent an illegal trade with her colonies that probably eventually exceeded the trade through legal channels. Portugal was still weaker, and the union of the two crowns after 1580 made her position worse because it exposed her to attack by Spain's enemies.

French, Dutch, and English interlopers began to appear in the West Indies early in the sixteenth century. Most of them were pirates, but they frequently traded with towns in Española and Cuba when smuggling seemed more profitable than robbery. They became more active after the settlement of the mainland, and they were often systematically encouraged by their own governments, even at times when the latter were at peace with Spain. The most famous of the early sea rovers were the Englishmen John Hawkins and Francis Drake. Hawkins made several voyages to the Indies after 1562 with cargoes of slaves he obtained by fair means or foul on the African coast, trading or plundering as the occasion offered. Drake, who was with Hawkins when the two were defeated and nearly captured by the Spanish Plate Fleet at Vera Cruz in 1568, later made several voyages on his own account, seizing Spanish ships and sacking towns along the American coast. One of his most notable exploits was the circumnavigation of the globe between 1577 and 1580—a voyage during which he looted towns and seized several ships along the South American west coast which had been thought safe from foreign attack. Drake was knighted by Queen Elizabeth, and in 1585 he was given command of an expedition that captured and plundered Santo Domingo and Cartagena. Eleven years later he died of fever after an unsuccessful effort to attack Panama.

The sixteenth-century interlopers were equally active along the Brazilian coast. The French threatened the very existence of the struggling Portuguese colonies by stirring up trouble among the Indians, and for several years, as we have seen, they held the region around Rio de Janeiro. The Englishmen Cavendish and Lancaster sacked several of the Brazilian towns in the last decade of the century. As a measure of protection against such attacks the authorities at Bahia undertook early in the seventeenth century to occupy the previously neglected coast north of Pernambuco. Settlements were made in Parahyba and Ceará, and in 1614 Jerónymo de Albuquerque drove out a group of French colonists who had built a fort in what is now Maranhão. Since it was difficult to govern the northern region from Bahia because the trade winds and the equatorial current made it hard for sailing vessels to weather Cape San Roque from the west, a separate "State of Maranhão" was set up in 1621. A number of industrious families from the Azores were brought in as colonists, and the new settlements were soon quite prosperous.

THE DUTCH IN BRAZIL

It was especially unfortunate for Brazil that union with Spain involved Portugal in the war between Spain and the Dutch. Merchants in the low countries, many of them persons of Portuguese-Jewish descent who had business relations with "new Christians" in Brazil, played an important part in the colony's commerce and were the chief distributors of Brazilian sugar in Europe. When they could no longer trade legitimately, they turned to smuggling and piracy. Many Portuguese Jews living in Holland became stockholders in the Dutch West India Company which was incorporated in 1621 to attack the Spanish-Portuguese monopoly in America.

In the seventeenth century, the Dutch started a general attack on the Spanish-Portuguese possessions. The West India Company's first venture was an expedition against Bahia in Brazil. The city was taken in 1624 because the Portuguese had made no preparations for its defense, but the Dutch were compelled to withdraw when a Spanish fleet appeared. For some years thereafter, the Company devoted its attention chiefly to the Caribbean, with results that will be described later. When its admiral, Piet Heyn, captured the entire Mexican treasure fleet in 1628, the Company was able to launch a more formidable attack on Brazil.

A force of nearly 8,000 men, with supplies for the establishment of a permanent colony, was this time sent against Pernambuco. The Portuguese were again unprepared, and Olinda and Recife, the chief towns of the province, were occupied with little difficulty. In the country districts the inhabitants offered more resistance, and patriot forces operating from a hamlet called the Arraial do Bom Jesus carried on guerrilla warfare for two years, with little help from the peninsula or from the royal officials elsewhere in Brazil. Finally, one of their leaders, a half-breed named Calabar, deserted to the enemy, and several Indian tribes which had hitherto resisted the invaders followed his example. The Dutch thereafter rapidly extended their control over an area that contained the majority of the population and the greater part of the wealth of Brazil, extending along the coast from the province of Maranhão in the north to the river São Francisco in the south.

In 1637, the West India Company sent Jan Mauritz, Count of Nassau, to govern the conquered territory. Nassau was a statesman who had liberal ideas and a keen interest in art and science. He completely reorganized the administration of the colony and encouraged trade by removing burdensome restrictions. His policy of religious toleration won the cooperation of many of the native inhabitants—who were further conciliated by being given a share in the government—and attracted to Pernambuco large numbers of Portuguese Jews whose wealth and business ability helped to make the district more prosperous than ever before. Many of these newcomers bought the confiscated plantations of Brazilians who refused to submit to Dutch rule. With the inflow of capital and more freedom of trade, sugar production greatly increased. The commerce in slaves, both Negro and Indian, also took on a new importance, especially after the West India Company occupied some of the principal Portuguese possessions on the coast of Africa. Nassau, nevertheless, met with much opposition from his own people, for the Calvinist ministers who came out with the invaders opposed his tolerant conduct, and the directors of the West India Company were by no means convinced that his liberal policy was calculated to produce the largest dividends. He was consequently removed in 1644.

Portugal had regained her independence in 1640 and had become an ally of Holland, but the Dutch government nevertheless continued to support the West India Company in Brazil. The government at Lisbon was too weak and too much in need of Dutch help at home to resist, and it did not dare to aid the colonists openly when the Brazilians themselves resumed the war after Nassau's removal. Nevertheless, the people of Maranhão were able to expel the Dutch from their province in 1644. The next year there was an insurrection in Pernambuco, led by João Fernandes Vieira, a rich merchant who had fought against the Dutch until the fall of the Arraial do Bom Jesus but who had later become one of Nassau's chief advisers. The war dragged on with varying fortunes for eight years. Though the Dutch were too busy with enemies in Europe to send large forces across the Atlantic, the Brazilians, in spite of victories in the field, were unable to take the enemy stronghold at Recife. Gradually the Portuguese government, which had secretly encouraged the revolt, grew somewhat bolder, and in 1649 it created the *Companhia Geral do Commercio do Brasil* for the dual purpose of establishing a convoy system to protect Brazilian trade and assisting in the recovery of the invaded provinces. In 1654 the Company's fleet supported the colonists in a successful attack on Recife, and the war was brought to an end. The Dutch formally abandoned their claim to Brazil in 1661, in return for money indemnities and trade privileges. The Brazilians never forgot that they had expelled the invaders by their own efforts, with little help from Portugal.

FOREIGN SETTLEMENTS IN THE WEST INDIES

In the Caribbean—"the Spanish Main"—the West India Company's operations had more lasting results. Dutch traders had long frequented the Venezuelan coast in search of salt, which they needed for curing the products of the great North Sea fisheries, and as early as 1616 there were successful Dutch plantations in Guiana. Between 1630 and 1640, the West India Company seized Curaçao and a few islands in the Lesser Antilles for use as bases for trade with the Spanish colonies and with the settlements that the British and French were now beginning to establish in the West Indies. The Dutch Company was an important factor in the success of these settlements for it bought their products and financed their plantations. When tobacco, which was the colonies' first product, became less profitable, the Company promoted the cultivation of sugar, which soon became the chief source of wealth in the West Indies, and brought in Negro slaves to provide the necessary labor.

The English and French settlers established themselves at first in islands which the Spanish had never occupied. The first English and French colonists who went to St. Kitts in 1624 and agreed to divide the island between them were dispersed by a Spanish attack in 1629, but they soon returned and gradually spread to the neighboring islands: the French to Martinique and Guadeloupe, and the English to many of the other islands, so that the whole chain of the Lesser Antilles was soon in non-Spanish hands. Barbados, meanwhile, was settled by the English in 1625. The English colonies grew rapidly in population because they profited from the same conditions in the home country that were causing emigration to Massachusetts and Virginia in the second quarter of the seventeenth century, but the French, though backed by a company sponsored by Cardinal Richelieu, did not become so prosperous until a few years later.

The Danish colony which was to become the Virgin Islands of the United States was founded in 1671 at the instigation of a group of Dutch traders who wished to have a neutral base of operations during a period when their own government was at war with France. They persuaded King Christian V to set up a Danish West India Company to occupy St. Thomas, where several Hollanders had taken refuge after their own island of St. Eustatius was taken by the French. St. Thomas soon became an important center for the slave trade, as well as a rendezvous for pirates.

SMUGGLING

In the seventeenth century the foreign governments that sought to breach the Spanish and Portuguese monopoly in the New World probably had less interest in acquiring territory than in obtaining a share in the commerce of the American colonies. The Spanish government, as we have seen, not only attempted to exclude foreigners from this commerce but confined legal trade to narrow channels to protect its own revenues and to benefit a few favored merchants. Portuguese policy was at first more liberal, but the privileges that the weak government at Lisbon was often compelled to extend to foreign merchants were restricted after the union with Spain in 1580. Both the Spanish and the Portuguese colonists were consequently eager for better opportunities to sell their products and for a chance to obtain the foreign goods which legal trade provided only in inadequate quantities and at exhorbitant prices. Smuggling was extremely profitable to all concerned, and even the royal officials frequently participated in it.

In the Caribbean, which was the gateway to Spain's rich mainland colonies, the leaders in the smuggling trade were the Dutch. Even before the organization of the West India Company, their ships that came to Venezuela for salt had brought European goods and had carried away cacao and tobacco. The royal authorities caught and hanged some of the smugglers and even prohibited tobacco growing in Venezuela to prevent further sales, but with little result. It was said, in fact, that the trade in cacao was so completely controlled by the Dutch that nearly all of the chocolate consumed in Spain itself passed through their hands. Hollanders also frequently visited Española to buy hides, and in 1605 the Spanish government sought to discourage them by compelling the inhabitants to abandon all of the towns on the north and west coasts of the island.

The activities of the Dutch and other north-European smugglers in the Caribbean were only one of the factors that led to the virtual breakdown of the Spanish commercial system during the seventeenth century. Portuguese smuggling in South America was another. Shipment of goods from Peru to Europe by way of Panama and the fleets was so expensive and difficult that the much longer alternate route to Buenos Aires and overland across the continent could actually be used with profit by those who wished to flout the law. The restrictions on the legal trade of Buenos Aires did not prevent illegal trade with Brazil, and some of the great merchants of Lima maintained agents in Brazil to arrange shipments by way of the River Plate. They found it profitable to employ their capital in this way in the intervals between the arrival of the galleons at Porto Bello, especially as there were times during the seventeenth century when the annual fleets did not sail.

Between 1580 and 1640, when the two kingdoms were united under the Spanish Crown, a large number of Portuguese settled in the Spanish colonies and took over much of the wholesale and retail trade. Many of these were of Jewish descent, and in 1635 all business in Peru was disrupted when the Inquisition arrested more than 80 persons, including most of the principal merchants of Lima, on charges of reverting to Hebrew religious practices. Eleven of the accused, after long-drawn-out proceedings, were burned at the stake, and many received less severe punishment. The Portuguese were again treated like other foreigners after 1640, but they continued their smuggling in the River Plate region. After 1680, Colonia do Sacramento, across the River Plate from Buenos Aires, was the great entrepôt for their trade. This establishment was a source of constant annoyance to the Spanish officials, and it was repeatedly seized by expeditions from Buenos Aires during the wars of the eighteenth century, only to be restored to Portugal when peace was made.

Smuggling could hardly have been carried on on so great a scale if many of the royal officials and the merchants who benefited from the restrictions on legal trade had not connived in defrauding the royal treasury. Even in the carefully supervised annual fleets, fraud in loading ships and manifesting cargoes seems to have been the rule rather than the exception. As Spain's industries declined, after the latter part of the sixteenth century, articles originally brought from foreign countries made up an increasing proportion of the exports from Seville to America. The shipment of such articles by Spanish firms was permitted, but many merchants of other nationalities, who could not legally take part in the American trade, also found ways of doing so, sometimes by acting through Spanish firms which merely lent their name to the transaction, and sometimes by loading goods directly from their own vessels in Cádiz Harbor, without the formality of registration. Gold and silver coming from the colonies found their way into foreign hands in the same manner. Official interference was avoided by bribery, or frequently by intimidation, for the Spanish government during the seventeenth century was too weak to risk offending other powers by confiscating the property of their subjects. Louis XIV of France even sent warships to Cádiz on more than one occasion as a warning not to molest French merchants in their illegal operations.

THE BUCCANEERS

Though Spain was unable to prevent foreign intrusions in parts of America that she had not effectively occupied, she refused for some time to recognize the existence of the English and French and Dutch colonies in the Caribbean. She was even more stubborn in her refusal to accede to the other powers' demands for trading rights in her own colonies. Since the other powers refused to respect her claim to exclusive rights in the Indies, and she insisted on it, it became customary to regard the Indies as outside the scope of treaties made with the Spanish government. Normal relations might exist within the "Lines of Amity," east of the meridian of the Azores and north of the Tropic of Cancer, but it became a common saying that there was "no peace beyond the line." Other European governments, even in time of peace, openly encouraged their subjects to prey on Spanish trade in the Indies.

The activities of the Providence Company are an example of the sort of enterprise that this situation made possible. Organized in 1629 by a group of Englishmen who were also prominent in the affairs of Virginia and New England, this company occupied Providence Island, off the east coast of Nicaragua, with the avowed purpose of using it as a base for piracy. It also established small settlements on the Central American coast. The Company hoped for a considerable Puritan immigration, but this did not materialize. Chiefly for this reason the venture was a failure, and the colony was destroyed by a Spanish expedition in 1641.

Other English and French colonies continued to offer bases and recruiting grounds for the pirates who became more and more numerous after the destruction of Spanish sea power. The great center for this activity was Tortuga, a small island off the north coast of Española which had been occupied some time before 1630 by a heterogeneous group of foreign outcasts and adventurers. The settlers had first been attracted by the good hunting on the nearby coast of Española, where great numbers of cattle and pigs had run wild after the partial abandonment of Santo Domingo by the Spaniards, and one of their main occupations was the supplying of dried meat and other provisions to passing pirates and smugglers. From their practice of curing this meat on a "boucan," or grill over a fire, they came to be called "buccaneers" —a term which was later applied to all of the seventeenth-century freebooters in the Caribbean. Piracy seems to have been merely a side line with the settlers at Tortuga at first, but they abandoned hunting for the more exciting and profitable "course" as the supply of game decreased. Their settlement, meanwhile, had gone through many vicissitudes. It had been repeatedly destroyed by Spanish raids, and there had been fights between the English and French parties among the buccaneers.

After being for a time under the control of the Providence Company, the island was ruled from 1641 to 1654 by a representative of the governor general of the French West Indies. By the middle of the century its inhabitants were a numerous and unruly population devoted almost entirely to piracy. They merely scattered when a Spanish expedition occupied the island in 1654 and returned a few months later when the Spanish forces were withdrawn to confront an English expedition that was attacking Santo Domingo.

This expedition had been sent by Cromwell, in time of peace and without warning to Spain, simply to conquer a part of the Spanish Main. It failed to take Santo Domingo, but the less strongly held island of Jamaica was occupied in 1655 and at once became the most important of the English possessions in the West Indies. In the war that followed this act of aggression, British naval forces under Admiral Blake captured or destroyed the greater part of the Porto Bello fleet off Cádiz in 1656 and destroyed the Mexican fleet at Santa Cruz in the Canaries in the following year, though not until the treasure had been safely hidden on land. Meanwhile the English forces in Jamaica were no less active. Spanish counterattacks were beaten off, and naval forces plundered several towns on the mainland. Even after the advent of peace in Europe, following the Restoration in England, the English authorities granted commissions to privateers for attacks on Spanish ships and settlements, and many of the buccaneers who had hitherto had their headquarters at Tortuga began to resort to Port Royal. The sea rovers were at first a welcome addition to the defensive forces of the new colony, and it was hoped that their depredations would compel Spain to grant the commercial privileges that had been the real objective of the West Indian expedition.

The occupation of Jamaica was thus followed by a reign of terror throughout the Spanish Main:

> Between the years 1655 and 1671 alone, the corsairs had sacked eighteen cities, four towns and more than thirty-five villages—Cumaná once, Cumanagote twice, Maracaibo and Gibraltar twice, Rio de la Hacha five times, Santa Marta three times, Tolu eight times, Porto Bello once, Chagre twice, Panama once, Santa Catalina twice, Granada in Nicaragua twice, Campeache three times, St. Jago de Cuba once, and other towns and villages in Cuba and Hispaniola for thirty leagues inland innumerable times.[1]

Many settlements in exposed localities were abandoned, and many others suffered an injury from which they never recovered. The most famous of the buccaneers' exploits was the destruction of Panama City in 1671 by Henry Morgan, who for this and similar achievements was knighted and made Lieutenant Governor of Jamaica.

---

[1] Haring, *Buccaneers in the West Indies in the XVII Century*, p. 267.

The buccaneers, however, were not desirable citizens, and the hope that their depredations would force Spain to relax the restrictions on the colonial trade soon proved illusory. The English government consequently entered into a treaty with Spain in 1670, by which it agreed to check their activities in return for the formal recognition of its sovereignty over the English West Indian colonies. For some years after this date piratical undertakings were sometimes secretly encouraged by the authorities at Jamaica, as well as by officials in the North American colonies, but open governmental support gradually ceased.

The freebooters continued to operate from Tortuga and other places in the western part of Española where there were by this time several settlements of French adventurers. These colonists had shaken off the control that the authorities at Jamaica had tried to exercise, and in 1664 the western end of the island was taken over by the French West India Company. The new Governor, Bertrand d'Ogeron, devoted himself with some success to the task of converting what had been little more than a nest of pirates into a flourishing agricultural colony. He not only encouraged the establishment of plantations but imported several shiploads of women from France as wives for the settlers. His regime laid the foundations for the prosperity that later made French Saint Domingue the richest of the West Indian colonies. As the influence of the home government increased, buccaneering was gradually suppressed there also, for French merchants, who contributed so large a proportion of the goods sent from Spain to the Indies, suffered as much as anyone else from attacks on Spanish merchant ships.

Thereafter buccaneering was no longer used as an instrument of national policy. Pirates were treated as outlaws by all nations. Some former corsairs took to cutting dyewood in the jungles of the Central American and Mexican coast, establishing small settlements which were later to be the basis for English territorial claims in that region. Others became planters. Sugar and tobacco cultivation was exceedingly profitable in the British and French colonies during the eighteenth century, and Jamaica and Saint Domingue had many great plantations worked by hundreds of Negro slaves. The owners of these had no desire for a continuance of the old unruly conditions. They still carried on a very extensive smuggling trade with the Spanish colonies; but the old idea that there was "no peace beyond the line" was gradually abandoned, and treaties between Spain and other powers applied in Europe and America alike.

CONDITIONS IN THE SPANISH COLONIES

The more important Spanish settlements were little affected by the foreign aggression that brought ruin and destruction to so many towns in the Caribbean. In Mexico and Peru the white and *mestizo* population gradually increased, more because the settlers had large families than because of any great immigration from Spain, and the Indian population was beginning to recover from the effects of the epidemics that had reduced it to a fraction of its former size in the latter part of the sixteenth century. There seem to have been no very great changes in the political and social institutions of the Spanish colonies, or in their way of life, between the time of Philip II and the advent of the Bourbons to the Spanish throne in 1700. The production of the mines, which gave the colonies their chief importance in European eyes, reached its peak at the end of the sixteenth century and seems to have declined rather rapidly after 1630.[2] Conditions in the colonies reflected the economic decline and the increasing governmental weakness and corruption in Spain. At the same time, if to a lesser extent, the colonists had a share in the literary and artistic activity that made the period a notable one in the history of the mother country. Finer churches and other buildings were erected, and painting reached the highest point that it was to attain during the colonial period.[3] In Mexico there appeared two of the most notable figures in Spanish literature: the poet Carlos de Sigüenza y Góngora, who was also a noted mathematician and engineer, and the lyric poet Sor Juana Inés de la Cruz.

GOVERNMENTAL CORRUPTION
AND INEFFICIENCY

There was little improvement in the government of the Spanish colonies. After the end of the sixteenth century practically all of the officials except the viceroys obtained their offices simply by purchase from the royal government, which sold appointments to the highest bidder. This was true even of the most responsible positions. The more important were usually sold in Spain, the others in the colonies. The new functionary's office thus represented an investment from which he naturally expected a financial return. There is little reason to suppose that the result was worse than if appointments had been dictated by favoritism and bribery, which would undoubtedly have been the alternative, but the sale of offices certainly did not promote efficiency or honesty.

Contemporary standards of official morality made graft and peculation inevitable under any system of appointment. Public office was regarded in Spain, as in many other European countries in the seventeenth and eighteenth centuries, primarily as an opportunity for self-enrichment. The whole character of the colonial system—the arbitrary

[2] See the table in Haring, *The Spanish Empire in America*, p. 268.
[3] *Ibid.*, p. 250.

power exercised by the Crown's representatives, the special privileges granted to favored persons and classes, and especially the restrictions on trade which made violations of the law extremely profitable—afforded an irresistible temptation to bribery and extortion. The viceroys themselves stooped at times to the establishment of commercial monopolies for their personal profit or accepted money in return for pardoning criminals. Among their subordinates, from the judges of the *audiencia* to the most humble clerk, corruption was universal and in most cases unpunished. The public treasury was defrauded in countless ways, and justice—or more frequently injustice—was for sale in the courts. Even private property was not safe from the rapacity of unscrupulous military or civil officials. The legal provisions designed to discourage official misconduct, through frequent inspections by members of the *audiencia* or specially appointed "visitors," and through the *residencias* which all officials had to undergo at the end of their terms, were of little value because they were usually carried out by officials who were themselves profiting by the practices that they were supposed to check. There was often a recognized customary price for a favorable report after a *residencia.*

The Spanish colonial administration was not only corrupt, but, judged by modern standards, inefficient. Some of the earlier viceroys, like Mendoza in Mexico and Francisco de Toledo in Peru, were able statesmen, but the majority, in the seventeenth century, were men of mediocre ability. The Crown's insistence that even unimportant questions must be decided in Spain discouraged local initiative and made it difficult for the best viceroys to accomplish much constructive work. Such centralization was the more impractical because communications between the colonies and the peninsula were slow and uncertain, especially when Spain's enemies controlled the seas, and communications between one colony and another in America often took many weeks. The lack of close contact between the home government and its representatives, combined with procrastination and red tape in the Council of the Indies, often caused matters requiring prompt decision to be discussed back and forth for years. On the other hand, the Crown was compelled to allow the colonial officials some latitude in enforcing royal decrees issued without full knowledge of the facts. The viceroys frequently nullified the king's commands by suspending laws until they could explain why their enforcement seemed undesirable, using the famous formula: "Let it be obeyed but not executed." Subordinate officials similarly evaded compliance with the viceroys' orders. Such practices could not but encourage insubordination and abuses of power.

INDIAN LABOR

There was some change in the situation of the Indians. The *mita* was still used in the mines of Peru, and drafts of forced labor were commonly employed in public works; but the owners of large farms and cattle ranches were endeavoring more and more to build up permanent labor forces on their own properties—either by giving the Indians bits of land, in return for which they worked a part of each week for the owner, or by a system of peonage, or debt slavery. The Indian who was persuaded, or forced, to accept a loan from the planter's agent could be compelled to work until it was paid, and there were few who could free themselves when they once became the victims of the system. Peonage was also used in the textile factories and in Mexico in the mines. It was probably less harmful to the natives than the *repartimiento* because it gave the employer an interest in perserving his Indians, but it resulted in virtual slavery. By the end of the seventeenth century it was probably the commonest form of relationship between employer and worker. At the same time a large proportion of the Indians continued to live in their own villages and more or less successfully defended their communal lands against the greed of nearby creole proprietors. In general, the lot of the Indians seems to have been a little easier in Mexico than in South America. Certainly work in the Mexican mines was less destructive, because communities of skilled workmen grew up around the mines and made the resort to forced labor less necessary.

THE FRONTIER MISSIONS

In most cases the Spaniards had originally established themselves in regions where there were settled, civilized Indian communities to support them. From the beginning, however, the religious orders had been interested in missionary work among the wilder natives on the frontiers. During and after the Conquest, Jesuits and Franciscans and other friars went into the wildest and most remote regions to preach the gospel with the same indomitable courage that inspired other Spanish explorers in the search for wealth and power. Many were killed by the natives or died of hunger and exhaustion, but others won the confidence of the wild tribes, taught them the rudiments of civilization, and brought them into touch with the Spanish community so that the royal authorities could peacefully establish control over them. Somewhat later, more elaborately organized frontier missions, directed and supported by the Crown, became the chief means through which the Spanish dominions were expanded. The friars were protected by military forces, and compulsion as well as persuasion were used to induce the Indians to give up their nomadic life and settle in permanent villages, or *reducciones,* where their economic and spiritual life could be supervised by the missionaries. The converts had little or no private property and worked for the benefit of the community as a whole, under constant supervision and direction. Such power as their own chiefs exercised was subject to the higher authority of the priests. Until they were considered sufficiently civilized to stand on their own feet, they were carefully kept from any contact with the Spanish community, and white settlers were excluded from their neighborhood.

The Indians were taught handicrafts and better agricultural methods, and the introduction of new animals and plants helped to do away with the danger of famine which had formerly been ever present. Many thousands in northern Mexico and the interior of South America were saved from extinction by slave-raiders or Spanish troops. In few cases, however, were the converts able to survive as organized communities after the missions were discontinued. In districts where Spanish colonization later took place, those who did not succumb to disease or mistreatment passed under the domination of white landowners or miners. Elsewhere they usually reverted more or less completely to savagery.

THE JESUITS IN PARAGUAY

The most famous missions were those of Paraguay. The Jesuits started work among the Guaranís along the upper Paraná River in the latter part of the sixteenth century, and they were especially authorized to Christianize the Indians of that region by a royal order issued in 1608. When their early settlements were destroyed some 20 years later by the raids of slave-hunting Paulistas from Brazil, they moved their converts south into territory which is now partly in southeastern Paraguay, partly in the Argentine province of Misiones, and partly in Brazil. Here they developed a theocratic community which was practically independent of the neighboring Spanish authorities. There were a score of *reducciones*, each under the paternalistic control of two or more missionaries, with a total population that eventually reached 100,000. The life and industry of the Indians were as closely regulated as in other missions, and efficient management made the settlements very prosperous. The creoles of Asunción and other nearby communities were bitterly hostile to the Jesuits, who protected the docile Guaranís from white exploitation and also sold their *yerba mate* and agricultural products in competition with those of the white settlements.

This hostility was frequently the cause of serious disorders in Paraguay. In the middle of the seventeenth century Bishop Cárdenas of Asunción, who was unfriendly to the Jesuits, became the ardent champion of the creoles. While serving temporarily as Governor of the province, he attempted to restrict the activities of the missions and then led the creoles in resistance to the new Governor who was sent to replace him. He was defeated by an army from the missions, for the Jesuits had been permitted to train and arm their Indians to repel further aggression by the Paulistas. The mission troops were also used occasionally by the Spanish authorities in other military operations in the River Plate region.

THE SEVENTEENTH CENTURY IN BRAZIL

In Brazil, the seventeenth century was an era of material progress and territorial expansion. The protracted struggle with the Dutch caused much destruction of life and property in northern Brazil, but it hardly affected the provinces that remained under Portuguese control. After the war there was a period of rapid development, and so many immigrants came from Portugal that the home government was concerned lest its European territory be depopulated. The growing importance of the settlements was recognized by the establishment of bishoprics in Maranhão, Rio de Janeiro, and Pernambuco, while the See of Bahia became an archbishopric. The increase in wealth and perhaps also the stimulating effect of contact with the Dutch brought changes in the intellectual and social life of the colonies. Education had hitherto been neglected, except for the primary schools under the Jesuits and the courses given rather irregularly for the training of priests, but in the latter part of the seventeenth century a number of young Brazilians went to Portugal to study at the University of Coimbra. Brazil nevertheless remained behind the Spanish colonies in the field of education, for there was no university in the Portuguese settlements.

The northern state of Maranhão also grew more prosperous in the second half of the seventeenth century, in spite of a series of disturbances provoked by the Jesuits' efforts to protect the Indians. Some of the planters of this region had obtained control of villages of peaceful Indians under conditions not unlike those in the Spanish colonies in the worst days of the *encomienda* system. Others had enslaved Indians by purchase or fraud or had taken them in forays on wild tribes. Slave hunting had led to constant warfare on the borders of the settlements, with all of the abuses that had been practiced in the southern provinces before the Indians near the settlements had been exterminated.

The natives' most determined defender was Father Antonio Vieira, the Superior of the Jesuit order, who was one of the most distinguished Portuguese writers and statesmen of his time. In 1655 Vieira obtained from the Crown full authority to control Indian relations in Brazil, and he proceeded energetically to free those who were illegally in bondage in Maranhão and to establish missions where the natives would be protected from the colonists. His activities aroused violent opposition, and in 1661 the settlers in Pará seized him and shipped him off to Lisbon.

Soon afterward, he fell from favor at court, but in 1680 he was able to persuade the King to enact a law forbidding the enslavement of Indians in Maranhão. Two years later, in order to encourage the importation of Negroes, a chartered company was granted a monopoly of the chief branches of trade in the northern provinces. These measures brought on another revolt under the leadership of one Manoel Beckman who seized control of the district around São Luiz and expelled both the Jesuits and the representatives of the Maranhão Company. The movement soon collapsed, as such movements usually did in colonial Brazil, because many of the participants lost interest after the first outburst of indignation. Beckman was executed, and the Jesuits were reinstated. On the other hand, the privileges of the commercial company were restricted, and the laws for the protection of the Indians were not enforced.

THE *BANDEIRANTES*

Negro slaves were gradually replacing the Indians on the sugar plantations of Bahia and Pernambuco, but there was still an active demand for Indian labor. Capturing natives to supply this demand was the principal occupation of the hardy, energetic inhabitants of São Paulo, themselves of mixed blood, whose territory was not suited to sugar planting and who seemed to prefer a wild, seminomadic life to more sedentary occupations. Since the natives of the nearby plateau were for the most part under the protection of the Jesuit missions, the Paulistas began soon after 1600 to carry their slave raids farther and farther into the interior, and the memory of their *bandeiras*, or expeditions, became an important part of Brazil's cultural heritage. Accompanied by their families, they would often remain in the wilderness for years at a time, stopping now and then to sow a crop when their supplies ran low, and returning with droves of Indians to be distributed among the sugar plantations along the coast. Their destruction of the earlier Jesuit Guaraní missions has already been mentioned. In many other sections, they all but wiped out the native population. The Jesuits asserted, probably with some exaggeration, that the *bandeirantes* enslaved 300,000 natives between 1614 and 1639.

The Paulistas explored great areas west and south of the older settlements, paving the way for Brazilian occupation of a considerable amount of territory that might otherwise have been claimed by Spain as lying west of the line of demarcation laid down by the Treaty of Tordesillas. At the end of the seventeenth century, they inaugurated a new era in the colonies' history by discovering rich gold deposits in what is now the State of Minas Geraes. Their conquest and settlement of Rio Grande do Sul was no less important, for it added to Brazil's territory a fertile area with a temperate climate which is one of the richer parts of the Republic today. It was after they had penetrated into Rio Grande do Sul that Portugal attempted to assure her possession of the entire region as far as the River Plate by establishing a military post at Colonia do Sacramento in 1680. The garrison was at once attacked and expelled by forces from Buenos Aires, just across the river; but Portugal protested to Spain, and an agreement was reached through the mediation of England, France, and the Pope by which the place was returned to Portugal pending an investigation to determine the exact location of the boundary fixed by the Treaty of Tordesillas. The line in reality passed to the east of the River Plate; but though Colonia was repeatedly captured by the Spanish in time of war, it was as often returned when peace was made, and it remained in Portuguese hands for nearly a century. The post did not give Portugal the hoped-for control of the rich country north of the River Plate estuary, which was gradually occupied during the eighteenth century by Spanish settlements, but it was important as a base for the smuggling trade with Peru.

PRODUCTION AND TRADE

Sugar was by far the most important product of the colonies in the seventeenth century, and during most of the century Brazil was the chief source of the world's supply of this commodity. Much of the crop was sold to other European countries, but the Portuguese government endeavored after it regained its independence from Spain to continue the same exclusive commercial system that the Spanish kings had introduced. We have already seen how the *Companhia Geral do Commercio do Brasil* was established in 1649 for the double purpose of protecting trade and aiding in the expulsion of the Dutch. The Company's capital was obtained partly by promising that money invested in it by "new Christians" would be exempt from seizure by the Inquisition. It undertook to send two well-armed fleets to America yearly, and these were to have a monopoly on the transportation of goods between Portugal and Brazil. At first it enjoyed a monopoly for the sale of the most important staple imports—codfish, wheat flour, oil, and wine—but this was discontinued because of complaints from the colonists. The Company rendered a useful service in its first years, but its privileges soon made it unpopular. It came more and more under the control of the royal government and was dissolved in 1720. The fleet system, however, was continued. The Maranhão Company, also mentioned previously, was no more successful. It was badly managed and continued to be extremely unpopular after the suppression of Beckman's revolt.

The effort to exclude other powers from Brazilian trade broke down for a time after the separation from Spain because Portugal was too weak to refuse the demands of the Dutch and English governments for commercial privileges. These concessions, however, were gradually made worthless by a systematic discrimination against foreigners, and by the early part of the eighteenth century, Brazil was as effectively closed to foreign commerce as were the Spanish possessions.

CHAPTER 5

The Last Century of Colonial Rule

THE LAST CENTURY of the colonial period saw notable changes in the Spanish possessions and in Brazil. For a time, at least, both of the home governments were better managed than they had been, and their increased efficiency was reflected in the administration of the colonies. Both were weak as compared with some of the other European powers, but the Spanish Bourbons' alliance with France and Portugal's alliance with England made their positions somewhat better than in the days when all other maritime nations were attacking their colonial empires. Though some of the more accessible American towns were captured or assaulted during the frequent wars of the eighteenth century, there was no such wanton destruction as the buccaneers had inflicted, and trade, at least in peace time, could be carried on with greater safety. In the Spanish colonies, some of the restrictions of the old commercial system were removed, and the creoles began to have more contact with the outside world.

ADMINISTRATIVE CHANGES IN THE SPANISH COLONIES

The earlier Bourbon kings made important changes in the administrative system in Spain, and in 1714 the Council of the Indies and the *Casa de Contratación* were subordinated to a Ministry of the Indies through which the royal government attempted to exercise a closer supervision over American affairs. Three years later a new viceroyalty was set up, with its seat at Bogotá, to govern New Granada, Venezuela, Quito, and Panama. This arrangement was later abandoned for a time but was made permanent in 1739. In 1776, Charles III (1759–1788) sent another viceroy to Buenos Aires to rule the River Plate provinces and the mining region of Upper Peru. The appointments were intended to strengthen the military defense of two increasingly important regions that had been somewhat neglected under the rule of the distant viceroys at Lima and Mexico.

Charles, who was the ablest of the Spanish Bourbon kings, also endeavored to make the local administration in the colonies more efficient. Beginning in 1764, the government of a few of the less important American provinces was entrusted to "intendants" who had more authority and responsibility than the old local officials. The arrangement worked well, and between 1782 and 1790 intendants replaced governors, *corregidores*, and *alcaldes mayores* throughout the colonies. The new officials were usually abler men than their predecessors and governed larger districts, with *subdelegados* under them in charge of smaller areas. They were still responsible to the viceroys, but they were the supreme representatives of the government in their own territory. One of their most important duties, to increase the royal revenues, was not calculated to make them popular with the colonists. In most cases they even deprived the city governments of what little authority and initiative the *cabildos* had formerly had.

The administrative changes were consequently of questionable value from the colonists' standpoint, and in any event they came too late to make any great change in the political heritage that was to shape the development of the Spanish American countries after independence. Their general effect, in fact, was to make the government more autocratic than it had been and to diminish the influence that some of the creoles had enjoyed through their position as great landowners or as members of the *cabildos* under a less centralized regime. Residents of the colonies now had practically no opportunity for political or administrative experience that would help them after independence. Furthermore, many of the worst abuses of the old system persisted. Charles III made some improvement in the government personnel, but the quality of the officials sent to America deteriorated under his incompetent successors.

At the same time, the Crown took measures to build up military forces in the colonies. Until the eighteenth century there had been few trained troops there. The principal settlements were in places where geographical barriers discouraged foreign attacks, but the seaports, especially in the Spanish Main, had suffered severely at the hands of Spain's enemies. After the Seven Years' War, a standing army and an organized militia were created. Both were officered and manned chiefly by creoles. Men of good family were eager to obtain commissions in these forces, and many of the military leaders who dominated Latin American politics after independence began their careers in this way.

THE EIGHTEENTH-CENTURY REVOLTS

The creoles were less enthusiastic about paying the costs of defense, and the government's effort to impose new taxes for this purpose was one of the chief causes of a series of revolts and conspiracies which fore-shadowed the revolution that took place in the next century. Small up-risings among the creoles or the Indians had occurred from time to time throughout the colonial period, but most of them had a purely local significance. Those that occurred during Charles III's reign revealed a new willingness to defy the royal authority. In 1765, for example, the populace of Quito, angered by the establishment of a liquor monopoly, drove all peninsular Spaniards from the city, and order was restored only by concessions to the insurgents and by the arrival of a strong Spanish garrison. In 1776 the imposition of new taxes in Peru, New Granada, and Chile caused riots in several places and gave rise to a rebellious spirit that soon found a more dangerous expression in Peru and New Granada.

In Peru, the spectacle of disorders among the upper class was one of the causes of the great Indian uprising that began in 1780. Its leader was José Gabriel Condorcanqui, the hereditary chief of a village near Cuzco, who had been officially recognized as the heir of the Inca royal family and who, unlike many *caciques*, had for years endeavored to obtain fairer treatment for his people. The Indians were still suffering under the cruelties of the *mita* and were shamelessly exploited by the officials. The *corregidores*, who had immediate jurisdiction over them, were permitted to sell goods to the Indians, as a means of giving them an incentive to regular work, and they often forced the Indians to buy useless articles—spectacles, silk stockings, and worn-out livestock—at exhorbitant prices. It was against these abuses that Condorcanqui revolted. Assuming the name of Tupac Amaru, he raised a large army which killed creole land-owners and destroyed property in much of Upper Peru. He himself was captured and executed in 1781; but his followers continued the struggle for two years more, and there was a frightful loss of life on both sides before the movement was suppressed. It was not entirely fruitless, for some of the worst abuses against the Indians were done away with after peace was restored. The *corregidores* themselves disappeared with the appointment of the intendants.

Of quite a different type was the revolt of the *Comuneros* in New Granada in 1781. In several towns of that province the creoles expressed their resentment against the new taxes by seizing control and organizing local governments which they called *comunes*. After some initial suc-cesses against the viceroy's troops, the insurgents proclaimed the inde-pendence of the colony and took steps to organize a republic. A number of Indians joined the movement under the leadership of a descendant of one of the Chibcha royal houses, and another group, in the province of

Pamplona, announced their allegiance to Tupac Amaru. Peace was restored after a few months through the mediation of the clergy, but not until after the *audiencia* had agreed to abolish the fiscal monopolies and to reduce or discontinue certain taxes. This agreement was repudiated after the rebels disbanded and the royal officials received reinforcements. Four of the leaders in the movement were executed.

THE MARQUIS DE POMBAL'S REFORMS IN BRAZIL

In Brazil the colonial administration had been weaker and less efficient than in the Spanish colonies. The Crown's representative at Bahia, whose title varied but who was usually a governor general between 1601 and 1714 and a viceroy thereafter, was nominally the head of the colonial administration, but inadequate means of communication made it difficult for him to exercise authority in the other captaincies. This was especially true of the northern provinces, and these, as we have seen, were made a separate "state" after 1621. Even in places like São Paulo and Rio de Janeiro the local governors usually received their orders directly from Lisbon and dealt with their own problems with little reference to their nominal superior at Bahia. In the absence of any effective control from outside, the local authorities were often corrupt and oppressive. The Portuguese government derived relatively little revenue from the colony, and little of what it did receive was spent for the benefit of Brazil or for the defense of the colony. The result of this neglect was evident during the War of the Spanish Succession, when French expeditions twice attacked Rio de Janeiro. The first one, in 1710, was driven off by the inhabitants after several public buildings had been burned, but the second a year later took and sacked the town.

The colonial government's incompetence was also manifested in events that occurred at about the same time in Pernambuco. Olinda, the Capital of this province and the home of the more important native families, had been built by Duarte Coelho on high ground at some distance from the place where ships customarily anchored, and many merchants had therefore established themselves at Recife, the "reef," which was more convenient to the port. Though this settlement had grown rapidly during and after the Dutch wars, it remained a part of the municipality of Olinda, and its inhabitants—most of them Portuguese immigrants—were excluded from any share in the local government. The *Mascates*, or peddlers, as the Brazilians derisively called these newcomers, had therefore persuaded the Crown in 1709 to make Recife a separate city. This led to violent quarrels. When the Governor attempted to arrest some of the more obstreperous native leaders, the people of Olinda expelled him from the province, and both sides took up arms. There was a year of savage fighting before a new Governor restored order by promising amnesty to both parties. Recife, generally called Pernambuco by English-speaking people, continued to grow in importance and soon far outstripped its onetime rival.

Between 1750 and 1777, the decline of Portugal was temporarily arrested under the vigorous administration of the Marquis of Pombal, the great minister of King José I. In the colonial sphere the most important change was the unification of Brazil, including Maranhão, under a viceroy who had real authority over the provincial governors. If this measure had not been adopted, there might well be several nations of Portuguese origin in America today instead of one. The Capital of the colony was moved in 1763 to Rio de Janeiro, which was by that time the chief city and the port through which the product of the gold and diamond mines reached the outside world. There were improvements in the administration of the finances and of justice, and official corruption was to some extent reduced. Pombal also promoted efficiency by ending the practice of appointing governors and other officials for terms of only three years, a limitation that had often deprived the Crown of the services of competent men just when they were becoming most useful.

THE EXPULSION OF THE JESUITS

One of the most important events that occurred in Spanish and Portuguese America while Charles III was King of Spain and the Marquis of Pombal was ruling Portugal was the expulsion of the Jesuits. The Jesuits were one of the wealthiest and most powerful of the religious orders, not only in the American colonies but throughout Catholic Europe. They maintained a high standard of discipline and personal conduct, but their conservatism brought them into conflict with the statesmen who were attempting to bring about political and economic reforms in several of the European countries. They were on especially bad terms with Pombal.

The "War of the Seven Reductions" in Paraguay particularly embittered the two governments against the Jesuit order. In 1750, Spain agreed to exchange seven of the Jesuit missions lying east of the Uruguay River for the Portuguese smuggling post at Colonia on the north side of the River Plate. The Indians, who remembered the raids of the Paulista slave-hunters, rose in revolt and were only subdued after a long and costly struggle. Both governments suspected the Jesuits of inciting their neophytes to resistance, and Pombal retaliated in 1755 by declaring the Indians in Maranhão free from all forms of tutelage, a step that promised to destroy the Jesuit missions in that area. The order was extended to all of Brazil in 1758, and in 1759 Pombal persuaded the King to banish the Jesuits both from Portugal and from her colonies.

In 1767 Charles III expelled the Jesuit order from Spain's possessions. His action caused a tremendous sensation in the American colonies.

Since there was some reason to fear that the creoles might resist the execution of the royal decree, all members of the order in each district were arrested secretly the same night and shipped immediately to Europe without regard for the hardship inflicted on the more aged and infirm priests in regions where travel was difficult. Their departure probably weakened rather than strengthened the Spanish government's position in the colonies. The Jesuits were somewhat less amenable to royal control than other branches of the Church because many of them were foreigners and because their highly centralized organization was directed by a general at Rome. But they were nevertheless one of the strongest links in the political-religious system that tied the colonies to Spain. Besides their missionary work, in other provinces as well as Paraguay, they had been the leaders in education and had had a great influence in the spiritual life of the white communities. Their wealth and organizing ability had made them an important element in the colonies' economic life. No other religious order was able to take their place, and most of their missions and schools were carried on less efficiently or abandoned after their expulsion. The populous and prosperous missions in Paraguay, placed under the administration of the civil authorities, were deserted by their inhabitants or degenerated into poverty-stricken Indian villages. In Brazil, many of the Indians from the Jesuit missions simply reverted to savagery.

CHANGES IN THE SPANISH
COMMERCIAL SYSTEM

The eighteenth century also brought far-reaching changes in the economic life of the American colonies. In the Spanish possessions, restrictions on trade with the mother country were gradually relaxed. It was clear by 1700 that these restrictions had had unfortunate results. The fleet system had indeed brought the treasure from the Indies safely to Spain on all but a very few occasions through a period of 150 years. On the other hand, the effort to confine trade to a few routes and to exclude foreigners from participation had simply diverted the greater part of the colonies' imports and exports into illegal channels. There were fewer and fewer ships in the fleets, and at times there were periods of some years when no fleets sailed.

Smuggling was still practiced everywhere, often with the connivance of the Crown's own representatives. Most of the officials were corrupt, and even if a viceroy or governor were himself honest he could not trust his subordinates. Early in the eighteenth century, for example, one of the viceroys of Peru determined to check the illegal importation of goods in the vicinity of Lima. After encountering many obstacles because of the secret efforts of other officials to protect the smugglers, he finally sent a subordinate to investigate the situation at a port where contraband goods were being introduced with the connivance of the local authorities. This man exacted a share in the profits which the smugglers were making and reported that he had found nothing out of the way. A second investigator followed the same course. A third, sent to confiscate a vessel which had just entered port from Mexico, found dissimulation impossible and was compelled to confiscate the ship and order the arrest of the port authorities. When the case came before the *audiencia*, the highest court in America, only a few of the culprits were punished, and they received very light sentences.[1]

Though the other European powers no longer encouraged buccaneering, they encouraged smuggling and endeavored when the opportunity offered to compel Spain to give them a share in the trade through legal channels. During the War of the Spanish Succession (1702–1713) when Spain and France were allies, French vessels sailed freely around Cape Horn to Peru and traded with other provinces. At the end of the war, England exacted from Spain the grant of the *asiento*, the contract for supplying slaves to the colonies, and with it the right to send one ship each year to the fair at Porto Bello. The South Sea Company, to which these privileges were ceded, built up a large trade. The *navío de permiso* often brought half as much merchandise to Porto Bello as the entire Spanish fleet, for she was accompanied by tenders which remained below the horizon during the day and replenished her stock of goods at night. The factories, or agencies, which the company established at several ports in connection with the *asiento* also carried on much smuggling. When Spain attempted to check these practices, the British government supported the company, and the "War of Jenkins' Ear" resulted in 1739. The Company's privileges were not restored when the war ended.

By this time, however, even the powerful merchants of the Seville *consulado* could not prevent changes in the commercial system. Seville was no longer an important seaport because silt had made the Guadalquivir too shallow for the larger ships of the seventeenth century, and after 1680 the fleets regularly sailed from the rival city of Cádiz. In 1717 the *Casa de Contratación* itself was moved to Cádiz.

A more important break with the past, under the Bourbon kings, was the establishment of several chartered companies to develop the trade of regions which had hitherto dealt chiefly with smugglers. Most of these were financed in Catalonia or in northern Spain rather than at Seville or Cádiz. They were given special privileges in the trade of one or more provinces and expected to organize forces to prevent smuggling there. The earliest was the Honduras Company, set up in 1714, and there were others in Venezuela, Habana, and Santo Domingo. The only successful one was the Caracas or Guipuzcoa Company which was given extensive privileges in Venezuela in 1728. This company's oppressive conduct and

[1] Juan and Ulloa, *Noticias Secretas de América* (London, 1826 ed.), p. 206.

its success in checking smuggling caused much dissatisfaction among the colonists, but it continued to control the trade of the province until 1781.

The merchant fleets were gradually discontinued. After 1740 traffic around Cape Horn to Peru was permitted, and the old route across the Isthmus of Panama practically ceased to be used. Thenceforth legitimate trade with all of the colonies except Mexico was carried on in "register ships" sailing alone. Until 1765 these were generally required to sail to and from Cádiz, but in that year several other Spanish ports were given permission to trade directly with the islands of the West Indies. Similar privileges were soon extended to other parts of the Empire, and after the famous free trade ordinance of 1778 trade with Spain was relatively free except in Venezuela, where the Caracas Company was still operating, and in Mexico. In 1789 the Mexican fleets were finally discontinued. All of the colonies were thereafter allowed to trade directly with the principal Spanish ports, and in 1790 the *Casa de Contratación* was abolished. Most of the restrictions on intercolonial trade were also lifted in the decade of the 1770's.

Spain, like other colonial powers, still attempted to forbid commerce between her possessions and other countries. During the eighteenth-century wars, however, the government not only was frequently obliged to make exceptions in favor of friendly powers but often found it impossible to prevent trade with merchants of hostile powers. When the British occupied Habana in 1762, and again when they seized Montevideo in 1807, hundreds of ships brought in merchandise and carried away the colonies' products. Ordinary smuggling also continued. The commercial ambitions of other nations—England, France, and the United States— were to have an important influence on the course of events when the colonies began their war for independence.

BRAZILIAN TRADE IN THE EIGHTEENTH CENTURY

By the beginning of the century, Portugal had withdrawn the special privileges that her weakness had compelled her to grant to other powers. Brazilian trade was confined to the fleet system that had been instituted after the Dutch wars. It was the English, however, who benefited chiefly from the monopoly, for the Methuen Treaty of 1703 gave England a dominant position in the trade of the mother country itself. Goods and even ships that came to Brazil were made in England and sent out for the account of English merchants, and a large part of the colony's exports went to pay for them.

The production of sugar, which had provided the principal export, was becoming less profitable because of competition from the recently established English and French plantations in the West Indies, but a new source of wealth developed after Paulista explorers found rich gold deposits in what is now the State of Minas Geraes. The discovery caused tremendous excitement. Many thousands of persons abandoned the older settlements, taking their slaves with them, and other thousands came from Portugal. These immigrants from Europe—the *Emboabas*, as the Brazilians called them—were soon engaged in a bloody contest with the Paulistas who considered the mines theirs by right of discovery. The newcomers were better led and better organized, and their chief, Nunes Viana, was for a time virtually the ruler of the mining district. Even the governor was at first refused permission to enter the district, and it was some time before the royal officials were able to assert their authority and to restore a semblance of order.

The Paulistas were somewhat consoled for their defeat in Minas Geraes when they discovered other rich gold mines in Matto Grosso in 1719 and in Goyaz in 1725. Still more important was the finding of diamonds in 1729 in the gold washings along some of the tributaries of the São Francisco River. The influx of population into the mining regions continued on a scale that seemed to threaten the depopulation of the agricultural districts of the coast, and great cities arose where there had been no inhabitants a few years before.

As in the Spanish colonies, the law required that one-fifth of all gold and silver extracted be paid to the king, but it was so difficult to collect these royalties in the early days of the gold rush that the Crown agreed to accept a relatively small lump-sum payment from the miners' organization. Later, the regular tax on gold was imposed for a time, but in 1735 it was replaced by a head tax on slaves employed in the mines. This was less easily evaded, but it encouraged wasteful methods of exploitation so that many of the richer placer deposits were exhausted before the end of the eighteenth century. The collection of the royalty on diamonds was still more difficult because the precious stones were so easily concealed. A head tax on slaves was therefore imposed in the diamond washings also, and this was gradually increased to an exorbitant amount in an effort to check the sharp drop in prices that had occurred when Brazilian stones began to flood the world's markets. In 1771 the government itself took over the control of production and excluded from the diamond district practically everyone but its own officials and workmen.

The Marquis of Pombal, in an effort to retain for Portugal part of the profits that English merchants were making from Brazilian trade, created two privileged commercial companies, one in Pará and Maranhão and the other in Pernambuco and Parahyba. The first seems to have encouraged the economic development of the northern provinces, but the Pernambuco company was oppressive and unpopular. Both were dissolved when Pombal fell from power in 1777. Some of the Marquis' other measures were more successful. The final extinction, by confiscation or purchase, of the proprietary rights of the sixteenth-century donatories and abolition of the fleet system, in 1765, were important steps toward greater freedom of trade.

Toward the end of the century, with the exhaustion of the richest placer deposits, gold mining decreased in importance. Backward and inefficient methods made the mines far less profitable than they might have been. On the other hand, the demand for Brazilian sugar increased—after a slave revolt destroyed the plantations in the French colony of Saint Domingue—and the planters along the coast were again prosperous.

SOCIAL CONDITIONS AT THE END OF THE COLONIAL PERIOD

At the end of the eighteenth century the Spanish and Portuguese colonies were richer and more populous than the states that had just attained their independence in North America. The North Americans had no source of wealth to compare with the silver mines of Mexico or the sugar plantations of Brazil, and their total population was no greater than that of Mexico alone. Mexico City and Rio de Janeiro were far larger than New York and Philadelphia.

The wealth of the colonies, however, was enjoyed by a relatively small privileged group. There was a striking contrast between the opulence of the upper class and the poverty and degradation of the masses of the people. The latter worked for the most part under some form of bondage on the properties of the relatively few families of European descent, who owned the mines and also the plantations and the cattle ranches that represented an even greater amount of wealth. Within the upper class itself there were sharp distinctions of social position and privilege: officials and immigrants from Europe considered themselves superior to the whites born in the colonies, and among the latter, wealth or inherited prestige gave certain families a pre-eminent position. Colonial society was thus divided into several sharply defined castes. Each was jealous of its prerogatives and looked down on the class below, and the policy of the governments—with their grants of special privileges to some and their discriminations against others—seemed deliberately designed to create hatreds and rivalries that would prevent unity in the colonial body politic. One of the practices that the Spanish creoles most resented was the sale to persons of mixed blood of the privilege of being regarded as white. Caste divisions were to be one of the factors that made it difficult to establish democratic institutions after independence.

In the Spanish colonies, several favored groups, including civil officials, the army, and persons connected with the Church, had a right to be tried by their own special courts, both in civil and in criminal cases. The *fueros*, as these exemptions from the jurisdiction of the ordinary courts were called, were extended until a traveler in Venezuela at the end of the colonial period reported that there were few white persons of any importance who could not claim one.[2] The military *fuero*, for example, extended to all members of the creole militia, even though they were not in active service, and the Church courts claimed jurisdiction over great numbers of persons who were not priests. The system led to many abuses, for the special tribunals were always inclined to favor members of their own order, and evil-doers often sought some minor military or ecclesiastical employment for the sake of the immunity it conferred. The *fueros* were ardently defended, and quarrels over questions of jurisdiction caused scandalous conflicts and, not infrequently, bloodshed. In Brazil the upper class had similar special privileges. Down to the end of the colonial period, the ownership of land was legally restricted to members of the white race [3]—a provision that did not prevent thousands of other persons from occupying land as squatters.

Another sort of discrimination set the upper class off from people of mixed blood. In the Spanish colonies the latter were forbidden to have any part in the exploitation of the Indians, and in the eighteenth century they were debarred by law, though not always in practice, from the universities and hence from the learned professions. Among the people of mixed blood, the *mestizos*, of Spanish-Indian descent, were in a better position than the mulattoes or the descendants of Indians and Negroes, for the latter were compelled to pay tribute, like the Indians and free Negroes, and their women were not permitted to wear gold, pearls, or silk, or to dress like those of the upper class. Such restrictions were perhaps not very rigidly enforced, but their existence on the statute book was humiliating. In spite of them, a large proportion of the people of mixed blood became useful members of the community. They formed the bulk of the artisan class in the cities, and many of them were overseers or foremen at the plantations and mines, or small independent farmers. They also served as mule-drivers and teamsters, and in other occupations one step above ordinary manual labor.

In Mexico and the Andean region the Indians still formed the great majority of the population. Many of them were by this time working as tenants or debt slaves on large *haciendas*, where they were regarded as a part of the owner's property. Others still lived in communities that had been able, with the help of the Spanish authorities, to keep at least a part of their communal lands. They still paid the tribute, or head tax, to the government, in amounts which in some places represented weeks or months of labor at the insignificant wages that they received, and they contributed heavily to the support of the Church, which exacted fees

[2] F. Depons, *Voyage à la partie orientale de la Terre-Ferme dans l'Amérique Méridionale,* Vol. II, p. 60.
[3] Smith, *Brazil, People and Institutions,* p. 474.

for baptisms and marriages and burials and numerous voluntary offerings. The local officials, as we have seen, exploited them mercilessly, although some of the worst abuses of power were stopped after Tupac Amaru's revolt. In general, they did the hard work for other groups in the community, and they received little in return. The distinguished scientist von Humboldt, visiting Mexico at the beginning of the nineteenth century, found them a miserable people, living on the least fertile lands, "indolent by nature and still more because of their situation in the community." We get much the same picture from the accounts of travelers who visited the other colonies.

Humboldt thought, however, that they were no worse off than the peasants in northern Europe in the same period. The fact that they offered so rich a field for exploitation indicates that many of them were relatively prosperous. Their condition varied from province to province, and it was improving somewhat at the end of the colonial period. The *encomiendas* were abolished legally in the eighteenth century, and the *mita* was tending to disappear. Some of the Indians were learning to work for wages, and voluntary labor, because better paid, was more efficient. After Tupac Amaru's revolt in Peru in 1780, forced sales to the Indians were discontinued. On the whole, the natives were probably better protected in their rights, and especially in the possession of their lands, than they were in the first century after the war for independence.

In Brazil most of the Indians in the vicinity of the Portuguese settlements had been exterminated or absorbed in the population of mixed blood. There were still some in the northern provinces. Theoretically, after Pombal's dissolution of the missions, they enjoyed the same rights as the Crown's other subjects, but the change in their legal status by no means ended their exploitation. Early in the nineteenth century, in fact, after the royal family had come to Brazil, a decree was issued permitting the practical enslavement for a term of years of Indians who revolted against the Portuguese authorities. This opened the door for widespread abuses, especially as many of the Indians who had theretofore led a peaceful life in the Jesuit missions had reverted to savagery and had occasionally committed depredations against the Portuguese settlements.

Two-fifths of the 3 to 3.5 million people in Brazil at the end of the colonial period were Negro slaves, who formed the labor force on the sugar plantations and in the mines. There were also many slaves on sugar and indigo plantations in the Spanish colonies, because the government had forbidden the use of Indian labor in such enterprises. The number of slaves was largest in the low-lying regions near the coasts, especially in the Caribbean area, but there were also some in the larger cities, where wealthy families had them as household servants. As we have seen, their treatment, as compared with that of the slaves in the British and French colonies, was relatively humane. They often obtained their freedom, through the piety of their masters or by earning money in their spare time, and there was consequently a large population of free Negroes.

Life in the colonies was not uneventful. Earthquakes and epidemics were frequent, and so too were violent and sometimes bloody quarrels between governors and bishops, or between natives of the colonies and immigrants from the peninsula. Rebellions and uprisings of Indians and slaves were not unknown, and many of the coastal settlements were terrorized by pirate raids in the seventeenth century and attacks by foreign naval forces in the eighteenth. The day-by-day existence of the colonists must nevertheless have been somewhat dull. Women, especially in Brazil, led a secluded life reminiscent of customs learned from the Moors. Few of them were given any education, and many persons thought it inadvisable to teach them to read and write, lest they waste their time on novels or engage in clandestine correspondence.

For the men of the upper class, one of the principal occupations was the incessant intrigue to curry favor with officials or other powerful persons who might aid in obtaining some valuable privilege from the government. Wealthy and influential people were continually called on to help or protect not only their less fortunate relatives and friends but also the multitude of dependents who attached themselves to each prominent family. There were frequent quarrels and lawsuits. Among the chief diversions were what in the Spanish colonies were called *tertulias:* informal gatherings of families and close friends for conversation in the evenings. For the men there were cockfighting and other forms of gambling, and for the whole family the very frequent religious festivals with their processions and fireworks. Outside of the larger cities, even the richer families lived very simply and had few comforts.

INTELLECTUAL LIFE IN THE SPANISH COLONIES

In general, only the members of the upper class received any formal education. In the Spanish colonies, a few schools for Indian boys were set up immediately after the Conquest; but the effort to train Indians as priests and leaders was soon abandoned, and the masses of the natives remained not only illiterate but ignorant of the Spanish language. Very few of the *mestizos* or mulattoes ever learned to read or write. Even the white families had scanty educational opportunities, except in the larger towns, where there were primary and secondary schools, most of them for boys. Most of the educational institutions were conducted by one or another of the religious orders, and all were controlled by the Church. The best schools were those of the Jesuits and the Dominicans.

The ecclesiastical authorities also attempted to make sure that the colonists did not read any harmful books. Books banned by the Inquisition could not legally be imported. An early decree forbidding shipment to the Indies of any but religious works was not enforced, but there was always an effort to exclude publications that might endanger religious orthodoxy or political loyalty. Large quantities of books were nevertheless brought in. It is probable that the colonists had access to about the same sort of literature that circulated in Spain itself. The permission of the Inquisition was also required for the publication of books in the colonies, but this did not prevent some notable literature from being produced there. In the sixteenth century, Spanish writers—most of them members of the Church—wrote several historical and geographical works that are still of value to scholars, and in the seventeenth century, as we have seen, Juana Inés de la Cruz and Carlos de Sigüenza y Góngora won a distinguished place in Spanish literature. Hundreds of lesser poets produced rather indifferent verse, marked by the artificiality characteristic of the period.

In the field of higher education, Spanish America was ahead of Anglo-Saxon America. The first university in the Western Hemisphere, at Mexico City, was formally opened in 1553, and the University of San Marcos at Lima, authorized by the same royal decree, opened some 23 years later. At the end of the eighteenth century there were eight major universities in the colonies and ten or more lesser ones. Theology, law, medicine, and philosophy were the chief subjects taught. Inevitably, curricula and teaching methods followed the medieval patterns that prevailed in European universities of the same period, and Aristotle, St. Thomas Aquinas, Duns Scotus, Galen, and Hippocrates were accepted as authorities who were not to be questioned. Nevertheless, the universities probably dealt with a wider range of subjects, and had a broader outlook, than the much smaller colleges in North America.

Most of the students were from the upper class, but there were scholarships for those who could not pay fees. The university community, which included not only the faculty and students but all doctors and masters living in the neighborhood, had a considerable amount of autonomy and important privileges, including the right to have misconduct and minor crimes of its members dealt with by the rector rather than by the ordinary courts. The rector was chosen each year by elected representatives of the community, and until late in the seventeenth century, the professors were chosen by the whole group of faculty, students, and degree-holders after a competition in which each candidate displayed his ability to hold forth on a passage selected at random from a textbook. The system had to be changed for much the same reasons that might make election of professors by the students inadvisable in a modern university. The students' dress and conduct were governed by detailed regulations, one of which forbid them to bring weapons into the classroom. Graduation was an elaborate and, for the candidate, an expensive ceremony. At Lima, at one period, the new doctor had to give expensive presents to all members of the university community and was also expected to put on a bullfight in the main plaza.[4]

The intellectual climate in the colonies naturally reflected that of Spain, which was slower than some of the other European countries to accept new ideas. Spaniards nevertheless felt the influence of the new currents of thought that changed the outlook of educated men everywhere in the eighteenth century, and the spirit of the Enlightenment was brought to America sooner than it might have been if the old restrictions on colonial trade and navigation had not been relaxed. As travel became less difficult and costly, some of the wealthier creoles were able to go abroad, and a few foreigners, including a small number of scientists and men of letters, came to America. There ensued an intellectual movement that was none the less notable because it was confined to a few centers. In the universities, students became familiar with the work of some of the modern philosophers and began to show a new willingness to question the old authorities. Educated men began to take a new interest in the natural sciences and to set up societies devoted to scientific and literary pursuits. Newspapers, like the *Mercurio Peruano* of Lima and the *Papel Periódico* of Bogotá, spread some of the new ideas.

DISCONTENT WITH SPANISH RULE

One of the effects of this new intellectual activity was to weaken Spain's hold on the colonies. She had thus far held them not so much by her own strength as by their traditional loyalty—a loyalty fostered by the isolation imposed by geographical and legal barriers to communication with the outside world, by the vast authority of the Church, and by the influence of the great merchants and landowners whose privileges depended upon the maintenance of the existing regime. These conservative forces were still powerful, but they were being undermined at the end of the eighteenth century by a rising spirit of discontent. Along with the new interest in science and literature, there inevitably came an interest in the political ideas that were circulating in Europe. Some travelers brought back books that would not have been permitted to circulate in the colonies and lent them secretly to their friends. Such books stimulated the imagination all the more because those found in possession of them might be severely punished. One of the chief duties of the Inquisition, in the eighteenth century, was to check the spread of subversive ideas, and it attempted to control the reading not only of ordinary people but of officials and members of the Church. In 1806, for example, when questions arose between Spain and the United States about the boundary of the Louisiana Purchase, a friar who had been designated to make a

---

[4] For an excellent account of the colonial university, on which much of the above is based, see John Tate Lanning, *Academic Culture in the Spanish Colonies.*

report on the question for the information of the King of Spain found it necessary to consult two foreign histories that the Inquisition had banned. He was refused permission to do so, though the Inquisition finally designated its own representatives to examine the books and extract such information as they considered useful.[5] Such rigid censorship, which extended to the works of many authors who were being widely read in other parts of the world including Spain itself, was an important factor in the colonies' intellectual backwardness.

Despite the efforts of the Inquisition and the civil authorities, seditious ideas continued to spread. Among those who were active in radical propaganda were José Antonio Rojas, a member of a wealthy Chilean family, and Antonio Nariño of Bogotá, who suffered a long imprisonment for circulating a few copies of a translation of *The Rights of Man*. In many places small groups began to dream of independence or actually to conspire to attain it. Their enthusiasm increased after the successful revolt in British North America and still more after the French revolution, for both of these events touched the imagination of thinking people throughout Spanish America. "Since the Peace of Versailles," wrote von Humboldt, "and especially since the year 1789, one often hears a person say proudly 'I am not a Spaniard at all, I am an American,' words which reveal a longstanding resentment." [6]

This resentment was felt by many people who knew little or nothing about foreign revolutionary philosophies. Each class had its own grievances. The Indians were still poverty-stricken and exploited, despite the abolition of the *encomienda* and the *mita* at the end of the eighteenth century. The *mestizos* and mulattoes were subject to legal discriminations which were humiliating if not very oppressive in practice. Even the creole aristocracy, with its wealth and privileges, was becoming dissatisfied as increased knowledge of other countries made the colonists more aware of the shortcomings of the Spanish regime. So long as trade was restricted to the ports of the mother country they still had no adequate markets for their products. The reforms in the political administration had not eliminated misgovernment and corruption. Taxation was if anything more burdensome than before because the establishment of a more effective governmental organization had been followed by efforts to obtain greater revenues for the royal treasury. These efforts, as we have seen, led to several revolts, and the cruel and treacherous treatment which was often meted out to the rebels, after they had been persuaded to lay down their arms, made the colonists still more bitter.

It should be said, perhaps, that the Spanish government was probably not a great deal worse than other European governments of the same

[5] Lea, *The Inquisition in the Spanish Dependencies*, p. 274.
[6] Von Humboldt, *Essai Politique sur le Royaume de la Nouvelle Espagne*, Vol. II, p. 3.

period. Corruption and favoritism and inefficiency characterized the public administration in most countries in the seventeenth and eighteenth centuries. They were possibly somewhat more prevalent in the Spanish administration, but on the other hand many of the higher officials who came to the Indies in the eighteenth century were able statesmen who were genuinely interested in the welfare of the colonies. This interest was evident in the building of roads and other public works, which had been neglected under earlier regimes. Even efficient government was less acceptable, however, when it was conducted, as it seemed to the creoles, by and for the benefit of a privileged group of foreigners.

The creoles' dislike of the peninsular Spaniards was in fact the chief source of discontent. The *peninsulares* still held most of the offices in the government except in the municipalities, and they often played a prominent part in these. They also monopolized the more lucrative positions in the Church, while the creoles served as poorly paid parish priests. The Crown gave them preference in appointments, not only because it wished to keep a closer hold on the colonies but because it was thought in Spain that the American climate had sapped the natives' energy and moral fiber. There was some basis for the idea that the creoles were less energetic and thrifty than many of the immigrants from the peninsula, for they also found it difficult to compete with the Spaniards in commerce. The result of all this was a bitter feeling of hostility between the two groups. Von Humboldt wrote at the beginning of the nineteenth century: [7]

> The most wretched European, without breeding and without intellectual culture, thinks himself superior to the whites born in the new continent; he knows that, with the aid of his compatriots and favored by the luck quite common in countries where fortunes are made as rapidly as they are lost, he can one day reach positions to which access is almost forbidden to the natives, even those distinguished by their talents, their learning, and their moral qualities.

It is not surprising that the creoles felt they were being exploited by an alien ruling class, and that even those who were sentimentally loyal to the king of Spain were eager to oust the king's local representatives and replace them by natives when the opportunity offered.

THE INFLUENCE OF THE ENLIGHTENMENT IN BRAZIL

Intellectually, Brazil was more backward in the eighteenth century than the Spanish American possessions. There was not a single printing press in the country, and the government's policy made it difficult to im-

[7] *Ibid.,* Vol. II, pp. 2–3.

port any but religious books. There were no institutions for higher education because the government thought it advisable as a matter of policy to force the Brazilians to go to Coimbra for university training. The colony's contact with countries other than Portugal had been cut off by the rigid policy of exclusion that had succeeded the more liberal policy of the earlier colonial period.

An increasing number of the richer Brazilians, however, were going abroad to study at Coimbra and other European centers of learning, and some of them came home with new ideas. There were signs of an intellectual awakening like that which was taking place in Mexico, Lima, and Bogotá. The authorities suppressed efforts to set up literary and scientific academies, fearing that they might become centers for the dissemination of subversive ideas, but several Brazilians nevertheless achieved some distinction as writers or scientists during the latter part of the eighteenth century. Especially notable was the appearance at Ouro Preto, the Capital of the mining district, of a group of young poets, some of whom, like Claudio Manoel da Costa, Gonzaga, and Alvarenga Peixoto, were "counted among the most illustrious of the Portuguese tongue." [8]

Several of the Minas poets were involved in the famous conspiracy of 1789, which was a movement for independence. The leaders were a small group of theorists who were inspired by French and North American revolutionary ideas, but they were supported by some of the miners in the province who resented an attempt by the government to collect a large amount of back royalties on their operations. Unfortunately for the conspirators, their plans were betrayed before they were ready for action, and the whole movement came to nothing. The principal leader, a young army officer best known by his nickname of Tiradentes, was executed and several of the other participants were exiled to Africa.

The Minas conspiracy, unimportant in itself, was new evidence of the same spirit which had found expression in Beckman's revolt and the war against the *Mascates* in Pernambuco. The Brazilians, with their long tradition of resistance to despotic authority and with the spirit of self-confidence which they had never lost since the time when they expelled the Dutch from their territory, were clearly not likely to remain indefinitely subject to a mother country which they were rapidly outstripping in wealth and population.

[8] M. Oliveira Lima, *Formation Historique de la Nationalité Brésilienne*, p. 123.

PART II

THE ERA OF
INDEPENDENCE

CHAPTER 6

The Achievement of Independence

DESPITE THE GROWING DISCONTENT with foreign rule and the rebellious spirit that showed itself in the eighteenth-century revolts, the independence of Spanish America and Brazil could hardly have come when it did had it not been for events in Europe. It was the involvement of the peninsular kingdoms in the Napoleonic wars that gave dissatisfied groups in the Spanish colonies an opportunity to take the control of affairs into their own hands and paved the way for the separation of Brazil from Portugal. Spain was an ally of France after 1795, and her naval power, like Napoleon's, was destroyed at the battle of Trafalgar in 1805. This gave England a control of the sea which decisively influenced ensuing events in America.

Brazil virtually ceased to be a colonial possession when the Portuguese royal family, sailing on a British fleet, took refuge there after French and Spanish troops invaded Portugal late in 1807. Rio de Janeiro became for the time being the Capital of the Portuguese empire, and the old relationship to the mother country was never completely restored. As we shall see, the efforts of a new Portuguese government to restore it led to Brazil's independence.

In the Spanish colonies, England's control of the sea made it impossible for the royal officials in America to look to the home government for support and encouraged the still very small groups of creoles who had been dreaming of independence. The first attempts to overthrow the Spanish regime, however, failed because the great majority of the inhabitants of the colonies that were attacked were not disposed to support the revolts.

FRANCISCO DE MIRANDA

One of these attempts was the expedition of Francisco de Miranda, the most famous of the "precursors" of Spanish American independence.

Miranda was born in Caracas in 1750. He entered the Spanish military service as a Captain at the age of twenty-two and took part in operations against England in Florida and the Bahamas during the American revolution. In 1782 he was accused of smuggling and other offenses while acting as aide to the Governor of Cuba, and he fled from the island when a military court was about to render a verdict against him. Thereafter he traveled in the United States, where he met Alexander Hamilton and Henry Knox, and in many parts of Europe, persistently endeavoring to persuade one or another of the powers to support a revolution in the Spanish colonies. He was given little official encouragement either in the United States or in France, though the revolutionary government at Paris at first seemed disposed to consider his project favorably. For a time he served as a Brigadier General in the French army, but in 1793, being unjustly suspected of treason, he was imprisoned for more than a year. In 1798 he went to England.

The British government apparently gave him a small pension, but it was not ready openly to support his plans in America. It perhaps aided him secretly in organizing the expedition of 200 men with which he sailed from New York in February, 1806, and Admiral Cochrane, a British officer who was later to become a prominent figure in the war for independence, helped him when he reached the West Indies. Miranda occupied the town of Coro in Venezuela, but he was soon forced to withdraw for lack of local support. There was much discontent in the colony, where 90 persons had been punished by death or imprisonment or exile after the discovery of a conspiracy headed by Manuel Gual and José María España in 1797; but the mass of the people were not ready to revolt and were still less willing to accept British in place of Spanish domination.

THE BRITISH IN THE RIVER PLATE, 1806–1807

In the meantime, in 1806, the British Admiral Sir Home Popham, who had been interested in Miranda's schemes, decided on his own initiative to attack the Spanish possessions in the River Plate. Crossing the Atlantic from the Cape of Good Hope, which he had just conquered from the Dutch, he landed 1,600 men under General Beresford at Buenos Aires. The Viceroy Sobremonte fled to Córdoba, but a force of creoles from Montevideo, commanded by Santiago Liniers, defeated the invaders and forced Beresford to surrender.

Popham was thus forced to withdraw, but the inhabitants of Buenos Aires realized that the British would undoubtedly make some attempt to avenge his defeat. In the expectation of a new attack, they convened a *cabildo abierto*, a large meeting of the city's principal inhabitants which the municipal authorities were traditionally empowered to convoke in time of emergency. This institution was to be used frequently in the colonies during the ensuing five years. In the Viceroy's absence, the *cabildo abierto* made plans for the colony's defense. Liniers, though he was of French birth and had previously held only a minor position in the Spanish navy, was elected Commander in Chief, and a force of creole militia was hastily organized. A part of this was the legion of *patricios* under Cornelio Saavedra, which was later to play an important rôle in the movement for independence. The *audiencia* took over the civil administration, and the Viceroy, when he returned to the city, was sent to defend Montevideo. He failed to hold this post when a much stronger British force arrived in February, 1807, but when the invaders moved on Buenos Aires in June, Liniers and the creoles put up a desperate fight. The poor management of General Whitelocke, the British Commander, placed his army in so dangerous a situation that he was compelled to surrender, thus ending the British invasion. The Viceroy was now deposed by another *cabildo abierto*, and Liniers took his place.

THE FIRST REVOLTS IN SPANISH AMERICA

The situation in Spain changed suddenly in 1808 when Napoleon forced King Charles and his son Ferdinand to relinquish their rights and placed his own brother Joseph Bonaparte on the throne. The Spaniards, awakening to the fact that the French troops that had come into the country were in reality an army of occupation, promptly rose in revolt and set up *juntas*, or local governing committees, in several parts of the country. Later in 1808, a *junta central* assumed direction of the movement in the name of Ferdinand, who was a prisoner in France. Much to the disappointment of Miranda, who had returned to London after his recent failure, the British government sent to the peninsula an army that had been about to go to America to prevent the control of the Spanish colonies from falling into French hands. The Spanish guerrillas co-operated with these forces, which were under the command of the future Duke of Wellington, but they could not prevent the French from occupying nearly all of Spain in the two years that followed.

With the dethronement of the King, the position of his representatives in America became precarious. The quarrels between different branches of the administration, which had always caused trouble, became more acute when there was no higher authority to whom they could be referred. Moreover, while most of the officials were loyal to Ferdinand, some, like many of their colleagues at home, were suspected of a willingness to make terms with the French. The creoles, though most of them sympathized with the patriots in Spain, saw their chance to obtain a greater participation in public affairs. Many of them felt that they had as much right as the people of Spain to set up *juntas* to exercise authority in the name of the captive King, and demands that they be permitted to do so were strongly supported by the radicals who secretly desired complete independence. On the other hand, the majority of the officials and peninsular Spaniards, and usually the more conservative part of the creole aristocracy, opposed any departure from the *status quo*.

There were disturbances in several colonies in 1808 and 1809. In 1808 the Viceroy of Mexico, hoping to increase his popularity, agreed at the request of the *ayuntamiento* at the Capital to give that body, with its creole membership, a share in the general government. This infuriated the *audiencia* and the peninsular Spaniards. The plan failed when the reactionaries kidnaped the Viceroy and removed him from office, but the affair left an aftermath of bitterness between the two parties. In Upper Peru, the *cabildo* of Charcas, with the support of several judges of the *audiencia*, deposed the President of that body in May, 1809, and invited other municipalities to join it in establishing *juntas* to govern in the name of Ferdinand. La Paz responded to the appeal, but the movement was suppressed in both cities by forces from Lima and Buenos Aires, and those implicated were punished with great cruelty. A similar affair occurred at Quito, where conspirators deposed the President and set up a *junta* which exercised authority until it was suppressed by loyal troops from Guayaquil.

In the River Plate, the ultraroyalist Governor of Montevideo, Francisco Xavier de Elío, organized a *junta* in 1808 to oppose the authority of Liniers, who had become Viceroy at Buenos Aires. The peninsular Spaniards distrusted Liniers because of his French birth and because he was supported by the creole militia that had repulsed the British invasion. A few months later the *peninsulares* in Buenos Aires itself attempted to remove him, but they were blocked by the resistance of the creole military leaders. These events intensified the already existing hostility between the people of Montevideo and Buenos Aires, but both recognized the authority of a new Viceroy appointed by the *junta central* in Spain, who arrived in July, 1809.

THE REVOLTS OF 1810 IN SOUTH AMERICA

In January, 1810, Ferdinand's cause seemed hopeless. The patriot *junta* had been forced to flee to Cádiz where it transferred what authority it still exercised to a "Council of Regency," named by itself. Many of those who had been most loyal to the monarchy began to feel that the colonies must now choose between French domination and independence, and both Spaniards and creoles realized that the supporters of the old regime in America could expect no further support from Spain. Those who wished to establish a new order had the opportunity for which they had been waiting.

The people of Venezuela were the first to act. In April, 1810, when reports of the apparently complete defeat of the Spanish patriots reached

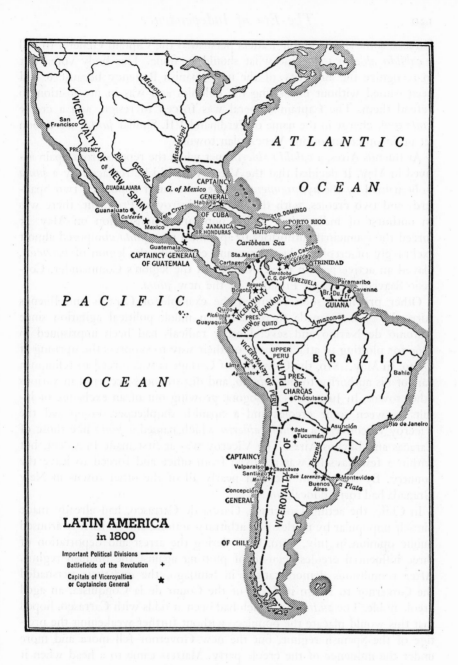

LATIN AMERICA
in 1800

Important Political Divisions - - - -

Battlefields of the Revolution +

Capitals of Viceroyalties or Captaincies General ★

Caracas, some of the creole leaders persuaded the Captain General to call a *cabildo abierto* to decide what should be done. This body voted not to recognize the authority of the new Spanish Regency because it had been named without consulting the colonies and was in no position to defend them. The Captain General was forced to resign, and a creole *junta* took charge in the name of Ferdinand VII. Similar *juntas* were soon set up in other important Venezuelan towns.

At Buenos Aires, a *cabildo abierto* met when the reports from Spain arrived in May. It decided that the Viceroy should be replaced by a *junta* to be named by the *ayuntamiento*. When the latter appointed two Spaniards and two creoles, with the former Viceroy as President, there was an outburst of indignation, and a popular demonstration on May 25 forced the municipal authorities to appoint a new *junta* composed almost exclusively of creoles. The militia, and especially the legion of *patricios*, played an active part in these events, and the legion's Commander, Cornelio Saavedra, became President of the new *junta*.

Other provinces soon followed the example of Caracas and Buenos Aires. In New Granada there had been much political agitation since Antonio de Nariño and several other radicals had been imprisoned in 1809 for plotting to attack troops on their way to suppress the uprising at Quito. In May, 1810, the Governor of Cartagena was forced to relinquish part of his authority to the *cabildo*, and disturbances occurred in various other towns. In July, riots at Bogotá, growing out of an exchange of insults between some creoles and a Spanish shopkeeper, compelled the Viceroy to convene a *cabildo abierto* which named a *junta* like those of Caracas and Buenos Aires. The Viceroy was at first made President, but within a few days he was removed from office and forced to leave the country. By the end of the year nearly all of the other towns in New Granada had formed local *juntas*.

In Chile, the acting Governor, García de Carrasco, had already made himself unpopular by tactless and arbitrary actions, and he further aroused public opinion in July, 1810, by ordering the arrest and deportation of three influential creoles accused of plotting against the Spanish regime. After tumultuous demonstrations in Santiago, the *audiencia* persuaded the Governor to resign in favor of the Count de la Conquista, an aged creole noble. The *audiencia*, which had been at odds with Carrasco, hoped that this would placate the populace without further weakening the prestige of the Spanish regime, but the new Governor fell more and more under the influence of the creole party. Matters came to a head when it was known that Elío, the Governor of Montevideo, had been transferred to Chile. An aroused populace demanded a *cabildo abierto*, and when this met on September 18 it set up a *junta* which at once entered into close relations with that at Buenos Aires.

By the latter part of 1810 the creoles had thus taken matters in their own hands in many of the more important South American provinces. Their actions made it clear that they did not intend that the old regime should return. In nearly every case the *juntas* in the chief cities invited other municipalities to send representatives to discuss a new form of government, and congresses met in response to these invitations in Venezuela, New Granada, and Chile. What the native leaders ostensibly contemplated was the creation of autonomous states under creole control but still nominally subject to the king; but many of them were already planning to seek complete independence, and republican ideas were gradually gaining ground among the people.

While these events were occurring, the *junta central* in Spain and the Regency that succeeded it had been attempting to obtain the support of the colonies in their struggle against Napoleon. In January, 1809, in recognition of expressions of sympathy and substantial financial aid from America, the *junta central* declared that the colonies were integral parts of the monarchy and invited each viceroyalty and captain-generalcy to send a delegate to be one of its members. A year later, provision was made for colonial representation in the new Spanish *cortes*, or parliament. In both cases, however, the procedure prescribed would in practice have left the choice of representatives to the royal officials, and the number of delegates would have been small compared with those allotted to the Spanish provinces. The creoles felt that their claim to equality had received little recognition. Furthermore, since the colonies legally belonged to the Crown and not to Spain, there were many who questioned the authority of a *junta* organized by the Spanish people without effective colonial representation, or of a Regency named by such a *junta*. Colonial resentment increased when it became known that the merchants of Cádiz had been able to procure the revocation in May, 1810, of a decree of the Regency that had authorized free trade between American ports and foreign countries. Subsequently, the *cortes* granted the colonists complete political equality with Spaniards and the right to be represented in future *cortes* in the same way as the people of the peninsula, but this action came too late. Even if it had come earlier, it would have meant little to the colonists so long as the government in Spain attempted to maintain in America a regime dominated by *peninsulares*.

The Spanish American revolution, however, was not so much a contest between the colonies and Spain as a civil war in the colonies themselves. Besides the relatively small but very influential group of peninsular Spaniards, there were powerful elements among the creoles which opposed the revolutionary movement because their own material welfare was bound up with the maintenance of the existing regime. Landowners, dependent on cheap, servile labor, were alarmed by the efforts of the radicals to win support from the lower classes. The creole aristocracy saw that it would be difficult to maintain its privileges without outside support, and its leaders had to weigh the advantage of throwing off Spanish control against the possibility that they themselves would be supplanted by the *mestizo* military chiefs who began to rise to prominence as the revolt got under way. There were, too, many who had moral scruples against rebellion. Though a number of priests were leaders among the revolutionists, the majority of the higher clergy were peninsular Spaniards, and the Church as an institution threw its vast influence into the scales on the loyalist side. Rebellion, in the minds of a large proportion of the faithful of all classes, was a crime against God as well as against the king.

It was the strength of these loyalist elements that made the struggle so long and uncertain. Natives of the colonies formed the greater part of the armies that supported the old regime. Before the war, creoles of good family had eagerly sought commissions in the regular army and the militia, and the rank and file of the forces in the colonies had been recruited locally. Some of these forces went over to the revolution, especially during the latter part of the war, but the people of many districts refused to join the movement. Peru, which had been the center of Spanish power and special privilege in South America, was a royalist stronghold until the end of the war.

At the same time, Spain sent a considerable number of troops to America during the war. Before 1815, while the Regency was still struggling to expel the French from the peninsula, it was able to despatch 15,000 soldiers to different parts of America, and an army of 10,000 sent after Ferdinand's restoration nearly put an end to the revolution in New Granada and Venezuela.

THE TWO PERIODS OF THE WAR

The story of the war in South America falls into two periods. During the first, the creole regimes in Venezuela, New Granada, Buenos Aires, and Chile were simply struggling for existence, weakened by rivalries among their leaders, and unable to win decisive victories over the royalists. Many places, even in those provinces, and nearly all of the territory now included in Peru, Bolivia, and Ecuador remained under Spanish control. This phase of the contest ended with the reinstatement of the Bourbons at Madrid and the restoration of Spanish authority almost everywhere except in the River Plate. The second began in 1817 when San Martín crossed the Andes to liberate Chile. Soon after this exploit Bolívar began to reorganize the scattered bands of revolutionists in the Orinoco Valley and to win victories in New Granada and Venezuela. Working independently and coming into contact with one another only when their objective had been almost accomplished, these two great leaders advanced from the south and from the north until the war was finally won in the highlands of Peru.

THE WAR IN THE NORTH, 1810–1816

Soon after its creation, the *junta* at Caracas sent three commissioners to London to ask recognition and aid from the British government. One of these was Andrés Bello, who was later to become one of the most famous writers and publicists of Spanish America. Another was Simón Bolívar, a wealthy young creole, who had traveled extensively in Europe during the years just before 1810 and had there become imbued with revolutionary ideas. The commissioners failed in their purpose, but in London they met Francisco de Miranda and established contact with the influential group whom he had already interested in the patriot cause. Miranda returned to Venezuela at the end of 1810 and at once became prominent in the Congress that met a few months later to consider the adoption of a new form of government. With Bolívar he worked zealously for the abandonment of any pretense of loyalty to Ferdinand VII and for a complete separation from Spain, and his efforts were crowned with success when the Congress voted a declaration of independence on July 5, 1811. In December of the same year a constitution was adopted, and Venezuela became a federal republic.

The new government was weakened by rivalries between the patriot leaders and the indifference or hostility of a large portion of the inhabitants, and its fate was sealed when a destructive earthquake occurred on March 26, 1812. The priests told the populace that the disaster was a punishment inflicted upon them by Providence for their rebellion. Many abandoned the patriot cause, and Domingo de Monteverde, a Spanish naval officer who had entered the province earlier in the same month with a force of 500 men, made rapid progress against the republican army under Miranda. On July 25, the latter entered into a capitulation which restored Spanish authority in return for a promise that the lives and property of the Venezuelans would be respected. The agreement was shamelessly violated after the rebels laid down their arms. Bolívar and his associates felt that Miranda had betrayed them, and when the leader was about to leave the country they seized him and turned him over to the royalists. The great precursor of independence died in a Spanish prison four years later. Bolívar, who was permitted to leave Venezuela under a passport from Monteverde, went to Cartagena to offer his assistance to the revolutionists there.

Cartagena had declared itself an independent republic in November, 1811, and several other provinces in New Granada had followed its example; but local jealousies made it impossible to set up a central government. The forces of the various towns were fighting among themselves as often as against the royalists who still held Santa Marta in the north and Popayán in the south. When Bolívar arrived at Cartagena, he was given command of a force with which he carried on successful minor operations against the royalists in the Magdalena Valley. Meanwhile the revolted provinces reached an agreement that made some measure of joint action possible, and Antonio Nariño, the President of Cundinamarca, undertook a campaign against Popayán while Bolívar attempted the reconquest of Venezuela. Nariño's campaign, successful at first, ended when he fell by accident into the hands of the enemy in May, 1814. Bolívar was hardly more successful. He overran Venezuela in 1813 and regained control of Caracas; there he was given the title of "Liberator" which was thereafter his proudest possession. A year later, however, he was driven out of the province by an army which had been recruited by a Spanish adventurer named Boves among the half-savage plainsmen of the Orinoco Valley. During this campaign the leaders on both sides resorted to the ruthless brutality which thenceforth characterized the war in all parts of South America. Bolívar proclaimed a "war to the death," threatening to kill all Spaniards even though they remained neutral, and in February, 1814, he ordered the summary execution of more than 800 prisoners in retaliation for the barbarous cruelties perpetrated by Boves against native patriots.

By this time the overthrow of Napoleon had restored Ferdinand VII to his throne, and the Spanish government was in a position to come to the royalists' assistance. In 1815 a force of somewhat more than 10,000 men sailed from Cádiz under the command of General Pablo Morillo. Cartagena was taken after a three months' siege, and the occupation of all New Granada followed. Many of the creole leaders were put to death, and the reconquered towns were treated with a harshness that did nothing to strengthen their loyalty. The revolution in the north collapsed. Bolívar fled to the West Indies, but a few of the other patriots escaped into the *llanos* east of the Andes, where they continued to carry on guerrilla operations.

FAILURE OF THE REVOLUTION IN CHILE

The regime set up by the creole leaders in Chile also had a brief and troubled existence. When the first Congress met in July, 1811, its members divided into conservative and radical factions. The conservatives were at first dominant, but in September a young military officer named José Miguel Carrera seized power and reorganized the Congress with a radical majority. Later in the same year, Carrera assumed dictatorial powers. The other patriot leaders opposed his actions, but most of them came to his support when the Viceroy of Peru sent Spanish officers to recruit an army in the still-loyal island of Chiloé early in 1813. These royalist forces occupied much of south central Chile during the next 12 months, but the fighting was indecisive and the Treaty of Lircai in May, 1814, provided for the withdrawal of the Spanish troops in return for the Chileans' promise to continue to recognize the sovereignty of Ferdinand VII.

This agreement was unsatisfactory to both sides. Carrera, who had been captured by the Spaniards during the war, returned to Santiago to protest against it and again seized control. Bernardo O'Higgins, another leader of the radical wing of the patriot party, organized a counter revolt. Civil war had already begun when word came that the Viceroy of Peru had also disapproved the treaty and was sending another army to Chile. O'Higgins at once placed himself under Carrera's orders, but the patriot forces were defeated at Rancagua on October 2, 1814. The two leaders, with 3,000 men, escaped across the Andes to Mendoza.

EVENTS IN THE RIVER PLATE

By 1816 the River Plate region was the only important part of Spanish America that had not been reconquered by the royalists. While the patriot movement was rising and falling in the north, a series of weak governments at Buenos Aires were endeavoring, with only partial success, to liberate the rest of the territory of the former viceroyalty. The *junta* set up in May, 1810, sent hastily recruited forces into several of the interior provinces. One which invaded Paraguay was defeated by the people of Asunción who did not wish to be ruled by Buenos Aires but who quietly removed the Spanish officials and set up an independent government of their own in 1811. Another force invaded the *Banda Oriental*, as Uruguay was then called. With the aid of local forces under José Artigas, it laid siege to Montevideo but suspended hostilities, by agreement with the royalists, when Portuguese forces entered the province from Brazil. A third army took Córdoba and then went on into Upper Peru. Several royalist commanders, including the former Viceroy Liniers, were executed by order of the *junta*, so that war without quarter became the practice in southern South America as in the north. The patriot army reached Lake Titicaca but was surprised and routed at Huaqui in June, 1811.

In the meantime there had been continual factional disputes at Buenos Aires. Mariano Moreno, the brilliant and enthusiastic secretary of the *junta*, resigned when the *junta*, led by Saavedra, voted to admit to its membership several deputies from the provinces. Moreno died soon afterward, while on his way to Europe on a diplomatic mission; but his followers continued to cause trouble, and in April, 1811, several of them were expelled from the *junta* after a military demonstration by the *Saavedristas*. After the defeat at Huaqui, Saavedra himself was exiled.

In September, 1811, the *junta*, which was too large for the effective conduct of business, transferred the executive power to a "triumvirate." This group soon dissolved the parent body and assumed full power, only to be ousted in October, 1812, by a barracks revolt that installed a new triumvirate. Among the leaders in this movement were José de San Martín and Carlos de Alvear, two creole officers formerly in the Spanish army who had recently arrived from Europe to offer their services in the cause of independence.

Military operations continued, with indifferent success. In the north, the royalists had taken the offensive. Manuel Belgrano checked their invasion by defeating them at Tucumán in September, 1812, and at Salta in February, 1813; but he was repulsed when he attempted to invade Upper Peru. In the *Banda Oriental*, hostilities against the Spaniards were renewed after British diplomatic pressure persuaded the Prince Regent at Rio de Janeiro to sign an armistice with Buenos Aires in May, 1812.

Artigas, the leader of the patriots in the *Banda Oriental*, had withdrawn from the province when the Portuguese invaded it. He took with him, by persuasion or by force, almost the whole population of the districts where his leadership was recognized, and for several months his followers and their families lived in a temporary camp at Ayuí, on the west bank of the Uruguay River, with trees and oxcarts as their only shelter. He then joined forces again with an army from Buenos Aires. A patriot victory at El Cerrito opened the way to Montevideo, but before the city could be taken, the success of the enterprise was threatened by a political dispute.

The government at Buenos Aires had thus far been controlled by the *porteños*, the people of the Capital, and this had caused much jealousy in the provinces. Artigas was the most prominent of the provincial leaders; and when the second triumvirate ordered the election of a Constituent Assembly to meet in 1813, he chose the delegates from the *Banda Oriental* and instructed them to advocate a "federal" republic in which the provinces would have complete autonomy. The Assembly, dominated by the *porteños*, refused to seat the Artigas delegates and ordered the election of new ones. Thereupon Artigas withdrew his troops from the army that was besieging Montevideo. His action began a war between "federalists" and "unitarians" which was to keep the whole River Plate region in a state of near-anarchy for many years.

Despite Artigas' action, the Assembly met, with delegates from most of the provinces, and adopted a series of measures that practically terminated the colonial regime in Argentina. The use of the royal coat of arms and the invocation of the king's name in official acts were abolished; entails and titles of nobility were suppressed; and the Indians were exempted from forced labor. All persons brought into the country or born there in the future were declared free, although the existing Negro slaves, of whom there were a considerable number, were not emancipated. Alvear and his associates were very influential in the work of the Assembly, and in January, 1814, Alvear's uncle, Gervasio Posadas, was elected to the newly created position of "Supreme Director of the United Provinces of the River Plate."

The Assembly did not adopt a constitution or make a specific declaration of independence. Many of the more conservative leaders, though they did not intend to permit the restoration of the old regime, felt that the best solution for the country's problems would be the establishment of a constitutional monarchy. One faction supported the aspirations of Carlota Joaquina, the ambitious and unprincipled sister of Ferdinand VII and the wife of the Prince Regent of Portugal. Carlota had accompanied her husband to Brazil and was carrying on intrigues from there with creole leaders in the River Plate and in Chile. The traditional antipathy to the Portuguese made her cause unpopular in Buenos Aires, and several persons were executed there after the discovery of a plot in her favor in 1812. There was less opposition to other members of the royal family. After the Bourbon restoration, Posadas' government sent representatives to Europe to seek to persuade a Spanish prince to accept the throne, but Ferdinand VII would not permit any of his relatives to consider their proposals.

Meanwhile, without Artigas' help, the *porteños* had taken Montevideo, depriving the royalists of their last stronghold in the River Plate region. If the city had not fallen when it did, it is very possible that the army which reconquered New Granada some months later might have been sent against Buenos Aires instead. The *porteños*, however, did not long hold the city, for Artigas drove them out of whole *Banda Oriental* in 1815.

Federalist *caudillos* in the other provinces joined Artigas in a general revolt against the government at Buenos Aires and formed a loose confederation under his leadership which included Entre Rios, Santa Fe, Corrientes, and Córdoba, as well as the *Banda Oriental*. The Uruguayan *caudillo* was for a time the most powerful figure in the River Plate region, but he was finally defeated by the Portuguese who again invaded the *Banda Oriental* and conquered the province after four years of fighting. Artigas was compelled to take refuge in Paraguay.

The other federalist leaders continued the war against the "unitarians." The *porteño* party continued to hold the Capital and some of the interior provinces, but it was weakened by factional quarrels and military reverses. Posadas was soon forced to resign, and several short-lived regimes followed. A third attempt to invade Upper Peru failed in 1815, and the royalists might well have conquered northern Argentina had it not been for the heroic resistance of Martín Güemes and his *gaucho* army, which held the frontier until the tide turned in favor of the patriot cause.

When a Congress representing the provinces that recognized the authority of the Buenos Aires government met early in 1816 at the northern city of Tucumán, the delegates decided to renew the effort to set up a constitutional monarchy. Belgrano, one of the chief *porteño* leaders, proposed the creation of an Inca dynasty, which might be expected to attract the support of the Indians of Peru, and this fantastic plan was seriously discussed. Negotiations were also resumed in Europe, and various candidates, including the future King Louis Philippe of France and Ferdinand VII's nephew, the Prince of Lucca, were considered. Although there was increasing popular opposition to the monarchical idea, these negotiations continued for some years; but they failed, as the earlier efforts did, because Ferdinand VII refused to give up his own claim to the throne.

The Congress also adopted a formal declaration of independence, on July 9, 1816, and elected Juan Martín de Pueyrredón Supreme Director of the United Provinces for a three-year term. The new government was still opposed by some of the federalist-controlled provinces, but for a time it had somewhat more prestige and authority than any of its predecessors. Its inauguration made possible the renewal of the war against Spain at a time when continued inaction might have meant the complete defeat of the patriot cause.

SAN MARTÍN AND THE LIBERATION IN CHILE

The war was renewed through the efforts of one determined leader. José de San Martín was born in 1778 in one of the old Paraguay missions, where his father commanded the Spanish garrison. The family returned to Spain while José was still very young, and the boy entered the royal army at the age of eleven. Twenty-two years later, after serving with distinction in Africa and in Europe, he had reached the rank of lieutenant colonel. Early in 1812 he arrived in Buenos Aires to offer his services to the revolutionary government. He was at once given a commission in the army and soon began to play an influential part in political as well as military affairs. Early in 1813 he distinguished himself by winning a battle at San Lorenzo which drove the royalists out of the littoral provinces. For a short time in 1814, after the failure of the second invasion of Upper Peru, he was made Commander in Chief of the forces in the north, but he soon asked to be relieved of this duty and a few months later obtained the governorship of the province of Cuyo, at the foot of the Andes in western Argentina. He seems already to have had in mind the idea of securing the independence of

South America by expelling the Spanish forces from Chile and then making an attack on Peru by sea. For two years he quietly matured his plans and trained his troops, and when his friend Pueyrredón became head of the government he obtained more effective help from the central authorities.

San Martín's passage of the Andes, in January, 1817, is one of the great exploits of military history. The transportation of an army with its supplies and artillery over difficult passes more than two miles above sea level was in itself a notable feat, made possible only by the care and thoroughness with which the Commander in Chief made his preparations and his skill in deceiving the enemy as to his intentions. Within a month he was able to unite his forces in the western valleys, and on February 12 he defeated the royalists at Chacabuco and forced them to evacuate Santiago. The Chileans received him with enthusiasm, for the stupidly repressive policy of the royal officials since 1814 had alienated many who had formerly opposed the patriot cause. After San Martín declined its invitation to assume charge of the government, a *cabildo abierto* at Santiago elected Bernado O'Higgins as Supreme Director, and on February 12, 1818, the independence of Chile was formally proclaimed. The Viceroy at Lima sent a new army under General Osorio to reconquer the province, and this force defeated the patriots at Cancha Rayada in March, 1818, but three weeks later, on April 5, San Martín won the decisive battle of Maipú. Thereafter small bodies of royalists held out in the south, especially in the island of Chiloé, but the Spaniards did not again threaten central Chile.

SAN MARTÍN IN PERU

The expedition against Peru, San Martín's next objective, would be possible only if the patriots obtained control of the sea. O'Higgins' government therefore set out to create a fleet. Several foreign ships, invited to go to Chile by the patriots' agents abroad, were purchased and put into service under British and North American officers. Among the latter was Captain Charles Whiting Wooster, formerly of the United States Navy, who played an active part in operations that broke the royalist blockade of Valparaiso and finally gave the patriots control of the sea on the South American west coast. Early in 1819 the fleet was placed under the command of Thomas Alexander, Lord Cochrane, a brilliant officer who had been discharged from the British navy after quarreling with his superiors and being convicted, perhaps unjustly, of financial irregularities. Eighteen months later, preparations for the expedition northward were completed.

By this time, San Martín's friends had lost control at Buenos Aires. Pueyrredón had met with increasing opposition from those who disapproved of the effort to set up a monarchy under a European prince, and his failure to act when the Portuguese invaded the *Banda Oriental* had cost him much prestige. When the Congress in 1819 adopted a constitution providing for a centralized form of government, opposition in the provinces rapidly increased. Pueyrredón, thoroughly discouraged, refused to accept a second term when his first expired in 1819, and the government was overthrown a year later when his successor, General Rondeau, was defeated by the federalists at the battle of Cepeda. The control of affairs passed into the hands of the local *caudillos* in each province, and for some years there was no effective central government. San Martín had refused to obey the unitarian regime's order to return to support it in the war, and he could expect no help from the federalists, who were his political enemies. On the other hand, he still had his own Army of the Andes, and he had the support of the Chilean government under O'Higgins.

Furthermore, events in Spain suddenly made the prospect for success seem brighter. In January, 1820, a Spanish army that was about to embark for America staged a mutiny at Cádiz and took the lead in a revolution that compelled Ferdinand to re-establish the liberal constitution of 1812. There seemed to be some ground to hope that the new regime in Spain might be willing to accept the independence of the revolted colonies, and it was clear at any rate that the royalist authorities were not likely to receive much help from Spain for the time being.

Escorted by Cochrane's fleet, San Martín sailed from Valparaiso in August, 1820, with somewhat more than 4,000 Argentine and Chilean troops. When he landed at Pisco, south of Lima, he found that the Viceroy had been instructed by the new Spanish government to endeavor to reach an agreement with him, and an armistice was arranged pending negotiations. The Viceroy proposed that the colonists accept the relatively favorable status which the Spanish constitution would have given them, but San Martín insisted on independence, though he was apparently willing to consider the establishment of an American constitutional monarchy under a Spanish prince. The negotiations consequently broke down. They were renewed some months later, after the Viceroy Pezuela had been removed by his own officers and General La Serna had been chosen in his place, but again they failed. Meanwhile there were minor military operations, and San Martín occupied points on the coast north of Lima. In July, 1821, La Serna abandoned the Capital and marched inland, permitting the invaders to occupy the city without resistance.

San Martín proclaimed the independence of Peru on July 28 and assumed dictatorial powers as "Protector" of the new state a few days later. His undertaking had thus far met with success. Several of the creole officers in the Spanish forces, including the Indian general Andrés

Santa Cruz, had gone over to the patriot side soon after the expedition landed. On the other hand, a large part of the people of Peru were still loyal to Spain, and there were strong royalist forces in the highlands. With the forces at his disposal, San Martín was in no position to carry the war to a conclusion, and he was compelled to mark time for some months while the now-triumphant patriot forces under Bolívar advanced from the north.

BOLÍVAR'S OPERATIONS IN VENEZUELA
1816–1819

Though the royal authority was re-established in the more settled parts of Venezuela after Bolívar's defeat in 1814, a few small bands kept up a guerrilla warfare in the plains of the Orinoco Valley, co-operating with the New Granadan patriots under Santander who had escaped into the sparsely inhabited *llanos* farther west after the reconquest of Bogotá. Bolívar himself fled to the West Indies. There he obtained help from President Pétion of Haiti, the little state that had freed itself from French rule 12 years before. He led an expedition to the Venezuelan coast in 1816, but dissensions among his followers and their inability to resist the stronger Spanish forces made the venture a failure. He returned to Haiti, where Pétion again helped him, and the end of 1816 found him back in Venezuela, now the recognized leader of the insurgent bands in that province.

During the next two years, while San Martín was freeing Chile from Spanish control, the revolution in Venezuela made little progress. Jealousies and open insubordination made Bolívar's task difficult. Spanish forces that attempted to invade the Orinoco Valley were repulsed, but Bolívar's troops were not strong enough to carry the war into the more populous mountain regions. After a serious defeat at La Puerta in March, 1818, the whole movement seemed certain to end in failure, but Bolívar refused to be discouraged. His army was gradually increasing as the people of the plains rallied to his standard. These wild, ignorant *llaneros* had made up the bulk of the armies that had driven Bolívar from Venezuela in 1814; but they had been alienated from the royalist cause by tactless treatment after Morillo arrived with his Spanish army, and many of them had become revolutionists. Under the leadership of the daring and popular José Páez, they became a formidable cavalry force. At the same time, Bolívar's agents abroad were persuading several hundred British and other foreigners to enlist in his army, and these played an important part in his subsequent campaigns. The Liberator's position was further strengthened when the Congress which he convened at Angostura in February, 1819, confirmed his appointment as Commander in Chief of the army and made him President of the Republic of Venezuela. Meanwhile, guerrilla warfare against the Spaniards had continued, and Bolívar was planning a daring new move that was to change the whole situation.

THE LIBERATION OF NEW GRANADA, VENEZUELA, AND ECUADOR

In June, 1819, in the midst of the rainy season, Bolívar made what seemed an almost impossible march into the upper Orinoco Valley to join the New Granadan patriots under Santander. The combined force then crossed the eastern range of the Andes to emerge on the plateau north of Bogotá. Only a daring and resourceful strategist could have conceived such a maneuver, and only a commander with Bolívar's qualities of leadership could have executed it. Its success was startling. Though the ill-clad and poorly equipped patriots had suffered terrifically from the cold and from the labor of marching through almost trackless country, they surprised and completely defeated a far superior Spanish force in the battle of Boyacá on August 7, and the victory gave Bolívar control of the most important part of New Granada. With a new base of operations and a new source of recruits and supplies, he was in a position to confront the main royalist army in Venezuela.

For the time being he did not follow up his advantage. Dissensions in the Congress at Angostura, where his enemies had obtained the upper hand, compelled him to make the long and dangerous journey back to the provisional Capital to restore his authority. Early in 1820, the news of the Spanish revolution arrived, and the royalist Commander made overtures for a treaty of peace. He offered to leave the patriot leaders in actual control of the provinces that had been liberated, provided the sovereignty of Spain be recognized, but Bolívar, like San Martín, insisted on complete independence. Hostilities were resumed even before the expiration of the six months' armistice which had been agreed upon.

Bolívar now marched eastward through the highlands from New Granada into Venezuela. On June 24, 1821, he won the second of the decisive victories of the war in the north at Carabobo. This practically freed Venezuela from Spanish rule, although Puerto Cabello, the last royalist stronghold in northern South America, was not captured until November, 1823.

The battles of Boyacá and Carabobo made the Republic of Colombia a reality. The existence of this new state, whose territory was to comprise New Granada, Venezuela, and the as-yet-unconquered Presidency of Quito, had been proclaimed by the Congress at Angostura in December, 1819, and Bolívar had been elected its first president. After the battle of Carabobo another Congress met at Cúcuta to confirm Bolívar's election and draw up a federal constitution. Bogotá soon afterward became the Capital. Great Colombia, as historians now call it, took its place in the family of nations when its government was recognized by the United States in 1822 and by Great Britain in 1824.

With Spanish resistance broken in New Granada and Venezuela, Bolívar was free to turn his attention southward. Early in 1821 he had sent Antonio José de Sucre by sea to Guayaquil, where the creoles had set up an independent government in the previous October. Sucre's first attempt to push into the interior was a costly failure, and Bolívar marched overland to his assistance. He was delayed for some months by the stubborn resistance of the inhabitants of Pasto, who had remained loyal to Spain, and in the meantime, on May 24, 1822, Sucre destroyed the Spanish forces in the region of Quito at the Battle of Pichincha. The Department of the Equator, "El Ecuador," thus became in fact as well as in name a part of Colombia. A few months before, on November 28, 1821, the inhabitants of Panama had thrown off their allegiance to Spain and adhered to the Colombian federation. With the loss of the Isthmus, it became more difficult for Spain to send reinforcements to the royalist commanders still in the field.

THE GUAYAQUIL CONFERENCE

Peru and Upper Peru were now the only important regions still occupied by Spanish armies. San Martín had made little progress after his occupation of Lima, and his situation was far from encouraging. Many of the people of Lima were still opposed to the revolution, and the military dictatorship which he had been obliged to establish was unpopular. It was impossible to expect large reinforcements from Argentina or Chile. There was much discontent among his own troops, and a quarrel with Lord Cochrane deprived him of the assistance of the Chilean squadron. A serious illness in November, 1821, added to his difficulties. Under the circumstances, he did not feel able to move against the Spaniards in the interior. The latter, he wrote Bolívar in 1822, had no less than 19,000 veteran troops, whereas the patriot forces could not put more than 8,500 men, mostly raw recruits, in the field at one time.

San Martín hoped to obtain from Bolívar the help he needed to bring the war to an end. Though he believed that Guayaquil should belong to Peru, he sent troops under General Santa Cruz to assist Sucre in the campaign that led to the battle of Pichincha, and he responded cordially to a letter from Bolívar offering support for a campaign in Peru. On July 26 and 27 of the same year the two leaders met in their famous conference at Guayaquil.

What took place was never fully revealed. San Martín apparently urged that a Colombian army be sent to Peru and offered to place himself under Bolívar's orders. Bolívar seems to have evaded a direct reply. His motives can only be guessed at. He was probably unwilling to share the glory of freeing Peru with another leader and skeptical of the possibility of whole-hearted co-operation. Furthermore, he disagreed emphatically with San Martín's idea that Peru should become a constitutional monarchy under a European prince, and he perhaps felt that this difference of opinion would lead to future trouble. There was no open break, but San Martín evidently left the conference convinced that Bolívar would not furnish the aid indispensable to the final liberation of Peru under any plan of joint action. With an unselfish patriotism that has few parallels in history, he decided to withdraw from the scene altogether, and when a Constituent Assembly met at Lima in September he resigned his authority as Protector and left the country.

San Martín went to Chile and thence to Argentina, but in both countries he found that political changes had left him with few friends and no influence. Practically penniless, he sailed for Europe in 1824. Five years later he went back to Buenos Aires but met with so unpleasant a reception that he immediately returned to Europe. He died in obscurity at Boulogne in 1850, and it was not until some years later that his great services to the cause of independence were fully recognized by his compatriots.

THE LAST STAGE OF THE WAR

Matters went badly in Peru after San Martín's departure. The Constituent Assembly entrusted the executive power to a weak *junta*, and in February, 1823, after the defeat of an expedition against the royalists, a military uprising forced the appointment of Colonel José de la Riva Agüero as President of the Republic. Soon afterward Bolívar sent Sucre with a strong force to assist the Peruvians, but internal dissensions continued. An army which Santa Cruz led into Upper Peru in May was almost completely destroyed. Even after Bolívar himself arrived at Callao on September 1 and was given dictatorial powers, the situation did not improve. The Liberator, prostrated by illness, found it difficult to maintain his authority because many people in Lima and many officers in the Peruvian army felt that Colombian military rule was hardly less objectionable than that of Spain. The Argentine troops that San Martín had left behind were also dissatisfied; and when they mutinied and permitted the royalists to reoccupy the fortress at Callao in February, 1824, Bolívar had to evacuate Lima and retire to Trujillo.

Within the year, however, the war ended in a complete victory for the patriot forces. Bolívar obtained reinforcements which enabled him to take the offensive. His enemies were weakened by the defection of General Olañeta in Upper Peru, who revolted against the Viceroy La Serna, an appointee of the liberal party, when it was learned that the absolutists had been restored to power in Spain. After Bolívar won an important victory at Junín on August 6, the royalists evacuated Lima. Sucre then took command of the army in the highlands, and on December 9, 1824, won the final great battle of the war at Ayacucho. The Viceroy was taken prisoner, and the remainder of the Spanish army capitulated. Olañeta attempted to hold out for a short time in Upper Peru but was abandoned by his troops and killed. Callao, which was still held by the royalists, surrendered on January 22, 1826, after a siege in which the defenders endured ghastly sufferings. Spain had lost South America, although the mother country did not recognize the independence of her former colonies until many years later.

Spain's other American colonies, with the exception of Cuba and Puerto Rico, had also attained their independence while Bolívar was still fighting in Peru. What happened in the other colonies will be described in later chapters.

HOW BRAZIL BECAME INDEPENDENT

While the Spanish colonies were taking advantage of the war in Europe to gain control of their own affairs, Brazil was enjoying most of the advantages of independence without having to fight for it. The arrival of the Portuguese royal family in the first days of 1808 made Rio de Janeiro the temporary Capital of the Portuguese empire. The advantages of the new situation were soon apparent, for a military school, a medical school, and a national bank were established, a newspaper was published, and the royal library of 60,000 volumes was thrown open to the public. Many foreigners began to visit Brazil, and the Prince Regent invited several French artists and scientists to make their home there. Rio de Janeiro and other ports were opened to the trade of all friendly nations, and goods of foreign manufacture began to replace the homemade articles which even wealthy families had previously been compelled to use. The lion's share of the new trade went to British merchants, who were given tariff preferences in a treaty signed in 1810.

The Prince Regent, who became King João VI on the death of his insane mother in 1816, was easygoing to the point of irresponsibility, but he had many statesmanlike qualities. Compared with the colonial regime, his government was enlightened and progressive, and his popularity was increased by an aggressive foreign policy. While his notoriously unfaithful wife Carlota Joaquina was intriguing to obtain a throne for herself in the revolted Spanish colonies, his own forces occupied French Guiana in the north and the *Banda Oriental* in the south. The former province was given up under pressure from the powers at the Congress of Vienna, but the latter, conquered between 1816 and 1820, continued to be a province of Brazil until 1828.

The presence of the Court entailed some disadvantages. The Brazilians now had to support not only the royal family but great numbers of the exiled nobility and thousands of Portuguese hangers-on, and the arrogance of the newcomers intensified the already existing hostility between natives and Portuguese. In Rio de Janeiro, pride at being the Capital and a lavish distribution of honors and titles did much to offset these causes of irritation, but elsewhere there was more discontent. In Pernambuco, where there had always been a strong spirit of local patriotism, a group that sought to set up a republic worked secretly for three years before the discovery of their plans forced them into open revolt in 1817. The movement met with little support outside of the province, and it lost many of its adherents in Pernambuco when the republican leaders advocated radical ideas that alarmed the landowning class. It was soon suppressed, and many of the participants were executed.

João became deeply attached to his new home and refused to return to Europe after Napoleon was overthrown. His continued absence caused much dissatisfaction in Portugal, especially as the abolition of the colonial trade monopoly had severely affected the country's commerce. At the same time, liberal revolutionary ideas had affected the army in Portugal as they had Spain, and in 1820, after the mutiny at Cádiz, the leaders of the troops at Lisbon and Oporto revolted and convoked a *cortes* to frame a constitution. The revolutionists had many supporters among the officers of the "auxiliary division" that had been brought to Brazil after the Pernambuco revolt, and on February 26, 1821, a military demonstration forced the King to promise to accept whatever constitution the *cortes* might adopt and to appoint a ministry satisfactory to the leaders of the troops.

Many Brazilians at first sympathized with the liberal movement, but their enthusiasm diminished when they realized that the new government intended to restore the old relationship between the colony and the mother country. One of the early acts of the *cortes* was to publish a manifesto attributing all of the misfortunes of the kingdom to the absence of the Court and the opening of Brazilian ports to the commerce of other nations. This became known in Brazil a few days after the demonstration of February 26, and the native leaders' alarm was intensified when the King reluctantly yielded to the pressure of his Portuguese advisers and announced his intention of returning to Lisbon.

João apparently hoped that the Brazilians would insist on his staying, and it was probably in the hope of obtaining their support that he convoked a meeting on April 20, 1821, of the electors who had been chosen at Rio de Janeiro as one of the first steps in the complicated process of selecting deputies to the *cortes*. The electors not only insisted that the King remain but also obtained from him a promise to put into effect at once a constitution like that of Spain. Historians have remarked that it is probable that neither the King nor the electors had read this document, but the purpose was to forestall the *cortes'* formulation of a constitution containing provisions harmful to Brazil. The King's action had barely been made known, however, when the Portuguese troops brutally attacked and dispersed the electors' meeting, and João was compelled to abrogate his decree. On April 26 he embarked for Portugal. His son, Pedro, who was suspected of having instigated the action of the Portuguese faction because he wished to be left to rule Brazil himself, was made Regent. Before sailing, João told Pedro that Brazil might soon become an independent nation and exhorted him to seize the Crown if this should occur.

João's parting counsel showed a clear perception of the political forces that were at work both in Portugal and in Brazil. The *cortes* at Lisbon, obsessed with a desire to restore the old colonial relationship, was as blind to realities as the Spanish *cortes* had been ten years before. The young Regent gave every evidence of a sincere desire to discharge his duties as his father's representative, but in April, 1821, the *cortes* destroyed his authority in the greater part of Brazil by inviting the people of each district to form provincial *juntas* corresponding directly with itself. The refusal of these bodies to remit the public revenues to Rio de Janeiro crippled the treasury, and matters became worse when the incompetently and dishonestly managed national bank was compelled to suspend specie payments. On September 29, the *cortes* decreed the abolition of the principal administrative and judicial tribunals that had been established at Rio de Janeiro during the residence of the Court. At the same time, it ordered Pedro himself to return to Portugal, traveling first through England, France, and Spain "to complete his political education." Later it voted to appoint a governor in each province who should receive his orders directly from Lisbon and decided to send additional troops to Brazil to enforce these decrees.

In Brazil these proceedings aroused increasing indignation. For the first time, political affairs were being discussed freely and publicly, especially in the numerous newspapers that had sprung up since the advent of constitutional government, and the native leaders, who were determined to prevent what they called "recolonization," decided that separation from Portugal was the only alternative. Among these were not only the liberals but also many conservatives who distrusted the radicalism of the *cortes* and feared that Pedro's leaving Brazil would result in anarchy. The clergy, most of whom were Brazilians, also supported the movement. The desire to obtain the help of these royalist groups, and the feeling that the maintenance of the dynasty offered the only hope of curbing the separatist tendencies that were already manifesting themselves in the provinces, led even those who would have preferred a republic to center their efforts on persuading the Prince to take the lead in making Brazil independent. They were encouraged to hope for success because Pedro, like many of the radical leaders, was a Mason.

It was difficult for these groups to achieve their purpose because the party that supported the *cortes* was in a strong position. Several thousand nobles and Portuguese merchants had left Brazil after the King's departure, but the troops of the "auxiliary division" were still stationed at Rio de Janeiro and Bahia. A part of the well-disciplined army trained by British officers during the peninsular war, these forces had an influence out of all proportion to their numerical strength. At Bahia, the Commander, supported by the Portuguese merchants resident in the city, openly refused to recognize Pedro's authority. At Rio de Janeiro a demonstration staged by the garrison in June, 1821, compelled Pedro to swear allegiance to the constitutional regime in Portugal and to dismiss his Chief Minister, who had aroused the officers' distrust.

The advocates of independence nevertheless soon gained the upper hand. When the *cortes* ordered Pedro to return to Europe the provincial *junta* of São Paulo presented an eloquent memorial urging him to defy the *cortes*, and another of like tenor bearing 8,000 signatures was laid before the Prince by the President of the Municipal Council of Rio de Janeiro. Impressed by this evidence of popular support, Pedro publicly declared on January 9, 1822, that he would remain in Brazil. The Portuguese troops were intimidated by the resolute attitude of a great concourse of townspeople and were finally prevailed upon to embark for Portugal, after receiving their pay for three months in advance. A few weeks later, when a Portuguese fleet came to carry Pedro back to Lisbon, it was not permitted to enter the harbor until the Commander had agreed to comply with Pedro's orders.

A new ministry was appointed at Rio de Janeiro, and José Bonifacio de Andrada, the President of the provincial *junta* at São Paulo, became Pedro's chief adviser. José Bonifacio [1] was perhaps the most notable Brazilian of his time. Born at Santos in 1763, he had attended the University of Coimbra and had traveled in several European countries studying mineralogy and metallurgy with the great authorities of the day. He afterward held official positions at Lisbon and fought at the head of a group of students against the French when they invaded Portugal in 1807. In 1819, he returned to Brazil. With the aid of his two brothers, Martim Francisco and Antonio Carlos, he soon became the

[1] In Brazil, Christian names, without the family name, are often used in speaking of well-known persons.

chief political leader in São Paulo. He was now to play a leading rôle in the political affairs of Brazil during one of the critical periods of the country's history.

Pedro's refusal to obey the *cortes'* command to leave Brazil made a final break merely a question of time. Though his authority was respected only in the southern provinces—Rio de Janeiro, Minas Geraes, São Paulo, and Rio Grande do Sul—and none of the others responded when the new ministry convened a council of *procuradores*, or representatives of the people, in February, 1822, he assumed the title of Perpetual Protector and Defender of Brazil on May 13 and, on June 3, issued a call for a Constituent Assembly. On September 7, 1822, while Pedro was visiting the Province of São Paulo, he received despatches which convinced him that the moment for a final decision had arrived. Drawing his sword, he dramatically cried "Independence or Death"— the *Grito de Ypiranga* which has ever since been commemorated as the Brazilian declaration of independence. His action was enthusiastically acclaimed in São Paulo and Rio de Janeiro, and on October 12 he was solemnly proclaimed constitutional Emperor of Brazil. Portuguese residents were given the alternative of accepting the new regime or leaving the country.

Under the energetic leadership of José Bonifacio, the imperial government rapidly extended its control over the provinces still in the hands of the Portuguese. Lord Cochrane, who had left Peru after his quarrel with San Martín, was employed to organize a navy, and other officers and seamen were brought out from England under contract. In July, 1823, forces sent by land and sea forced the Portuguese to evacuate Bahia, and by September the provinces north of Cape São Roque, which had been in a state of near-anarchy since 1820, submitted to Cochrane's fleet. The Portuguese Commander at Montevideo soon afterward surrendered. The *cortes* was no longer in a position to support its adherents, for it had itself been swept away by a counterrevolution.

CHAPTER 7

The Problems of the
New Republics

EVEN AFTER the decisive victory at Ayacucho, the independence of the former Spanish colonies was far from secure. Civil strife which began in each of the new states before the Spanish forces were expelled from their last strongholds cast serious doubt on their ability to manage their own affairs. Many of those who wanted independence had from the first doubted the possibility of setting up stable governments under native leadership and had worked for a monarchy under a European prince. Their projects had been defeated, not only by Ferdinand's obstinacy but also because the majority of the people were against them. However imperfectly most of the citizens of the new nations, and most of their leaders, understood what republican government really meant, they were determined to establish republics.

THE MONROE DOCTRINE

It was by no means certain that they would be permitted to solve their internal problems without foreign interference. A spirit of reaction dominated much of Europe, and the principal continental powers were banded together in the Holy Alliance to suppress liberal ideas. After the French army, acting as the agent of the Alliance, destroyed the constitutional regime in Spain in 1823 and again made Ferdinand an absolute monarch, the danger of a similar intervention in Spanish America seemed to increase. The idea was discussed by the allied powers at some of their conferences.

Fortunately, the danger was less serious than it seemed. The new states had friends as well as enemies in foreign countries. Believers in political liberty were enthusiastic over the establishment of a new group of free republics, and mercantile and shipping interests were eager to share in their trade. Other nations had an exaggerated idea of the wealth of Spanish America and high hopes for the opening of great markets there, once the restrictions of the Spanish colonial system had been broken down. From 1810 on, British, North American, and French vessels appeared in increasing numbers at ports under patriot control. British merchants helped the patriots obtain arms and supplies during the war, and after independence, Mexico, Central America, Colombia, Buenos Aires, and Chile were able to float government loans in the London market. Much money was subscribed also for stock in companies formed to take over mines abandoned by Spanish interests. Many of these ventures were wild speculations, and most of them resulted disastrously; but they laid the foundations for a British financial ascendency in Latin America which was to last until the twentieth century. They were an assurance that the new nations would have British support against any effort to deprive them of their independence.

The United States was interested in Latin American trade but still more interested in the success of the revolution for political reasons. The natural sympathy for colonists striving for their independence was increased by the desire to be rid of a neighbor whose presence was likely to drag the United States into the complications of European politics. The government at Washington sent agents on several occasions to maintain informal relations with the revolutionists, and after 1816 Henry Clay, the Speaker of the House of Representatives, ardently advocated the formal recognition of the new republics. The Monroe administration delayed action, chiefly because it desired first to obtain Spain's ratification of the treaty for the cession of Florida; but in 1822 the way was clear, and Manuel Torres was formally received as the chargé d'affaires of Colombia. The establishment of diplomatic relations with the other republics followed.

Both Great Britain and the United States were thus opposed to any foreign intervention on behalf of Spain, and early in 1823, Canning, the British Foreign Secretary, suggested to the American Minister in London that the two governments unite in a declaration designed to discourage any action by the Holy Alliance. President Monroe and his advisers, however, decided that the United States should act alone.

In a discussion with Russia of the latter's territorial claims in Alaska, the United States had already laid down the principle that the American continents were "henceforth not to be considered as subjects for future colonization by any European powers." In his message to Congress on December 2, 1823, Monroe set forth more fully the doctrine which was thenceforth to bear his name. The political system of the powers of the Holy Alliance, he said, was essentially different from that of America, and the United States would "consider any attempt on their

part to extend their system to any portion of this hemisphere as dangerous to our peace and safety." The United States would not interfere
with any existing European colony, but it would view as an unfriendly
act any European intervention to oppress or control the destiny of the
American republics whose independence it had recognized.

We now know that the danger of European intervention had probably disappeared before this message was read. None of the powers
of the Holy Alliance was really prepared to send forces to America.
The French government, which had intervened in Spain, would have
been glad to see republicanism destroyed in the new states but at the
same time wished to maintain trade relations with them. It was interested in efforts to establish European monarchies because that would
achieve both purposes.[1] In October, 1823, in response to a British inquiry, it disclaimed any intent to interfere between Spain and her former
colonies. After this there was little danger that any other power would
act. The enunciation of the Monroe Doctrine was nevertheless an event
of the greatest importance, for it became and has continued to be the
basis for the policy of the United States in the Western Hemisphere.

BOLÍVAR AND THE PANAMA CONFERENCE

Monroe's message met with warm approval in Spanish America, and
shortly before the battle of Ayacucho, Bolívar proposed that a Congress be held at Panama to discuss measures to assure respect for the
principles that the President had set forth. Colombia already had treaties
of alliance with most of the other revolutionary governments, but Bolívar
hoped that a closer confederation might be achieved. He invited not
only the Spanish American states, but also the United States, Great
Britain, and Brazil. By June, 1826, representatives from Colombia, Peru,
Mexico, Central America, and Great Britain, as well as an unofficial delegate from Holland, had gathered on the Isthmus. The governments of
Buenos Aires and Paraguay declined the invitation. Brazil accepted but
did not attend, and Chile, Bolivia, and the United States were delayed
in appointing delegates. At Washington, the delay was caused by a
long factional dispute in Congress. When representatives were finally
appointed, one of them died en route, and the other did not go to Panama, though he later went to Mexico in the hope of attending the proposed second conference there.

The Congress at Panama accomplished little, because national jealousies made any real union impracticable. The Spanish American delegates signed treaties providing for a confederation, for future congresses,
and for joint military action under certain conditions, but these were
never ratified by any of the states except Colombia. Because of the unhealthful climate at Panama, the Congress adjourned after a few months

[1] See Dexter Perkins, *The Monroe Doctrine, 1823–1826*, pp. 105 ff.

with the intention of reconvening at Tacubaya near Mexico City. This second meeting never took place. Bolívar was bitterly disappointed, but the failure of his plan for a new international order in the Western Hemisphere was a small matter compared with the other disappointments that he was to suffer during the next five years.

THE BOLIVARIAN REPUBLICS AND THE *CONSTITUCIÓN VITALICIA*

The Liberator was still President of Great Colombia, though he had left the administration of affairs there in the hands of the Vice-President, Santander. He was also exercising dictatorial powers in Peru, while Sucre, his most trusted lieutenant, controlled Upper Peru, which was soon to become the Republic of Bolivia. The area where his leadership was accepted included by far the greater part of the wealth and population of Spanish South America, for Argentina and Chile were as yet relatively unimportant countries. He was at the height of his power and prestige, and the future of the newly liberated republics seemed to rest in his hands. In his efforts to establish the new governments on a firm basis, however, he faced obstacles which no one man could possibly overcome—obstacles which he himself saw more clearly than most of his contemporaries. The political inexperience of his fellow citizens, the violent local jealousies that prevented co-operation between the liberated countries, and a growing opposition to his own power were to make the last years of his life an anticlimax and a failure.

Bolívar had given much thought to the internal political problems of the new republics, and his conception of the form of government that they should adopt was embodied in the famous constitution which he drew up in 1826 for Bolivia, the new state that had been set up in the region formerly called Upper Peru. This region had been governed from Buenos Aires between 1776 and 1810, and from Lima during the revolution, and both the River Plate provinces and Peru claimed the territory after independence. When Bolívar's able lieutenant Sucre occupied the country, however, he found a strong local desire for independence, and an Assembly that he convened voted in August, 1825, to set up a separate republic bearing the name of Bolívar. The Liberator, after some hesitation, gave his approval and accepted the Assembly's invitation to write a constitution for the new state.

The result was a constitution that provided for a life-president, responsible to no other authority, and empowered to name his own successor. The vice-president was the responsible head of the administration, subject to impeachment by congress and the supreme court. The judiciary was completely independent. There was a complicated procedure for the appointment of local officials, but no provision for real local self-government. The legislative power was divided between three chambers: the tribunes, serving four years; the senators, serving eight years; and the censors, elected for life. Each had the exclusive right to initiate laws on certain subjects, and the approval of two chambers sufficed to make a law effective. The congress was largely self-perpetuating, since the chambers filled vacancies in their own membership from lists of three candidates presented by the "electors": a group chosen every four years by the votes of those citizens who could read and write. Though there were detailed provisions for the exercise of the right of ecclesiastical patronage by the government, non-Catholics, according to Bolívar's draft, were to have freedom of worship. This provision was too advanced for the members of the Bolivian Constituent Assembly, who insisted upon the inclusion of a provision forbidding the public exercise of any but the Catholic religion.

With all its cumbersome and obviously unworkable features this so-called *constitución vitalicia* in some respects more nearly responded to the realities of the political situation of Latin America in 1826 than did the constitutions modeled upon that of the United States which several other countries adopted. It at least recognized that the people of the new republics were not yet ready for democratic institutions and that only a strong, permanent executive could give permanent stability to their governments. It might be argued that the regime that the constitution was designed to establish would have been fully as representative as most of the governments that did flourish in the Bolivarian republics during the next half-century. Its adoption, however, would have made it more difficult for the people of these republics to obtain the political experience which was indispensable for the evolution of the democratic institutions that most of the people of the new states were determined to achieve. The *constitución vitalicia* was certain to be opposed by many who saw in it only a device for the perpetuation of the Liberator's personal power.

The constitution was adopted in Bolivia in November, 1826. Sucre, who had been ruling there since the end of the war, was persuaded by the inhabitants to become the Republic's first President, but he consented to serve only for two years because he was anxious to return to the fiancée whom he had left at Quito. About the same time a similar constitution was adopted by a plebiscite in Peru, and Bolívar was proclaimed President for life. The Liberator seemed well on his way to the achievement of his ambition to unite the countries that he had freed in a great "Confederation of the Andes" with himself at its head.

THE FAILURE OF BOLÍVAR'S PLANS

Disillusionment came almost immediately. A breakdown of discipline soon began to diminish the effectiveness of the troops who had followed

Bolívar loyally during the war but who were demoralized by inaction and the monotony of barracks life. Many of them were paid irregularly, or not at all, and many of them, like the Colombians and Argentines in Bolivia and Peru, were far from their homes in an atmosphere that soon became unfriendly. Some of their leaders began to yield to the temptation to make themselves the heads of independent governments in the districts under their command. Bolívar's personal influence was still great, but he could not be everywhere at once in a confederation where travel from one region to another required weeks or months.

In 1826 Bolívar was forced to return to Colombia to deal with a revolt led by General Páez who had quarreled with Santander, the acting President at Bogotá. As soon as he left Lima, his authority in Peru began to crumble. The Peruvians had little desire to be governed by a man whom they regarded as a foreigner, and they were offended by the creation of a separate state in Bolivia which they regarded as part of their own territory. General Andrés Santa Cruz, who was left in charge at Lima, went forward with the adoption of the *constitución vitalicia*, but growing opposition soon forced him to set it aside and convoke an Assembly to frame another. When this body set up a new government under General La Mar in July, 1827, Bolívar made no effort to reassert his authority.

The Liberator again took over the presidency of Colombia and patched up the quarrel between Páez and the central government, but his popularity rapidly diminished. As we shall see in a subsequent chapter, the Bolivarian constitution was rejected, and the Liberator's last years as President were a period of increasing turmoil. Sucre was expelled from Bolivia in 1828 with the aid of Peruvian troops, and in the same year there was a war between Colombia and Peru which was short and inconclusive because internal troubles in both countries made the continuance of hostilities difficult. In 1830, Great Colombia disintegrated. Páez set up a separate republic in Venezuela, and Juan José Flores, the military Commander in Ecuador, followed his example. Bolívar refused to continue in office and died in December, 1830, just before he was to have sailed for Europe. In his last days, he felt that all his work had been in vain and that only the darkest future awaited the countries that he had freed.

OBSTACLES TO DEMOCRATIC GOVERNMENT

Many Spanish Americans and many foreign observers shared the Liberator's discouragement about the future of the new states. Throughout the former Spanish colonies, military despotism and factional strife seemed to make republican constitutions a mockery. As we shall see in subsequent chapters, Mexico was gradually sinking into a state of near-anarchy after the overthrow of Iturbide's improvised empire, and the Central Americans had been no more successful in their attempt to set up a federal republic. In the River Plate region, civil strife had been almost continuous even during the war with Spain. The hostility of the provinces to Buenos Aires prevented the establishment of a national government in Argentina, and Uruguay became an independent state only after a costly war between the Argentine provinces and Brazil. Chile, on the other side of the Andes, had passed through a period of turmoil and had hardly yet begun to settle down under the autocratic regime of Portales. Chile enjoyed relative peace after 1830, but in nearly all of the other countries disorder and misrule continued for a generation or more to retard internal progress and to invite foreign intervention. The establishment of orderly political institutions was the great problem that the Latin American states must solve if they were to take their place among the progressive communities of the modern world.

In most parts of Spanish America, the victorious revolutionists set up republican governments with constitutions like that of the United States. They hardly realized the difficulty of making such governments work in countries where the structure of society was entirely different. In Spanish America the system of caste and special privilege that had been nurtured by the home government as a means of preventing its subjects from uniting against it survived the revolution and made the establishment of political democracy impossible. Subject races, exploited and oppressed by those who had economic and political power, formed the great mass of the population. The revolution made little change for the better in the situation of the Indians. The *encomienda* and the *mita* had disappeared, but debt-slavery and lack of land of his own kept the rural laborer dependent on the creole proprietors. The Negroes also were still in bondage in most of the countries where they formed any large proportion of the working class, for they were not fully emancipated in Colombia, Venezuela, Ecuador, and Peru until after the middle of the nineteenth century. The *mestizos*, though their condition had probably improved during the revolution, were for the most part poor and ignorant. Wealth, education, and social position were virtually the monopoly of the creole aristocracy, still predominantly Spanish in descent though many successful soldiers of humble origin and mixed blood joined its ranks during and after the war. It was this class that dominated political affairs in the new republics. Its power and its relations to other social groups varied somewhat from country to country. Conditions in Peru or Mexico, for example, were different from those in regions where the Indian population was less numerous, and these differences were to become more important as time went on.

The creole leaders wanted to set up governments that could maintain order and assure the liberties for which the colonies had fought, but few of them were equipped by education or experience for the task that confronted them. The new governments were grievously handicapped by the lack of men qualified to fill official positions, and even the able statesmen that emerged in some of the republics, like Santander in Great Colombia and Rivadavia in Argentina, could accomplish relatively little because they did not have competent subordinates. After the revolution there were few persons who had even a limited experience in public administration because the creoles had been excluded from any participation in the autocratic regime imposed upon them by the mother country. Even the municipal councils, where the creoles could hold office, were not democratic institutions, for most of the members either bought or inherited their positions. The *cabildos* played an important rôle in the early days of the movement for independence; but their aristocratic traditions made them suspect to the patriot leaders, and most of them were soon dissolved or reorganized. Practically all of the machinery of organized government had thus been swept away. It was difficult to rebuild it because one of the effects of the colonial system had been to prevent the growth of any spirit of local initiative and to engender a lack of self-confidence.

The new governments were also handicapped by lack of funds. Some important sources of revenue, like the royalties from mining, had dried up during the war. It was not easy to replace the relatively efficient Spanish machinery for tax collection, and even after the fiscal system had been reorganized, recurrent disorders often prevented the collection of revenues in large parts of the country. Furthermore, the armies almost everywhere absorbed by far the greater part of the money that the government did have, and consequently little was available for more useful purposes or even for the payment of civilian employees.

Unfortunately, some of the worst traditions of the old regime had survived the war for independence. The Spanish officials had been closely, if not very effectively, supervised in matters of interest to the Crown, but they were often arbitrary and greedy tyrants in their dealings with the people under them. Their example, since it represented the only form of government that the colonists knew, was naturally followed by many of their creole successors, despite the efforts of men like Bolívar, San Martín, and Sucre to enforce higher standards of conduct. The whole community had been demoralized by the brutal cruelty of the war, and many of the military chieftains had been accustomed to oppress and rob friends and enemies alike on the pretext of military necessity. They continued after peace was restored to look upon public office chiefly as an opportunity for personal profit. Many of them showed no inclination to give up the power that they enjoyed, and this was as true of the lesser officials as it was of leaders like Bolívar and Páez and Flores. Even where civilian statesmen were able to exercise some influence in the central governments, the provincial governors were usually military men, and the local *comandante*, with a few barefooted soldiers, was apt to be the real ruler of the smaller towns and villages.

It was difficult under such conditions to operate a complicated system of government taken over from people of a different race and temperament. The very principles on which the new system rested were unfamiliar. Under the Spanish regime there had been no real separation of powers. Viceroys, *audiencias*, and many local officials had exercised political and military authority, had issued orders that had the force of law, and had acted as judges. The native presidents who replaced them expected to exercise the same sort of authority, and usually did so. It was difficult for them, or for their fellow citizens, to grasp the concept of a president and congress and judiciary, each acting independently in its own sphere, and when authority was further divided between the central government and the states—as it was in several countries where jealousy of the provinces toward the capital led to the adoption of a federal system—conflicts over jurisdiction became still more frequent. There was no accumulated experience or body of precedents to aid in settling such conflicts, and few of the political leaders had the forbearance or the spirit of co-operation that might have made compromises possible. The tradition of authoritarian government in fact led the people to expect that the man in power would impose his will on those around him, and a president who failed to do so ran the risk of being thought weak. The situation was simply made worse when inexperienced theorists inserted in some of the new constitutions provisions that enabled minorities to block the election of a president or to paralyze the legislature. Often a resort to force seemed the only way to settle disputes between political factions or between different branches of the government.

ELECTIONS

Under most of the early constitutions, the franchise was restricted to those who had a considerable amount of property, as it was at that time in many other countries. Even the upper classes, however, hardly knew how to exercise their civil rights. Often they had no opportunity to do so, for elections were dispensed with or made a mere farce by military leaders who had fought their way to power and had no intention of relinquishing their authority. More often, perhaps, in the first years of independence, the government made a sincere attempt to hold a real election, but the result was almost always unsatisfactory. Disputes inevitably arose over the qualifications of voters, the counting of the ballots, and the frauds committed by both sides. Since there were no impartial courts to decide such matters, these quarrels led to violence, and it was only natural that the intervention of the authorities to restore order should usually benefit the friends of the government. If higher officials honestly attempted to assure fair play, as many of them did, they could not control their subordinates, who had no desire to lose their positions by permitting the party to be defeated. In short, it was impossible for the Spanish Americans to learn overnight to use democratic procedures which had been developed elsewhere as the result of centuries of practice and under conditions far more favorable to success.

It soon became the practice for the party in power to control the electoral process so completely that the victory of the official candidate was a matter of course. By tactics that ranged all the way from intimidation and petty police persecution to exile or murder, the government made it difficult for its opponents to conduct a campaign against it. On election day they were excluded from the polls by force while the government's supporters voted as often as they chose. If necessary, the ballots were dishonestly counted, or the results were arbitrarily changed by the president or congress. Under such circumstances, the opposition frequently did not attempt to contest the election at all. Defeat, even by fraud and violence, hurt the prestige of the leaders in the eyes of their followers. It was hardly worthwhile to expose the party workers to arrest and mistreatment, or to use funds that might better be saved to buy arms and ammunition.

In a situation where an unpopular government could only be changed by violent means, revolution became an accepted and almost a necessary part of the political system. Those in power consequently tended to regard any opposition as an incitement to disorder. For their own protection they imprisoned or exiled leaders whom they regarded as dangerous and kept lesser opponents under constant surveillance. At the first indication of trouble, the government would proclaim a "state of siege," which suspended the citizens' constitutional rights and permitted arbitrary arrests. The lot of members of the party not in power was a hard one. They were the first victims when forced loans were needed for military purposes, and they were persecuted in a great variety of other ways, partly from mere hatred and partly with the deliberate purpose of diminishing their political influence. Political murders, with or without some pretense of following legal forms, were not uncommon. Such treatment often made revolution, with all its dangers, preferable to continued submission, and the result was a vicious circle of revolt to escape from oppression and oppression to prevent revolt.

MILITARY DOMINANCE: THE *CAUDILLO*

With military force the final arbiter, both in disputes between different branches of the government and in the elections, the leaders of the army became the real rulers of the country. Presidents were set up and deposed, and congresses were intimidated or dissolved by barracks revolutions. The losing party, if strong enough, sought to nullify the action of the troops at the capital by taking up arms in other parts of the country. *Golpes de cuartel,* as the barracks revolutions were called, and general civil wars were the two ways in which changes of government were normally brought about during the first half-century of independence.

The men who thus came into power were rarely fitted by character or training to cope with the problems which confronted the new governments. In Peru and Mexico most of the army officers were creoles of the upper class who had served in the Spanish army or militia. In the other countries, many of them were men who had risen from the ranks during the war for independence. After the war, the officers were a powerful privileged caste, subject to trial only by military courts, and drawing at least a portion of their pay even when not on active service. Except in very rare instances, it was the officers alone who directed the army's political activities. A part of the enlisted men were professional soldiers, but the great majority of the rank and file were ignorant Indians or *mestizos,* ill-paid and ill-treated, who had been recruited by force and were serving only because they did not know how to escape. The standing armies were usually small and always inefficient, but they were influential in time of peace because they were the only organized military force.

When civil war came, improvised forces were hastily recruited by both parties. It was here that the *caudillo* played a leading rôle. The *caudillo* was a leader, a man who could command the personal loyalty of a sufficiently large group of friends and followers to make him an important military or political figure. He represented the inclination to exalt personal leadership which has always been a Spanish trait. He might be either a professional soldier, popular among the subordinate officers or the rank and file of the army, or a landowner backed by the tenants and laborers on his own and neighboring estates, or even a politician whose eloquence or other gifts procured him a following. In the earlier period he was usually a hero of the war for independence. Almost always, whether a professional soldier or not, he held high military rank. If his influence was confined to one locality or to one small group, he was usually himself a follower of some more powerful *caudillo* to whom he was bound by ties of friendship and the expectation of favors to be received. His interest in politics, in most cases, was primarily a selfish one—to obtain power and the perquisites of power. Though almost always an ardent member of one of the great political parties, it was not uncommon to find him shifting his allegiance from one camp to another when such action seemed likely to be profitable.

The *caudillos* drew their followers both from the upper class and from the *mestizo* element. Even the creole landowners seemed more interested in partisan political advantage than in the maintenance of peace, for the theft of a year's corn crop or the loss of some cattle from their carelessly managed *haciendas* was often a less serious misfortune than the defeat of the party to which they belonged. This was especially true in countries where backward economic conditions made office-holding more attractive than productive enterprise. The increasingly numerous *mestizos* had even less interest in stable government. A revolution might mean starvation, or death in battle, but it offered a welcome change from the monotony and hardship of daily life and an opportunity for plunder and excitement. Ignorant and excitable, the people of mixed blood were easily stirred up by political agitators and formed the majority of those who served voluntarily in the revolutionary armies. The majority of the soldiers, probably, were involuntary recruits—*mestizos* or Indians who were simply caught and pressed into service by the first commander who found them.

POLITICAL PARTIES

The military *caudillos* who ruled most of the Latin American countries in the period after independence were usually allied with and supported by civilian political groups who regarded them as a dangerous but indispensable instrument for maintaining their own party in power. The civil wars often seemed on the surface to be mere contests for offices and spoils, but they could not have assumed such proportions as they did had it not been for controversies over social and political issues which divided the ruling class, and to some extent the other classes also, into hostile factions.

Usually there were two parties. Whether they called themselves conservatives and liberals, or centralists and federalists, the differences between them were much the same from one country to another. In one camp were many of the landowners and the higher clergy, with their followers among the lower classes, who clung to the surviving features of the colonial social organization, defended the prerogatives of the Church, and distrusted democratic institutions. This group naturally included most of the ex-loyalists, and it was especially strong in cities that had formerly been centers of Spanish power. Primarily interested in the maintenance of the existing order, it tended to favor a strong, centralized government and often supported military leaders from less privileged classes, like Páez in Venezuela or Flores in Ecuador, when their dictatorships seemed to offer the best means of preserving peace.

Opposed to the conservatives were the advocates of more advanced ideas, including a fraction of the landowning class and many merchants and professional men, often of mixed blood, who resented the creole aristocracy's claim to social pre-eminence. Since the Church was on the other side, the liberals were anticlerical. Frequently they advocated a "federal" or decentralized form of government in order to capitalize upon the jealousy of the provinces toward the capital. The position of the Church and the question of centralization or decentralization in government were usually the two great issues in the political struggles of the first half-century of independence.

THE CHURCH

Catholicism was the state religion, and in most of the republics no other sect was officially tolerated in the first years of independence. It is true that the Church had suffered losses during the war against Spain. Many creole priests had sided with the patriots; but most of the higher clergy were royalists, and the majority of the bishops had either abandoned or been expelled from their dioceses. Without them the clergy was leaderless, and their number rapidly decreased because it was impossible to consecrate new priests. Within a few years, however, this condition was corrected. Though the Papacy long refused to recognize the new republican governments, or to admit their claim to the right of patronage, ways were found to fill the vacant sees and appoint new priests.

The Church dominated the minds and consciences of the masses of the people and controlled many aspects of their personal lives as it had during the colonial period. It still virtually monopolized education, though several countries made not-very-successful efforts to establish state schools. The prerogatives of the clergy, with their special courts and exemptions from taxation, were little affected by the revolution, and the efforts of some of the new governments to curtail these *fueros* were vigorously resisted. It was inevitable that the Church should be an object of attack by leaders imbued with nineteenth-century liberal ideas, especially as its wealth was always a temptation to governments chronically in financial straits. Its attempt to defend itself by supporting the conservative party intensified the liberals' anticlericalism. On the other hand, the liberals' determination to confiscate ecclesiastical property, to abolish the *fueros*, and to bring education, marriage, and burial under lay control seemed sacrilegious to the more devout portion of the community. Conflicts over questions of this sort, where irreconcilable and tenaciously held personal convictions were involved, could have appalling consequences.

LOCALISMO

The question of federalism likewise aroused violent animosities, because it had its origin in the spirit of *localismo*, or narrow local patriotism, which seems characteristic of the Spanish people. In each country, the inhabitants of the provinces were jealous of the metropolis and predisposed to revolt against any administration functioning there. It was this separatist spirit that defeated Bolívar's project for a Confederation of the Andes and broke up Great Colombia. It caused the Federal Republic of Central America to dissolve into five little states and brought years of bloodshed to the River Plate region. *Localismo* was a disturbing influence even in lesser political units, for the smaller towns in each district were jealous of the more important ones and often carried on inherited feuds with each other. In many places, in fact, party divisions became a matter of locality rather than of principle, and a town would be predominantly "conservative" or "liberal" simply because a neighboring town adhered to the opposite faction.

Where the advocates of federalism got the upper hand and forced the adoption of constitutions that gave a greater measure of self-government to the provinces or states, the change rarely worked as its sponsors hoped it would. Even presidents from the federalist party were apt to interfere continually in local matters, whatever the constitution might say, because they could not permit opponents or potential opponents to use the state administration as a base for building up a political influence that might challenge their leadership. In the few cases where the state governments did have any real independence, the result was to reduce the central government to impotence and to increase rather than decrease internal disorder.

GEOGRAPHICAL HANDICAPS

Geography played a large part in keeping the spirit of *localismo* alive and was an obstacle in other ways both to stable government and to economic progress. The great mountain ranges in Mexico and Central America and the Andes in South America made travel difficult between the highland communities, where most of the people lived, and between these communities and the coast. Tropical jungles, on the east side of the continent, were an even greater barrier to communication. Except in a very few places, the only roads were rough mule-trails, or paths passable only by men on foot, so that journeys from the national capitals to provincial cities required days or even weeks. Ocean currents and wind conditions often made travel by sea difficult. Ships from abroad could reach the important communities on the west coast only by making the long and dangerous voyage around the southern tip of the continent, and commerce was further handicapped by the fact that there were very few good natural harbors on that coast, either in South or in Central America.

The lack of means of communication made it difficult to create a sentiment of national unity and encouraged revolts against the central governments. A revolution could get well under way before the authorities at the capital even heard of it, and the transport of troops to restore order was a slow and dangerous business. The lack of roads and ports also discouraged production, for mines and plantations could not be operated profitably unless their products could reach a market. In the turbulent years after independence, few of the new governments could do anything to remedy this situation. It was not until the second half of the nineteenth century that a period of relative stability and an influx of foreign capital made road and railroad building and port improvement possible. What was accomplished, however, was only a fraction of what needed to be done, and the improvement of communications is still an urgent problem in most Latin American states.

CONSEQUENCES OF INTERNAL DISORDER

When attempts to change the government led to armed conflicts between the political parties, the consequences were often disastrous. In the chapters that follow, many civil wars will be mentioned and passed over in one or two brief sentences. It would be impossible to describe each one in detail, but the reader will have but an inadequate picture of the history of Latin America if he does not realize what each of these internal struggles meant to the country where it occurred. Aside from the loss of life, often out of all proportion to the number of troops engaged, there was much suffering among noncombatants. The armies lived off the country, killing cattle and seizing other food wherever they went, and agriculture and industry were paralyzed because able-bodied men who did not join in the fighting went into hiding to avoid recruiting parties. With the roads unsafe for travel, internal trade ceased, and imports and exports, upon which the government revenues depended, fell off. The regular forces on both sides looted and committed other outrages, especially in districts where the people were not in sympathy with them, and irregular guerrillas, many of them mere bandits, terrorized regions outside of the zone of major operations. Too often the country found itself at the mercy of the worst elements in the population, under the irresponsible authority of men whose only claim to importance was their ability to command an ignorant and cruel soldiery. After a war, the general demoralization and the hatreds engendered by political executions and other atrocities made it difficult to establish real peace even when one party won a decisive victory.

Internal disorders also embroiled the Latin American states in dangerous international controversies. Europeans and North Americans as well as natives suffered personal injuries and losses of property, and the aftermath of every civil war was a flood of damage claims. Though these were frequently of doubtful validity and usually grossly exaggerated, they were energetically supported by the claimants' governments. In many cases settlements were affected by agreement or arbitration, but in others continued disorder and financial mismanagement made payment impossible. Then foreign powers sent warships, blockaded ports, or even landed troops to force compliance with their demands. Such interventions involved serious dangers, for they might easily lead to a more permanent occupation as one did in Mexico in 1862.

Each of the former Spanish colonies had to contend with the problems described in this chapter. The history of Brazil was different because the empire gave the country a long period of peace at the very time when the other states were suffering most from internal disorder, but after the Republic was set up political conditions were basically much like those in the rest of South America. Social inequalities and illiteracy and the absence of a tradition of free government made it hard to hold real elections, and those who wanted a change of administration usually had to resort to military force to attain it. Fortunately, the fall of the empire came at a time when Brazil, like the other countries, was enjoying a prosperity that for some decades tended to discourage revolutionary movements.

PROGRESS TOWARD STABILITY

The close relationship between economic and social progress and the attainment of political stability makes it necessary to emphasize political development in any study of Latin American history. Without internal peace it was impossible to attract foreign capital for road and railroad building, or to develop natural resources, or to free a part of the revenues of the government for popular education and public health work. At the same time, stability itself was a result of economic and social progress and was much more easily attained in countries where rich natural resources were available or where the racial make-up of the population facilitated the improvement of the situation of the masses of the people.

Stable government was not necessarily democratic government, but the economic progress that often accompanied stability helped to build up powerful groups that were more interested in the maintenance of peace than in the fortunes of any political faction and who were consequently interested in finding some means other than civil war for determining who would control the government. The alternative to violence was the holding of free elections. There were other conceivable alternatives, like monarchical rule or totalitarianism, but they had little chance of acceptance because the majority of the people had no sympathy for the philosophies behind them. The people did want republican institutions, and even in the countries where political conditions were most backward there were few dictators who did not feel compelled to maintain the outward appearance of constitutional government and to go through the form of holding regular elections. As the masses acquired more political experience and influence, it was inevitable that elections should become more than a form.

Any attempt to show how the Hispanic American nations as a group endeavored to deal with their political and social and economic problems is made difficult by the fact that each country presents a different picture. Dissimilarities in the make-up of the population, in natural resources, and in facilities for contact with the outside world combined with accidents of history to make progress uneven. Nevertheless, if we look at the area as a whole, we can see certain broad trends in its development.

Very roughly, we may divide the story of this development into three periods. In the first, which comprised approximately the first half-century after independence, most of the new republics were ruled by *caudillos* who came into power and stayed in power by the use of force and whose followers usually supported them for purely personal reasons. Though men of this type for the most part seemed more interested in the enjoyment of power than in political programs, they usually worked with one or another of the political parties. Throughout the period there was intermittent strife between the two political parties, "conservatives" and "liberals," usually with the relations between Church and State or federalism as against centralized control as the chief issues. There was substantial economic progress in some countries, as in Argentina and Peru, but in general, commerce and the development of natural resources were discouraged by costly civil wars and by the preoccupation of the ruling classes with political conflicts.

In the second period, during the last part of the nineteenth century and the first part of the twentieth, many of the republics had relatively stable and efficient governments, and there was a notable increase in production and exports. Argentina, Brazil, Chile, and Mexico became important factors in world trade. They also benefited from large investments of foreign capital, and in the River Plate and Brazil there was a great wave of immigration from Europe. The older political issues were still troublesome and in some places caused bloody conflicts during the first part of the period, but by the turn of the century they had lost much of their importance. In many countries a new issue arose with the increasing demand for more democratic political institutions, and in several of them, first in Uruguay and then in Costa Rica, Argentina, Chile, and Colombia, the holding of free elections seemed to mark the advent of real republican government.

It is more difficult to describe the third period because we are too close to it. One of its characteristics is the rising influence of social groups that formerly had little voice in national affairs. The growth of industry and the greater participation of natives in business activities are creating a new middle class between the landholding upper class and the industrial and agricultural laborers, and both this group and the workers—especially where they are organized in labor unions—have become more articulate and more active in politics. Both have been dissatisfied with existing economic and social conditions. They have insisted that the governments embark on programs of economic development designed to provide increased opportunities and a better standard of living, and they have usually advocated programs of extreme economic nationalism.

Their influence has not always promoted governmental stability or democratic procedures. Not infrequently they have given their support to leaders who won it by promising social change and who seized and held power by force. Those who disagree with them have also resorted to forceful methods to keep the governments in more conservative hands. In the 1930's and during much of the postwar period there were more dictatorships in Latin America than there were in the first years of the century. By 1960, however, it seemed probable that this was a passing phase and that the traditional determination to achieve democratic government was reasserting itself. In recent years, elections in most of the Latin American countries have been held under freer conditions, and with the participation of a far greater number of voters, than ever before. At the end of 1959, there were only three or four dictatorships in all of Latin America.

PART III

THE RIVER PLATE
AND CHILE

FROM THE TIME when the Spanish empire broke up into a number of independent states, it is difficult to deal with the history of the area as a whole. There had been differences among the colonies, in the makeup of population and in geographical conditions, and these were accentuated when the outward uniformity of the colonial regime disappeared and each state began to deal with its own peculiar problems. We can discern common factors and trends in the development of Spanish America since 1824, but when we attempt to generalize about these we must note so many exceptions and qualifications that any attempt to write their history without breaking it down into the history of separate states becomes vague and confused.

The countries that advanced most during the first century of independence were those of the South Temperate Zone, a region that was relatively unimportant in colonial times. The absence of a settled, easily conquered Indian population, which had made this area unattractive to settlers in search of easy wealth, was one of the factors that helped this progress. There was little Indian blood in the people of Argentina and Uruguay, and the native element in central Chile, though much larger, was to a great extent assimilated. The southern republics thus did not have to contend with problems that confronted countries where the masses were of a separate race, speaking different languages, and working under various forms of servitude. For this reason, and because of their climate, they were more attractive to a new type of settlers who began to come during the nineteenth century, and European immigration played an important part in their development.

Another important factor was the development of foreign trade. Buenos Aires, Montevideo, and Valparaiso, which had been virtually closed to overseas shipping until nearly the end of the colonial period, became important commercial centers soon after independence. In the last quarter of the nineteenth century exports of meat from Argentina and Uruguay and of nitrate from Chile made the southern region the most prosperous part of Spanish America. This prosperity attracted foreign investment and made possible the building of railroads and the still-more-intensive development of natural resources. It also made for political stability because people who are making money are rarely disposed to revolt and a government that has ample revenues is usually a strong one.

With a more homogeneous population and higher standards of living, it was easier for the southern countries to develop democratic political institutions. A larger proportion of their people could be reached by education and could take an intelligent interest in politics. This interest, coupled with a growing desire for internal peace, strengthened a demand for freer elections as a substitute for revolutions. By the end of the first quarter of the twentieth century, Argentina, Uruguay, and Chile seemed to have achieved truly republican forms of government. There was a retrogression to older political practices during the depression years, but it was short-lived in the case of Uruguay and Chile. Argentina did not return to democratic government until after the fall of Perón in 1955.

In Paraguay, the situation is different. The masses of the people are of Indian or mixed blood, and the country has less natural wealth. Two disastrous wars with South American neighbors retarded political and economic progress. Paraguay is included in this section, however, because it is geographically a part of the River Plate region and because of its very close economic and political relations with Argentina.

CHAPTER 8

The Argentine Republic

ARGENTINA IN 1810

ARGENTINA, more than a third the size of the continental United States, stretches some 2,300 miles from the tropics in the north to a latitude corresponding to that of Labrador in the south. Except for the Andean foothills in the west and northwest, it is one great almost unbroken plain. Much of it is unattractive as a home for human beings. The Gran Chaco is a tropical jungle, and much of the west is an arid desert. The vast reaches of Patagonia are of some value for sheep raising, but they can hardly support any large population. The region which has made Argentina what it is, is the *pampa*—the fertile, well-watered central area some 600 miles square, where the agricultural products of the temperate zone can be produced and where an equable climate permits cattle to graze throughout the year. It is here, north, south, and west of Buenos Aires, that the greater part of the Republic's population is concentrated.

This region attracted few settlers during the colonial period because its primitive and intractable Indians were poor material for the sort of exploitation that enriched the *encomenderos* and the religious orders in Peru and Mexico. It was cut off from the rest of the world by the restrictions of the Spanish colonial system, though the effect of these restrictions was somewhat lessened by smuggling, from the Portuguese outpost at Colonia and through the depot that the English maintained at Buenos Aires between 1715 and 1739 for the importation of slaves, under the *asiento* treaty.[1] After 1776, however, when Buenos Aires became the Capital of a viceroyalty that included modern Paraguay, Uruguay, and Bolivia, as well as the present territory of Argentina, the city had begun to grow in population and importance. In 1810 it was thought to have 45,000 inhabitants, though it was still an ill-paved, dirty town, with few decent houses and an inadequate supply of food and water. Even as a

[1] See above, p. 110.

seaport, it left much to be desired, for vessels had to anchor several miles out and goods and passengers were carried ashore in lighters and high-wheeled carts.

The other Argentine towns were described by an English traveler a few years later as mere secluded villages. The more important of them were hundreds of miles from Buenos Aires, in the western part of the country near the foothills of the Andes and in the far northwest on the road to Upper Peru. Outside of these settlements, the same traveler wrote: "although a few individuals are either scattered along the path, which traverses these vast plains, or are living together in small groups, yet the general state of the country is the same as it has been since the first year of its creation." [2]

GAUCHOS AND INDIANS

These scattered country people were the *gauchos* of the *pampas*. Around each settlement were great unfenced *estancias*, or ranches, where from time to time the half-wild cattle were captured and slaughtered. This was the work of *gauchos* who gave the herds the small amount of care they received. Living in crudely built, one-room huts furnished with bullocks' skulls in place of chairs, and subsisting mainly on meat and water, these Argentine cowboys were a lawless lot, much given to personal violence and without great respect for property rights. The majority of them, perhaps, had never visited a town. The isolation in which they lived precluded any influence of church or school, but foreign travelers invariably admired their never-failing courtesy and hospitality, their reckless courage, and their marvelous horsemanship. A large proportion of them were of mixed blood, for there was a strong Indian strain among the Argentine people in 1810, and many Negro slaves had been brought into the country during the eighteenth century.

Only a small part of modern Argentina had any European settlers at all. A short two days' horseback journey south from Buenos Aires and a much shorter distance north of Santa Fe brought the traveler to regions still held by the Indians. Some of these lived a comparatively civilized life in settled villages and maintained generally friendly relations with their white neighbors; others were predatory nomads. Driving with them large herds of horses, which served not only for remounts but for food, the hostile tribes often traveled hundreds of miles to raid small settlements or *estancias*. The Araucanians from southern Chile were especially active in stealing cattle for sale in the Spanish settlements on the western side of the Andes. Indian depredations grew much worse during the political disorders of the first years of independence, when the authorities were unable to maintain adequate forces along the frontier; and some of the

[2] Head, *Notes on the Pampas*, p. 4.

tribes who had previously been friendly took up arms because the increased demand for hides for export led the white ranchers to encroach on their land. In the province of Santa Fe their raids were so frequent and so destructive that many formerly prosperous districts were almost completely depopulated.

OBSTACLES TO UNITY

Travelers between one town and another were thus continually exposed to attacks by Indians or other robbers. The great distances and the lack of improved roads also discouraged intercourse and trade between the different settlements. Heavier goods were transported across the *pampas* in carts drawn by several yoke of oxen which usually required seven weeks or more to reach Mendoza from Buenos Aires. Persons with little baggage, however, could make the same journey in a few days, traveling at a breakneck gallop, mounted or in a springless carriage, with frequent changes of horses. Wayfarers slept under the stars, or in a comfortless, vermin-infested post-hut, and depended for food on cattle lassoed along the road. It was apparently considered proper to kill these animals if the hide, the only part that had a market value, was left where the owner could recover it.

Aside from difficulties of intercommunication, there were other factors which complicated the task of welding the Argentine provinces into a united nation. The viceroyalty of La Plata had been a political rather than an economic unit. Mendoza and San Juan and San Luis, which had originally been settled from Chile, had closer relations with Santiago than with Buenos Aires, and the provinces of the northwest had a similar connection with Peru. The prosperity of Buenos Aires' neighbor Santa Fe also depended on its commerce with Upper Peru and especially on the breeding of mules for use in the Peruvian mines. In each of these cases, the war for independence cut off important trade relationships, and the provinces were not happy to find themselves compelled to carry on their commerce through Buenos Aires. They did not profit so much as Buenos Aires did from the new freedom of trade with foreign countries because the competition of cheaper goods from Europe ruined many of their small local industries while the charges imposed by the *porteño* merchants diminished the profits that they might have made from their exports. Furthermore Buenos Aires' refusal to permit foreign ships to use the Paraná River prevented the development of ports in the interior.[3] There were differences of opinion on other matters that contributed to the provinces' reluctance to submit themselves to a central government dominated by the group in control at the Capital. The anticlerical policy of the early

[3] For a full discussion of these matters see Miron Burgin, *The Economic Aspects of Argentine Federalism, 1820–1852.*

governments at Buenos Aires seemed outrageous to interior communities like Jujuy, where an American adventurer serving as a colonel in the army was imprisoned for three months for inadvertently failing to fall on his knees as the Eucharist was carried through the streets,[4] and there was much opposition to the *porteño* leaders' monarchical projects. Most of the thinking people in the provinces wanted a national government, because they realized that the provinces were too poor and too weak to stand on their own feet; but they wanted a "federal" government that would leave them free to manage their own local affairs and that would protect them from exploitation by the Capital.

The "unitarian" party was less numerous, but it was powerful. The city of Buenos Aires and the province of the same name were the most populous and by far the wealthiest part of the new nation, and the part that profited most from the opening of trade with foreign countries. The *porteño* officials and merchants and army officers who had taken over the machinery of government and the control of the military forces at the time of the revolt against Spain could avail themselves of the preponderant influence of the province and its great economic resources so long as they controlled its administration, even though many of the landowners outside of the city were more disposed to side with the federalists. They also had influential allies among the merchants and intellectual leaders in some of the provinces. We saw in Chapter 6, however, how their efforts to set up a strong central government were successfully resisted by the federalists while the war against Spain was still in progress, and how the unitarian regime set up by the Congress of Tucumán was overthrown early in 1820.

FEDERALISTS AND UNITARIANS, 1820–1829

After the federalist victory there was no central government in Argentina. At Buenos Aires, there were nine months of turmoil, with repeated changes in the local administration. The vigorous resistance of the people of the province frustrated the federalist leaders' effort to install Carlos de Alvear as Governor, but Estanislao López, the *caudillo* of Santa Fe, continued to maintain an army in Buenos Aires' territory and to interfere in local affairs. The situation improved after General Martín Rodríguez became Governor in September, 1820. López was compelled to withdraw his troops and accepted 25,000 head of cattle as the price of an alliance, and the people of Buenos Aires were again free to manage their own affairs. Both in the military operations that put him in power, and in the not inconsiderable task of collecting the cattle for the war indemnity to López, Rodríguez' most helpful collaborator was a young landowner named Juan Manuel de Rosas.

[4] King, *Twenty-four Years in the Argentine Republic* (New York ed.), pp. 116 ff.

Both parties had joined in defending the province's autonomy, but it was the unitarians who controlled its new provincial government. Rodríguez' Minister of State was Bernardino Rivadavia, who had just returned from a long stay in Europe and whose liberal ideas were reflected in the administration's policy. The public administration and the courts were reorganized, and a university was founded at Buenos Aires. Several measures against the Church, including the abolition of the ecclesiastical *fuero*, provoked a small uprising in Buenos Aires which was repressed with some severity. Except for this affair, the province enjoyed a relative tranquility. The government's growing prestige abroad enabled it to obtain a $3,000,000 loan in England for port works and other improvements, pledging the province's vast holdings of public lands as security. This arrangement prevented the sale of the land at a time when the expansion of cattle raising caused much demand for it, but Rivadavia met the problem by his system of *"emphyteusis,"* under which the land was leased at fixed rentals for 20-year periods.

The rest of the country hardly shared in Buenos Aires' growing prosperity. Most of the other provinces were by this time controlled by the leaders of the *montoneras*, undisciplined hordes of *gaucho* cavalry which began to appear on the *pampas* in the first years of independence. Freedom of trade had brought economic changes which made the *gauchos'* lot harder and which were eventually to compel them to give up altogether their wild, free life on the plains. When the landowners had a better export market for their hides and salt beef, they were less willing to have their cattle killed indiscriminately, and the one food on which the country people depended became difficult to get. This forced the *gauchos* into more regular work for the landowners, and their dependence was increased by the need for protection against the more and more frequent raids of the wild Indians. With their intense love of personal freedom, many preferred to join the first leader who promised a chance for excitement and plunder in a military campaign. The *caudillos* whom they brought to power were in some cases influential members of the local landholding aristocracy, in others wild, ignorant adventurers. The struggles of rival leaders to attain power and the frequent conflicts between the provincial governments contributed to the poverty and backwardness that prevailed throughout the interior.

Despite the strong spirit of *localismo* and the antagonism between the interior and Buenos Aires, most of the provincial leaders had at least as much interest as the *porteños* in the establishment of a national government. The "quadrilateral treaty" of 1822 united Buenos Aires, Sante Fe, Entre Ríos, and Corrientes in a loose defensive alliance against a feared attack from Brazil, and the other provinces entrusted the conduct of foreign relations to Buenos Aires, so that the United States entered into diplomatic relations with the administration there when it recognized

Argentina's independence in the same year. In December, 1824, after General Las Heras succeeded Rodríguez as Governor, a Congress representing all of the provinces met at Buenos Aires to frame a constitution. Disputes between the unitarians and the federalists made it impossible to agree on the form that the new government should take; but the outbreak of a war with Brazil convinced both parties that the country must have some central executive authority, and in February, 1826, Rivadavia was elected President of the United Provinces of the River Plate.

It will be remembered that the Portuguese conquered the *Banda Oriental* between 1816 and 1820. The territory continued to form a province of Brazil after that country became independent, and many of its leaders took refuge in Buenos Aires. In April, 1825, a small band of these, the famous "Thirty-Three," crossed the river and started an insurrection; and a few months later an Assembly meeting in the territory which they controlled voted to reunite the province with Argentina. When the Congress at Buenos Aires approved their action, Brazil declared war. A hastily organized Argentine squadron under Admiral Brown, an Irish soldier of fortune, defeated the Brazilian fleet in the River Plate, and land forces from Buenos Aires, with smaller contingents from other provinces, won an important victory at Ituzaingó in February, 1827.

Political dissensions prevented the Argentines from following up these successes. The provinces rejected the constitution which the Congress adopted in July, 1826, and Rivadavia lost much support in Buenos Aires when he procured the adoption of a law separating the Capital city from the province to create a federal district. Confronted by these difficulties, Rivadavia accepted British mediation to bring about peace with Brazil. When the Argentine representative signed a treaty recognizing the *Banda Oriental* as Brazilian territory the unpopularity of the government increased, even though Rivadavia repudiated the agreement and prepared to continue the war. In July, 1827, the President resigned. His successor, Vicente López, stayed in office only long enough to dissolve the Congress and what was left of the national administration.

Manuel Dorrego, who became Governor of Buenos Aires, continued the war with Brazil until 1828 when both sides were compelled by British diplomatic pressure to accept a peace treaty that made Uruguay an independent nation. Three months later Dorrego was overthrown and executed by unitarian forces returning from the *Banda Oriental,* and his friend Juan Manuel de Rosas at once started a counterrevolution. The federalists, under Rosas' leadership, took control of Buenos Aires province, but in the meantime, the unitarian General José María Paz occupied Córdoba and defeated the federalists in several of the western provinces. The civil war thus started involved most of Argentina and lasted for three years, until Paz was accidentally captured in May, 1831. At its end, federalist *caudillos* were in power throughout the country.

THE ARGENTINE CONFEDERATION
UNDER ROSAS

Rosas, who became Governor of Buenos Aires in 1829, was a member of a distinguished family and was himself a successful businessman. He had spent much of his life among the *gauchos* and Indians of the frontier, adopting their ways and winning their admiration by his strength and courage and brilliant horsemanship. He had large estates in the southern part of Buenos Aires province, where he maintained a private army to defend his own properties and those of his neighbors against the raids of hostile Indians. He was the idol of the small farmers in the neighborhood, and he was popular among the artisans and workers of the city of Buenos Aires. During his first term in office, the people of the province enjoyed a welcome tranquility, despite the civil war in the interior, and at its end the legislature begged him to accept another. Rosas declined and instead organized a great campaign against the Indians which opened a new part of the *pampas* to white settlement and increased his own prestige. When he was again persistently urged to accept the governorship, he finally consented, in 1835, but only after insisting on a plebiscite in which the voters gave him dictatorial powers.

For the next 16 years, Rosas was the real ruler of Argentina. The federalist *caudillos* in the other provinces were soon compelled to accept his leadership. His chief potential rivals, in 1835, were Estanislao López of Santa Fe and Facundo Quiroga, a *gaucho* leader who had a great following in the Northwest. In 1835 Quiroga was killed while passing through Córdoba, where López' lieutenants the Reynafé brothers were in control. Rosas was accused by his enemies of instigating the murder, but he made the crime the excuse for overthrowing the Reynafés and putting one of his own followers in their place. After this affair, López' influence was so impaired that he was thenceforth little more than a lieutenant of the Governor of Buenos Aires.

Rosas opposed all efforts to set up a central government for Argentina because he feared that Buenos Aires might be deprived of the large revenue that it derived from levying customs duties on the trade of the entire country,[5] a revenue that helped to make his position far stronger than that of the other provincial leaders. The other provinces, however, delegated to Rosas the direction of foreign relations and national defense and a measure of authority in other matters of concern to the Confederation as a whole. Theoretically, the provinces were otherwise autonomous. In fact, Argentina became unified as it had not been since independence, and a national point of view began to take the place of the intense provincialism of the earlier period. The suppression of local guerrilla warfare and

[5] Burgin, *op. cit.*, pp. 148 ff.

banditry made the roads safer for travel, and agriculture and stock raising flourished.

From the beginning, Rosas' government at Buenos Aires was a dictatorship which dealt harshly with its opponents. The execution of political enemies had been a common practice since independence, but none of the earlier governments had practiced such systematic brutality in suppressing conspiracies and revolts. The official motto, "Long live the Argentine Confederation; death to the savage unitarians" appeared in all public documents. People were killed or tortured merely because they fell under suspicion, and an unofficial band of cutthroats called the *Mazorca* and an extensive spy system helped to maintain a reign of terror. Opponents who escaped by flight lost all of their property, and it was alleged that many were compelled to leave the country by threats and mistreatment simply to make possible the confiscation of their estates. Rosas' system was perhaps no more atrocious than many others which have flourished in the Western Hemisphere, but it attracted much attention abroad and gave him an unenviable distinction as the classic example of Latin American tyranny.

Rosas was constantly embroiled in conflicts with other governments. In 1837–1838 he was at war with Santa Cruz, the ruler of Bolivia and Peru, and a little later he was involved in desultory hostilities with Paraguay. Much more important was his intervention in Uruguay. Rivera, the first President of that Republic, had angered Rosas by granting asylum to a number of Argentine political exiles, and in 1836 when Rivera revolted against his successor, Oribe, Rosas came to the latter's support. This was the beginning of a long struggle which was soon complicated by a conflict with France.

THE FRANCO-BRITISH INTERVENTION

For several years there had been a dispute with France over a law requiring all foreigners in Buenos Aires to serve in the provincial militia. There had also been trouble over pecuniary claims. Rosas arrogantly refused to settle these questions, and in 1838 the French government, partly for internal political reasons, decided to take a more aggressive course. It first established a blockade of Buenos Aires. When this produced no result, pressure was applied in the shape of aid to Rosas' enemies. Oribe was driven out of Montevideo, and a joint French-Uruguayan expedition seized Martín García Island which commanded river navigation on the Paraná. The trade of Buenos Aires was severely affected, but Rosas refused to yield. French efforts to overthrow him by supporting a unitarian revolution were a miserable failure, though they provoked a troublesome civil war in the littoral provinces. By 1840, political developments at home and in the Near East made the French government ready to withdraw from an adventure which was clearly unprofitable, and a treaty was signed under which the French claims were to be arbitrated and the blockade withdrawn.

The civil war in Uruguay and the unitarian revolt in Argentina had by this time merged into one conflict, in which the principal armies on both sides were operating in Argentine territory. The decisive battle between Oribe and Rivera, the rival claimant to the presidency of Uruguay, took place in Entre Ríos after the agreement with France. Oribe, who won, soon got control of all of Uruguay except Montevideo and began a long-drawn-out siege of that city which will be described in Chapter 9.

The French government alleged that Rosas' continued aid to Oribe was a violation of the recently concluded treaty, and the British government also objected to the protracted war because it hurt foreign trade. In 1845 both powers intervened to help Rivera's party, the *colorados* in Montevideo. Their warships blockaded Buenos Aires, and a British expedition attempted, with little success, to go up the Paraná River to help a short-lived unitarian revolution in Corrientes. Though the blockade cut off Buenos Aires' trade and reduced his income, Rosas refused to come to terms, and his successful resistance greatly increased his prestige in Argentina. Pressure from the numerous British merchants in Buenos Aires and friction with France finally convinced the British government that its policy was a failure, and in spite of Rosas' rejection of all conciliatory proposals it withdrew its forces in July, 1847. French intervention ceased a year later, after the fall of King Louis Philippe.

THE FALL OF ROSAS

The government of Brazil, which had no wish to see Rosas control Uruguay, had given some help to the *riveristas* during the siege of Montevideo, and it was clear that Oribe's occupation of the city, which seemed merely a question of time after the failure of the Anglo-French intervention, would make worse the existing tension between Brazil and Argentina. Rosas forced the issue by breaking off relations when the imperial government failed to check incursions from its territory into northern Uruguay. He apparently counted on enthusiastic national support for a conflict against a traditional enemy, but in May, 1851, Justo José de Urquiza, the powerful Governor of Entre Ríos, repudiated the dictator's leadership and led an army into Uruguay. Oribe was quickly compelled to agree to the formation of a compromise government that joined with Brazil and Entre Ríos in the war against Rosas. The allied forces, accompanied by many of the Argentine exiles in Montevideo, defeated the Argentine army at Monte Caseros on February 3, 1852, and Rosas fled to England where he lived in poverty until his death 25 years later.

SEPARATION AND REUNION OF BUENOS AIRES
1852–1862

The other provincial governors, though most of them had taken no part in his revolt, accepted Urquiza as the new leader of the country. They welcomed his plans for establishing a federal government and for opening the rivers of the country to commerce. Rosas, as we have seen, had opposed both ideas because they would have decreased the predominant power of Buenos Aires, and for the same reason Urquiza's policy was opposed both by the *porteño* exiles who had taken control of Buenos Aires and by the still-influential local federalist party. Reports that Urquiza intended to revive Rivadavia's project for separating the city from the province of Buenos Aires widened the split.

On May 31, 1852, all of the provincial governors signed the Agreement of San Nicolás which recognized Urquiza as the military Commander of the Confederation and authorized him to use a portion of the customs receipts at Buenos Aires pending the holding of a constitutional convention. The unpopularity of this agreement in Buenos Aires caused the resignation of Dr. Vicente López, whom Urquiza had selected as Governor of the province. Urquiza then assumed control of the city, but when the *porteños* revolted and set up a new government in September he withdrew his troops without attempting to suppress the movement. A few months later he supported a federalist attempt at counterrevolution, but this failed when the foreign officer who commanded his naval force was bribed to betray him.

The province of Buenos Aires was consequently not represented in the convention that met at Santa Fe in November, 1852, to draw up the constitution which was to govern Argentina's political life for nearly 100 years. The work of the delegates was much influenced by the views of the Argentine jurist J. B. Alberdi, who had published a book examining the reasons for earlier failures to attain national stability and reached the conclusion that what the country needed was a federal government that would have sufficient power to maintain order and unity and would at the same time meet the provinces' aspirations for local autonomy. The constitution which was very much like that of the United States was signed on May 1, 1853, and on March 5, 1854, Urquiza was inaugurated as President.

The convention voted to separate Buenos Aires from its province and to place the city under the direct control of the federal government, but the measure did not go into effect because the province refused to ratify the constitution. For the next nine years, the Argentine Confederation, with its Capital at Paraná in Entre Ríos, and the province of Buenos Aires were separate independent states. Both made progress during this period. Much attention was devoted to education, and foreign trade increased.

One of Urquiza's most important acts was the signature of treaties in 1853 with Great Britain, France, and the United States by which the Paraná and Uruguay Rivers were opened to international commerce. The 1850's also saw the beginning of the great influx of immigrants which was soon to transform the nation's social and economic life. Several thousand British arrived to take up sheep raising, and agricultural colonies were established by Swiss and other Europeans in Santa Fe and Entre Ríos. At Buenos Aires, the control of affairs remained in the hands of the *porteño* group, most of whom had been exiles during the Rosas regime. Though the opening of the rivers made possible the development of other ports, the city still dominated the trade of the River Plate area, and the province continued to be wealthier and more populous than its neighbors.

It was hardly possible for the two states to continue indefinitely as separate political units. There was still a feeling of common nationality, and the *porteños* had allies among the "liberals" of other provinces, just as federalists still had many partisans in Buenos Aires. The commercial dependence of the other provinces on Buenos Aires and their desire for a share in the customs duties made an eventual reunion almost inevitable. Though Urquiza gave up the effort to control Buenos Aires and good relations were temporarily established, a new conflict arose after 1856 from the Confederation's attempt to increase foreign trade at Rosario by imposing discriminatory duties on foreign goods transhipped at Buenos Aires. The government at Buenos Aires decreed retaliatory measures, and war soon followed. Urquiza defeated the Buenos Aires army under General Mitre at Cepeda on October 23, 1859, but then agreed to a compromise under which Buenos Aires would enter the Confederation after changes had been made in the constitution.

There was a resurgence of bad feeling, when the *porteños* were accused of fomenting revolts to put their friends in power in some of the other provinces. When the federal Congress refused to seat the delegates from Buenos Aires, ostensibly on the ground that they had not been elected in accord with the constitution, but in reality to prevent the liberals from having a majority, both sides prepared for war. Santiago Derqui, who had become President of the Confederation in March, 1860, entrusted the command of the federal army to Urquiza, who was not friendly to the new government and who seems to have permitted Mitre to defeat him at Pavón on September 17, 1861. Mitre assumed control of the national government, and in October, 1862, he was elected President of what was thenceforth the Argentine Republic.

THE PRESIDENCY OF MITRE

Bartolomé Mitre was the first of a group of able presidents under whose leadership the political and economic life of Argentina was to be completely transformed during the latter half of the nineteenth century. Though only forty-one at the time of his election, he had already had a notable career. For several years, beginning when he was barely seventeen, he had taken part in the defense of Montevideo against Rosas. Later he fought in civil wars in Bolivia and directed newspapers there and in Chile, returning to Argentina in time to command an artillery force at Monte Caseros. He was the most influential leader of the party that upheld the autonomy of Buenos Aires against Urquiza and the Confederation, but he welcomed national unity on terms that seemed to safeguard the interests of Buenos Aires. He was not only a statesman and soldier, but a prolific poet, a journalist, and a historian. *La Nación* of Buenos Aires, which he founded, is an important newspaper today, and his books on San Martín and Belgrano are still used by students of South American history.

As President, Mitre was compelled to deal with several difficult problems. The transfer of the national government to Buenos Aires raised again the "Capital" question that had repeatedly caused trouble in the past, and Mitre's proposal to make the city of Buenos Aires a federal district was vigorously opposed by the provincial legislature. As a compromise, the national government was finally permitted to stay temporarily in Buenos Aires without interfering with the autonomy of the province, an arrangement that proved unsatisfactory and led to armed conflict some years later.

A more difficult problem was the establishment of the new government's authority outside of Buenos Aires. Many of the provinces were still ruled by the federalist governors who had been in office under Rosas. Urquiza, the most important of these, was permitted to continue as ruler of Entre Ríos, but in some other provinces there were serious disturbances before the new administration succeeded in installing regimes that it could control. For some months in 1863–1864 *montoneras* led by a federalist *caudillo* named Peñaloza, commonly called "El Chacho," carried on a civil war in the northwest.

The most serious test of the new government's stability was the war with Paraguay, between 1865 and 1870, which will be described more fully in Chapter 10. Argentina was drawn into this conflict when Francisco Solano López' troops marched through Corrientes to attack Brazil and Mitre himself for a time commanded the allied Argentine-Brazilian-Uruguayan armies. As the war dragged on with few successes to offset the great expense and the heavy allied losses, there was much discontent, and the President had to suppress two small revolts in the interior. In 1868 he turned over the conduct of the Paraguayan operations to the Brazilian Marshal Caxias and returned to Buenos Aires for the final months of his presidential term.

SARMIENTO AND AVELLANEDA

The reverses in the war cost Mitre much popular support, and a rival faction won the provincial election in Buenos Aires in 1868. The President was thus in no position to dictate the choice of his successor, and Alsina, the new Governor of Buenos Aires, joined with leaders in some of the other provinces to bring about the election of Domingo Faustino Sarmiento, who had been a close associate of the *porteño* group but was a native of San Juan. Sarmiento had been one of the most prominent of the political exiles who had opposed Rosas, and he was the author of a number of books that still have an outstanding place in the literature of the American continent, among them his classic book on Facundo Quiroga. He believed passionately that the progress of Argentina depended on the destruction of the culture the *gaucho caudillos* typified and its replacement by European and North American customs and ways of thought. Sarmiento's chief interest was in the field of education. He had taught school for several years as an exile in Chile and Bolivia and had had charge of public instruction in Buenos Aires when the province was a separate state. During the last years of Mitre's administration, he had been Minister at Washington, where he devoted much time to a study of the educational institutions which he regarded as the basis of North American prosperity. He became a friend and admirer of Horace Mann and was much influenced by the latter's ideas, and he engaged a number of teachers from the United States to work in the normal schools that he established when he became President. Thanks to his efforts, the Argentine educational system became one of the best in South America.

The "Córdoba league," the group of provincial governors who had backed Sarmiento, supported Nicolás Avellaneda of Tucumán for the presidency in 1874 and procured his victory by the mixture of fraud and violence that generally characterized South American elections in the nineteenth century. Mitre, who was the *porteño* candidate, promptly revolted, but was defeated after a short campaign and pardoned by the government. This lenient treatment was a marked contrast to the brutal cruelty with which participants in unsuccessful uprisings had been treated, not only in Rosas' time but under the *porteño* governments, and it seemed to mark a hopeful change in the political atmosphere. Avellaneda, who had been Sarmiento's Minister of Public Instruction, continued the educational work of his predecessor. By this time the national government seemed to have acquired a real stability, and its prestige was rapidly increasing, at home and abroad.

The most important event of Avellaneda's administration was the final conquest of the rich *pampa* south and west of Buenos Aires. The Indians, who had been kept under control by force and bribery so long as Rosas was in power, had resumed their raids when the army was withdrawn to take part in the frequent civil wars after 1851, and early in Sarmiento's term they burned *estancias* and stole cattle along a great section of the frontier. The government's efforts to check them were unsuccessful until General Julio Roca, in 1878–1879, led an army into their territory and systematically exterminated most of the Argentine tribes. His operations opened up a great tract of new and fertile land for stock raising and agriculture. Unfortunately, most of this was sold in large tracts to speculators or influential politicians instead of being made available to the immigrants who were then arriving in ever greater numbers from Europe.

THE CREATION OF THE FEDERAL DISTRICT

The status of the national Capital, still unsettled, was a constant danger to the Republic's tranquility. The presence of the federal and provincial authorities in the same city led to much friction, especially after the federal government passed into the hands of a group whom the *porteños* regarded as outsiders. There was always a possibility that the leaders in Buenos Aires might attempt to regain by revolution the dominant position they had enjoyed under Mitre. This did occur in 1880, when Carlos Tejedor, the Governor of Buenos Aires, was a candidate for the presidency in opposition to General Roca, who had the support of Avellaneda and most of the other provincial administrations.

Since Roca's victory was a foregone conclusion, unless the *porteños* resorted to force, Tejedor began to recruit and drill troops. Open warfare began in June, 1880. The federal government withdrew to Belgrano, in the suburbs; but after a sharp conflict, its forces compelled the insurgents to surrender. The city of Buenos Aires was now separated from the province and made a federal district, in which only the central government exercised authority. The province, with a new Capital at La Plata, continued to be one of the most important sections of the Republic, but it could no longer hope, after its dismemberment, to dominate the nation's affairs. A political issue that had caused trouble from the first years of independence thus virtually disappeared.

THE BEGINNING OF MODERN ARGENTINA

In 1880 Argentina was still a relatively backward country. There was more security for life and property than there had been 20 years earlier, but travelers still compared the Republic unfavorably in this respect with Brazil. Buenos Aires was becoming a prosperous modern city, but there had been less change in the interior. Many of the provinces were ruled by unprogressive oligarchies of great landowners or by military *caudillos*, and the federal government in its frequent interventions in their affairs showed more interest in keeping its own friends in power than in promoting better administration. Local revolts and Indian raids had helped to discourage agriculture and stock raising. Even in the more prosperous regions little land was under cultivation, and the cattle which formed the country's chief wealth were raised mainly for their hides and to make *tasajo*, or jerked beef.

Already, however, the Republic was beginning the astonishingly rapid economic development that was to continue through the next generation. The most notable changes took place in the livestock industry. The appearance of refrigerator ships, in 1877, made possible the shipment of frozen beef, and later of chilled beef, to the European markets, where there was a rapidly increasing demand for meat products. Some years earlier, many of the *estancieros* had begun to import fine cattle from abroad and to regulate breeding, and with this innovation came the fencing of the ranges, the growing of alfalfa for feed, and the transformation of the nomadic, liberty-loving *gaucho* into a paid hand on the *estancia*. Roca's conquest of the *pampa* greatly increased the area available for cattle raising, and it made Patagonia safer for settlers so that sheep raising soon became an important occupation there.

A substantial beginning had been made in railroad construction. Starting in 1863, the North American promoter William Wheelwright, working with British capital, built a line from Rosario to Córdoba, and this was later extended to Tucumán. There were shorter lines elsewhere, especially in the province of Buenos Aires, so that the country had a total of 1,500 miles of railway in 1880. The promoters were in most cases given grants of land along the right of way, much of which they sold in small holdings to foreign immigrants. The newcomers devoted themselves mainly to tilling the soil, an occupation always uncongenial to the *gaucho*, and about 1880 the Republic began, for the first time, to export wheat instead of importing it for local consumption.

Progress was more rapid after 1880. Roca strengthened the power of the central government by a firm but at the same time conciliatory policy. In the six years of his administration, railway mileage more than doubled; the tonnage of ships calling at Argentine ports increased threefold; and immigration, encouraged by peaceful conditions and reports of the country's prosperity, reached figures hitherto unknown. Land values went up rapidly and many of the *estancieros* found themselves wealthy. The province of Buenos Aires, which occupied the more fertile portion of the *pampa* and which had successfully asserted a claim to the best part of the lands recently conquered from the Indians, profited far more by this development than did the interior provinces.

JUÁREZ CELMÁN AND THE REVOLT OF 1890

This phenomenal prosperity continued into the first years of the term of Dr. Miguel Juárez Celmán, who succeeded Roca in 1886, but it was soon followed by a reaction. Reckless speculation had created unsound business conditions, and the policy of the government, under the new administration, made matters worse. The new President was a brother-in-law of Roca, but the latter's influence was soon superseded by that of Juárez' other associates, many of whom were incompetent and corrupt. There was an orgy of graft and extravagance, made possible partly by borrowing abroad and partly by large issues of unsecured paper money, and when business conditions began to grow worse, the Republic's credit was seriously affected. The financial crisis brought on political troubles.

The "Córdoba" group was still unpopular in Buenos Aires, and even the powerful foreign commercial and financial interests encouraged a movement of protest that gained more and more adherents in the Capital despite persecution by the police. The government's opponents organized the *Unión Cívica,* made up of many of the old *porteños* led by Mitre, and a new group of younger leaders. The movement received much support among the common people, who wanted to oust the landholding oligarchy from the control of the government. Mitre endeavored to confine the actions of the *Unión Cívica* to a peaceful protest; but the more radical element were not satisfied with this, and in July, 1890, a part of the army joined them in a revolt at Buenos Aires. After two days of fighting in the city streets, the movement was suppressed, but the government was so discredited that Juárez Celmán was compelled to turn over his authority to the Vice-President, Carlos Pellegrini. During the two years that ensued before another election, the country passed through a severe commercial depression which might have been still more serious had it not been for Pellegrini's efforts to reform the government's finances and preserve its credit.

THE *UNIÓN CÍVICA RADICAL*

The leader of the revolt in 1890 had been Leandro N. Alem, an ardent democrat whose father had been executed as a supporter of Rosas after the dictator's fall. After the failure of the revolt, Alem parted company with the more conservative group in the *Unión Cívica* and continued his agitation for political reform as the head of the *Unión Cívica Radical* which soon came to be called the radical party and which has ever since been a powerful factor in Argentine politics. He demanded especially the holding of free elections.

There was if anything less political and social democracy in Argentina in 1890 than there had been during the war of independence. The central government had become more stable, and somewhat more civilized in dealing with its opponents, but its growing prestige and the general prosperity that made all classes inclined to accept the established order rather than risk the destructive effects of civil war had made it easier for the landholding oligarchy, supported by the commercial interests in Buenos Aires, to maintain itself in power. There were factional disputes within the ruling group, but the mass of the people had less participation in political affairs than in the more turbulent earlier period. As in other Latin American countries, elections were almost always won by the party in power.

The provincial governors were by this time little more than agents of the President of the Republic. Railroad construction had unified the country economically and socially, and it was easy to send troops promptly to any area where disaffection appeared. Though the provisions of the Argentine constitution governing relations between the central government and the provinces were very similar to those of the constitution of the United States, they were applied in practice in a very different spirit, and the federal authorities repeatedly intervened in local affairs simply to remove administrations that were politically obnoxious to them and that were in a position, through the control of elections, to embarrass the party in power at Buenos Aires. The influence of the central government was also increased by its greatly superior financial resources which enabled it to carry out public works that local authorities were too poor to undertake.

In the last years of the century, economic progress was bringing into existence forces that would make impossible the indefinite continuance of the old political regime. As the thousands of immigrants from Italy and Spain were assimilated, they and their children, who were loyal Argentines, added an intelligent and politically conscious element to the electorate. This element and the native middle class that was gradually arising in the larger cities were beginning to demand a more influential rôle in public affairs. It was these groups that made up the rank and file of the radical party and that supported the party's persistent agitation for electoral reform.

POLITICAL EVENTS, 1892–1910

The threat posed by the radicals caused the leaders of the oligarchy to draw closer together, and in 1892 Roca and Mitre, who had been political enemies, formed a coalition, called the *acuerdo*, to support Luis Sáenz Peña for the presidency. The government assured his election by declaring martial law and arresting Alem and his more prominent followers. The new President found his task a hard one. The economic depression had severely affected the country, and there was much discontent. A radical revolt in 1893 was suppressed by the army under the leadership of Roca, but in January, 1895, continued political difficulties led Sáenz Peña to turn over his office to Vice-President José Evaristo Uriburu. Roca and Mitre continued to support the administration, and Roca, as the official candidate, was elected to the presidency in 1898.

Many Argentines felt that there should be a military leader like Roca at the head of the government because the country seemed on the verge of war with Chile. There had long been a controversy over the boundary between the two republics. In 1881, with the aid of the United States, they had agreed that the island of Tierra del Fuego should be divided between them and that the boundary north of the 52nd parallel should run "where the highest peaks of the Andes divide the watershed." When it was discovered that the watershed was actually some miles east of the highest peaks, there was another dispute. Fortunately, a peaceful agreement was reached during Roca's administration. The boundary in the north, in the *Puno de Atacama*, was fixed in 1899 by an arbitral commission headed by W. I. Buchanan, the American Minister at Buenos Aires, and the rest of the line was adjusted three years later, after another period of acute tension, by the arbitration of the King of England. In 1904 the establishment of a lasting peace between the two countries was signalized by the erection of the great statue of the Christ of the Andes in the Uspallata Pass. In the meantime, another boundary dispute, with Brazil over the eastern part of the Misiones Territory, had been settled by an arbitral award handed down by President Grover Cleveland in 1895.

Manuel Quintana, the administration candidate, was elected President in 1904, but he died in 1906 and was succeeded by the Vice-President, José Figueroa Alcorta. The country's prosperity continued, but political conditions were somewhat more disturbed than while Roca's firm hand guided the ship of state. Both the radicals and other political factions endeavored to embarrass the government, and Figueroa Alcorta found it necessary to disperse a hostile Congress by force early in 1908—an affair which demonstrated the difference between the working of republican institutions in Argentina and in the United States. He also intervened in several provinces to strengthen the federal administration's political control.

The radicals, meanwhile, continued their agitation for electoral reform. Alem committed suicide in 1896, but his nephew Hipólito Irigoyen took over the leadership of the party and built it into a formidable organization. Though it was clearly one of the strongest political groups, it refused to present candidates in the presidential elections and from time to time staged revolts. Though these were rather easily suppressed, because the ruling class was little inclined to tolerate disturbances that would interfere with farming and business, it was becoming more and more evident that something must be done to meet the radicals' demands. Figueroa Alcorta, before the end of his term, held a number of conferences with Irigoyen in an effort to reach an agreement, and his successor, Roque Sáenz Peña, came into office in 1910 pledged to a program of electoral reform.

ELECTORAL REFORM

The new President was an idealist who had had a romantic career. As a youth, he served as a volunteer in the Peruvian army during the war against Chile. In 1892 he was a candidate for the presidency, but withdrew when his own father was nominated by the *acuerdo*. He had a distinguished record of public service in other positions at home and abroad, and his experience in other countries helped to convince him of the necessity to create real democratic institutions in Argentina. Though he knew that the change would end the domination of his own class, he pushed through the Congress the electoral law of 1912 which established for the first time the secret ballot and effectively provided for freedom of the suffrage. All citizens were to be allowed to vote, and minorities were given proportional representation.

Progressive electoral laws have often been enacted in Latin American countries without actually changing the character of the electoral process because neither the authorities nor the people were prepared to make democratic institutions a reality. In Argentina, the reform came in response to a widespread and insistent demand, and the new law was enforced by a President who sincerely wished to make its provisions effective. In the congressional elections of 1912, more than 640,000 citizens cast votes. The radical party participated, and several of its candidates were successful. The significance of the change was not diminished by the fact that the democratic ideal was still far from attainment, that bribery to some extent took the place of coercion as a means of obtaining votes, and that more than a third of the people were still illiterate.

Sáenz Peña, who had been ill for some time, died in August, 1914, and was succeeded by Vice-President Victorino de la Plaza, whose main concern during his short term of office was the economic dislocation caused by the European war. The sudden falling off in foreign trade and in the government's revenues caused grave difficulties for a time, but by 1916 exports were booming, with sales of meat and wheat to the allies.

HIPÓLITO IRIGOYEN

In the presidential election of 1916, the radical party, with Hipólito Irigoyen as its candidate, won by a narrow margin. The overturn brought into office a group of men who had little experience either in administrative positions or in Congress. Many of the radical leaders were members of old and distinguished families, but the rank and file represented the middle class which had hitherto been excluded from political life. Irigoyen himself was a remarkable character. He had been active in politics for more than 40 years, and for the preceding 25 had carried on a constant agitation, sometimes violent, sometimes peaceful, for more democratic methods of government. He had made some money in cattle raising, and when he held public office, in his earlier years as a teacher in the state schools and later as President, he is said to have given all his salary to charity. Though he almost never made a speech he had a tremendous following among the common people. When elected President he rode to his inauguration in a streetcar, and he continued to live in a modest flat, always accessible to the humblest visitors.

The radical party, despite its name, did not attempt to make any great changes, though some progressive labor legislation was adopted. Irigoyen kept the conduct of affairs in his own hands even more than his predecessors had and delegated little authority to the members of his Cabinet. His party's continued control was assured by several interventions in the provinces to remove governments controlled by the old regime.

Marcelo de Alvear, another radical, was elected to succeed Irigoyen in 1922. The country continued at peace, but the new President was much embarrassed, especially in his relations with Congress, by a split in his own party growing out of his attempt to assert his independence of Irigoyen's leadership. A few of the radicals, who came to be known as *anti-personalistas*, supported his administration, but the great majority of the party were *personalistas*, or unconditional adherents of the former President. In 1928, in fact, when Irigoyen announced his willingness to be re-elected to the presidency, he easily defeated the administration's candidate, without making an active campaign.

THE REVOLUTION OF 1930

By this time the radical chieftain was an old man, and defects as an administrator which had already been evident during his first term made his second period in office a dismal failure. Though it was no longer possible for him to attend personally to every detail, he refused to delegate authority. Government business of every kind was paralyzed. Important offices remained unfilled, and the treasury's failure to pay current bills hurt businessmen and made worse the effects of the world depression, which had greatly reduced the country's exports. A general feeling that a change was imperative found expression in the revolution of September 6, 1930, when the military forces, with the support of many civilian political leaders, ousted the President and proclaimed a provisional government under General José Uriburu. Irigoyen was arrested and remained in confinement for more than a year.

It soon became clear that the new government, though it was supported by many of the *anti-personalista* radicals, really represented the conservative political groups that had dominated the administration before 1916, and there was much opposition to its policies. In April, 1931, the *personalistas* won a provincial election in Buenos Aires, but the government annulled the result and intervened in 12 of the 14 provinces to assure its control of the electoral machinery. Alvear, now reconciled with the *personalistas* and recognized as their leader, was exiled after a small radical revolt in July, and the government decreed that no one who had supported Irigoyen's regime or who had opposed the objectives of the 1930 revolution was eligible for public office. When the radicals nominated Alvear as their candidate for the presidency, the government declared the nomination void because the constitution prohibited the election of an ex-president until six years had elapsed after the end of his term. The radicals consequently did not participate in the election of November, 1931, and General Agustín Justo, the government's candidate, easily defeated a candidate put forward by some of the other opposition parties.

POLITICAL EVENTS, 1931–1945

The new President, who was inaugurated in February, 1932, was an *antipersonalista* who had been a Cabinet Minister under Alvear. He took office at a difficult time, for the economic depression was at its worst and the uncompromising hostility of the *personalistas* made the political situation tense. The government kept the country under a "state of siege" during much of 1933 and 1934. As the economic situation slowly improved and exports increased, Justo gradually relaxed the dictatorial controls that he and his predecessor had maintained, and the political atmosphere became somewhat more tranquil.

There were nevertheless complaints of intimidation and fraud in the presidential election of 1937 when Roberto Ortíz, the official candidate, defeated Alvear, who was again nominated by the radicals. Ortíz represented the same coalition of *antipersonalistas* and conservatives that had backed Justo, but in 1940 he broke with the conservatives, and united most of the radicals under his own leadership. Radical gains in the congressional election of the same year strengthened his position; but in July, 1940, illness compelled him to turn over the government to the conservative Vice-President, Ramón Castillo. The continuance of conservative domination seemed assured when Ortíz died in 1942.

Castillo's government was ostensibly neutral in the European war, but it favored the Axis in many ways, and his delegates to the Rio de Janeiro conference in January, 1942, prevented the passage of a resolution calling for an immediate severance of relations between the American republics and Germany and Japan.[6] His policy was opposed by many landowners and merchants, who were traditionally friendly to Britain. It nevertheless

[6] See below, p. 504.

seemed improbable that the division among the conservatives would prevent the victory of his candidate Robustiano Patrón Costas in the presidential election that was to take place in 1943, especially as interparty jealousies prevented the radicals and socialists from co-operating effectively against him.

The election did not take place, because the army removed Castillo in June, 1943, and installed a military government. At first it seemed possible that the revolt might bring a change in foreign policy, for General Arturo Rawson, the provisional President, was known to be friendly to the democracies. Within a few days, however, Rawson was ousted and replaced by General Pedro Ramírez, who had been Castillo's Minister of War, and who set up a military dictatorship that was even more friendly to the Axis than Castillo's administration. Argentina's territory became a base for espionage and sabotage, and the government was even accused of conniving with German agents to bring about revolutions in other American states. There was little real change in the government's attitude after Ramírez yielded to the pressure of public opinion and broke relations with the Axis powers on January 26, 1944, especially as the pro-German group reasserted its supremacy on February 24 by forcing Ramírez to turn over the presidency to General Edelmiro Farrell.

The United States and most of the other American governments refused to recognize the new regime. This diplomatic isolation became more embarassing as it grew clear that the Axis was losing the war, and in March, 1945, Farrell sought to end it by declaring war on Germany and Japan and by subscribing to the agreements that the other American republics had adopted at the recent conference at Mexico City.[7] Even then, however, he showed little willingness to take action against Axis interests in Argentina. His failure to keep his promises and the new American Ambassador's openly expressed disapproval of his undemocratic policies again strained relations with the United States.

THE RISE OF PERÓN

The most powerful figure in Farrell's government was Colonel Juan Domingo Perón. Perón had a strong following in the army as leader of a nationalistic clique that called itself the *Grupo Oficiales Unidos* (GOU) which had played a prominent part in the 1943 and 1944 revolutions. As head of the labor department in Ramírez' administration he had also made himself popular among the working people by promises of higher wages and other favors. After the 1944 revolution his influence steadily increased, and it seemed clear that he would soon be the real head of the government if his progress were not stopped.

Some of the more conservative officers in the army attempted to stop

[7] See below, pp. 506–7.

it in October, 1945, when they staged a coup d'état and forced Farrell to confine Perón on Martín García Island. The purpose of the movement was apparently to establish a more democratic government; but its civilian leaders were prevented by their disagreements and irresolution from taking advantage of the opportunity, and riots organized by labor unions in Buenos Aires encouraged Farrell to release Perón and to oust the ministry that had been imposed on him. The way was thus clear for Perón to be the official candidate for the presidency in February, 1946, and he defeated José P. Tamborini, the nominee of the opposition parties, by 1,479,-000 votes to 1,210,000 in a relatively free election. Some votes were probably influenced when the State Department at Washington, 12 days before the election, issued a "blue book" based on captured German documents which showed how Perón and other Argentine officials had been involved in intrigues with Axis representatives during the war. It was a devastating indictment of the government's policies, both foreign and domestic, but its publication may have swung to Perón the votes of many persons who resented outside interference in the country's affairs.

THE PERÓN REGIME

It soon became clear that the new President intended to control the country's political and economic life more completely than any of his predecessors. Elections continued to be held, and the minority parties had a number of representatives in Congress; but in other respects the regime moved closer and closer to totalitarianism. In September, 1946, four of the five judges of the Supreme Court were impeached on the ground that they had recognized *de facto* governments in 1930 and 1943, a charge that seemed particularly cynical in view of Perón's own participation in the 1943 revolt. Political criticism became more dangerous after a law passed in 1949 made "disrespect" of government officials a crime, and the opposition press was intimidated or suppressed. *La Prensa* of Buenos Aires, the country's most important newspaper, which had been politically independent, was taken from its owners and nationalized in 1951. The universities, formerly autonomous, were brought under government control, and hundreds of professors were replaced by faithful *peronistas*. In 1951, after the constitution of 1853 had been replaced by a new one that increased the power of the executive and did away with the prohibition against presidential re-election, Perón ran for a second term and defeated Ricardo Balbín, the candidate of the opposition parties. The voting was free and peaceful, probably because the President was confident that he could win without the use of force or fraud.

Perón at this time was at the height of his power. He had the greater part of the army behind him, partly because he had increased its pay and favored it in many other ways, especially in giving important government positions to its officers, and partly because he was popular with the common soldiers. He also had the support of the Church, which had welcomed the establishment of compulsory religious education in the public schools after the revolution of 1943. His great strength, however, lay in the devotion of the masses of the working people, the *descamisados* or "shirtless ones," who looked on him as their champion against the aristocracy that had ruled Argentina in the past. The social legislation that he sponsored and the arbitrary increases of wages that he forced on employers helped him to retain the loyalty of the rank and file of the labor unions, despite the fact that he systematically broke down the unions' independence and eliminated labor leaders who did not unquestioningly follow his orders.

In his appeal to the masses, Perón had an invaluable asset in his attractive and energetic wife. Eva Perón was herself popular with the workers, and the welfare foundation which she established, with contributions levied on the labor unions and on businessmen, handed out great sums in small amounts to needy persons. Her rising influence disturbed some of the administration's supporters, and the army was said to have blocked a plan to have her elected Vice-President of the Republic in 1951. When she died in 1952, there was a tremendous and spectacular display of public mourning.

The improvement of living conditions for the common man was but one aspect of Perón's economic program. Another was the attainment of Argentina's "economic independence" by eliminating the influence of foreign capital and building up industrial production. Cattle raising and agriculture, which were the basis of the power of the landowning aristocracy, were less favored. An official trade promotion agency, called the IAPI, bought meat and grain from the producers at low prices fixed by the government and sold them abroad at much higher ones; and the profits thus obtained, as well as the great backlog of sterling and dollar exchange that had come from the excess of exports during the World War were used to buy properties hitherto owned by foreigners and to promote industrialization. The purchase of the British railways, for $600,000,000 was the most important step in a program of "nationalization" that embraced many other public utilities and much of the country's banking and insurance system. For a time, the government had such great sums at its disposal that it was able to retire the entire foreign bonded debt and to make large loans to other Latin American and European countries, for political reasons or to promote Argentine trade.

Such policies, of course, could not be continued indefinitely, especially as many of the officials who carried them out were also bent on enriching themselves. The wartime backlog was soon exhausted, and discouragement among the stock raisers and farmers brought a decline in exports. In 1950, Perón was compelled to obtain a loan of $125,000,000 from the United

States to pay for goods that had been imported. Inflation began to be a serious problem, and food prices were subsidized to allay discontent among the workers. Industrial production, as well as agricultural production, slowed down, and the country sank into an economic stagnation that was to last for several years.

From the start, a large proportion of the Argentine people opposed Perón and were disgusted by the corruption and the increasingly totalitarian character of his regime. Many officers in the armed forces, and especially in the navy, shared this feeling, and even in the ranks of organized labor there was resentment at the subordination of the unions to the government's political ends and to the elimination of leaders who were not subservient to the dictatorship. Opposition increased when Perón broke with the Catholic Church and issued decrees legalizing prostitution and divorce. Tension increased rapidly after an abortive revolt in June, 1955, and when the garrison at Córdoba started a revolution on September 16, 1955, the rest of the armed forces joined it. Within a few days, Perón was compelled to flee to Paraguay.

THE RESTORATION OF
DEMOCRATIC GOVERNMENT

General Eduardo Lonardi became provisional President; but in November, 1955, the Consultative Council, an unofficial body representing the principal anti-Peronist parties, forced him to turn over the office to General Pedro Aramburu. The constitution of 1853 was restored, and the new government worked valiantly to re-establish republican government. The task was a difficult one, for the armed forces were by no means united, and the Peronist party, which was outlawed, was still formidable. A part of the armed forces, supported apparently by the *peronistas*, staged an unsuccessful revolt in June, 1956, and there was another uprising in February, 1957. Repeated strikes prevented economic recovery. Quarrels among the democratic parties made the situation worse, and when a Constituent Assembly met in September, 1957, it accomplished little because the withdrawal of several groups of delegates left it without a quorum.

Aramburu nevertheless gave the country the most orderly presidential election that it had seen in many years in February, 1958. The principal candidates, Ricardo Balbín and Árturo Frondizi, were leaders of rival sections of the radical party. The *peronistas* were not allowed to participate as a party, and they supported Frondizi, who had been one of the more active critics of the provisional government. Frondizi won and was inaugurated on May 1, 1958.

The new administration faced many of the same problems that had confronted Aramburu. Neither agriculture nor industry had recovered from the effects of Perón's policies. There was a large deficit in the federal budget, and issues of paper money were steadily reducing the purchasing power of the peso. A rapid increase in the cost of living caused much labor unrest and led to strikes which made matters worse. The politicial situation was also uncertain. The armed forces, whose support was indispensable to the government's stability, were distrustful of the President, and there were times when it seemed possible that they might attempt to remove him. The *peronistas*, though they had helped Frondizi to be elected, lost no opportunity to make trouble, especially in the labor unions, where they still had much power. The extreme nationalists, who had also backed the President, objected when he enlisted the help of an international group of oil companies to assist the state monopoly to increase petroleum production. There was also opposition when the government embarked on an economic stabilization program which promised to cause some temporary hardship but was obviously needed if the rapidly worsening inflation was to be brought under control. The program was supported by the International Monetary Fund and by financial aid from the United States, and at the end of 1959 it seemed possible that it might start the country on the road to economic recovery.

Argentina is still basically one of the richest and most progressive of the American republics. The fertility of the *pampa*, the ease with which roads and railroads could be built between the centers of population, and the homogeneity of her people have all contributed to her prosperity. Few Latin American countries have a higher per capita income and foreign trade. The population of 20,000,000 is less than that of Brazil or Mexico, but the general level of education and well-being is higher than in those countries.

Except in the west and northwest the people are overwhelmingly of European descent. Immigration has played a large part in the country's growth, for it is estimated that 3,500,000 people came to Argentina as permanent residents between 1810 and 1930. Italians and Spaniards, both easily assimilated, formed by far the larger part of the new arrivals. Unfortunately, many of the immigrants congregated in the larger cities, living in crowded and unsanitary tenements, and those who went to the rural districts became laborers or tenant farmers rather than landowners. The wealthy Argentine families have been reluctant to break up their great estates even when they could not themselves utilize the land to best advantage. Nevertheless, the Republic's social problems seem less difficult of solution than those of its neighbors which have large Indian populations.

CHAPTER 9

Uruguay

THE *Banda Oriental*, the gently rolling country east of the River Uruguay, was the last important region of South America to be occupied by settlers of European descent. Until late in the colonial period it was held by the warlike, seminomadic Charruas, a people very similar to the tribes of the Argentine *pampas* and, like them, inveterate enemies of the white man. Expeditions from Buenos Aires frequently hunted wild cattle there in the seventeenth and eighteenth centuries, but the first European settlement was Colonia which the Portuguese established in 1680 as a base for the smuggling trade. Montevideo was founded in 1726 by the Governor of Buenos Aires, as an outpost to prevent further penetration from Brazil. As late as 1751 the town had less than 1,000 inhabitants, but the presence of a fort and garrison made it possible for colonists to settle in the country roundabout, and the interior was gradually occupied by creole cattle ranchers and their half-wild *gaucho* employees. The Indians were pushed back and finally exterminated, leaving little trace of their blood in the people who took their place. After the Portuguese were expelled from Colonia in 1777, the entire region came under the control of Spain, as a part of the viceroyalty of Buenos Aires.

The *Orientales*, as we have seen, played a leading part in the recapture of Buenos Aires from the British in 1806. In the following year Montevideo and other points along the coast were occupied for seven months by Sir Samuel Auchmuty's forces. Several hundred English merchants followed close on the heels of the army, and *La Estrella del Sur*, a newspaper issued by the invaders as a vehicle for propaganda against Spain, spread ideas which profoundly influenced the thought of the hitherto isolated creole community. Nevertheless Montevideo later became the chief center of resistance to independence in the River Plate region. Spanish influence was strong there because it was still primarily a military post and because localistic jealousy made the creoles unwilling to follow the leadership of Buenos Aires.

ARTIGAS

The revolutionary spirit was stronger in other parts of the *Banda Oriental* where the movement for independence was led by José Artigas, the national hero of Uruguay. Artigas had served for many years as Captain in a cavalry force organized by the Spanish authorities to maintain a semblance of order among the turbulent people of the interior and had taken a distinguished part in the resistance to the British invasion. After the revolution in Buenos Aires he offered his services to the patriot *junta*, and when Belgrano marched against the Spanish force at Montevideo in 1811, Artigas preceded him, recruiting forces among the *gauchos* and bandits of the interior and winning a victory at Las Piedras which opened the way to Montevideo.

The patriot forces had to withdraw when an army from Brazil invaded the *Banda Oriental*, but Artigas and his allies again moved against Montevideo after British diplomatic intervention caused the Portuguese to withdraw. The events that followed—the break between Artigas and the Buenos Aires *junta*, the subsequent war between unitarians and federalists throughout the River Plate region, and the establishment of Artigas' control over much of what is now the Argentine Republic—have been described in Chapter 6. The Portuguese invasion of the *Banda Oriental* in 1816 made the struggle a three-cornered one, and Artigas was defeated by the Portuguese at Tacuarembó in January, 1820, at the very time when other federalist leaders were winning decisive successes against the unitarians. After this battle many of his Uruguayan supporters went over to the Portuguese. Even his allies in the littoral provinces turned against him, and Artigas took refuge in Paraguay, where he lived as a simple farmer until his death in 1850. The *Banda Oriental* became a province of Portugal, and after 1822 of the new empire of Brazil.

Though many of the province's more conservative people seemed willing to accept this situation as preferable to the disorder of the past ten years, most of the *orientales* were unhappy under foreign rule. A separatist movement in 1822–1823 was suppressed, and many of the participants had to flee to Buenos Aires. In 1825, a small band of exiles, the famous "Thirty-Three," recrossed the River and started a revolt that met with a general response. Their most important recruit was Fructuoso Rivera, a former lieutenant of Artigas, who had held an important military command under Brazil. Rivera had a great following among the *gauchos*, and with his help the patriots soon controlled enough of the *Banda Oriental* to convene a representative Assembly. This chose Juan Antonio Lavalleja, the leader of the Thirty-Three, as Governor of the province and voted to join the

Argentine Federation—an act that brought on the three-years' war between Argentina and Brazil mentioned in Chapter 8. In 1828, the mediation of England brought about the conclusion of a treaty that established the independence of the *Banda Oriental*.

INDEPENDENCE

The total population of the new "República Oriental del Uruguay" was probably less than 75,000, of whom about one-fifth lived in Montevideo. The cattle which were the country's chief wealth had been greatly reduced by long years of warfare, and the only exports were small quantities of hides and jerked beef. Few of the citizens had even the rudiments of an education. Darwin, in 1832, found that the people of Colonia were proud of their representatives in Congress because all could at least sign their names, and he tells of falling in with a mail carrier whose route included several of the more important towns of the Republic but whose whole load consisted of two letters.[1] The establishment of a stable government, based on the republican constitution that the Congress adopted in 1830, would clearly be a difficult task.

Ignorance and poverty were not the only problems that confronted the people of the new state. Uruguay's position on the border between Portuguese and Spanish America had made her territory a battleground for a century and a half before 1828, and for many years thereafter frequent armed intervention by one or the other of her stronger neighbors prevented her people from settling their own problems. In the 1830's and 1840's, Argentine interference and the strife between Rosas and the European powers caused a long and costly civil war in Uruguay. In the 1850's and 1860's, Argentine interference continued, though it became less frequent, and Brazil repeatedly intervened in the Republic's affairs.

BLANCOS AND COLORADOS

The factional strife which invited this foreign intervention began even before the end of the war for independence. Rivera, who was the chief commander of the army, showed little respect for Lavalleja's authority, and when the time came to elect a new governor a conflict seemed imminent. The Assembly compromised by naming General Rondeau who soon found his position intolerable and resigned. Lavalleja was then chosen to serve until the new constitution took effect, but Rivera remained in control of the army and was thus able to assure his own election as the first President of the Republic in 1830.

[1] Darwin, *Journal of Researches into the Geology and Natural History of the Various Countries Visited During the Voyage of H.M.S. Beagle Around the World* (Everyman's ed.), pp. 136–137.

Rivera was a typical *gaucho caudillo*, a fine horseman, a daring military leader, and a man who commanded the enthusiastic loyalty of his followers. He was less successful as an administrator. There was much criticism of his government because many of his associates were men who, like himself, had held positions under the Brazilian regime, and because some of them were corrupt. The dissatisfaction found expression in a number of minor conspiracies and revolts, but Rivera nevertheless served his four-year term and retained control of the army after he passed on the presidency in 1835 to Manuel Oribe, another member of the Thirty-Three. When Oribe brought some of his predecessor's opponents into the government and then attempted to remove Rivera from his position in the army, there was a civil war. It was in this conflict that the two factions adopted the emblems that were thenceforth to give names to the historic political parties of Uruguay: Oribe's followers became the *blancos*, or whites, and Rivera's the *colorados*, or reds. Rivera defeated Oribe in 1838 and was installed as President in 1839.

THE GREAT WAR

Rivera's victorious army included a number of unitarian refugees from Buenos Aires, and he was aided in the civil war by the French naval forces that were blockading that city. He was thus aligned with Rosas' enemies, and early in 1839 he declared war on the Argentine dictator. Rosas supported Oribe, who still claimed the presidency, and after the French withdrew from the River Plate in 1840, the *blancos*, with Rosas' help, got control of practically all of Uruguay except Montevideo. In 1843 they began the long siege of the city, which is one of the famous events of Uruguay's history.

The *colorados* were able to hold out because the port was kept open by the Anglo-French forces that resumed the blockade of Buenos Aires in 1845. Oribe's army was not strong enough or well enough equipped to take it by storm, and there were in fact long periods when there were virtually no military operations at all. On the defense side, much of the fighting was done by foreigners, for there had been so much French, Italian, and Spanish immigration in the years just before the siege that a majority of the city's people were by this time of foreign birth. Especially active were a French Basque legion, 3,000 strong, and a smaller contingent of Italians under Giuseppe Garibaldi, who was later to become a hero in his own country. Rivera, who gave up the presidency when his term expired in 1843, played little part in the last years of the war. He left the country when his army in the interior was defeated in 1845, and when he returned and seized control at Montevideo in 1846 he was soon deposed and exiled. The defense government, from 1843 on, was headed by Joaquín Suárez as provisional President.

When Britain and France tired of their unsuccessful effort to bring Rosas to terms and abandoned the blockade of Buenos Aires, the authorities at Montevideo were compelled to agree to an armistice which was virtually a surrender, but before the terms of this agreement could be carried out the coalition of Brazil and Urquiza against Rosas brought another sudden change in the situation. A large part of Oribe's army deserted when a force from Entre Ríos invaded Uruguay in 1851, and later in the same year the two Uruguayan parties agreed to a treaty under which both were to be represented in a new Uruguayan Congress and a citizen acceptable to both was to become president. In 1852 a small force of Uruguayan troops joined the allied army that defeated Rosas at Monte Caseros.

Montevideo suffered surprisingly little from the long siege. Its inhabitants continued their normal social life, and the theaters were open and well patronized. Communication by land with the interior was by no means entirely cut off, and the Anglo-French squadrons gave the city free access to the sea. During the blockade of Buenos Aires, in fact, Montevideo became the commercial center of the River Plate, and its merchants enjoyed unusual prosperity. But for the rest of the nation, the "Great War," as it is called in Uruguay, was a calamity. Farmers and cattle raisers suffered much from military operations and from banditry, and the products of regions controlled by Oribe could not be shipped out through the Anglo-French blockade. For more than ten years no funds had been available for education or public works.

BRAZILIAN AND ARGENTINE INTERVENTION

In the treaties of alliance under which the two governments had joined in the war against Rosas, Brazil had promised to give the new regime at Montevideo both financial and military support. The imperial government had also taken advantage of the situation to arrange a boundary settlement favorable to Brazil's claims, and a dispute over the ratification of this agreement led to the overthrow in 1853 of Juan Francisco Giró, a *blanco* who had been elected President in the preceding year by an almost unanimous vote of the bipartisan Congress. Colonel Venancio Flores, a *colorado*, became President, but in 1855 he was ousted by a dissident faction in his own party. Flores then made an alliance with Oribe which put a *blanco*, Gabriel Antonio Pereyra, in the presidency in 1856. These changes occurred in the presence of a Brazilian army of 4,000 men that had been sent to maintain order in Uruguay, and there was more than a suspicion that they had been brought about by Brazilian intrigues.

Since the Great War, many of the Republic's leaders had been trying to promote the "fusion" between the *blancos* and the *colorados* that had been agreed on in the peace treaty of 1851. There was no real difference in the programs of the two parties, although the *colorados*, as a result of the war, had more following among the townspeople in Montevideo and the *blancos* were stronger among the landowners in the interior. There were greater differences within each party, and especially among the *colorados*, arising from a revolt against the influence of the *caudillos* who had dominated Uruguay's politics since independence with the support of their *gaucho* followers. It was a combination of the *principistas* or reformers in both parties that forced Flores to resign in 1855, and it was to combat their influence that Flores and Oribe, the principal *caudillos*, joined forces to make Pereyra President in 1856. Pereyra attempted to maintain a neutral position between the two parties, but he had to suppress a revolt by a faction of the *colorados* in 1857–1858, and the execution of most of the leaders of the movement after their surrender left much bitter feeling.

Bernardo P. Berro, another *blanco* who was elected President in 1860, attempted to continue his predecessor's nonpartisan policy, with no more success. In 1863, Flores and other *colorado* leaders invaded the country with the help of the Argentine government, which took this way of paying for their recent services in Mitre's army. Their revolution made little progress until after the end of Berro's term, when the Brazilian government also intervened to help them and the *blanco* provisional government was compelled to surrender. It was this intervention that led López, the ruler of Paraguay, to declare war on Brazil and Argentina. Uruguay, as the ally of these two countries, was involved in the long war that followed, but not in a way that greatly affected her internal affairs.

Flores ruled as a dictator until 1868, when he was murdered just as arrangements were being made for the election of one of his supporters as constitutional President. He had been bitterly opposed by the *blancos* and by the insurgents in his own party, and Lorenzo Batlle, a moderate *colorado* who became President in 1868 had an even more difficult time. After suppressing attempted revolutions fomented by both of the factions in his own party, he was confronted by a much more formidable *blanco* revolt in 1870. There was a destructive civil war that lasted until 1872, when Argentine mediation brought about a peace settlement that gave the insurgents control of four of the Republic's departments, or provinces, and $500,000 in cash.

POLITICAL AND ECONOMIC PROGRESS

This arrangement set the precedent for a series of deals in which offices and money were used to placate the *blancos* and dissuade them from revolt. The *blancos*, since the "Great War," were pre-eminently the rural party, and the great landowners who led them were less disposed to object to the control of the national government by the politicians in Montevideo if they themselves were permitted to rule their own districts. Such compromises were less costly than armed conflict, and they tended gradually to allay the enmity between the two parties and to make possible the establishment of a more stable government. For a generation to come, political disputes were settled by force rather than by the ballot; but revolutions became less frequent and less destructive.

This improvement in political conditions was in part the result of social and economic changes somewhat similar to those which were taking place in Argentina. As in that country, the *gauchos*, who had made up the armies led by *caudillos* like Rivera and Lavalleja, were gradually disappearing as the increasing European demand for meat and other pastoral products led property owners to abandon the old careless methods of stock raising. The character of the population was changing in other ways also, for 170,000 foreigners entered the country between 1861 and 1874.[2] The total population, which had fallen from an estimated 200,000 in 1840 to 132,000 in 1852, had grown to 420,000 in 1872, with a quarter of the total in the city of Montevideo. Foreign commerce had developed proportionately. The great Liebig plant for the preparation of preserved meats and meat extract had been established at Fray Bentos in 1861, and the first railroad had been begun in 1867. Landowners and merchants, as in Argentina, were becoming more interested in developing their properties and businesses than in politics and consequently less tolerant of revolutionary disturbances. The governments that ruled Uruguay for some years after 1872 were more dictatorial in their methods than their predecessors, and there was less rather than more freedom of the press and of political activity; but the relative absence of disorder made it possible for the country to continue this material progress and paved the way for the later development of democratic institutions.

"THE ERA OF PROFESSIONAL SOLDIERS"

A Uruguayan historian characterizes the political change which took place at this time as the end of the age of the *caudillos* and the beginning of the era of the "professional soldiers." [3] With the improvement in weapons and military techniques, the standing army had become more powerful, and those who controlled it had a distinct advantage in any conflict with old-style political leaders at the head of improvised forces recruited among their friends and partisans. The army was also more powerful than the civilian leaders in both parties who were striving for a more democratic government. There was a strong popular reaction against *caudillismo* and militarism after the civil war of 1870–1872, and the civilian

[2] These figures are from Acevedo, *Manual de Historia Uruguaya*, p. 146. It is impossible to ascertain the net increase from immigration because the number of foreigners who returned to Europe during the same period is not known.
[3] *Ibid.*, p. 125.

groups had some success in the election of 1872—the first election in the country's history in which the public at large showed an active interest.[4] Their adherents in the Assembly made much trouble for José Ellauri, who was chosen as President, and in 1875, when there were disturbances in connection with local elections, the army took control. Pedro Varela, who became provisional President, suppressed a revolt of the *principistas* in both parties; but he could not check the rising influence of Colonel Lorenzo Latorre, the leader of the army, and in 1876 Latorre ousted him and set up a military dictatorship.

Latorre maintained order and did something to correct the hitherto chaotic condition of the government's finances. The most important accomplishment of his administration was the reform of the educational system, under the leadership of José Pedro Varela. Uruguay, like her neighbors, had been backward in this respect, for the average attendance in the public schools in 1877 was only about 12,000.[5] The increase in the number of schools and students and, even more, the improvement in the quality of instruction were important factors in the political change that was to occur some years later. Latorre's regime in fact saw a marked increase in intellectual activities of all sorts, for his repression of political activity tended to divert the energies of the former ruling class into other lines. He was nevertheless able to remain in power only by a reign of terror. His chief opponents were openly murdered or simply disappeared, and their less important followers were imprisoned. In 1880, discouraged by popular opposition and signs of disaffection in the army, and finding himself in financial difficulties despite his careful management of the national treasury, he resigned. He was "disillusioned," he stated in a manifesto, "to the point of thinking that ours is an ungovernable country."

Latorre had probably hoped that the groups that wanted stable government would demand his continuance in power, but after the President of the Senate took over the executive authority, in accord with the constitution, the new Minister of War, Colonel Máximo Santos, emerged as the real head of the government. Santos, who had himself elected President in 1882, was no less dictatorial than his predecessor, and his arbitrary acts aroused much resentment. He suppressed armed revolts, but when he attempted to stay in power after the end of his term he found himself politically isolated and was compelled to offer positions in his Cabinet to members of a bipartisan group that had been organized to oppose him. Soon afterward, he resigned.

The "era of professional soldiers" had ended. Another army officer, General Máximo Tájes, became President in 1886, but he was not a dictator. The influence of the army was diminished by disbanding some of the

[4] J. E. Pivel Devoto, "Uruguay Independiente," in Ballesteros, *Historia de América*, Vol. XXI, p. 566.

[5] *Ibid.*, p. 223.

regiments that had been most active in conspiracies and revolts, and the influential members of the Cabinet were *colorado* civilian leaders who were determined to restore civilian government.

POLITICAL EVENTS, 1890–1903

Dr. Julio Herrera y Obes, who had been Tájes' Minister of Government, was elected President in 1890. His administration was made difficult by the effects of the world depression, but he too served out his term without having to suppress any serious armed uprisings. His successor, Juan Idiarte Borda, who took office in 1894, was less fortunate. Since 1890, the *blancos*, or "nationalists," as they now called themselves, had been completely excluded from the government and had not even had all of the local offices that they had been promised under the peace agreement of 1872. In 1897, they revolted, demanding a larger share in the administration and a reform of the electoral laws. Idiarte Borda refused to make concessions, but after he was assassinated in August, 1897, the provisional President, Juan Lindolfo Cuestas, yielded to the strong popular desire for a compromise peace. It was agreed that the minority party should have a greater participation in the conduct of elections, and that it should control the local government in six departments—nearly a third of the country. The *blancos* were given $200,000 for "expenses of pacification."

Cuestas, after dissolving an intransigent *colorado* Assembly and having a new one elected, was chosen as President for a term beginning in 1899. In the new Congress, the *blancos* were given a number of seats by agreement, anticipating the working of a new electoral law that provided for minority representation in future legislatures. The more extreme *colorados*, on the other hand, were excluded. Though there were obvious disadvantages in a situation where the *blanco* leaders in a part of the Republic's territory were virtually independent of the central government, the peace settlement of 1897 seemed a long step toward more stable and democratic government.

JOSÉ BATLLE Y ORDÓÑEZ

In 1903 the Congress elected as President a man whose personality was to dominate Uruguayan politics for many years to come. José Batlle y Ordóñez, the son of the ex-President Lorenzo Batlle, was the leader of the liberal wing of the *colorado* party. In his newspaper *El Día*, founded in 1886, he had vigorously combated Santos' dictatorship and urged political and social reforms. He came into office with support from both of the traditional political parties, but before he could begin to carry out his program he had to contend with one final civil war of the old type.

Batlle had promised to honor the long-standing agreements between the two parties; but there was a split in the nationalist party, and its chief leaders were indignant when the new President appointed members of the dissident group to two of the six departmental governorships to which the party was entitled. Concessions by Batlle placated them for a time; but new disputes arose, and in January, 1904, they revolted under the leadership of Aparicio Saravia who had taken a prominent part in the wars of 1870 and 1897. After several months of fighting and much loss of life, they accepted a general amnesty, a payment of $100,000, and a promise of constitutional and electoral reform; but they were deprived of the control that they had hitherto exercised in a large part of the Republic's territory. The position of the central government was thus greatly strengthened. Its stability was not again seriously threatened by general revolts of the old type, and the small uprisings that occurred from time to time were easily put down because they received little popular support. The incentive to revolt became less after the turn of the century because elections were better conducted and the lot of the opposition party improved in other respects. The press enjoyed almost complete freedom, and opponents of the government were not exiled or imprisoned for political activity. Uruguay became one of the most democratic states in the Western Hemisphere.

Partly because of the effects of the civil war, Batlle accomplished little in the way of political or social reform during his first administration, though he did make important improvements in the country's school system. In 1911, however, he was elected for a second term, after Claudio Williman, a somewhat more conservative *colorado*, had been President in the intervening period. He at once embarked on a program that sought to break down the power of foreign capital in Uruguay and to improve the lot of the native laborer, by a series of measures which seemed more radical in the early 1900's than they would today. The Bank of the Republic, established by the government in 1896, greatly expanded its operations, and in 1912 the government bought control of the Mortgage Bank of Uruguay. Through these two institutions the government sought to encourage small savings, provided rural credit, encouraged construction, and helped small farmers, steadily extending its control over the Republic's financial and economic life. In 1911 the government set up a State Insurance Bank to compete with foreign companies and gradually to take over a monopoly of certain lines of insurance, and in 1912 the production of electric light and power was made a state monopoly. Batlle also attempted to create a national system of railways and highways to diminish the power of the foreign-owned lines, but in this he was less successful.

In the field of labor legislation Batlle's proposals met with more opposition. An 8-hour day, with a 48-hour week, was made compulsory in all industrial establishments in 1915, but the law was difficult to enforce.

Further reforms were blocked for the time being by conservative opposition to the growing influence of the Montevideo labor unions, but after the end of Batlle's second term, and while his influence was still powerful, old-age and retirement pensions, compulsory workmen's compensation insurance, and minimum wages for rural laborers were established.[6]

THE CONSTITUTION OF 1917

Meanwhile there had been much discussion of proposals for constitutional reform. Many leaders in both parties wished to see a decrease in the autocratic power of the president and a fairer opportunity for all political groups to participate in public affairs. There had been much controversy, however, as to the character of the changes which should be made. Batlle advocated the establishment of a "collegiate executive" of nine citizens to take the place of the president. The nationalists, as the *blancos* now called themselves, wished to retain a president but to make the cabinet responsible to congress under a parliamentary form of government. On the other hand, a strong faction among the *colorados*, who later called themselves *riveristas*, opposed any radical change.

A constitutional convention was elected in 1916, after Batlle had turned the presidency over to his friend Feliciano Viera (1915–1919). The opponents of a "collegiate" executive won a majority of the seats, but a few months later another election gave the advocates of the plan control of the regular congress. The leaders of the two historic political parties then agreed on a compromise, which was incorporated in the constitution of 1917. The Republic continued to have a president, who controlled foreign affairs, national defense, and the maintenance of order; but the other duties of the executive—the preparation of the budget, the direction of education, public works, public health activities, and other administrative functions—were entrusted to a popularly elected National Council of Administration. This had nine members, each serving for six years, and one of the three members chosen biennially was always to be an adherent of the minority party. The president was elected by direct vote of the people, rather than by the congress as under the earlier constitution. The principle of proportional representation was applied in the congress and in the local elective bodies as well as in the National Council of Administration. The secret ballot was introduced; voting became compulsory; and the government was decentralized to some extent by providing for popularly elected local assemblies and administrative councils.

This constitution was in force from 1919 to 1933. Dr. Baltasar Brum, who had achieved much prestige as Foreign Minister under President

[6] S. Hanson, *Utopia in Uruguay*, is the best account of these economic and social reforms.

Viera, succeeded the latter in 1919 and was followed by José Serrato (1923–1927) and Juan Campisteguy (1927–1931). Uruguay, like Argentina and Chile, seemed to have passed beyond the era of revolutionary disturbances. Though the *batllista* wing of the still-divided *colorado* party continued to control the administration by a small margin of votes, the elections were conducted under conditions that gave little real cause for complaint, and the number of voters increased from 46,000 in 1905 to 318,000 in 1930. The opposition always had a substantial representation in the administrative council and in the congress. The government's business enterprises were on the whole well managed, and their number increased. A national meat-packing plant was established in 1928 in an effort to assure better prices to producers of livestock, and a government corporation called the *Ancap*, set up in 1931, took over the monopoly of the manufacture and sale of alcohol and went into competition with private companies in the sale of petroleum products. When Batlle y Ordóñez died in 1929, many of the reforms he had fought for seemed to be accomplished.

THE REVOLUTION OF 1933

The divided authority created by the constitution of 1917 was a handicap to effective governmental action when the world depression caused suffering and discontent in Uruguay as it did in other countries. President Gabriel Terra, who was elected in 1931 as the *batllista* candidate, quarreled with the National Council of Administration and obtained support from the *riveristas* and from Luis Alberto de Herrera, the leader of the largest faction in the nationalist party, in a movement to abolish it. On March 30, 1933, after the Council and the Congress refused to approve certain measures that the President had taken on the preceding day, both bodies were dissolved by force and Terra assumed dictatorial power.

A convention that met a year later framed a new constitution abolishing the administrative council but requiring that the minority party have half of the membership of the senate and three out of the nine positions in the president's cabinet. The same convention elected Terra as President for a new four-year term. Though the conservative property-owning classes had more influence in the new regime than they had enjoyed while the *batllistas* were in power, Terra did not abandon his predecessors' social and economic reforms, and if anything the government moved farther in the direction of state socialism. On the other hand, his political policy was more repressive than any which Uruguay had known since the beginning of the century. The publication of opposition newspapers was prohibited, and individual liberty was restricted in other respects, especially after the suppression of a small revolt in 1935.

Nevertheless the presidential election of 1938, at the end of Terra's term, was held under fairly normal conditions. The unusually large popular vote of 357,000 was rather evenly divided between three candidates, two of them *colorados* and the third a nationalist. Under Uruguay's peculiar electoral system, all ballots cast for any of a party's candidates are credited to the one who receives the largest vote, and this gave the victory to the leading *colorado*, General Alfredo Baldomir. With his inauguration, normal republican government was restored.

THE SECOND WORLD WAR

The Second World War caused political complications in Uruguay as it did in Argentina. From the start, the government supported the democracies and co-operated with the United States. In May, 1940, it discovered that Germans in the Republic were plotting to seize military control and suppressed the plot by prompt action. During the crisis, the United States rushed two cruisers to Montevideo as an evidence of moral support, and Brazil aided the government with military supplies. In the summer of 1941 Uruguay proposed to the other nations of the Hemisphere that an American country at war with a non-American power should not be treated as a belligerent—a principle that was generally adopted by the American republics after Japan attacked the United States. The government's policy was savagely opposed by the Herrera wing of the nationalist party, which was openly supported by Argentina; and the fact that the nationalists had three members of the Cabinet and half of the Senate under the 1934 constitution made it possible for them to obstruct many measures which the administration wished to take.

To eliminate this obstruction, President Baldomir arbitrarily dissolved the Congress in February, 1942, and ruled with the aid of an appointed Council of State during the next 12 months. In the meantime the constitution was amended and a new President and Congress were elected by popular vote. Baldomir's successor was another *colorado*, Juan José Amézaga (1943–1947) who continued Uruguay's policy of co-operation with the democratic powers during the war. The *herreristas*, supported by both political and economic pressure from Argentina, continued to make trouble for the government, but lend-lease from the United States and loans from the Export-Import Bank helped to strengthen the government's position. Uruguay formally declared war on the Axis powers on February 21, 1945.

Tomas Berreta, a *batllista colorado*, was elected for the term beginning in 1947; but he died after five months in office, and Vice-President Luis Batlle Berres, the nephew of Batlle y Ordóñez and himself one of the most influential *colorado* leaders, served the rest of the term which ended in 1951.

RETURN TO COLLEGIATE GOVERNMENT

Andrés Martínez Trueba, who became President in 1951, proposed at the beginning of his term that his office be abolished and that the country adopt the "collegiate" form of government urged many years before by Batlle y Ordóñez. Herrera and other *blanco* leaders supported the idea, and a detailed plan was worked out in an agreement between the majority factions of the two parties. Other groups opposed the change, and it was approved by a rather narrow margin in a plebiscite in December, 1951. This time, the National Council of Government was given all of the powers formerly exercised by the President. It was to have nine members, six from the majority party and three from the strongest minority party, all elected at one time from the country at large, serving for four-year terms and ineligible for immediate re-election. The presidency of the Council was to rotate annually among the representatives of the majority party. By a special provision, however, it was made possible for Martínez Trueba to preside over the Council until 1955 when popularly elected members were to replace the first incumbents, chosen by the Congress. Ministers, appointed by the Council, were to head the executive departments. The Congress, of course, retained the legislative power. The new government was installed on March 1, 1952.

Though still divided, the *colorado* party had a majority in the Council during the next six years and continued the social and economic policies that had started under Batlle y Ordóñez. The faction led by Luis Batlle Berres obtained control in the election of 1954. Political quarrels, however, hampered the Council's work, and discontent increased as the economic situation deteriorated. Wool exports, the country's most important source of income, fell off with a sharp drop in prices in the world market, and exports of meat and hides also declined. A subsidy to encourage the planting of wheat had caused so much land to be taken out of pasture that the number of cattle had decreased; and at the same time price controls on meat encouraged large-scale smuggling to nearby countries, with the result that the British and North American packing plants were compelled to close because they could not buy cattle at prices that made operation possible. The decline in exports made it more difficult to finance the government's social services and to obtain needed goods from abroad. A rapid increase in the cost of living, with its accompaniment of frequent and costly strikes, made matters worse.

The situation increased dissatisfaction with the collegiate form of government, but a move to return to the presidential system was defeated in 1958, partly because rival proposals were presented. The election did, however, end the long tenure of power by the *colorado* party and diminished the dominance of the government by politicians from Montevideo. The rural wing of the nationalist party, the *blancos*, obtained a majority in the

National Council, but internal feuds within the party made the political outlook uncertain when the new councilors took office. Luis Alberto de Herrera, who had led the *blancos* for more than half a century, died a few months after the victory, in April, 1959. The new administration had hardly taken office when disastrous floods ruined crops and killed livestock in a large part of the Republic's territory.

Though one of the smallest of the American Republics, with less than 3,000,000 inhabitants, Uruguay's success in achieving and maintaining democratic government has given her an influential voice in the councils of the hemisphere. As in Argentina, a homogeneous population and a good educational system have encouraged political and economic progress. Unfortunately, much of this progress has primarily benefited Montevideo, where about a third of the people live. In the rural districts, wages and standards of living are far lower than in the city. The social legislation of the past 50 years has mainly helped the urban working classes, and most of the great army of government employees work in the city.

CHAPTER 10

Paraguay

▧▧▧▧▧▧▧▧▧▧▧▧▧▧▧▧▧▧▧▧▧▧▧▧▧
▧▧▧▧▧▧▧▧▧▧▧▧▧▧▧▧▧▧▧▧▧▧▧▧▧

PARAGUAY BEFORE 1810

THE SURVIVORS of Mendoza's ill-fated expedition to the River Plate, who settled at Asunción in 1541, found the Guaranís of the interior less intractable than the fierce Indians of the *pampas*. The Paraguayan tribes lived in settled villages, practicing agriculture in a crude way as a supplement to hunting and fishing, but they had no government beyond that of the *caciques* and village councils in each small community. They were easily conquered and most of those on the east bank of the Paraguay, in the immediate vicinity of Asunción, were apportioned among the settlers in *encomiendas*. Since there were relatively few Spaniards, and no mines or other enterprises in which the intensive use of forced labor was profitable, the Indians seem to have been less cruelly exploited than in some other parts of the continent. Great numbers of them, in fact, were protected from abuse at the hands of the creoles because they were gathered in the Jesuit missions to the southeast. A large proportion survived, and *Guaraní*, rather than Spanish, is generally spoken in rural Paraguay today. Even the upper class was largely of mixed blood, because few women came to Asunción from Spain.

It required more than two weeks for a hardy traveler, on horseback, to reach Asunción from Buenos Aires, which was itself an out-of-the-way place during the colonial period. Sailing vessels, the only means of transporting goods, required three months for the voyage upstream on the Paraná and Paraguay Rivers. Economic development was further retarded by the competition of the Jesuit missions and by internal commotions, for which popular hatred of the Jesuits was at least partly responsible. Until 1779, when coined money is said to have been first introduced by the tobacco monopoly, all trade was by barter, and even postage was paid in *yerba mate*, cotton, or tobacco.[1] *Yerba mate*, or Paraguay tea,

[1] Félix de Azara, *Geografía Física y Esférica de las Provincias del Paraguay y Misiones Guaraníes*, p. 431.

which was consumed in great quantities in the other River Plate provinces, was the chief export during the colonial period.

At the beginning of the nineteenth century the population was probably between 100,000 and 200,000. Asunción, with some 10,000 inhabitants, was little more than a large village. Such few schools as existed were of the most elementary sort, and there were said to be only two natives of the country who had had the advantage of an education outside of Paraguay. The colony was consequently almost untouched by the intellectual revival that changed the outlook of the creoles in many other parts of Spanish America in the latter part of the eighteenth century, or by the revolutionary propaganda that had been one of its consequences.

INDEPENDENCE

There was thus little enthusiasm in Paraguay when the creoles at Buenos Aires overthrew the viceregal government in May, 1810. An Assembly of the principal inhabitants of Asunción, convened by the Governor, decided to recognize the authority of the regency at Cádiz rather than that of the *porteño junta*, and traditional dislike of Buenos Aires made it easy to raise an army to repulse Belgrano when he attempted to invade Paraguay some months later. Nevertheless, Belgrano, who remained in the country for a time after his capitulation, made friends with the creole officers who commanded the Paraguayan troops, and through his efforts a revolutionary party rapidly grew up. In May, 1811, a military revolt forced the Governor to transfer power to a *junta* composed of himself, another Spanish officer, and the influential creole Dr. Gaspar Rodríguez de Francia. A month later the Governor's intrigues with emissaries of the Portuguese Princess Carlota caused a second uprising by which he and the pro-Spanish *cabildo* were deprived of all authority. A Congress met to appoint a new *junta* of five, including Francia and Fulgencio Yegros, who had come into prominence as a leader of the army that defeated Belgrano.

The government at Buenos Aires still hoped to bring all of the former viceroyalty under its authority, and there were some leaders at Asunción who favored a union. Francia, however, opposed the idea. The *junta*'s proposal for a confederation, which foreshadowed the later demands of the Argentine federalists, was rejected at Buenos Aires, but in October, 1811, the two governments signed a treaty of alliance which recognized Paraguay's autonomy. Their relations nevertheless rapidly deteriorated. Paraguay refused to send troops to help in the war against the Spaniards in the *Banda Oriental*, and Buenos Aires retaliated with measures against Paraguay's trade.

Conflicts between those who desired and those who opposed a closer union with Buenos Aires and the intrigues of the still influential Spanish party caused much political tension at Asunción. Francia, at odds with the leaders of the army, withdrew from the *junta* in December, 1811. This weakened the *junta*, and when relations with Buenos Aires seemed to be approaching a crisis in November, 1812, he was persuaded to return. He insisted however, that a part of the army and half of the nation's war materials should be under his immediate control, and that a Congress be summoned to deal with pending problems.

Unlike the earlier congresses, whose members had been representatives of municipal and ecclesiastical corporations and other important persons invited by the government, the body that met in 1813 was, in part at least, chosen by popular election. The majority of its 1,000 members were from the rural districts, where Francia's influence was predominant, and there was little opposition to the measures that Francia proposed. One of these was a rejection of Buenos Aires' invitation to send delegates to the Constituent Assembly that was to attempt to set up a government for the United Provinces. Another was a constitution that placed the government of Paraguay in the hands of two consuls, to hold office for one year. Each consul was to have command of half of the army, and they were to take turns as head of the administration. Francia and Fulgencio Yegros were elected to these positions, and Francia arranged that he should have the first and, consequently, the third four-month turn, so that he was in charge at the end of the year. He was thus able to push his colleague aside, and a Congress that met in 1814 made him sole dictator for five years. Another Congress, in 1816, made him dictator for life. From 1816 until his death, "El Supremo," as he required his people to call him, exercised an unquestioned and unlimited authority.

FRANCIA

Francia is said to have been the son of a Spanish army officer and a creole lady of distinguished family.[2] In his youth he studied theology at the University of Córdoba, which was the chief center of learning in eastern South America. After his return to Asunción he practiced law and eagerly read such philosophical and scientific books as he was able to obtain. Though he was unsociable and apparently had little personal charm or capacity for friendship, his courageous and disinterested defense of the interests of poor and friendless litigants had brought him a large popular following, and his reputation for great learning had increased his prestige. Before 1810 he had held various positions in the municipal government at Asunción. With the advent of independence he had shown himself an able administrator and a shrewd and resourceful politician, in a community where politics was an untried art.

After he became dictator, Francia rigorously suppressed political activ-

[2] For a review of the evidence on this point, about which there have been many conflicting statements, see Blas Garay, *La Revolución de la Independencia del Paraguay* (Madrid, 1897), Appendix B.

ity of any sort. No congresses met after 1816, and all criticism of the government was severely punished. Those merely suspected of unfriendliness were exiled to an unhealthful penal colony in the north. There was much discontent among the creole aristocracy, who were systematically mistreated and impoverished, and among the former leaders of the army, who were kept under close surveillance. In 1820 a formidable conspiracy against the dictator was discovered, involving most of the leaders in the movement for independence. A great number of prominent citizens were arrested, and more than 100 were shot. Hundreds of others were kept in prison, some of them until the dictator's death nearly 20 years later. All of the Spaniards in the country, including the bishop and the ex-Governor Velazco, were jailed and released only after paying heavy fines. Thereafter no one ventured to oppose the government, and anyone whose education or standing in the community might make him the object of suspicion strove to remain in a prudent obscurity.

Francia took no advice and had no trusted collaborators. He himself decided every detail of policy and closely supervised every branch of the administration including the courts. The Church was made completely subservient to his authority when the Spanish bishop was replaced by a vicar general named by the government, and no one in the army was given a rank higher than captain. After 1830, when the calculated cruelty of the dictator's policy had done its work, there were fewer arrests and executions. The majority of the Paraguayans were probably not unhappy under his rule, but no one ventured to discuss public affairs. The country was at least governed with relative efficiency and complete honesty, for Francia had no interest in money for himself and severely punished graft among his subordinates.

For a quarter-century, Paraguay was practically cut off from the outside world. Francia was determined to keep the country from being contaminated by the disorder that reigned in the rest of the River Plate region, and he was suspicious of foreigners and foreign governments. Other governments' efforts to establish diplomatic relations were rebuffed, and their communications were simply left unanswered. Their representatives were rarely permitted to visit Asunción. Few other travelers were permitted to enter the Republic, and those who did were often refused permission to leave. A group of British and other foreigners who had been held in Paraguay for varying periods were rescued only by diplomatic intervention in 1825, and M. Bonpland, a French naturalist who was kidnaped while experimenting with the cultivation of *yerba mate* in the nearby Argentine province of Corrientes was compelled to live for nine years in a small Paraguayan village. Few natives were permitted to travel abroad, and no one but the dictator could receive foreign magazines and newspapers. Books, however, could be imported, after Francia himself had examined them.[3]

[3] *Ibid.,* p. 73.

Some imports were necessary, if only to supply the government's troops with munitions. Foreign vessels were therefore occasionally permitted to come as far as Pilar, the first port on the Paraguay River, and merchants from Brazil were encouraged to visit Itapúa, now called Encarnación, on the Paraná. Much of the trade was carried on for the account of the government itself and the rest under its close supervision. The amount was always small, for conditions along the lower Paraná, where local *caudillos* were likely to confiscate any ship passing the ports under their control, would in any event have discouraged traffic on the river. The Paraguayans were thus compelled to develop local manufactures, though of a very crude sort, and to increase their production of foodstuffs, instead of cultivating *mate* for export. They at least enjoyed peace and a primitive plenty at a time when the rest of the River Plate area was periodically being laid waste by civil war.

CARLOS ANTONIO LÓPEZ

Francia maintained his amazing ascendancy over the minds and bodies of the Paraguayans until his death at an advanced age on September 20, 1840. As there was no provision for the choice of his successor, the commanders of the troops at Asunción joined with the *cabildo* in establishing a military *junta* to govern the country pending the election of a Congress. In the confused period that followed, while barracks revolts set up and overturned new *juntas*, a civilian named Carlos Antonio López gradually emerged as the most influential political leader. He was one of two Consuls elected for a three-year term by a Congress that met in 1841, and in 1844 he became President. A constitution adopted in the same year gave him practically unlimited power, subject only to the control of Congresses meeting at five-year intervals.

López, a self-trained lawyer, was one of the few educated Paraguayans who had not incurred Francia's suspicious enmity. He had prudently remained in obscurity until 1840, but when the dictator died he soon acquired much influence with the ignorant and politically inexperienced military leaders who attempted to take over the control of affairs. Paraguay made some progress under his leadership. The system of taxation and the judiciary were reorganized, and the first newspaper, a government organ, edited and for the most part written by the President himself, began publication in 1845. The country gradually emerged from the isolation that Francia had imposed. Rosas, who still professed to regard Paraguay as a rebellious member of the Argentine Confederation, for some years obstructed intercourse with the outside world by way of the Paraná, but after his fall the river was opened to commerce. In 1853 Paraguay was formally recognized by the United States and several European powers. Foreign trade gradually increased, though it was still subject to burdensome restrictions and the most important products, like *yerba mate*, lumber, and hides, were controlled by government monopolies. Steamship service was established between Asunción and Buenos Aires, and the construction of a railway line was begun at Asunción.

Closer contact with the outside world had some disadvantages. Paraguay became involved in the troubled international politics of the River Plate, and for some years was intermittently at war with Rosas. Boundary disputes, both with Argentina and with Brazil, became acute and forced the government to build up its military forces. There were also unpleasant controversies with France and England and the United States, arising from the claims of businessmen or adventurers who had disagreements with López. When Paraguayan forts fired on the U.S.S. *Water Witch* in 1855, killing several members of her crew, a serious conflict was averted only by the mediation of President Urquiza of Argentina.

López showed somewhat more respect for constitutional forms than Francia, and was less cruel in his treatment of suspected enemies, but he permitted no more freedom of political discussion. All persons of any importance were subject to a constant and humiliating surveillance, and no one openly opposed the President's evident intention to remain in power for life and to secure the succession for his son Francisco. A constitutional amendment in fact empowered the President to designate the person to take office in case of his death. The younger López, who was already in command of the army, consequently asserted his right to the presidency when his father died in 1862, and the Congress, overawed by a display of military force, promptly confirmed him in his position.

FRANCISCO SOLANO LÓPEZ AND THE PARAGUAYAN WAR

Francisco Solano López had been brought up in the enjoyment of irresponsible power. The old President had been notoriously slow to check the lawless and licentious conduct of his sons, and Francisco, as the oldest, had been trained from early youth to regard himself as the future ruler of Paraguay. His chief ambition, apparently, was to achieve fame as a soldier. When only nineteen he had been given nominal command of an army during the intermittent conflict with Rosas. Seven years later, while in Europe as his father's Minister Plenipotentiary, he visited the allied camps in the Crimea and came home fired with the idea of making Paraguay a great military power. He also brought with him an Irish mistress, Madame Lynch, to whose influence the Paraguayans attributed some of his most reckless acts. Partly at least because of his insistence, much of the nation's resources had been devoted to building up the army and accumulating stores of war supplies, and skilled foreign workmen had been employed in the construction of an iron foundry, a powder factory, and an arsenal to make the country partly self-sufficient in the production of munitions. In 1862 the country had a larger standing army than any of its neighbors. There was some justification for these preparations in the fact that Paraguay had boundary disputes with both Brazil and Argentina, but there is little reason to suppose that war with those countries would have occurred if Francisco López had not deliberately provoked it.

From the time he took office, the new President was obsessed by the idea that Paraguay should play a more influential rôle in the affairs of the River Plate region. He feared, or professed to fear, that Argentina and Brazil had designs on the independence of both Paraguay and Uruguay, and when the two stronger governments interfered to help Flores' revolt against the government at Montevideo in 1863 he made a vigorous protest. In 1864, when the Emperor Dom Pedro sent troops into Uruguay, he declared war on Brazil. He planned to send his army into Brazil through the province of Misiones, which was claimed by Paraguay but occupied by Argentina, and when President Mitre refused to consent, he attacked the Argentine province of Corrientes.

López had been in communication with Governor Urquiza of Entre Ríos, whose party had recently been defeated at Pavón, and he hoped that the federalist provinces in Argentina would revolt against the new government at Buenos Aires. He also seems to have hoped for a slave uprising when his forces entered Brazil. In both cases his expectations were disappointed, and it was soon clear that his folly and ignorance had involved his people in a hopeless struggle against a group of enemies so superior in manpower and resources that even his better-trained army gave him only a temporary advantage. Argentina, Brazil, and the *colorado* government of Uruguay signed a treaty of alliance against him in May, 1865. In September their forces captured a Paraguayan army that had crossed Misiones and invaded Rio Grande do Sul, and seven months later they were ready to invade Paraguay itself.

During the next two years the allies made little progress. Their fleet, under the Brazilian Admiral Tamandaré, won an overwhelming naval superiority on the Paraguay River by its victory at Riachuelo in June, 1865, but neither it nor the land forces commanded by President Mitre were able to force their way past the strong Paraguayan forts at Humaitá. Long delays were caused by indecision and inefficiency and by internal disturbances in Argentina which compelled Mitre to return to Buenos Aires. Uruguay's help became negligible after Flores was assassinated. The Paraguayan forces, however, were weakened by many months of desperate fighting, and in 1868, after the allied fleet had forced its way past Humaitá, López was compelled to withdraw to new positions farther up the river. These also were taken after a hard struggle, and on December 31 the allies occupied Asunción. There was another long delay before the new Allied Commander, the Brazilian Emperor's son-in-law the Count d'Eu, was ready to pursue López still farther north. By this time the Paraguayans could offer little resistance. López fled into the forests of the north, where he fell into the hands of the Brazilians on March 1, 1870, and was killed as he resisted capture. Madame Lynch, who had remained with him to the end, returned to Europe.

The results of the war were appalling. The Paraguayan people had fought with desperate bravery, and nearly every male in the country, including young boys and old men, had stayed with the colors to the bitter end. Many thousands had been killed in battle, and a far greater number had died of disease or starvation. Out of a population of probably somewhat over half a million in 1865, only 221,079 were counted by the census in 1871; and all but 28,746 of these were women and children. Agriculture had been neglected, and nearly all the cattle had been killed for food. The upper class had suffered even more severely than the peasants, for López had treated the leading families of Asunción with insane cruelty during the final months of the war and had executed hundreds of people whom he suspected of conspiring against him. Among them were his own brothers and brothers-in-law. Many others, including the wives and families of those who incurred his displeasure, died from torture or harsh treatment.

THE PERIOD OF RECOVERY

In 1869, after the allies occupied Asunción, they permitted a *junta* of three Paraguayans to set up a provisional government and call together a convention which adopted a republican constitution. Both Brazil and Argentina demanded large war indemnities and proceeded to settle in their own favor the long-standing boundary disputes, so that Paraguay lost a considerable area in the north to Brazil and recognized Argentine ownership of Misiones, where the Jesuits had had their famous missions. Argentina also demanded a large part of what is now the Paraguayan Chaco; but this claim was submitted to arbitration, and an award handed down by President Hayes at Washington in 1878 gave much of the territory to Paraguay.

It was difficult to set up a republican government in a country which had for such a long time submitted tranquilly to autocratic rule. No postwar president exercised the absolute power that Francia and the two López' had wielded, but it was many years before any substantial part of the population began to participate in political affairs. Until 1876, the country was occupied by Brazilian troops whose commanders frequently interfered in the conduct of the government and were at least partly responsible for the overthrow of two or three of the short-lived regimes that controlled the country until Juan Bautista Gill became President with their support in 1874. Gill was murdered some months after the Brazilians withdrew, and thereafter the leaders of the small, poorly trained army were in control. Elections were a mere formality, and there were no real political parties until 1887.

The most influential of the military leaders was General Bernardino Caballero, who had been one of the heroes of the war against the Triple Alliance. Caballero supported Cándido Barreiro, who became President in 1878, and took control of the government himself when Barreiro died in 1880. He continued to be powerful during the administrations of Patricio Escobar, another war hero (1886–1890), and Juan González (1890–1892). After 1892 another faction of the *colorado* party, as the dominant group now called itself, obtained control for some years, but Caballero again placed one of his associates in the presidency in 1902. Throughout the 30 years after the war there were frequent revolts or attempted uprisings by parts of the army and by the opposition "liberal" party, but the factions that struggled for power were composed of relatively small groups of politicians and army officers.

There were thus no general civil wars to delay the slow and painful process of recovery to which the surviving Paraguayans were courageously addressing themselves. Though few men had come back from the war, the women cultivated the fields, and internal commerce slowly revived. Foreigners began to invest capital in stock raising and the exploitation of forest products like *yerba mate* and *quebracho*, and a considerable influx of Italians and other Europeans helped to fill the gaps in the upper class left by López' insensate executions. By the end of the century, Paraguay had recovered from the worst effects of the war. It was still one of the poorer and more isolated parts of South America, and the continual political disturbances at Asunción had made it difficult for the government to cope with the problems that remained to be solved.

POLITICAL EVENTS, 1904–1932

The *colorados*, or "republicans," who had been in power since 1877, lost control of the government in 1904 when President Juan Antonio Ezcurra was ousted by a popular revolt. The advent of their rivals, the liberals, made little difference in political conditions. A succession of presidents held office for periods of a year or two, only to be driven out by dissensions within their own party. In the 20 years from 1904 to 1924, only one chief executive, Eduardo Schaerer (1912–1916), succeeded in remaining in office through his constitutional term. Dr. Schaerer's administration was notable for the completion of the railroad from Asunción to Encarnación on the Paraná, where it connects by ferry with the Argentine line to Buenos Aires. After 1924 there was a period of relative tranquility during the administrations of Eligio Ayala (1924–1928) and José Guggiari (1928–

1932). Under Guggiari's successor, Eusebio Ayala, internal political events were pushed into the background by another foreign war.

THE CHACO WAR

The Gran Chaco, an almost uninhabited region of more than 100,000 square miles west of the Paraguay River, had long been in dispute between Paraguay and Bolivia. Though most of the territory was of no value for agriculture or stock raising, both countries stubbornly maintained their claim to it; and several efforts to bring them to an agreement, either for arbitration or for a compromise boundary line, failed. Both pushed farther and farther into the disputed territory with chains of small forts, which were soon dangerously close to one another. In December, 1928, the Paraguayans destroyed a Bolivian post at Vanguardia. Prompt action by a Pan American conference on conciliation and arbitration, that happened to be meeting at Washington, delayed the outbreak of hostilities for the time being, but in June, 1932, new clashes occurred in the Chaco, and the fighting soon developed into a full-fledged war. Appeals for peace from all of the other American republics and from the President of the Council of the League of Nations went unheeded.

The fighting continued for three years. Bolivia had a larger and better-equipped army, but the hot climate of the Chaco caused terrible suffering among the Indians from the high plateau. Paraguay's untrained and ill-equipped recruits were at least accustomed to the tropical climate, and the earlier fighting was in regions far from any Bolivian town but relatively near the settled part of Paraguay. After some initial reverses, therefore, the Paraguayans at the end of 1933 began an offensive that gradually pushed the Bolivians back across the Chaco and almost out of the territory in dispute. In the first months of 1935 they occupied part of the oil-bearing region of eastern Bolivia, but here they were too far from their own bases and were soon forced back by counterattacks.

The League of Nations and the other American states persistently endeavored to stop the war, and in June, 1935, with military operations at a stalemate, the United States and several of the South American governments were finally able to bring about a truce. The armies on both sides were disbanded, but the conclusion of a treaty of peace was delayed for more than three years by the intransigence of both belligerents. When the treaty was finally signed, on July 21, 1938, it gave most of the Chaco to Paraguay but gave Bolivia access to the upper Paraguay River and provided that she should have the use of Puerto Casado in the Paraguayan Chaco as a free port.

The war had been costly to both belligerents. One hundred thousand men are said to have died in the course of the fighting. In Paraguay, the maintenance of the army, and later the demoralization inseparable from its demobilization, severely affected production and exports. By the end of the war, the already-depreciated paper currency had lost five-sixths of its value. Living costs had risen rapidly; government salaries were far in arrears; and there was a moratorium on debts.

RECENT EVENTS

There was much discontent among the officers of the army, who feared that many of their number would be discharged with the advent of peace, and in February, 1936, a group of officers led by Colonel Rafael Franco ousted President Ayala and took control of the government. Franco sought the support of the labor unions, the university students, and the soldiers returning from the war for a program of state socialism and economic nationalism; but he could not maintain harmony among these groups, and in August, 1937, he was forced to resign. Félix Paíva became provisional President, with a Cabinet selected by agreement between the liberal party and the army. Neither group was satisfied with this arrangement, and in 1939 General José Félix Estigarribia was elected President. Estigarribia had been the Commander of the army in the Chaco, and it was hoped that his prestige and popularity would enable him to end the disorders that had plagued the country since the end of the war. Unfortunately, the new President was killed in an airplane accident in September, 1940.

General Higinio Morínigo, the Minister of War, became provisional President and soon made it clear that he intended to rule as a military dictator. He imprisoned or exiled many of the civilian politicians, and in 1943 he held an election with himself as the only candidate. There were several plots and revolts, and some politically inspired labor disturbances, but the support of the army enabled him to remain in power. Though Paraguay was especially vulnerable to economic and political pressure from Argentina, he broke diplomatic relations with the Axis powers in January, 1942. Lend-lease assistance and loans from the Export-Import Bank, and also a substantial loan from Brazil, helped him to maintain a policy of co-operation with the democracies. A part of the army, however, sympathized with the military clique at Buenos Aires and caused the President some embarrassment. The army lost some of its influence in July, 1946, when Morínigo permitted several of the civilian political parties to resume activity and appointed a Cabinet in which the *colorados* and the *febreristas*, or followers of Colonel Franco, were represented. This Cabinet resigned in January, 1947, however, and two months later the *febreristas*, with some communist support, started a civil war. The fighting continued until August, but the government was finally victorious.

A presidential election was held at the end of Morínigo's term in 1948. With the leaders of the recent revolt and many other politicians still in exile, the *colorados*, who now dominated the administration, were the only party in a position to participate. Even they were sharply divided, and the nomination of Morínigo's Finance Minister, Natalicio González, was forced on the party convention by high-handed methods. After the election, there was still some uncertainty about the President's willingness to step down, and in June, 1948, he was ousted by a military *coup*. A provisional administration took over until González' inauguration in August.

This was the first of a series of governmental changes caused by continued factional quarrels within the *colorado* party. González suppressed an uprising in the army in October, 1948, but in January, 1949, he was removed, without fighting, by members of his own Cabinet. General Raimundo Rolón, his successor, was ousted by a similar movement in February, and Felipe Molas López, who became provisional President and was then elected constitutional President, was forced to resign in September in favor of the veteran statesman Federico Chaves. Chaves was formally elected President in 1950 and re-elected in 1953.

There was still dissension within the dominant *colorado* party, and in 1954 the Chief of Staff of the Army, General Alfredo Stroessner, ousted Chavez and held an election in which he himself was the sole candidate for the presidency. The new government repressed all open opposition and imprisoned or exiled many of the country's political leaders, including some *colorados*. There were several revolts in the next few years, but none succeeded.

General Stroessner was inaugurated for a second term in 1958. In 1959, when his administration was attracting embarrassing attention abroad as the only remaining dictatorship in South America, he announced a program of political reform: the lifting of the state of siege, a political amnesty, more freedom of expression, and the convening of a constitutional convention. The state of siege was lifted, for a short period, but renewed disturbances apparently led the President to postpone for the time being the other measures that he had promised.

Though the railroad and the airplane have improved communications with the outside world, Paraguay is still an isolated and backward country. With about 1,600,000 inhabitants, it is the least populous of the South American republics. Only a small fraction of its arable land is under cultivation, and its exports—chiefly cotton, *quebracho* extract, meat, hides, and *yerba mate*—amount to but a few dollars per capita. There has been little foreign investment, and there are few important agricultural or industrial enterprises. The upper class, since 1870 largely of foreign descent, are politicians, professional men, and merchants rather than great landowners. In the country districts, standards of living are low, and most of the people speak *Guaraní* rather than Spanish. Peonage, or debt slavery, is said to be common.

CHAPTER 11

Chile

▨▨▨▨▨▨▨▨▨▨▨▨▨▨▨▨▨▨▨▨▨▨▨▨▨▨▨▨

THE TERRITORY OF CHILE is a narrow mountainous strip between the summits of the Andes and the Pacific, stretching some 2,500 miles from the boundary of Peru to Cape Horn. At the beginning of the nineteenth century, only one small part of the country—the temperate, fertile Central Valley between Santiago and Concepción—had any considerable population. North of the Valley there was an almost rainless desert, with rich mineral resources that were nearly untouched, and to the south a region potentially attractive to white settlers was still held by the savage Araucanians, who had carried on an intermittent warfare with the Spanish throughout the colonial period. There were some small European settlements south of the Indian country, around Valdivia and in Chiloé, but beyond these the heavily forested, excessively rainy mountains were practically uninhabited.

The population at the time of independence was probably between one-half and three-quarters of a million. The colony had attracted few Spanish immigrants, for no important mines had been found there, and geographical isolation, as well as the constant Indian wars, had retarded its development. Cattle raising was still the chief occupation, though some wheat was grown for export to Peru. There were almost no improved roads, and the towns were small. In the southern part of the Central Valley, farms and settlements were still raided from time to time by the Araucanians.

In the Valley itself, a considerable proportion of the people were *mestizos*. The Indians north of the Bío-Bío River had been partly civilized by the Incas and lived a more settled life than the wild tribes farther south, and they had been divided among the colonists in *encomiendas* when Chile was conquered. Both they and the numerous slaves taken during the Araucanian wars had been assimilated into the white community, but their descendants still formed the bulk of the laboring class. Most of them were *inquilinos*, or tenant farmers, who worked for the creole landowners in payment for the small plots of ground they were allowed to cultivate. Their condition was hardly better than that of the Indians in other countries, for their wages, when they received any, were extremely low and they were bound to their employer's service by a system of peonage. Though they were miserably poor and underfed, custom and necessity led them to accept their lot as a matter of course, and most of them were personally devoted to their *patrones*. Each *hacendado* ruled like a feudal lord on his own estates, settling disputes and punishing minor crimes without the intervention of the public authorities.

The landowning aristocracy was a compact, class-conscious group which was to dominate public affairs in Chile for more than a century after independence. Some of its members were descendants of the first settlers, others of more recent arrivals. During the eighteenth century there had been a number of immigrants from the Basque provinces and other parts of northern Spain, and the Republic's historians attribute to this thrifty, industrious element many of the qualities that characterize Chilean society today. The landowners seemed to take more interest in the management of their properties than in most of the Spanish colonies, and until late in the colonial period many of them actually lived on their *haciendas*. There was thus little of the hostility between city and country which helped to make the early history of the River Plate republics so turbulent. Local jealousies, though by no means absent, were also less important as a political factor because the great estates were concentrated in a relatively small area and the Province of Santiago was far more populous than the regions to the north and south.

O'HIGGINS

There was nevertheless much political strife in the first years of independence. Bernardo O'Higgins, who had been installed as *Director Supremo* after San Martín's victory at Chacabuco, remained in power from 1817 until 1823. His chief opponents were the still-strong Carrera faction. Juan José and Luis Carrera were executed at Mendoza in 1818 by local authorities friendly to O'Higgins, but José Miguel, the most influential of the three brothers, continued his efforts to overthrow the government until he himself was put to death in Argentina in 1821. The loss of their leaders did not make the other members of the party less unfriendly to the government, and as time went on the Director's popularity with other groups was undermined by opposition to his policies.

O'Higgins, who had lived in Europe, realized better than most of his compatriots how backward Chilean society was. He promoted education and attempted, against increasing opposition from the clergy and the aristocracy, to change local institutions and customs that he deemed unsuitable in a democracy. At the same time he governed as a military dictator, sharing his authority only with a Senate of five members appointed by himself. Though there was an increasingly strong demand for a more representative government, no Congress was convened until 1822; and when one finally did meet in that year the Director selected its members and the Assembly adopted a constitution that was clearly designed to extend his dictatorship. Discontent with the progress of San Martín's efforts to liberate Peru also undermined O'Higgins' prestige, and in January, 1823, a military revolt led by General Ramón Freire forced the Director to resign.

LIBERALISM AND FEDERALISM

Freire, who became Supreme Director, was popular with the army and with the civilian leaders, but the very qualities that inspired confidence —his moderation in dealing with political opponents and his freedom from selfish ambition—hampered him in meeting an increasingly difficult situation. The constitution adopted in 1823, which restricted the authority of the executive and placed the real power in the hands of Congress, was so obviously unworkable that Freire was soon compelled to suspend it and to assume dictatorial powers with the consent of the congressional leaders themselves. Efforts to frame a new constitution were frustrated by partisan squabbles, and Freire finally became discouraged and resigned in 1826. The principal achievement of his troubled term in office was the conquest of the island of Chiloé which had remained under Spanish control until this time.

The new Constituent Assembly that now met was controlled by advocates of "federalism" led by José Miguel Infante. As in the River Plate, there were many persons who thought that governmental decentralization would make for democracy—an idea that was welcomed by the great landowners because it would give them more independence in their own domains. When the Assembly met, Infante and his followers proceeded to put their ideas into execution. Hastily drawn and ill-considered laws divided the Republic into eight provinces and provided for the selection of all provincial and local authorities, including parish priests, by popular election. The only result was factional strife and confusion. Disputes over boundaries, quarrels between rival towns, and the utter inability of the inexperienced local political leaders to cope with the problems which suddenly confronted them soon discredited the new system. The country was drifting into anarchy when Freire reluctantly agreed to accept the office of President in January, 1827. He soon resigned again and was succeeded by the Vice-President, Francisco Antonio Pinto.

A new constitution restored some of the authority of the central government, but the administration was beset by financial difficulties and had to contend with frequent mutinies in the army. Party strife also became increasingly violent. The old personal factions, the *O'Higginistas* and the *Carreristas*, had given place after 1823 to new political groups: the conservatives, popularly known as *pelucones*, and the liberals, or *pipiolos*. The latter supported Pinto and were able to bring about his re-election in 1829, but a dispute over the vice-presidency, for which no candidate received a majority, brought on a civil war. The government fell when the conservatives under General Joaquín Prieto defeated its forces on April 17, 1830, at the bloody battle of Lircai.

PORTALES

The outstanding figure in the regime that thus came into power was Diego Portales, a businessman who had only recently begun to take an interest in politics. Portales' firm had undertaken in 1824 to provide funds for the service of the government's foreign debt, in return for a lease of the fiscal monopoly of tobacco and certain other commodities. The venture had been a failure that involved him in a series of disputes with the liberal officials and led him to throw his support to the conservatives. By 1829 he was the recognized leader of the opposition.

In the new provisional government he assumed control of practically all branches of the administration. The army was purged of officers who were not in sympathy with the dominant party, and its power for mischief was decreased by strengthening the civil militia. Prompt and ruthless punishment of criminals did much to check the banditry which had grown to be an intolerable curse in the country districts. Government expenses were reduced; the customs service was reorganized to produce more revenue; and political disturbances were suppressed with a heavy hand. The freedom of the press which had existed under the liberal regime became a thing of the past.

Refusing to be a candidate himself, Portales was largely responsible for the election of General Prieto as President of the Republic in 1831. Thereafter he devoted himself to his private business for some years, except for a brief period when he served as Governor of Valparaiso. His influence in the administration, however, was hardly less than if he had held office, and the autocratic, highly centralized government which existed in Chile during the following 30 years was the result of his passion for order and his determination to make the authority of the state respected. His political views were reflected in the constitution of 1833 which was to remain in force for nearly a century. The president, chosen by indirect election for a five-year term, controlled all branches of the administration and was given broad powers, especially in dealing with political disorder. At the same time the judiciary was strengthened and its independence safeguarded. All vestiges of the federal system disappeared, for provincial and local affairs were placed in the hands of agents of the central government, though the municipal councils continued to be elective. Catholicism was made the state religion, and the public exercise of any other was forbidden.

Under the liberal regime there had been an effort, if a not-very-successful one, to hold free elections. After 1833, the official candidates were nearly always victorious. Literacy and property qualifications restricted the suffrage to an insignificant fraction of the population, and the government's authority and prestige, backed if necessary by the use of force, made successful opposition almost impossible. The government was not, however, a mere military despotism, for legal forms were generally observed and the courts and the congress enjoyed a measure of independence. It derived its real strength from the support of the Church and the majority of the aristocracy, who were by this time ready to sacrifice some of their liberty if they could obtain relief from the disturbed conditions which had marked the past six years of political experimentation.

As the end of Prieto's first term approached, a few conservatives who objected to Portales' high-handed methods joined with the liberals in advocating the presidential candidacy of Manuel Renjifo, the Minister of Finance. Portales at once emerged from his retirement, became Minister of War, and proceeded to exercise dictatorial power. Prieto was re-elected, and a liberal revolt under General Freire, who came from Peru with an expedition that seized the island of Chiloé, was suppressed.

Since Freire had received help from Andrés Santa Cruz, the ruler of the Peru-Bolivian Confederation, the Chilean government, in November, 1836, declared war on its northern neighbors. Santa Cruz tried to avert the conflict by proposing arbitration, but Portales was implacable. Chile's relations with Peru had been embittered by the growing commercial rivalry between Valparaiso and Callao and by disputes over the repayment of money spent by Chile in helping to liberate Peru from Spain; and the Chileans were alarmed by the union of Peru with Bolivia, which threatened to destroy the balance of power on the west coast. Nevertheless there was opposition to the war in Chile, and Portales' harsh repression of criticism increased the government's unpopularity. After Portales was murdered by mutinous troops near Valparaiso in June, 1837, there was a revulsion of feeling which helped to unite the people behind the war effort. The first expedition sent against Peru failed, but the second one, under General Manuel Bulnes, destroyed Santa Cruz' forces at Yungay on January 20, 1839, and put an end to the Peru-Bolivian Confederation.

THE ADMINISTRATIONS OF BULNES AND MONTT

After Portales' death there was a reaction against his intolerant policies, and several of his personal enemies returned to political life. There was still no great change in the autocratic, centralized political system that he had established. General Bulnes, whose military exploits made him the logical candidate, was elected President in 1841 and served two five-year terms. During these, the country's wealth and trade rapidly increased. Mining prospered, especially with the exploitation of the rich silver deposits that had been discovered at Chañarcillo in 1832, and the discovery of gold in California opened a market for Chilean wheat and other agricultural products. Valparaiso, with its state-owned warehouses where goods might be stored pending shipment to other ports, became the great entrepôt of the South Pacific and a base of supplies for North American whalers. William Wheelwright, the North American who was later to build the first Argentine railroad, took a leading part in many important enterprises in Chile in this period: railroad building, the establishment of an electric telegraph system, and the introduction of gaslighting and better water supplies in the towns. Through his efforts, the first steamship line from Europe to Chile began service in 1840.

The Chilean aristocracy had hitherto shown little interest in literary pursuits, or indeed in any but the most rudimentary education, but the first years of Bulnes' administration saw the beginning of an intellectual movement which was soon to have an important effect upon the Republic's political life. The inspiration came from a group of distinguished foreigners, which included Andrés Bello, the great Venezuelan, and several of the more prominent exiled opponents of the Argentine dictator Rosas. By their writing and teaching, the visitors aroused the younger generation of Chileans to a new interest in literature and a receptiveness to new ideas. Bello was the first Rector of the University of Chile, opened in 1843, and Sarmiento, the future President of Argentina, the first director of the normal school established about the same time in an effort to raise the lamentably low level of instruction in the primary schools. Much was accomplished in this direction, though education continued to be the privilege of the upper and middle classes and more than six-sevenths of the Republic's inhabitants were still illiterate in 1854.

One result of this intellectual movement was the rise of a new liberal party which sought to make the government more democratic. Inspired by the European revolutions of 1848, this group became especially active toward the close of Bulnes' second term. The *Sociedad de la Igualdad*, organized by Francisco Bilbao, even promoted political demonstrations among the workmen of Santiago. The government resorted to its usual weapons—the declaration of a state of siege, the muzzling of the press, and the deportation of the chief liberal leaders—and when an uprising occurred in Santiago in April, 1851, it was suppressed with a heavy loss of life. After Manuel Montt, the official candidate, was elected in the same year to succeed Bulnes, his defeated rival, General José María de la Cruz, led another revolt. This was not suppressed until 2,000 Chileans had been killed and 1,500 wounded in the desperately fought battle of Loncomilla.

Montt, unlike his predecessors, was neither a professional soldier nor a great landowner. The son of a poor family, he had been educated on a scholarship in the National Institute and had later taught and served as Rector there. While still a young man he had attracted the attention of Portales, who drew him into the government service. In 1840, at the age of thirty-one, he had become Minister of the Interior. His chief interest was in public instruction, and the number of government schools was greatly increased during his two terms as President. Railroad and highway construction were also pushed forward and the colonization of the region around Valdivia and Osorno, south of the Araucanian country, was encouraged. Many German immigrants settled in this region, and many of their descendants live there today.

Some of Montt's policies aroused opposition among the more conservative part of the aristocracy. The abolition of the law of primogeniture, by which he hoped to bring about the gradual division of the great entailed estates, was approved by Congress in the face of opposition by many of the landowners, and a conflict with the Church increased his difficulties. The Church, both during the colonial period and after independence, had been far more influential in Chile than in the River Plate region, and it had been a powerful ally of the conservative government since 1830. As in other Latin American countries, however, it had refused to admit that the Republic had inherited the control over the ecclesiastical administration which the Papacy had granted to the King of Spain. Disputes over the right of patronage had embarrassed each of Montt's predecessors. The Church had also clung to many of the special privileges that it had enjoyed under the Spanish regime, and its attitude grew more aggressive under the energetic leadership of Rafael Valdivieso who became Archbishop of Santiago in 1848. A particularly violent controversy involving the jurisdiction of the ecclesiastical courts occurred in 1856. Thereafter the proclerical party joined forces with the more radical wing of the liberals to oppose the President. The less extreme conservatives and liberals, on the other hand, supported the administration.

The antigovernment coalition was especially determined to prevent the election of Antonio Varas as Montt's successor. Varas, who was also a former schoolteacher from a poor family, was a lifelong friend of the President, and it had been clear for some time that he would be the official candidate in 1861. He was known to be unfriendly to the Church, and many of the liberals opposed him because they thought that he, like Montt, represented the authoritarian tradition of Portales. The coalition knew, however, that it could not hope to defeat him by peaceful means, and it consequently resorted to a revolt in 1859. The movement was suppressed; but Varas withdrew his candidacy in the interest of harmony and José Joaquín Pérez, an administration liberal, was elected with the support of all factions.

THE BEGINNINGS OF PARTY GOVERNMENT

Pérez' ten years in office were tranquil ones, except for a brief period in 1865–1866 when Chile, as an ally of Peru and Bolivia, became involved in an inconclusive war with Spain.[1] During this conflict, Spanish forces blockaded the coast and bombarded Valparaiso, but hostilities ended with the withdrawal of the enemy squadron. There was no internal disorder. As in Argentina, the prosperity that the country had begun to enjoy led the upper classes to oppose any movement which seemed likely to disturb the peace.

As commerce and mining developed, successful businessmen began to exercise more influence in public affairs. They usually allied themselves politically with the more liberal groups in the landowning class, and their influence was one of the factors that gradually brought about a change in the character of the Chilean government. Between 1830 and 1861, the president was virtually a dictator. Congress had little independent authority because the president controlled the election of its members. The fact that its members could hold other official positions without resigning their seats gave the administration another means of assuring a friendly majority. Opposition groups consequently had little chance to influence policy except through revolt, and the government tended to regard any unfriendly political activity as seditious and subversive. After 1861, the political parties became stronger and more independent, and the presidents began to find it necessary to rely on a party or a coalition for support in the congress. Pérez, for example, after an unsuccessful attempt to govern with a cabinet representing several shades of opinion, fell back on the liberal-conservative coalition that had opposed Montt. Under his successor, Federico Errázuriz Zañartu (1871–1876), the coalition broke up, and the liberals came into power.

The liberals, though weakened by factional quarrels, were able to carry out some of the reforms that they had been advocating during the past 20 years. A constitutional amendment adopted in 1871 had prohibited the election of a president for two successive periods, and further amendments now diminished the power of the executive and paved the way for the ascendancy that congress was to exercise at a later date. One of the most important forbade members of congress to hold other offices, except in the cabinet. New laws gave the press more freedom and made it somewhat more difficult for the administration to control elections. The anticlerical tendencies of the liberal party, which had been held in check so long as its various factions were co-operating with conservative groups for

[1] See below, pp. 255–6.

selfish political ends, also found expression. The measures actually adopted, restricting the jurisdiction of the church courts and setting aside portions of the cemeteries for the burial of non-Catholics, did not go very far, but they aroused violent opposition among the clergy and misgiving among the more devout supporters of the government.

Toward the end of Errázuriz' term, and during that of Aníbal Pinto (1876–1881), Chile felt the effects of the world depression of the '70's. Many mining companies failed, and the service of the foreign debt, increased by new loans contracted during the recent period of prosperity, became difficult. In 1878 the government was compelled to relieve the banks of their obligation to convert their notes into coin upon demand. Thus began the paper-money regime which was to be a feature of Chile's economy for many years to come.

THE WAR OF THE PACIFIC

In the midst of this financial crisis the country became involved in a foreign war. For some time, Chilean companies backed by British capital had been working the guano and nitrate deposits along the desert coast of Tarapacá and Atacama, and their activities had led to disputes with Peru and Bolivia, which owned these provinces. Peru and Bolivia had entered into a secret alliance against Chile in 1873, and two years later Peru expropriated the Chilean nitrate properties in Tarapacá without making any substantial arrangement for compensation. Chile did not resist, but in 1879, when Bolivia took action against the nitrate producers, the Chilean government declared war on both countries.

The boundary between Chile and Bolivia, like so many others in the former Spanish colonies, had not been fixed at the time of independence, but in 1866 a treaty had fixed it at 24° south latitude and had provided that the two countries should share the exploitation of guano and mineral deposits betwen 23° and 25° and divide the export taxes on products from that area. This treaty was replaced in 1874 by one in which Chile gave Bolivia full control over the region north of 24°, where the principal nitrate deposits were, in return for Bolivia's promise not to increase taxes on the Chilean producers for a period of 25 years. Bolivia nevertheless imposed a new tax on the export of nitrate from Atacama in 1878 and seized the property of the Anglo-Chilean company, which was the chief producer in the region, when it refused to pay. Chile retaliated by occupying Antofagasta in February, 1879. Two months later Chile declared war against Peru, which refused to abrogate the alliance of 1873.

The War of the Pacific, which thus began, was to have far-reaching effects on each of the three participants. The outcome at first seemed doubtful. The combined population of the allies far exceeded that of Chile, but Chile had a better trained and equipped army, and a far more

TERRITORY UNDER DISPUTE IN THE
WAR OF THE PACIFIC

powerful navy. Since it was difficult to move troops along the desert coast of the nitrate region, the control of the sea was of the utmost importance. One of Peru's two ironclads was destroyed in the hard-fought battle of Iquique on May 21, 1879, but the other, the *Huáscar*, commanded by Admiral Grau, defied the Chilean navy for several months. When it was finally captured on October 8, in the battle of Angamos, a Chilean army went north by sea to occupy Tarapacá. The Peruvian forces, after some fighting, retreated along the base of the Andes to Arica, and on May 26, 1880, the armies of the northern allies were defeated at Tacna. This put Bolivia out of the war, and Peru's last hope of checking the Chilean advance vanished when a small force defending the Morro of Arica was destroyed in a surprise attack on June 7. The Chilean navy began a ruthless destruction of towns and plantations along the Peruvian coast, and Callao was blockaded.

Nevertheless, neither Peru nor Bolivia would accede to Chile's demand for the cession of the nitrate provinces when the government of the United States attempted to bring the belligerents to an agreement in October, 1880. The Chilean army consequently occupied Lima early in 1881 after a short but violent conflict. Peru was powerless to offer further resistance.

It was more than two years before a Peruvian government agreed to make peace. When the Treaty of Ancón was finally signed on October 20, 1883, Peru gave up Tarapacá and agreed that Chile should occupy the provinces of Tacna and Arica for ten years. After that a plebiscite was to determine their final disposition, and the country which won them was to pay the other $10,000,000. The failure of the two powers to agree on conditions for holding this plebiscite made the Tacna-Arica question an obstacle to good relations between them during the ensuing 45 years. A truce with Bolivia was signed in 1884, leaving Chile in possession of Antofagasta and the rest of the Bolivian seacoast, but no formal treaty was concluded until 1904.

AFTER THE WAR

Chile emerged from the war one of the richest and most powerful of the South American republics. Her foreign trade, already large, was tremendously increased. Her new provinces contained great deposits of copper and other minerals as well as nitrate, and the development of their resources, as well as the new market which they offered for agricultural products from the south, made the country more prosperous than ever before. The export taxes on nitrate alone gave the government a large part of its revenue. It was chiefly the mercantile and landowning classes, however, which benefited, for the *inquilino* laborers of the interior continued to work for a bare subsistence. Their wages, paid in depreciating paper money, increased little while prices were soaring, and the miners and landowners opposed any change in a currency system that enabled them to obtain labor more and more cheaply while they sold their products abroad for gold. The workers in the newly acquired nitrate fields fared little better. Their wages were somewhat higher; but life in the desert was difficult at best, and at many plants they were badly housed and exploited through company stores.

One of the important events of the years just after the war was the final conquest of the Araucanians. The Indians had made trouble during the civil wars of 1851 and 1859, when the insurgents enlisted their help, and in 1861 the government began a systematic military occupation of their territory. There was a new revolt in 1868, which lasted three years, and another in 1880 after troops were withdrawn from the frontier for service in Peru. At the end of the war, a strong force was sent into the Indians' territory. Several new towns were established, and the few Araucanians who remained at the end of the military operations were confined to reservations, where some thousands of them still live.

There was also a revival of the conflict between Church and State. When Archbishop Valdivieso died in 1878, the Pope refused to accept a priest of pronounced liberal views whom the Chilean government proposed as his successor. This revived the old dispute about the *patronato* and led Domingo Santa María, who succeeded Pinto in 1881, to order that the apostolic delegate be handed his passports. The liberal majority in Congress then passed laws freeing public cemeteries from Church control, making civil marriage compulsory, and providing that the official registry of births, marriages, and deaths should be maintained by the civil authorities rather than by the parish priests. The clergy retaliated by refusing to participate in burials in public cemeteries, and the government forbade burials in places under ecclesiastical control. The conservatives, and devout Catholics generally, supported the Church, and feeling ran so high that an outbreak of violence seemed imminent. Fortunately, a compromise which made possible the installation of a new archbishop was worked out by José Manuel Balmaceda, who became President in 1886.

BALMACEDA AND THE CIVIL WAR

Balmaceda was one of the most popular leaders of the liberal party, and he was able for a time to persuade the various factions of the party to work together. A great increase in the government's revenues, derived from the expanding nitrate industry, made possible an extensive program of public works, and the administration seemed a notably successful one until the approach of another presidential election caused violent dissensions among its supporters. Balmaceda's own candidate, Enrique Sanfuentes, met with strong opposition. Since it was still practically impossible to defeat a candidate supported by the president and his ministers, the groups that did not want Sanfuentes attempted to force changes in the cabinet that would deprive him of the government's help.

It had by this time become the accepted practice for the president to select his cabinet in such a way as to command the support of a parliamentary majority, and recent political changes had made it more difficult for him to do so without consulting the views of the party leaders. The congress had become more independent, and the law forbidding its members to hold other official positions had deprived the president of one of his chief means of influencing them. Whether the executive or the legislature would dominate if there were a conflict between them was nevertheless an open question, which Balmaceda's opponents now forced to an issue. The President tried in vain to restore harmony. Sanfuentes withdrew his candidacy, and changes were made in the Cabinet; but the new Ministers quarreled among themselves and resigned, and Balmaceda replaced them with his own adherents. The Congress then suspended action on the appropriations for the coming year and adjourned. Balmaceda, facing a situation where there was no legal authorization for any payments from the treasury, announced that the budget for the preceding year would remain in force.

This frankly unconstitutional procedure precipitated the most costly civil war in Chile's history. On January 7, 1891, a majority of the members of Congress issued a statement declaring the President removed from office. They were supported by the navy, but the army remained loyal to Balmaceda. Again it was the control of the sea which decided the issue, for the insurgents seized the nitrate provinces, where they could not be attacked by land, and used the proceeds of the export taxes to equip an army of their own. They also obtained funds, apparently, from British nitrate interests which had been alarmed by Balmaceda's proposal for the nationalization of the industry.[2] In August the insurgent forces defeated those of the government in two important battles near Valparaiso, and Balmaceda turned over the executive power to General Baquedano. Three weeks later he committed suicide in the Argentine legation, where he had been given asylum. The war had cost some 10,000 lives and many millions of dollars, and both Santiago and Valparaiso had been looted by mobs before the new authorities could restore order.

Several incidents during the revolution led the insurgents to accuse the United States of partiality to Balmaceda, and their resentment increased when the American Minister gave asylum to several members of the defeated party after the war. In the midst of the controversy caused by the Minister's action, in October, 1891, a mob at Valparaiso killed two sailors from the U.S.S. *Baltimore* and injured five others. The ship's commanding officer reported that the sailors had given no provocation and that the

[2] Hardy, "British Nitrates and the Balmaceda Revolution," *Pacific Historical Review*, Vol. 17, p. 165.

police of Valparaiso had been partly responsible for what occurred. Chile at first refused the American government's demand for reparation, and a situation already bad became worse when a cable from the foreign office at Santiago, couched in offensive terms, was made public by the Chilean Minister at Washington. The Chilean government insisted that the American sailors had been at fault and that the Valparaiso police had conducted themselves properly, but it yielded to the demands of the United States when President Harrison asked authority from Congress to use force if necessary to obtain satisfaction. The incident was closed by the payment of an indemnity of $75,000, but it left an aftermath of bitterness in Chile which long clouded the relations between the two countries.

THE ERA OF PARLIAMENTARY GOVERNMENT

The revolution of 1891 effected a radical change in the character of the Chilean government. The president became little more than a figurehead. Though the constitution was not changed, the congress in fact became the dominant power, ruling through cabinet ministers who remained in office only so long as they had the support of majorities in both houses. The result was unfortunate. Congressional majorities could be obtained only by forming combinations among the numerous political factions, which worked together only so long as it suited their selfish interests and were likely to desert the government when minor quarrels arose. Cabinets thus came and went with a rapidity that discouraged efficiency and made impossible any continuity of policy.

The members of congress continued for the most part to be representatives of the landholding aristocracy that had dominated the country's political life since independence. The masses of the people had little more voice in political affairs than before. The control of elections was taken from the president and entrusted to local communal governments, but these were dominated by the local landowners. Under the new system, the use of force and intimidation became less common, but bribery increased. The corruption of the electorate became so much a matter of custom that instances are recorded where the indignant citizens rose en masse and stoned the houses of the party leaders because agreements between the parties had made an electoral contest unnecessary and thus deprived the voters of what they regarded as a normal source of income.[3]

The defects of the parliamentary system might have been felt more acutely had it not been for the prosperity that the country enjoyed until after the end of the First World War. The civil war of 1891 and the world depression that followed it were only temporary setbacks to Chile's economic development. By the end of the century, foreign trade was again

[3] Galdames, *Estudio de la Historia de Chile*, 7th ed., p. 447.

increasing at a phenomenal rate. The export taxes on nitrate gave the government an ample revenue which made for political stability, though at the same time it encouraged extravagance and corruption. Another source of wealth opened up when the great copper mines of El Teniente and Chuquicamata, developed by American capital, began production in 1911 and 1915.

This prosperity made it more difficult to defend the continuance of the system of depreciating paper currency, which was profitable for the miners and landowners but inconvenient for commerce. A plan to stabilize the currency was adopted in 1892. Six years later, however, when the boundary controversy with Argentina threatened to lead to war, the government seized on its heavy military expenditures as an excuse to abandon the plan and the paper peso again became inconvertible.

Little need be said of the presidents who held office between 1891 and 1920. Jorge Montt, who had commanded the insurgent navy during the civil war was elected in 1891; he was followed by Federico Errázuriz Echáurren (1896–1901) and Jermán Riesco (1901–1906). The chief event of Riesco's administration was an earthquake that destroyed most of Valparaiso and much of Santiago, with the loss of several thousand lives. Pedro Montt, the next President, was elected by a coalition that hoped that he might check some of the abuses of the parliamentary system, which had been somewhat discredited by the resignation of 17 successive cabinets during the preceding five years; but he was hardly more successful in this respect than his predecessors. After Montt died in 1910, neither Ramón Barros Luco (1910–1915) nor Juan Luis Sanfuentes (1915–1920) attempted to challenge the supremacy of Congress. During their administrations the World War brought a great wave of prosperity, with high prices for nitrate and copper. Chile remained neutral throughout the conflict.

POLITICAL CHANGES, 1918–1926

Under the leadership of a few hundred landowning families, Chile in 1918 had enjoyed a longer period of relatively stable government and good administration than any other country in South America. Even the defects of the parliamentary system did not seriously affect its internal tranquility. Nevertheless, increasingly influential groups were dissatisfied with the existing political situation. With the development of mining and manufacturing and the growth of large cities, there had arisen a class of merchants, manufacturers, and professional men who had little connection with the old aristocracy. There was also a host of graduates from the free public schools and the universities who could find little opportunity for employment in the already overcrowded professions. Many of these had taken an active part in politics as party workers, and had held positions in the government; but they were hostile as a class to a political system that limited their opportunities for advancement.

The situation was in many ways similar to that which led to the victory of the radical party in Argentina in 1916, but in Chile it had more serious implications because of the discontent among the laboring class. The *in-quilinos* on the farms in the Central Valley still seemed to accept their hard lot submissively, but the thousands of workers who had left the *haciendas* for employment in the mines or in the cities were less tract-able. Their wages were higher than those of the *inquilinos;* but they were still low, and their purchasing power was diminished by the depreciation of the paper peso. The constantly changing governments at Santiago had done little for them, and only a few employers, like the American copper companies, had shown an interest in bettering their living conditions. Radical agitators, both native and foreign, thus found the laboring class a fertile field for disruptive propaganda. One result had been a number of industrial strikes, often accompanied by violence and bloodshed, which had been brutally suppressed by the police and the army. Labor had neither the leaders nor the organization to enable it to assume an independ-ent rôle in politics, but it was ready to join enthusiastically with other discontented groups that were seeking a change.

The leader of the revolt against the old regime was Arturo Alessandri. Alessandri came into prominence in 1915 when he ran for Senator in Tarapacá and advocated labor legislation and social reforms with an elo-quence that won him an enthusiastic following among the workers in the nitrate fields. When the election of 1918 brought into Congress a number of new members whose views were similar to his, he became for a time the head of the Cabinet under Sanfuentes. In 1920 he ran for the presidency, frankly appealing to the middle classes and the labor organizations for support against the aristocracy. Nearly all the old political groups joined in the *Unión Nacional* to oppose him, with Luis Barros Borgoño as their candidate. There was talk of civil war when disputed elections in several districts cast doubt on the final result, but the Congress avoided serious trouble by referring the disputes to a "tribunal of honor" in which the two parties were equally represented. The result was Alessandri's election by a margin of one electoral vote.

Alessandri's supporters, the Liberal Alliance, obtained control of the Chamber of Deputies, but the conservatives retained a majority in the Senate which forced one cabinet after another to resign. The President's projects for social and political reforms were blocked, and there was a long controversy before the Congress ratified the Washington protocol of 1922, by which Chile and Peru agreed to submit the Tacna-Arica ques-tion to arbitration by the President of the United States. Meanwhile, in-creasing artificial nitrate production in foreign countries was injuring the country's chief industry and chief source of public revenue, and many thousands of unemployed laborers from the nitrate fields were crowding into Santiago and Valparaiso. Alessandri's position became constantly more difficult. Even after the government's open intervention in the elections of 1924 gave the Liberal Alliance control of both houses of Congress, the approval of reforms sought by the administration was delayed by endless debates.

The crisis came in September, 1924, when the Cabinet, in an effort to obtain support in the Congress, introduced a bill providing that the Congressmen should receive salaries. They had hitherto been unpaid, for members of the aristocracy had been willing to spend large amounts for the honor of serving as senators or deputies; and the fact that the new measure was needed if men who were not rich were to have an opportunity to serve honorably in the legislative body did not seem to justify its taking precedence over needed social reforms. When the Congress voted the bill, the younger officers of the army, whose own pay was two months in arrears, vociferously expressed their disapproval. On September 4, with at least the passive support of their superiors, their representatives visited the President and compelled him to appoint a new Cabinet composed of military leaders. The Congress, intimidated by the threat of force, promptly passed a number of the reform measures that had long been under discussion.

Alessandri, feeling the army's seizure of power made his own position untenable, took refuge in the American embassy and then went to Argentina, availing himself of a leave of absence granted by the Congress. A *junta* of high-ranking military men took control. Its members, chosen because of their rank, were more conservative than the group of young officers who had staged the demonstration in Congress and who had a strong following in the army. The new government, in fact, was warmly welcomed by the aristocracy, and the parties that had been defeated in 1920 put forward one of their most reactionary leaders as their candidate for the presidency. The prospect of a return to the old regime naturally aroused much opposition. The younger officers, especially, felt that they had been betrayed, and in January, 1925, they arrested the members of the governmental *junta* and invited Alessandri to return to complete his legal term of office. The President was given an enthusiastic reception when he reached Santiago.

Alessandri then attempted to put an end to the parliamentary form of government. A new constitution, drawn up by a committee and ratified by plebiscite, restored much of the authority that the president had had before 1891. Its provisions greatly curtailed the power of congress to interfere with the executive branch of the government. Its members could no longer hold office in the cabinet, and the ministers were made independent of congressional approval. The requirement that tax laws and laws fixing the strength of the military establishment be voted annually was abolished, and the budget was to become effective in the form proposed by the president if the legislature failed to act upon it within a given time. The constitution also provided for the complete separation of Church and State, and for important reforms in the judiciary. The president was to be elected by direct popular vote for a six-year term. These changes did away with some of the practices that had been an obstacle to effective government during the preceding 34 years. Later presidents still found it advisable to make changes in their cabinets from time to time to hold the support of a congressional majority, but they were no longer so completely at the mercy of the leaders of the numerous factions represented in the legislative body.

It was some years, however, before Chile again enjoyed orderly constitutional government. Alessandri resigned after a few months because he could not control his Minister of War, Colonel Carlos Ibáñez. Ibáñez, who had been the leader of the group that invited the President to return, aspired to succeed him, but after Alessandri's resignation he gave up his candidacy, under strong pressure from the civilian political leaders. He nevertheless continued as Minister of War in the Cabinet of Emilio Figueroa Larrain, who was inaugurated in December, 1925. His power steadily increased, and in May, 1927, he forced Figueroa to resign and took the presidency himself.

IBÁÑEZ DICTATORSHIP

The new regime was more dictatorial than any that had ruled Chile since 1861, but many citizens were by this time disposed to support a strong government, even at the cost of political liberty. They were dismayed by the breakdown of Chile's traditional governmental stability and alarmed by the specter of class warfare, which had seemed to become more imminent as the discontented groups that put Alessandri in office in 1920 found themselves disappointed in their expectations. The new President was acceptable to many people in these groups, because of his stand for social reform, but at the same time his evident determination and ability to maintain order won him the adherence of the conservatives. Such opposition as there was found little opportunity for expression. The press was muzzled, and political opponents were imprisoned or exiled. The Congress was compelled to accept the President's orders, and in the election of 1930 the official candidates for senator and deputy were returned without opposition as the result of an interparty agreement.

The most notable event of Ibáñez' administration was the final settlement of the Tacna-Arica question. The plebiscite that was to have decided the final position of these provinces had never been held because the two governments could not agree on the conditions which should govern it.

When the question was submitted to arbitration under the protocol signed at Washington in 1922, the President of the United States decided in 1925 that the plebiscite should be held. General Pershing was appointed President of a Commission to supervise the vote, but both he and his successor General Lassiter reported that the conduct of the Chilean authorities in the two provinces would make a fair election impossible. The plebiscite was consequently abandoned. Soon afterward, however, the United States resumed its efforts to bring about a settlement, and an agreement for the division of the disputed territory was signed in 1929. Chile kept Arica, and Peru received Tacna with an indemnity of $6,000,000. Friendly relations were thus established between the two republics for the first time in half a century.

At home, Ibáñez attempted to carry further the program of social reform that Alessandri had advocated. Advanced labor laws were enacted, and a modest agrarian program was started. Primary instruction, which had been made obligatory by law in 1920, was extended and improved in quality, so that the number of illiterates over seven years of age decreased from 37 out of each 100 in 1920 to 25 in 1930.[4] At the same time the government financed an ambitious program of public works by loans contracted in the United States and Europe. The inflow of new money, combined with measures for the stabilization of the currency, did much to raise wages and living standards, and a general prosperity was one element in the government's strength.

DEPRESSION AND DISORDER, 1931–1932

Ibáñez' regime collapsed when this prosperity ended. The depression of the early 1930's affected Chile with peculiar severity. The government's revenues, derived chiefly from import and export duties, fell off sharply with the decline of trade. The inflow of foreign capital ceased, and thousands of men employed on the public works program lost their jobs. Other thousands were thrown out of work at the mines, as nitrate, iodine, and copper, the three commodities that made up four-fifths of the country's exports, became almost unsalable. The situation of the nitrate industry was especially discouraging because of the competition of synthetic nitrogen. Unimportant before the European war, the extraction of nitrogen from the atmosphere had increased until by 1926 it supplied the major part of the world's requirements, and foreign governments were protecting and subsidizing the new industry in an effort to assure an adequate domestic supply for military purposes. Ibáñez, with the aid of North American capital, endeavored to meet this competition by combining the Chilean producers in one great company and substituting new scientific methods of treating the ore for the old wasteful and expensive Shanks process; but

_____
[4] *Sinópsis geográfica-estadística de la República de Chile* (1933), p. 87.

the *Cosach*, as the new company was called, suffered heavy losses when the depression came.

As conditions grew worse, opposition to the government increased. The movement which overthrew Ibáñez was an emphatic demonstration of popular discontent rather than an armed revolt. It began with rioting by the university students in Santiago in the latter part of July, 1931. A day or two later, the lawyers, engineers, schoolteachers, and even the physicians went on strike; and soon afterward the labor unions, which had hitherto supported the government, joined in the demand for a change. On July 26, Ibáñez resigned. Three months later Juan Estéban Montero, with the support of most of the organized political parties, defeated Alessandri in a presidential election.

The new administration faced a difficult situation. Montero, who had accepted his position reluctantly, was unwilling to adopt vigorous measures to maintain his authority. Alessandri and his friends were able to turn the labor unions and other radical groups against him, so that he was soon supported only by the conservatives. The economic situation was growing worse, and the government's finances were disorganized. For the first time since the days of Portales, Chile defaulted on the service of the foreign debt. The Chilean peso was depreciating until by September, 1932, it was worth less than one-sixth of its former value. Unemployment caused much suffering.

The administration had little support from the armed forces. The army, which since 1924 had given up its traditional aloofness from politics and its traditional support of the constituted government, was reluctant to relinquish the influence which it had been exercising. Many of its officers objected to the President's conservative policy. There were several military plots, and in June, 1932, the head of the air force, Colonel Marmaduke Grove, led a popular movement that forced Montero to resign. Grove, however, was soon forced to leave the country, and Carlos Dávila became provisional President and attempted to inaugurate a radical socialist regime. After three months of near-anarchy, another military revolt brought in a provisional administration pledged to restore the constitutional order. The country returned to more normal conditions with the election of Arturo Alessandri as President in October, 1932.

ALESSANDRI'S SECOND ADMINISTRATION

Alessandri was supported, rather unenthusiastically, by a majority of the old ruling class because they feared him less than they feared his principal opponent, the socialist Marmaduke Grove. He thus took office in December, 1932, under conditions very different from those at the beginning of his first term. The right-wing parties had majorities in both houses of Congress, and for some time the President openly accepted the backing of the *milicia republicana*, a private army organized by influential civilians in 1932 to oppose the revolutionary activities of the radical elements in the regular army and to protect the established order against the growing danger from the communists and other extremists. He was able to suppress a number of disturbances fomented by the extremists, and conditions became somewhat more stable as the worst effects of the depression disappeared.

Even with the gradual revival of prosperity, grave economic and social problems remained. The nitrate industry had not recovered. Chile had supplied 55 per cent of the world's nitrogen in 1913, 23 per cent in 1929, 4 per cent in 1933, and only 8 per cent in 1938. Other export industries were not flourishing. The peso recovered only a part of its value, and imports still had to be restricted. The rapid growth of local manufacturing only partially offset the effect on local standards of living, and labor suffered especially because wages had not increased as the value of the *peso* fell. Discontent among the lower classes remained a serious political problem.

Alessandri succeeded in pushing through some measures for the improvement of the condition of the laborers and the *inquilinos*, but his efforts were hampered by conservative opposition. He received more support in measures directed against foreign capital. The *Cosach*, sponsored by North American interests, was dissolved early in his term. The nitrate companies resumed operations as separate concerns, but they were compelled to sell their product through a government agency which retained 25 per cent of the profits in lieu of the former export tax. The American-owned Chile Electric Company was compelled to accept an increased measure of government control. These and many similar measures were a response to a widespread feeling of popular hostility to foreign "economic imperialism" which found expression in other Latin American countries as well as Chile during and after the depression.

THE ERA OF THE POPULAR FRONT

In 1936, the radical party, to which Alessandri had formerly belonged, joined with the socialists and the communists in a "popular front" which supported a veteran radical leader, Pedro Aguirre Cerda, in the presidential election of 1938. The more conservative parties nominated Gustavo Ross, a liberal, who had been Alessandri's Minister of Finance. The Chilean nazis, who advocated fascist ideas but disclaimed any connection with European fascism, supported ex-President Carlos Ibáñez, but he withdrew his candidacy after some of his supporters attempted a *coup d'état* and were slaughtered by the police. The nazis then supported the popular front, and Aguirre Cerda defeated Ross by 220,000 to 213,000 votes.

Early in 1939, an earthquake killed more than 25,000 people in the region around Chillán and destroyed much property. The government was still struggling with the task of reconstruction when the outbreak of war in Europe brought new problems. In 1941, the government's situation became more difficult when the socialists refused to co-operate further with the communists in the popular front. Nevertheless, when Aguirre Cerda died a few months later, Juan Antonio Ríos, the left-wing candidate for the presidency, defeated ex-President Ibáñez, who was put forward by the conservatives.

Partly because of a desire to remain on good terms with Argentina, and partly from fear of a possible Japanese attack on her coast, Chile refused to break relations with the Axis powers immediately after Pearl Harbor when all of the other Latin American countries except Argentina did so. This caused some resentment in Washington, but in January, 1943, the Ríos administration changed its policy and co-operated in the war effort. It took measures against the German and Japanese agents in Chile and obtained lend-lease and other aid from the United States. It declared war on Japan in April, 1945.

Ríos' death in June, 1946, made a new presidential election necessary. Since no candidate received a majority of the popular vote, the choice went to Congress, where some of the conservative groups joined in the selection of Gabriel González Videla, who had been the candidate of the radicals and the communists and one wing of the socialists. In recognition of this support, the new President appointed three liberals as well as three communists to his first Cabinet. Such diverse elements could hardly work together; and in April, 1947, the liberals resigned and the President formed a new Cabinet from which the communists also were excluded.

The communists, who controlled most of the stronger labor unions, retaliated by organizing a series of dangerous and costly strikes. The worst of these, in the coal mines near Concepción in October, 1947, was finally suppressed by the army. The government charged that these strikes had been fomented by Soviet agents and broke off relations with Russia and Czechoslovakia. At the same time many communist officials were removed, and some hundreds of the party's leaders were arrested. In July, 1948, the Congress outlawed the party and forbade its members to vote or hold office.

The communists continued to be a formidable political force, though they were compelled to work underground, and the government also faced opposition from the extreme right. In November, 1948, ex-President Ibáñez and a former Governor of Santiago were arrested on charges of plotting a revolt in connivance with agents of the Argentine government. The chief cause of discontent was the worsening economic situation, and especially the phenomenal rise in living costs caused by the depreciation of the paper currency. Chile suffered more than most of her neighbors from the inflation that prevailed through South America in the postwar period.

RECENT ADMINISTRATIONS

The economic situation and a reaction against the corruption that had crept into the government under the leftist administration were chiefly responsible for the victory of Ibáñez in the presidential election of 1952. The new President did not revert to the dictatorial practices that had characterized his earlier administration, but on the other hand he disappointed those who hoped that he would carry through a vigorous program of reform. His advanced age—he was seventy-five when he took office—perhaps accounted for his lack of vigor. His effort to put into effect a stabilization program recommended by a private North American financial mission met with much resistance. Conditions improved somewhat in 1956, when copper prices were high, but a sharp decline in the copper market soon afterward made the situation worse than ever. Before the end of Ibáñez' term, the cost of living was at least 25 times what it had been in 1946, and a dollar would buy 1,000 Chilean pesos. The desperate situation of the working people was reflected in continual and costly strikes.

Economic problems were thus again an important issue in the election of 1958. There were four principal candidates. Jorge Alessandri, the son of the former President but a successful businessman rather than a politician, was supported by the conservative parties. Salvador Allende, the socialist leader, was nominated by the *Frente de Acción Popular,* a left-wing coalition. This included the communists, who were still not permitted to register as a party in the 1958 election, though a law passed in the last months of Ibáñez' administration authorized them to function as a party in the future. A center group, the Christian democrats, supported Eduardo Frei. The radical party, with little hope for victory, nominated Luis Bossay. As there was no majority in the popular election, the Congress had to choose between the two leaders, Alessandri, with 387,297 votes out of a total of 1,245,526, and Allende, with 352,915. Traditionally, in such cases, the Congress voted for the candidate who had a plurality, and though the other parties had seemed at times during the campaign to be working together to defeat him, Alessandri was elected.

The new President took office in November, 1958, with a Cabinet of businessmen and technical experts, few of whom had been prominent in any of the political parties. In April, 1959, he obtained from Congress a very broad grant of authority for one year to reorganize the administration and to make changes in the monetary and banking system and other economic institutions. Strong measures were clearly needed, for the government's budget showed a tremendous deficit and the cost of living was still rising rapidly. The first months of Alessandri's administration, however, raised hopes that the painful process of checking inflation might have begun, but terrifically destructive earthquakes in 1960 created new problems.

Chile today has somewhat more than 7,000,000 inhabitants. This is a small number compared with the population of some of the other South American countries, but few of the others have so large a per capita foreign trade. The Republic is one of the world's chief producers of copper, and its prosperity depends largely on the fluctuating price of that metal. Iron ore has also become an important export in recent years, and nitrate, which was formerly the chief source of wealth, is still shipped abroad in large amounts. Excessive dependence on the world market for a few products, however, exposes the country's economy to dislocation when commodity prices fall, and during the past 30 years the government has been endeavoring, with some success, to promote local industries, which now supply many goods once purchased abroad.

Chile's already-serious social problems have been much aggravated by inflation. A measure of inflation, as we have seen, has characterized the economy since the War of the Pacific, and for a long time was even welcomed by the groups that controlled the government. In recent years, however, the situation has grown infinitely worse. Wages have gone up far less rapidly than prices, and the workers in mining and industry, with their low living standards, are a prey to disease and alcoholism, and to communist propaganda. Efforts to improve their condition by legislation have been only partly effective. The social security system, for example, has been administered in an inefficient and exceedingly costly way. Furthermore, these efforts have chiefly benefited the urban workers. The situation of the *inquilinos* in the interior is still not very different from what it was in the nineteenth century, for most of the land is still held in large estates and wages are excessively low. Progress toward better social conditions, however, will be difficult until the government has been able to bring the inflation under control.

PART IV

THE REPUBLICS OF THE
CENTRAL ANDES

In Chapter I we spoke of the divergence in political and social development caused by the dissimilarities in the character of the aboriginal Indian populations of the various countries of Latin America. One striking illustration of this divergence is the contrast between the republics of the south temperate zone and those of the Central Andes: Peru, Bolivia and Ecuador. Unlike the River Plate, the Andean region was the home of populous, civilized native communities before the Conquest. Today it has a small upper class of Spanish descent and a much larger group of mixed race, but the majority of the people, taking the region as a whole, are Indians. Most of them live in their own communities, where they speak *Quechua* or *Aymara* rather than Spanish.

In the first years of the twentieth century, the *encomienda* and the *mita* had long since disappeared, but custom and economic necessity still compelled the Indians to work for the white families and the Church, who owned most of the better land. Some were paid very small wages; others gave several days of labor each week in return for the use of the plot of ground on which they produced their own food. Peonage, or debt-slavery, survived in many places, despite laws forbidding it. In some regions, Indian families were required as a part of their customary payments to the landlord to furnish a certain number of *pongos*, or household servants, to work either at the *hacienda* or in the landlord's city house—an arrangement reminiscent of the "personal service" which the Spanish government vainly attempted to abolish in the sixteenth century.

The ignorance and poverty which helped to keep the Indian in subjection to his landlord also exposed him to exploitation at the hands of officials, priests, and private individuals, and a local expression, *gamonalismo,* was used to describe the manifold forms of extortion practiced against him. In one respect, at least, the Indians' situation seems to have become worse after independence, for many of the *ayllus* or village communities which possessed lands under royal grants during the colonial period lost a part or all of them through fraud or violence after the control of the governments passed into the hands of the white upper class.

Fortunately, as we shall see, some of the political leaders in the Andean countries have taken an interest in the Indians' problems in recent years, and the situation is now improving. Nevertheless, it is difficult for the Indians to become integrated into the national community because of their poverty and ignorance as well as the prejudices and language barriers that cut them off from other groups. Their depressed condition is an obstacle to the political and economic progress of the country as a whole.

Another obstacle to the progress of the Andean republics is their geography. High mountain ranges cut off the coast from the interior and isolate the valleys and plateaus where most of the people live. The topography made road and railroad building expensive, and until the advent of the airplane, journeys from one section to another were often a matter of many days or even weeks. Isolation has fostered *localismo* and made more difficult the establishment of stable national governments.

CHAPTER 12

Peru

FIRST YEARS OF INDEPENDENCE

In 1795, there were 1,249,723 inhabitants in the area now known as Peru, according to a contemporary census.[1] Lima had been the great center of Spanish power in America earlier in the colonial period, but the establishment of separate viceroyalties in New Granada and the River Plate, the changes in commercial legislation, and the decreasing production of the mines had diminished the relative importance of the city and the province of which it was the Capital. The country had nevertheless been the chief stronghold of the loyalists during the war for independence. The creole nobility and other privileged classes had little sympathy for the revolution, and the Indians, though they fought as unwilling conscripts on both sides, were on the whole more inclined to support the royal authority. The patriot party was too weak to win independence without outside help, which came first from Chile and then from Colombia. It lacked effective leadership and popular support when it was compelled to assume the responsibility for organizing a national government.

We have seen how Bolívar, who was ruling Peru at the end of the war, failed in his attempt to make the Republic a part of his Confederation of the Andes. Within a few months after his departure from Lima in 1826 to deal with the crisis in Colombia, the Peruvian leaders set aside the *constitución vitalicia*. General Andrés Santa Cruz, whom the Liberator had left in charge of the government, was compelled to convene a Constituent Assembly. When this met in June, 1827, its leading spirit was the veteran patriot Luna Pizarro, a priest who had been one of the earliest advocates of Peruvian independence but who had opposed both San Martín and Bolívar. Through his influence, General José de la Mar was elected President of the Republic, while Santa Cruz accepted a diplomatic appointment abroad.

[1] Basadre, *Historia de la República del Perú*, p. 13.

MILITARY DOMINANCE, 1827–1835

La Mar was the first of a series of soldier-presidents. The control of the government after Bolívar's departure naturally fell into the hands of military leaders because years of constant warfare had accustomed the people to regard armed force as the only basis of authority and because there was no other group sufficiently strong to dispute their predominance. The creole aristocracy had been discredited by its adherence to the royalist cause, and even the civilian leaders who participated in the revolution— and who were active in politics as "liberals" after independence—had little popular following. Some of them, like Luna Pizarro, were influential as advisers or aides to the military *caudillos,* but they could not obtain power for themselves. For some 40 years after independence, Peru's political life was dominated by the "marshals of Ayacucho"—the group of officers who had risen to prominence during the revolution. Most of them, including Santa Cruz, La Mar, Gamarra, Orbegoso, and Castilla, had served in the Spanish army during the earlier years of the war but had joined San Martín in 1820–1821. They were professional soldiers rather than political leaders, and it was their ability to command the loyalty of their troops, rather than any popularity in the civilian community, that gave them their power. Their rivalries and conflicts caused Charles Darwin to observe in 1835 that "no state in South America, since the declaration of independence, has suffered more from anarchy than Peru." [2]

Soon after La Mar took office, he found himself involved in a war with Colombia. Bolívar had acquiesced in Peru's withdrawal from his Confederation, but the Liberator's lieutenants still held Guayaquil, which was claimed by Peru, and also Bolivia, which many of the leaders at Lima regarded as part of their country. In 1828, Agustín Gamarra, the military commander at Cuzco, invaded Bolivia without orders from La Mar and overthrew Sucre's government. Sucre avenged himself a few months later by defeating a Peruvian army in Ecuador. The conflict ended because internal disturbances in both countries made it difficult to continue fighting.

In Peru, Gamarra overthrew La Mar and was President from 1829 until 1833, despite several efforts to turn him out. There was one especially sensational affair at Lima when one of his lieutenants who tried to seize power during the President's absence from the city was driven from the country by Gamarra's energetic wife. There was further trouble with Bolivia, where Santa Cruz had become President and was intriguing with dissatisfied elements in Peru, but Chilean mediation prevented an outbreak of war. Gamarra nevertheless completed his constitutional term. His government was not so despotic as some of the other regimes that flourished

[2] Darwin, *Journal of Researches into the Geology and Natural History of the Various Countries Visited During the Voyage of H.M.S. Beagle Around the World* (Everyman's ed.), p. 352.

at the same time in Latin America. Political opponents, though frequently imprisoned or exiled, enjoyed some freedom of expression in the Congress and in the press, and elections were less effectively controlled than in more recent times.

In 1833, in fact, the President was unable to bring about the election of General Bermúdez, whom he had chosen as his successor. No candidate received a majority of the popular vote and the Constituent Assembly, acting under the leadership of Luna Pizarro, chose General Luis José Orbegoso as provisional President.

Orbegoso was a creole of Spanish descent, more in sympathy with the aims of the civilian liberal group than were *mestizo caudillos* like Gamarra and Santa Cruz. It was hoped that his election would diminish the influence of the army in the government. He had been in office only a few days when the troops at Lima under Gamarra's leadership attempted to depose him and would have done so if the inhabitants of the city had not rallied to his support. In 1835, another revolt, led by a young *caudillo* named Felipe Santiago de Salaverry, spread rapidly through the country. Orbegoso was compelled to seek help from Santa Cruz, and in the fighting that ensued Salaverry was defeated and put to death.

SANTA CRUZ' CONFEDERATION

Santa Cruz was now able to realize a long-standing ambition to unite Peru and Bolivia under his own leadership. To make the partnership better balanced, Peru was divided into two states, with Orbegoso as President in the north and General Ramón Herrera in the south, and these were joined with Bolivia in a Confederation which Santa Cruz ruled as "Protector," with virtually unlimited powers. The union does not seem to have been generally popular either in Peru or Bolivia. Santa Cruz had won the respect of the propertied classes in both countries by his efficient administration in Bolivia, and the Inca blood that he claimed to have inherited through his mother gave him prestige among the Indians on both sides of the frontier; but in each country there was a fear that the union would mean domination by the other.

The Confederation was thus weakened by internal dissatisfaction when it was attacked by foreign enemies from two sides. An army sent by Rosas of Argentina was easily defeated, but the war with Chile, described in Chapter 11, ended with Santa Cruz' defeat at Yungay in January, 1839. The Confederation was dissolved, and Gamarra, who had returned with the Chilean army, again became President of Peru.

The next five years were a period of great disorder. Santa Cruz' adherents were still powerful in Bolivia, and their leader, from his exile in Guayaquil, endeavored to foment revolts in Peru. When Gamarra, in an attempt to bring Bolivia under his control, invaded that country, he was killed in the battle of Ingavi in 1841. Several military *caudillos* resumed the struggle for control, and a series of short-lived regimes rose and fell at Lima while civil war raged throughout the country. Finally, in July, 1844, Ramón Castilla, a professional soldier who had participated in most of the internal struggles since independence, emerged as master of the situation.

RAMÓN CASTILLA

Castilla's advent to power marked a turning point in Peru's history. Between 1827 and 1844 the country had made little progress. Many of the customs and institutions of the colonial period still survived. The Indians paid tribute as in the days of the viceroys, and Negroes were still in slavery, though San Martín and later lawgivers had decreed the freedom of children born after the revolution. The colonial aristocracy were impoverished by a quarter-century of near-anarchy, but they still had their great entailed estates and their social pre-eminence. Even in manners and dress, the people were only just beginning to feel the influence of nineteenth-century Europe. In some respects, indeed, the country was more backward than in Spanish times. In 1835, Darwin had found Lima "in a wretched state of decay," with streets nearly unpaved and heaped everywhere with filth.

Much of this changed in the 18 years when Castilla dominated Peru's political life. The new President was an able administrator, and he showed more respect than most of his predecessors for the authority of Congress and the freedom of the press. His relatively tolerant policy did much to placate the opposition. The chief factor making for stability and economic progress, however, was the wealth that began to flow in from the export of *guano*. The great deposits of bird manure on the islands along the coast, though used by the Indians before the Conquest, had received little attention during the colonial period; but when their value as a fertilizer was demonstrated by Baron de Liebig in Germany in 1840, *guano* almost immediately became Peru's most important export. The deposits were nationalized in 1842, and for several years contracts for their exploitation provided the major part of the government's revenue. The foreign debt, long in default, was refunded and it was possible for the first time to undertake the construction of much-needed public works. Many great private fortunes were also built up, for contracts for exporting *guano* were often granted on terms that were more favorable to the contractor than to the government. At the same time, Wheelwright's new steamship line, starting service in 1840, aided commerce in general and encouraged travel to the United States and Europe.

At the end of his first term, Castilla permitted an active contest between several candidates for the presidency; but there was much violence in the election, and General José Rufino Echenique, who had the government's support, was the victor. Echenique soon fell out with Castilla, and his position was also weakened by financial scandals. Early in 1854 Castilla placed himself at the head of a popular revolt. Most of the army remained loyal to the government; but the revolution succeeded, after nearly a year of fighting, and Castilla again became president.

Among the political groups that made the revolution a success were the leaders of a new liberal movement. Like the similar movement in Chile, this was in part a reflection of the European revolutions of 1848. It was also a protest against militarism. The liberals had opposed Echenique's election in 1851, and they now joined with Castilla to overthrow him. It was they who persuaded Castilla to issue two decrees of historic importance while the war was still in progress. One of these, early in 1854, freed the Indians from the tribute that had been imposed on them early in the colonial period, a tax by which the poorest and most oppressed part of the population had provided approximately a quarter of the government's revenue. Its abolition assured the revolution of the support of the Indians and had an important effect on its outcome. The other, issued some months later, abolished slavery. This affected fewer people, for there had been only about 40,000 Negro slaves in Peru in the latter part of the colonial period,[3] and all persons born after independence were theoretically free, under a decree issued by San Martín in 1821. This decree, however, had not been fully enforced, and there had even been some importation of slaves from other South American countries in the period just before 1854. The *guano* revenues made it possible to pay compensation to the owners of some 25,000 slaves who were emancipated.

The liberals were strongly represented in the national convention which met after the war to revise the constitution, and they were able to bring about the enactment of a few mildly anticlerical measures, restricting the ecclesiastical *fuero* and ending the collection of ecclesiastical taxes by the state. Their relations with Castilla, however, were somewhat strained, and in 1857 the President dissolved the convention by force. Thereafter he relied on the conservatives for support. Castilla was re-elected and continued as President until 1862. Neither a revolt at Arequipa in 1856, which was put down only after an eight-months' siege of the city had caused much suffering, nor a flare-up of the boundary dispute with Ecuador in 1859 seriously affected the prosperity the country was enjoying.

THE WAR WITH SPAIN

Grand Marshal Miguel de San Román was elected without opposition to succeed Castilla in 1862, but he died a few months after his inauguration. The Vice-President, General Juan Antonio Pezet, had not been in office

[3] Basadre, *op. cit.*, p. 251.

long when relations with Spain, already strained by disputes over pecuniary claims and by the Peruvian government's outspoken disapproval of the Spanish interventions in Mexico and Santo Domingo, were made worse by the "Talambo affair." A group of Basque immigrants, who had complained of mistreatment at the hands of the wealthy planters who had brought them to Peru, were brutally attacked by native laborers. No real effort was made to bring the offenders to justice, and when a Spanish "Royal Commissioner" was sent to Lima to demand satisfaction, the government refused to deal with him because it considered his title offensive. In April, 1864, a Spanish fleet seized the Chincha Islands, which were the site of some of the richest *guano* deposits. Pezet agreed to pay an indemnity, in order to obtain the return of the Islands, but public opinion was so outraged by his surrender that the government was overthrown in 1865 by a revolution under General Mariano Ignacio Prado.

Prado's revolt had at least the moral support of Chile, which itself declared war on Spain in September, 1865. In December, Chile and Peru signed an offensive and defensive alliance to which Ecuador and Bolivia later adhered. The war was short and inconclusive. Valparaiso was bombarded in March, 1866, and an attack on Callao on May 2 was repulsed, in a bloody combat that is one of the famous events in Peru's history.

Prado ruled as dictator for more than a year, with the support of many of the liberal leaders. His effort to carry out a program of administrative and financial reform met with much opposition, and his position improved little after a Constituent Assembly was elected in 1866. An attempted revolution led by Castilla in 1867 failed when the ex-President died in the middle of the campaign, but another, in 1868, made Colonel José Balta President of the Republic.

THE CLIMAX OF THE GUANO ERA

The *guano* trade, which had made Peru one of the richest of the American republics, had not been an unmixed blessing. The inflow of money had greatly increased the government's income and had made possible such reforms as the abolition of Indian tributes and the emancipation of the slaves; but it had also encouraged extravagance and corruption. Most of the benefit, in fact, had gone to private individuals—both Peruvians and foreigners—who could obtain contracts for the sale of the *guano* abroad. The government's share had been great enough to cause the abandonment of any real effort to collect other taxes, but it was not great enough to meet the vastly increased expenditures that had come to seem necessary. When Balta took office, in fact, he was confronted with the prospect of a formidable budgetary deficit.

Nicolás Piérola, the new Minister of Finance, who was later to be one of the country's great leaders, proposed a radical solution. Despite the opposition of the local interests that had benefited from the old system, he obtained approval of a contract with Dreyfus Brothers, in Paris, under which this firm would have the sole right to sell *guano* and in return would advance large sums for the government's immediate needs and would assume the service of the foreign debt. The new system gave the government a larger share in the *guano* income and made it possible for the government to float new large foreign loans for public works.

Balta's administration was in fact a period of great prosperity. Several important railway lines were built, under the direction of the American Henry Meiggs, and agricultural production was increased, especially on the coast. The labor problem, which had become acute in the coastal valleys even before slavery was abolished, was partly solved by the importation of Chinese coolies, most of them under contracts that compelled them to labor for long terms of years at low wages. Nearly 85,000 of these unfortunate people were brought in between 1861 and 1875, when a treaty with China forbade any but voluntary migration,[4] and their descendants form a considerable part of the population of the Peruvian coast today.

THE RISE OF THE *CIVILISTA* PARTY

In the first 50 years of independence, most of Peru's presidents were members of one military group. There were violent personal rivalries within the group, but for the greater part of the period, one faction, led first by Gamarra and then by Castilla, dominated the government. There had indeed been no long periods of personal dictatorship, for, except in the one case of Castilla's re-election in 1858, each president had withdrawn at the end of one term. The congress, too, had somewhat more authority and freedom of action than the Buenos Aires legislature, for example, had under Rosas. Elections were sometimes vigorously contested, even though relatively few of the citizens voted and the victory of the official candidate was almost certain. The dominant faction's control of the government, as we have seen, had been repeatedly challenged by armed revolt. One of the most influential opposition *caudillos* in Castilla's time had been Colonel Manuel Ignacio de Vivanco, who was supported by an aristocratic group that wished to see a more authoritarian government modeled on Portales' regime in Chile. Another, somewhat more important group was that of the civilian liberals, who had from time to time achieved a measure of political power only to lose it in a resurgence of militarism. La Mar and Orbegoso, whom the liberals placed in the presidency, were unable to control the other army chiefs, and both Castilla and Prado worked with the liberals for a short time, but then broke with them.

With the growth of trade and the emergence of a new wealthy class

[4] Ugarte, *Bosquejo de la historia económica del Perú*, pp. 60–63.

of merchants and plantation owners, there was increasing dissatisfaction with military rule. Abuses of power during Balta's administration, and especially the corruption and financial mismanagement that characterized his government, brought this feeling to a head during the electoral campaign of 1872 when Manuel Pardo, a successful young businessman who had already served with distinction in several official positions, organized the *partido civil* to combat the official candidate. The election, despite much violence and fraud, gave Pardo a majority, and his success was assured when it became clear that his followers would control Congress, where the final decision would be made. It was the first time since 1833 that the official candidate had been defeated.

Balta accepted the result of the popular vote, but Tomás Gutiérrez, the Minister of War, made a desperate effort to keep the army in power. Balta was arrested, and soon afterward murdered, while the army chiefs sought to set up a military dictatorship. The people of Lima and Callao, however, revolted as they had in 1834, and the usurper and two of his brothers were killed. Soon afterward Pardo assumed the presidency.

FINANCIAL TROUBLES, 1872–1878

Peru's first period of civilian government was not a happy one. Pardo diminished the importance of the army by establishing a national guard, and he encouraged education and attempted to bring about other useful reforms; but he was handicapped by financial difficulties. The government's expenditures, increased by the still-uncompleted railroad program, were far in excess of its revenues, and the proceeds of the *guano* sales were by this time entirely mortgaged to foreign bondholders. The collapse that a reckless fiscal policy made inevitable was hastened by the world depression. In 1875 the banks were compelled to suspend specie payments, and the government defaulted on its foreign debt. There were several small revolts. Financial and business conditions continued to grow worse in the first years of the administration of General Prado, the ex-President, whom Pardo accepted as the official candidate in 1876 when it appeared that a *civilista* could not be elected without a violent conflict.

The drop in the price of *guano*, which was a major element in the country's financial difficulties, was caused partly by the competition of nitrate from the Peruvian province of Tarapacá and the Bolivian province of Atacama. Pardo had attempted in 1873 to control this competition by setting up a sales monopoly for Peruvian nitrate, but this effort was blocked by the Chilean and European interests that were exploiting the principal deposits. In 1875 he decided to expropriate the producing companies, despite the fact that the government was in no position to compensate the owners. These policies, combined with Bolivia's treatment of the nitrate producers, brought on the war with Chile which has been described in Chapter 11.

THE WAR WITH CHILE

The War of the Pacific found Peru woefully unprepared. Neither the army, which Pardo had reduced for internal political reasons, nor the navy were a match for Chile's well-equipped forces. Bolivia could give little help. The Chilean advance was held up for some months by Admiral Grau's daring operations at sea, but after the *Huáscar* was sunk the enemy easily overran Tarapacá. In December, 1879, President Prado suddenly embarked for Europe to purchase munitions. Nicolás de Piérola, an audacious political agitator who had been Finance Minister under Balta and had later led several unsuccessful uprisings against the *civilista* regime, seized control of the government but was no more successful than his predecessor in checking the Chilean advance. Tacna and Arica were lost, and an effort to end the war through the mediation of the United States failed. When Lima was occupied by a Chilean army in January, 1881, Piérola withdrew into the interior where he continued for some months to lead an ineffective opposition to the invaders.

At Lima a government headed by Dr. Francisco García Calderón was set up under the protection of the Chilean Commander. The new administration, however, refused to accept Chile's demands, partly at least because it hoped for diplomatic support from the United States. After a few months, when the Peruvian generals in the interior had recognized García Calderón's authority and had begun to act in his name, the President was arrested and deported to Chile. The Peruvian leaders kept up their opposition for another year, but at the end of 1882, after Chilean expeditions had dispersed the forces of some of the other chiefs, General Miguel Iglesias assumed the presidency and agreed to the invaders' terms. By the treaty signed on October 20, 1883, Peru lost Tarapacá and agreed to a temporary Chilean occupation of Tacna and Arica—a provision which, as we have already seen, was a source of friction for many years. The Chilean army of occupation was withdrawn in 1884, after the treaty had been ratified.

RECOVERY, 1884–1899

The military chiefs who had opposed a surrender accepted the treaty with Chile as an accomplished fact; but they continued to combat Iglesias, and late in 1885 General Andrés Avelino Cáceres overthrew the government after several months of hard fighting. During Cáceres' term as President, from 1886 to 1890, Peru began to recover slowly from the demoralization and impoverishment caused by the war. The Chileans had levied heavy contributions on the people of the occupied districts and had carried off or destroyed much valuable property. Many of the rich valleys along the coast had been systematically laid waste. The *guano* deposits which remained to Peru were now of relatively little value, and such income as they still produced was pledged to foreign creditors.

One of the most urgent problems was the reorganization of the public finances. With annual revenues of less than $6,000,000, hardly a third of what they had been 15 years earlier, the government could barely meet the most necessary expenses of administration, to say nothing of paying interest on its $150,000,000 foreign debt. After prolonged negotiations, an arrangement with the British bondholders was reached in 1889. The government was relieved of responsibility for its outstanding bonds and in return ceded the state railways to the bondholders for 66 years. It further agreed to pay 80,000 pounds sterling annually for 33 years and to give the bondholders a right to extract and export a total amount of 3,000,000 tons of *guano*.

Cáceres had the support of many of the *civilistas*, but Nicolás de Piérola, who for more than two decades had been opposing militarism and advocating democratic reforms, made a vigorous bid for the presidency in 1890. The government cut short his campaign by imprisoning him and brought about the victory of the official candidate, Colonel Remigio Morales Bermúdez, who was President until 1894 but who met with increasing opposition in the Congress and from the civilian political leaders. The situation grew much worse when Morales died, and Cáceres' adherents resorted to illegal and oppressive measures to bring about their leader's election for the next term. There was a general demand for a return to civilian government, and the *civilistas* joined the *pierolistas* in a revolt that succeeded after three days of savage fighting in the streets of Lima.

Piérola, who was President from 1895 until 1899, gave Peru an efficient government which hastened the process of recovery. The depreciated and fluctuating currency was stabilized; public works were constructed; and the army was again brought under the government's control. A return of military domination was made more difficult by a law promulgated in 1896 which entrusted the conduct of elections to boards chosen chiefly by the legislative and judicial branches of the government.

CIVILIAN GOVERNMENTS, 1899–1919

Eduardo de Romaña, supported by the *pierolista-civilista* coalition, became President in 1899 and was followed by a *civilista*, Manuel Candamo, in 1903. When Candamo died, after eight months in office, José Pardo was chosen to take his place, after a hotly contested election. Pardo, the son of the first *civilista* President, was an able man who carried out a number of constructive measures and especially attempted to build up the neglected . public school system. At the end of his term in 1908 Peru had enjoyed 13 years of practically unbroken peace, and the country was sharing in the prosperity that most of South America was enjoying.

Augusto B. Leguía, a businessman who had been Minister of Finance under Candamo and Pardo, was elected as the official candidate in 1908, but he soon broke with his former associates and established a semidictatorial personal regime. A revolt by Piérola's followers was suppressed in 1909, and vigorous measures were taken against other opposing political leaders. Leguía nevertheless failed when he attempted to have his friend Antero Aspíllaga chosen as his successor in 1912. The elections were unusually disorderly, and when Congress met, it annulled them and chose the *piero-lista* candidate, Guillermo Billinghurst, as the new Chief Executive.

Billinghurst had much popular support at the outset of his administration, but he lost most of this during his first year in office. After a quarrel with Congress and an unfortunate effort to compromise the Tacna-Arica dispute with Chile, he was overthrown in February, 1914, by a group of military leaders working in connivance with the *civilistas*. Colonel Oscar Benavides assumed charge of the government temporarily, and in August, 1915, José Pardo was again inaugurated as constitutional President. The high prices of petroleum, copper, sugar, and cotton during the European war made Peru unusually prosperous in his four years in office. The sympathies of the government were openly on the side of the United States after that country entered the conflict, and Pardo severed diplomatic relations with Germany in October, 1917.

THE DICTATORSHIP OF LEGUÍA

At the end of Pardo's second term, the *civilista* party, which has been described as "a fusion of a plutocratic class with a part of the hereditary nobility," [5] had been in power, except for short intervals, for nearly a quarter-century. The wealth of its membership was a factor in its success because bribery had tended to replace force and intimidation in the elections after Piérola's reforms assured more freedom in the voting. The party's influence, however, was being undermined by social and economic changes somewhat like those that were weakening the political aristocracies of Argentina and Chile. The Indians still had no part in the nation's political life; but the working people and the lower middle classes in the cities were taking more interest in matters of government, and it was among them that Piérola's "democratic" party, in opposition since 1903, found many of its supporters. There were also increasing numbers of business and professional men who had no family or other connections with the *civilista* group and resented its monopoly of political power, and their

[5] Basadre, *Perú: Problema y Posibilidad*, p. 95.

importance increased during the war years when many new fortunes were created. In 1919 most of these elements opposed to the party in power supported ex-President Leguía, who won the election despite the government's efforts in behalf of its own candidate. Since there was some reason to fear that the Congress might attempt to upset the result when it made the final canvass of the vote, Leguía's followers seized the presidential palace by force and installed their leader in power shortly before the end of Pardo's constitutional term.

This *coup d'état* inaugurated a dictatorship that lasted 11 years. Leguía's popularity, combined with the general prosperity of the 1920's, enabled him to override all opposition. Constitutional changes first extended his term to five years and then legalized his re-election in 1924 and 1929. His opponents were powerless in the face of his efficient military and police forces and his active secret service. Those who did attempt to revolt received harsh treatment. In many ways, however, Leguía was an enlightened and progressive ruler. The most important event of his administration was the settlement of the Tacna-Arica controversy which had so long embittered Peru's relations with Chile. At home, something was done to improve the position of the working classes; an educational mission was brought from the United States; and irrigation systems, harbor improvements, and other public works were constructed. Funds were obtained by floating large loans abroad. Unfortunately the inflow of capital and the governmental and private extravagance which it encouraged made the reaction all the more severe when the depression set in.

RECENT ADMINISTRATIONS

Leguía, like Irigoyen and Ibáñez, fell in the wave of revolutions that marked the first years of the depression. On August 22, 1930, the military commander at Arequipa, Colonel Luis M. Sánchez Cerro, rose in revolt. The attitude of the army chiefs and of public opinion at Lima made resistance impossible, and on August 25 Leguía resigned to spend the last years of his life in prison. Sánchez Cerro became provisional President. Though he was forced to resign six months later, he returned to power as President after an election in 1931. He had to suppress several revolutionary movements and brought Peru close to war with Colombia in 1932–1933 by his support of a group of Peruvians who had seized a piece of Colombian territory in the Amazon region. Peace was made with Colombia, but internal disturbances in Peru continued after Sánchez Cerro was assassinated and General Oscar Benavides became President in 1933.

After the fall of Leguía, the strongest opposition party was the *"Apra"* (*Asociación Popular Revolucionaria Americana*), a radical group which had been organized originally as an international movement against foreign imperialism, political and economic. The *Apra*'s founder, Victor

Raúl Haya de la Torre, was one of the candidates in the presidential election of 1931. He had many adherents in Peru, and an outbreak of his followers in the northern highland region was suppressed with some difficulty in March, 1933. Thereafter the party was virtually outlawed, and its leaders were imprisoned or exiled; but it continued to make trouble.

Haya de la Torre was not permitted to be a candidate in the presidential election of 1936 because the government maintained that he represented an international organization rather than a Peruvian political party. The *apristas* consequently voted for Luis Antonio Eguiguren, another radical opposition leader, and their support gave him a majority over the official candidate, Jorge Prado. Before the votes were officially counted, however, a Constituent Assembly annulled the election and extended Benavides' term for three additional years. A revival of business helped to make the general political situation more tranquil, and there was no effective resistance to the government's high-handed action. A number of *apristas* were nevertheless arrested and held in jail for long periods. Benavides exercised dictatorial powers, since the annulment of the elections left the country without a congress, and in 1939 constitutional amendments greatly increasing the authority of future presidents were adopted by plebiscite.

Later in the same year, Manuel Prado y Ugarteche was chosen as Benavides' successor in an election in which the *apristas* were again debarred from participation. Prado was in office throughout World War II. His government broke off relations with the Axis in January, 1942, and its policy of co-operation with the United States met with little opposition from other political groups. An increased demand for the country's copper and other products, combined with substantial financial aid from the United States, helped the economic situation, and there was little political disorder. Congress granted the President extraordinary powers for the duration of the war, and the principal opposition parties, including the *Apra*, were not permitted to carry on even normal political activities.

With the approaching victory of the democracies in Europe, there was an increasing public demand in many Latin American countries for more democratic government. This trend affected Peru, and the election of 1945 was one of the freest in the Republic's history. A direct conflict between the *apristas* and the conservative-military group that controlled the government was avoided when both Haya de la Torre and ex-President Benavides withdrew their candidacies. The *apristas* joined with some of the other antiadministration parties in a "national democratic front," and their votes were chiefly responsible for the election of José Luis Bustamante y Rivero, who became President in July, 1945. With a near-majority in Congress, they were the most powerful element in the new administration.

The *Apra*, like most native radical parties in Latin America, was hostile to communism. Its attitude toward the United States had changed, and it now advocated co-operation with American capital to develop Peru's natural resources as well as a series of measures for the improvement of social conditions in Peru. Everything that it stood for, however, was opposed by the conservatives, both in Congress and in Bustamante's Cabinet, and the President's position was made more and more difficult by the savage conflict between the two groups. Matters became worse in January, 1947, when the *apristas* were accused of instigating the murder of one of the owners of a newspaper which opposed them, and the party's three representatives in the President's Cabinet resigned. The loss of their support weakened the administration, and when the conservative Senators prevented Congress from functioning, by refusing to attend meetings, the government was all but paralyzed. Things came to a head after an unsuccessful revolt, said to have been instigated by the *apristas*, in October, 1948. A part of the army, accusing Bustamante of leniency to his former allies, overthrew him on October 29, and General Manuel Odría became provisional President. There was a general purge of *aprista* office-holders, and when an election was held in July, 1950, no opposition candidacies were permitted and Odría became President.

Odría ruled as a dictator during the ensuing six years. There were relatively few serious disturbances, and no opposition political parties were permitted to function. Haya de la Torre, after spending many months in asylum in the Colombian Embassy, where he became the center of a much publicized diplomatic controversy, went into exile and was not permitted to return. The country was prosperous and suffered less than most of its neighbors from the inflation after the Second World War. At the end of his term, Odría declined to be a candidate for the next one, and held a free election in 1956 in which the candidate whom he favored ran a poor third. More than 1,200,000 votes were cast, showing that a far larger part of the people had participated than in other recent contests in Peru. The victor was ex-President Manuel Prado y Ugarteche, to whom the still-outlawed *apristas* had thrown their support late in the campaign.

With some 10,000,000 inhabitants, Peru is one of the more important countries of South America. Petroleum in the north, cotton and sugar in the irrigated coastal valleys, and copper from the mines of Cerro de Pasco have greatly increased the volume of her export trade since the beginning of the century. Most of this economic development has benefited the coast, where the bulk of the population is white or *mestizo*, rather than the mountain region where the Indians live. In the *sierra*, conditions have changed less, though road building in recent years has brought many of the towns into closer contact with the outside world. The *sierra* is still primarily a region of great *haciendas*, worked by Indians, and to a lesser extent of small, isolated Indian communities. Great numbers of the Indians have left the highlands for the coast, where they have become assimilated socially in the *mestizo* class, but those who remain still live and work under much the same conditions as in colonial times.

The outlook for the Indians has nevertheless become brighter in recent years. Peruvian public opinion has awakened to the importance of the problem that they present, and the *apristas'* advocacy of social reform is one of the factors that has won them a large following. Recent governments have shown more interest in checking some forms of oppression that were formerly customary, and the Indians themselves have shown more disposition to stand up for their rights. Those who go to the coast find freer working conditions and better wages. In the *sierra*, many of the ancient *ayllus*, or landowning communities, continue to exist despite the encroachments of the *haciendas* and the efforts made in the early days of the Republic to force the distribution of their lands among the individual members. The improvement of the Indian's condition and his integration into the body politic are the most important problems that Peru must solve in the not distant future.

CHAPTER 13

Bolivia

THERE ARE FEW sections of South America where civilized communities contend with greater geographical and climatic handicaps than in Bolivia. Much of the great plateau, 12 to 14 thousand feet above sea level and bordered by higher snow-covered peaks, is too cold and arid for agriculture, but a considerable number of people live there, some of them working in the mines on which the nation's economy largely depends, and others tending flocks of llamas and alpacas that graze on the sparse vegetation. There are other centers of population around the edges of the bleak tableland, in the more temperate valleys on the eastern slopes and near La Paz and Lake Titicaca where the prehistoric city of Tiahuanaco flourished and where hardy plants like potatoes and *quinoa* can be cultivated, though with constant danger of crop failure from cold or drought. Most of the great area east of the Andes is sparsely inhabited. Much of it is either tropical jungle or hot, low-lying plains, but there are portions, like the region around Santa Cruz de la Sierra, which are more fertile and have a better climate.

What is now Bolivia had a large Indian population before the Conquest, and its mineral wealth made it one of the most valued Spanish possessions during the colonial period. At the time of independence, however, the output of the once fabulously rich silver mines had virtually ceased, and other forms of mineral wealth which have since become important had not been developed. The population, greatly reduced by the cruelties of the *mita*, had been further diminished after 1809 by 15 years of particularly savage civil strife. There were probably somewhat less than 1,000,000 people in the country in 1825.

The majority of these were Indians, either Quechuas like the people of southern Peru or the more sullen and intractable Aymaras. Like their Peruvian neighbors they still spoke their native dialects and retained many of their primitive customs. Exploited and oppressed by the officials and landowners, undernourished and suffering constantly from the cold, their lot was even harder than that of the natives in other parts of the Andean region. In several places, especially in the more remote and unproductive regions, they had been allowed to retain their ancient communal agricultural system; but elsewhere their lands and much of their livestock had passed into the hands of the descendants of the *conquistadores*, and they themselves had become debt-slaves or tenant farmers, obliged by law or custom to work for the benefit of the landowner. Above the Indians in the social scale, but only slightly less ignorant and primitive in their way of living, were the Spanish-speaking *cholos*, or *mestizos*, some of them farmers, others artisans or small tradesmen in the towns.

Both the Indians and the *cholos* far outnumbered the people of more or less pure Spanish blood, who lived in the small isolated towns. Though a few of the creoles had studied at the ancient University of Chuquisaca, their general standard of intellectual attainment was low. The meager revenues from their estates, worked by the Indians under *cholo* overseers with little or no attention on the part of the owners, made it possible for them to live in idleness, but with few comforts and fewer diversions. Only a handful had any conception of conditions beyond the mountains and deserts which cut off the plateau from the outside world.

FIRST YEARS OF INDEPENDENCE

Since the provinces of the plateau had been governed from Buenos Aires between 1776 and 1810, and from Lima during the revolution, both the Argentine Confederation and Peru claimed the territory when Spanish resistance collapsed after the battle of Ayacucho. When Bolívar's lieutenant Sucre occupied the country, however, he found a strong sentiment for independence, and an Assembly that he convened voted in August, 1825, to establish a separate republic bearing the name of Bolívar. The Liberator, though he at first opposed the independence movement, accepted the Assembly's invitation to draw up a constitution for the new state. The draft that he submitted was accepted but with one important change: the delegates could not agree with Bolívar's rather liberal views about religion and insisted upon an article prohibiting the public exercise of any but the Roman Catholic cult. The other provisions of the *constitución vitalicia* have been described in Chapter 7.

Sucre, though he himself urged the selection of a native Bolivian, was chosen President and reluctantly consented to serve for a period of two years. The Venezuelan general had been the real ruler of the country since the end of the war. His tactful leadership had made the orderly establishment of the new Republic possible, and he had already reorganized the administrative and fiscal system. He had also begun to build up a school system, but the effort to implant the educational methods of ancient Sparta, sponsored by Bolívar's old teacher Simón Rodríguez, does not seem to have been a great success.[1] Sucre had remained in Bolivia, however, only from a sense of duty, and he was eager to return to Quito to be married. Never ambitious on his own account, he made no attempt to build up a personal regime as other lieutenants of Bolívar were already doing in Venezuela and Ecuador.

His position grew more difficult after the collapse of the Liberator's authority in Peru. The new rulers of that country intrigued against him, and his own soldiers were becoming homesick. Sucre was wounded when some of them mutinied at Chuquisaca in April, 1828, and could offer little resistance when the Peruvian General Gamarra invaded Bolivia. In July he assented to a treaty that required him to leave the country with his Colombian troops. Andrés Santa Cruz, who was at the time in Chile, was chosen by the Congress as his successor.

Santa Cruz, who had already figured prominently in events in Peru, was a *mestizo*, claiming descent on his mother's side from the royal family of the Incas. Born on the shore of Lake Titicaca, he had a great following among the Indians on both sides of the Peru-Bolivian frontier. He fought on the Spanish side during the greater part of the war for independence, as did most of the Peruvian generals, but joined San Martín's army in 1821. Later, as we have already seen, he served under Bolívar and governed Peru for a short time as the Liberator's lieutenant.

There was much disorder, fomented by Gamarra's intrigues, before Santa Cruz reached Bolivia, and General Velasco, the acting President, was overthrown and then restored by barracks revolts. The hostility of the populace finally forced Gamarra to withdraw his army, and when the President-Elect assumed power in May, 1829, the war between Peru and Colombia had ended for the time being the danger of a new invasion. One of Santa Cruz' first acts was to set aside the Bolivarian constitution. His regime was a dictatorship, but it was nevertheless one of the best governments in Latin America and without question the best government that Bolivia was to have for many years. His able administration and careful financial management won him much support while his sagacious but firm handling of opponents prevented disorder. A large and well-disciplined army further strengthened his hand, and for several years the country enjoyed a measure of prosperity. We have already seen how this state of affairs impressed the propertied classes in Peru and helped to make possible a union of the two countries, with Santa Cruz as "Protector," which was proclaimed in 1836 but was destroyed by Chilean intervention in 1839.[2]

Even before the defeat of Santa Cruz' army at Yungay, his leadership had been repudiated by his subordinates in Bolivia, and he was compelled to dissolve the Confederation and go into exile. General José Miguel de

---

[1] Pinilla, *La Creación de Bolivia*, pp. 269–270.
[2] See above, pp. 228, 253.

Velasco, who had been provisional President in 1828–1829 and President of the State of Bolivia under the Confederation, became head of the government. Popular, but inept and easygoing, he was soon struggling against revolts fomented by other military leaders. When his government was overthrown by the partisans of Santa Cruz in 1841, the Peruvian President Gamarra at once invaded Bolivia to prevent his old enemy's return to power and supported a revolution under General José Ballivián. The latter, however, demanded that the Peruvians withdraw, and in the ensuing fighting Garmarra was defeated and killed at the battle of Ingavi.

Under Ballivián, who became President, the country had six years of comparative tranquility. In 1845, after negotiations with the three governments of Bolivia, Peru, and Chile, Santa Cruz was persuaded to cease his efforts to return to power and to take up residence in Europe with a generous pension. Other conspirators were promptly executed. The administration did something, though not very much, in the way of building roads and improving education. Not one school had been open in Bolivia in 1841, but some 4,000 pupils, still a pitifully small number, were receiving instruction a few years later.[3] A few foreign scientists and teachers were brought to the country, and the first real newspaper was established. Unfortunately, even the very moderate progress that the Republic was making under Ballivián ceased under his immediate successors.

THE ERA OF MILITARY DESPOTISM, 1847–1879

Ballivián was overthrown in 1847 by a military mutiny under Colonel Manuel Isidoro Belzu. Velasco again became President, but he had been in office only a few months when Belzu led a revolt and assumed power himself. Belzu's administration was the first of a series of sanguinary and corrupt despotisms which have few parallels in the history of Latin America. A professional soldier, uneducated and with no conception of the responsibilities attaching to his high office, the new President was typical of the military *caudillos* who were the leading figures in Bolivian politics during the next 30 years. Since the expulsion of Sucre, nearly every change of government had been the result of a mutiny in the army, and every officer of the higher ranks had come to regard himself as a potential dictator. Most of them were more or less illiterate ruffians who had entered the army as common soldiers. Personal bravery, lack of scruples, and a readiness to kill an enemy in cold blood were the qualities which seemed to assure success. Civilian leaders, though they held important posts in the cabinet and congress, played a secondary rôle. There were no real political parties, and even the purely personal factions that surrounded each *caudillo* were frequently disrupted by jealousy or treachery. The constant interference of Peru, whether by armed intervention or by

[3] Argüedas, *Historia general de Bolivia*, p. 117.

intrigue, made matters worse, as did the spirit of *localismo*, which found expression in the rivalries and antipathies between the different towns.

Belzu, himself of humble birth, sought popularity by appealing to class hatred. Mobs were encouraged to sack the properties of his opponents among the upper class, and the *cholos* were encouraged to regard themselves as the new rulers of the country. The President became the idol of the *pueblo*, the turbulent artisans of the towns. He was nevertheless continually beset by conspiracies and revolts, which were not discouraged by the brutal punishment of enemies who fell into his hands. On one occasion he was nearly killed by would-be assassins, and the Council of Ministers, during his convalescence, shot not only those implicated in the plot but also the President of Congress and other high officials of whom they were jealous for political reasons. In 1855 Belzu wearied of the struggle to remain in power and presented his resignation, informing Congress that "Bolivia has become ungovernable." Actually, he probably intended to retain control by passing on the presidency to his son-in-law Jorge Córdoba, a soldier of even more obscure origin, but Córdoba was ousted in 1857 by a revolt led by José María Linares.

Linares, unlike his predecessors, was a civilian, respected for his upright character and his intellectual attainments. He had been acting President for a short time in 1848 and then had led one revolution after another, sacrificing much of his personal fortune in the effort to restore what he believed to be the constitutional order. Once in power, however, he was little less arbitrary and ruthless than his predecessors. His energetic but often ill-considered attack on long-standing political and social abuses made many enemies, and he was finally betrayed by two of his own ministers, who seized power by a *coup d'état* and sent him into exile in 1861.

A new Congress, chosen in an election more nearly free than any since the time of Sucre, made General José María de Achá President. Achá chose his Cabinet from several political factions and apparently made a real attempt to govern constitutionally, but his tolerant policy merely encouraged intrigue and revolt. Shocking scenes occurred in La Paz, where more than 60 political prisoners, including ex-President Córdoba, were massacred to thwart a rumored jail-delivery. The President, like most of the military *caudillos*, was ignorant and incompetent, but he remained in office until the end of 1864 when his close associate, Mariano Melgarejo, ousted him by a barracks revolt.

Melgarejo, starting as a common soldier, had risen to high position in the army, and consequently in the government, chiefly by his audacity and complete lack of scruples. He established his authority only after a sharp struggle with several other leaders, including Belzu. This *caudillo*, still popular with the *cholo* class, defeated the new government's forces and occupied La Paz, but Melgarejo went into the city with a handful of followers and killed Belzu with his own hand. In power the new President showed a complete contempt for legal restraints and private rights. No congress met for a period of four years, and any manifestation of opposition was cruelly suppressed. During his frequent periods of drunkenness, in fact, Melgarejo was guilty of atrocities that shocked even his unprincipled associates. He had no scruples about using public funds to gratify his vices or to enrich his friends. Many of these obtained lands that had belonged to the Indians after Melgarejo issued a decree requiring that the property of the native communities should be divided among their members. Melgarejo was also inept and careless in dealing with the increasingly dangerous dispute with Chile, which was later to cost Bolivia much of her territory.

Melgarejo was overthrown in 1871 by another professional soldier named Agustín Morales. Though hardly less ignorant and dissolute than his predecessor, the new President attempted at first to obtain the support of the better elements and permitted the restoration of a semblance of constitutional government. When he was killed in a brawl with his own nephew in 1872, a rich merchant, Tomás Frías, became provisional President and held an election in which Adolfo Ballivián was chosen as President. Ballivián was a well-educated army officer who had supported Linares. He had good intentions, but he could accomplish little; and shortly before his death from illness in 1874 he turned over the government to Frías, who was Vice-President. The interval of civilian government was a brief one, for General Hilarión Daza, the Minister of War, overthrew Frías in 1876.

THE WAR WITH CHILE

Bolivia was even less ready than Peru to face the war with Chile, which began in Daza's administration. The country's rulers, absorbed in a bloody struggle to gain or hold power, had paid little attention to the threatening situation that was developing in the south. There had never been any close connection between the interior and the inaccessible coastal province of Antofagasta, because Arica, in Peru, had been the chief port for such foreign commerce as the Republic had. Ballivián had urged the purchase of arms, but his proposals had been defeated in Congress. The army, though it dominated the country's internal politics, was insignificant compared with that of Chile and lacked modern weapons and real training. Neither Daza nor his predecessors seem to have realized this, and they recklessly allowed the quarrel with Chile over the taxation of foreign nitrate companies to develop into armed conflict.

The story of the war has been told in Chapter 11. Daza at first took command of the Bolivian army, but his troops revolted in December, 1879, after he abandoned his allies in Tarapacá, and an uprising in the interior made General Narcisco Campero President of the Republic. In

May, 1880, the allied forces under Campero's command were routed at Tacna. So far as Bolivia was concerned the war was over, though Campero endeavored to raise a new force in the interior. Chile took the rich nitrate fields of Antofagasta, and Bolivia became a landlocked country. The Bolivians never reconciled themselves to the loss of their access to the sea, and their resentment continued to be a dangerous element in the international politics of South America even after a formal treaty of peace was signed with Chile in 1904.

PROGRESS AFTER THE WAR

Both economic and political conditions improved after the war. The country was more prosperous, thanks to a revival of silver mining, and it was ruled by men of a better type. The sharp differences of opinion over the question of continuing the war or accepting defeat led to the rise of political parties which for the first time were something more than mere personal factions. Though the question of war or peace was at first the only important issue, these new parties soon began to take sides on other matters. The conservatives, who opposed a resumption of the struggle, had somewhat the same relation to the Church as the parties of the same name in other countries, and the liberals—the war party—were mildly anticlerical. The religious question, however, never became so acute as in some other Latin American countries.

The liberals' chief leaders were Campero and General Eliodoro Camacho, another war hero. Their chief opponent was Aniceto Arce, who was Vice-President under Campero but was exiled when he opposed the continuance of the war. It is interesting to note that all three of these leaders, unlike most of the earlier Bolivian statesmen, knew something of the outside world from long residence in Europe, an experience that increased their prestige with their fellow citizens. In the election of 1884, Camacho and Arce were the liberal and conservative candidates, but a third contender, the wealthy silver miner Gregorio Pacheco, bought votes on a large scale and obtained a plurality. The decision went to Congress, and a deal between Arce and Pacheco made the latter President and assured Arce's election as the official candidate for the term beginning in 1888.

Pacheco, though he was an estimable citizen, generally respected for his philanthropies, was a mediocre President. His four years in office were nevertheless peaceful, chiefly because of Camacho's unwillingness to risk a return to the disorder and militarism of the prewar period. Camacho's attitude changed, however, after Arce was elected in 1888 by a combination of bribery and governmental interference, and after a small military uprising caused the government to adopt harsh measures against the liberal leaders. There were conspiracies and small revolts throughout the new President's term. Arce was nevertheless able to complete the railroad connecting Oruro with the coast at Antofagasta and to build a number of cart roads. Both the railroad and the highways were of inestimable importance to a country where llamas and pack mules had hitherto been practically the only means of transport.

In the election of 1892 the liberals, who again nominated Camacho, and also ex-President Pacheco's "democratic" party, opposed Arce's candidate Mariano Baptista. The popular vote was very evenly divided, but Baptista's success was assured when the government declared a state of siege and arrested or expelled several liberal members of Congress, which was to make the final decision. Baptista had distinguished himself by his able conduct of several delicate diplomatic negotiations under the preceding administration, and he had won tremendous prestige by his oratory; but he accomplished little as President. There was increasing opposition to the long-continued domination of the conservative party, and under Baptista's successor, Severo Fernández Alonso, who took office in 1896, this found expression in a revolt that returned the liberals to power.

The occasion was a quarrel over the location of the national Capital. Sucre, the ancient Chuquisaca, was constitutionally the seat of the government as it had been in colonial times, but in practice presidents had often found it more convenient to carry on the administration from other cities and the congress had customarily met alternately in the northern and central and southern sections of the Republic, as a concession to localistic spirit. Proposals to move the Capital to some place less inaccessible than Sucre had frequently aroused controversy. La Paz, as the largest and most important town, had been especially insistent on its claims, and when the Congress voted late in 1898 to make Sucre the Capital permanently, the people of La Paz rose in revolt. The government's forces were defeated, after some months of particularly savage fighting, and Colonel José María Pando, who had been the liberal candidate in the election of 1896, became President. Though Sucre continued legally to be the Capital, the government offices were moved to La Paz and have remained there.

LIBERAL ADMINISTRATIONS, 1899–1920

In Pando's administration, Bolivia nearly became involved in war with Brazil over the Acre territory. The Bolivian government had found it very difficult to maintain any control over the unruly adventurers of various nationalities who were gathering rubber in this distant jungle area, and it accused the local Brazilian authorities of encouraging revolts there. It consequently proposed to entrust the control of the territory to an Anglo-American company headed by Percival Farquhar. Brazil opposed this measure, and the dispute was settled in 1903 by the cession of the Acre to Brazil and the payment to Bolivia of £2,000,000 sterling to be used for railroad building.

The liberals were in power from 1899 until 1920, controlling elections by much the same means as their conservative predecessors. The progressive and able Ismael Montes was President from 1904 until 1909 and again from 1913 until 1917, after Eliodoro Villazón served the intervening term. During this time Bolivia enjoyed the longest period of internal peace in her history. Tin production, which became important at the turn of the century, increased until the Republic was producing a quarter of the world's supply, and new copper and lead mines helped to bring about a rapid increase in foreign trade. Railroad construction did much to encourage this economic development, and also to promote internal stability by bringing some of the hitherto isolated, mutually hostile provincial towns within easier reach of the Capital. A line from Lake Titicaca to the heights above La Paz, completed in 1903, provided a connection by rail and lake steamer with the Peruvian port of Mollendo, and in 1913 lines were completed from La Paz to Oruro, connecting with the existing railroad to Antofagasta, and from La Paz to Arica. The latter was built by Chile under one of the provisions of a treaty of peace which finally replaced the truce that ended the War of the Pacific. By the end of Montes' second term, most of the Republic's larger cities had railroad service.

Montes' continued dominance of the government and of the liberal party was unsatisfactory to many of the party's other leaders, and some of them, including the ex-President Pando, formed a new party—which they called "republican"—to oppose him. A law passed during Montes' second term, which gave one bank the sole right of note issue and brought on a crisis in the business of all of the other banks, increased the feeling against him, especially as economic conditions were adversely affected by the war in Europe. The government's prestige was further hurt by a suspicion that it was responsible for the murder of Pando in 1917, although the charges against it were never substantiated. The republicans failed to defeat the administration candidate, José Gutiérrez Guerra, in the election of 1917, but they easily overturned the government, with the aid of a part of the army, in 1920.

POLITICAL EVENTS, 1920–1931

Though most of the army had taken no part in the revolt, it recognized the authority of the civilian *junta* that assumed control. There was dissension within the *junta*, and Bautista Saavedra, who was elected President by a national convention in which the liberals were not represented, had to contend with opposition from his former associates as well as from the defeated party. Constitutional guarantees were suspended under the so-called "state of siege" during the greater part of his term, and there was little freedom of the press. He nevertheless continued the liberal administrations' efforts to improve the schools and the transportation system, and he sponsored some labor legislation of a mildly progressive nature.

In 1925, Saavedra supported José Gabino Villanueva as the official candidate in an election in which the opposition parties did not vote. He annulled the election, however, when Villanueva showed a disposition to conciliate some of Saavedra's enemies. Saavedra continued actually to control the government, after nominally turning his office over to a provisional President, until Hernando Siles, another prominent leader of the republican party, took office as constitutional President in 1926. Siles, who had been one of the prominent leaders of the republican party, began his administration by lifting the state of siege and proclaiming an amnesty, and his period in office, was somewhat more tranquil than his predecessor's.

Both Saavedra and Siles contracted large loans in the United States, increasing the foreign debt from approximately $6,000,000 to more than $60,000,000. Some beneficial results were obtained from this great expenditure, including especially the completion of a connecting link between Bolivia's railway system and that of Argentina, but much of the money went for nonproductive purposes, to buy arms and munitions, or simply to meet the chronic deficits in the budget. To obtain the loans the country pledged nearly all of its principal revenues and entrusted the supervision of their collection to a permanent fiscal commission, nominated partly by North American bankers. This arrangement broke down during the depression when the Republic stopped service on its foreign debt.

Toward the end of his term, Siles turned over his authority to a provisional President and became a candidate for re-election, attempting to evade a constitutional prohibition that all of his predecessors had been compelled to respect. An aroused public opinion, supported by part of the army, overthrew him in May, 1930, and a military *junta* took over the government. Daniel Salamanca, one of the country's most respected civilian political leaders, was inaugurated as President in March, 1931.

THE CHACO WAR AND ITS AFTERMATH

The war with Paraguay, which has been described in Chapter 10, began in 1932. The Bolivian government had been preparing for the conflict for some years, and much of the proceeds of the foreign loans, which were supposed to provide funds for public works, had in fact been spent on the army. Though the territory in dispute was of very little real value, it had been impossible to bring about a peaceful settlement, partly because public opinion in any Latin American country is always sensitive about any relinquishment of rights to territory, and partly because of the Bolivians' obsession with the desire for an outlet to the sea, which they might conceivably obtain through ports in the Chaco on the Paraguay River. In the peace settlement, after three years of inconclusive fighting, Bolivia did obtain a strip of territory on the upper reaches of the Paraguay which could be of little use to her in the foreseeable future.

In every other respect, the war was a disaster. The cost in human life and money was terrific. Bolivian soldiers, taken from the cold highlands into the low, hot plains where the fighting took place, suffered much more than their opponents. The drafting of men into the army caused a shortage of labor that crippled mining and agriculture, and the inflation of the currency caused much hardship.

As a result of the war, the army became more active in politics than it had been for half a century. In 1934, when President Salamanca went to the Chaco and attempted to dismiss the Commander in Chief, General Peñaranda, the army arrested him, and the Vice-President José Luis Tejada Sorzano assumed power at La Paz. After the fighting ended, there was much discontent. A new radical party, composed largely of students and demobilized soldiers, overthrew Tejada Sorzano in May, 1936, and installed the Chief of the General Staff, Colonel David Toro, as the head of what professed to be a socialist regime. Toro involved Bolivia in a dispute with the United States when he expropriated the properties of the Standard Oil Company in March, 1937, and some of his other policies brought on conflicts with powerful Bolivian mining and banking interests. These local interests helped to overthrow him in July, 1937, but his successor, another army officer named German Busch, adopted policies that seemed equally dangerous to the business community. When Busch committed suicide, or was murdered, in August, 1939, there was a reaction. The army remained in control for a time, but in March, 1940, with the election of General Enrique Peñaranda as President, the constitutional order was restored with the more conservative political groups in control.

POLITICAL CONFLICTS, 1940–1951

During the Second World War, Bolivia's internal politics became a matter of importance to the outside world. Bolivian tin became indispensable to the allied war effort after Japan conquered Malaya, and the country's other strategic minerals were desperately needed. The Peñaranda government was pro-ally, and in July, 1941, it expelled the German Minister after the discovery of a subversive conspiracy in which the German legation was involved. After Pearl Harbor, the government obtained aid from the United States in the form of lend-lease and Export-Import Bank loans and settled the chief source of disagreement between the two countries by paying the Standard Oil Company $1,500,000 for its expropriated properties. The President declared war on the Axis powers in April, 1943. Meanwhile, the government was struggling with increasingly grave internal problems. While the mining industry was enjoying great profits, inflation was making worse the already-bad situation of the Indians who worked in the mines. Public opinion, in Bolivia and abroad, was shocked when a number of striking miners were killed by the army at Cataví in December, 1942.

In December, 1943, a group of army officers joined with the newly organized National Revolutionary Movement, the M.N.R. to overthrow the Peñaranda government. The new administration, headed by Lieutenant Colonel Gualberto Villaroel was at first refused recognition by the United States and most of the other American republics because it was known that the revolt had been planned with the co-operation of the Argentine government and German agents in Buenos Aires. Villaroel finally obtained recognition by promising to co-operate with the democracies, but his internal policies, and especially his brutal treatment of his opponents, aroused much hatred. In July, 1946, a popular uprising, which the army did not try to check, overthrew the government, and Villaroel himself was seized by a mob and hanged from a lamp post in La Paz.

A provisional government held fairly orderly elections, in which there were two candidates. Enrique Herzog, who won by a small margin, was inaugurated as President in March, 1947. His administration was strongly opposed by the M.N.R. and other leftist groups, and there was much disorder, some of it political and some caused by continuing unrest among the mine workers. An M.N.R. revolt in 1949 was suppressed only after much fighting in several parts of the Republic. Shortly after this revolt, Dr. Herzog, who was ill, resigned and the Congress chose Mamerto Urriolagoitia as his successor.

"THE NATIONAL REVOLUTION"

In the election of 1951, Dr. Victor Paz Estenssoro, the leader of the M.N.R. received more votes than any other candidate, but the government claimed that he did not have an absolute majority. In such cases, the constitution required that the choice be made by Congress, but Urriolagoitia, determined that the M.N.R. should not come into power, resigned and turned the government over to the army. In April, 1952, however, the M.N.R., with the help of the national police, turned out the military *junta*, and Paz assumed the presidency.

The "national revolution" of 1952 paved the way for social and economic changes not unlike those that had taken place in Mexico a generation earlier. The M.N.R. relied for support chiefly on the organized workers and the peasants, whom it won over by its agrarian program, and it armed both groups as a safeguard against a conservative reaction. The old army was dissolved and only gradually replaced by a new force that the government hoped to be able to trust. A decree in 1952 abolished the literacy test for voters, which had until then disqualified more than four-fifths of the Indians, so that the masses of the people for the first time began to participate in elections. Organized labor began to have a powerful influence in government policy.

The agrarian reform was instituted during the first year of the new administration. Hundreds of thousands of Indians immediately became the owners of the little plots that they had been cultivating in return for their labor on the *haciendas*. The government also began to divide the large estates, and especially those that were inefficiently exploited by absentee landlords, compensating the former owners with government bonds. It encouraged co-operative farming by the new holders, but permitted individual operation where the Indians preferred it. As in Mexico, the reform proceeded slowly and met with many obstacles, one being the government's poverty which made it impossible to supply the new landowners with needed tools and working capital.

In October, 1952, the new administration expropriated the properties of the three largest tin-mining companies, the Patiño, Aramayo, and Hochschild groups. The mining companies, in which there was much North American capital, had been accused of supporting and financing the M.N.R.'s opponents, and there had been much criticism of labor conditions in their camps. The exploitation of the properties was turned over to a government corporation. The former owners were promised compensation, and in 1953 the government made a temporary arrangement to pay them a portion of the receipts from tin and wolfram exports, pending a final agreement on the total amount. The result of the expropriation, from an economic point of view, was unfortunate. The government could not supply the new management with the capital that it needed, and the withdrawal of most of the foreign employees left the mines with few qualified engineers and technicians. At the same time the management was compelled for political reasons to employ far more workers than it needed. Falling tin prices in the world market made matters worse.

Decreasing revenue from tin exports was an important factor in the inflation which soon became the government's most threatening problem. Not long after the revolution of 1952, the value of the paper currency began to fall precipitately. The American dollar, which would buy about 200 *bolivianos* in 1952, bought more than 10,000 in 1956. When the government sought to mitigate the effect of the resulting rise in prices, by controls and subsidies and especially by permitting the importation of food and industrial raw materials at the old official rate of 190 to the dollar, vast quantities of manufactured goods and agricultural products were smuggled across the frontiers into countries where prices were higher, and it became increasingly difficult to buy anything in the open market in Bolivia. The cost of the subsidies, meanwhile, increased the already-tremendous government deficit and led to further issues of paper money.

President Hernan Siles Suazo, who was elected to succeed Paz in 1956, made a heroic effort to bring the situation under control. In December, 1956, he announced a stabilization program which had been formulated with the advice of a North American financial expert. Deficits in the government's budget were to be reduced by a sharp cut in expenditures. Price controls and subsidies on consumer goods were to be eliminated, and import and exchange controls were to be abolished. Wages and salaries were to be increased to meet the expected increase in prices but were then to be frozen for one year. When the program was put into effect, prices rose, but goods at once reappeared in the markets. Buyers no longer had to stand in line for hours in an attempt, often unsuccessful, to buy the day's food. The *boliviano* rose from 15,000 to 7,500 to the dollar and remained relatively stable during the next few years. Some groups in the community were hurt, and there was much angry criticism from some of the other M.N.R. leaders as well as from the opposition parties, but the President courageously went forward with the program. Its execution would not have been possible if the United States had not provided $17,500,000 for the stabilization of the *boliviano*, in addition to the many millions that it was giving the government each year for other purposes.

As President Siles' term approached its end in 1960, the prospect for the immediate future still seemed uncertain. Despite its great mineral resources, Bolivia is one of the poorest of the American republics. Many Bolivians would have been near starvation in the past few years if the United States had not provided large grants for the purchase of food. The great majority of the country's inhabitants, who now number between 3,000,000 and 3,500,000, are still concentrated in the bleak and generally infertile highland region. Recent changes, including the agrarian program, have probably improved the state of the peasants, who form the great majority of the population, but it will be difficult to look for substantial progress until the national income can be increased by the development of new sources of wealth.

The increase and the diversification of production has been one of the chief objectives of the revolutionary governments. Though the results of their efforts have hardly offset the bad situation in the tin industry, much has been accomplished. Oil production by the government's petroleum corporation has increased until it more than supplies local consumption, and several North American companies have been encouraged to carry on exploration and drilling, in the hope that large oil exports will one day solve many of the Republic's problems. A great and apparently potentially rich area in the temperate plateau east of the Andes was made accessible by the completion of the road from Cochabamba to Santa Cruz de la Sierra. The government is attempting to encourage colonists from the plateau to settle this region, and substantial amounts of rice and sugar are already being produced there.

Both the United States and the United Nations have helped in the government's economic program. In addition to its grants for other purposes, the United States has helped to finance *servicios,* staffed by Bolivians and North Americans, which have worked in agricultural development, road building and maintenance, public health, and education. Many Bolivians have been brought to the United States each year for professional or technical training. The United Nations has provided smaller grants of money and has assisted in the agrarian program and many other matters through technical experts attached to the various ministries. Bolivia in fact offers the outstanding example in the western hemisphere of inter-American and international co-operation.

In June, 1960, Victor Paz Estenssoro was elected to succeed Siles as President.

CHAPTER 14

Ecuador

ECUADOR in many ways resembles the other Central Andean countries. Most of her people are descendants of the civilized tribes that formed part of the Inca empire. A large proportion of them still speak *Quechua* and live in a chain of high valleys between the two ranges of the Andes, working under much the same conditions as the Indians of Peru. In Ecuador, however, the highland region lacks the mineral wealth of the mountains farther south, and its inhabitants, though they supply themselves with most of the products needed to maintain a very simple standard of living, contribute little to foreign trade. Most of the country's exports—cacao, bananas, ivory nuts, coffee, rice, Panama hats, and gold—come from the coastal plain along the Pacific, which is wider and has a heavier rainfall than Peru. The coast has a considerable population of mixed Spanish, Negro, and Indian descent, and Guayaquil, the chief seaport, is the Republic's largest city. Steep, jungle-covered mountains make communication between this region and the interior very difficult, and the separation of the country into two sections, with different interests and different points of view, has encouraged *localismo* and has made it more difficult to establish a stable government.

Though the presidency of Quito had close relations with Peru, it became a part of the viceroyalty of New Granada in the eighteenth century and was thus claimed as a part of Bolívar's Republic of Colombia when that state was created. Colombian control was assured after Sucre defeated the royalists at Pichincha. Those who preferred independence were helpless in the face of the Liberator's prestige and popularity, especially as the country was occupied by veteran troops from Colombia and Venezuela. In one respect, at least, the future Republic of Ecuador profited from the union, for the people of Quito, without outside help, could hardly have resisted Peru's claim to Guayaquil which was the only seaport accessible to them and which was consequently indispensable to their existence as a separate state.

FLORES AND ROCAFUERTE

The military commander in Ecuador in 1830 was General Juan José Flores, a thirty-year-old Venezuelan who had been a soldier from the time he was fifteen, first in the royalist army and then in Bolívar's forces. Flores had won Bolívar's confidence by handling several difficult assignments with tact and courage, and in 1824 the Liberator left him in charge of the government at Quito. Though of obscure origin and almost illiterate, he married into one of the Capital's best families and made many friends among the creole aristocracy. He thus had some local support to offset the resentment of the *Quiteños* at being ruled by a foreigner with the support of foreign troops. He was apparently loyal to Bolívar so long as the Liberator retained control at Bogotá, but he lost no time in seizing power for himself when it became apparent that Great Colombia was breaking up. At his instigation, the more prominent citizens of Quito met in May, 1830, to declare Ecuador independent, and some months later a Constituent Assembly elected him President of the Republic.

It was not long before organized opposition appeared. One of the leaders was Colonel Hall, an ardent English liberal who had settled in Quito after serving in the patriot army. Hall encouraged a group of young patriots to start a newspaper called *El Quiteño Libre* in 1833, and when this began to denounce the government as a foreign military despotism and to criticize its corrupt administration of the finances, Flores suppressed the paper and arrested those connected with it. Hall and several of his associates were murdered. The "nationalists" then revolted, but their military chief, Vicente Rocafuerte, soon fell into the government's hands.

Instead of shooting his captive, Flores promised him the presidency for the next term. Rocafuerte, who thus became the head of the government in 1835, was a wealthy creole from Guayaquil. He had spent much of his life abroad, first in school, then as an American deputy in the Spanish *Cortes*, and later as a diplomatic representative of Mexico in England. His writings on political subjects had won him some distinction. The nationalist group had eagerly accepted his leadership when he returned to his own country, but they turned against him when he made his deal with Flores. His administration was little more than a continuation of the preceding regime because Flores remained in command of the army and frequently interfered in political affairs. The government's energy was absorbed in maintaining order, and its treatment of opponents was so harsh that there were many who welcomed Flores' return to the presidency in 1839. Flores' second administration, however, was more corrupt and arbitrary than Rocafuerte's. He ruled without a congress, after quarreling with the legislative body in 1840, and in 1843 he changed the constitution and brought about his own re-election, with increased powers, for a new term of eight years. This caused a break with Rocafuerte, who had expected to be

President himself. Further unpopular actions such as the imposition of a general head tax and the granting of freedom of worship to non-Catholics strengthened the opposition, and when a revolution broke out in Guayaquil on March 6, 1845, the government collapsed. Flores accepted $20,000 and a pension in return for his agreement to leave Ecuador for two years.

FOREIGN INTERFERENCE AND
INTERNAL DISORDER, 1845–1860

The "March revolution" was not only a revolt against a dictatorship maintained by foreign troops but a revolt against militarism in general. Unfortunately, it was as difficult for the civilian leaders to set up a government based on law as it was at the time in most of the Spanish American republics. They were soon confronted by a resurgence of militarism under native leaders, and they also had to contend with interference from more powerful nations, which for some years was to be a disturbing factor in the Republic's political life.

During the administration of Vicente Ramón Roca, who was elected President in 1845, the government was much alarmed by Flores' efforts to bring about a counterrevolution with the help of Spain. The ex-President apparently obtained the support of the Queen Mother María Cristina by holding out hopes of establishing a Spanish prince as ruler at Quito, and he was able to recruit a large force in Europe. The plan collapsed when the South American Ministers at London persuaded the British government to seize three ships that were to have carried the expedition to America, but the threat of a Spanish reconquest of Ecuador greatly alarmed the Republic's neighbors and led to the meeting of an American Congress at Lima in 1847 to consider plans for mutual defense.

At the end of Roca's term in 1849, the Congress was unable to elect a successor because neither of the leading candidates could obtain the two-thirds majority that the constitution required. The Vice-President, Manuel de Ascasubi, took charge, but a year later the army took control under the leadership of General José María Urbina. Urbina installed Diego Noboa as President, but in 1851, when Noboa nearly brought on a war with Colombia by giving asylum to the Jesuits who had just been expelled from that country, Urbina ousted him and assumed power himself. The new President forced the Jesuits to leave and adopted a mildly anticlerical policy in other respects. This aroused the antagonism of the conservative government of Peru, which helped the ever-active Flores in an unsuccessful counterrevolution.

These events and, especially, the repercussions of the bitter Church-State conflict in Colombia gave a new meaning to the party divisions in Ecuador where the names *conservative* and *liberal* had hitherto been used as convenient labels by the friends and enemies of Flores without signifying any great differences in ideology. Urbina adopted several of the policies espoused by liberals in the neighboring countries. The influence of the Church was still strong enough to prevent any serious attack on its prerogatives; but in 1854 Negro slavery was abolished, and a little later the Indians were freed from the tribute that had been imposed on them early in the colonial period. Many of the emancipated Negroes were recruited into the army where their loyalty to their benefactor increased Urbina's personal power.

Urbina retained control of the army when he installed General Francisco Robles as his successor in 1856. There was still much opposition to the government from those who disliked military rule, and a flare-up of the long-standing boundary dispute with Peru made matters worse. In 1858, when Robles proposed to discharge a part of the debt inherited from Great Colombia by giving the bondholders lands in the disputed territory, Peru blockaded Guayaquil and supported a revolt in Ecuador led by General Franco. The conservatives also took up arms against the government, and after a bloody three-sided struggle, the conservative leader, Gabriel García Moreno, became President in 1861.

THE DICTATORSHIP OF GARCÍA MORENO

Ecuador had made little progress in 40 years of independence. The cities were declining in population, and public buildings were falling into decay. There was little foreign commerce. The only road from the interior to the coast was the trail from Quito to Guayaquil, passable only for pack mules, and this was closed to traffic six or eight months each year by the rains. Though slavery and tributes had been abolished, both Negroes and Indians were still working for insignificant wages under a peonage system established by law, exploited and oppressed as in colonial times by landowners, priests, and officials. The sanguinary struggles between rival military leaders had taken a heavy toll in life and property. Many were beginning to feel that a monarchy under a foreign prince might be better than continued anarchy, and García Moreno himself made unsuccessful efforts to make Ecuador a protectorate of France during the civil war in 1859.[1]

The country was more peaceful under García Moreno's heavyhanded dictatorship. The new ruler was not a professional soldier but a lawyer. Since his father was a loyal Spaniard, the family property had been confiscated during the revolution, and García Moreno himself grew up in poverty. A charitable friar took charge of his education, and his intellectual ability, combined with utter fearlessness and indefatigable energy, soon made him one of the leaders of the younger generation. He be-

[1] Howe, *García Moreno's Efforts to Unite Ecuador and France, Hispanic American Historical Review*, Vol. 16, p. 257.

came active in politics at an early age, first as a "nationalist" against Flores and later as a conservative against Urbina and Robles. For a time, as a political exile, he studied in France. He now came into power with Flores' support, but the old *caudillo* had little influence in his administration. The new President centered all authority in his own hands. Opponents and even peaceful critics were shot or imprisoned without regard to legal forms, and counterrevolutionary movements under Urbina and other liberals were suppressed with ferocious energy. The Congress was reduced to obedience when several of its more independent members were sent into exile, and the press was permitted no freedom.

García Moreno dominated Ecuadorean politics for 15 years. Since the constitution forbade re-election, he permitted Gerónimo Carrión, the liberal candidate, to become President in 1865 but dictated the appointment of his Cabinet and made him little more than a figurehead. In 1867, when Carrión allowed Congress to get out of hand, García Moreno demanded his resignation and installed another liberal, Javier Espinosa, in his place. As the election of 1869 approached, and several presidential candidates appeared, Espinosa attempted to remain neutral and was promptly ousted by the army. A few months later García Moreno again became President under a new constitution which gave him a six-year term and greatly increased his authority.

The clergy gave García Moreno the same sort of support that they had given the Spanish authorities in colonial times. Despite the infiltration of foreign ideas since independence, the Church still had much influence with the masses of the people, and even the liberals had not dared to abrogate the constitutional provision against the public exercise of any but the Catholic religion. Monasteries and other pious foundations owned great amounts of land and had great economic power. García Moreno was himself extremely devout, at least in outward practice, and he systematically built up the Church's influence as a means of maintaining his own power. A concordat promulgated in 1863 gave the ecclesiastical authorities control over the publication and importation of books and supervision of all education. At the same time, the President was relentless, though largely unsuccessful, in his effort to eradicate the abuses that had grown up among the native clergy since the separation from Spain.

In many respects, García Moreno was a statesman of vision and constructive ability, honest in his management of public funds, and an indefatigable worker. He gave much attention to the improvement and beautification of the cities of the Republic and also to popular education, entrusting to the Jesuits the direction of the secondary schools and bringing Christian Brothers from France to take charge of primary instruction. The number of children in school increased threefold, and the quality of the teaching, theretofore grievously neglected, was improved. Equally

important, perhaps, was the building of a cart road from Quito to Guayaquil, which revolutionized transportation between the coast and the interior.

POLITICAL EVENTS, 1875–1895

García Moreno was assassinated in 1875 by a group of political conspirators. His War Minister, who had perhaps been involved in the plot
against him, seized control but was soon overthrown by a popular uprising in Quito, and Antonio Borrero, a liberal with many friends among
the conservatives, became President after the first really free election
in the country's history. Borrero attempted to follow a conciliatory policy,
but the liberals turned against him when he refused to call a convention
to change the reactionary constitution that García Moreno had imposed.
The military group that had supported Urbina overthrew him in 1876, and
General José Ignacio de Veintemilla became President.

Veintemilla, supported by a well-paid and well-equipped army, remained in power for seven years. Unusual prosperity, the effect of high
prices for cacao and other products, made his position stronger, but many
of the civilian political leaders resented the return of military rule and
the corruption that accompanied it. In 1883, when the President attempted
to stay in office after his term expired, both the liberals and the conservatives revolted. The army stood by Veintemilla, and there were six
months of fighting before the government was overthrown. There was
another, shorter, civil war when a Constituent Assembly elected an extreme conservative as President and the liberals again took up arms; but
the revolt was suppressed, and many of its leaders were shot.

José María Plácido Caamaño, the new President, attempted to return
to the authoritarian methods of García Moreno and to restore the close
alliance between State and Church. His reactionary policy was too much
for many members of his own party, and the "progressives," as the more
moderate conservatives called themselves, were able to obtain control of
the government in the election of 1888, with Antonio Flores, the son of
the founder of the Republic, as their candidate. Flores was a well-educated
man who had lived much abroad. The four years of his administration
were peaceful, and he was able to permit a greater freedom of the press
and of political activity than had been customary in Ecuador and to devote
a part of the government's resources to public works. Luis Cordero, another progressive who became President in 1892, was less able and less
popular. He was forced out of office by a noisy scandal in 1895 when
Ecuadorean officials were involved in the improper transfer of the warship *Esmeralda* from the Chilean to the Ecuadorean flag and then to Japan,
which was at war with China. The weak interim government that followed
was unable to suppress a revolution started by the liberals, and after some

months of fighting the insurgents, led by General Eloy Alfaro, took control.

ALFARO AND HIS SUCCESSORS, 1895–1920

Alfaro, who was to be the chief figure in the Republic's politics during the next 17 years, had been active as a conspirator and revolutionist since García Moreno's first administration. For some time, he had been in exile at Panama where he built up a fortune in private business. A close friend of the great Ecuadorean liberal thinker Juan Montalvo, he had a more definite political philosophy than many of the earlier leaders, to whom "liberalism" had been little more than a convenient party label, and he headed a wing of his party that called themselves "liberal radicals." His anticlerical views made him especially objectionable in the eyes of the conservatives, who attempted a counterrevolution, with aid from Colombia, soon after he took control. Alfaro was nevertheless able to avoid an acute conflict with the Church during his first term as President (1897–1901), even though the Law of Patronage, enacted in 1899, gave the civil authorities a large measure of control over the Church.

A series of anticlerical measures, including laws authorizing the practice of other cults, permitting civil marriage and divorce, and expropriating much church property, were enacted under Alfaro's successor, General Leonidas Plaza (1901–1905), and a new constitution, with no provision making Catholicism the state religion, was adopted in 1906. By this time Alfaro was again in power, for he forcibly ejected Plaza's successor, Lizardo García, within a few months after the latter took office. His second term was much more troubled than his first, for he was compelled to suppress a number of conspiracies and revolts, and a revival of the boundary dispute threatened for a time to bring on war with Peru. It was nevertheless possible to complete the railroad from Guayaquil to Quito, upon which Alfaro had concentrated much of his energy during his first term. The new line was of the greatest value not only from an economic but from a political standpoint, but the bonds issued to finance it soon went into default, with unfortunate effects upon the country's credit.

Emilio Estrada, "elected, as usual, by the soldiers and public employes,"[2] succeeded to the presidency in 1911. Alfaro attempted at the last minute to prevent the new Chief Executive from taking office, because of the latter's ill health; but he had by this time many enemies even in his own party, and a revolt of the troops and populace at Quito sent him into exile. When Estrada died suddenly four months later, Alfaro made a new bid for power but was captured by government troops led by his old associate General Plaza. In January, 1912, the ex-President was dragged from his prison at Quito and killed by a mob in the streets. Many of the

[2] Reyes, *Historia de la República del Ecuador,* p. 272.

other liberal leaders were massacred at the same time, and a prominent presidential candidate, Julio Andrada, was murdered soon afterward.

General Plaza, who had been a close friend of Alfaro but had later become the head of a rival wing of the liberal party, became President. He was forced to suppress an uprising by Alfaro's former partisans and had to contend with the temporary dislocation of trade and finance that came with the outbreak of the European war, but he was able to serve out his term. Under his successor, Alfredo Baquerizo Moreno (1916–1920), both economic and political conditions improved. The question of Church and State had by this time lost much of its importance as a political issue, and the government made no effort to influence the selection of a new archbishop when the venerable González Suárez died in 1917.[3]

The most important event of Baquerizo's administration was the sanitation of Guayaquil. The presence of endemic yellow fever and the danger from other tropical diseases had long made shipmasters reluctant to dock at this city, which was the Republic's chief port, and it was clear that a continuance of these conditions would deprive Ecuador of many of the benefits anticipated from the opening of the Panama Canal. The work of sanitation, which included especially the eradication of yellow fever, was carried out with the help of the Rockefeller Foundation.

PARTY STRIFE, 1920–1948

José Luis Tamayo, President from 1920 to 1924, was a liberal, like his predecessors, but he appointed many conservatives to positions in the administration. He was opposed, on the other hand, by a growing element in his own party which believed that the banks, and especially the Banco Comercial y Agrícola of Guayaquil, were exercising an undue influence in the country's politics in order to maintain their privilege of issuing irredeemable paper money. The depreciation of the currency and the resultant increase in the cost of living caused much hardship. In 1922–1923 there were riots at Guayaquil and in the interior, with many deaths. Popular discontent increased as time went on, and in 1925, when the next President, Dr. Gonzalo Córdoba, was forced to withdraw because of illness, the army seized power and there was a period of confusion and weak government by *juntas* before Dr. Isidro Ayora became provisional President, with virtually dictatorial powers, in 1926.

The new administration restored order and invited a mission headed by Professor Kemmerer of Princeton University to draw up plans for a central bank and for the stabilization of the currency. Ayora delayed the establishment of constitutional government until these and other reforms were carried out. In 1928, he called a Constituent Assembly which elected him President and framed a new constitution. Soon afterward, however,

[3] *Ibid.*, p. 279.

the prosperity that had made the administration popular disappeared with the advent of the depression. The program of financial reform broke down, and increasing discontent forced Ayora to resign, after a popular demonstration against him, in 1931.

During the next four years, governments rose and fell with kaleidoscopic rapidity. There was a free election in 1931 in which the conservatives' candidate, Neptalí Bonifaz, faced several liberal rivals. Bonifaz won, partly apparently with the votes of the women, who had been enfranchised by the constitution of 1928 and who were more responsive to the influence of the clergy than their husbands. When the liberals in Congress found excuses for disqualifying him, his supporters revolted but were defeated after four days of fighting at Quito in which 1,000 persons died.[4] The liberals continued to control the administration, but one President after another was forced out by quarrels with Congress and insubordination in the army.

Finally, in 1935, when it seemed likely that the conservatives would win an approaching presidential election, the Minister of Government, who was temporarily in power, asked the army to set up a dictatorship. Federico Páez, whom the army selected, struggled for two years against increasing opposition—working first with the radical groups, including the new socialist party, and then turning to more conservative elements—before he was ejected by his own Minister of War, Alberto Enríquez. The latter, after promulgating a series of radical measures that increased tension between the political parties and alarmed foreign business interests, was forced to resign in 1938, and three provisional administrations held office for short periods before Carlos Arroyo del Rio, a "liberal radical," was elected constitutional President in 1940.

A few months later a flare-up of the boundary dispute with Peru developed into a real though undeclared war. The United States, Argentina, and Brazil offered their mediation, but it was some months before they were successful in establishing a neutral zone that stopped the fighting. While the Foreign Ministers of the American republics were meeting at Rio de Janeiro early in 1942 to consider the situation created by Japan's attack on the United States, Ecuador and Peru were persuaded to agree on a definite boundary. Though the treaty met with violent opposition in Ecuador, Arroyo del Rio weathered the storm and co-operated effectively with the United States in the war. Bases in the Galápagos Islands and at Salinas on the mainland did much to facilitate the defense of the Panama Canal. In return, Ecuador received lend-lease and loans from the Export-Import Bank, and a development corporation established with the help of the United States carried on a program of public health work and road building and did much for the rehabilitation of the coastal province of El Oro, which had been devastated by Peruvian troops.

[4] Reyes, *Breve Historia General del Ecuador*, Vol. II, p. 430.

In May, 1944, as the time for a new presidential election approached, a revolt in Guayaquil and a general strike in Quito forced Arroyo del Rio to resign. A *junta* representing all of the opposition parties, from the conservatives to the communists, took control, and José María Velasco Ibarra was proclaimed President. Velasco Ibarra had been considered a left-wing radical; but he had disagreements with the communists and socialists, and after 1945 he worked chiefly with the conservatives. In August, 1947, he was removed by the army in a bloodless *coup* and a series of temporary presidents held office for short periods.

The activities of radical groups like the socialists and communists and the continual strife between the various factions that arose after the breakup of the old liberal party helped to account for the political disorders of the period after the First World War, but the underlying cause was probably dissatisfaction with economic and social conditions. The Republic had but a small share in the wealth that increasing foreign commerce brought to other South American countries, and it was especially unfortunate in the vicissitudes that befell its one important export crop, cacao. Ecuador was for many years the chief source of the world's supply of chocolate, and a steady increase in the output of her plantations from the time of García Moreno until 1916 brought the country a modest prosperity which was reflected in the relative stability of the government during much of the period. After 1916, the *monilia* and witches'-broom diseases wrought havoc with the crop, and exports were less than half the amount shipped abroad during the First World War. The other products of the coast—tagua nuts (for making buttons) and Panama hats, the best of which come from Ecuador—were relatively less important, and the highland region supplied little for export.

PROGRESS TOWARD
DEMOCRATIC GOVERNMENT

After 1948 the government became more stable, and there was a series of orderly elections in which substantial numbers of voters participated. In the first of these, in June, 1948, Galo Plaza Lasso, supported by a coalition of the liberal parties, won by a narrow margin. The new President was a graduate of Cornell who had distinguished himself as Ambassador in Washington during the Second World War. Though he was compelled to suppress a revolt in 1950, his administration was relatively peaceful, and he was the first Chief Executive in a quarter-century to serve a full term.

Plaza's successor, ex-President Velasco Ibarra, was also in office for four years. In the 1956 election, there were four candidates, three of them representing various liberal factions. The conservative, Camilo Ponce Enríquez, won, though he obtained less than a third of the popular votes. Ecuador has been more prosperous in recent years. The country has become the world's greatest exporter of bananas, and coffee is also shipped abroad in large amounts. There has been less development of industry, but on the other hand the country has to a great extent avoided the inflation that accompanied efforts to promote rapid industrialization in some of the countries farther south.

The lack of adequate means of transportation between the coast and the Sierra is still an economic and political handicap and has helped to perpetuate the deep-seated jealousy between the two regions. It is not an accident that so many of the country's revolutions have started in Guayaquil, the coastal metropolis. The building of the railroad between that city and Quito and, more recently, the construction of automobile roads have improved matters to some extent, but the highlands of the interior are still one of the most isolated inhabited portions of South America.

Half of the Republic's 3,900,000 people are Indians, most of whom work on the properties of the white upper class. The *huasipungo* in the highlands is still bound to the soil, by custom if not by law, and the number of laborers attached to a *hacienda* is one of the most important elements in its market value. In 1857, when Indian tributes were abolished, the civil code legalized a system of *concertaje*, or debt-slavery, which persisted in practice even after imprisonment for debt was legally abolished in 1918 and does not seem to have disappeared entirely today. Standards of living are still low. The condition of the Indians is still one of Ecuador's major unsolved problems.

At an election in June, 1960, ex-President Velasco Ibarra defeated several other candidates for the presidency for the term 1960-1964.

PART V

THE NORTH COAST

COLOMBIA AND VENEZUELA are neither predominantly Indian countries like the Central Andean republics nor predominantly European like Argentina and Uruguay. The descendants of the Chibchas and other tribes that lived in the northern part of South America before the Conquest have for the most part given up their native languages and cultures. They still form a substantial fraction of the population, and the non-European element was increased after the Conquest by a considerable importation of African slaves; but both Indians and Negroes have been assimilated into the Spanish-speaking community. People of Spanish descent still own much of the land and direct public affairs, but other groups are by no means excluded from political life. As ardent members of the traditional parties in Colombia or as followers of local *caudillos* in Venezuela, they took an active part in the civil wars that retarded progress in both countries in the nineteenth century and have participated still more actively in the hardly less-violent conflicts of recent years.

The political development of the two countries has been quite different. In Colombia, to a greater extent than in most Latin American countries, political strife has centered around ideas rather than personalities, and conflicts between opposing schools of thought as to forms of government, and more especially as to the relations between Church and State, have been the real cause rather than merely the pretext for civil war. This concern with ideas seems to be one expression of an intense individualism which has affected political institutions in other ways, making for an intolerance of any curb on freedom of expression or political action, and at the same time frequently impairing party cohesion and discipline. It helps to explain why dictatorships of the ordinary Latin American type have seldom flourished in Colombia. In Venezuela, on the other hand, *personalismo* has been the chief factor in political life, and a series of dictators have ruled the country during most of the period since independence. This divergence between two neighboring countries which are otherwise similar in so many ways seems to stem from differences in the character of the people, arising partly, perhaps, from differences in the character of the Spanish immigration during the colonial period.

CHAPTER 15

Colombia

GEOGRAPHICAL PROBLEMS

COLOMBIA'S DEVELOPMENT, like Bolivia's and Ecuador's, has been influenced by isolation imposed by geography. Nearly all of the principal settlements except the ancient coast towns of Cartagena and Santa Marta are in the inaccessible plateaus and valleys of the Andean highlands. The Andes, at their northern end, form three great ranges, one along the west coast, another between the deep valleys of the Cauca and the Magdalena Rivers, and the third east of the Magdalena, which extends along the north coast into Venezuela. There are two chief centers of population: in the west in the central range and the rich Cauca Valley, and in the east on the broad plateau of Bogotá. The mountains and the jungles of the lowlands have made it difficult to build roads and railroads, and even today the lack of adequate means of transportation is one of the Republic's chief problems.

In the first years of independence, communication was exceedingly difficult between the two chief centers of population, and between these centers and the coast. As late as 1842 there was not even a mule train from the Cauca Valley to Bogotá; travelers from the west regularly went over the Quindío pass in the central range on the backs of men, a nine days' trip on a dangerous footpath, and then climbed four days more on horseback from the hot and unhealthful Magdalena Valley to Bogotá, 8,563 feet above sea level. Between the interior and the ports on the north coast, through which passed such commerce as the country had with Europe and North America, all traffic was by small boats on the Magdalena River. The rapidity of the voyage depended—as it does now—on the depth of the water, which changed from day to day, and on the boatmen's luck in avoiding snags and sandbanks. Land travel through the swamps and forests of the Valley was impossible. When General William Henry Harrison went to Colombia as American Minister in 1828 he considered himself fortunate in completing in six weeks the canoe trip from the coast to Honda, where travelers obtained horses for the ascent to Bogotá.[1] Under such conditions there could be little contact with the outside world, and within the Republic the spirit of *localismo* was unusually intense.

GREAT COLOMBIA

At the beginning of the nineteenth century New Granada proper probably had somewhat more than 1,000,000 people. Except on the coast and in the Cauca Valley, where there were many Negro slaves, the majority were of Indian blood, but the descendants of the Chibchas and other aboriginal tribes had for the most part adopted the language and religion of their conquerors and did not form a separate community as in Peru or Mexico. In the cities, the principal families were of Spanish descent, and it was they who dominated the country economically and politically.

We saw in Chapter 6 how local jealousies helped to defeat the first movement for independence in New Granada between 1810 and 1816. During the reign of terror after the reconquest, the small bands of patriots who escaped to the *llanos* of the interior co-operated with Bolívar's Venezuelan troops in the guerrilla warfare that kept the movement for independence alive during the next three years. When the Liberator crossed the Andes and won the decisive victory of Boyacá in 1819, New Granada was again free, and Bolívar was naturally elected to the presidency when the Republic of Colombia was created by the Congress of Angostura in the same year. The new state, which historians have called Great Colombia, was to include not only New Granada and Venezuela but also the province of Quito, which was freed from Spanish control three years later. Its government was given a more definite organization by a Constituent Assembly that met at Cúcuta in 1821, and Bolívar was re-elected, with Francisco de Paula Santander as Vice-President. During the next five years, the Vice-President administered the government at Bogotá while Bolívar was winning the war for independence in Quito and Peru.

Santander had entered the patriot army as a young man at the beginning of the revolution and had been the leader of the force from New Granada that had joined Bolívar in the *llanos* in the dark days after 1816. Though an able and at times a cruel soldier, he was a statesman by temperament, liberal in his views, hard working, and personally honest. Under his leadership, the country had a more truly republican government than any of its South American neighbors, with free elections and a free press and a Congress that often opposed the Executive's proposals. Factional strife was kept within bounds by the President's moderation in dealing with controversial questions, such as the relationship between Church and State. The public administration and the tax system were reorganized. Santander

[1] Scruggs, *The Colombian and Venezuelan Republics*, p. 45.

had ambitious plans for economic development and for the advancement of education, but it was impossible to accomplish very much while the war in Peru took so much money and manpower. The government was in fact always in financial difficulties, except for a short time while it was spending the proceeds of a large loan contracted in London.

Santander's government was less popular in Venezuela and Ecuador than in New Granada. The people of the outlying provinces disliked being ruled from Bogotá and felt that they had little part in the administration. The Congress was largely dominated by *granadinos* because the expense and hardships of the journey to the Capital often discouraged other deputies from attending its sessions.[2] The separatist spirit and opposition to Santander personally were especially evident in Venezuela, and they found expression in 1825 when Páez, who was the military Commander at Caracas, joined with other dissatisfied leaders in urging Bolívar to supplant the government at Bogotá by a personal dictatorship. The Liberator refused to consider this proposal, and in 1826, when the Congress at Bogotá ordered Páez to appear before it to answer charges of arbitrary conduct in recruiting troops, the *llanero* leader headed a rebellion. Peace was restored when Bolívar returned from Peru in response to Santander's urgent summons; but Páez retained his position, and the prestige of the central government suffered.

Meanwhile, news of Bolívar's plans for the perpetuation of his control over Bolivia and Peru under the *constitución vitalicia* reached Bogotá, and a violent conflict of opinion arose between advocates and opponents of a similar arrangement for Colombia. Bolívar himself continued ostensibly to support the constitution of Cúcuta; but several municipalities were encouraged by his friends to demand the establishment of a life-presidency, and there was soon a definite break between the Liberator and Santander, who headed the party opposing the scheme. Both the President and the Vice-President had been re-elected in 1826, and Bolívar personally took over the executive power in 1827.

The next three years were the tragic period of the Liberator's career. His popularity declined, and a convention which met at Ocaña in 1828 to attempt to devise a more workable constitution than that of 1821 broke up because a majority of the delegates opposed his proposal for a strong centralized government with a president elected for an eight-year term. Bolívar then suspended the constitution of 1821 and assumed dictatorial power in an effort to curb the disorders that were breaking out in many of the provinces. On September 25, 1828, he barely escaped being assassinated in his house by a well-organized group of conspirators, and 14 participants in the plot were executed. The war with Peru in 1828–1829, and revolts in Popayán and Medellín made the situation worse. So discouraging did the outlook become that the Council

[2] Bushnell, *The Santander Regime in Gran Colombia*, pp. 51–52.

of Ministers endeavored in 1829 to obtain the support of the English and French governments for a plan by which Bolívar would rule Colombia in his lifetime but would be succeeded by a European prince. Nothing came of this proposal which was unpopular in Colombia and was apparently opposed by Bolívar himself.

When Bolívar suspended the constitution of Cúcuta in 1828, he issued a call for a new Constituent Assembly. Before this met in January, 1830, Páez placed himself at the head of a separatist movement in Venezuela, and his example was followed by Juan José Flores whom Bolívar had left in command of the troops at Quito. Venezuela and Ecuador thus became independent republics. At Bogotá Bolívar refused to continue in office, and the Assembly elected Joaquín Mosquera as President. It voted an expression of gratitude to Bolívar and granted him a life pension of $30,000 annually.

The Liberator, ill and discouraged, left Bogotá in May, 1830, intending to go to Europe. At Cartagena he received the sad news of the murder of General Sucre who had been his most faithful and perhaps his ablest lieutenant. Before he could sail from the coast his illness became worse, and on December 17, 1830, he died at the *quinta* of San Pedro Alejandrino near Santa Marta.

THE ADMINISTRATIONS OF
SANTANDER AND MÁRQUEZ

A few months earlier a movement that had as its ostensible purpose the restoration of Bolívar's authority had overthrown the government at Bogotá. General Rafael Urdaneta assumed control with the support of the local garrison; but revolts throughout the country ousted this purely military regime, and a new Congress was elected. In February, 1832, a constitution for "the Republic of New Granada" was adopted, and in the following month Santander, who had been in exile since 1828, was elected to the presidency.

For a time things went well. Despite the dissatisfaction of many of Bolívar's former followers, the new government was popular, and the President displayed the same administrative ability that marked his first term. The government's financial difficulties were somewhat relieved by economies and good management, and the school system was improved. There was no serious disturbance when a new President was elected in 1837. Santander did not attempt to impose a candidate, and when none received a majority of the popular vote, the Congress chose Dr. José Ignacio de Márquez, though he had been supported by political groups unfriendly to the outgoing administration. The country remained tranquil, except for two unimportant military mutinies, through the first two years of the new President's term, for the opposition, led by Santander until his death in

1840, confined itself to constitutional methods. During this period, Márquez concluded an agreement with Venezuela and Ecuador for the apportionment of the old Colombian foreign debt, now increased by many years' unpaid interest, and endeavored to re-establish the country's credit by a partial resumption of payments.

By this time the political leaders were beginning to form the two political parties that have ever since divided the Colombian people. Santander and his followers were "liberals," while the group that supported Márquez, which included many of Bolívar's friends, was the nucleus of the conservative party. Rivalry between the two factions gradually became more bitter, and the difficulty of maintaining order was increased by the strong spirit of *localismo* inevitable in a country where communication between the Capital and the outlying provinces was so difficult. The first revolt occurred in July, 1839, in the old royalist stronghold of Pasto, where the populace objected to the government's closing four almost-deserted monasteries. Soon after this was suppressed, General José María Obando, who had been the unsuccessful candidate in the election of 1837, led another uprising near Popayán. He too was defeated, but in the meantime several local *caudillos* in other sections started revolts on their own account. While the army was dealing with these, revolutionists attacked Bogotá but were repulsed by the determined resistance of the townspeople. Fighting continued for two years, with results generally favorable to the government, before peace was restored through the mediation of the British Chargé d'Affaires. The war had caused much destruction of crops and livestock and had cost many thousands of lives.

CONSERVATIVES AND LIBERALS, 1842–1857

After the civil war of 1840–1842 the dominant political group began to develop the characteristic policies of the conservative party. Under the leadership of General Pedro Alcántara Herrán, who was elected President in 1841 while he was still leading the army in the field, there was a reaction from the liberal political philosophy that had prevailed in the time of Santander. A new constitution adopted in 1843 strengthened the authority of the central government at the expense of individual and local liberties, and the freedom of the press was restricted. Closer relations were established with the Church. The Jesuits, excluded from the country since the royal edict of 1767, were invited to return, and the clergy were given a larger part in the educational system. In the schools, such studies as Roman law and the humanities were substituted for subjects like constitutional law and parliamentary procedure, which were considered dangerous.[3]

Herrán's successor was General Tomás Cipriano de Mosquera, who was the candidate of the more extreme conservatives, including the army

[3] Arboleda, *Historia Contemporánea de Colombia*, Vol. II, p. 93.

and the Church. During Mosquera's term (1845–1849) the liberal party began to recover from the effects of its defeat in 1842, and there was much political agitation in Congress and in the press. The Jesuits especially were the target for violent partisan attacks. The hopes of the opposition were raised by the overthrow of the conservative regimes in Ecuador and Venezuela and also by a split which developed in the government party at home as the time for new elections approached. As in Chile and Peru, public opinion was stirred by the French revolution of 1848, and many of the younger generation enthusiastically espoused European radical ideas. In the presidential election of 1849, the liberal candidate General José Hilario López received a substantial plurality, though not a majority, and the final choice, as usual, fell to Congress. In that body there was a small conservative majority, but popular demonstrations in and around the church where Congress met so intimidated its members that López was elected after four ballots. The situation was well described by the President of the Chamber, who wrote on his ballot: "I vote for General José Hilario López so that the deputies may not be assassinated."

The new regime embarked on a series of radical reforms. It expelled the Jesuits and adopted other anticlerical measures, and when the ecclesiastical authorities protested, it exiled the Archbishop and two bishops. In 1851 it abolished slavery, with compensation to the owners. The Congress of Cúcuta had provided that children born in bondage should be free at the age of eighteen, but there were still some 26,000 slaves in the country at the time of the census of 1843. The government also abolished the death penalty for political offenses and established freedom of the press.

The government's program intensified the antagonism between the two parties, and the conservatives revolted in several places in 1851. They were defeated, but violent political agitation continued. Young people in both parties, aroused to a new interest in public affairs by the events of 1848–1849, had organized political societies which often engaged in sanguinary brawls or small uprisings and sometimes degenerated into criminal gangs that made life and property unsafe in large sections of the country. The worst of these were liberal clubs, whose members took advantage of the government's unwillingness to curb its own partisans. There was, however, a growing division within the dominant party. The *gólgotas*, the more aristocratic but at the same time the more radical wing, controlled Congress, while the President was supported by the *democráticos*, who had many followers among the artisan class. Each faction had its own clubs, and there were frequent clashes between them. When López objected to the provisions for freedom of religion and the press and for universal secret suffrage which the Congress insisted on incorporating in the new constitution of 1853, there was an open break. This led to a bitter contest in the presidential election of the same year, even though the conservatives refrained from voting.

The government's candidate, the veteran *caudillo* José María Obando, was elected, with the support of the army and the *democráticos*. The *gólgotas* continued to control Congress, and strife between the two groups, intensified by class hatred, soon made the new President's position intolerable. In April, 1854, the troops at Bogotá seized control and offered to make him dictator; but he declined, and a military government was set up under General Melo. This in turn was overthrown, after a short but bloody struggle, by a coalition of prominent men in both parties, inspired by the repugnance to dictatorship that has characterized the Colombians even in the most difficult periods of their history. A bipartisan government was established under Manuel María Mallarino to serve the remainder of Obando's term, and in 1857 the conservative leader Mariano Ospina, who had received 96,000 votes in the popular election as against 82,000 for his liberal opponent and 32,000 for General Mosquera, became President.

THE PERIOD OF FEDERALISM

Much of the disorder from which Colombia had suffered since 1848 had been caused by local jealousies and by the central government's inability to maintain contact with the outlying provinces. Many leaders in both parties had consequently begun to look on "federalism," an increase in local autonomy, as a solution for the country's political ills. A long step in this direction had been taken in the constitution of 1853 which gave each of the 35 provinces the right to elect its own governor and control its local affairs. Subsequent laws gradually grouped the provinces into states with greater powers of self-rule, and a new constitution adopted in 1858 provided for still further decentralization. Ospina found himself powerless to suppress the continual revolts within individual states or the not-infrequent wars between states, and his ineffectual attempts to assert the federal government's authority merely made matters worse. At the same time, the general removal of liberal officeholders and the return of the Jesuits intensified partisan bitterness.

Local revolutions, some liberal and some conservative, directed against the party that happened to be in power in each state, were going on in many parts of the country in 1859, and in 1860 a country-wide civil war began. Ex-President Mosquera, now Governor of the state of Cauca, quarreled with the conservatives and joined forces with the liberals under General Obando, and the struggle continued until the end of 1862. Mosquera became the leader of the revolution after Obando's death. His army was finally victorious, and among his first acts when he entered Bogotá were a series of harsh measures against the Church which showed, and perhaps were intended to show, how completely he had abandoned his former political associates.

Mosquera had long been known as a brilliant but erratic soldier, unscrupulous, ambitious, and often cruel. Many of the other leaders of the revolution distrusted him, and their fear that he might attempt to remain in power indefinitely colored all of the proceedings of the Constituent Assembly which met at Río Negro in 1863. It was not possible to prevent his election to the presidency; but his term was made to expire in the following year, and it was provided that future presidents should be chosen for two-year periods and should not be eligible for immediate re-election. The desire to curb his authority, as well as the still-strong sentiment for federalism, was evident in provisions that still further restricted the powers of the national executive and increased those of the states. The delegates sought to preclude the possibility of a reaction against the federal system by providing that amendments might be adopted only by unanimous vote of the states in the national Senate.

Mosquera, with his personal following and his prestige in the army, continued to be powerful and was again elected to the presidency in 1866. In the following year, after a violent quarrel with Congress, he attempted to establish a dictatorship but was overthrown and sent into exile. Thereafter the control of the government was in the hands of the former *gólgotas*, who now called themselves "radicals."

The liberal party remained in power for 20 years after 1863 under the Río Negro constitution. Throughout this time the central government had little prestige or effective authority, and it would serve no purpose to enumerate the presidents who were either chosen legally for the short two-year term or installed provisionally for still shorter periods after successful revolutions. There was continual disorder and at times virtual anarchy. Civil wars on a national scale were infrequent because subversive movements generally had as their purpose the control of individual states, but more than 40 local armed conflicts are said to have occurred during the two decades.[4]

Curiously enough, it was during this same period, when political conditions were at their worst, that Colombia became one of the chief intellectual centers of South America. Literary pursuits had received little attention during the earlier years of the Republic, but there had been a revival of interest about 1843. Poets like Gregorio Gutiérrez González (1826–1872), José Eusebio Caro (1817–1853), José Joaquín Ortiz (1814–1892), and Julio Arboleda (1817–1862) helped to justify the *Bogotanos'* description of their city as "the Athens of America." Jorge Isaacs (1837–1895), the author of "María," was a famous novelist as well as a poet, and Rufino José Cuervo (1844–1911), who passed most of his life in Paris, was one of the greatest of Spanish philologists.

RAFAEL NÚÑEZ

The division within the liberal party continued, and in 1880 the so-called independents wrested control from the radicals who had dom-

[4] Henao y Arrubla, *Historia de Colombia*, 5th ed., p. 674.

inated the administration since 1866. The independents' leader, Rafael Núñez, was elected President for the term 1880–1882 and was again elected in 1884. In that year he was supported not only by the independents but by the conservatives, and it was the latter who saved the government from defeat when the radicals rose against it in 1885. The President, who had at first attempted to govern with a Cabinet representing all political groups, was compelled thenceforth to rely on his new allies for support, and the suppression of the revolt marked the beginning of a long period of conservative supremacy.

Núñez was a poet and a writer on public affairs as well as a statesman. He believed that the abandonment of the unsuccessful experiment in federalism and the establishment of a strong centralized government were indispensable if Colombia was to achieve the economic progress which several of the more stable South American countries were by this time enjoying. His political ideas were embodied in the new constitution of 1886, which was drawn up by a "National Council of Delegates" after the Río Negro code had arbitrarily been set aside. The states became departments under governors appointed and removed by the president, and their separate codes of laws were replaced by national codes. The president was elected for six years instead of two and was given greatly increased powers. The new government's policies were equally reactionary. The Church, which Núñez looked to as a powerful factor in maintaining order, was given control over the national school system. Elections were far from free, and the liberty of the press was restricted.

Though Núñez was nominally President until his death in 1894, he actually discharged the duties of the office only for a few brief periods. The rest of the time he lived in Cartagena, wielding a controlling influence in political affairs but leaving the work of administration to others. Carlos Holguín, a militant conservative, was the active head of the government from 1888 until 1892. He was succeeded by Miguel Caro, who was elected Vice-President in 1892 and became President after Núñez died.

CIVIL WAR AND TERRITORIAL DISMEMBERMENT, 1895–1903

The disappearance of the leader whose prestige had been its chief support was a blow to the conservative regime. Before the election of 1892, rivalries between the "historic conservatives" and the "nationalists," among whom were the former independent liberals, had badly split the dominant party. Núñez' influence had procured a victory for the nationalists, but the opposition liberals were encouraged to a new activity by the divisions among their opponents. The fear that the liberals would resort to arms led the government to close their newspapers and to exile or imprison many of their leaders. When they did revolt early in 1895 they were rapidly defeated by government forces under General Rafael Reyes, but the end of the war did not restore tranquility.

An agreement between the two conservative factions made possible the election of Manuel Sanclemente and José Manuel Marroquín as President and Vice-President in 1898. Sanclemente, who was an old man in bad health, at first permitted Marroquín to assume the presidency. The new Chief Executive made a real effort to diminish political tension and placate the opposition. "The evils which threaten Colombia, and which already afflict her," he said in his inaugural address, "are not much less serious than the consequences of a foreign invasion." [5] When he proposed a number of concrete reforms, including an improvement in electoral methods and greater freedom for the press, the nationalists opposed them and prevailed upon Sanclemente to assume power himself. This revived the feud within the party and weakened the administration, which further lost prestige when Sanclemente's illness compelled him to leave Bogotá for a lower altitude.

The liberals seized the opportunity to revolt, and in 1899 the Republic was plunged into the longest and most sanguinary civil war in its history. After July, 1900, when the *históricos* removed Sanclemente by a *coup d'état* and installed Marroquín as President, the government gradually got the upper hand, but fighting continued throughout the country until 1902. It has been asserted that 100,000 men were killed in battle, to say nothing of the loss of life from other causes. [6] When the revolutionists finally signed treaties of peace, commerce and industry were paralyzed, and the government was practically bankrupt. The paper dollar, already depreciated before the war, was worth one cent in gold.

A year later Colombia suffered another calamity. The secession of Panama, to be discussed in more detail in Chapter 20, was not only a material loss but a blow to the national pride. It intensified the revulsion inspired by the terrific consequences of the recent internal conflict because thinking people realized that the recurrent civil wars, in which the Isthmus had always been a battleground, had created the conditions which made foreign intervention there possible.

THE CONSERVATIVE ERA, 1904–1930

The loss of Panama, in fact, marked a turning point in the Republic's history, the beginning of a long era of internal peace. As in other Latin American countries, the change was partly the result of economic development. The production of coffee, which had been the principal export since the 1880's, was increasing rapidly. Since coffee was grown

[5] *Ibid.*, p. 754.
[6] *Ibid.*, p. 760.

chiefly on small farms, rather than on large plantations as in Brazil, the industry was creating a substantial class of prosperous peasant proprietors who had everything to gain by the maintenance of peace. Other classes too were becoming more dependent on foreign trade and felt the effects of civil war more than in the days when each region was relatively self-sufficient. There was a growing realization that the country was far behind many of its neighbors in commerce and transportation and in the development of its resources, and that there could be little improvement in these respects until foreign capital should be attracted by more stable political conditions.

Party rivalries by no means disappeared, but their bitterness was somewhat alleviated by new political practices. General Rafael Reyes, who became President in 1904, had been out of the country during the recent war and had fewer enemies in the defeated party than most of his associates. He was thus in a position to attempt a policy of conciliation, and one of his first acts was to name two prominent liberals to his Cabinet. When a number of conservative senators and deputies objected to these appointments, he dissolved Congress and replaced it by a more amenable "National Assembly" chosen by the departmental councils. This extra-legal body proceeded to adopt several important amendments to the constitution, among them a provision for proportional representation in Congress and other elective bodies which assured the liberals an opportunity to share in the task of government. The minority was thus encouraged to contest elections instead of devoting its energies to preparing for revolt, and the electoral machinery, though still defective, was gradually improved as the public began to show more interest in exercising its right to vote.

Under Reyes' leadership, the country recovered rapidly from the effects of the war. New roads and railways were built, especially in the highlands and between the plateau of Bogotá and the Magdalena River, and coffee production increased. The currency was reorganized and stabilized. An agreement for the resumption of service on the foreign debt restored the nation's credit and made it possible to obtain loans for public works. The new regime was more autocratic than any that Colombia had had in modern times, but it was for some years accepted with comparatively little opposition by a people weary of disorder and civil strife.

Opposition increased, however, when the National Assembly voted to extend Reyes' term to December 31, 1914, and still more after he negotiated the tripartite treaties of 1909, by which Colombia agreed to recognize the independence of Panama in return for concessions from that country and from the United States. Ratification of these agreements was violently opposed, and there were vociferous demands that they be submitted to a Constitutional Congress rather than to the hand-picked National Assembly. In the face of demonstrations in the Capital, which showed that public opinion was strongly aroused, Reyes withdrew the treaties and consented to the election of a Congress to meet in February, 1910. This concession hurt the government's prestige without placating its opponents, and in June, 1909, Reyes quietly left the Capital and resigned. Many of the laws that he had sponsored were declared void, but a Constituent Assembly which met in 1910 made permanent the arrangement for minority representation in Congress.

The same Assembly elected Carlos Restrepo, a conservative, as President for the term 1910–1914. Restrepo was the candidate of the *Unión Republicana*, the bipartisan coalition which had opposed Reyes; but this broke up before 1914, and the conservatives took control. The liberals, however, still had a substantial representation in Congress, and under Restrepo and his immediate successors, José Vicente Concha (1914–1918) and Marco Fidel Suárez (1918–1921), liberals served in the Cabinet. There was thus some co-operation between the two parties. At the same time there was more freedom of speech and of the press, and political persecution was unusual. Elections began to approximate a real expression of the wishes of the citizenry, though complaints of highhanded or fraudulent practices in behalf of the official candidates by no means ceased.

Relations with the United States had been clouded since 1903 by the bitter feeling aroused by the Panama affair. The failure of the tripartite treaties of 1909 if anything made the situation worse, but negotiations between the two governments continued. A new treaty, in which the United States expressed "sincere regret" for what had happened and promised to pay an indemnity of $25,000,000, was signed in 1914, but ratification was delayed for several years by opposition in the United States Senate to anything in the nature of an apology.

President Suárez finally agreed to the elimination of the expression of regret in 1919, but the United States Senate's approval was then delayed because the Colombian government issued a decree similar to the constitutional provision that had recently deprived American companies of property rights in subsoil deposits in Mexico.[7] After the decree was declared to be contrary to the Colombian constitutiton and was replaced by a new law, the treaty was ratified early in 1922. Suárez' concessions, however, were so violently criticized that he turned over the presidency in 1921 to General Holguín, the first *designado*.

The election of 1922 was a real contest, for the liberals, who had not usually presented presidential candidates, united in support of General Benjamín Herrera. They were defeated by 413,000 votes to 256,000, and General Pedro Nel Ospina, the conservative choice, was President from 1922 until 1926. Under him, and under his successor Dr. Miguel Abadía Méndez, the country was unusually prosperous. Brazil's coffee valorization helped the Colombian producers by increasing world prices, and the

[7] See below, Chapter 19.

product of the recently developed oil fields furnished a new export. Business in general was stimulated by the inflow of capital from abroad. The treaty indemnity from the United States was paid in annual installments of $5,000,000 between 1922 and 1926, and still greater sums were obtained by borrowing in New York. The central government and several departments and municipalities contracted foreign loans for public works and other purposes, and new road and railroad construction began in nearly every section of the country.

THE LIBERALS IN POWER, 1930–1946

The inflation that accompanied the spending of such great sums made worse the collapse that came with the world depression. Reaction had already set in when it became time to elect a new president in 1930. The conservative regime faced the same situation which caused the overthrow of several other Latin American governments in that year, and the party's chance of success was further diminished by internal feuds. Two factions supported rival candidates for the nomination, and the Archbishop of Bogotá, who usually had much influence in the party's councils, wavered uncertainly between them.

The liberals decided at the last minute to take advantage of the situation. With the support of many conservatives, they nominated Enrique Olaya Herrera, who had served brilliantly as Minister at Washington during the past two administrations, and who now returned to Colombia for a short but effective campaign. Addressing voters in all parts of the country in person or by radio, Dr. Olaya advocated a program of political and social reform which met with an enthusiastic response. He was elected by a large majority, and the 45 years of conservative rule ended.

The orderly manner in which the liberals were permitted to take over the administration and the moderate policy which they pursued after their victory showed how much political conditions in Colombia had changed. The constitution of 1886 and even the concordat with the Papacy remained in force. There was no serious disturbance of public order, though the economic crisis grew increasingly acute during the first years of the new administration. The effects of the depression were aggravated in 1932 by heavy expenditures on military preparations occasioned by the Leticia controversy with Peru,[8] and the government was compelled to reduce payments on the foreign debt and to float large internal loans. Despite these difficulties, Olaya retained his personal popularity and, thanks in part at least to his able leadership, the country escaped the political vicissitudes that marked the depression period in some of the other republics.

Many conservatives held official positions under the Olaya government,

[8] See above, p. 262.

but in 1934 their leaders decided to abstain altogether from the presidential election, in which they would clearly have little chance for success, and not even to take advantage of the constitutional provisions which would have assured them a number of seats in Congress. The administration that came into power in that year was thus exclusively liberal, and the new President, Alfonso López, had no political obligations to elements outside his own party. Abandoning Olaya's conciliatory policy, he put into effect some of the reforms that liberal leaders had long advocated. Constitutional amendments deprived the Church of its control over public instruction and opened the way to a larger measure of government control over foreign and native business enterprises, and negotiations were begun with the Holy See for changes in the concordat in order to make possible the institution of civil marriage, supervision of cemeteries by the government, and other reforms. Efforts were made to expand the public school system and to provide for much needed public health work, and 1,000 miles or more of new roads were built. A reform of the tax system, with much-increased levies on business and private wealth, helped to provide funds.

Ex-President Olaya was to have been the liberal candidate to succeed López, but his sudden death in 1937 upset the plans of the party leaders and brought on a conflict between the moderate and radical wings of the party. Though López supported the radicals, Eduardo Santos, a moderate, obtained the liberal nomination in 1938 and was chosen President in an orderly election in which the conservatives again refused to vote. His administration co-operated with the United States in the war, in the face of strong resistance from Laureano Gómez, the conservative leader, who was openly pro-German. The conservatives again participated in elections in 1939, and from that time on they held the balance of power in Congress as between the two liberal factions. In 1942, they supported the moderate liberal candidate instead of nominating one of their own, but the coalition was defeated by ex-President López, who was the candidate of the radical wing.

López' second administration was a period of violent political agitation. His followers failed to obtain a majority in Congress, and his position was further weakened by accusations of improper conduct directed against some of his associates. In July, 1944, there were several minor revolts, and the President himself was kidnaped and held prisoner for a short time by disloyal army officers at Pasto. A state of siege was imposed, and Gómez, the conservative leader, was forced to leave the country. Finally, in 1945, López resigned and Alberto Lleras Camargo became provisional President. Dr. Lleras was one of the ablest and most generally trusted of the Republic's statesmen, but he could not check the personal rivalries and the increasing partisan bitterness that were soon to make Colombia's recent progress toward democratic government seem illusory.

THE BREAKDOWN AND RESTORATION OF CONSTITUTIONAL GOVERNMENT

The division within the liberal party continued, and in the presidential election of 1946, the conservative candidate Mariano Ospina Pérez was victorious, with 523,000 votes, as against 401,000 for Gabriel Turbay, the candidate of the right-wing liberals, and 332,000 for the left-wing candidate Jorge Elíecer Gaitán. The liberals still had a majority in Congress. The new President attempted to govern with a bipartisan Cabinet; but labor troubles and the postwar inflation made his position difficult, and political unrest continued. Early in 1948 there were disturbances in some of the provinces, and the liberals withdrew their Ministers from the Cabinet. The opposition party became much more aggressive after both liberal factions agreed to support Jorge Gaitán for the presidency in 1950.

On April 9, 1948, while the Ninth Conference of American States was meeting at Bogotá, Gaitán was murdered, apparently by a personal enemy. The left-wing leader had been extremely popular among the laboring class, and within a few minutes angry mobs were killing, looting, and wrecking government buildings. For a time it seemed that the government would fall, but the co-operation of the chief liberal leaders, who agreed to the formation of a Coalition Cabinet, made it possible to restore order after hours of anarchy. It was officially reported that 1,200 persons were killed in Bogotá and 300 more in similar riots elsewhere,[9] and the material damage ran into hundreds of millions of dollars. The small Colombian communist party had been active in the riots, although it probably had not planned the affair, and Colombia broke off diplomatic relations with Russia some weeks later. The Inter-American Conference continued its sessions, though the building in which it had been meeting was destroyed by the mob.

The liberals again withdrew from Ospina's Cabinet in May, 1949, and the political situation rapidly grew worse. For several months there were almost daily reports of killings resulting from party hatreds. Ospina's successor was to have been elected in June, 1950, but in September, 1949, the liberal majority in Congress passed over the President's veto a bill advancing the date in order to have the election while Congress was in session. This caused further bad feeling. Ospina offered to turn the government over to a bipartisan commission which would rule the country until 1954; but this proposal was unacceptable to the extreme elements in both parties, and early in November the President imposed a state of siege. Dario Echandía, the liberal candidate, thereupon withdrew, and on November 27 the conservative leader Laureano Gómez was elected without opposition for the presidential term beginning August 7, 1950.

[9] *The New York Times,* April 22, 1948.

By this time party strife in many parts of the Republic had reached a point where no one in the smaller towns and villages felt safe. Armed bands of liberals or conservatives were murdering members of the opposite party, and thousands of refugees were seeking safety in the cities. A "state of siege" was declared, but the situation seemed to have passed beyond the control of the government and the party leaders, and each outrage inspired a new desire for revenge. After Gómez fell ill in 1952 and Roberto Urdaneta became acting President, the situation was worse than ever. Many people in both parties were willing to support Lieutenant Colonel Gustavo Rojas Pinilla when he ousted the government by a military *coup* in 1953 and announced a policy of conciliation.

Rojas was elected President by a Constituent Assembly in 1954, and for a time conditions improved. Very soon, however, the new government's dictatorial conduct aroused distrust and hostility among Rojas' fellow conservatives as well as among the liberals. In 1956 the chief leaders of the two parties, Laureano Gómez and Alberto Lleras Camargo, met in Spain and agreed to work together to restore democratic government. Some months afterward, when Rojas announced that he intended to have a hand-picked Constituent Assembly vote him another term in office, he met with vigorous opposition from both political parties and from the Church, and in May, 1957, he resigned and left the country. A military *junta* took over the government.

The internal disorder, which had again become serious in the last months of the dictatorship, continued for a time, and the provisional government's existence was threatened by military plots inspired by Rojas and his friends; but the bipartisan agreement for the restoration of democratic government had strong popular support. In December, 1957, some 4,000,000 men and women went to the polls to approve the constitutional amendments that Gómez and Lleras Camargo proposed. These provided that the two parties should have equal representation in the president's cabinet and in the national and provincial legislatures. Catholicism was to be recognized as the national religion. Ten per cent of the central government's budget was to be set aside for education. Under the amended constitution, the first congressional elections in ten years were held in March, 1958, and the presidential election in May.

The interparty agreement had provided that the first president should be a conservative; but internal feuds prevented the conservatives from choosing a candidate, and they agreed to support Lleras Camargo, who was inaugurated in August, 1958. Thereafter, fighting in the interior gradually subsided, and wise fiscal and economic policies strengthened the new government's position. At the end of 1959, the country seemed to have regained much of the prosperity that it enjoyed before the political crisis.

With more than 13,000,000 people, Colombia ranks fourth in population among the Latin American republics. It produces more coffee than any other country in the world except Brazil. The development of its economic potentialities, however, is still held back by lack of adequate transportation for which the country's geography is largely responsible. Serious political and social problems also remain to be solved. Though Colombia is one of the four or five Latin American countries that have made the greatest progress toward truly republican government, the events of the past ten years show the strength of the explosive tendencies in her political life. The poverty and illiteracy prevalent in many sections of the country will have to be ameliorated before these tendencies become less dangerous.

CHAPTER 16

Venezuela

VENEZUELA IN 1821

THERE WERE PROBABLY about 700,000 people in Venezuela at the end of the war for independence. Most of these, like their descendants today, lived in the pleasant, temperate valleys of the Andean range which crosses the country from west to east within a few miles of the Caribbean coast. There were also settlements on the coast and in the hot lowlands around Lake Maracaibo. Another region of some economic importance was the *llanos* or plains of the Orinoco Valley, alternately parched by the sun or drenched by torrential rains, where half-savage *mestizo* cowboys tended cattle belonging to creole families in the highlands. The great area south of the Orinoco was unoccupied and almost unexplored.

As in many other Latin American countries, the upper class were the landowners of Spanish descent, who lived in the towns and left the management of their properties to overseers. Most of the labor on the farms, especially in the neighborhood of Caracas, was done by Negro slaves. The majority of the country's inhabitants were of colored blood, for, except in the western part of the highlands, few Indians had survived. The Venezuelan provinces, in colonial times, had been backward in many respects as compared with New Spain or Peru. At the beginning of the nineteenth century there were no roads over which even an oxcart could travel between the chief agricultural regions and the seaports, and travelers reported that there were no wheeled vehicles even in Caracas. Schools were few in number and poor in quality, and there had been no printing press in the country until Miranda brought one with his filibustering expedition of 1806.[1]

During the war for independence, Venezuela probably suffered more than any other South American country. Twice freed and twice reconquered before the final patriot victory at Carabobo, the people of the high-

[1] González Guinán, *Historia de Venezuela*, Vol. II, p. 31.

lands experienced both the horrors of Bolívar's "war to the death" and the brutality of the Spanish reaction. In the *llanos* many years of guerrilla warfare had greatly depleted the herds of cattle. A large proportion of the able-bodied men were compelled to abandon agriculture and stock raising to take part in the conflict, and several thousand left the country to accompany Bolívar in his campaigns for the liberation of New Granada, Ecuador, and Peru. Many of these did not return at the end of the war, for Venezuelan leaders like Sucre, Flores, and Bolívar himself remained abroad as rulers of other South American countries, relying largely upon their Venezuelan troops for support.

In Venezuela itself, the military caste, looking to the public treasury for support and insisting upon the maintenance of its special privileges, dominated the country's political life for many years after independence. Local *caudillos* in each district either exercised power as representatives of the central government or conspired to revolt against it. They were intolerant of civilian control and had little respect for any law save that of force. The parties that they headed were built around personalities and held together chiefly by a desire for office or a thirst for revenge for past persecutions. Questions of principle played a secondary rôle, though certain issues, like federalism, were sometimes used as a means of winning popular support. Even the problem of Church and State, so productive of strife in Colombia, was of secondary importance in Venezuela because the Church had lost much of its prestige and authority by the end of the war for independence. Such conditions are peculiarly favorable to the growth of dictatorships, and the Republic was ruled throughout the first century of its history by a series of "strong men."

PÁEZ

The first of these was the *llanero* general, José Antonio Páez. As Commander of the military forces in the Caracas district, Páez was the most prominent figure in Venezuela during the period when the country formed a part of Great Colombia. He had been restive under the authority of the government at Bogotá, and in 1826, as we have seen, he headed a separatist revolt. This collapsed when Bolívar returned from Peru to reassert his own authority, but Páez came out of the affair with undiminished prestige. He encouraged the separatist tendencies, which became stronger as Bolívar's popularity declined; and in 1829, when the people of each locality were invited to express their opinion as to changes which should be made in the Colombian constitution, the majority of the towns in Venezuela declared for complete independence under his leadership. Early in 1830, Páez set up a provisional government and summoned a convention to draft a constitution. Secession was accomplished practically without bloodshed because the authorities at Bogotá were powerless to resist, but there was a rather formidable though unsuccessful revolt in Venezuela early in 1831 under the leadership of General José Tadeo Monagas.

This revolt represented various elements of discord that continued to make trouble. One was the jealousy of Páez' military rivals, many of whom had opposed the secession movement out of loyalty to Bolívar. Another was the ever-present jealousy of the provincial towns toward Caracas which found expression in the demand for federalism—the slogan of many revolts in years to come. A third cause of dissension was the opposition of the clergy to the new constitution because it did away with some of the special privileges of the Church and contained no special provisions safeguarding the Catholic faith.

The four years that followed were relatively peaceful. Though Páez was a daring and brilliant soldier, with little education, but a great capacity for leadership, he maintained his pre-eminence as much by his prestige and popularity as by force. The country enjoyed a more truly republican government than it was to know for a century to come. The Congress and the press were relatively independent, and the elections were actively contested with comparatively little official interference. Unfortunately, this situation did not continue after Dr. José Vargas was elected to succeed Páez at the end of the latter's term.

Vargas was a civilian who had been supported by the richer landowners and merchants in an effort to diminish the power of the military caste, but he soon found himself unable to cope with the responsibilities he had very unwillingly assumed. Within a few months he had been driven from office by an uprising in the army. Páez, who had retired quietly to his farm, hastily recruited a new force which restored the constitutional order, but he did not approve Vargas' action in shooting or exiling several of the rebel leaders, and further friction between the two men compelled Vargas to resign in 1836. The government was administered by vice-presidents more amenable to Páez' influence until 1839 when Páez himself again became President. He was succeeded in 1843 by his associate, General Carlos Soublette.

There was by this time a rising opposition to Páez' long-continued predominance. In 1840, Antonio Leocadio Guzmán, formerly one of the *caudillo*'s chief advisers, had organized the liberal party to avenge himself for the loss of his position in the government. Hard times helped him to build up a following, and he attracted support from various dissatisfied elements including especially the friends of the still-exiled participants in the revolts of 1831 and 1835. Though overwhelmingly defeated in the election of 1842, the liberals became stronger during Soublette's term, and the conservatives, or followers of Páez, won the vice-presidential election of 1844 and the presidential election of 1846–1847 only by using force and fraud to an extent that had not formerly been necessary. The contest between the two parties, though almost entirely a matter of personalities rather than principles, aroused a new interest in political affairs, and the landowning aristocracy, hitherto glad to follow Páez' leadership in the interests of peace, divided into factions.

THE MONAGAS BROTHERS

In 1846, each party split its vote among several presidential candidates, and the final decision, in the absence of a majority, went to Congress. The victor was General José Tadeo Monagas, the chief *caudillo* in the eastern provinces, whom Páez supported in the final days of the campaign despite the fact that Monagas had once been his most formidable opponent. The new President soon showed that he did not intend to be a figurehead like his predecessors. After co-operating with Páez for some months, he broke with the conservatives and turned to the liberals for support. When the Congress attempted to impeach him in 1848, a mob invaded its meeting place and killed three of the deputies. This outrage, and the celebration of its anniversary as an official holiday, increased the bitterness between the two parties, but Páez was defeated and exiled when he revolted.

Monagas had his brother, José Gregorio Monagas, elected President for the period 1851–1855, despite opposition from both parties. Serious disturbances resulted, especially in 1853 and 1854, and it was in the hope of diverting attention from the political situation that the President forced through Congress in 1854 a law for the complete abolition of slavery with compensation to the owners. There were still some 13,000 slaves and 27,000 *manumisos*, or persons born of slave mothers and bound to serve their masters until the age of twenty-five. In the same year José Tadeo Monagas was elected to the presidency for a second term. The government had now become a dictatorship, with elections a mere form and with increasing restrictions on the freedom of the press. In 1857, after making the necessary changes in the constitution, Monagas had himself elected for a new term of six years.

CIVIL WAR AND FEDERALISM, 1858–1872

A year later the government was overthrown by a revolt of members of both parties. The titular leader, General Julián Castro, was one of Monagas' own military commanders who was promised the presidency because his aid was necessary to success. He had little personal following, and his government lasted barely 12 months before the conservative leaders to whom he entrusted the control of the army arrested and imprisoned him. The liberals were already in revolt under the leadership of General Juan C. Falcón, and the veteran Páez, despite much opposition within his own party, returned from exile to take command of the conservative army. In 1861 Páez proclaimed himself dictator, but a series of liberal victories forced him to agree to a treaty of peace in 1863 by which Falcón assumed the presidency. Páez again went to the United States and died there ten years later at the age of eighty-three.

Since the liberals at the beginning of the war had proclaimed their adherence to "federalism," the states now set up autonomous governments, and in 1864 a federal constitution was adopted. The result was as unfortunate as in Colombia. There were constant disorders within the states and quarrels between them, as well as less frequent uprisings against the central government. Falcón was popular, but he was a poor administrator; and his dislike of official life at Caracas led him to entrust the actual exercise of power to others during much of his term.

A "blue" revolution, so called from the color that its army adopted, put José Tadeo Monagas in the presidency in 1868; but he died after a few months, and his son José Ruperto succeeded him. The liberals, now called the "yellow" party, soon revolted. In April, 1870, they took Caracas. The war continued in other sections for two years more, but the "blues" were finally beaten. After 14 years of almost continual strife the country was more than ready for a period of peace. It was to enjoy this under the rule of Antonio Guzmán Blanco.

GUZMÁN BLANCO

Guzmán Blanco, the son of Antonio Leocadio Guzmán, had been Falcón's ablest lieutenant in the five-years' war, and by 1870 he had become the leader of the liberal party. Within a short time after the "yellow" victory, he built up a more absolute power than any former ruler of the Republic had enjoyed. The states, retaining their prerogatives on paper, were ruled in fact by puppets entirely subservient to his will, and all branches of the national government were controlled in the same way. Opposition, or even criticism, was sternly punished. At the same time roads and railroads were built; ports were improved; and the larger cities were modernized and beautified. No earlier ruler had done so much to promote material progress. None, on the other hand, had gone to such lengths of self-glorification. The President caused statues of himself to be erected everywhere, and it was indiscreet to make a speech or publish a book that did not render a tribute of adulation to "The Illustrious American, Regenerator of Venezuela." The dictator and his relatives accumulated great private fortunes; but his administration was relatively efficient, and the situation of the national treasury was better than under his predecessors. The country benefited from the establishment of peace and for some years submitted to his firm rule with little evidence of discontent.

At the beginning of Guzmán Blanco's regime, there was a new conflict with the Church. The Archbishop of Caracas was expelled from Venezuela in 1870 because he made difficulties about celebrating a *Te Deum* in honor of one of the "yellow" victories. In the years that followed, the few remaining convents and the seminary at Caracas were closed; civil marriage was authorized; and the cemeteries were placed under lay control. On one occasion the dictator even threatened to set up a national church independent of Rome, but his attitude became less hostile after the offending Archbishop resigned.

In 1877 Guzmán Blanco made his friend Francisco Linares Alcántara President and himself went to Europe. Linares' death and a revolt that followed forced him to resume control of the government. He was again President from 1879 until 1884. In 1881 he brought about the adoption of a new constitution, ostensibly modeled on that of Switzerland, that provided that the Chief Executive should be chosen for a two-year term and should not be eligible for re-election. After 1884 he spent much time in Paris, sending his orders by mail and cable to lieutenants who successively occupied the presidency.

The popularity that Guzmán Blanco enjoyed in 1870 had vanished by 1888, and Dr. Rojas Paúl, who was elected President by order of the dictator in that year, was enthusiastically supported by public opinion when he began to show an unexpected independence. Guzmán Blanco's wishes were flouted, first by the disapproval of concessions that he had granted in Paris and then by bringing to Venezuela the body of his old enemy, General Páez, for burial in the national pantheon. Other exiles were allowed to return, and the press was permitted to discuss political questions. The authorities endeavored to avoid an open break; but the populace tumultuously prevented the celebration of Guzmán Blanco's Saint's Day and the anniversaries of his victories, which had previously been national holidays, and in October, 1889, his numerous statues were destroyed by simultaneous mob action in all sections of the Republic. Thereafter the ex-dictator wisely remained abroad, though he made futile attempts to foment a counterrevolution.

CRESPO'S ADMINISTRATION AND THE GUIANA BOUNDARY DISPUTE

Dr. Andueza Palacio, who succeeded Rojas Paúl in 1890, was overthrown two years later by General Joaquín Crespo. The latter, a professional soldier from the *llanos*, gave the country a period of comparative peace from 1894 to 1898. His administration was notable chiefly for the sensational controversy over the boundary between Venezuela and British Guiana. The question was an old one, but it had recently become acute with the discovery of gold in the disputed territory. The British government refused to arbitrate it unless a large area was recognized in advance as a part of the Guiana colony. The United States intervened in the dispute because it considered that any European occupation of territory legally belonging to Venezuela would be a violation of the Monroe Doctrine, and in 1895 Secretary of State Olney demanded that the British government submit the question to arbitration. When the British government made an unsatisfactory reply, President Cleveland proposed to Congress the appointment of a commission to investigate the dispute. He indicated that the United States would determine for itself what was the rightful boundary and would use force, if necessary, to compel its acceptance. This arrogant stand might have brought the United States and Great Britain very close to war, but the government at London was occupied with more important problems elsewhere and soon agreed to an arbitration with Venezuela. An award handed down in 1899 decided the controversy without granting the extreme demands of either party.

CIPRIANO CASTRO

Crespo peacefully turned over his office to General Ignacio Andrade in 1898 but was killed soon afterward leading the government forces against one of several revolutions that again plunged the country into anarchy. Even when an agreement between the various military leaders placed General Cipriano Castro in the presidency in 1899, new revolts occurred, and it was not until 1903 that something approaching order was established. Castro, an unscrupulous and greedy politician, supported chiefly by the army and by associates who profited from his corrupt financial practices, remained in power as dictator until 1908.

Castro is best remembered for his offensive treatment of foreign powers. Controversies with other nations over debts and claims had embarrassed the Venezuelan government since the days of Páez, and the recent civil wars had caused new injuries to foreign life and property for which Castro arrogantly refused to make compensation. At the end of 1902, therefore, British, German, and Italian naval forces blockaded the Venezuelan coast, seized four gunboats, and bombarded Puerto Cabello. Since the governments concerned had previously assured the United States that no seizure of territory was contemplated, President Roosevelt did not consider it proper to object to their action; but he exerted his good offices to persuade all concerned to agree to an arbitration of claims, and the blockade was raised early in 1903. The incident had an important influence, as we shall see later, upon the general Caribbean policy of the United States. Apparently it had less effect on Castro, for new violations of foreign rights kept his administration in hot water in later years.

JUAN VICENTE GÓMEZ

Castro's chief aid was Juan Vicente Gómez who had been one of the ablest military leaders in the civil wars between 1899 and 1903 and had continued to be powerful despite Castro's growing jealousy. Late in 1908, when the President was compelled to go abroad for medical treatment, Gómez was left in charge. He at once made himself master of the situation, and Castro was defeated when he attempted to return at the head of a revolution.

During the next 27 years Gómez ruled Venezuela with a heavy hand. He was not President continuously, but he retained command of the army and with it a complete control of the government during the periods when he allowed straw men like Dr. Márquez Bustillos, from 1914 to 1922, and Dr. Juan Baustista Pérez, from 1929 to 1931, to exercise the executive power. He also dominated the governments of the states, finally amending the constitution to give himself the right to appoint their presidents by decree. Opponents were treated with severity and often, it is said, with fiendish cruelty. The press was compelled to praise the ruler and his policies, and an elaborate spy system made criticism dangerous. The army, well trained and equipped with modern weapons, prevented resistance by a people who were entirely deprived of firearms. Political parties disappeared, and revolutionary movements, after the first years, were few and unimportant.

Gómez had little or no education, but his energy and acumen had made him a prosperous cattleman before his entry into politics. As dictator he showed himself a keen judge of men, and he was able to obtain the cooperation of many of the country's best minds. His administration was lawless and corrupt, but the country derived some material benefit from it. While the dictator and many of his relatives were growing rich by graft or extortion, roads were improved, something was done for education, and the entire foreign debt was paid off. The amazing growth of the petroleum industry made the government rich during the last decades of the Gómez regime. Anglo-Dutch and, later, North American companies began to exploit the rich oil deposits around Lake Maracaibo immediately after the First World War, and within ten years Venezuela had become one of the great sources of the world's supply.

RECENT GOVERNMENTS

When Gómez died, at the age of eighty, in December, 1935, General Eleázar López Contreras, the Minister of War, became provisional President. The new administration, to the surprise of many observers, was able to survive the violent popular reaction that followed the removal of the dictator's control. Much of the property of Gómez and his relatives was destroyed or looted by mobs, and sanguinary riots occurred in Caracas; but the removal of several high officials hated for their connection with the Gómez regime prevented more serious outbreaks. The army supported the new order, as did many influential groups which were primarily interested in the maintenance of peace. Some of the most objectionable features of the Gómez regime were done away with, and free elections for a new Congress were promised. Meanwhile the old hand-picked Gómez Congress elected López Contreras as constitutional President.

Continuing prosperity made the new government's task easier, but there was opposition from liberal and radical groups, and in 1937 the opposition parties won an unexpected victory in the congressional elections. López Contreras thereupon arrested several of the newly elected deputies and senators, accusing them of being communists, and a little later expelled from the country a large number of leftist leaders. Thereafter the government encountered less opposition, and it was able in 1941 to obtain a large majority in the Congress which, under the constitution, was to elect the next President. López Contreras did not attempt to succeed himself, and in the same year General Isaías Medina, a veteran soldier who had until recently been Minister of War, was installed as his successor.

Venezuela's support of the democracies in the World War was particularly important because of her oil production, and the government's policy of co-operation strengthened its position. As the end of Medina's term approached, however, the political situation became increasingly uncertain. The *Acción Democrática*, a radical party, had developed much strength, but it had no chance to win because the next president would be named not by the people but by Congress. None of the candidates who seemed likely to be chosen by the government had any great popular following, and many of the younger officers in the army were dissatisfied with the leadership of the group of generals who had been in control since the days of Gómez. In October, 1945, some of these officers ousted Medina and set up a provisional government headed by Rómulo Betancourt, the leader of the *Acción Democrática*.

A popularly elected Assembly drew up a more democratic constitution, and in December, 1947, the internationally famous novelist Rómulo Gallegos was elected President. The new regime had much popular support, but it had little opportunity to carry out the liberal program that its leaders advocated. Its failure to maintain order and eliminate official corruption weakened its position, and it was soon involved in a dispute with the army, which demanded a larger share in the government. In November, 1948, the army revolted and established a military *junta* headed by Lieutenant Colonel Carlos Delgado Chalbaud. Many political leaders were jailed, and the *Acción Democrática* was outlawed.

Rivalries within the *junta* led to the murder of Delgado Chalbaud in 1950 and the rise to power of another of its members, Colonel Marcos Pérez Jiménez. In 1952 the voters were asked to elect another Assembly to revise the constitution. The *Acción Democrática* and the communists were not allowed to participate, but two other opposition parties, the Christian democratic *"Copei"* and the more radical *U.R.D.*, nominated slates of candidates. The government hampered their campaigns in many

ways, but when the counting of the ballots began, it appeared that the
U.R.D. had obtained more votes than the government party. The *junta*
immediately imposed a censorship on election news and arrested several
of the opposition leaders, and candidates whom it supported were seated
in the new Assembly.

In the meantime, the other members of the *junta* resigned, and Pérez
Jiménez became provisional President. In April, 1953, after election by the
Assembly, he was inaugurated as President for a five-year term. His government was an undisguised dictatorship. His position was stronger because of the vast sums that he had at his disposal from the oil revenues. In
addition to its 50 per cent share in the profits of the oil industry, the government obtained more than $667,000,000 in 1956–1957 by the sale of
concessions to explore lands as yet undeveloped. By this time, furthermore, oil was no longer the country's only important export, for 1954
saw the first shipments of iron ore from the extensive deposits in the
Orinoco basin, and these rapidly increased.

Much of the government's revenue was spent for roads and education
and other useful purposes and also to carry out grandiose building projects
in Caracas. At the same time, great amounts went into the pockets of persons connected with the government. This corruption, more flagrant and
on a greater scale than under previous administrations, increased the resentment caused by the dictator's disregard of the constitution and the
cruel treatment of his opponents.

Even the army became restive when Pérez Jiménez went through the
motions of a plebiscite in December, 1957, and had himself re-elected
as President for a five-year term. For a time he resisted pressure from his
fellow officers to make changes in his government, but when labor staged
a general strike in January, 1958, he was forced to resign and a *junta*
headed by Admiral Wolfgang Larrazábal took control. There was some
fighting in Caracas, and in the months that followed counterrevolutionary
plots made the situation uncertain. In May, 1958, the provisional government's failure to control a mob in Caracas led to the most shocking incident
that occurred during Vice-President Nixon's good will visit to Latin
America.

Nevertheless, preparations for an election went forward. The leaders
of the principal parties, the *Acción Democrática*, the *Copei*, and the
U.R.D., attempted to form a coalition to avert a contest, but they could
not agree on a candidate. Each consequently presented its own ticket, but
they did agree to carry on their campaigns in a way that would not engender ill feeling and to co-operate in the new administration. Admiral
Larrazábal, who resigned as President of the *junta* shortly before the election and who was supported by a coalition that included the *U.R.D.* and
the communists, was popular in Caracas and seemed likely to win. When
the election was held in December, 1958, however, the *Acción Democrática*

candidate, Rómulo Betancourt, defeated Larrazábal and the *Copei* leader, Rafael Caldera. President Betancourt took office in February, 1959, with a Cabinet in which both of the other major parties were represented.

Though Venezuela has only about 6,000,000 people, the Republic's oil and more recently its exports of iron ore have given it an important place in the world's economy. Its oil production, which has reached approximately a billion barrels annually in recent years, exceeds that of any country except the United States. The wealth brought by oil, however, has not been an unmixed blessing. Some thousands of workers in the industry enjoy wages that are very high by Latin American standards, and many other people share in one way or another in their prosperity; but the income of many workers in other occupations and of the peasants in the country districts is smaller in relation to the fantastically high cost of living for which the industry is chiefly responsible. The whole economy has been distorted. Agriculture, which is still the occupation of the masses of the people, is backward, and the country does not produce enough food for its own use. Efforts of the governments before 1958 to invest the income from oil in programs for economic development were not entirely successful, partly because of official corruption and the tendency to spend money on ostentatious public works in the cities.

After the fall of Pérez Jiménez, one of the most important problems that confronted the new government was the determination of its policy toward the oil industry. The spirit of economic nationalism that has led so many other Latin American countries to take measures unfriendly to foreign capital is also strong in Venezuela, and Pérez Jiménez' alleged friendliness to the oil companies was one reason for his unpopularity. The provisional government imposed new taxes on the industry in an effort to increase its already-large share in its profits, and the *Acción Democrática* government when it came into office indicated that it proposed to take further measures toward this objective.

PART VI

BRAZIL

WITH AN AREA nearly as great as that of the United States, Brazil occupies almost half of the South American continent, and its population of 63,000,000 is not very much less than that of all its Spanish American neighbors put together. In the number of its people, in fact, the country today ranks seventh among the nations of the world. In its potentiality for further growth it perhaps ranks still higher, for it has great, as yet little-exploited, mineral resources and much still-sparsely-occupied land suitable for grazing and farming. Settlement until recent times has been confined to a narrow strip on or near the coast, and it is only within the last few years that the rapidly increasing population has begun to push back into the interior.

Most of Brazil is tropical or subtropical. There are only a few regions, like the State of Ceará in the northeast, where the rainfall is not at least adequate. Much of the Republic's territory lies in the Amazon Valley, where the jungle and the heavy rainfall have discouraged settlement, but there are still greater areas of plateau of moderate altitude with a comfortable climate.

We have already seen that the history of the Portuguese settlements in America was different in many ways from that of their Spanish neighbors. From the beginning, they were somewhat less completely dominated by the home government and had less help from Europe in their long struggles against foreign aggression. The exploration and occupation of the interior of the continent, carried on in Spanish America by a combination of military and missionary activity directed by the Crown, was left in Brazil to local enterprise. The memory of frequent revolts against the royal authority, of conflicts with the French and the Dutch, and of the exploits of the *bandeirantes* gave the Brazilians something very like a national tradition before the country became independent.

Other factors, historical and psychological, helped to make the country different from the Spanish American republics. One was the attitude toward religion. The Portuguese had less of the crusading spirit that played so great a rôle in the Spanish Conquest. This was evident in their treatment of the Indians and in a less energetic effort to exclude suspected heretics from the colony. The Church never became so powerful or so wealthy as in the Spanish colonies, and its position has not been an important political issue since independence. Some of the other differences are harder to define. The Brazilian seems somewhat more tolerant, in other matters besides religion, and has less of the sensitive pride that often complicates political relations among people of Spanish descent. The spirit of *localismo* is less evident, though by no means absent. If it had been as strong as in Spanish America, it would hardly have been possible for the Brazilian settlements, strung thinly along 4,800 miles of coast, to emerge as a united nation.

CHAPTER 17

Brazil:
Empire and Republic

THE REIGN OF PEDRO I

BRAZIL WAS FORTUNATE in becoming independent and setting up a relatively stable government without the long-drawn-out internal strife that caused so much destruction and bloodshed in the Spanish American republics during the nineteenth century. The transition from a colonial status to independence had really begun when the arrival of the Court in 1808 made Rio de Janeiro the Capital of the Portuguese empire. No very great changes either in political or in social institutions followed the formal separation from the mother country in 1822. The presence of a Prince whom the people were accustomed to accept as their ruler helped to avert the strife between rival military leaders and between advocates of different forms of government which for some time prevented orderly progress in other parts of South America.

There were nevertheless problems to solve before the stability of the new regime could be assured. The movement for independence had been supported chiefly in Rio de Janeiro and São Paulo. In some of the other provinces there was opposition to the break with Portugal, and though this had been suppressed it was clear that the maintenance of the government's authority in the whole of the empire's vast territory might not be easy. Northern Brazil had always had closer connections with Portugal than with Rio de Janeiro, and the provinces of the extreme south, with their *gaucho* population, had more in common with the people of the River Plate area than with tropical Brazil. In several provinces there were groups who were unenthusiastic about the new government because they would have preferred a republic. Another element of weakness was the antipathy of the natives to the peninsular Portuguese who still controlled much of the country's trade and surrounded the Emperor as friends and advisers.

Both Pedro I and his Brazilian supporters wished to set up a constitutional monarchy, with an elected parliament. In attempting to operate such a regime, however, the Brazilians faced the same sort of obstacles that confronted their Spanish-speaking neighbors. Few even among the upper class had more than the barest rudiments of an education. Half of the population were Negroes, for the most part slaves, and a large proportion of the other half were persons of mixed blood who had until very recently been treated by the law as an inferior caste. In the larger cities, the visits of foreigners and the increase of commercial contacts with the outside world were already modifying colonial customs and points of view, but in the country the change was less apparent. The owners of the great plantations were often petty despots. Not only their own slaves but also the free people of the neighborhood looked to them for support and protection, and it was from among them that the government usually appointed the *capitão mór*, who was its representative in each rural district. Under such conditions it was if anything more difficult to hold real elections than it was elsewhere in Latin America.

The Emperor's first Cabinet, headed by José Bonifacio de Andrada, had shown energy and competence in overcoming the resistance to independence, but it was less fortunate in handling day-by-day political problems. José Bonifacio was tactless and arbitrary in dealing with political opponents and was accused of using his position to persecute personal enemies. His attacks on the freedom of the press and the establishment of an extensive system of political espionage increased his unpopularity. Even the Masonic lodges, in which the Andradas had hitherto been prominent, were closed when their members ventured to criticize the government's actions. The Emperor, who was himself perhaps somewhat jealous of his Minister's great prestige and authority, was finally persuaded to dismiss him in July, 1823.

In the meantime an Assembly had met in April, 1823, to draft a constitution. Its members had already shown a disposition to disagree with the Emperor about the powers that the Throne should exercise, and they became more aggressive after the Andradas assumed the leadership of the opposition. Relations became so strained that Pedro dissolved the Assembly by force on November 12 and deported the three Andrada brothers to France. He then appointed a Commission of ten members, who proceeded to draw up the constitution that was to remain in force until the advent of the Republic in 1889.

The new code guaranteed personal liberty and freedom of the press and abolished all privileges of rank and caste. It provided for a chamber of deputies elected for four years and a senate chosen by the Emperor from lists submitted by the electoral colleges and holding office for life.

A measure of self-government was granted to the provinces and munici-palities. On the whole the constitution was a liberal one by comparison with those of other monarchical states and also by comparison with that which had been under consideration by the recently disbanded Assembly. It nevertheless gave the Emperor very great power, for he not only ap-pointed one branch of the legislature but was free to choose his cabinet without regard to the wishes of parliament. These provisions and the way in which the constitution had been imposed on the country increased the strength of the liberal opposition that had made itself felt in the Con-stituent Assembly.

In Pernambuco, in fact, the liberals revolted in 1824 and proclaimed the establishment of a republic called the "Confederation of the Equator." This was to have included all northern Brazil, but the movement received little support in the neighboring provinces. A reaction soon occurred in Pernambuco itself, and after Pedro's forces occupied Recife, with the aid of Admiral Cochrane's fleet, other places that had revolted were soon reduced. This campaign marked the end of Cochrane's career in South America. He had had a dispute with his employers over the disposition of prizes taken in his earlier operations, and he now proceeded to settle his account with the imperial government by seizing Maranhão, where he took about $100,000 from the customhouse. He then sailed away to England on one of Pedro's vessels.

Despite the constitution, Pedro continued to rule almost as though he were an absolute monarch. The first meeting of the legislative chambers was delayed on various pretexts until 1826, and though regular sessions were held thereafter the views of the people's representatives received little consideration. The deputies were at first too much in awe of the imperial authority to assert their prerogatives effectively; but they grew bolder as the government's difficulties increased, and the majority were openly critical and unfriendly in the sessions of 1827, 1828, and 1829. Pedro's attempts to placate the opposition by appointing ministers friendly to the leaders in parliament had little effect.

The war with Argentina, which grew out of the revolt of the Spanish-speaking inhabitants of the *Banda Oriental*, helped to weaken Pedro's position. The conflict dragged on for three years, from 1825 to 1828, be-fore it was finally ended by British mediation. Its conduct reflected little credit on the incompetently led imperial army and navy, and its chief result, so far as Brazil was concerned, was the impoverishment of the treasury and a decrease in the prestige of the government.

At the same time, several other factors were helping to destroy the popularity that the Emperor had once enjoyed. The chief cause of discon-tent was the feeling that his government was not truly Brazilian. The Emperor was still surrounded by Portuguese advisers and army officers who had remained in Brazil from personal loyalty or from other motives, and the few natives whom he took into his confidence were for the most part conservatives and ultraroyalist members of the newly created nobility who had little political following. There had been much criticism of an agreement negotiated through British mediation in 1825 by which Pedro assumed part of the Portuguese debt in return for the mother country's recognition of Brazil's independence, and the Brazilians had disliked his preoccupation with efforts to have his daughter Maria da Gloria recognized as Queen of Portugal after João's death in 1826. To make matters worse, Pedro's personal conduct was undignified to the point of vulgarity. Even the far from puritanical Brazilians were shocked by his treatment of his wife and the influence which his mistress, the Marchioness of Santos, was permitted to exercise in public affairs. These matters were discussed passionately and often scurrilously in the newspapers, for the government had by this time relaxed its restrictions on the press. By far the most important of the opposition papers was the *Aurora Fluminense*, founded in 1827 by Evaristo Ferreira da Veiga who was one of the leaders in the liberal movement.

When the term of the first deputies expired and a new Chamber met in May, 1830, it was clear that a crisis was at hand. The greater number of the new members were frankly hostile to the Emperor and his advisers, for the technique of controlled elections, by which the government in later times always obtained a majority, had not yet been developed. Pedro made some concessions that merely encouraged his adversaries, and the news of the July revolution in Paris helped to arouse the liberals' enthusiasm. There was an outburst of popular indignation when a radical Italian journalist named Badaró was murdered at São Paulo in November, supposedly by order of the imperial judge. The Emperor made a belated effort to placate public opinion by appointing a Cabinet of native Brazilians; he then, in April, 1831, committed the final error of replacing these Ministers by members of his own immediate circle. A mob gathered to demand that the former Cabinet be reinstated, and many of the troops whose officers had been won over by the radical leaders joined in the movement. Pedro at first refused to yield, but on the early morning of April 7 he suddenly signed an abdication in favor of his five-year-old son, Pedro de Alcantara, and named José Bonifacio de Andrada as his children's guardian. Immediately afterward he embarked for Europe on a British warship. Those members of the Parliament who happened to be in the Capital elected a Regency of three members to rule in the name of the new Emperor during his minority.

THE REGENCY

The nine years that followed the revolution of 1831 were a period of factional strife at Rio de Janeiro and disorder in the provinces. The first

Regency was supported by the moderate liberals, and especially by Evaristo da Veiga's "Society for the Defense of Liberty and National Independence" which organized behind the government the native commercial and landholding interests. It was opposed both by the *exaltados,* or radical federalists and republicans, and by the still-powerful Portuguese element, allied with many conservative Brazilians, like José Bonifacio de Andrada, who sought the restoration of Pedro I. Both of these groups made repeated attempts to overthrow the new regime. Revolts at the capital were suppressed by the firm hand of Diogo Antonio Feijó, a priest who was Minister of Justice during the first years of the Regency and became sole Regent, superseding the commission of three, in 1835. The government's position in the Capital and in the nearby provinces was strengthened by the creation of a national guard which was more reliable than the poorly trained and undisciplined army. There was more difficulty in maintaining order in other parts of the empire where radical agitators stirred up trouble by appealing to local jealousies and arousing popular hostility to the Portuguese who controlled much of the trade in the larger seaports. There were rebellions in many of the northern provinces, and especially in Pará, where the insurgents defied the government's authority for several years. Since a desire for more local autonomy seemed to be one of the chief causes of these disorders, the government attempted to placate federalist sentiment in 1834 by an *ato adicional,* or amendment to the constitution, which authorized the election of provincial legislative assemblies and made other changes advocated by the liberals.

This concession did not prevent the worst local civil war in Brazil's history, the "Guerra dos Farrapos" in Rio Grande do Sul, which began in 1835. In customs and way of life, the cattle raisers and *gauchos* of Rio Grande do Sul were far closer to their neighbors in Uruguay and Argentina than to the people of the Brazilian provinces where the economy was based on slavery. There was much intermingling of the people on both sides of the frontier, and *caudillos* in one region frequently took part in civil strife in the other, as indeed they continued to do throughout the nineteenth century. The *Riograndenses* had been influenced by the republican ideals of the River Plate region, and one object of the revolt in 1835 was to set up a republican government in their own territory. The war was carried on chiefly by bands of *gaucho* guerrillas, and it dragged on for years without decisive victories for either side.

The government's inability to cope with the situation in Rio Grande do Sul helped to bring about a change in the Regency in 1837. Feijó's inflexible disposition and somewhat radical ideas had already alienated many of the more moderate liberals, and many of these had joined a new conservative party, organized under the leadership of Bernardo Pereira de Vasconcellos. This also attracted the support of most of Pedro I's partisans after the ex-Emperor died in 1834. Other liberals continued to support the Regent, and were joined by many of the *exaltados*, but the government lost prestige as the public grew tired of continued political strife. In 1837, when Feijó found a majority of the Parliament against him, he quietly turned over the Regency to the conservative leader, Araujo Lima.

The new government was hardly more successful than its predecessor. The war continued in the south, while fresh revolts occurred in Bahia and Maranhão. Araujo Lima's reactionary policy, and especially the restriction of the limited autonomy granted to the provinces in 1834, increased the feeling of discontent, and early in 1840 the liberal leaders began a campaign to have the fourteen-year-old Emperor declared old enough to rule. Their immediate purpose was to do away with the conservative Regency, but they were supported by many influential people who hoped that the factional struggle for control of the government would lose its violent character when the nation had a ruler independent of either political party. Under the leadership of the two surviving Andradas, for José Bonifacio died in 1838, the movement soon had the support of a majority in the Chamber of Deputies. The Regent at first temporized and then attempted to adjourn the Parliament. This was the signal for a bloodless revolution. The two Chambers met in defiance of the Regent's order, obtained the Emperor's consent, and on July 23, 1840 proclaimed him of age to rule in his own name.

THE REIGN OF PEDRO II

Under the new Emperor, Brazil was to enjoy a long period of internal peace. Despite his youth, Pedro II soon showed a surprising capacity to give the country precisely the kind of government that its political and social development seemed to demand. Educated by conscientious tutors under a strict regime that left him little opportunity for contact with the court influences which had shaped his father's character, he grew up to be serious-minded, irreproachable in his private life, and indefatigable in the performance of what he considered his duty. He was keenly interested in art, science, and literature, well informed though not profound or brilliant, an able and intelligent ruler if not a great statesman. His subjects loved him for his simplicity and his democratic ways even when they regarded his weaknesses with tolerant amusement or criticized his official acts with all the freedom permitted by a broad-minded and tolerant policy toward the press.

Though the new regime was welcomed by the great majority of the people, it was several years before the political disturbances inherited from the Regency were suppressed. Factional rivalry was still virulent. The Andradas, who had formed a Ministry after their victory in 1840, soon disagreed with the Emperor, and when a new conservative Cabinet dissolved the liberal-controlled Chamber of Deputies, revolts broke out in São Paulo and Minas Geraes. They were suppressed by General Luiz Alves de Lima e Silva, later known as the Duke of Caxias. In 1845, by a succession of military victories followed by the promise of a general armistice, Caxias also ended the ten-year war in Rio Grande do Sul.

At the Capital, the liberals returned to power in 1844 but were again forced to give way to the conservatives in 1848. This was the occasion for the last serious disturbance of Dom Pedro's reign, the *"praieira"* revolt in Pernambuco. The liberal officials in that province had made political rivalries more acute than usual during their recent tenure of power by openly encouraging a campaign of terrorism against resident Portuguese merchants, and they now attempted to prevent the conservatives from assuming control of local affairs. The revolt was suppressed after a few months of fighting. A newly established coastwise steamship service which carried troops rapidly to disaffected areas facilitated the task of restoring order.

The Emperor had by this time begun to exercise the great personal influence that kept party strife within bounds during the remainder of his reign. The radicals and federalists who had inspired the rebellions against the Regency lost their influence, and the slave-owning landed aristocracy dominated local affairs in most of the provinces. The leading figures in this group, in the first years of Pedro's reign, were the sugar barons of Bahia and Pernambuco, but after the middle of the nineteenth century the development of great coffee plantations, in the mountains back of Rio de Janeiro, and a little later in São Paulo, created a new aristocracy in the central provinces. Most of the political leaders came from the landholding class. They formed two parties, which called themselves liberal and conservative; but there was no great difference in their objectives, and neither had any large popular following. For several years in the 1850's the Emperor governed with "cabinets of conciliation" representing both groups. Later he usually called on one or the other to assume the responsibility of administration, but the fall of a cabinet meant little more than a change in personnel and caused no disturbance of public order. The defeated party could withdraw peacefully because it knew that the system would assure its return to power within a few years.

The Emperor was the real head of the government, making the most important decisions and carefully supervising his ministers' work. It was he rather than the voters who decided which party should be in power. The ministers were drawn from the group that had a majority in the Chamber, but it was a simple matter to dissolve this body and obtain a new one with a majority favorable to the other party when the Emperor felt that the time for a political change had arrived. Elections were no more free than in other South American countries, but Dom Pedro endeavored to rule in harmony with public opinion, and his government perhaps approached the ideal of a constitutional monarchy as nearly as the political education of the Brazilians permitted. The Senate, whose members were carefully selected by the Emperor from lists presented by the provincial electors, became a highly respected body, though an exceedingly conservative one. Dom Pedro's influence and his untiring attention to the details of administration made the government more efficient and less corrupt than its predecessors, at least so far as the higher officials were concerned. Among the lower ranks of officeholders the bad practices inherited from the colonial regime seem to have persisted to a greater degree.

The most troublesome question that confronted the empire after the establishment of internal peace was the continued existence of the African slave trade. In 1826 Pedro I had been compelled by pressure from Great Britain and as a condition for the recognition of Brazilian independence to agree by treaty to stop this traffic. It was made illegal in 1830, but foreign vessels continued to bring many thousands of Negroes each year, with the connivance of the Brazilian officials. The planters felt that they must have new slaves if they were to continue to produce sugar and coffee, for the Negro population of Brazil had never held its own by natural increase. The continued existence of the trade was a constant source of friction with Great Britain, and in 1845, when Brazil refused to renew the treaty of 1826, the British parliament passed the Aberdeen Act, which permitted the condemnation of slave ships by British admiralty courts rather than by the joint commissions that had acted under the treaty. Five years later it authorized its cruisers to seize such ships even in Brazilian territorial waters. Confronted by this threat, Dom Pedro insisted on the passage of the Queiroz law of 1850 which effectively suppressed the trade.

In dealing with his South American neighbors, Dom Pedro's policy was a somewhat aggressive one. His interventions in the River Plate region between 1850 and 1870 have been mentioned in earlier chapters. Brazil's participation in the movement that overthrew Rosas in 1852 cost the empire little and gave it for the time being a preponderant influence in eastern South America, but another intervention in Uruguay 12 years later brought on the long conflict with López of Paraguay, in which the imperial army lost 33,000 men and the government spent several hundred millions of dollars. At its close, in 1870, Brazil was exhausted morally and financially, but the Emperor's prestige, somewhat shaken by the reverses in the earlier years of the war, was restored by final victory.

The war only temporarily interrupted the empire's economic progress. In the second half of the nineteenth century, European immigrants began to arrive in considerable numbers, especially in the southern provinces. Rio de Janeiro, Minas Geraes, and São Paulo were henceforth more important than the older settlements in the north, where the cultivation of sugar, tobacco, and cotton was no longer so profitable as in the first years after independence. Coffee had become the empire's chief export, and it was in this period that Brazil began to supply more of this commodity to the world's market than all other countries combined. With internal peace and a growing foreign trade, both population and national wealth increased rapidly. The first railroads were built, and small industries were established. The chief figure in the country's economic development under the empire was the Baron de Mauá, who organized companies for the construction of railways, public utilities, and industrial ventures and controlled banks in Brazil and nearby countries.

WHY THE EMPIRE FELL

A traveler who visited South America in 1881 was much impressed by the contrast between Brazil and other countries on the east coast of South America. Despite the continued existence of slavery and the mixture of races among its people, the empire seemed "really civilized," with a government that appeared to be securely established and far better able to maintain order than those of the River Plate republics.[1] To such an observer, the monarchy must have seemed responsible for much of the difference. It would have been difficult for him to suppose that the Emperor would soon be overthrown, for few contemporary rulers were apparently more beloved by their own people or more highly regarded in foreign countries.

Several factors were nevertheless working to weaken the dynasty's position. Many businessmen felt that Dom Pedro had failed to grasp the importance of the new economic problems that had come with the growth of population and trade, and many of the political leaders criticized his government as undemocratic and ultraconservative. Before 1870, a reorganized and more aggressive liberal party began to demand electoral reforms and to work for the abolition of slavery, objectives with which the Emperor had much sympathy but which he did not consider immediately attainable. While opposition was thus growing among the progressive elements, many conservatives were becoming lukewarm, if not hostile. Among these were the more devout Catholics. Dom Pedro was extremely tolerant in religious matters, but at the same time he firmly maintained the government's authority over the Church. Ecclesiastical questions gave little trouble until a conflict between some of the clergy and the Freemasons—brought on by Pope Pius IX's condemnation of the Masonic order—aroused much public excitement in the early 1870's. When the bishops of Pará and Pernambuco ordered the *irmandades*, or lay religious fraternities, to expel all Masons from their membership and sought to force compliance by laying interdicts, the government intervened, and the two bishops were imprisoned for disobedience in 1874. This caused a

[1] Knight, *Cruise of the Falcon*, p. 333.

great scandal, and the release of the bishops a few months later in response to the pressure of public opinion did not help the Emperor's prestige.

The growing feeling that the imperial government was an anachronism that had outlived its usefulness was increased by the unpopularity of the Princess Isabel, who was Dom Pedro's prospective successor, and by the dislike of the Brazilians for her French husband, the Count d'Eu. There were relatively few Brazilians who advocated a revolution during the Emperor's lifetime, for he was still personally popular, but an increasing number looked forward to the establishment of a republic after his death. Since 1870, a small but vociferous republican party had carried on propaganda with little interference from the imperial authorities. This group acquired some importance in São Paulo and Minas Geraes, and Dom Pedro's rapidly failing health encouraged it to intensify its activities. The avowed republicans were probably a small minority, but there was a strong desire among the educated classes generally for political reforms of some sort.

The event that did most to alienate the class to whom the dynasty might normally have looked to support was the abolition of slavery. Slavery had been done away with in nearly all other civilized countries, and there was a strong abolition movement in Brazil. In 1871 the government had forced through Parliament the Rio Branco law which declared all children born thereafter legally free, though requiring them to work for their mothers' owners until the age of twenty-one. This satisfied the advocates of emancipation for the time being, but after 1878 there was a vigorous campaign for complete abolition, led by Joaquim Nabuco. In 1884 the provinces of Ceará and Amazonas freed slaves in their territory by local action, and in 1885 the imperial Parliament freed all slaves over sixty years of age. Thousands more were emancipated by the voluntary action of their masters, so that whereas a quarter or more of the inhabitants of Brazil had been in servitude in 1865 there were approximately 700,000 in a population of 15,000,000 in 1888. Many of these were becoming unruly. In São Paulo great numbers simply abandoned the plantations, assisted and protected by emancipation sympathizers, and the army refused to help the civil police to capture them.

Dom Pedro disliked slavery, and he suffered keenly from the criticism directed against Brazil in foreign countries; but he had not been inclined to force any sudden and radical solution of the problem because of the economic interests involved. His daughter Isabel was less cautious and more ardent in her zeal for emancipation. In 1888, when the Princess was acting as Regent while her father was making one of his occasional visits to Europe, a bill freeing all slaves was proposed by the Crown and passed by a large majority in both chambers. Since there was no provision for compensation, the owners were deprived at one stroke of property worth hundreds of millions of dollars. The "Golden Law," as the Brazilians called the measure, was tremendously popular with the masses of the people, but it ruined many landowners who could not readily find a new labor supply for their plantations.

When the Emperor returned from Europe, he was welcomed affectionately, as usual, but it was clear even to him that the dynasty's position was gravely weakened. He himself was ill, and his mental powers were apparently failing. He had always said that he would not resist if his people desired to abolish the monarchy, but he sought to avert the threatened revolution by making concessions. The Viscount of Ouro Preto, who became Prime Minister in June, 1889, proposed a series of constitutional changes, among them the granting of autonomy to the provinces, the extension of the suffrage, and the abolition of life tenure in the Senate. His program was defeated in Parliament, and though a new election, controlled by the customary methods, gave the Cabinet a majority, it was clear by this time that even radical reforms could not restore the dynasty's popularity. The civilian population, however, was apathetic rather than actively rebellious, and the sudden fall of the empire was brought about by a revolt in the army with very little civilian participation.

Discipline in the army had been deteriorating since the death of the Duke of Caxias, the empire's greatest soldier, in 1880. Brazilian army officers had customarily participated in politics, and their partisan activities had sometimes brought them into conflicts with the War Ministry in a way that encouraged a dangerous spirit of insubordination. There had been repeated violations of an order issued in 1884 prohibiting them from making public statements on controversial subjects without prior approval by the Ministry, and the government had been timid and ineffective in its efforts to deal with the offenders. At the same time, much republican propaganda had been spread among the younger officers by the teachings of Benjamin Constant Botelho de Magelhães, a popular professor in the military school at Rio de Janeiro.

On November 15, 1889, when the Ouro Preto Cabinet attempted to send some of the more disaffected regiments into distant provinces and to offset the influence of the professional soldiers by strengthening the national guard, a portion of the garrison at Rio de Janeiro, led by General Deodoro da Fonseca, seized control of the city. There was almost no bloodshed because the Adjutant General, Floriano Peixoto, refused to obey the Cabinet's order to resist. The army leaders originally planned merely to overthrow the Cabinet without displacing the Emperor, but Benjamin Constant and other radical leaders persuaded Deodoro to abolish the monarchy altogether. The Emperor was deposed and sent into exile. A Federal Republic, the United States of Brazil, was proclaimed, and Deodoro became the head of the "provisional government by the army and the navy, in the name of the nation."

MILITARY GOVERNMENTS, 1889–1894

The Republic had been established by a part of the army, with only a small amount of support from civilian leaders. There was little effective opposition from the old ruling class, and the masses of the people accepted it rather apathetically. The new President relied for support chiefly on his popularity with the army. His Cabinet included distinguished civilians like Ruy Barbosa, who was one of the country's most eminent jurists, and the future President Campos Salles, but it was inexperienced and hampered in its work by internal differences. It nevertheless reorganized the national and local administration and carried out a number of other reforms, among them the separation of Church and State. A Constituent Assembly which met in November, 1890, drew up a constitution much like that of the United States, converting the provinces into self-governing states. It also elected Deodoro President of the Republic.

Deodoro was an able soldier, with a reputation for personal honesty, but he showed little skill in dealing with political questions. There was much opposition to his autocratic methods, and he met with a growing resistance in the Assembly which had now become the first federal Congress. The President finally dissolved the Congress by military force and announced that he was assuming dictatorial powers to frustrate a plot for the restoration of the monarchy. This provoked a revolutionary outbreak in Rio Grande do Sul, and there were lesser disturbances in several other provinces. In November, 1891, when the navy turned its guns on Rio de Janeiro and demanded his resignation, Deodoro quietly turned over his office to the Vice-President, General Floriano Peixoto.

Peixoto had the army behind him and was able by persuasion or coercion to command the support of a majority in the Congress, but he was unpopular with the conservative groups and with the business community. The navy, whose officers came mainly from the old aristocracy, was jealous of the army's preponderance in the government, and in September, 1893, the entire fleet revolted under the leadership of Admiral Custodio de Mello who had headed the uprising of 1891. The insurgents controlled the harbor of Rio de Janeiro for six months, but the commanders of several North American and European warships prevented them from bombarding the city or blockading the port. De Mello finally left Rio de Janeiro with a part of his forces to co-operate with a revolutionary movement led by Gumercindo Saraiva in Rio Grande do Sul. The insurgents obtained control of much of southern Brazil, but they failed to follow up their successes with a movement on the Capital. Admiral Saldanha da Gama, who had been left in command of the insurgents there, had meanwhile made it known that he favored the re-establishment of the monarchy, and his attitude cost the rebels many supporters even though there was little evidence that the other leaders had the same purpose. In March, 1894, when several new warships purchased abroad by the government arrived off the harbor, the movement collapsed. A large number of those implicated in the revolt were put to death by the federal authorities.

REPUBLICAN GOVERNMENTS, 1894–1914

The presidential election of 1894 was held while the revolt was still in progress. Prudente de Moraes, one of the original republican leaders from São Paulo, was the official and consequently the successful candidate, for the early republican governments controlled elections at least as effectively as the imperial government did. Peixoto, who was ill, did not attempt to remain in power himself or to perpetuate the control of the army, and the inauguration of an able civilian President gave the republican regime a prestige that it had not thus far had. Nevertheless, the new President had to deal with many troublesome questions. Financial problems inherited from his predecessors became all but insoluble as the effects of the world depression of the '90's made themselves felt, and there were several unsuccessful uprisings in the army, which resented its loss of political power. Some of the participants in the recent revolt continued guerrilla warfare in Rio Grande do Sul until August, 1895. In 1896 a group of religious fanatics in the back country of Bahia, led by one Antonio Maciel, generally called Antonio Conselheiro, came into conflict with the authorities, and order was not restored until several federal expeditionary forces had been ingloriously defeated and a great amount of money had been wasted. In 1897 a conspiracy to assassinate the President himself, instigated by military officers and rival politicians, resulted in the death of the Minister of War.

In spite of these difficulties, Prudente de Moraes maintained the prestige of the federal government, and his successors had less trouble with internal disorder. By 1898 economic conditions were improving. Dr. Manoel Ferras de Campos Salles, who became President in that year, was able to put the finances in relatively good order, for the first time in the Republic's history. Under his successor, Dr. Francisco de Paula Rodrigues Alves (1902–1906) municipal improvements enhanced the great natural beauty of Rio de Janeiro, and a campaign against yellow fever, directed by the Brazilian physician Oswaldo Cruz, made the Capital a safer place to live. During the same period the Baron of Rio Branco began his long and brilliant service as Minister of Foreign Affairs, in the course of which he settled by arbitration or friendly agreement nearly all of the boundary disputes that were a potential source of trouble between Brazil and other South American republics. Continued prosperity during the administration of Affonso

Augusto Moreira Penna, who was elected to the presidency in 1906, made it possible to stabilize the fluctuating and depreciated paper currency which had been a handicap to commerce since the days of the empire.

Most of the civilian political leaders, in the first years of the Republic, were members of the same landholding aristocracy that had furnished the statesmen and politicians of the empire. The republican party was the only important political party, but it was divided into factions, and political control after 1900 passed more and more into the hands of oligarchies that dominated politics and controlled elections in some of the larger states. Of these, São Paulo and Minas Geraes were the most important. The smaller states had less influence because their local administrations were dominated by the group in control at the Capital and the federal government did not hesitate to interfere in their affairs when such action seemed desirable for political reasons. The first three civilian presidents were from São Paulo, which had been the original center of the republican movement, and Penna was a native of Minas Geraes.

There were many political leaders in other states who resented this state of affairs, and there was much discontent in the army, which had never resigned itself entirely to the loss of the power that it enjoyed before 1894. The opponents of the São Paulo–Minas Geraes coalition obtained control temporarily after Affonso Penna died in 1909 and the Vice-President, Nilo Peçanha, took his place. Through the machinations of Pinheiro Machado, the political boss of Rio Grande do Sul, a congressional caucus chose Marshall Hermes da Fonseca, a nephew of Deodoro and a native of Rio Grande do Sul, as the official candidate. Those who opposed a return of military domination supported Ruy Barbosa, but official pressure decided the election as it always did. Hermes da Fonseca's administration was corrupt and inefficient, and there were several small uprisings in the navy and among other discontented groups, but he served out his term from 1910 to 1914. The São Paulo–Minas Geraes coalition returned to power in 1914 when Wenceslau Braz Pereira Gomes of Minas Geraes was chosen by the administration as the next President.

COFFEE, RUBBER, AND IMMIGRATION

As in most of the Latin American countries, political events in Brazil in the last years of the nineteenth and the first years of the twentieth century were of less interest than the economic progress which was rapidly giving the Western Hemisphere a new importance in world affairs. Coffee and rubber were doing for Brazil in these years what meat and grain were doing for Argentina, and a great wave of immigration was having the same effect as in the River Plate countries. The arrival of some 3,000,000 European laborers, most of them from Italy, Portugal, and Spain, more than offset any bad economic effect from the abolition of slavery, for the newcomers were far more useful, especially on the coffee plantations, than slave labor had been. Like the earlier immigrants, most of them came to São Paulo and the less developed regions farther south.

Coffee was still the most important export, and Brazil was by this time furnishing three-fourths of the total world supply of this commodity. During the last decade of the nineteenth century coffee production outran consumption, and prices fell. To check the decline, the State of São Paulo prohibited planting of new trees for a period of ten years after 1902. In 1906, with the co-operation of the federal government and with financial help from London and New York bankers, the State undertook the first of a series of experiments in "valorization," buying up a large amount of coffee and withholding it from the market until prices improved. The success of this scheme and of a similar operation during the European war led in 1922 to the adoption of a permanent plan of control which has continued in one form or another to the present time.

Rubber, in the first decade of the century, was an almost equally important export. For generations the greater part of the world's supply had been obtained from the wild trees of the Amazon Valley, and with the increasing use of bicycles, and later of automobiles, the demand rapidly increased. Many thousands of laborers from the drought-ridden state of Ceará and other nearby districts were employed in gathering it. Manáos, a riverport 1,000 miles from the sea, became a large city. After 1912, however, the plantations of the Far East, with their cheap labor, began to produce great quantities of rubber, and the Brazilian product, gathered under great difficulties from scattered trees in the tropical jungle, ceased to be an important item in world trade.

A large amount of sugar, consumed chiefly in Brazil itself, was still raised in Pernambuco, and the cultivation of cacao and tobacco was important in Bahia. These older communities, however, had advanced less rapidly than those of the south, and they had been more severely affected by the abolition of slavery. Their population was still predominantly of Negro blood, and their hotter climate made them less attractive to immigrants. They had shared to a relatively small extent in the new railroad mileage that had been built since the fall of the empire. The south had definitely become the most important section of the Republic. Minas Geraes and São Paulo had populations larger than those of most of the independent Latin American countries, and Rio Grande do Sul, with its growing cattle industry, had more influence in Brazilian affairs than Pernambuco.

POLITICAL EVENTS, 1914–1930

The First World War affected Brazil as it did her neighbors. When it started, imports and exports fell off and with them the government's revenues. The conversion office was closed, and new paper money was issued to meet current expenditures. The export trade, however, soon revived, and the inconveniences caused by the dislocation of ocean transport and the shortage of goods were offset by an increased demand for products like cotton and sugar. Since Brazil declared war on Germany in 1917, her government was represented at the Peace Conference, and she became one of the first members of the Council of the League of Nations. She left the League in 1926, however, when the other powers refused to make her position in the Council a permanent one.

Ex-President Rodrigues Alves was elected to succeed Wenceslau Braz in 1918; but he died at the beginning of his term, and Epitacio da Silva Pessoa of Parahyba, who had distinguished himself as the head of the Brazilian delegation at Versailles, was chosen in his place. The new administration embarked upon an ambitious program of public works, financed in part by foreign borrowing. This involved the government in difficulties when depression followed the brief postwar boom. There was a sharp contest in the election of 1922. Ex-President Nilo Peçanha was the opposition candidate, put forward by the same political-military group that had been in power between 1910 and 1914. When he was defeated by Arthur da Silva Bernardes, who had the support of the administration, there was some talk of revolution. Small uprisings did occur in the army as the result of a conspiracy headed by Hermes da Fonseca, but they were suppressed before Bernardes' inauguration. A much more serious revolt took place in July, 1924, when a portion of the army seized the city of São Paulo and held it for three weeks before loyal troops were able to gain the upper hand. Other disturbances frequently compelled the government to establish martial law in one region or another during the remainder of Dr. Bernardes' term, but after Dr. Washington Luis Pereira de Souza became President in 1926, business conditions improved with higher coffee prices, and the political situation was more tranquil.

THE COLLAPSE OF COFFEE VALORIZATION AND THE REVOLUTION OF 1930

Unfortunately the prosperity of the coffee industry was partly factitious. During the postwar depression, the federal government again attempted to stabilize the market, and in 1922 an Institute for the Permanent Defense of Coffee was established. Two years later this national organization turned the problem over to a state institute in São Paulo, which worked with the co-operation of similar bodies in other Brazilian states. In order to maintain prices, the amounts exported each month were limited by compelling growers to ship their production to warehouses in the interior, from which it was forwarded to the ports in amounts determined in accordance with the condition of the market. Loans were made to the planters on coffee that had not yet been sold, and production was not restricted.

On the contrary, it tended to increase because prices were artificially maintained at a high level and direct purchases were made by the Coffee Institute when the market needed support.

Two very large crops in succession, in 1927–1928 and 1928–1929, finally caused a tremendous oversupply at a time when increasing tightness in the world's money markets made it difficult to continue the foreign borrowing by which the system of valorization had been maintained. In October, 1929, the world price of coffee suddenly collapsed, bringing ruin to planters and merchants and gravely affecting the government's financial situation. The catastrophe had serious political repercussions because the plan of valorization was the work of the same group of political leaders in São Paulo who controlled the federal administration under Washington Luis.

Washington Luis made matters worse when he put forward another *Paulista*, Julio Prestes, as the official candidate in the election in 1930. This was a departure from the arrangement by which the dominant political groups in São Paulo and Minas Geraes had maintained their supremacy in federal affairs and had taken turns in presenting candidates for the presidency, and the leaders in Minas Geraes consequently threw their support to Getulio Vargas, the Governor of Rio Grande do Sul. The party in power, however, controlled the administrations and the electoral machinery in nearly all of the other states and was victorious by a popular vote of 1,089,000 to 735,000.

The losers seemed inclined at first to accept the result peaceably, but their attitude changed when several of their party who had apparently been elected to Congress were counted out by the board that canvassed the returns, and when the federal authorities intervened in Parahyba to set up a state administration controlled by their own partisans. On October 3, 1930, revolts began simultaneously in Rio Grande do Sul, Minas Geraes, and Parahyba. A civil war involving much of the Republic's territory seemed imminent. Before very much fighting had actually occurred, however, a group of military leaders seized control at Rio de Janeiro and São Paulo, establishing a provisional *junta* which some days later recognized Getulio Vargas as provisional President.

GETULIO VARGAS

Dr. Vargas ruled Brazil during the next 15 years. When he first took control, all federal, state, and local legislative bodies were dissolved, and the constitutional guarantees were suspended. The arbitrary conduct of the young military officers who served as interventors in most of the states aroused much dissatisfaction even in the provisional President's own party. In May, 1932, however, public opinion was somewhat mollified by an announcement that a Constituent Assembly would be convened, and the people of São Paulo received little help from other states when they made a desperate effort to recover their ascendancy in the federal government by armed revolt the following July. Fortunately, the war was a short one, and the insurgents surrendered early in October. Though the chief leaders were exiled, the defeated party was treated with a moderation that did much to facilitate a return to normal conditions.

The Constituent Assembly met in November, 1933, after an election in which the secret ballot was used for the first time in Brazil's history. The administration apparently made an effort to assure freedom and fair play, and opposition parties were well represented, though the majority of the delegates were supporters of the government. The new constitution, promulgated on July 16, 1934, differed in several respects from that of 1891, especially in its provisions for advanced social legislation and in the restrictions that it imposed on participation by foreigners in business and in the learned professions.

The Assembly elected Vargas President for the term 1934–1938, and in the months that followed, the state governments were reorganized and the constitutional order was generally restored. The economic situation improved, but political conditions were still unsettled. Besides the old factions centering around leaders in the various states, two extremist parties, the communists and the fascistic *integralistas,* had made their appearance. The communists were accused of inciting a radical revolt in the army and navy, which was put down with much bloodshed in November, 1935. Thereafter the party was driven underground, and its leader, Luiz Carlos Prestes, was sentenced to a long term in jail. The *integralistas,* on the other hand, co-operated for some time with the Vargas administration.

In 1937, political agitation increased with the approach of the time for the election of a new president. The most prominent candidate was Salles Oliveira, a former Governor of São Paulo; but he was not acceptable to Vargas, and his chances were diminished when his ally, Governor Flores da Cunha of Rio Grande do Sul, was driven from power by a federal intervention. Under the constitution, Vargas could not be re-elected to succeed himself, but on November 10, 1937, he settled the problem by setting aside the constitution and proclaiming a new one that extended his term for six years. The new fundamental law gave the executive very extraordinary powers. Its most remarkable provision, perhaps, was that it should not go into full effect until the President should see fit to submit it for popular approval in a plebiscite. In the meantime, under its emergency provisions, the President was to legislate by decree and to take such actions as he saw fit to maintain order. Since the plebiscite was never held, Vargas was the absolute ruler of Brazil until he left office in 1945.

Unlike most Latin American dictatorships, the *Estado Novo,* as the new regime called itself, made little pretense of being republican in form. For a time, some of the President's advisers seemed inclined to adopt the ideas and methods of European totalitarianism, but Vargas himself was too shrewd a politician to espouse a philosophy that was repugnant to most of his fellow citizens. The native fascists, the *integralistas* who had supported him in the *coup d'état*, were given little part in the new government, and when they attempted to kill the President and seize power in May, 1938, several hundred were imprisoned. Thereafter neither they nor the communists gave the regime much trouble. All other political parties were dissolved by order of the government, and the freedom of the press was greatly restricted.

The establishment of the dictatorship met with surprisingly little opposition. Vargas was popular personally, and he was able to obtain the co-operation of many other influential leaders. The common people felt that an effort was at last being made to improve their situation, for the new constitution contained several provisions intended to benefit the working man. The propertied classes were glad to have a strong government, especially in view of the increasingly threatening international situation.

The rise of fascism in Europe was a greater danger to Brazil than to most of the other American republics. In the southern states of Rio Grande do Sul, Santa Catarina, and Paraná, there were perhaps a million people of German descent who, unlike the Italian and Spanish immigrants, had retained their own language and to some extent their loyalty to the mother country. Nazi propaganda, backed by economic coercion, had been alarmingly successful among these people, and by the end of 1937 there was a strong potential fifth column throughout the region. In April, 1938, Vargas issued a decree-law forbidding foreigners to engage in any sort of political activity. The need for this was emphasized when officials of the German legation at Rio de Janeiro were implicated in the *integralista* revolt a month later and the German Minister was declared *persona non grata*. Later decrees forbade the maintenance of schools by foreign minorities and sought in other ways to force the rapid assimilation of the German population.

The loss of the European coffee markets after the outbreak of the war in 1939 was a severe blow, but the Inter-American Coffee Agreement made it somewhat less serious.[2] Shipments of many other products to the United States increased. Brazil's manganese and quartz crystals and other strategic materials were of great value in the war effort. A program of road and railroad building helped to relieve unemployment, and a loan from the United States Export-Import Bank made possible the erection of a large steel mill. Brazil declared war on Italy and Germany in August, 1942, and sent troops to the front in Italy. The airfields in her territory were extremely important to the United States in maintaining communication across the Atlantic during the operations in North Africa and Europe.

[2] See below, p. 504.

POSTWAR ADMINISTRATIONS

Vargas refused to consider the holding of elections while the war was in progress, but he promised that constitutional government would be restored with the return of peace. In February, 1945, however, the pressure of public opinion compelled him to relax the ban on political activity and to agree to call a presidential election. There were two principal candidates: General Eurico Gaspar Dutra, the Minister of War, and General Eduardo Gomes, who had the support of some of the more liberal elements. Dutra was supposedly the government's candidate; but there were many who doubted whether Vargas would actually step down when the time came, and this skepticism increased when Vargas apparently accepted the support of the communist leader, Luiz Carlos Prestes, who was released from jail in April with other political prisoners. A repetition of what had happened in 1937 was prevented when the army forced Vargas to resign in October, 1945, and the Chief Justice of the Supreme Court took over as provisional President. General Dutra was elected to the presidency five weeks later and was inaugurated on January 31, 1946. There was little complaint about the fairness of the voting, in which more than 5,000,000 citizens took part. A new constitution, in 1946, restored a normal republican form of government and gave back to the states some of the autonomy that they had lost under the highly centralized *estado novo*.

The constitution also authorized the suppression of undemocratic political parties, and the communist party—which had polled more than half a million votes in December, 1945—was declared outlawed in May, 1947. The government seized its offices and took over the direction of the Brazilian Workers Confederation which had been under communist control. In October, after the Moscow press published articles which insulted President Dutra, Brazil broke off diplomatic relations with Soviet Russia. The communists nevertheless continued to participate in political affairs, and in November, 1947, their leader, Prestes, and ex-President Vargas campaigned side by side against the government-supported candidates in local elections in São Paulo. Some communists continued to serve in Congress until that body expelled Prestes from the Senate and 15 deputies from the lower House in January, 1948.

Vargas, who still had a great following, returned to the presidency in 1951, after a free and orderly election. He owed his victory, apparently, to the votes of people who were dissatisfied with existing economic and social conditions and to the suffering caused by inflation which had become a serious problem since the end of the war. He could do nothing, however, to improve the situation. Inflation grew worse, and a $300,000,-000 loan from the United States in 1953 only helped matters temporarily. Opposition to the President consequently increased and became more bitter. The crisis came when the government was accused of complicity in the attempted murder of an opposition newspaper man. There were loud demands that the President resign, and even the Cabinet urged him to withdraw temporarily. Instead, Vargas killed himself, in August, 1954.

The Vice-President, João Cafe Filho, took over the government and presided over another orderly election in which Dr. Juscelino Kubitschek was chosen as President. There was a brief flurry of excitement in the interval between the election and the inauguration, when Cafe resigned because of illness and General Teixeira Lott, who had been Minister of War, ousted the speaker of the Chamber of Deputies, who was the constitutional successor. Order was restored after the Congress chose a new provisional President, and the constitutional President was inaugurated on January 31, 1956.

At the beginning of his term Dr. Kubitschek announced that the objective of his administration would be a broad program of industrial and agricultural development. In the two decades before 1956, Brazilian industrial production had been increasing very rapidly, and São Paulo had become one of the great industrial centers of the continent. Agricultural production had also grown with the settlement of large hitherto unoccupied areas in the interior. The very rapidity of the country's development, however, had created grave economic and social problems.

The most serious of these was the inflation which had caused trouble for earlier administrations and which grew even worse after 1956. Great issues of paper money, much of it issued to cover continuing deficits in the government's budget, caused a sharp fall in the value of the *milreis*, and coffee prices, which were extraordinarily high in 1954, fell rapidly in the years that followed, despite the government's costly efforts to support them. It was increasingly difficult to pay for the imports that the country needed, and the rise in the cost of living caused labor unrest that manifested itself in strikes and disorders.

The government's plans for further development called for a considerable investment of new capital. Large sums were obtained as loans from the government of the United States, although Brazilian dissatisfaction with the amount that the United States felt able to provide and with the terms on which it was offered caused some friction between the two governments. Much private capital was also obtained, and more would have been available had it not been for the strong spirit of economic nationalism that prevailed in Brazilian political circles. This spirit, for example, precluded the enlistment of help from foreign oil companies to increase Brazil's petroleum production, at a time when great amounts of much-needed foreign exchange were being used for oil imports. The expropriation of some of the foreign companies already working in the country was a further deterrent to new investment.

One of Dr. Kubitschek's major projects was the construction of a new capital city far in the interior, in a region that was as yet sparsely settled.

There was much opposition to this, especially in Rio de Janeiro, but great sums were spent on what promised to be an imaginatively planned and beautiful home for future governments. The federal authorities began to move to Brasilia in April, 1960.

With its great area and rapidly increasing population, Brazil has a great potentiality for further growth. The country is still the world's principal source of coffee, though the increased production of cotton and other agricultural products has decreased the excessive dependence on this one crop. Industrial production is still increasing rapidly, and there are great as-yet-undeveloped mineral resources. Wealth, however, is unevenly divided. The Amazon Valley, with its heavy rainfall and large areas where much of the natural plant food has been leached from the soil by the rains, can hardly support a large population in the foreseeable future. Much of the *sertao*, the inland plateau in the northeast, is drought-ridden. The southern states, with their good farm land, are far more prosperous than the tropical north. Even in the south, however, standards of living are low among the masses of the people, and malnutrition, bad housing, disease, and illiteracy are obstacles to the development of political democracy and an encouragement to the growth of communism. It is these conditions that recent governments have endeavored to better by their programs of development.

PART VII

MEXICO

THE HISTORY OF THE COUNTRIES north of the Isthmus of Panama is more intimately connected with our own than is the history of the South American republics. This is especially true of Mexico, the only Latin American state with which we have a land frontier. The course of events in Mexico has repeatedly been affected by its proximity to the United States, and relations with Mexico have frequently been an issue in our domestic politics.

This is not the only reason why the history of Mexico is especially interesting to the North American student. With a population larger than that of any other Latin American state except Brazil, our southern neighbor is one of the most important nations of the hemisphere. Furthermore, its troubled history illustrates with peculiar vividness the character of the political and social problems that have complicated the development of many of the other countries of Spanish origin: the difficulty of establishing stable republican institutions, the conflict between Church and State, and above all the social tensions arising from the presence of an unassimilated, exploited Indian population. The Mexicans have made a real effort to solve some of these problems, and their experience, whether of success or of failure, is important to anyone who wishes to understand the problems of the other countries where somewhat similar conditions exist.

CHAPTER 18

Mexico, 1810-1911

MEXICO IN 1810

AT THE BEGINNING OF THE NINETEENTH CENTURY, New Spain was the richest and most important of the Spanish American colonies. Its population of 6,000,000 was greater than that of New Granada and Peru put together and had only recently been surpassed by that of the rapidly growing United States. Mexico City, with about 135,000 inhabitants, was probably the largest city of the Western World, with public institutions such as the School of Mines, the Academy of Fine Arts, and the Botanical Garden that had no peers in North or South America. It had always been one of the chief intellectual centers of the continent, and there had been an especially active interest in literature, art, and science from the latter part of the eighteenth century. The viceroyalty of which it was the Capital produced two-thirds of the world's silver, and many great fortunes had been made from its mines. Agriculture also flourished, for the mines furnished a large market and there was also a considerable export of sugar. New Spain's revenues helped to support the governments of some of the less prosperous colonies and left a large surplus to be remitted to Spain.

The chief beneficiaries of this prosperity were the people of Spanish descent, who made up hardly more than 15 per cent of the total population. As in other parts of Spanish America, it was they who owned the best lands and most of the mines. The *mestizos*, mostly artisans or day laborers, were set apart from the white aristocracy by caste prejudices and legal disabilities, and many thousands of them, especially in the larger cities, lived in abject poverty. The Indians probably outnumbered both of the other groups. In the mining regions, at least, they were better off than in South America because the miners were comparatively well paid and compulsory labor was less common. The eminent traveler von Humboldt thought that the Mexican Indians in general were probably better off than the serfs in Russia and northern Germany, but he nevertheless

349

gave a dismal picture of their condition.[1] Most of them were still in a state of tutelage, living on the properties of white landowners or in separate villages under the often despotic government of officials of their own race, and legally incapable of signing contracts or incurring debts of more than three dollars.

THE *GRITO DE DOLORES*

The struggle for independence in Mexico began in the same year that saw the first successful uprisings in Spanish South America. As in Caracas and Buenos Aires, some of the creoles saw in Napoleon's conquest of Spain an opportunity to free America from the rule of the peninsular Spaniards who monopolized the higher positions in the government and the Church. A group of conspirators at Querétaro had for some time been discussing plans for a revolt when the betrayal of their conspiracy forced them into a premature uprising. The leader of the movement was Miguel Hidalgo y Costilla, a creole priest at nearby Dolores, who had long been suspected of radical views and had a devoted following among his parishioners.

On September 16, 1810, Hidalgo summoned his followers to revolt, professing allegiance to Ferdinand VII but demanding creole supremacy and the abolition of Indian tributes and caste distinctions. *El Grito de Dolores,* the "cry of Dolores," met with an immediate response among the country people aroundabout, and Hidalgo was soon at the head of a great mob of Indians and *mestizos.* He occupied the provincial Capital of Guanajuato and two or three other cities; but his undisciplined followers could not be converted into an effective fighting force, and the outrages they committed horrified many people who might otherwise have sympathized with a movement for independence. Early in 1811, his army was defeated and dispersed by the Viceroy's troops, and Hidalgo was captured and put to death.

Insurgent bands nevertheless remained in the field in several parts of the country. Another creole priest, José María Morelos, emerged as their most prominent leader. It soon became evident that the movement had the sympathy of a large part of the Mexican people, for when the Viceroy was compelled to promulgate the Spanish constitution of 1812, which provided for freedom of the press, there was an outburst of subversive writings which soon compelled him to suspend its operation. For a time in 1812 and 1813, the royal authorities hardly controlled any part of the country except the larger towns and principal ports. The revolutionary movement, however, was weakened by rivalries among its leaders, and the hardships that followed the paralyzation of trade and the closing of the mines and the larger agricultural enterprises caused many persons who disliked the

[1] Von Humboldt, *Political Essay on New Spain,* Vol. I (New York ed., 1811), p. 134.

Spanish regime to support the authorities in their efforts to restore order. As in the other colonies, creoles made up the greater part of the armies on both sides. The Viceroy gradually got the upper hand, and late in 1815 Morelos was captured and shot. During the next few years most of the other insurgent leaders accepted the government's offer of amnesty.

ITURBIDE

Though many of the creoles continued secretly to wish for independence, the separation from Spain, when it came, was largely the work of the most reactionary group among the peninsular Spaniards. After the Spanish revolution of 1820, the extreme conservatives saw the home government controlled by people whose ideas were as odious as those of the creole insurgents. The radical *cortes*, which a mutinous army compelled Ferdinand VII to convoke, adopted a series of measures which were especially obnoxious to the Church: the Inquisition was abolished; tithes were suppressed; and much ecclesiastical property was sequestrated. Many of the higher clergy felt that independence would be a lesser evil than the execution of such a program, and some of the most prominent officials of the Church entered into a conspiracy to prevent the constitution from being enforced in Mexico. They chose as their instrument Agustín de Iturbide, a creole officer in the Spanish army who had distinguished himself in the fighting against the insurgents but had recently been summoned to Mexico City to answer charges of misconduct. Apparently through their influence, Iturbide was given command of a force that was to march against Vicente Guerrero, the leader of the most important band of rebels still in the field.

Iturbide probably hoped to defeat Guerrero and then to initiate his separatist movement, but reverses in the first weeks of the campaign led him to adopt a different course. He entered into negotiations with Guerrero, and on February 24, 1821, the two leaders agreed on joint action to attain independence. The "Plan of Iguala" provided that Mexico should become a constitutional empire under the rule of Ferdinand VII or some other European prince chosen by a Mexican *cortes*. The Catholic Church and the privileges of the clergy would be maintained, and all of the country's inhabitants would be equal before the law. These promises, skillfully designed to attract support from all parties, caused the agreement to be called the "Plan of the Three Guarantees": independence, religion, and union. "Union" meant not only the abolition of legal discrimination against the "castes" and the Indians but equality and co-operation between creoles and peninsular Spaniards.

The Viceroy rejected Iturbide's invitation to be a member of the *junta* that was to govern the country until the new Emperor arrived, but he took no energetic action to suppress the revolt. As the weeks passed, a large part of the government's troops, including many Spanish officers who opposed the liberal revolution at home, went over to the Plan of Iguala. The Army of the Three Guarantees had control of practically all of the country outside of Mexico City when a new Viceroy, Juan O'Dónoju, arrived at the end of July and felt compelled to sign the Treaty of Córdoba which accepted the program of the revolution. O'Dónoju became a member of the Regency that took control of the government of Mexico, but he died soon afterward, and the Crown's repudiation of his actions showed that there was little hope of Ferdinand's agreeing to become Emperor of Mexico himself or to permit a member of his family to do so.

A Regency headed by Iturbide assumed control of the government and called for the election of a Constitutional Assembly, which met in February, 1822. Since the Regency apparently made little effort to dictate the choice of the members, the Assembly included representatives of several points of view: bourbonists who still hoped that a Spanish prince would take the throne, republicans, and personal followers of Iturbide. It at once began to quarrel with the Regency, usually over minor matters, and its relations with Iturbide became still more unfriendly when it replaced three members of the Regency with persons whom he did not trust.

A proposal to forbid members of the Regency to have command of troops brought on a crisis. Iturbide, who was Commander in Chief of the army and navy as well as head of the Regency, had no intention of giving up either position. He had strong support among the conservative leaders and especially among the clergy, and he was popular with the common people of Mexico City. His supporters now encouraged him to seek the throne for himself, for the treaty of Córdoba had provided that another person might be chosen if no Spanish prince were available. In May, 1822, street demonstrations by the soldiers and populace, and forceful measures against some of the more recalcitrant deputies, compelled the Assembly to elect him as Emperor.

Agustín I reigned less than a year. He had much support at first, but the republicans and most of the bourbonists opposed him. The pomp with which he attempted to surround the new monarchy exposed him to ridicule, always a fatal weapon in Latin America, and financial troubles made his situation more difficult. He attempted to rule as a constitutional monarch, but his quarrels with the Assembly were soon resumed, and after he imprisoned a number of the deputies, and then in October dissolved the Assembly itself, public opinion turned against him. In December, a young officer named Antonio López de Santa Anna, who had been one of the Emperor's most outspoken supporters, revolted at Vera Cruz. Several of the leaders who had fought for independence before the Plan of Iguala, and who had long resented Iturbide's pre-eminence, joined the movement, and its success was assured when the powerful Scottish-rite Masons, whose membership included many of the officers in the imperial army, decided to support it.

On February 19, 1823, Iturbide abdicated and was permitted to go into exile with the promise of a pension. The Assembly, which the Emperor had convened in a last-minute effort at reconciliation, appointed three generals to head the new government. Their authority was challenged by mutinous military leaders in some of the provinces, but in most cases they were able to avert fighting by negotiation. Iturbide's friends staged a small revolt in July, 1824, but it soon collapsed, and when the ex-Emperor himself landed on the Mexican coast soon afterward he was captured and shot.

THE FIRST YEARS OF THE REPUBLIC

Most of the leaders were now agreed that Mexico should be a republic, but there was a difference of opinion about the form that the new government should take. The conservatives, including the former bourbonists and most of the Masons, wanted a centralized regime which would continue the ascendancy of the creole aristocracy in Mexico City, but many of the leaders in the provincial towns advocated a federal regime. Most of the revolutionists of the period before 1821 were in this group, as was the increasingly influential liberal party. The Assembly was chosen by a cumbersome system of indirect election, which left the control largely in the hands of the local groups, and the result was a victory for the federalists, who drew up a constitution that divided the country into 19 states and resembled in other ways the constitution of the United States. In October, 1824, Guadelupe Victoria and Nicolás Bravo, both of them heroes of the war for independence in the dark days before the Plan of Iguala, were inaugurated as President and Vice-President.

Victoria, whose real name was Manuel Félix Fernández, was a man of no great ability, but he was popular and honest. He gradually restored order in some of the states where local factions had been fighting for the control of the state government, and the government's financial difficulties, which had been a grave source of weakness under Iturbide, were relieved by the gradual recovery of mining and commerce and by two loans obtained from bankers in London. The long years of disorder after 1810 and the departure of most of the Spanish capitalists who had financed the miners had greatly reduced silver production, but many of the mines were now reopened by British and other capitalists. The Republic recovered the free use of its chief port when the Spanish garrison that still held the Castle of San Juan de Ulua at Vera Cruz was compelled to withdraw in November, 1825.

The most active political groups, during Victoria's administration, were the rival Masonic lodges. Since the Scottish-rite Masons, or *escoceses,* who had taken a leading part in the overthrow of Iturbide, were for the most part centralists, the federalists, with the encouragement of the government, organized the York-rite, or *yorquino*, lodges in 1825. One of their most active supporters was the first American Minister to Mexico, the active but not always judicious Joel Poinsett, who disliked the *escoceses* for their conservatism and because he thought that they were under the influence of the British Minister. Poinsett's political activity aroused much criticism, and when the *escoceses* revolted in 1828, under the leadership of Vice-President Bravo, one of their demands was for his expulsion.

The failure of this revolt, and the exile of its leaders, destroyed the influence of the Scottish-rite lodges, but the movement proved to be the first of a series of disturbances that undid much of the progress achieved in the first years of Victoria's administration. As in many of the other Spanish American countries, political inexperience and habits that had developed through years of revolutionary violence made it difficult to settle political disputes by peaceful means. It was as difficult to hold satisfactory elections as it was elsewhere. If fair elections could have been held, so that the government that emerged from them had a clear claim to legality, public opinion might have restrained the defeated party from attempting to reverse the outcome by force; but when the validity of the election could be challenged the government's moral position was weaker. There had been little difficulty about the election of 1824 because Victoria had great popular support, but the choice of his successor was a different matter.

Victoria's own candidate, Gómez Pedraza, was supported by one faction of the *yorquinos* and by many of the *escoceses*, but he had less popular following than his rival Vicente Guerrero, who was the Grand Master of the York-rite lodges and was backed by the more radical groups, including Poinsett. The election was by the state legislatures, a small majority of which voted for Gómez Pedraza. The defeated party, on the other hand, obtained a majority in the Chamber of Deputies, which was elected by popular vote, and claimed that the defeat of their presidential candidate had been brought about by fraud and official interference. They were supported by Santa Anna and other military leaders, who after a short civil war compelled the government to recognize Guerrero as President-elect.

One of the issues raised by the revolutionists to obtain popular support was a demand for the expulsion of the peninsular Spaniards. The animosity between creoles and *peninsulares*, which had been a principal cause of the revolts in South America, was also a strong force in Mexico, but it found less overt expression there in the first years of independence because members of the two groups had worked together to bring about the separation from Spain. Prominent Spaniards had taken part in the conspiracy that led to the Plan of Iguala and had held important positions in the government and in the army under the Empire. The *yorquinos* had insisted on

Victoria's removing all Spanish officials in the civil government and in the army, and since 1821 many merchants and many of the capitalists who financed the mining industry had been leaving the country. In the last days of his administration the Congress decreed that all Spaniards should leave Mexico.

The revolution of 1828, like the revolt against Spain and the overthrow of Iturbide, was the work of officers of the regular army, and for many years after 1828 political disputes were decided not by the ballot but by the intervention of professional soldiers who were usually more interested in obtaining power and the perquisites of office than in questions of policy. The army had deteriorated in discipline and efficiency since 1821, but it was still better organized than any other group that aspired to power. The officers had for the most part been trained in the Spanish army or militia. They had participated in the sudden change of front that made independence possible and had helped to set up and then overthrow the imperial government. They were ready to seek advancement and personal profit through further ventures of the same sort and to espouse any cause that seemed likely to further their ambitions. In the words of a contemporary American diplomat, the army was "the greatest nuisance, and the most insuperable barrier to the prosperity and progress of Mexico." [2] It consumed an inordinate proportion of the public revenue, despite the fact that the common soldiers—unfortunate Indians or *mestizos* recruited by force—received but a small part of their nominal pay; and its *fuero*, or exemption from the jurisdiction of the civil courts, gave its members a privileged position which was frequently abused.

SANTA ANNA

The principal figure in the army was Antonio López de Santa Anna. Santa Anna had been a junior officer in the Spanish army at the time of the Plan of Iguala but had risen rapidly to high rank through the favor of Iturbide. In 1823 he had a prominent part in the revolt against the Emperor. For a quarter-century after 1828, he dominated Mexican politics. Crafty and unscrupulous, with few convictions and little administrative ability, he derived his influence from a popularity among the troops which survived misfortunes that would completely have discredited another leader. He enjoyed power but not the responsibility of exercising it, and he often permitted others to assume the presidency while he retained military control. His political views were flexible. In his earlier years he was usually on the side of the liberals, but he became the champion of the conservatives and helped to maintain the supremacy of the aristocracy and the Church when that course seemed more likely to forward his own ambitions.

[2] W. Thompson, *Recollections of Mexico*, p. 168.

Santa Anna was responsible for a series of revolts that brought the country to a condition approaching anarchy in the years following 1829. He soon turned against Guerrero, who proved weak and incompetent and whose mixed blood and radical views made him disliked by the aristocracy. The President was compelled to abandon the Capital, after some fighting, and the Vice-President, Anastasio Bustamante, took office early in 1830 with conservative support. Guerrero attempted to continue the struggle but was treacherously captured and executed—an act that aroused indignation among the liberals and helped to bring on a new revolt in 1832. Again Santa Anna was the leader, this time supporting Gómez Pedraza who still claimed that he had been elected as constitutional President in 1828. The latter was installed in office for the few remaining months of the four-year term, and for the new period, starting in 1833, Santa Anna himself was elected, with a liberal Vice-President and an overwhelmingly liberal congress.

By this time the *escoceses* and the *yorquinos* had ceased to exist as political organizations, and the parties that contended for power called themselves conservatives, or centralists, and liberals, or federalists. The conservatives, as might be expected, were especially strong in Mexico City, where many of the most influential members of the old creole upper class, the owners of great entailed estates and the richer miners and merchants, had their homes. They were opposed by the same elements that formed the liberal party in other Latin American countries: intellectuals of the upper class who advocated liberal ideas for their own sake; middle-class professional men and small merchants, often of *mestizo* origin; and leaders in other parts of the country who felt that the provinces were being exploited commercially and politically by powerful groups in Mexico City and who were eager to obtain more control over their own local affairs. At first the question of "federalism" as against "centralism" had been the principal political issue, but after 1833 a bitter conflict developed over the relationship between Church and State.

The Church's hold on the Mexican people had been less affected by the separation from Spain than in some other countries where it opposed the movement for independence. In Mexico, many of the leaders in the war after 1810 had been creole priests, and the Plan of Iguala had owed its success largely to the support of some of the higher clergy. The Church's influence had been somewhat reduced after 1821 because the Papacy refused to recognize Mexico's independence and would not agree with the new government on appointments to fill the places of bishops who had died or returned to Spain; but a compromise in 1831 made it possible to fill the vacant sees. The ecclesiastical authorities were now less amenable to political control than they had been when the Spanish kings exercised the *patronato*, but the government still enforced the payment of Church dues and recognized the Church's *fueros*—its exemption from taxation and the right of its members to be tried in its own courts. In its effort to protect these privileges, and especially to protect its great wealth, which was a perennial temptation to a government always in desperate need of money, the Church was inevitably drawn into politics. It naturally supported the conservatives, especially as many of the leaders on the other side were opposed on principle to the continuance of the close relationship between Church and State.

One of the most radical of the anticlerical leaders was Valentín Gómez Farías who became Vice-President after the revolution of 1832. Gómez Farías took charge of the government for long periods in the first year of the new administration, while Santa Anna either led the troops against revolting conservatives or enjoyed life at his country estate, and under his leadership, the Congress enacted a series of anticlerical laws. Indian missions and their property were brought under government control; the government ceased to use its authority to compel the payment of tithes or the fulfillment of monastic vows; and the right to exercise the *patronato* was reasserted. Each of these measures was violently opposed by the clergy and the conservatives, who revolted in the summer of 1833 but were defeated after several months of fighting. Santa Anna supported the constitutional regime at this time, but when it became apparent that the liberals had lost the support of public opinion by going too fast and too far he threw in his lot with the forces of reaction. Resuming the presidency in April, 1834, he dissolved the Congress, removed liberal state governors, and arbitrarily abrogated many of the recently enacted laws. Gómez Farías was forced to flee the country.

A new Congresss, dominated by the conservatives, met in 1835. The federal form of government was abolished, and the constitution of 1824 was replaced by the so-called "Seven Laws" of 1836. These provided that the president should be elected for an eight-year term but hedged him about with restrictions that showed the civilian politicians' distrust of Santa Anna, among them being a provision for a *"poder conservador"* to maintain the equilibrium between the executive, the legislative, and the judiciary. The new fundamental law seems to have been satisfactory to no one, but even a more workable form of government would hardly have received a fair trial in the midst of the internal and external difficulties that beset the Republic during the next few years.

The worst of these was the revolt in Texas. Before the end of the Spanish regime the Viceroy had given Moses Austin permission to establish a colony of Roman Catholics in Texas. This grant was confirmed by Iturbide, and later by the republican government, when Stephen Austin took up the enterprise after his father's death. Similar grants were made to other persons, and several thousand North Americans settled in the region during the 1820's. Their presence soon became a source of concern, especially in view of the United States government's openly expressed desire to acquire the territory. Mexican efforts to restrict immigration and to bring the colonists under more effective control increased the tension between the newcomers and the authorities, and an attempt to prohibit slavery in the territory produced no result. The colonists were especially resentful when Texas was united with Coahuila as one state in 1830. Encouraged by the continual party strife in Mexico, they revolted in 1835, and in April, 1836, they defeated the Mexican forces at San Jacinto and captured Santa Anna himself. A treaty they made with their prisoner was repudiated by the government at Mexico City; but the latter was in no position to carry on further military operations, and Texas became an independent republic.

Despite these events, the conservatives remained in control at Mexico City, and their position was somewhat strengthened when both Spain and the Papacy recognized Mexico's independence in 1837. Nevertheless Anastasio Bustamante, who became President in 1837, had to contend with continued internal disorder, and aggression from abroad soon made matters worse. Many foreigners had been injured in one way or another during the continual strife of the preceding 15 years. Their governments had insistently pressed demands for compensation, but with little result, and in 1838 France sent a fleet to Vera Cruz and summarily demanded payment of claims amounting to $600,000. It will be remembered that the French government was at this same time endeavoring to restore its waning prestige at home by aggressive action against Rosas in the River Plate. When Bustamante rejected the demand, Vera Cruz was occupied, and other ports were blockaded. This "Pastry War," so called because one of the French claims was that of a baker whose shop had been sacked, was finally ended through British mediation when Mexico agreed to pay the sum demanded.

Santa Anna commanded the Mexican forces in their unsuccessful resistance at Vera Cruz, and a fortunate wound, which compelled the amputation of one leg, restored his popularity. Very soon he was again plotting to resume power. For a time he supported Bustamante in suppressing the persistent revolts of the federalists, but in 1841, under the "Plan of Tacubaya," he again seized control of the government. He had by this time definitely aligned himself with the centralist party, and a new Constituent Assembly was dissolved when it showed federalist tendencies. In its place a hand-picked Assembly of notables drew up a new constitution, the *Bases Orgánicas* of 1843, which was no more liberal than the "Seven Laws" but did away with some of their more impractical features. Santa Anna was elected President in 1844, but he continued, as on other occasions, to spend much time on his country estate while Valentín Canalizo, as acting President, struggled with federalist disaffection and a rising opposition in Congress. The government fell before the end of the year, and José Joaquín Herrera was installed as provisional President.

He in turn was overthrown late in 1845 by General Mariano Paredes, who had revolted against Santa Anna in 1844 but now reappeared as the leader of a conservative reaction.

THE WAR WITH THE UNITED STATES

The ostensible purpose of Paredes' revolt was to set up a government that would take a firm stand against the United States. Relations between the two countries, long clouded by Mexican suspicion of American territorial ambitions and made worse by blundering diplomacy and disputes over claims, had been especially strained since the revolt of Texas. Mexico resented the recognition of Texan independence by the United States in 1837, and a number of incidents increased the hostile feeling on both sides. When Texas was annexed to the United States by joint resolution of Congress in March, 1845, a conflict became all but inevitable, for the Mexican government had announced as early as 1843 that such an act would be regarded as a declaration of war. First Herrera and then Paredes refused to receive an American Commissioner sent to attempt a peaceful settlement. In February, 1846, General Zachary Taylor was ordered to move into territory between the Nueces River and the Rio Grande which, the Mexicans claimed, had never formed a part of Texas. In April, hostilities began. The untrained and poorly equipped Mexican troops were defeated in several battles; and before the end of 1846 Taylor occupied much of northern Mexico, and other American forces took possession of New Mexico and California.

At the Capital the government was weakened by the chronic lack of funds and by internal dissension. Paredes' popularity declined, especially after his chief adviser, the centralist leader Lucas Alamán, openly advocated the establishment of a monarchy. This was an idea that many of the reactionary conservatives had never given up, but the proposal aroused the opposition of all the republican elements. The controversy that ensued gave Santa Anna the opportunity for which he had been waiting. This time he sought the support of the federalists, though he worked chiefly, as always, through his friends in the army. In 1846 there were uprisings in his favor in different sections of the country, and in August General Salas "pronounced" for him at Mexico City and overthrew the Paredes regime. Santa Anna himself landed at Vera Cruz a few days later. He was allowed to pass through the American blockading squadron because President Polk was given to understand that he would accept American proposals for peace if he were allowed to resume power, but once in Mexico he took command of the army and prepared to resist the invaders. He was no more successful than his predecessor, and in February, 1847, he was defeated by Taylor in the battle of Buena Vista near Saltillo.

Meanwhile his associates at Mexico City were making efforts to strengthen the national defense. In their desperate need for money they turned to the Church, which had retained much of its wealth while the commercial stagnation and disorder of the past quarter-century were causing the great private fortunes of an earlier period to dwindle away. In January, 1847, the Congress authorized the government to raise $15,-000,000 by mortgaging or selling Church property, an act which aroused a storm of opposition from the clergy and their supporters. Santa Anna, though elected to the presidency, had characteristically refrained from taking office in order that Gómez Farías, who was again Vice-President, might assume the responsibility for a policy certain to be dangerous politically; and when it became evident that public opinion would not support the government's action, he returned to Mexico City, compromised with the Church for a payment of $2,000,000, and eliminated Gómez Farías by causing the office of Vice-President to be abolished.

Since Taylor's victories in the north had not brought Mexico to terms, another American army under General Winfield Scott landed in March, 1847, at Vera Cruz. By September, after much fighting, it had occupied Mexico City, and on February 2, 1848, representatives of the two nations signed the Treaty of Guadelupe Hidalgo. Texas, New Mexico, and California became a part of the United States, which paid $15,000,000 by way of compensation. In July the American army was withdrawn.

POLITICAL AND RELIGIOUS CONFLICT, 1848–1860

Santa Anna was compelled to relinquish his authority after the loss of Mexico City. First Manuel de la Peña, the President of the Supreme Court, then General Anaya, and then De la Peña again, occupied the presidency while peace negotiations were going on. In June, 1848, General José Joaquín Herrera became President by election, serving under the federalist constitution of 1824 which Santa Anna had re-established. A moderate liberal, supported by the influential elements that had advocated the conclusion of peace with the United States, Herrera earnestly endeavored to repair the damage wrought by the war. He had assumed office with great reluctance, for the difficulties he faced seemed well-nigh insuperable. The finances, as usual, were in a bad state, and foreign claims continued to cause trouble. During the war the already weak prestige of the central government in the more remote sections of the country diminished still further, and the wild Indians in several regions were committing depredations against towns and *haciendas*. A race war in Yucatán, where the Maya took up arms against the officials and *hacendados* who had oppressed them since the Spanish Conquest, caused heavy losses of life and property. At the same time, both the extreme conservatives led by Paredes and the *"santanistas"* staged unsuccessful revolts. Nevertheless Herrera served out his legal term and passed on the presidency in 1851 to his constitutionally elected successor, General Mariano Arista.

Arista, without his predecessor's ability and prestige, was less fortunate. There were controversies in some of the states over the religious question, which Herrera had kept in the background, and there was much discontent in the army because the number of officers and men had been reduced for the sake of economy. Even the liberals gave the administration little support. Revolts and disorders gradually made its position untenable, and in January, 1853, Arista resigned.

A few weeks later Santa Anna returned from exile to assume the presidency. With conservative support, he set aside the constitution, dissolved the national Congress and the state Legislatures, and finally in December, 1853, proclaimed himself dictator for an indefinite term with power to name his own successor. This arrogant assumption of supreme power and the unpopular sale to the United States of the Mesilla Valley, "The Gadsden Purchase," soon brought on a reaction. Early in 1854, General Juan Álvarez and Colonel Ignacio Comonfort started a revolt in the State of Guerrero under the Plan of Ayutla, appealing to the liberals for support. Indecisive fighting went on for more than a year until Santa Anna, deserted by many of his followers, decided to take refuge abroad. His flight permitted the insurgents to take over the government and marked the end of his active influence in Mexican politics.

The revolution of Ayutla marked the beginning of a new phase in the struggle between the groups that had hitherto dominated Mexico's political life and the less privileged groups that were now demanding a voice in the government. The chief issue was the relationship between Church and State. The Church had continued to be active in politics, partly because it constantly had to defend its property against needy federal and state governments, but the liberals, after their unfortunate experience in 1833–1834, had shown little disposition to attack it during the brief periods when they were in power. The revolution now brought into office men who were determined to assume a more aggressive policy.

The most important of these was the full-blooded Indian, Benito Juárez. Born of poor parents in a Zapotec village near Oaxaca, Juárez entered the service of a white family in that city while still a child and so aroused the interest of his employer that he was given unusual opportunities to obtain an education. Though at first destined for the priesthood, he soon left the seminary to take up the study of law, and in 1829, at the age of twenty-three, he entered local politics as a member of a *yorquino* lodge. From then on he was an active liberal, first in his own state of Oaxaca and then at Mexico City. As a representative of the middle-class element which was challenging the political pre-eminence of the old creole families, he was to be the chief figure in Mexico's political life during the next quarter-century, as Santa Anna had been in the preceding period.

Juárez was a member of the Cabinet under General Álvarez, whom the revolutionists installed as provisional President, and was the author of a law promulgated in November, 1855, which limited the jurisdiction of both the ecclesiastical and the military courts. This was an attack on the cherished *fueros* of the clergy and the professional officer caste in the army. Since most of the leaders of the army had supported Santa Anna, it was natural that the liberals should try to curb its privileges and diminish its capacity for mischief, but the *Ley Juárez* was also bitterly resented by the portion of the military forces that was supporting the new government. The storm that it aroused was one of the reasons that General Álvarez, an honest but not very competent provincial *caudillo*, was forced to turn over the presidency to Comonfort in December, 1855.

Comonfort was more moderate in his liberalism, but his associates continued to push the reform program. In June, 1856, the Congress enacted the *Ley Lerdo*, drafted by Miguel Lerdo de Tejada, which required the Church to sell all real estate not actually used for religious purposes and also required the Indian communities to distribute their lands among their members. The liberals hoped to build up an independent class of small farmers, but the result was unfortunate because the Indians as individuals were more easily robbed of their property or persuaded to sell it. Another anticlerical measure, the *Ley Iglesias* of April, 1857, deprived the Church of its control over cemeteries. Another law compelled the clergy to perform services gratuitously for impoverished parishioners. Meanwhile the new constitution of 1857 had been drawn up, and the principles of the *Ley Juárez* and the *Ley Lerdo* had been incorporated in it, together with other provisions for which the liberals had contended: a federal form of government; manhood suffrage; and freedom of speech, of teaching, and of the press.

The Church furiously opposed the whole reform program. Revolts inspired by the clergy at Puebla and elsewhere were suppressed, but unrest continued. The Archbishop of Mexico excommunicated all persons taking oath to support the new constitution, and the Pope approved his stand. The liberal party itself was still divided, and those who approved the new laws were probably a minority of the nation as a whole. A reaction was inevitable, and the conservatives had their opportunity when Comonfort quarreled with the majority in the Congress. The President at first accepted the aid of a group of conservative army officers in abolishing the new constitution and assuming dictatorial powers, but he was soon afterward deserted by his new friends and compelled to leave the country. Félix Zuloaga, the chief of the army, was installed as provisional President early in 1858, while Juárez, claiming the presidency as Comonfort's constitutional successor, placed himself at the head of a liberal counterrevolt.

For the next three years the "War of the Reform" deluged Mexico in blood. Juárez, defeated in the interior north and west of Mexico City, fled by way of the west coast and Panama to Vera Cruz, where he established his Capital. Thenceforth the fortunes of war favored first one side and then the other. Zuloaga resigned late in 1858 and was replaced by the brilliant young General Miguel Miramón. After the inexcusable murder of a number of prisoners by the conservative General Márquez in 1859, captured officers were regularly executed by both sides. The bitterness between the two parties increased when Juárez issued decrees confiscating all ecclesiastical property except Church buildings, suppressing monasteries, and instituting civil marriage in districts under liberal control. While the conservatives had the sympathy of several European powers, Juárez was supported by the United States, and an attack on Vera Cruz was frustrated in 1860 by the intervention of American warships. By the end of that year the conservatives had been decisively defeated, and the liberals had taken possession of Mexico City. A few months later, after an election, Juárez took office as constitutional President.

THE FRENCH INTERVENTION

The conservatives continued guerrilla warfare in the interior, and while Juárez was still struggling to establish order a new danger appeared from abroad. During the long civil war, military requisitions, destruction of property, forced loans, and outrages against individuals had greatly increased the already-large amount of foreign claims. The treasury had no money even for the service of the bonded debt, and when the Congress voted to suspend all debt payments for two years Great Britain, France, and Spain signed an agreement for a joint intervention to obtain reparation for injuries to their citizens and to compel Mexico to meet her financial obligations. The United States was invited to take part, but declined.

The three-power treaty of October 31, 1861, ostensibly barred any interference in Mexico's internal political affairs, but it was evident from the first that at least two of the signatories had other purposes in mind than the mere protection of their citizens' financial interests. The Spanish government had openly supported the conservatives during the War of the Reform, and its ambassador had been expelled from Mexico after the liberal victory. For three years Spain had been toying with the idea of restoring its control over what had once been its richest colony. Napoleon III, on the other hand, had ambitions of his own. Encouraged by the Civil War in the United States, which made North American interference unlikely, he had been intriguing with some of the Mexican conservatives to set up a foreign monarchy under French protection, and Maximilian of Hapsburg, the brother of Emperor Franz Joseph of Austria, had already been chosen as its head. These two powers were thus working at cross purposes with each other and with Great Britain, which was interested solely in the collection of claims. Although British participation in the intervention was confined to naval action, both France and Spain sent considerable bodies of troops.

A Spanish fleet seized Vera Cruz in December, 1861, and French and British forces arrived soon afterward. Juárez entered into negotiations and agreed that the allied forces might march inland from the fever-infested coast while the discussions continued. In the ensuing conferences, the French Commissioner took a position that made any peaceful settlement impossible. His most indefensible demand, perhaps, was for full payment of the Jecker claim, based on a $16,800,000 bond issue agreed to by Miramón shortly before his government collapsed. Only a small portion of the proceeds of the loan had ever reached Mexico, and the French action in espousing the claim was the more scandalous because Jecker himself was a Swiss citizen at the time the loan was made and had only recently acquired French nationality under suspicious circumstances. The British and Spanish representatives were unwilling to support such a demand, and their increasing realization of the divergence of views between the three allies led them to withdraw with their forces, leaving France to continue the intervention alone.

Napoleon's real purpose now became evident. General Juan Almonte, one of the leaders of the group that sought foreign intervention, was permitted to proclaim himself President of the Republic under the protection of the French troops, and the latter marched inland toward Mexico City, despite their earlier promise to withdraw to the coast if negotiations failed. At Puebla, however, they were defeated with heavy losses by a Mexican army under General Zaragoza, in a battle which made May 5 one of the great anniversaries in Mexican history. The invaders' advance was held up for nearly a year—a delay which in the long run proved fatal to their designs.

Resistance became more difficult after General Forey arrived with 30,000 fresh troops, and the French occupied Mexico City in June, 1863. An "Assembly of Notables," convoked by the invaders, voted on July 8 to establish a hereditary monarchy and to offer the crown to Maximilian or to some other Catholic prince proposed by Napoleon III. In the meantime a Regency headed by Almonte nominally assumed the executive power, though those parts of the country occupied by the invaders were in reality under French military rule. Juárez and his associates continued to fight in the interior and for a time held a large part of the country.

After insisting that the invitation of the Assembly of Notables be ratified by a plebiscite, which of course was a farce, Maximilian accepted the throne on April 10, 1864. At the same time he signed a convention with Napoleon by which the latter promised military support during the first years of the new regime, to be paid for by the Mexican treasury, and obtained a loan on exorbitant terms with the aid of English bankers. Encouraged by these arrangements, he and his wife, the Belgian princess Carlota, entered Mexico City on June 12, 1864.

The new Emperor, still in his thirty-second year, was an affable, well-educated prince, who had served as Commander in Chief of the Austrian navy and as Governor-General of Lombardy-Venice. In the latter post he had shown a mildly liberal disposition which enhanced his prestige in Europe but made him less rather than better fitted for the enterprise he was now undertaking. Such support as he had in Mexico came from the conservatives, who were already disillusioned because the French Commander had refused to restore the property that the Church had had to sell under the *Ley Lerdo*. He further alienated the more extreme members of this party when he attempted to establish a free press and to obtain liberal support by an offer of amnesty. The conservative leaders were also jealous of the continued dominance of French officers in military affairs, and the situation was not improved by the organization of an imperial force of Austrian and Belgian volunteers. The liberals, on the other hand, showed little interest in Maximilian's efforts to conciliate them, even though some prominent members of the party, to the disgust of their opponents, were given important posts in the government. Their resistance stiffened when Maximilian changed his policy and ordered that those who opposed the government should be treated as bandits. Consequently internal strife continued with all the savagery that had marked the War of the Reform.

For a time the French armies were generally successful. Juárez was forced back until he was compelled to establish his Capital at El Paso on the Texas frontier, and Porfirio Díaz, who had held most of the country south of the Capital, surrendered at Oaxaca in February, 1865. By this time, however, the Civil War, which had compelled the United States to maintain an outward neutrality, was approaching an end, and the government at Washington made it clear that it would not permit the French protectorate to continue. Confronted by the threat of American intervention, and influenced also by the situation in Europe, Napoleon III decided early in 1866 to withdraw his troops from the adventure within the next two years. Thenceforth the defense of the imperial interests was left more and more to Mexican troops, and the tide of battle turned in favor of the liberals. Maximilian's pleas for continued French aid fell on deaf ears. He was disposed to abdicate; but the extreme conservatives persuaded him to make a final stand with their support, and in February, 1867, he went to Querétaro at the head of his army. He was besieged there by superior liberal forces, but he resisted until the city was taken through treachery on May 14. A month later he was condemned to death and shot, in spite of the remonstrances of foreign diplomatic representatives.

THE LIBERALS IN POWER, 1867–1877

Juárez, who had continued at the head of the revolutionary government after the expiration of his term in 1865, was re-elected President in 1867. He attempted to give the country a genuinely republican government. It was some months, however, before many of the guerrilla bands in the interior laid down their arms. The regional *caudillos* who had carried on the war more or less independently in many of the provinces continued to rule their own districts. Several of them were restive under Juárez' attempts to control them, and at Mexico City the President's opponents caused him some embarrassment. Both the Congress and the newspapers had a freedom unknown under previous administrations, and much of the government's energy was dissipated in political controversies. The President was criticized for ruling with a small coterie of old friends, and many of the men who had fought in the recent war were displeased because much of the army was disbanded without giving the soldiers the rewards that they considered due them. Juárez was nevertheless again re-elected in 1871, this time by the Congress, which had to make the choice when none of three candidates obtained a majority of the popular vote.

Porfirio Díaz, who had been a candidate both in 1867 and in 1871, started a revolt when it became evident that he had lost the election. He was defeated, but many of his partisans were still under arms when Juárez died suddenly on July 18, 1872, and Sebastián Lerdo de Tejada, the President of the Supreme Court, took his place. Díaz accepted the new regime, and the country was relatively peaceful during the next three years. In 1874, several of the radical antiecclesiastical measures promulgated by Juárez during the War of the Reform were incorporated in the constitution.

THE DÍAZ REGIME

Lerdo, though popular at the beginning of his term, was unable to hold the support of the mutually jealous factions within the liberal party, and when he sought re-election Díaz ousted him in 1876 and became constitutional President in May, 1877. Several revolts by Lerdo's followers were suppressed, and order was gradually established. At the end of his term, since a man who had made "no re-election" his battle cry in two revolutions could hardly be a candidate for re-election himself, Díaz placed his friend General Manuel González at the head of the government. From Díaz' point of view the choice was a good one, for the new President was able to repress opposition but made himself so unpopular by unwise and corrupt financial measures that he could not have opposed Díaz' return to power if he had wished to.

Díaz resumed the presidency in 1884, to begin one of the longest periods of personal rule in the history of Latin America. The constitutional prohibition which he had felt compelled to respect in 1880 was done away with, and he was re-elected as a matter of course at the end of each successive term until he was ousted by revolution in 1911.

Porfirio Díaz was born in Oaxaca in 1830. His father, a minor employee in a commercial house, was white or nearly white; his mother half Indian. Despite the family's poverty, he received some education, studying at one time for the Church and later for the law. He began his active participation in politics, as a liberal, during the revolution of Ayutla. Later he served as Governor of Tehuantepec, which he held for the *juaristas* during the War of the Reform, and was one of the outstanding heroes of the struggle against the empire. After the restoration of the Republic his restless ambition and frequent revolts had turned against him most of the people who were interested in peace and orderly progress, but he had a great following among the middle and lower classes. In office he showed a political astuteness, combined with a firmness of purpose and a ruthless energy, that disarmed, or crushed, any serious opposition. He owed his long tenure of power partly to these qualities and partly to the rapidly increasing prosperity that Mexico enjoyed under his rule. As in other Latin American countries, political rivalries became less acute as the ruling class turned their attention to new opportunities created by the growth of foreign commerce and the development of the country's natural resources.

Díaz gave positions in his government to rivals in the liberal party and to many former conservatives, including some who had co-operated with Maximilian. The Church, still influential despite its losses, became more friendly when he showed a willingness to relax the enforcement of the laws of reform, and it gradually recovered some of its property and much of its importance as a social force. Party enmities lost much of their virulence, and those who sought governmental favors found it more profitable, and far safer, to court the dictator than to organize a revolution. The revolts that occurred were quickly crushed and their leaders killed. In 1879, nine persons accused of conspiracy were executed without trial at Vera Cruz. Such acts of cruelty might merely have provoked further outbreaks under other circumstances, but they were effective in discouraging disorder when the great majority of thinking people were sick of civil war. The disappearance of armed political opposition was followed by the elimination of banditry, long the curse of the Mexican countryside. A well-trained rural police, recruited largely from former professional revolutionists and highwaymen, made life and property, at least for the upper classes and foreigners, safer than in many parts of the United States and Europe.

For the first time the government of Mexico became a real personal dictatorship. Hitherto the local *caudillos* who controlled the state governments had had much independent power. The dominant party in Mexico City had naturally sought to assure the control of the states by its own partisans, by armed intervention if necessary, but it had often been compelled to compromise with the local leaders and to purchase rather than to command their support. It was the state governors who had in practice controlled the electoral machinery—a fact which explains the occurrence of disputed elections in a country where there was little real freedom to vote. Under Díaz this situation changed. The power of local *caudillos* was systematically undermined and finally destroyed, and the state governors became mere subordinates of the President, named and removed at his pleasure. Elections, as in the past, were a mere form so far as the voters were concerned, but the outcome was now dictated from Mexico City. There was thus no longer any opposition group in Congress. The press, which had enjoyed freedom under Juárez and Lerdo, was brought into line by a combination of repressive measures and bribery.

Díaz carefully prevented any other member of his government from building up a prestige that might threaten his own power. By promptly relegating to obscurity lieutenants who became too influential, and by fomenting jealousies and rivalries in his official family, as well as by exiling or terrorizing potential opponents, he made sure that there was no one in Mexico who could successfully aspire to replace him in the government. The only group that attempted to influence his policies were the so-called *científicos*, originally a loose association of young deputies who attempted rather ineffectively to bring about political reforms while outwardly supporting the administration and enjoying many favors at its hands. Their importance as a political factor does not appear to have been great, but one of their leaders, José Limantour, was Minister of Finance for a long period and in this capacity was largely responsible for the dictatorship's most important achievements.

The Republic's finances, when Díaz succeeded González in 1884, were in the chaotic condition that had been normal since independence. Expenditures far exceeded receipts; salaries were unpaid; and the foreign debt was in default. By economy and better administration, matters were soon much improved. After Limantour became Minister of Finance in 1893 a series of brilliantly successful financial reforms were carried out. The old burdensome taxes inherited from the Spanish regime and especially the internal customs duties were abolished or modified. The budget showed a surplus, for practically the first time in the country's history, and the currency was placed on a gold basis. Mexico's credit became so well established that it was possible to issue bonds abroad with a coupon rate of 4 per cent—a rate which no other Latin American country had hitherto been able to approach. With the aid of borrowed money the government was able to purchase a controlling interest in the majority of the country's railway lines after 1904.

One reason for the general prosperity that made these achievements possible was a great influx of foreign capital. Foreign mining enterprises again made Mexico the world's chief silver producer, and the country was second only to the United States in the production of copper. Railroad building also made remarkable progress, until there were nearly 25,000 kilometers of railways in the Republic in 1911, as compared with 691 kilometers in 1876.[3] Industrial plants of many kinds, most of them, it is true, leading an artificial existence behind high customs barriers, were established in the principal cities. The country's foreign commerce increased fivefold, and the petroleum industry, just becoming established at the end of the Díaz regime, gave promise of far greater exports in the future. Most of the new undertakings were financed and managed by foreigners; but the benefits of material progress accrued also to many thousands of Mexicans, and the Republic appeared to foreign observers to be one of the most fortunate of the American republics when the centenary of the *grito de Dolores* was celebrated in 1910.

Beneath the surface, however, there was much discontent. The monopoly of public office by Díaz and the clique that surrounded him irritated other people who had political ambitions. A more acute feeling of unrest was growing among the common people. On the great plantations, the Indian and *mestizo* laborers were still subject to a peonage system which had kept their wages practically unchanged for a century while increases in prices depressed their already low standard of living. More and more of the country people had become debt-slaves during the preceding 50 years because the *haciendas* had been steadily expanding at the expense of the small landholders and the village communities. As in Peru and Bolivia, but probably to an even greater extent, the Indian had been systematically despoiled by those who had wealth or political power. The constitution of 1857, which required the division of village communal holdings as well as the sale of Church property, had facilitated this process; and other laws of the Díaz period, providing ostensibly for the surveying of the national domain, had permitted favored individuals to build up vast estates on lands which theoretically belonged to the nation but which in fact had long been occupied by Indian or *mestizo* farmers. The peasants' lot was thus becoming harder than ever at a time when the rest of the country was enjoying an unheard of prosperity, and they were ripe for revolt as soon as the dictator's grip should weaken. Their desperate determination to recover their lands made the agrarian question the most pressing political problem in Mexico under the revolutionary governments which followed Díaz.

Since much of the land had passed into the hands of foreigners, discontent among the peasants tended to take on an antiforeign character. This was also true of the less acute but still active discontent among the laborers in mining and industry. The employer, in most cases a North American or a European, was usually supported by the army and police in dealing with labor agitators or strikes, and he often profited by tariff protection and other special privileges. Díaz sought to encourage the investment of capital as a means of developing the country, but many of his fellow

[3] Rabasa, *L'Évolution Historique du Mexique*, p. 165.

citizens were dismayed to see the control of the Republic's economic life and natural resources pass out of Mexican hands. A change in this situation became another of the chief objectives of the political groups that were to come into power after the long period of turmoil that followed the overthrow of Díaz in 1911.

CHAPTER 19

Mexico Since 1911

THE MISERY of the landless peasantry, the growing dislike of foreign economic interests, and the increasing discontent among the new class of industrial laborers, found expression after 1910 in a long-drawn-out revolt against all that the Díaz regime stood for. A revolt which at first seemed purposeless and hardly different from earlier struggles for power among ambitious military leaders, it gradually took the form of a real social revolution. During the ensuing 30 years, the agrarian program and the rising power of organized labor transformed the Republic's economic life. The period of the Mexican Revolution is one of the most interesting in the history of Latin America.

THE END OF THE DÍAZ REGIME

As Díaz approached the end of his sixth consecutive term, Mexico appeared to be one of the wealthiest and most stable of the American republics. To all outward appearances the President was at the height of his prestige, even though it was obvious that a ruler who was about to celebrate his eightieth birthday could not continue indefinitely at the head of the government. For a generation no important political group had dared to challenge his authority. Occasional minor revolutionary movements had been promptly and easily suppressed before they could take advantage of the prevailing discontent.

The election of 1910 might have been as uneventful as its predecessors had it not been for the interview which Díaz permitted an American writer named Creelman to publish in *Pearson's Magazine* in March, 1908. Mexico, the President said, was now ripe for democracy, and he would welcome the establishment of an opposition party and the holding of a free election. This statement, evidently intended only for foreign consumption, caused a sensation in Mexico. After its publication the government could not well prevent an unwontedly free discussion of political affairs in the Mexican press. Few ventured openly to oppose the President's re-election, but a movement was soon under way to make Díaz' lieutenant, General Bernardo Reyes, Vice-President, instead of Ramón Corral, the official candidate. When Reyes was sent off on a mission to Europe, many of his supporters backed Francisco Madero, who had the temerity to accept an opposition nomination for the presidency. Though Madero was arrested and later forced to flee to the United States, his campaign, following that of Reyes, afforded an opportunity for political agitation, and the President lost prestige when he failed to show his accustomed vigor in suppressing any sign of discontent or resistance.

After Díaz and Corral were re-elected, Madero, from his refuge in Texas, issued a call for a revolt to begin on November 20, 1910. The movement had no effective organization or leadership; but there were small local rebellions in many parts of the country, and it soon became evident that the government did not have the will or the power to suppress them. There was surprisingly little real fighting. After the rebels' first important success, the capture of Ciudad Juárez on the American border in May, 1911, Díaz agreed to turn the government over to Francisco de la Barra, the Minister of Foreign Affairs, with a Cabinet named by the revolutionists. Díaz left Mexico, and in November, after an election, Madero became President.

MADERO AND HUERTA

Madero was a member of a wealthy landowning family in the north of Mexico. He had no previous administrative or military experience. As the man who had dared to become a presidential candidate when the rest of the nation was still in awe of the dictator, he had naturally become the titular head of the revolution, but he had taken little part in actual military operations. Unfortunately he had few qualifications for his new office. He lacked the political skill and the ruthless energy that had kept his predecessor in power. He was a man of high ideals, more sensitive than most of the aristocracy to the distress of the Mexican masses, but he had only vague ideas about economic and social reform. A promise in his revolutionary program to restore land to the dispossessed peasantry had brought his movement much support among the country people, but he did little to carry out the promise after he took office. His popularity rapidly diminished, and rivalries among his supporters weakened his administration. There were a number of small revolts, led by partisans of the Díaz regime or by dissatisfied leaders of Madero's own party, and in the State of Morelos, Emiliano Zapata and his followers began their long, desperate struggle to regain the land for the peasants. Businessmen and property owners, dismayed by the government's inability to maintain order, began to wish for a return of the strong hand of the old regime.

It was the army, still commanded by officers who had served the dictatorship, that overthrew the new government. Félix Díaz, the dictator's nephew, and General Bernardo Reyes had been imprisoned in the Capital after participating in earlier revolts. On February 9, 1913, they were released by mutinous troops who seized control of several strong points in the city. Reyes was killed in the ensuing fighting, but for ten days Félix Díaz and the forces at the presidential palace carried on an artillery duel in the heart of the Capital. The destruction of noncombatant lives and property seemed the more shocking when it transpired that the commander of Madero's troops, Victoriano Huerta, was in league with the rebels and was simply awaiting a favorable opportunity to betray those of his comrades who were still loyal. On February 18 Huerta imprisoned Madero and the Vice-President, Pino Suárez. After negotiations in which members of the diplomatic corps participated, the President and Vice-President reluctantly agreed to resign in return for a promise that they would be permitted to leave the country.

Huerta, with the approval of Congress, at once assumed the presidency. A few days later Madero and Pino Suárez were murdered by the officials who had them in custody. Though this and several other equally brutal acts foreshadowed the character of the new administration, it received support from conservatives and from foreign interests which hoped for a restoration of a strong government. Within a few months it had been recognized by the principal powers of Europe, though not by the United States.

President Wilson refused to countenance what he considered an inexcusable usurpation of power. Recalling the American Ambassador, who had been openly sympathetic with the Huerta regime, he sent John Lind as his personal representative to propose the establishment of a constitutional government by means of an election in which Huerta would not be a candidate. Huerta not only rejected this suggestion but showed his disregard for legality by suspending the constitution, dissolving the Congress, and imprisoning several of its members. Wilson thereupon announced that nothing done by the dictator would be regarded as legal and endeavored to persuade foreign governments to withdraw diplomatic support from his regime. The British government's reluctance to do so caused some friction between the two powers. Meanwhile, some of Madero's supporters, under the leadership of Venustiano Carranza, had started a counterrevolution, calling themselves "constitutionalists." In February, 1914, the United States' embargo on the shipment of arms to Mexico, which had been imposed in 1912, was lifted in order to help them.

On April 9, 1914, an incident at Tampico afforded the occasion for a more effective intervention. When a boat's crew from the U.S.S. *Dolphin* was landing for supplies, some of Huerta's soldiers arrested them and held them for more than an hour before higher officials ordered their release and offered an apology. Huerta himself expressed regret, but when Admiral Mayo demanded a salute to the American flag he refused to comply except under conditions which were deemed unacceptable. On April 20 Wilson laid the matter before Congress and asked approval for the use of armed force to compel Huerta to recognize "the rights and dignity of the United States." Before Congress had time to act, however, word arrived that a German steamer was about to land arms for Huerta at Vera Cruz, and on April 21 American forces occupied that port after severe fighting with Mexican troops. Huerta considered this an act of war and dismissed the American Chargé d'Affaires. Evan Carranza, who stood to gain most from the action of the United States, protested and demanded that the American forces be withdrawn.

A real war might have ensued if Argentina, Brazil, and Chile had not offered their mediation, which was promptly accepted. A conference which met at Niagara Falls in May attempted to work out a plan for a government acceptable to all parties, but its efforts were frustrated by the intransigence of the rapidly advancing revolutionists. Carranza, who did not participate officially in the conference, would not even agree to an armistice, and the United States sympathized with him in his insistence that the civil war could be ended only by a constitutionalist victory. Meanwhile the position of Huerta steadily became more desperate, and on July 15, 1914, he resigned in favor of Francisco Carbajal, the President of the Supreme Court. A month later, when the constitutionalist army occupied Mexico City, Carranza formally assumed the "Executive Authority of the Mexican Republic."

CARRANZA AND VILLA

Unfortunately, Huerta's fall did not end the civil war. The 12 months that followed were one of the most chaotic periods in Mexico's history. Francisco Villa, who had won several important battles for Carranza, had already become restive under the "First Chief's" leadership, and in September, 1914, he revolted and joined forces with Emiliano Zapata who was still carrying on his own revolt in Morelos. Under the influence of the two leaders, a convention of generals designated Eulalio Gutiérrez as provisional President, and Carranza was forced to withdraw to Vera Cruz which had just been evacuated by the American forces. Gutiérrez in turn quarreled with the other generals and was succeeded as titular head of the "convention government" by Roque González Garza and then by Lagos Cházaro. Mexico City was taken and retaken by the contending factions, and the large foreign population there, as well as the Mexican residents, suffered from food shortages and disease and from the tyranny of irresponsible military leaders. In some districts of the interior, conditions were even worse. Foreign mining and oil interests complained of lack of protection, and many North Americans and Europeans were mis-treated or killed. It became more and more difficult for the United States government to maintain its policy of "watchful waiting."

In June, 1915, President Wilson publicly called on the Mexican factions to come to an agreement, saying that the United States would otherwise lend "active moral support" to some leader who could restore order. Somewhat later several of the other American republics joined with the United States in proposing the establishment of a provisional government and the holding of elections. Villa agreed, but Carranza, whose troops were by this time getting the upper hand, was as unco-operative as always. Nevertheless, the governments which had made the proposal decided in October to recognize Carranza, and the United States imposed an embargo on the shipment of arms to other factions which materially aided the con-stitutionalist regime in establishing its control over the greater part of Mexico.

Peace did not come at once. Zapata's followers in Morelos did not lay down their arms until after their leader was killed by treachery in 1919. Villa, defeated in battle, continued to operate near the American frontier and showed his resentment at the recognition of Carranza by atrocities against Americans and other foreigners. On March 9, 1916, he attacked Columbus, New Mexico, killing 17 Americans and burning a part of the town. This compelled the United States to act, and a force under General Pershing was sent into Mexico to capture the bandit leader. The expedi-tion failed, partly because Carranza refused to co-operate and in fact assumed a definitely hostile attitude. Pershing's force was withdrawn in February, 1917, when it became clear that war with Germany was im-minent.

Carranza's unfriendliness to the United States, which had been evi-denced even when he was profiting from North American diplomatic sup-port, did not abate during the World War. His government was neutral but distinctly unco-operative. There is no evidence, however, that he took seriously the famous Zimmermann note, delivered by the German Minister in Mexico, which proposed that he enter the war on the German side in order to regain California and New Mexico.

THE CONSTITUTION OF 1917

By this time the Carranza government had made some progress in re-storing order in the interior, and a constitutional convention represent-ing the various factions which supported it had met at Querétaro. The result of this body's labors was the constitution of 1917, which embodied most of the ideas that inspired the revolutionary movement. It had become clear by 1917 that the fall of the Díaz regime and subsequent events had aroused hopes and aspirations which must be satisfied before any government could hope to command lasting popular support. Many of the military chieftains were determined to destroy the oppressive features of the old regime, and even those who, like Carranza, were chiefly interested in obtaining power for themselves had made promises of reform which could not be ignored.

The land question was especially urgent. In the general disorder of the preceding few years, the peasants had seized and divided the large estates in many sections of the country and had fought savagely under leaders like Zapata to destroy the power of the landlords in other districts. Madero and several of the later revolutionists had promised agrarian reform, more often perhaps in the hope of attracting followers than from conviction, and in 1915 Carranza issued a decree providing for the restoration of lands unjustly taken from the villages and for the granting of lands to villages which owned none. Article 27 of the new constitution adopted this decree as the basis for a radical program of agrarian reform. It declared null and void the legal proceedings by which many of the villages had been deprived of their communal lands since 1856, and provided that villages which could not establish a legal right to lands should receive them by "dotation." The nation assumed the obligation to divide large estates for this purpose.

By Article 27 the Republic also claimed the ownership of all minerals and subsoil deposits—a provision which particularly affected the growing foreign oil industry. Minerals in the Spanish colonies had always belonged to the government, whoever the owner of the surface might be, but in Mexico a series of laws during the Díaz regime had apparently changed this rule with respect to hydrocarbons such as coal and petroleum and had made it possible to acquire the ownership of subsoil deposits by buying the land under which they lay. The oil companies had acquired most of their properties in this manner. Their interests were consequently jeopardized, and their situation was made still worse by another clause of the same article which provided that foreigners, if they were to own land or obtain concessions for the development of natural resources, must agree to forego the protection of their own governments.

Another important part of the new constitution was Article 123, which contained a long series of provisions, culled from the most advanced legislation of other countries, dealing with labor and social welfare. Among other innovations it authorized the government to establish an eight-hour day, restrictions on the labor of women and children, minimum wages, a right to share in profits, and compensation for accidents and industrial diseases. The laborers' right to organize and to strike was established, and provision was made for the arbitration of disputes. These provisions affected only the relatively small industrial laboring class in the cities and the mines, but their importance increased as new industries were established. A clause that abolished peonage, or debt-slavery, benefited an immensely greater number, for it did away with a device by which the masses of the rural population had been kept in servitude to the land-owners since the seventeenth century.

In other articles, the Church was treated even more harshly than in the "Laws of Reform." It was forbidden to conduct primary schools. The state legislatures were authorized to limit the number of priests in each district, and title to all Church property was vested in the nation.

Many of the provisions of the constitution could not be put into effect until the Mexican Congress had passed legislation to implement them, and it was in some cases many years before the Congress acted. Nevertheless they were a promise to the landless peon and the working man, and most of the program that they represented was carried out by Carranza's successors.

At the same time they were a threat to foreign interests and a new disturbing factor in the Republic's already strained relations with the United States. Though President Wilson perceived more clearly than most foreign statesmen that the revolutionary movement was fundamentally a struggle to establish more tolerable conditions of life for the poorer classes, and consequently persisted in his policy of nonintervention despite terrific pressure at home and almost intolerable provocation in Mexico, the American government could not be indifferent to provisions that threatened severe injury to legally acquired American property rights. Carranza, both before and after the recognition of his government, assured the United States that foreign property would be respected, but he soon gave evidence of an intention to apply Article 27 of the new constitution in a way hardly consistent with these pledges. A tax decree issued in February, 1918, which required the oil companies to recognize the Mexican government's ownership of the petroleum in the subsoil, gave rise to a diplomatic controversy which had not been settled when Carranza's government fell.

OBREGÓN AND THE QUESTION OF RECOGNITION

Carranza's successor was to be elected in the summer of 1920. General Álvaro Obregón, the government's chief military leader, was apparently the strongest candidate, and when the President attempted to bring about the election of his friend Ignacio Bonillas, Obregón's friends revolted. Carranza, abandoned by most of his followers, was murdered, and Obregón was elected President.

The United States delayed recognition of the new government in an effort to obtain assurances that American property rights would be respected. Secretary of State Hughes proposed a treaty that would prevent the confiscatory application of Article 27 of the new constitution, but

Obregón considered this impossible for political reasons. In 1923, however, the so-called Bucareli Conference, meeting at Mexico City, agreed on a compromise solution. All pending claims were to be arbitrated, and the United States reluctantly consented to permit its citizens to be paid in bonds, within certain limitations, for land taken in connection with the agrarian program. There was no agreement on the basic question of the legal ownership of petroleum deposits, but the commissioners achieved a temporary working arrangement. The Mexican Supreme Court, in the case of the Texas Company, had decided that Article 27 did not deprive the owner of the surface of his right to the oil in the ground, provided that he had shown by some "positive act" an intent to exploit this oil, and this principle, expanded to apply also to lands which the foreign companies had bought for future use, was finally accepted, though with reservations, by the American government.

Recognition was thus obtained. Its practical value became apparent when Adolfo de la Huerta, formerly a member of Obregón's Cabinet but now an opposition candidate for the presidency, started a revolt in the latter part of 1923. The movement was a formidable one, supported by a large part of the army as well as by the still-powerful conservative groups, including the clergy and the great landowners. It was soon suppressed, however, by the energetic action of General Plutarco Elías Calles, aided by arms purchased from the government of the United States.

CALLES AND HIS SUCCESSORS, 1924–1934

Calles, who was the official and consequently the successful candidate for the presidency in 1924, was a close friend of Obregón and one of the most prominent leaders in the revolutionary party. Soon after he took office it became clear that he would push the revolution's program of economic and social reform more actively than his predecessors. Laws injecting fresh vigor into the agrarian program and restricting the right of foreigners to inherit agricultural property alarmed foreign landowners, and a new petroleum law violated the 1923 agreement with the United States. These measures, combined with Mexican efforts to frustrate the policy of the United States in Nicaragua,[1] brought on a new crisis in Mexican-American relations.

Matters were made worse by a sudden flare-up of the religious question. Though the revolutionary governments had done little to implement the anticlerical articles of the 1917 constitution, their attitude toward the Church had been unfriendly, and a number of minor incidents had stirred up bitter feeling. On April 21, 1926, the bishops of the Republic issued a statement condemning the constitutional provisions affecting the Church, and the government promptly retaliated by decrees and laws putting

[1] See below, p. 428.

some of the provisions into effect. Catholic schools and convents were closed, and all priests were required to register with the government. The Church refused to comply, and a league of Catholic laymen announced a campaign to paralyze the economic life of the nation by restricting purchases to the barest necessities. In many sections of the country small armed bands rose in rebellion, and there was much loss of life before order was restored in July, 1927. The Knights of Columbus and other Catholic organizations in the United States gave the Church much moral support in the conflict, and the *Cristeros*, as the rebels were called, were undoubtedly encouraged by a belief that the numerous controversies between the United States and the Calles government would weaken the latter's position.

Fortunately, more friendly relations between the two countries were restored after 1927, when Dwight Morrow was appointed American Ambassador. The most objectionable provision of the petroleum law, the requirement that oil companies apply for 50-year concessions to confirm their acquired rights, was declared unconstitutional by the Mexican Supreme Court, and an amended law, giving them concessions unlimited as to time, was enacted early in 1928. A more conciliatory attitude on both sides facilitated the handling of other pending matters, and even the religious question became temporarily less acute as the result of a compromise worked out through Morrow's informal good offices.

Obregón was elected to succeed Calles in 1928; but he was assassinated by a religious fanatic before his inauguration, and Emilio Portes Gil was installed as provisional President by Congress. Calles refused to remain in office; but he continued to be the chief leader of the revolutionary party, and his influence dominated the government during the next six years. He took command of the army to suppress a revolt by a group of dissatisfied generals in March, 1929. Three years later, when he became dissatisfied with the conduct of Pascual Ortíz Rubio, who had been elected in 1929 to serve the balance of Obregón's term, the President was compelled to resign, and Abelardo Rodríguez took his place. The policy of the government during this period was relatively conservative, for Calles and some of his associates, as they grew older and acquired personal wealth, seemed less interested in social and economic reform.

There was nevertheless a revival of the conflict with the Church, touched off by a great demonstration at the shrine of the Virgin of Guadalupe in December, 1931. In the months that followed, the federal authorities limited the number of priests in the Capital city and the territories to one for every 50,000 people. Many of the states took similar or even more drastic action. Feeling ran especially high after the government amended the constitution in 1934 to require that all education should be "socialistic" in character, and for a time civil war again seemed imminent.

An important faction in the revolutionary party opposed the growing conservatism of Calles and his associates, and in 1934 this group persuaded the older leaders to put forward Lázaro Cárdenas as the official candidate for the presidency. The new Chief Executive had been in office only a short time before he repudiated Calles' leadership and sent the ex-President into exile. The six years of Cárdenas' term were to be the most radical period of the revolution, marked by vigorous efforts to give land to the peasants and to improve the condition of labor, and also by unprecedented attacks on foreign economic interests in Mexico.

CÁRDENAS AND THE AGRARIAN REFORM

A considerable amount of land had already been redistributed, especially during the administrations of Calles and Portes Gil. By the end of 1933 nearly 19,000,000 acres had been allotted to villages containing 750,000 families.[2] For the most part, this had been accomplished by "dotation," or grants of land from expropriated large estates, rather than by the restitution to the villages of lands unjustly taken. The government theoretically proposed to compensate the original owners of the land thus distributed, but payments had been made in only a few cases, and then usually in bonds which had little market value. The *ejido*, as the tract granted to each village was called, was usually in part pasture or woodland, for the common use of the inhabitants, and in part crop land which was divided among the heads of families under restrictions designed to prevent them from selling their holdings.

Obstacles of many sorts had hampered the execution of the agrarian program. The examination and disposition of so many thousands of cases was a difficult matter, especially as it was complicated by governmental red tape, friction between federal and state authorities, factional politics, and official corruption. There was tenacious opposition from other conservative groups as well as the landlords, and also from foreign governments which objected to the seizure of their nationals' property without compensation. Even the villages which received land did not always seem to benefit, for the plot given to each family was often too small for its support and the lack of tools and machinery prevented efficient cultivation. The government endeavored to provide capital for the new landowners through the establishment of an agricultural bank and the encouragement of co-operatives, but lack of money and administrative difficulties made its efforts only partly successful.

Cárdenas did not overcome these obstacles, but he went ahead aggressively in spite of them. Local conservative opposition, which had often taken the form of violence and intimidation, was discouraged by arming the peasants to enable them to defend themselves and incidentally to support the administration in case of need. Foreign diplomatic opposition

[2] Simpson, *The Ejido*, pp. 170–171.

was less effective after the adoption of the "Good Neighbor" policy by the United States, especially as the two governments reached an agreement in 1938 for the eventual compensation of Americans who had lost their land. By 1940 it was said that between 60,000,000 and 70,000,000 acres of land had been distributed among nearly 2,000,000 heads of families since 1915.[3] Peasants who did not receive land benefited from the government's fairly successful efforts to abolish peonage and to check exploitation by company stores.

INCREASING POWER OF ORGANIZED LABOR

The situation of the industrial workers had also improved under Cárdenas' predecessors. The provisions of the 1917 constitution encouraged the organization of labor unions, and labor leaders played an increasingly prominent rôle in politics. The *Confederación Regional Obrera Mexicana*, the C.R.O.M., which was a national federation embracing most of the larger unions, helped Obregón to overthrow Carranza in 1920, and its leader, Luis Morones, was a powerful figure in the Obregón administration. In the years that followed, many of the benefits promised by the constitution were actually attained. In 1931 a federal labor law provided for collective labor contracts, enforceable by boards of conciliation and arbitration, which greatly strengthened the position of the worker as against the employer. The law also provided for the fixing of minimum wages in the various sections of the country, and specific minimum wages were in fact established in the federal district and in many of the states in 1934.

Meanwhile there had been internal dissensions in the labor movement, and the influence of Morones had declined. A more radical group supported Cárdenas for the presidency, and after the formation in 1936 of the *Confederación de Trabajadores de Mexico*, the C.T.M., Vicente Lombardo Toledano was the most powerful of the country's labor leaders. Lombardo Toledano, who had been a teacher and a writer, was an avowed Marxist, and his evident purpose was to substitute labor management for capitalist control throughout Mexican industry.

In carrying out this program, he had effective support from President Cárdenas. The national railways, in which the government had had a majority stock interest since the time of Díaz, were expropriated in 1937 and turned over to the railroad workers' union for operation in 1938. Other less important concerns were expropriated in much the same manner, and in some cases where strikes or other labor trouble made operation of an enterprise unprofitable, the government forbade the closing of the plant and exerted pressure on the owners to surrender it to the workers. Foreign interests suffered especially, because the elimination of foreign eco-

[3] *Seis Años de Gobierno al Servicio de México, 1934-1940,* p. 330.

nomic control was as important a part of the revolutionary policy as the improvement of the condition of the workers. In 1940 Lombardo Toledano claimed that syndicates of the C.T.M. were managing street railways, buses, and other municipal services, several sugar mills and textile factories, and all of the Mexican ships carrying on commerce in the Gulf of Mexico, as well as the railroads.[4] The program of socialization might have gone farther had it not been for practical difficulties. Inefficient management, lack of discipline, and inability to obtain capital made operation by the workers' co-operatives unsatisfactory, and the railways, especially, were in a deplorable state by the end of Cárdenas' term.

THE EXPROPRIATION OF THE OIL COMPANIES

One of the most important events of the Cárdenas administration was the expropriation of the North American and British oil companies. These still represented one of the largest foreign investments in the Republic, though the production of the Mexican fields was relatively far less important than it had been. The oil companies, like other foreign interests, had to contend with the increasingly aggressive spirit of the labor unions, and in May, 1937, their workers went on strike to obtain higher wages and other benefits, including a share in the management of the industry. When the Federal Board of Conciliation and Arbitration ordered the companies to accept terms that they considered confiscatory, they refused, and on March 18, 1938, Cárdenas expropriated the property of all the larger foreign-owned concerns. The administration of the nationalized industry was entrusted to an official organization in which the labor unions had a considerable voice.

Since there was little probability that Mexico could or would make any adequate payment for the seized properties, the expropriation brought a vigorous protest from the United States and led to a break in diplomatic relations with Great Britain. The government at Washington, which had been buying newly mined Mexican silver at prices far above its market value, ceased to do so. This severely affected the country's economy, and at the same time the export of oil became difficult because the companies that had formerly operated in Mexico controlled most of the world's tanker tonnage. Some shipments were made to Germany and Italy, but these ceased with the outbreak of war in Europe. In the oil fields, production fell off, and costs increased under the new management. The government, however, was enthusiastically supported by public opinion, and these economic difficulties did not seriously weaken its position.

[4] Lombardo Toledano, in *Annals of the American Academy of Political and Social Science*, Vol. 208 (May, 1940), pp. 52–53.

THE ELECTION OF 1940

The official candidate for the presidency in 1940 was General Manuel Ávila Camacho, who had been Secretary of War in Cárdenas' Cabinet. His chief rival, General Juan Andreu Almazán, was also a member of the revolutionary party. Almazán received much conservative support, as well as some backing from labor unions that had had disgreements with Cárdenas. The government did not prevent its opponents from carrying on an active campaign; but on election day many of the usual abuses appeared, and there were disputes and minor disturbances at the polls. Though some observers thought that Almazán had received a majority of the votes, the official count gave an overwhelming victory to Ávila Camacho. There was talk of revolution, but Almazán's withdrawal prevented an armed conflict.

MEXICO AND THE SECOND WORLD WAR

When war broke out in 1939 Mexican public opinion sided with the democracies, and the labor unions, despite the communist leanings of some of their leaders, took a strong stand against the Axis even during the period when Russia was co-operating with Germany. Relations with the United States, during Ávila Camacho's administration, became more friendly than they had been for many years. American forces were permitted to use Mexican airfields and other military facilities in transporting planes to Panama, and the United States was assured of a preferential position in obtaining the important strategic raw materials that Mexico produced. In November, 1941, a series of agreements settled many of the outstanding problems between the two governments. It was arranged that the indemnity to the American oil companies should be decided by experts representing the governments, and the companies were subsequently awarded $23,995,991. This was far less than the $130,000,000 they had demanded, but it settled the controversy. Provision was made for the settlement of other claims and for substantial loans to Mexico by the Export-Import Bank, and silver purchases were resumed.

Mexico was one of the first American states to break diplomatic relations with the Axis after Pearl Harbor, and on June 1, 1942, the Republic declared war and began to take part in antisubmarine operations in the Gulf of Mexico. Three years later an air squadron was sent to the Far East, making Mexico one of the two Latin American countries that actually sent troops to the fighting front.[5] Meanwhile, by agreement between the two governments, more than 100,000 Mexicans entered the United States to work on the railroads and in the harvests. There was a close co-operation in many other aspects of the war effort.

[5] The other was Brazil.

POSTWAR ADMINISTRATIONS

After 1946 the dominant political group called itself the *Partido Revolucionario Institucional*. The change in name signified a change in its attitude. The Mexicans continued to speak of the "Revolution" as a continuing movement, but the policies of the postwar governments were quite different from those of Calles and Cárdenas. Under Ávila Camacho, himself a Catholic, there had been little friction with the Church, and this situation continued under his successors. The breaking up of large landholdings was almost stopped, and there was a friendlier attitude toward foreign capital. Military influence in the government diminished somewhat. Ávila Camacho's successor, Miguel Alemán (1946–1952), was the first civilian elected to the presidency since Madero, and the next two Presidents, Adolfo Ruiz Cortines (1952–1958) and Adolfo López Mateos (1958–   ) were members of the civilian bureaucracy.

In the elections of the postwar period, there were opposition candidates, but the government always won. None of the opposition candidates, however, seemed to have enough popular following to arouse fear of a serious attempt to reverse the result by revolution. The official candidates for the presidency and also apparently the candidates for other offices, including those in the states and the municipalities, were chosen by a small group of leaders at the Capital. Many Mexicans nevertheless felt that the country had made real progress toward more democratic government. The press enjoyed a considerable amount of freedom, and increasing numbers of voters went to the polls.

The poverty and ignorance of the masses of the people continued to be Mexico's chief problem. Though most of the revolutionary governments showed much interest in education, they were handicapped by lack of funds and the shortage of trained teachers. The conflict with the Church forced the closing of many of the schools that had formerly existed. Much was nevertheless accomplished. Between 1920 and 1925, when José Vasconcelos was Secretary of Public Instruction, thousands of new schools were established in rural communities, and there was a special effort to improve the status of the hitherto despised and neglected Indian. Adults as well as children were taught to read and write and were also given instruction in better agricultural methods and simple trades. Later administrations continued the work, and in 1944 a law required each literate Mexican to teach one other person to read and write. In 1957, however, 50 per cent of the Mexican people were still said to be illiterate, and there were hundreds of thousands of children who had no opportunity to attend school.

The postwar governments devoted much of their attention to increasing the country's agricultural production. The distribution of land to peasants who did not have the capital or the skill to utilize it effectively had done little to remedy the Republic's chronic food shortage, and the rapid increase of the population made the problem a pressing one. After the war, the amount of arable land was considerably increased by irrigation and drainage projects, some of them on an impressive scale. The production of corn and other food crops was greatly increased as the result of a program, inaugurated by the Rockefeller Foundation, to develop varieties better suited to local conditions. At the same time cotton and coffee growing were expanded so that these products took the place of minerals as the Republic's chief exports.

There was also a notable increase in manufacturing. The government took an active part in the establishment and expansion of power plants and factories through its development corporation, the *Nacional Financiera,* and the United States helped with loans from the Export-Import Bank. Much private foreign capital also came into the country, a considerable part of it in mixed companies in which Mexicans had a large interest. Foreign capital continued to dominate the mining industry, which was still an important source of wealth. Petroleum, on the other hand, was a government monopoly. Oil exports were no longer significant, but the fact that Mexico produced almost enough for its own needs was an element of strength in the economy.

An important source of wealth was the tourist trade, which increased rapidly after the war. In the 1950's, visitors from the United States each year left in the country half as many dollars as the Republic received from all its exports. Another smaller item in the foreign exchange budget was the money brought home by the many thousands of Mexicans who went annually to the United States to work in the harvest in the southwest. Agreements between the two governments regulated this immigration and provided for the protection of the workers while in the United States, but there were also many "wetbacks" who crossed the border illegally.

In general, the period 1945–1960 was one of remarkable economic progress. Rapid industrial development brought some inflation, reflected in higher living costs and a decline in the exchange value of the peso, but the inflation was far less serious than in some of the South American republics. The Secretary of State for Finance and Public Credit was able to report in 1958 that the average Mexican's real income had nearly doubled between 1939 and 1956, and agricultural production had increased two and one-half times. Manufacturing had grown to a point where the output was greater than that of the country's farms.[6] Continued progress, however, would be necessary, not only to give the Mexican people an adequate standard of living but to provide for the rapid increase in the country's population.

[6] Antonio Carrillo Flores, in *Foreign Affairs,* Vol. 36 (April, 1958), pp. 491 ff.

PART VIII

THE CARIBBEAN REGION

THE HISTORY of the Central American and West Indian Republics, like that of Mexico, has been much influenced by their relations with the United States. The American government has inevitably been interested in the affairs of countries so close to it and to the strategically and commercially important Isthmian transit routes. The United States has always considered it essential for the national security that the Central American and West Indian Republics should not fall under the control of any foreign power.

In the nineteenth century several other nations also had important interests in the Caribbean. Spain still held Cuba and Puerto Rico, and Great Britain, France, the Netherlands, and Denmark owned most of the other islands. Great Britain, in British Honduras, had a foothold on the mainland of Central America and for a time in the middle years of the century attempted to extend her control to other portions of the Isthmus with a view to controlling the projected Nicaragua canal. She abandoned this effort after a diplomatic controversy with the United States, but the British navy, with its strong bases, continued to be the predominant military factor in the Caribbean until the rise of the German navy caused the British government tacitly to relinquish its commanding position to the United States in the last decade of the century.

After the Spanish American war, and particularly after the United States decided to build the canal at Panama, our relations with the Caribbean states took on a new importance. The canal could be used safely only so long as its approaches were kept clear of potential enemies. The existing European colonies were no longer a cause for concern, because they had lost much of their economic importance and were in friendly hands, but the situation would be different if any foreign power should undertake to obtain new possessions and thus make the Caribbean the scene of a contest for territory and spheres of influence like the contests that were going on at the end of the nineteenth century in Africa and the Far East. Rightly or wrongly, many American statesmen of the period before the First World War believed that Germany and perhaps other powers had their eyes on the Caribbean as a field for imperial adventures and would not be indisposed to challenge the Monroe Doctrine should a favorable opportunity arise.

Internal disorder and financial mismanagement had already exposed Latin American countries to aggression on many occasions. Mexico had suffered twice from foreign invasions to collect claims, and Honduras and Nicaragua had nearly lost portions of their territory because they were too weak to resist British encroachments on the Mosquito Coast. Other countries had frequently been compelled by force to adjust pecuniary claims or to pay indemnities for the mistreatment of foreigners, and foreign troops had repeatedly been landed to protect lives and property in times of civil disturbance. Such occurrences had been especially common in the Caribbean because the countries of that region were the smallest and weakest—and some of them were among the most turbulent—of the American republics. It was always possible that a European intervention of this sort might be made the pretext for a more permanent occupation.

In the early 1900's the right of a nation to intervene in the affairs of a weaker state to protect the lives and property of its own nationals was too firmly established in international practice to be challenged easily. The American government thought the Caribbean countries would be safe from intervention only when the conditions that invited intervention were rectified, and it consequently endeavored to help its neighbors to rectify them. When it made Cuba independent, it insisted that the new Republic agree to the Platt Amendment, which gave the United States a right to intervene to maintain a government that could protect life, property, and individual liberty. The same idea found expression in Theodore Roosevelt's corollary to the Monroe Doctrine: that the United States, if it wished to prevent European interference in the Western Hemisphere, must help its neighbors to do away with the political instability and financial mismanagement that invited interference. Unfortunately, efforts to eliminate political instability and financial mismanagement involved the American government itself in an increasing interference in the internal affairs of several of its neighbors and led in several cases to armed intervention. This caused bad feeling throughout Latin America and aroused justified concern in the United States.

Other considerations also influenced American policy in the Caribbean in the first decades of the present century. Much American capital was being invested in sugar companies in Cuba, in banana farms in Central America, and in mines and oil fields and railroads. Many American citizens were living there, employed in the management of these enterprises or in commerce. Relations with the Caribbean governments were frequently complicated by controversies over the rights of American companies, and warships were often sent to protect resident North Americans when disturbances occurred. Concern for the safety of its citizens and their interests gave the United States an additional reason for wishing to see stable political conditions in the area. There is little foundation, however, for the frequently expressed idea that the promotion of economic interests was one of the primary objectives of American intervention. In most of the countries where the United States actually intervened, American investments were relatively insignificant.

The improvement of health conditions was an important objective. In the nineteenth century, epidemics of yellow fever, brought in from Cuba and other Caribbean countries, had repeatedly caused a heavy loss of life at American Gulf ports and even at times in Philadelphia and New York. With increasing contact the danger became greater. It was also imperative to protect the Canal Zone against infection from nearby countries. The United States consequently insisted upon measures to improve sanitary conditions in Panama and in Cuba, and at a later date the Public Health Service was one of the most important Treaty Services in Haiti. A greater number of people benefited from the magnificent work done in tropical America by the International Health Division of the Rockefeller Foundation, which co-operated with several Latin American states in campaigns against yellow fever, hookworm, and other menaces to health.

We shall discuss what happened in each country in the chapters that follow, but the story will be easier to understand if we have in mind the way in which United States policy was developing in the region as a whole during the period after the Spanish American war. In Theodore Roosevelt's administration, the United States interfered in the internal affairs of Caribbean states only when immediate action seemed necessary to correct a bad situation. The Dominican customs receivership was established to avert the apparently imminent seizure of one or more ports by European powers. An American provisional government was set up in Cuba after the constituted authorities refused to continue in office, but it was discontinued as soon as needed reforms were effected and a new election held. In Central America international conflicts were ended by North American and Mexican mediation, and relations between the five countries were placed on a new basis under the Washington treaties. The Taft administration, with Mr. Knox as Secretary of State, went farther. Under the so-called "preventive policy" it constantly interfered in the internal affairs of Caribbean countries on the theory that it was better to remedy conditions likely to cause civil war or foreign complications than to wait for crises to arise. It did not hesitate to threaten the use of force when its advice was not heeded, and its armed intervention in Nicaragua involved the United States in responsibilities which were troublesome for many years to come. It especially sought to extend to other countries the same sort of financial control that until 1911 had seemed so helpful to the Dominican Republic. It was the effort to promote financial stability and economic development, through American loans secured by customs collectorships, that caused Taft's policy to be called "Dollar Diplomacy."

There was no great change in the policy of the United States when Woodrow Wilson became President in 1913. There was perhaps less emphasis on the protection of American economic interests, but there was a greater insistence on the maintenance of constitutional forms and democratic practices. Governments that came into power by methods openly illegal were refused recognition and in some cases were forced out of office. Carrying farther an idea already developed under the preceding administration, Wilson and his advisers attempted to attack the basic causes of Caribbean political instability by insisting on the establishment of efficient police forces, the reform of financial administration, and the adoption of broad programs of economic rehabilitation, all under the direction of North American advisers. When these objectives could not be accomplished by diplomatic pressure, there was a resort to force. Haiti was occupied by American marines in 1915, and the Haitian government was compelled to sign a treaty giving the United States control of several important branches of its administration. A year later a military government was set up in the Dominican Republic. American intervention in the Caribbean had reached its high point at the end of President Wilson's term in 1921.

Thereafter there was a gradual change in policy. In the decade that followed the World War, when no European power was in a position to challenge the Monroe Doctrine, the Roosevelt corollary lost much of its significance. It became apparent, furthermore, that the policies hitherto followed were repugnant to Latin American public opinion and were becoming increasingly unpopular in the United States. Gradually the responsibilities already assumed were liquidated. There was less active interference in the internal affairs of Cuba and Panama, and the American forces were withdrawn from the Dominican Republic in 1924 and from Nicaragua in 1925. Unfortunately the second intervention in Nicaragua in 1926 and the continuance of the treaty regime in Haiti tended to obscure the fact that a change in policy was occurring. North American "imperialism" continued to provide material for hostile propaganda in Latin America, even though President Hoover's policies between 1929 and 1933 made it clear that the United States was determined to avoid further interference in the internal affairs of Caribbean countries. Latin American suspicion of the United States only began to diminish after President Franklin Roosevelt formally pledged the American government to a policy of nonintervention in 1933.

The basic objectives of American policy in the Caribbean are the same today as they were a half-century ago: to help the Caribbean countries to achieve stable, democratic governments and to improve the conditions under which their people live. In recent years, however, the United States has sought to attain these objectives by programs of co-operation and direct financial aid, which will be discussed in a later chapter.

CHAPTER 20

Panama and the Canal

EARLY CANAL PROJECTS

THE FIRST PROPOSAL for a waterway between the Caribbean Sea and the Pacific was made soon after the discovery of the Central American Isthmus. Its discussion was forbidden in Spain, where the land barrier was looked on as the best protection of the rich colonies on the South American west coast, but the idea was revived after independence. Several projects for construction were brought forward after 1825, and especially after North American settlers began to pour into California. Despite the hardships involved and the danger of death from yellow fever and malaria, many travelers went from the eastern seaboard to the gold fields by way of Panama or Nicaragua before the opening of the transcontinental railway in the United States.

Panama and Nicaragua offered the most feasible of several canal routes that were advocated. At Panama, where the traffic between Spain and Peru crossed in colonial times, the Isthmus reaches its narrowest point, and the mountainous backbone of the continent sinks to an altitude of a few hundred feet. In Nicaragua the divide is still lower, and the San Juan River and the great lake provide a natural waterway for small vessels from the Caribbean to a point within a few miles of the Pacific. Both routes involved tremendous engineering problems, the magnitude of which was hardly realized until construction actually began.

Both routes were in countries that could not possibly build the canal themselves. It was clear that it would have to be built by foreign enterprise, and the question who would control it was important not only to the United States but to other powers. Great Britain, as the principal maritime and commercial nation, had a very special interest in an enterprise that would provide a new trade route to South America and the Orient as well as to California, and after the war between the United States and Mexico, British efforts to obtain control of the Nicaragua route led to a long-drawn-out diplomatic conflict.[1] One result of this was the Clayton-Bulwer Treaty of 1850, in which Great Britain and the United States agreed that neither would seek to control any canal that might be built.

The government of New Granada, or Colombia, to which the Isthmus of Panama belonged, also realized the dangers involved in international rivalries over the canal routes; and in 1846, after vainly attempting to obtain similar agreements with other countries, it entered into a treaty with the United States by which that government guaranteed the neutrality of the Isthmus and New Granada's sovereignty there. In return the United States was granted the right of free transit by any existing or future means of transport. This was not an exclusive privilege, but it gave the United States a special position on the Isthmus, especially as the Colombian government in subsequent years frequently asked American intervention to keep the transit routes open in time of civil war. During the period when the transit route was being used by travelers going to California, and especially after an American company completed the railroad across the Isthmus in 1855, American influence on the Isthmus increased.

THE FRENCH CANAL COMPANY

Nevertheless the first effort to build a canal at Panama was made by a French company that obtained a concession from Colombia in 1878 and started work in 1880. Ferdinand de Lesseps, the builder of the Suez Canal, was the leading spirit in the enterprise, and a large capital was obtained by popular subscription. The undertaking was regarded with little favor in the United States. President Hayes informed Congress in 1880 that "the policy of this country is a canal under American control," but opposition diminished when American capital and a few important American politicians were given an interest in the company.

The company originally planned to build a waterway at sea level, but it found that this would involve far more work and expense than the engineers had estimated, and a lock canal was decided upon instead. Even so, the company's resources, depleted by extravagance and gross mismanagement, were unequal to the task, and the terrific loss of life among its employees from yellow fever and other diseases made the continuance of the work almost impossible. Though a substantial amount of excavation was accomplished, de Lesseps' company failed in 1888, and the new company which took over its rights and property had too little capital to carry on work of any importance. When the question of selling its interests to the United States arose, the company valued them at $109,-000,000.

[1] See below, pp. 409-11.

THE AMERICAN GOVERNMENT
UNDERTAKES THE TASK

The collapse of the French effort and the failure of a North American company which was incorporated by act of Congress in 1889 to build a canal in Nicaragua made it evident that the canal could not be built by private enterprise. There was a growing feeling that the American government itself would have to undertake the work, and this increased after 1898 when the battleship *Oregon,* which was in the Pacific at the outbreak of the Spanish American War, had to round Cape Horn to join the fleet in the West Indies.

The Hay-Pauncefote Treaty, signed in 1901, freed the United States from the restrictions of the Clayton-Bulwer Treaty, and the Congress appointed a commission to make a new study of the Panama and Nicaragua routes. The commission recommended that the former be adopted if the French company would sell its rights for $40,000,000, and if a satisfactory agreement could be made with Colombia. The French company reluctantly agreed to sell, and the Spooner Act of June 28, 1902, authorized the President to build the canal at Panama, if Colombia consented, or in Nicaragua if no prompt agreement could be made with Colombia. The Hay-Herrán Treaty, signed in January, 1903, provided that Colombia would authorize the French company to sell its rights to the United States and would grant to the United States the use of a zone ten kilometers wide for the construction of a canal. Colombia was to receive $10,000,000 and in addition an annuity of $250,000 starting nine years after the ratification of the treaty. The Congress at Bogotá, however, refused to approve this agreement, apparently because it hoped that a delay might make it possible to obtain more favorable terms from the French company or from the United States.

THE PANAMA REVOLUTION

There was much disappointment in Panama when the rejection of the treaty made it seem probable that the canal would be built in Nicaragua. The people of the Isthmus had always depended for their livelihood on the transit trade. Panama's prosperity had declined in the latter part of the colonial period when the galleons no longer came to the great fair at Porto Bello. It revived somewhat in the days of the gold rush to California, but the opening of transcontinental lines in the north again left the Isthmus in a backwater so far as international trade was concerned. The Panamanians enjoyed another short period of prosperity while the French company was at work, and they looked forward eagerly to the resumption of construction by the United States.

Well-informed people were consequently not surprised when a group of revolutionists, with the support of the Commander of the local garrison, seized control of Panama City on November 3, 1903, and declared the independence of the Republic of Panama. The revolutionary conspiracy had originated with persons connected with the Panama Railroad, which then belonged to the French canal company, and it had apparently been encouraged in its earlier stages by William Nelson Cromwell, the French company's representative in New York. Cromwell later disassociated himself from the project, but Philippe Bunau-Varilla, an engineer formerly connected with the French company, then took over its promotion and financing. Just before the revolt occurred, when a Colombian force arrived at Colón, the local officials of the railroad prevented it from crossing the Isthmus by withholding a train.

Bunau-Varilla had promised the revolutionists help from the United States. He later asserted that he had done this without any assurances from American officials, and President Roosevelt vehemently denied that the United States government had done anything to instigate the revolt. He did, however, prevent Colombia from suppressing it. Four days after the revolt the United States formally recognized the government of Panama, and a treaty signed at Washington on November 18 guaranteed the independence of the new republic and ended any possibility of Colombia's reconquering the Isthmus.

The events just described were the subject of much controversy. President Roosevelt's action was defended on the ground that the construction of the canal was an urgent necessity, that it was being prevented by the obstructive conduct of Colombia, and that the people of Panama had a right to revolt against an action which "threatened their most vital interests with destruction and the interests of the whole world with grave injury." [2] The United States claimed that its course was justified by the provisions of the Treaty of 1846. On the other hand, there was much criticism both in Latin America and in the United States. In retrospect, it seems difficult to justify the American government's action. We have already seen that a $25,000,000 indemnity was later paid to Colombia in recognition of the injury she had suffered.

THE CANAL TREATY

The Treaty of November 18, besides guaranteeing the independence of Panama, provided for the construction of a canal by the United States. Negotiated by M. Bunau-Varilla, who had been appointed the new Republic's Minister at Washington, it granted more extensive privileges than Colombia had been willing to concede. The United States was given

[2] Secretary Hay to the Colombian Minister, *Foreign Relations of the United States* (1903), p. 302.

the perpetual "use, occupation, and control" of a Zone ten miles wide, and the right to take such additional lands as might be needed for the construction, maintenance, operation, sanitation, and protection of the canal. The cities of Panama and Colón, at either end of the canal route, were not included in the Zone, but the United States was to have the right to intervene if necessary to maintain public order in them. Panama, in return, received $10,000,000, with the promise of an additional payment of $250,000 annually to begin nine years after the treaty went into effect.

The situation of the new Republic of Panama was a peculiar one. Its territory extended some 200 miles on either side of the transit route; but the region to the east was still held by unconquered Indian tribes, and that to the west was undeveloped and thinly populated. Economic and political life centered in two cities, Panama and Colón, which were separated only by imaginary lines from North American towns in the Zone. Until a corridor connecting Panama with the Republic's territory to the east was created in 1914, both cities were entirely surrounded on the land side by the Zone. Their prosperity depended on the canal. On the other hand, Panaman co-operation, especially in such matters as sanitation and military defense, was essential to the operation of the canal. Relations with the United States were bound to be extremely close, and many delicate questions, often involving vital interests of both countries, were certain to arise.

THE FIRST YEARS OF THE REPUBLIC

A *junta* named by the municipality of Panama City took over the government at the time of the revolution, and in January, 1904, a Convention met to frame a constitution. One provision of this authorized the United States to intervene in any part of the Republic if necessary to maintain order. The Convention chose Dr. Manuel Amador Guerrero, the leader of the revolution, as President of the Republic. His administration was at first supported by a coalition of the two political parties that Panama had inherited from Colombia, but the liberals soon became dissatisfied and induced the Commander of the army to threaten a *coup d'état*. The American Minister's intervention prevented a conflict, and the army was soon afterward disbanded and replaced by a civilian police.

Meanwhile work on the canal had begun. The most urgent problem at the outset was the conquest of yellow fever and malaria, which had been major causes of the French company's failure. Since this could not be accomplished without strict sanitary controls in Panama City and Colón, the treaty of 1903 had given the United States a virtually unlimited authority with respect to public health measures in these municipalities, and early in 1905 the Panaman government turned over to the Zone authorities the administration of sanitary regulations in both cities. Under the direction of Dr. William C. Gorgas of the United States Army, yellow fever was promptly eradicated. Malaria, a hardly less formidable enemy to human welfare, was brought under control in the areas near the settlements. For the first time in its history, the Isthmus became a safe place to live.

Another question involving the rights of the United States under the canal treaty was not so easily settled. In June, 1904, President Roosevelt formally opened the Canal Zone to commerce and established customhouses and post offices there. There was a storm of protest in Panama, for it was clear that the merchants of the Republic would be deprived of much business and the government would lose much of its revenue if commerce were allowed in the Zone. The Panama government took the position that the treaty gave the United States only such rights in the Zone as it needed for the "construction, maintenance, operation, sanitation, and protection" of the canal, and insisted upon a narrow interpretation of these rights. The United States, on the other hand, pointed out that Article III of the treaty gave it "all the rights, power and authority within the zone . . . which the United States would possess and exercise if it were the sovereign of the territory." Nevertheless, it disclaimed any desire to inflict unnecessary hardship on Panama, and when Secretary of War Taft visited the Isthmus in the fall of 1904 a compromise was arranged. Thereafter imports into the Zone were limited in general to goods for the use of persons working on the canal or for sale to vessels passing through, and the general public was not permitted to trade at the commissaries the American authorities established. This arrangement was satisfactory in principle to both governments, but it did not prevent disputes over the operation of the commissaries from embittering their relations at frequent intervals in succeeding years.

Work on the canal began rather slowly, but after 1907 it was pushed forward more energetically under the direction of Colonel George W. Goethals. Some thousands of North Americans and a much larger number of Negro laborers from the British and French West Indies were brought to the Isthmus to work on the project. Large communities grew up at either end of the waterway, close to Panama City and Colón, with schools, club houses, and commissaries maintained by the United States government. Many other North Americans and several thousand colored West Indians settled in the territory of the Republic. The Panaman cities flourished on the great sums of money spent in the Isthmus during the construction period and on the tourist trade after the canal was opened to commerce in 1914.

The canal itself is one of the great achievements of modern engineering. At either end, three locks raise ships to Gatun Lake, an artificial body of water created by damming the Chagres River at Gatun and flooding 164 square miles in the center of the Zone. South of the lake vessels pass through a cut, 300 feet deep, from which tremendous quantities of earth were removed before troublesome landslides were brought under control. The transit, from Cristóbal on the Caribbean to Balboa on the Pacific, requires about six hours. The waterway at once became one of the world's principal trade routes. It benefited especially the countries of the west coast of South and Central America, which now had readier access to the eastern United States and Europe with more frequent and adequate steamship services. It also became an important link in the domestic communication system of the United States, for it was cheaper to send many commodities by sea via Panama than overland by rail. Equally significant, from the standpoint of the United States, was the usefulness of the canal from a military point of view.

INTERNAL POLITICS, 1906–1924

The people of Panama had little experience with self-government during their connection with Colombia, and the extraordinary geographical and economic situation created by the canal was hardly conducive to orderly political development. In the first years of independence there was much factional strife among the small groups of politically minded persons in Panama City and Colón, and on several occasions disorder that would have interfered with work on the canal was only averted by the influence of the United States. The American government was at first rather reluctant to interfere in Panaman internal affairs. When new members of Congress were to be chosen in 1906, it informed the Panaman leaders that it did not undertake to guarantee the holding of free elections; but it was soon compelled to change its attitude and to threaten to intervene if peace were disturbed. Its representatives then helped to bring about an agreement between the contending parties.

In the presidential election of 1908, when a coalition of liberals and conservatives opposed President Amador's choice of Ricardo Arias as his successor, both parties asked that an American commission be appointed to hear electoral complaints. The Amador government, however, joined in this request reluctantly, in response to diplomatic pressure, and before the election Arias withdrew his candidacy. José Domingo de Obaldía consequently became President in 1908. He died in 1910 and was succeeded by Pablo Arosemena. There was a new threat of disorder as the election of 1912 approached. The liberals, now in opposition, had a majority in Congress and could thus name the electoral boards. On the other hand Arosemena and the conservatives could count on the police. Under these circumstances both sides appealed for American supervision, and a committee of American officials, with more than 200 assistants, took charge of the election. Before the voting the administration party withdrew from the contest, claiming that it had not received fair treatment, and Dr. Belisario Porras, the leader of the liberal party, became President.

Dr. Porras dominated Panaman politics during the next 12 years. He declined to accept American supervision of the election of 1916, and the opposition consequently refused to participate. His follower Ramón Valdés became President, but died two years later. Thereafter Porras was again elected acting-President, but only after a violent controversy during which American troops took over the policing of Panama City and Colón.

The United States intervened on this occasion, not only to prevent political disorders but for other reasons. It had long been dissatisfied with conditions in the Panaman police force. There had been a series of clashes between police and American soldiers or sailors, some of which had ended in fatalities, and in 1916 the American legation had insisted that the Panaman government take away the rifles with which the police had been armed. During the European war, when a large number of troops were stationed in the Canal Zone, the failure to control drug-selling and other undesirable activities had been a further cause for complaint. These conditions were now remedied, and an American instructor already in the employ of the Panaman government was given authority to effect a thoroughgoing reform of the police force. At the same time, the United States insisted on reforms in the government's financial administration, and an American "Fiscal Agent," nominated by the United States, served for some years as a sort of financial adviser and comptroller.

Dr. Porras was re-elected in 1920, after the United States refused to interfere. The chief event of his administration was a short war with Costa Rica. The boundary between the two countries had long been in dispute, and in 1914 Panama had refused to accept an arbitral decision by Chief Justice White of the United States Supreme Court and had continued to hold the Coto region on the Pacific coast which White had awarded to Costa Rica. After long negotiations, in which the United States urged Panama to accept the award, Costa Rica invaded Coto in 1921. Her forces were defeated by an improvised army composed chiefly of Panama City policemen, and at this point hostilities were checked by the diplomatic intervention of the United States. Some months later, acting under the authority which it claimed as the guarantor of Panama's independence, the United States insisted that Costa Rica be permitted to occupy the Coto region without resistance. This action caused much bitterness against the United States; but Panama's relations with Costa Rica soon improved, and the boundary question was finally settled by a treaty signed in 1941.

RELATIONS WITH THE UNITED STATES
1924–1936

In 1924 the United States abrogated the Taft Agreement of 1904, which was intended only as a *modus vivendi* while the canal was being built. This raised again the whole problem of commercial operations in the Canal Zone. Rudolfo Chiari, who had become President in 1924, consequently negotiated a new agreement with the United States covering the commissary question and several others that had arisen since 1903, but the treaty, signed in 1926, was defeated in the Panaman Congress, chiefly because Porras, who had quarreled with his successor, wished to embarass the new administration. Negotiations for a new agreement began soon afterward, but it was several years before one was signed. In the meantime, however, the United States of its own accord continued to exclude private business from the Canal Zone and to confine sales at the commissaries to persons connected with the canal or ships passing through.

During the 1920's changes that were taking place in the general Caribbean policy of the United States were reflected in a growing disinclination to interfere in internal affairs in Panama. Elections were conducted without American supervision after 1918, and the powers of the American Inspector General of Police and the Fiscal Agent were gradually curtailed after 1922. Except for one brief period in 1925, American troops were not again called on to maintain order in Panaman territory.

By this time party lines had broken down, and politics had become almost entirely a matter of personalities and desire for office. Since the government's control of elections made it difficult if not impossible for an opposition candidate to win, a small group had been able to perpetuate itself in power, and there were increasing corruption and inefficiency. Discontent with this situation, aggravated by the effects of the world depression, was especially evident during the administration of Florencio Harmodio Arosemena who succeeded Chiari in 1928. On January 2, 1931, a group of the President's opponents suddenly seized control of Panama City. There was some fighting, in which several policemen were killed, but the United States did not intervene. Afterward, however, the American Minister used his good offices to bring about a settlement which had the outward appearance of constitutionality, and the United States continued normal diplomatic relations with the new provisional regime headed by Dr. Ricardo Alfaro. In 1932 Harmodio Arias, one of the leaders of the revolution, was elected President.

A new treaty with the United States, which made important concessions to Panama's national pride and material interests, was signed on March 2, 1936. The United States abrogated its formal guarantee of Panaman independence and gave up its right to intervene to maintain order in Panama City and Colón. It also accepted important limitations on its freedom of action in the Canal Zone, in which only employees of the United States and persons connected with the operation of the canal were henceforth to be permitted to live. It gave up the right to take additional land outside of the Zone for canal purposes and ceded to Panama a corridor connecting the city of Colón with the rest of the Republic's territory. A dispute that had arisen when the United States devalued the dollar and attempted to pay the canal annuity in the new currency was settled by an agreement that the annuity should be the equivalent in gold of the former payment.

One of the more important provisions of the new treaty was Article X which provided that in case of war or threat of aggression the two governments would act to protect their common interests and would consult regarding any measures that either government considered necessary, if these measures affected the territory of the other. Under the old treaty, the United States had claimed the right to use Panama territory for military purposes in any way that seemed necessary, and a reluctance to give up full freedom of action in defending the canal led the United States Senate to delay its approval. By an exchange of notes in February, 1939, however, Panama agreed that maneuvers of American troops in territory adjacent to the Zone were an essential measure of preparedness and that in an emergency the United States might take action to defend the canal in advance of consultation between the two governments. This clarified the situation, and in July, 1939, the treaty was ratified and went into effect.

POLITICAL EVENTS, 1936–1952

The election at which Harmodio Arias' successor was chosen in 1936 was one of the most closely contested in the history of the Republic. The official candidate, Juan Demóstenes Arosemena, was declared ineligible for technical reasons by the National Elections Jury; but the President insisted upon Arosemena's right to run and, after the voting, removed one member of the jury to procure a majority which would declare him elected. On the face of the returns, Arosemena received a small majority over his principal opponent, Domingo Díaz, but the latter's supporters loudly impugned the fairness of the final count.

Arosemena died in December, 1939, and Dr. Augusto Boyd served out the few remaining months of the presidential term. In the election of 1940 Dr. Arnulfo Arias, Harmodio Arias' brother, was the government candidate. His opponent, Dr. Ricardo Alfaro, withdrew from the race in May after several of his supporters had been arrested and others had been compelled to flee into the Canal Zone. A few months after Arias took office a constitutional change extending his term to six years gave color to charges that he was setting up a dictatorship with fascist tendencies. The suspicion that he inclined toward totalitarianism increased in October, 1941, when he forbade the arming of Panama merchant ships. This was an act of some importance, because a large number of vessels owned by companies in the United States had been registered under the Panama flag and several had been sunk in the war zone.

On the day after this decree was issued, Arias secretly flew to Habana, where, as he later said, he wished to consult an oculist. His Cabinet, discovering that he had left the country without obtaining the necessary permission from Congress, promptly declared that he had forfeited the presidency and installed Ricardo Adolfo de la Guardia in his place. The change took place without disorder, and the new administration made it clear that it proposed to co-operate with the United States in questions of hemisphere defense. An agreement signed in 1942 gave the United States the use of a number of military bases in the Republic's territory in return for the transfer to Panama of the water and sewer systems and much valuable real estate in Panama City and Colón. In January, 1943, de la Guardia's term of office was extended for two additional years. During this period Arias' followers provoked minor disturbances, and a quarrel with Congress caused the President to dissolve that body and suspend the constitution. His friends controlled a Constituent Assembly that met in 1945 and chose Enrique Jiménez as provisional President.

During the war the United States had used more than 130 areas in Panaman territory for military purposes. It relinquished most of these after 1945, but it wished to retain some that were important to the defense of the canal; in December, 1947, after long negotiations, the two governments signed an agreement giving the American government a ten-year lease on the important Rio Hato air base and a five-year lease on 13 other sites. When this was submitted to the Panaman Congress, however, there were turbulent anti-American demonstrations in Panama City, and the agreement was unanimously rejected. The United States at once abandoned the military installations outside of the Canal Zone.

In 1948, in the first regular presidential election after 1940, the government's candidate Domingo Díaz was opposed by ex-President Arnulfo Arias, who was supported by the extreme nationalist and anti-United States groups. The result was disputed, but the National Elections Jury proclaimed Díaz the victor. Díaz died in August, 1949, however, and a few months later his successor, Daniel Chanis, was ousted by the Chief of Police, Colonel José Remón. The latter then arranged to have the Elections Jury recount the votes cast in 1948, and Arias was proclaimed President.

Arias' dictatorial government aroused much discontent, and this found expression in May, 1951, in riots and a general strike. When Colonel Remón refused his support, Arias was overthrown and imprisoned, and a year later Remón himself was elected President. The advent to power of the Commander of the Police was disturbing to believers in democracy; but both Remón and his wife Cecilia, who was also active in politics, had much popular following, and many hoped that the new administration would end the disturbances that had plagued Panama ever since the United States had adopted a policy of nonintervention.

RECENT RELATIONS WITH THE
UNITED STATES

Remón negotiated a new agreement with the United States dealing with some of the matters that had recently caused bad feeling in Panama. The Panamanians were especially bitter about the employment policies of the canal, a matter that had received little attention in earlier treaty negotiations because few Panamanians worked for the canal in its first years. In the construction period the engineers and skilled laborers came chiefly from the United States, and manual labor was recruited among the Negroes of the British and French West Indies. The North Americans were paid high wages in "gold," which meant United States dollars, and had many other privileges intended to compensate them for living under strange conditions in a difficult climate, while the West Indians, coming from places were labor was cheap, were glad to work for much less and were paid in "silver," or local currency. The "gold" and "silver" employees had separate living quarters and schools and other facilities, and even a "silver" employee who had special skills or outstanding ability could rarely aspire to the same pay as a North American who was doing similar work. The Panaman leaders, who themselves discriminated against the West Indians in the terminal cities and had no desire to see local wage scales forced up, long regarded this situation with indifference, but later, when the children of the immigrants were native Panaman citizens, their treatment in the Zone became a political issue. There was also an increasing resentment at the Zone's segregation policies among the original inhabitants of the Isthmus, most of whom were partly of African descent.

The labor problem was one of the questions covered by an agreement made public on January 25, 1955, after more than a year of negotiation. The United States promised to seek legislation that would authorize one basic wage scale for all North American and Panaman employees of the canal and would bring Panaman employees under the Civil Service Retirement Act. It further pledged itself to give Panaman citizens equal opportunities for employment in any position in the Zone for which they were qualified, unless security considerations required the appointment of a North American. An act of Congress authorizing this revolutionary change in Zone policy was signed by the President of the United States on July 25, 1958.

In the same agreement, the United States promised to ask Congress to transfer to Panama real estate in Panama City and Colon valued at $25,000,000 and to appropriate money for a highway bridge over the canal at Balboa, which would provide better access to the Republic's territory west of the canal. Congress later approved both proposals. A treaty, signed on the day when the agreement was made public, made other concessions to Panama, among them an increase in the canal annuity from $430,000 to $1,930,000 and an assurance that business operations in the Canal Zone would be further restricted in order to help Panaman merchants. In return, the United States received a 15-year lease on the Rio Hato area which it had wished to retain as an air base after the War.

On January 2, 1955, just as the negotiations with the United States were being concluded, Remón was assassinated. Vice-President José Ramón Guizado took his place, but a few days later a lawyer named Rubén Miró revealed that he had shot the President and implicated Guizado in his confession. Guizado was impeached by the National Assembly and sentenced to six years and eight months in prison, and the Second Vice-President, Ricardo Arias, became head of the government.

In an election held in May, 1956, Ernesto de la Guardia, a successful businessman, was the official candidate. The new administration faced many of the same problems that had made the situation of its predecessors so difficult. In the absence of an electoral system that assured fair play, political opposition was always likely to take the form of revolutionary conspiracy, and frequent strikes and riots were a danger to the government's stability. One revolutionary attempt, launched from Cuba, was checked when the timely interposition of the Organization of American states discouraged any further support from outside.

Relations with the United States were troubled by the three-year delay in obtaining congressional approval of the new agreements at Washington, and even after Congress acted there were complaints that Panamanians were not receiving fully equal treatment in the canal's employment policy. There were also demands that the United States give Panama a share in the tolls-revenue of the canal, in addition to the recently increased fixed payment, and that Panama's claim to sovereignty over the Zone should receive more recognition. On two occasions in November, 1959, many persons were injured when nationalist mobs attempted to invade the Canal Zone for the announced purpose of raising the Panaman flag there.

In May, 1960, Roberto Chiari was elected to succeed de la Guardia as President.

CHAPTER 21

Central America, 1821-1900

THE COUNTRY AND THE PEOPLE

THE FIVE CENTRAL AMERICAN PROVINCES, today the Republics of Guatemala, El Salvador, Honduras, Nicaragua, and Costa Rica, were ruled in colonial times by a Captain General at Guatemala City, with governors under him in each province. Their principal settlements, in the volcanic region on the western side of the Isthmus, were cut off from the east coast by high mountains and tropical jungle, and though the San Juan River gave access to the interior in Nicaragua, its dangerous bar and troublesome rapids diminished its value as a trade route. On the Pacific side there were few good ports. The provinces had had some economic importance during the colonial period because they produced a considerable part of the world's supply of indigo, but the prosperity of this industry was affected by new foreign competition in the first years of the nineteenth century.[1] They nevertheless had relatively little contact with the outside world, and most of the towns were small and unprogressive. The whole area probably had somewhat over a million inhabitants at the time of independence, the majority of them in Guatemala.

There were, and still are, important differences in the character of the population of the various sections of the Isthmus. In Guatemala, the great majority of the people are Indians of Maya stock, who still speak their native languages and until recently were exploited and oppressed by the government and the landowners much as the natives were in the Andean countries and central Mexico. The ignorance and poverty of the Indians were obstacles to democratic progress, and the governments of Guatemala until very recently have usually been dictatorships resting on the support of the army. In El Salvador, Honduras, and Nicaragua

[1] Robert S. Smith, "Indigo Production and Trade in Colonial Guatemala," *Hispanic American Historical Review*, Vol. XXXIX (1959), pp. 181 ff.

the aboriginal population, less advanced and less numerous before the Conquest, was more completely assimilated, and the masses of the people, as well as many of the principal families, are of mixed blood. In Honduras and Nicaragua especially, the landowning aristocracy has been less powerful, and the common people have taken more interest in politics. A larger proportion of them have participated in the civil wars, and the damage done by internal strife has been correspondingly greater. In Costa Rica, on the other hand, there were still fewer Indians, and only an insignificant number survived the first years of Spanish domination. The lack of a native labor supply made the colony unattractive to immigrants, but those who did come were hardy farmers whose descendants today are an industrious people more completely European in blood than those of any other Latin American country except Uruguay and Argentina. Concentrated in one small area in their central plateau, and able because of their geographical position to remain aloof from the continual conflicts between the other states, the Costa Ricans attained a truly republican government earlier than most of the Latin American republics.

CENTRAL AMERICAN INDEPENDENCE

The Central American provinces were at first little affected by the movement for independence in the other colonies. There were a few small revolutionary disturbances between 1811 and 1814, but the inhabitants as a whole seemed content to maintain the connection with Spain. The creole leaders who felt otherwise had little following. After 1820, however, freedom of speech and press under the new Spanish constitution gave the more radical element an opportunity to advocate changes in the colonial political and social organization. This alarmed the conservatives and the clergy, who were already shocked by the conduct of the liberal government in Spain, and made them less averse to breaking away from the mother country if they could thereby retain their own prerogatives. Iturbide's revolt in Mexico set the example and precipitated their action. Their movement met with little resistance because the acting Captain General, Gabino Gaínza, proved willing to work with the advocates of independence in return for their promise to make him head of the new government.

On September 15, 1821, an assembly of royal officials, high ecclesiastical dignitaries, and prominent creoles met in Guatemala City to declare the independence of Central America. Gaínza retained his position but shared power with a *junta consultiva* of influential citizens. Both the conservatives and the more radical revolutionary leaders took part in the proceedings, but it was not long before the existence of the new regime was threatened by internal disputes. The liberals objected to the predominance of the conservatives in the *junta* and to the *junta*'s efforts to control the election of the Congress that was to decide upon a permanent form of government. The conservatives were divided among themselves, and the Spanish Governors of Honduras and Nicaragua, who were unfriendly to Gaínza, threw off his authority and announced their adherence to Iturbide's Plan of Iguala.

The idea of annexation to Mexico was taken up by other conservatives, and especially by those who opposed the establishment of a republic, and in November Iturbide announced his intention of sending troops to support his partisans. The latter hastily obtained approval of their scheme by a majority of the municipal councils throughout the five provinces, and on January 5, 1822, the union with Mexico was proclaimed. General Filísola, who was sent by Iturbide to take charge of the government, was well received in Guatemala. He encountered more resistance in El Salvador, where republican sentiment was especially strong, and where the Congress, in the hope of obtaining outside help, voted to seek admission to the North American Union. Before this request could reach Washington, however, the city of San Salvador was occupied by the imperial troops. The union of Central America with Mexico lasted a little more than a year, for Filísola relinquished his authority when Iturbide fell in February, 1823.

THE FEDERAL REPUBLIC

A Central American Congress which Filísola convoked named a triumvirate to take charge of the administration. While this *junta*, weakened by quarrels among its members and handicapped by lack of money, strove to maintain a semblance of organized government, the Congress drew up a federal constitution. There were to be a president and a congress at Guatemala City, with state governments in each of the provinces. A limited suffrage and a cumbersome indirect system of voting assured the maintenance of power in the hands of the wealthier and better-educated class. Catholicism was made the state religion, and the public exercise of all others was prohibited. Negro slavery, never a very important institution in Central America, was abolished.

In 1825 Manuel José Arce became President of the Republic. Arce was a liberal, but he soon quarreled with the liberal majority in the legislative body and sought conservative support. His term of office was a stormy one. It proved impossible for the federal and state authorities to exist side by side in harmony in Guatemala City, and minor quarrels over questions of jurisdiction culminated in the forcible ousting of the liberal state Governor and his replacement by a conservative. Meanwhile the Congress was paralyzed by party strife, and the federal authorities were reduced to impotence by disorders in the states. The people of the city of San Salvador, angered by their failure to obtain the creation of a new diocese in their state, and led by Father Delgado, the disappointed aspirant to the bishopric, rose in revolt in 1827. They were joined by disaffected groups in other states, and there ensued two years of general civil war which finally ended in the government's defeat. The leader of the victorious liberal army was Francisco Morazán, a native of Honduras, who was barely thirty years old.

Morazán was elected to the presidency of Central America in 1830. His party obtained control of all the state governments, but within a few months the conservatives resumed the war. Revolts were suppressed in Guatemala and Honduras, but only after severe fighting. There was renewed friction between the federal and the state authorities in Guatemala City, and when Morazán decided to move his headquarters to San Salvador, where the liberal party was stronger, he met with armed resistance from the state government there. He nevertheless made San Salvador the Capital of the Republic in 1834. Soon afterward he was re-elected as President; but his prestige was waning, and the Federal Republic itself was disintegrating. In 1838 the national Congress dissolved and declared the states free to adopt any form of government they desired. In 1840, after more than a year of renewed civil war, Morazán was defeated by the forces of Nicaragua, Honduras, and Guatemala and went into exile.

THE AFTERMATH OF THE FEDERATION

The attempt to unite Central America under one government had thus failed. The people of the Isthmus were no better prepared to make a success of democratic institutions than their neighbors in Mexico, and their political inexperience made it especially difficult to operate the complicated machinery of a federal system. The central government's task was complicated by the lack of means of communication between the states, and still more by the intensity of the localistic spirit which made the people of the provincial towns and villages jealous of the national Capital and caused dissensions within the states.

Attempts to reunite Central America after Morazán's downfall were uniformly unsuccessful. In Guatemala, many of the great families and the clergy preferred a local government under their own control to the uncertainties of a revived federation. In Costa Rica there was an equally strong separatist feeling. Geographical isolation had enabled the Costa Ricans to avoid participation in the civil wars which destroyed the federal republic, and they had no desire to become involved in new complications. In El Salvador, Honduras, and Nicaragua, on the other hand, unionist sentiment was stronger, and these states repeatedly endeavored to set up a new federal government, even though only the three of them participated in it. In 1842 they did establish a loose confederation, which broke up two years later when they started fighting among themselves. In 1849 they made another attempt, inspired by the desire for mutual defense against the British encroachments on the Mosquito Coast, which will be described below. The Central Council which they set up had little power, and when an effort was made to strengthen it in 1852 the whole project failed. Thereafter interest in the union seemed to decline, but it revived from time to time in later years.

Unfortunately the political enmities formed during the federal period persisted after the union was dissolved, and liberals and conservatives in each country continued to support their former associates in the others and to aid them in time of civil strife. International wars frequently occurred simply because two states were ruled by administrations of different political complexions, for each government was tempted to aid revolutionary movements against the other if only to forestall similar action by its neighbor. The weaker states naturally suffered most from this practice. For many years after the breakdown of the federation, the political history of El Salvador, Honduras, and Nicaragua was little more than a confused story of internal and international conflicts, provoked usually by the interference of Guatemala.

RAFAEL CARRERA

In Guatemala, more than in the other countries, the political parties were divided on real issues. Lines were drawn much as they were in Mexico, with the clergy, the remnants of the colonial nobility, and many of the great landowners and rich merchants on the conservative side, and creole and *mestizo* professional men and other groups who had a less privileged position in colonial times forming the liberal party. The hostility between the two groups became acute during the last years of the federal republic. The liberals, when they came into power with Morazán, suppressed the monastic orders and enacted other anticlerical measures which encountered violent opposition.

The conservatives had their opportunity when an epidemic of cholera broke out in 1837. By spreading a story that the government was poisoning the wells to destroy the natives and make way for Protestant immigrants from England, they provoked a popular uprising in the isolated mountain region east of Guatemala City, where most of the peasants were *ladinos*, or *mestizos*. The leader was an illiterate youth named Rafael Carrera, who became the Chief General on the conservative side in the civil war that followed. It was this conflict that caused the breakup of the Central American Federation. The liberals, weakened by their own factional quarrels, were driven out of Guatemala City, and when they attempted to set up the separate state of Los Altos in the western part of the country they were defeated there. By 1840 the conservatives were in full control. Their leaders, however, found themselves at the mercy of the chieftain of the half-savage horde that had won the victory for them, and though others occupied the presidency, Carrera remained at the head of the army and was the real ruler of the country. In 1844 he took the presidency himself. He was forced to resign in 1848 but returned to power a year later. In 1854 he made himself President for life and ruled as dictator until his death in 1865.

Carrera gave Guatemala a period of relative tranquility. His power rested chiefly on the blind devotion of his peasant followers and the loyalty of a well-paid army, but he was also supported by native and foreign property owners who desired the maintenance of peace and by the Church, which again became a powerful political force. The liberals' anticlerical legislation was repealed, and the Jesuits and other religious orders were invited to return.

Guatemala's neighbors enjoyed less internal peace, and their difficulties were made worse by Carrera's continual interference in their internal affairs. In 1840 a Guatemalan army defeated the liberal regime that had supported Morazán in El Salvador and placed that country under the *de facto* control of a military leader named Francisco Malespín. In the same way, a conservative government was set up in Honduras. Personal quarrels, however, prevented any lasting co-operation between the rulers of the three states, and in 1844–1845 all of them, and Nicaragua as well, were involved in a general war which was both an international conflict and an internal struggle in each state. In El Salvador, the liberals came into control for a brief period, were overthrown in 1851 by Carrera, and then returned to power in 1860 under the popular and able Gerardo Barrios. In 1863 a new Guatemalan intervention replaced Barrios by Francisco Dueñas. In Honduras the story was much the same; Francisco Ferrera, an ally of Carrera, dominated the government through his control of the army until 1852. In that year Trinidad Cabañas, a liberal, became President. In 1855 Cabañas was overthrown by Carrera and was succeeded by General Santos Guardiola. The latter was assassinated in 1862, and a year later the liberals, who had regained power, were driven out by Guatemalan and Nicaraguan intervention.

ANGLO-AMERICAN RIVALRY IN NICARAGUA

Nicaragua not only took part in many of the conflicts between her northern neighbors but suffered constantly from internal strife made more virulent by the inveterate enmity between the two chief cities, León and Granada. León was the liberal center, Granada the conservative, and all differences of policy or principle were lost sight of in what became simply a regional feud. There were levelheaded leaders in both cities who endeavored to bring about harmony, but their efforts were frustrated by popular hatreds and by the machinations of military leaders who profited from the continuance of disorder. The heads of the army, rather than the numerous "Chiefs of State" who succeeded one another for two-year terms, were the real rulers of the country. Casto Fonseca, a liberal, was *comandante de armas* until 1845 when the conservatives, with their allies from Honduras and El Salvador, barbarously sacked León and killed many of its inhabitants.

During the next 12 years, Nicaragua was the victim of aggression from outside of Central America. It will be remembered that one of the two practicable trans-Isthmian canal routes lay within her territory, and that Great Britain and the United States were both interested in controlling these routes. The British had had a foothold in Central America since the seventeenth century when buccaneers from Jamaica frequently cut dyewoods on the mainland, at times when piracy was unprofitable or too dangerous, and established small settlements which the Spaniards were never able completely to destroy. Belize, or British Honduras, became a British colony after the independence of Central America, and in the 1830's British authorities at Jamaica set up a protectorate over the Mosquitos, a primitive people of mixed Indian and Negro blood who lived along the coast of northeastern Nicaragua and eastern Honduras. In the same period they occupied the Bay Islands off the coast of Honduras. This gradual encroachment met with little resistance, but in 1848, British forces, acting in the name of the Mosquito King, provoked a diplomatic crisis by seizing San Juan del Norte at the mouth of the San Juan River.

San Juan del Norte, or Greytown, had never been considered a part of the Mosquito protectorate, and the obvious purpose of the seizure was to obtain control of the eastern end of the prospective canal route. The United States, more than ever interested in the canal project since the acquisition of California, made a vigorous protest. In the ensuing negotiations it became clear that each government was actuated primarily by fear of the other's intentions. It was consequently possible to reach an agreement, in the Clayton-Bulwer Treaty of 1850, that neither would "obtain or maintain" any exclusive control over the proposed waterway or occupy any part of Central America. The British soon afterward evacuated San Juan del Norte, and disputes about the application of the treaty to other British-held territories were gradually settled by further negotiation. The Bay Islands were returned to Honduras in 1859, and the Mosquito protectorate was relinquished in 1860 under a treaty with Nicaragua which stipulated that the Indians should govern themselves in a reservation that did not include the territory at the mouth of the San Juan River.

San Juan del Norte became the eastern terminus of a trans-Isthmian passenger service established by the Accessory Transit Company for the benefit of travelers between New York and California. Large numbers of persons used the small steamers the company operated on the San Juan River and Lake Nicaragua and the carriages that covered the short distance between the lake and the Pacific, for crossing the Isthmus, either in Nicaragua or in Panama, was on the whole less dangerous and difficult than going overland through the United States. This American concern soon became involved in a sensational series of events in Nicaragua.

WILLIAM WALKER AND THE FILIBUSTERS

After the conservative victory in 1845, the Capital of Nicaragua was moved to Masaya and then to Managua, both of them small towns near Granada, but a few years later the new *comandante de armas*, Trinidad Muñoz, broke with the conservatives and re-established the Capital at León. When the conservatives regained power in 1851, with help from Honduras and Costa Rica, they first vainly attempted to set up a coalition government and then subjected the liberals to a repressive regime which goaded the people of León into revolt in 1854. Carrera intervened on the conservative side, and the liberals turned for help to a band of "filibusters" recruited in the United States by one William Walker.

Walker came to Nicaragua in June, 1855, with 58 men. In October he seized Granada by a surprise attack, and the conservative leaders, though their army was undefeated, made peace in order to save their families from mistreatment. A conservative became President, but Walker was made commander of the army. Disbanding the native troops, he soon made it clear that he proposed to rule the country with his "American Phalanx"; and in 1856, after the leaders of both parties had started a revolt against him, he had himself "elected" President of Nicaragua. By this time hundreds of adventurers were coming to Nicaragua to join his forces. His activities aroused much interest in the United States, both because they seemed likely to defeat British efforts to obtain control of the canal route and because many persons in the South hoped that he would eventually bring Nicaragua into the Union as a new slave state.

Walker's most useful ally was the Accessory Transit Company. He made a mistake, however, when he supported a group within this company that was trying to wrest control from its former president, Cornelius Vanderbilt. When Walker cancelled the company's concession and granted a new one to his friends, Vanderbilt quickly avenged himself. By this time armies from all of the other Central American states as well as forces representing both parties in Nicaragua were marching against the intruders. While Walker was preparing to make a stand against these enemies in western Nicaragua, Vanderbilt's steamers on the San Juan River and the great lake helped a Costa Rican force to cut off his communications with New York. The filibusters held out against overwhelming odds for several months; but they lost heavily from disease and desertion, and on May 1, 1857, Walker surrendered to the Commander of an American warship. Twice in the next three years he attempted to return to Central America with filibustering expeditions, but his career ended when he was captured and executed in northern Honduras in 1860.

In Nicaragua, both parties were under arms at the end of the war and ready to fight for control, but they reached an agreement when Costa Rica attempted to retain some territory claimed by Nicaragua on the San Juan River. Máximo Jerez, the liberal leader, consented to the establishment of a conservative government under Tomás Martínez, and the country settled down to a long period of relative peace.

COSTA RICA, 1821–1870

Though they took an active part in the war against Walker, the people of Costa Rica were usually able to remain aloof from the political struggles that kept the neighboring countries in a state of turmoil. Most of the Costa Ricans lived in or near four little towns, all within a few miles of one another on a pleasant plateau in the interior. Descended from sturdy North Spanish peasants who had come to the colony because they were not afraid to work with their hands, the majority were small farmers, ignorant and conservative but industrious and self-respecting. There were few wealthy landowners and, at the other end of the scale, few Indians or Negroes.

Even in the first years of independence, the Costa Ricans suffered less from internal political strife than did their neighbors. There were brief struggles between the various towns, arising from disputes over the location of the Capital, and there were periodic revolts and *coups d'état* provoked by factional rivalry; but they caused relatively little bloodshed or destruction of property. Political affairs were dominated by a few prominent families, among whom the Montealegres and the Moras, heads of rival groups, were the most important. Juan Mora was the first President, serving from 1825 until 1833.

One of the most notable of the country's early presidents was Braulio Carrillo, who held office from 1835 to 1837 and from 1838 until 1842. It was he who first promoted the growing of coffee, which soon became the chief export, and his subdivision of the common lands formerly held by the towns considerably increased the number of small landowners. It was these peasant proprietors, more interested in farming than in politics and strongly averse to civil war, that gave the country a political and social stability that made it different from its neighbors. Carrillo was an able administrator, but his dictatorial methods, and especially his attempt to make himself President for life, made him unpopular. His own troops deserted him when Francisco Morazán landed in Costa Rica to start a revolution in 1842.

Morazán still aspired to restore the federal republic of which he had recently been the head, but when he began to raise money and recruit men for an attack on the other states the Costa Ricans turned against him and put him to death. There followed seven years of factional quarreling and frequent governmental changes. The government became more stable under the firm hand of Juan Rafael Mora, who became President in 1849 and who distinguished himself in the war against the filibusters in Nicaragua. When Mora was overthrown and shot, after ten years in office, the old rivalry between his family and the Montealegres again threatened to cause a civil war; but a compromise was reached, and the country was fairly peaceful under the administrations of Jesús Jiménez (1863–1866) and José María Castro (1866–1868). The army, under two leaders named Blanco and Salazar, exercised much influence in the government during this period.

THE LIBERAL REGIME IN GUATEMALA

The long period of conservative domination in northern Central America ended in 1871 when the liberals overthrew Vicente Cerna who was President of Guatemala after Carrera died in 1865. Miguel García Granados became President, but the most powerful member of the government was the military leader of the recent revolt, Justo Rufino Barrios. It was Barrios who brought about the expulsion of the Jesuits and the confiscation of the property of the monastic orders. In 1873, García Granados withdrew, and Barrios took over the presidency, to rule as dictator until his death 12 years later. With a strong popular following, he crushed all opposition and destroyed the political influence of the Church and the conservative aristocracy. He built some roads and attempted to improve the public schools, and during his administration the country's first railroad was built between Guatemala City and the Pacific port of San José. His vigorous promotion of the cultivation of coffee increased the country's wealth but made worse the situation of the Indians, who were robbed of much of their land and forced to work on the new plantations.

In February, 1885, Barrios proclaimed the reconstitution of a united Central American republic, with himself as provisional President and Military Commander. In taking this step, he apparently hoped to have the support of El Salvador and Honduras, for liberal regimes had come into power with his help in these countries immediately after the Guatemalan revolution of 1871 and he had interfered from time to time to bring about further changes of government. President Bográn in Honduras did support him, but Zaldívar of El Salvador opposed the project and prepared to resist. Barrios marched to attack him and was killed in battle at Chalchuapa on the frontier.

The liberal regime was by this time so firmly established in Guatemala that even the death of its leader did not upset it. As in many other Latin American countries during this period, the development of agriculture and foreign trade made for political stability. Coffee growing had become an important industry, in which foreign as well as native capital was invested, and the planters exercised a powerful influence to prevent civil strife which would interfere with the harvesting of their crops. Manuel Lisandro Barillas, one of the *designados*, succeeded Barrios and was able to make himself President for the next term. In 1892 a comparatively free election placed José María Reyna Barrios, a nephew of Justo Rufino, at the head of the government. When he was assassinated in 1898, the first *designado*, Manuel Estrada Cabrera, assumed power. This was the beginning of a cruel and unprogressive dictatorship which was to last until 1920.

EL SALVADOR AND HONDURAS

El Salvador also was enjoying prosperity with a rapid increase in coffee production and was moving slowly toward more stable political conditions. After 1885 the country suffered relatively little from outside interference in its political affairs. Rafael Zaldívar, who had been one of Justo Rufino Barrios' closest allies before they separated over the question of the Union, was overthrown soon after the battle of Chalchuapa and was succeeded by Francisco Menéndez. When the latter died in 1890, the two Ezeta brothers seized control and maintained a rather barbarous military despotism until they were ousted in 1894. Under Rafael Gutiérrez, the next President, El Salvador joined with Honduras and Nicaragua in an attempt to set up a "Greater Republic of Central America." A treaty signed in 1895 provided for a "Diet" which was to conduct the three states' foreign relations and draft a federal constitution. In 1898, a Federal Council met at Amapala, Honduras, to assume the general government. At this point, however, the opponents of the union revolted in El Salvador and General Tomás Regalado became President.

Honduras, with little coffee production, was less prosperous and was the weakest and most backward of the five republics. Her stronger neighbors continued to interfere in her internal politics. Guatemalan intervention put Ponciano Leiva in the presidency in 1873, forced him out in 1876, and in 1883 forced the resignation of his successor, Marco Aurelio Soto.

Luis Bográn was President from 1883 until 1891. Thereafter presidents followed one another in quick succession until 1894, when Policarpo Bonilla, an ardent liberal, came into office with the aid of President Zelaya of Nicaragua. Bonilla was followed by another liberal, General Terencio Sierra, in 1899.

NICARAGUA

The conservatives ruled Nicaragua until 1893. The Granada aristocracy was a homogeneous, well-organized group whose leaders succeeded one another in the presidency by agreement and followed a conciliatory policy toward the liberals. The country made some material progress, though less than Guatemala or El Salvador. As time went on, however, the prolonged domination of one small group was increasingly distasteful to the people of León and to the country at large. The first serious dissension within the oligarchy was the signal for a successful liberal revolt headed by a young leader from Managua named José Santos Zelaya, who set up a personal dictatorship that was to last 16 years.

COSTA RICA

The liberal victories in the northern countries had their counterpart in Costa Rica in 1870 when an army officer named Tomás Guardia overthrew the government, exiled the leaders of the political groups that had hitherto competed for control, and set up a regime in which the Moras and the Montealegres had no part. Guardia dominated affairs, though not always as President, until his death in 1882, and was succeeded in power first by his close friend Próspero Fernández and three years later by the latter's son-in-law, Bernardo Soto. Soto's administration was especially notable for the establishment of free compulsory education in the principal towns and villages of the Republic, under the direction of his Minister Mauro Fernández.

In 1889 an aroused public opinion compelled Soto to permit the holding of a real election, probably the first in the history of Central America, in which the opposition candidate, José Joaquín Rodríguez, was chosen as President. Despite its origin, the new administration, supported by the Church, was practically a dictatorship, and Rodríguez' successor, Rafael Yglesias, was put in office for two terms (1894–1902) by the electoral methods formerly in vogue. Yglesias, however, was an able ruler, and the country owed much to his progressive policy. When he left office, Costa Rica, despite its small area and scanty population, was a well-governed and peaceful community where an increasingly intelligent public opinion would very soon demand a government republican in fact as well as in form. The completion of a railroad from the interior to the east coast in 1890 and the growth of banana cultivation, which brought with it the establishment of regular, fast steamship service to foreign ports, brought the Costa Ricans into closer contact with the United States and Europe.

CENTRAL AMERICA AT THE TURN OF THE CENTURY

Elsewhere in Central America the prospect was not so bright. Coffee brought prosperity to the upper class in Guatemala, but the Indians were on the whole worse off than when Thomas Gage gave so sad an account of their condition in the seventeenth century. As coffee planting developed, much of their land was taken, often by force or fraud, and Justo Rufino Barrios and his successors sought to help the new industry by extending and making more effective the systems of forced labor which had always existed. As in colonial times, Indian villages were compelled to furnish groups of laborers, called "mandamientos," when local planters needed them. Still worse, from the Indians' point of view, was the peonage system, enforced by law, under which laborers were tricked or forced into debt and then compelled to work for wages which in 1916 were equivalent to from five to eight cents per day in United States currency.

In El Salvador, Honduras, and Nicaragua, the *mestizo* laboring class was better off, but wages and standards of living were low and tropical diseases made miserable the lives of a large part of the population. In El Salvador, as in Guatemala, the rapid increase in coffee production had benefited principally the landowning aristocracy. In Nicaragua there had been less agricultural development, in Honduras almost none. In all three countries disorder and governmental poverty made it difficult to establish schools or to take other measures to improve the lot of the common people. The great majority were probably little better qualified to be citizens of free republics than they had been in 1821. Despite the trend toward greater stability in the last years of the century, changes of government by revolution or *coup d'état* were still the rule rather than the exception, and constant interference by the various states in one another's internal affairs brought on frequent international conflicts.

Except in Honduras, the principal Central American cities were by this time connected by railroad with the west coast, but they still had relatively little contact with the outside world because steamship service on the Pacific was infrequent and irregular. Comparatively few Central Americans were able to study or travel abroad, and few foreigners came to the Isthmus. Foreigners had built the railroads and developed several small mines and some of the coffee plantations, but the total amount of their investments was not very great. In general the Isthmus was one of the more backward parts of Latin America at the turn of the century.

CHAPTER 22

Central America Since 1900

IN THE FIRST DECADES of the twentieth century the internal history of the Central American republics was much influenced by the new policies that the United States adopted after it began to build the canal at Panama. The American government endeavored especially to put an end to the intermittent warfare that discouraged economic progress and frequently threatened to embroil the Central American governments in conflicts with European powers. Its efforts to promote internal and international peace in the five states began with friendly mediation but soon developed into a more active interference and in Nicaragua led to armed intervention.

After 1900, the Central American countries began to have more contact with the outside world. With the opening of the Panama Canal in 1914, many more steamers, including passenger vessels bound for San Francisco or New York, began to call at the west coast ports to land goods or pick up coffee. About the same time the automobile came into more general use, and the building of improved highways brought places like Tegucigalpa, the Capital of Honduras, and Quezaltenango, the second city of Guatemala, within fairly easy reach of the coast. The automobile opened up many sections of Central America where goods had formerly been transported on muleback or on the backs of men. The advent of regular air services after 1929 revolutionized travel between Central America and the United States.

THE BANANA INDUSTRY

Another important development was the growth of the banana industry. Minor C. Keith, a North American, began to plant bananas in Costa Rica in 1872 to provide paying freight for a railroad that he was building from the east coast to San José, and when the line finally reached the Capital in 1890 the export of bananas from Port Limon, its eastern terminus, had already become an important business. Keith later established plantations in Colombia and Panama, and in 1899 he joined with other banana interests in creating the United Fruit Company. This concern extended its operations to Guatemala in 1906 and soon afterward to Honduras, where two other American firms also had plantations. Wherever they operated, the fruit companies established lines of fast steamers that carried passengers as well as fruit and built railroads to bring bananas to the ports. In Guatemala as well as in Costa Rica, these lines were extended into the interior. Service from Guatemala City to Puerto Barrios on the Caribbean was opened in 1908, and a branch from the same line reached San Salvador in 1929.

The banana industry brought great tracts of hitherto uninhabited jungle under cultivation, and bananas became the principal export, after coffee, in the trade of the Isthmus. The plantations at first were operated largely with imported Negro labor from the West Indies, but as time went on they employed many natives of the country at relatively high wages. Many other natives grew bananas on small farms for sale to the fruit companies. The fruit companies dominated the economic life of the areas where they operated, but since these were usually remote from the main centers of population their activities had less effect on the community as a whole. Nevertheless the terms of their concessions and their relations with the laborers and small farmers dependent on them gave rise to many disputes, and they were often accused of interfering in local politics.

The centers of production in the banana industry shifted from time to time because disease usually invaded the plantations after some years of cultivation, destroying much of the value of the great investment in farms, railroads, and port facilities and depriving the local population of its chief source of livelihood. One producing area after another was virtually abandoned while new ones were developed. Research eventually made it possible to control the principal diseases, but only at a cost that made commercial banana production more than ever an undertaking for large, well-financed companies.

The earlier banana plantations were on the lowlands of the Caribbean coast. Costa Rica was the most important Central American producer before the First World War but then gave place to Honduras which exported 31,000,000 stems in 1932. By 1955, with the development of plantations on the Pacific side of the Isthmus, Costa Rica was again in the lead, but Honduran production, after a sharp decline, had risen to a point where it constituted half of the country's exports. Large plantations had also been established on the Pacific coast in Guatemala. On most of their properties the fruit companies provided modern housing and hospitals for the workers. They nevertheless were frequently involved in conflicts over wages and labor conditions.

POLITICAL CONDITIONS

Economic progress led to increased political stability in some of the five republics. In Costa Rica, where most of the people were of Spanish descent and coffee had brought prosperity to thousands of small land-owners rather than merely to a few wealthy families, Ascensión Esquivel was made President by an agreement between the political parties in 1902, and his successors, Cleto González Víquez (1906–1910) and Ricardo Jiménez (1910–1914), were chosen at free elections. Both were able statesmen who governed by law rather than by force. There was complete liberty of the press, and no persecution of political enemies. With internal tranquility and orderly administration, the country enjoyed as truly republican institutions as any in Latin America, and the Costa Ricans proudly boasted that they had more schoolteachers than soldiers.

El Salvador had a fairly efficient and progressive, though not a democratic, government. Each president surrendered his office at the end of his term, but it was almost always to a successor of his own choice. Regalado, the leader of the revolution that broke up the union with Honduras and Nicaragua in 1898, was President until 1903, and was followed by Pedro José Escalón (1903–1907), Fernando Figueroa (1907–1911), and Manuel Enrique Araujo (1911–1913). Araujo was assassinated, and Carlos Meléndez, the Vice-President, succeeded him. This was the beginning of a long period of rule by one family, for Carlos Meléndez was re-elected in 1915, his brother, Jorge Meléndez, became President in 1919, and his brother-in-law, Alfonso Quiñónez, followed in 1923. During this period there were no important revolts, and the country made substantial material progress. Roads were built; the schools were improved; and the coffee industry flourished.

In Guatemala, Manuel Estrada Cabrera was President from 1898 until 1920. An astute and unprincipled politician, without personal popularity and apparently with no aspiration beyond merely staying in office, his regime was a despotism maintained by a reign of terror. All classes were demoralized by an omnipresent spy system, and elections were the merest farce. Little or nothing was accomplished in the way of public works or social welfare, but the maintenance of order and the government's support of the increasingly oppressive peonage system made the regime acceptable to native and foreign property interests. The old party lines had broken down, and the landowners were inclined to frown on efforts to provoke civil war because it would endanger their prosperity. There was nevertheless much discontent, and the dictator was constantly apprehensive that his enemies might organize a revolution in one of the neighboring countries. He was especially suspicious of José Santos Zelaya, the ruler of Nicaragua.

In Nicaragua there had been less economic progress, and the traditional political rivalry between León and Granada continued unabated. A citizen was born a liberal or a conservative and trained to regard members of the opposite group as enemies. Zelaya, a liberal, had come into power in 1893 after a long period of conservative rule. A native of Managua, he at first did not have the full support of the leaders at León, but he skillfully played off one group against another and even obtained some conservative support. The more militant conservative leaders revolted time after time but were always defeated. Zelaya's regime was despotic and corrupt, but he had much popular support. By the turn of the century his ambition to be the dominant figure in Central American politics was arousing apprehension in other countries as well as Guatemala.

In a struggle between Zelaya and Estrada Cabrera, Honduras was certain to be the first victim. Honduras was the poorest and weakest of the Central American states, and the interference of her stronger neighbors, who had frequently instigated or aided revolutions against her government, had kept party hostility alive. Zelaya had helped the liberals to come into power in 1894, but in 1903 they were ousted by the conservatives led by Manuel Bonilla.

Each of the four northern governments had enemies, many of them in exile, who were eagerly attempting to overthrow it. Without free elections, the only hope for a change was by armed revolt. The customary method of starting a revolution was to obtain arms and a base for operations in a neighboring country. Each government consequently felt unsafe so long as a neighboring government was in unfriendly hands, and in the first years of the century most of the presidents distrusted and feared one another. It was this situation that led the United States to take a more active interest in Central American affairs.

THE 1907 TREATIES

In 1906, when a war broke out between Guatemala on one side and Honduras and El Salvador on the other, Secretary of State Root invoked the co-operation of Mexico, and the two governments interposed their friendly mediation to restore peace. A few months later a general Central American peace conference met in Costa Rica but accomplished nothing because Zelaya not only refused to take part in it but started a war against Honduras which ended with the installation of Zelaya's friend Miguel Dávila as President of that country. The Nicaraguan dictator then attempted to foment a revolution in El Salvador, as a step toward uniting all Central America under his own leadership. When Guatemala prepared to intervene, a war involving most of Central America seemed inevitable.

The United States and Mexico again interposed and invited all of the five republics to attend a conference at Washington, which met in 1907 and drew up a series of treaties that seemed to promise a new era in Central America. One provided that all disputes between the five governments should be submitted to a permanent court made up of one judge from each state. Another neutralized Honduras so that her territory would no longer be a battleground for her stronger neighbors. Each government promised to restrict the activities of political refugees from other states and not to encourage revolutionary movements. Several other treaties sought to bring about closer co-operation in economic and cultural activities, as a first step toward the reconstitution of a united Central America.

The new treaties might have assured peace if the signatory governments had acted in good faith, but neither Zelaya nor Estrada Cabrera showed any disposition to take them seriously. Zelaya continued to send filibustering expeditions against El Salvador, despite a joint American-Mexican naval patrol of the west coast, and the United States finally ordered its forces to intercept them. On the other hand, Guatemala and El Salvador were accused of aiding revolutionists who invaded Honduras. There would have been a new war involving all four states if the United States and Mexico had not made strong representations and suggested that the Honduran situation be dealt with by the new Central American Court. This tribunal absolved Guatemala and El Salvador of responsibility for the invasion. Unfortunately it seemed clear that political or other considerations had influenced the votes of the judges, and the affair seriously hurt the Court's prestige.

DOLLAR DIPLOMACY

Secretary of State Knox, who succeeded Root in 1909, went farther than his predecessor in his efforts to restore peace in Central America. A few years earlier the Dominican Republic had entrusted the collection of its customs duties, which were the chief source of revenue in all of the Caribbean countries, to North American officials. Thereafter it had enjoyed several years of relative peace, because the government had more money and because its relationship with the United States seemed to discourage revolution. Knox thought that a similar arrangement would produce the same result in the weaker states in Central America, especially as it would make it possible to obtain loans to promote the economic development which was a prerequisite for political progress. President Taft spoke of this idea as a policy of substituting dollars for bullets in order to maintain order, and the policy came to be called "Dollar Diplomacy."

Since the weakness of Honduras seemed to be one of the chief causes of international wars in Central America, Knox proposed to set up a customs collectorship there, and at the same time to insist, forcefully if necessary, that that country's neutrality be respected by its neighbors. He had special reasons for urging financial reform in Honduras because the British government was at the time insisting that the Republic resume service on two loans which had been contracted under rather scandalous circumstances in London between 1867 and 1870 and which had long been in default. The State Department enlisted the co-operation of American bankers, and after long negotiations the British bondholders agreed to accept somewhat less than four cents on the dollar from funds to be provided by an American loan secured by a customs collectorship. A treaty providing for the collectorship was then negotiated with a very reluctant Honduran government and signed January 10, 1911. The plan had to be abandoned, however, when it failed to obtain approval either by the Honduran Congress or by the United States Senate.

While the Honduras treaty was still being negotiated, a revolution in Nicaragua made possible the establishment of an American customs collectorship in that country. The events of the revolution were the first chapter in a long and unhappy story of North American involvement in Nicaragua's internal affairs. By the latter part of 1909 relations between the United States and Zelaya's government were strained almost to the breaking point, for there had been acrimonious disputes over claims and other matters as well as constant friction over Zelaya's efforts to promote revolutions in other countries. The State Department was thus predisposed to sympathize with a revolt that started on the east coast of Nicaragua in October of that year, and it openly took sides after Zelaya ordered the execution of two American soldiers of fortune serving with the revolutionists. Knox wrote the Nicaraguan Chargé d'Affaires that the Zelaya regime was "a blot upon the history of Nicaragua" and expressed the conviction that the revolution represented "the ideals and the will of a majority of the Nicaraguan people." Diplomatic relations were broken off and were not resumed even after Zelaya resigned the presidency in favor of Dr. José Madriz, a generally respected liberal from León. When the revolutionists were defeated in the interior and driven back to their original base at Bluefields, the American Naval Commander refused to permit the government forces to attack them there, on the ground that fighting in the town would destroy the property of Americans and other foreigners. Soon afterward, in August, 1910, Madriz' regime collapsed, chiefly because its supporters felt that the attitude of the United States made their cause hopeless.

The victorious revolutionists set up a government at Managua, but it was clear that their regime was not likely to survive without outside help. There was much rivalry and distrust between the leaders, and the Zelayista liberals, still numerically strong, were united in their determination to return to power. It was only through the good offices of Thomas C. Dawson, the representative of the United States, that the revolutionary leaders agreed that Juan J. Estrada should be provisional President for two years. At the same time they agreed that a foreign loan, secured by a customs collectorship, should be obtained for public works and for the payment of claims.

A treaty similar to the pending treaty with Honduras was signed on June 6, 1911, and while it was awaiting ratification two New York banking firms which obtained the contract for the proposed loan made a small short-term advance to meet Nicaragua's most pressing needs. To secure this, the collection of the customs was at once turned over to an American citizen nominated by them. They also helped to set up a National Bank and to reform the depreciated paper currency, so that they were already deeply involved in Nicaragua's affairs when it became clear that the United States Senate would not approve either the Nicaraguan or the Honduran treaty and that the proposed large loan was consequently impossible. Since the Nicaraguan government's financial situation was steadily deteriorating, the bankers could not recover the money they had already advanced and in fact had to make small additional loans during the next two years. The customs collectorship continued, and in 1913 the bankers bought from the government a 51 per cent interest in the National Bank and in the Pacific Railroad, both of which they were already managing.

The political situation, meanwhile, had grown steadily worse. In May, 1911, Luis Mena, the Minister of War, forced Estrada to resign. The Vice-President, Adolfo Díaz, became the nominal head of the government, but Mena continued to control the army and to prepare the way for his own assumption of the presidency for the next term. He was opposed by a strong faction in the conservative party led by General Emiliano Chamorro, and this group supported Díaz when he ousted Mena from the Cabinet in July, 1912. Mena, however, had most of the army behind him, and the revolt which he started seemed certain to succeed when the liberals also took up arms against Díaz. The President consequently asked the United States for help. American marines who were sent to Nicaragua to protect foreign lives and property did not at first intervene in the fighting, but their presence, and the United States' emphatic public condemnation of Mena's action caused most of the rebels to lay down their arms. Those who did not were finally defeated by American forces. Seven American soldiers were killed during the intervention.

For 13 years after this a legation guard of about 100 American marines was stationed at Managua as a symbol of the determination of the United States to uphold the existing government. Its presence enabled the conservative party to remain in power despite growing opposition. Adolfo Díaz was re-elected as President and was succeeded by Emiliano Chamorro in 1917, after the American Minister informed the liberal candidate that he would not be recognized if elected. Diego Manuel Chamorro, a relative of Emiliano, became President in 1921.

Economically, Nicaragua benefited somewhat from the State Department's policy, despite the failure of the loan treaty. An efficient customs service was created, the fluctuating and rapidly depreciating paper currency was stabilized, and service on the British debt, in default after the revolution, was resumed. The government nevertheless was constantly in financial difficulties, and payments for supplies and salaries were always in arrears. When the European war temporarily dislocated the country's commerce in 1914, both the New York bankers and the English bondholders were compelled to agree to a suspension of payments due them, and even the new currency system seemed about to break down.

Partly with the idea of affording some financial relief to the Nicaraguan government, the United States entered into the Bryan-Chamorro Treaty of 1914 which provided for the payment of $3,000,000 to Nicaragua in return for the exclusive right to construct a trans-Isthmian canal in her territory. The United States was also to obtain naval bases in the Gulf of Fonseca and on the Corn Islands in the Caribbean Sea. This agreement brought angry protests from Costa Rica and El Salvador. Costa Rica maintained that she had a right to be consulted before Nicaragua made any grant for canal purposes in the San Juan River, and El Salvador claimed that a naval base in the Gulf of Fonseca would violate her rights. Both countries brought suit against Nicaragua in the Central American Court of Justice.

When the Court criticized Nicaragua for entering into the Treaty, though without declaring the Treaty itself invalid, Nicaragua withdrew from the convention under which the Court operated. An important part of the peace machinery set up by the 1907 treaties thus disappeared. The Court had accomplished little of value in ten years of existence, but it was unfortunate that the United States should have been partly responsible for its demise. The naval bases contemplated by the Bryan-Chamorro Treaty were never established, and even today there is no immediate prospect that the canal will be built.

The $3,000,000 was paid to Nicaragua, but only after a long dispute as to the way in which it would be used. The bankers, relying on promises by Nicaragua, maintained that their claims and those of the British bondholders should be paid first, but the Department of State insisted that other American creditors should have equal consideration. A compromise was finally reached in the Financial Plan of 1917, which limited the Nicaraguan government's current expenditures to a fixed sum each month and made the balance of its revenues available for the payment of debts. The operation of this plan, and of a similar plan adopted in 1920, was supervised by a High Commissioner appointed by the Secretary of State at Washington. There was thus for some years a considerable measure of American control over Nicaragua's finances. Under both plans large sums were available for debt payment, and by 1924 the government had discharged its debts to the American bankers and repurchased the latter's stock in the National Bank and the national railroad. Even after the bankers had no further financial interest in Nicaragua, however, they continued for several years, at the government's request, to manage both of these companies.

PRESIDENT WILSON'S NONRECOGNITION POLICY

For some years after the American intervention in Nicaragua in 1912, Central America was relatively peaceful. President Wilson's announced policy of refusing to recognize governments coming into power by force discouraged potential trouble makers, and the United States' vigorous diplomatic insistence on the observance of the 1907 treaties deterred the Central American states from helping revolutions in neighboring countries. If revolts did occur, they frequently subsided when an American warship appeared at the nearest port. The policy of the United States thus tended to support any regime that outwardly observed constitutional forms, and in all of the republics except Costa Rica elections continued to be little more than a sham. Estrada Cabrera remained in undisputed control in Guatemala, while groups of political leaders passed on the presidency from one to another in Nicaragua and El Salvador. In Honduras, the conservatives, who had ousted Zelaya's friend Dávila in 1910, remained in control until 1919, first under Manuel Bonilla and after 1915 under Francisco Bertrand.

The first test of President Wilson's nonrecognition policy in Central America came, strangely enough, in Costa Rica. Alfredo González, who was made President of that country by the Congress in 1914 after no one had received a majority of the popular vote, made many enemies by his advocacy of taxes on wealth; and in January, 1917, he was ousted by a *golpe de cuartel* led by his own Minister of War, Federico Tinoco. Though most of the other political leaders co-operated with the new regime, the United States denounced it and warned American citizens against business dealings with the usurper. Tinoco nevertheless maintained a corrupt and oppressive dictatorship for two years until he was overthrown by revolution in 1919. Julio Acosta, the leader of the revolt, was elected President, and Costa Rica resumed her orderly political life.

POLITICAL EVENTS, 1919–1923

The Tinoco affair and a successful liberal revolution in Honduras in 1919 disturbed the relative tranquility that the Isthmus had been enjoying, and in 1920 another revolt put an end to Estrada Cabrera's dictatorship in Guatemala. The political party that took power in Guatemala, with Carlos Herrera as President, had been organized—ostensibly at least —to promote the union of Central America which was still the aspiration of many Central American patriots, and in June, 1921, Honduras and El Salvador joined with Guatemala in setting up a provisional Federal Council at Tegucigalpa. Before the new government began to exercise any authority, however, a military revolt in Guatemala drove the unionists from power and killed the project. By this time there were political unrest and a revival of international tensions throughout the Isthmus. The governments of Honduras and El Salvador were unfriendly to the new regime in Guatemala, and Honduras and Nicaragua were each accusing the other of encouraging revolutionary activity on the frontier. The 1907 treaties, which had been relied on to prevent friction of this sort, seemed to have lost their efficacy.

The United States consequently invited the five republics to a conference at Washington at which a new set of Central American treaties was signed early in 1923. These were in general similar to the treaties of 1907, except that a new court, consisting of a panel of Central American and foreign judges from which the parties to a dispute could select a tribunal in each case which arose, took the place of the five permanent, politically appointed judges of the old court. The pledges to settle all disputes by peaceful means and not to permit aid to be given to revolutionists conspiring against the government of another Central American country were reiterated, and machinery for enforcing these pledges was provided in the form of international commissions of inquiry to investigate disputes. The United States became a party to the convention that provided for these commissions.

The new treaties also contained in more explicit form a provision which had appeared in the 1907 treaties but which had had little application in practice. The five countries agreed not to recognize a revolutionary government in a Central American state until there had been a free election— and not even then if one of the leaders of the revolution or a person who had been a high official of the recently overthrown regime became president. Revolutions were thus to be made unattractive by preventing those who led them, or officials who took part in a *golpe de cuartel*, from enjoying the fruits of victory. The significance of the provision was enhanced when the United States announced that it would follow the same principle in its own policy in Central America.

The nonrecognition provision was first invoked after a protracted and destructive civil war in Honduras which overthrew President López Gutiérrez and brought the conservatives back into power in 1924. The fighting was ended and a provisional government established through the mediation of the United States. The chief leader of the conservatives, General Tiburcio Carías, had been the party's candidate in the election of

1923 and now expected to become President as a matter of course when new elections were held; but he was compelled to withdraw when the United States declared that he would not be recognized if elected. Dr. Paz Barahona, another conservative but a civilian, became President instead.

THE SECOND INTERVENTION IN NICARAGUA

Another application of the nonrecognition principle, in 1926, helped to involve the United States in one of the most unfortunate episodes of its Caribbean policy. Nicaragua was still ruled by the conservative party, which had been able to remain in power because the presence of the legation guard discouraged revolution. The Department of State had for some time felt that this situation was indefensible, but it knew that a withdrawal of the guard would almost certainly precipitate a civil war. It had unsuccessfully urged the Nicaraguan government to hold a free election in 1920, and after President Diego Manuel Chamorro took office it insisted that he employ an American expert to draw up a new electoral law and assist in its application. In November, 1923, the United States informed the Nicaraguan government that it intended to withdraw the legation guard when Chamorro's successor took office in January, 1925. Secretary Hughes pointed out that the new government should be in a strong position if it were the result of a really free election, and he offered the assistance of American experts not only in holding the election but also in training an efficient constabulary to maintain order after the marines were withdrawn.

While this note was in the mail, President Chamorro died. The Vice-President, Bartolomé Martínez, was a member of a minority faction in the conservative party, and his accession radically changed the political situation. When the other conservative leaders refused to support his candidacy for re-election, he made an alliance with the liberals. He had to relinquish his own presidential aspirations when the United States pointed out that his election would violate the Nicaraguan constitution, but he continued to oppose Emiliano Chamorro, who was the candidate of the conservative party, and supported a coalition that nominated Carlos Solórzano, a conservative, as President and Dr. Juan B. Sacasa, a liberal, as Vice-President. When the date of the election approached, he refused to accept any further assistance from Dr. Harold Dodds, who had drafted the electoral law and supervised the registration of voters. No one was surprised when Solórzano defeated Chamorro in the election.

The legation guard was not removed at once, because Solórzano asked that it remain pending the organization of the police force suggested in the American note of November, 1923. When the government showed little real interest in the police force, however, the marines were withdrawn, in August, 1925. Disturbances began almost immediately. The new President had little ability, and his administration was weakened by the rivalry between the conservative and liberal officeholders. In August, two liberals withdrew from the Cabinet after a military demonstration led by the President's brother-in-law, and in October Emiliano Chamorro seized control, forced the Vice-President to leave the country, and had the Congress elect himself as first *designado*. Chamorro thus assumed the presidency when Solórzano was "given" a leave of absence early in 1926.

In accord with the 1923 Treaty, the United States and the other Central American states refused to recognize the new regime. This encouraged the liberals to resist, and a revolt which they started on the east coast developed into one of the most savagely fought civil wars in the Republic's history. The United States' disapproval of Chamorro hampered its efforts to restore peace, but it finally persuaded Chamorro to withdraw; and in November, 1926, the Congress chose Adolfo Díaz as President. The United States recognized him; but the liberals continued the war, and Dr. Sacasa, who returned to Nicaragua in December, set up a rival government on the east coast. When Mexico recognized Sacasa and sent him arms, the situation became more serious.

American marines had already landed at several places on the east coast to protect foreigners, and in January, 1927, the legation guard was re-established at Managua. After Díaz was recognized, the American government sold him arms and helped him to obtain a loan in New York. With this aid, he could maintain himself in the west, but he was not strong enough to carry the war to the revolutionists on the east coast. Meanwhile marauding brigands made life intolerable for noncombatants in many regions outside the zones of military operations.

The war seemed thus to be developing into a stalemate, and in April, 1927, President Coolidge sent Henry L. Stimson to Nicaragua to insist on a settlement. After brief negotiations, both sides agreed to surrender their arms to the American forces in return for a promise that the United States would supervise a free election in 1928. To assure fair play, a constabulary was to be trained by American officers, and until this was ready for service the American marines were to maintain order. Díaz continued as President, but liberals were restored to many of the positions which they had held in the coalition government before Chamorro's *coup d'état*.

In the negotiations that led to this settlement the liberals were represented by General José María Moncada, the principal leader of the revolutionary army. Sacasa and his civilian advisers were inclined to object to the arrangement, but they made no effort to prolong the war. The greater part of the forces on both sides cheerfully surrendered their weapons, and a few recalcitrants were forcibly disarmed. The population as a whole was relieved and pleased that the war had ended. It seemed probable that the program of pacification would be carried through without great difficulty, until Augusto César Sandino suddenly attacked and very nearly overwhelmed a garrison of American marines and Nicaraguan constabulary at Ocotal in July.

Sandino, one of Moncada's lesser generals, had refused to disband his force and had escaped into the sparsely inhabited region of northern Nicaragua. For several years he carried on guerrilla warfare there against the Nicaraguan police and the American marines, who were obligated under the Stimson agreement to help the Nicaraguan government maintain order. He never had more than a few hundred men under arms, but the mountainous, heavily forested terrain made it difficult to catch him. As he attracted more and more attention by ambushing small patrols or raiding unprotected villages and plantations, he won much sympathy in Latin America and among anti-imperialists in the United States. His movement did much to create hostile feeling toward the United States in other parts of the Hemisphere.

Sandino's operations had less effect in Nicaragua itself. Peace was restored in the more important sections of the country, and the new constabulary, the *Guardia Nacional*, became a fairly efficient body under its American officers. The presidential election, supervised by General Frank R. McCoy, was held late in 1928 under conditions satisfactory to both parties. General Moncada was the liberal candidate, and Señor Adolfo Benard was nominated by the conservatives after the United States had pointed out that the Nicaraguan constitution would make General Chamorro's election illegal. Moncada won and was peacefully inaugurated on January 1, 1929.

Shortly before the election both candidates agreed that the winner would ask for American supervision of the election of 1932, hoping in this way to diminish the possibility of renewed party strife in the meantime. Moncada not only honored this agreement but also arranged to have American officers conduct the congressional election in 1930. In both cases the liberals won, despite some dissension within the party. The President who took office in January, 1933, was Dr. Juan Bautista Sacasa, the titular leader of the revolt of 1926–1927.

Sandino continued to make trouble. In 1931, when an earthquake destroyed Managua and killed nearly 1,000 people, he took advantage of the general confusion to sack Cabo Gracias on the east coast, murdering nine North Americans and a number of other civilians. In January, 1933, however, the last of the American marines were withdrawn from Nicaragua, and the objective for which the rebels had ostensibly been fighting was accomplished. At the same time Sandino was confronted by an agreement between the liberals and conservatives to co-operate energetically against him, and in February, 1933, he made peace with the Nicaraguan government.

EVENTS IN THE OTHER COUNTRIES, 1923–1933

Elsewhere in the Isthmus, the decade that followed the Washington conference of 1922–1923 was a period of relative prosperity and some progress toward democratic institutions. The United States' moral support of constituted governments discouraged revolutions, and Guatemala, El Salvador, and Costa Rica obtained loans in New York for public works and municipal improvements. Honduras became for a time the world's greatest producer of bananas.

In Costa Rica, democracy seemed firmly established. Ex-President Ricardo Jiménez succeeded Julio Acosta in 1924, and another of the country's elder statesmen, Cleto González Víquez, was elected in 1928. When Jiménez was re-elected in 1932, one of the defeated candidates attempted a revolt but surrendered after three days of fighting in the Capital. In Honduras, there were two free elections, in each of which the opposition candidate won. Vicente Mejía Colindres succeeded Paz Barahona in 1929, and Tiburcio Carías, the conservative leader, became President in 1933.

In El Salvador, there was increasing dissatisfaction with the continued dominance of the Meléndez-Quiñónez family. Pío Romero Bosque, who was made President by Alfonso Quiñónez in 1927, repudiated his predecessor's leadership and held a relatively free election at the end of his term in 1931. Arturo Araujo became President, but he was removed a few months later by General Maximiliano Martínez, his Minister of War. The other Central American countries and the United States refused to recognize Martínez because he was ineligible under the 1923 treaty, but he remained in power, after suppressing with much bloodshed a revolt in which there seems to have been a considerable communist participation.

The government of Guatemala was still a military dictatorship. José Manuel Orellana, who became President after the defeat of the unionists in 1921, died in 1926, and another General, Lázaro Chacón, ruled until he was incapacitated by illness in 1930. After some disorder, General Jorge Ubico set up a dictatorship which was to last for 13 years.

CENTRAL AMERICA AND THE GOOD NEIGHBOR POLICY

The policy of the United States from the time of the Washington conference of 1907 had done much to promote peace in Central America. International wars seemed to have become a thing of the past, and the nonrecognition of revolutionary governments had discouraged internal disorder. In 1933, three of the five republics had presidents who had been chosen in real elections. Foreign interference, however, was unpalatable even when it took place at the request of the local leaders, and the Nicaraguan affair, especially, aroused fear and distrust throughout Central

America. The policy of intervention was also increasingly unpopular in the United States. The American government had shown an increasing reluctance to resort to force in the Caribbean even before the Nicaraguan civil war, and this trend was accentuated after 1929. After 1933, when President Franklin Roosevelt proclaimed the Good Neighbor Policy and formally renounced the use of intervention, the United States generally refrained from attempting to influence the course of political events in Central America even by diplomatic action.

Except in Costa Rica, where León Cortés was peacefully elected President in 1936 and Rafael Angel Calderón Guardia in 1940, all of the Central American republics were ruled by dictators in the later 1930's and in the first years of the Second World War. Martínez remained in power in El Salvador and was recognized by his neighbors and the United States in 1934. Ubico, in Guatemala, was in many ways a progressive ruler, but he sternly repressed all opposition. Carías, though he had obtained the presidency by a free election, established a relatively mild dictatorship in Honduras and remained in office until 1948 after suppressing several liberal revolts.

In Nicaragua, the prospect for peace seemed fairly bright when the American marines left in 1933. The two political parties not only cooperated in bringing Sandino to terms but worked out agreements intended to provide guarantees of electoral freedom and minority representation in Congress and in other government offices. Before the necessary constitutional amendments could be adopted, however, unforeseen developments caused the plan to miscarry.

Sandino had been permitted to maintain a small private army in the north and had begun to carry on radical propaganda in the interior, capitalizing on the prestige that he had built up during his resistance to the United States. His activities were particularly offensive to the leaders of the *Guardia Nacional*, who resented the lenient treatment accorded him by the armistice, and on February 21, 1934, members of this force killed him and his brother just after Augusto Sandino had dined with President Sacasa. The President attempted to have the murderers punished but failed because the *guardia* Commander, General Anastacio Somoza, assumed responsibility for their act. It became clear that the constabulary, created to support the constitutional government, had become the government's master. Soon afterward, in fact, Somoza forced Sacasa to resign and made himself President. At the end of his term in 1939 a Constituent Assembly did away with the constitutional prohibition against re-election and voted to continue him in office until 1947.

All of the Central American states profited from the aid that the United States gave its Latin American allies during the war. Each government declared war immediately after Pearl Harbor and co-operated in measures for the defense of the Panama Canal. The United States spent much money on road building, air bases, and projects for developing the production of rubber and other strategic raw materials. An effort was made to open the Pan American Highway for overland traffic to the Canal Zone, but this project was still far from complete at the end of the war. North American expenditures gave the governments larger financial resources and offset the dislocation of normal trade, though they also contributed to an inflation that caused trouble when the war was over.

THE RISE AND FALL OF THE
COMMUNIST REGIME IN GUATEMALA

The new forces that affected the political and social life of many of the larger Latin American countries after the war—the increasing dissatisfaction with low living standards, the rising power of organized labor, and the disruptive influence of international communism—were felt also in Central America. In most parts of the Isthmus, however, they had less effect than in countries like Mexico and Argentina. The small area and population of the Central American states discouraged industrial development, and the great majority of the people continued to live in rural districts and to make their living from agriculture. There was nevertheless evidence of discontent with political and social conditions that had improved relatively little since independence.

The most sensational events of the postwar period occurred in Guatemala. In July, 1944, a series of strikes and minor disorders, in which the university students took a leading part, forced Ubico to turn over the executive power to a *junta* representing the army, and in October this government was overthrown by some of the younger army officers working with the civilian liberals. A month later, Juan José Arévalo was elected President.

Arévalo was a schoolteacher who had been living for the past ten years in Argentina and was little known except by reputation in Guatemala. He was supported by the university students and other advanced liberals and, more importantly, by the army, which was led by the officers who had taken part in the revolution. Under his leadership, the revolutionary party carried out a small part of its promised program. Advanced labor and social security laws were enacted, chiefly for the benefit of the industrial workers in the towns and the employees on the United Fruit Company's banana farms, and there was some improvement in the situation of the Indians. Under Ubico, the peonage statute had been replaced by a law that compelled each Indian to work a certain number of days in the year, but with somewhat more freedom in choosing employers and bargaining for wages. This "vagrancy" law was repealed by the Arévalo administration, and the Indian, theoretically at least, became a free man. His wages, though still pitifully small, increased considerably. There was also, for a time, more political freedom. Opposition parties participated in local elections and occasionally won them. There were nevertheless several small revolts during Arévalo's term, and tension increased as the time for a presidential election approached.

The principal candidates were the two military leaders of the 1944 revolution: Colonel Francisco Arana and Colonel Jacobo Arbenz. When Arana was eliminated by assassination, Arbenz was easily elected, but he faced not only the opposition of the conservatives but the hostility of many army officers who blamed him for the murder of his rival. He consequently turned for support to the communist leaders, with whom he already had close personal relations. Foreign communist agents and a few very young Guatemalan converts had begun soon after 1944 to take over the leadership of the newly organized labor unions and to form political groups which ostensibly supported the aims of the 1944 revolution. Under Arbenz their influence rapidly increased, and within two or three years they had a dominant influence in the government.

In 1952, Arbenz promulgated an agrarian reform law. The numerous coffee plantations taken over from German owners during the war were to be divided among the peasants, and large proprietors were to be compelled to give up land tilled by sharecroppers and uncultivated land. The owners were to be compensated with government bonds. The communists obtained control of the administration of the program and set out to use it as a means of obtaining control of the Indian and *mestizo* peasants, most of whom probably had only the vaguest idea of what was taking place. When the Supreme Court questioned the constitutionality of the arbitrary procedures that were being adopted, four of its members were promptly impeached and removed by the Congress. The first important application of the law was the expropriation of several hundred thousand acres belonging to the United Fruit Company, and the Guatemalan government angrily rejected a request from the United States that the company receive adequate compensation.

The United States and Guatemala's Central American neighbors watched these developments with growing alarm. At the inter-American conference at Caracas in 1954, however, an effort by the United States to arouse the other American states to a realization of the danger in the situation was only partly successful.[1] In May of the same year, when a ship from Poland landed arms at a Guatemalan port, the United States sent arms to Honduras and Nicaragua, to enable the governments of those countries to protect themselves.

In June a small revolutionary army under Lieutenant Colonel Carlos Castilla Armas invaded Guatemala from Honduras, and rebel planes bombed Guatemala City. Arbenz and his communist friends, meanwhile, had inaugurated a reign of terror in Guatemala, torturing or murdering

[1] See below, p. 518.

great numbers of active anticommunists. The Guatemalan government asked the Security Council of the United Nations to intervene and openly requested the support of Russia. It also laid the matter before the Organization of American States, but as both bodies were beginning to consider the matter the army forced Arbenz to resign. A few days later the American Ambassador persuaded the army leaders to permit Castilla to take control of the government. The communists and other unfriendly critics charged that Honduras and Nicaragua, and also the United States, had aided Castilla in ways that were inconsistent with the inter-American treaties outlawing intervention by one state in the affairs of another.

Castilla became constitutional President, after going through the form of an election. He had much popular following, but he had trouble with the radicals and the always-turbulent university students on the one hand and with the conservatives on the other. Nevertheless the country began to recover from the ruinous state in which the communists left it. A new agrarian program was inaugurated, though without notable success, and something was done in the way of road building and economic development. Guatemala's prospects seemed brighter than they had for many years, when the President was assassinated in July, 1957.

The Vice-President took charge of the government. An election held a few months later produced a large majority for Chief Justice Miguel Ortíz, who had the administration's backing, but the principal opposition candidate, Miguel Ydígoras, claimed that the election had been fraudulent and led riots in Guatemala City which caused the army to take control and annul the result. A new vote, in January, 1958, gave Ydígoras a plurality, but not a majority, and soon afterward the Congress chose him as President. His government, supported by the groups that had been prominent in business and public life before the 1944 revolution, was expected to be somewhat more conservative than its immediate predecessors.

EL SALVADOR AND HONDURAS

Martínez, like Ubico, fell from power when the approaching victory of the democracies in Europe weakened the position of several of the Latin American dictatorships. In April, 1944, just after a Constituent Assembly extended the President's term for another five years, there was an unsuccessful military revolt which destroyed a large area in the heart of the Capital, and a month later a general strike forced Martínez to resign. The civilian liberals, who had been largely responsible for the movement, were shouldered aside when a new government was formed, and provisional military regimes administered the government until the army made Salvador Castaneda Castro President in 1945. Continued political tension forced the new administration to maintain a "state of siege," with constitutional guarantees suspended, during the greater part of the next three years. In 1948 Castaneda was ousted by a part of the army.

Lieutenant Colonel Oscar Osorio, a leader of this group, was elected President in 1950. During the six years of his term, despite the subversive efforts of the communists in Guatemala, the country was fairly tranquil, and the government was able to devote more attention to constructive policies. Its most important project was the Lempa River dam, which vastly increased the country's supply of electric power and made possible the eventual development of light industries, much needed in a country so densely populated as El Salvador. Financial and technical aid from the United States government and the World Bank helped the government in this project and in the development of agriculture, and high coffee prices made the country unusually prosperous. Osorio's associate José María Lemus became President in 1956. Though the treatment of the opposition in the election showed that there had been less progress toward democracy than in other directions, the new administration seemed as stable as its predecessor, and it continued its predecessor's economic policies.

In Honduras, Carías voluntarily declined to be a candidate in 1948 but imposed the election of Juan Manuel Gálvez as his successor. The new President restored the political freedoms denied under the dictatorship and endeavored to carry out a rather modest program of economic development. In 1954, however, a general strike, starting on the American banana plantations on the north coast and later spreading to other foreign and Honduran-owned companies, disastrously affected the country's economy. Communists and the communist-controlled radio in Guatemala encouraged the movement and obstructed efforts to effect a settlement by negotiation. The workers had no experienced noncommunist leaders because earlier governments had not permitted the formation of unions. For a time, North Americans and other foreigners seemed to be in grave danger, but the President, with the support of many of his political opponents, succeeded in maintaining order, and after some months the strike was settled by substantial concessions to the workers. Thereafter, labor unions were permitted and in fact encouraged by the government.

There was further trouble when presidential elections were held later in 1954. Carías was the candidate of the "national" party, but he was opposed by a dissident wing of that party and by the liberals. Gálvez attempted to assure a free vote, but there was much bitterness and some violence during the campaign. Since Ramón Villeda Morales, the liberal candidate, received only 48 per cent of the vote, the decision rested with Congress, which was unable to act because the two "national" groups prevented a quorum. At this point Gálvez fell ill. The Vice-President, Julio Lozano, annulled the election and assumed dictatorial power, pending the meeting of a Constituent Assembly. All parties apparently acquiesced in his action; but they grew restive when it began to appear that Lozano was maneuvering to remain in power indefinitely, and in October, 1956, a group of young army officers seized control. Soon afterward Villeda Morales was elected President for the term beginning January 1, 1958.

COSTA RICA

In Costa Rica there was criticism of the way in which the government brought about the election of Teodoro Picado as Calderón Guardia's successor in 1944, and dissatisfaction increased when it seemed probable that Calderón would return to the presidency by the same methods in 1948. After clashes between the people and the police and a general strike, Picado agreed to measures that would assure fairness in the voting, and in February, 1948, Otilio Ulate, the opposition candidate, obtained a substantial majority in the election. When the Congress annulled the election, Ulate's supporters revolted, under the leadership of José Figueres, who had organized a small military force on his plantation in the interior. In the fighting that ensued, the communists, whose leader Manuel Mora had supported Calderón, took an active part and for a time controlled one of the barracks and the airfield at San José. Mora continued to resist after Picado agreed to turn over the government, but was finally persuaded by the diplomatic corps to surrender.

With Ulate's consent, a *junta* headed by Figueres took charge of the government to restore order. The communists were obviously plotting a revolt, and in December, 1948, *Calderonistas* invaded the country from Nicaragua. The movement collapsed when the Organization of American States sent a commission to investigate Costa Rica's charge that Somoza was aiding it. In the months that followed, a new constitution was drawn up, and congressional elections were held; consequently conditions were fairly normal when Ulate was inaugurated as President in November, 1949. Ulate's term was a period of solid economic progress, encouraged by his government's sound fiscal policy. At its end in 1953 Figueres was elected President by an overwhelming majority.

Figueres, who was by this time one of the most prominent of the advanced liberal leaders in Latin America, was feared and disliked by many of the more conservative people in Costa Rica, but his administration brought no very great changes. His most notable accomplishment was the negotiation of a new contract with the United Fruit Company which gave Costa Rica a far greater share in the company's profits. His relations with the United States were friendly, but there was a revival of his bitter personal feud with President Somoza of Nicaragua.

In recruiting forces for his revolution in 1948, Figueres had gathered around him a number of political exiles from other Caribbean countries who called themselves the "Caribbean legion." This group was said to look forward to the overthrow of several of the dictatorships in Central America and the West Indies, counting on help from "democratic" governments like those of Guatemala and Cuba, and the O.A.S. commission which investigated the Costa Rican-Nicaraguan conflict in 1949 criticized Figueres for harboring it. In 1954, Somoza asserted that members of the legion, with Figueres' help, had taken part in a plot to assassinate him. A few months later the O.A.S. was again compelled to take steps to discourage an invasion of Costa Rica from Nicaragua.

In the election of 1957, Mario Echandi, the candidate of Figueres' opponents, was elected President after a fairly close but orderly contest.

NICARAGUA

Somoza continued to rule Nicaragua. Early in 1947 he permitted Leonardo Arguello to be elected President, but he retained command of the *Guardia Nacional;* and when Arguello showed an unexpected independence he replaced him with Victor Manuel Román y Reyes. Most of the other American governments disapproved these actions and refused for a time to recognize the new administration, but Somoza was too firmly entrenched in power to be seriously affected by their attitude, and in 1950 he again assumed the presidency. During his long tenure of power, there was little freedom of the press, and opponents were sometimes treated roughly; but there was somewhat more freedom of expression and less official terrorism than under most Latin American dictatorships. Somoza had much popular support and was even able to obtain the co-operation of many of the leaders of the conservative party. Nicaragua prospered as never before because the maintenance of peace encouraged agriculture and cattle raising. Cotton growing provided an important new source of wealth. New roads brought the farmers closer to their markets. The President himself became one of the richest men in Central America.

Somoza placed his two sons in key positions in the government, and when he himself was assassinated in 1956 Luis took over the presidency and Anastacio, Jr., continued as chief of the *Guardia Nacional.* They encountered surprisingly little resistance. Luis took his father's place as the liberal nominee in the election of 1957, in which most of the conservatives refused to participate. As constitutional President, he endeavored to give his government a more liberal appearance, permitting more freedom of the press and even sponsoring a constitutional amendment that would prevent his own re-election, or the election of his brother, at the end of his term. The overthrow of the "Somoza dynasty" nevertheless became one of the prime objectives of the "democratic" groups that began an active campaign against all Latin American dictatorships after Fidel Castro's victory in Cuba in 1959.

CHAPTER 23

Cuba

CUBA IN THE 19TH CENTURY

CUBA and the smaller island of Puerto Rico were the only Spanish possessions in America that did not become independent in the first quarter of the nineteenth century. Apparently their people had less desire to break away from the mother country than had the people of Venezuela or the River Plate, even though they complained of many of the same abuses that inspired the revolts elsewhere. One reason, especially in the case of Cuba, was the prosperity that they were enjoying. The British occupation of Habana in 1762, during the Seven Years' War, had opened that port to foreign ships, and a sudden outburst of commercial activity revealed for the first time the colony's potential wealth. After the British withdrew, restrictions on trade with Spain were somewhat relaxed, and at times during the Napoleonic wars foreign vessels were freely admitted to Cuban ports. After 1818 commerce with other countries was generally authorized, though on less favorable terms than commerce with Spain. Meanwhile, beginning in the last years of the eighteenth century, there had been a phenomenal increase in production. After the slave revolt in French Saint Domingue, and the destruction of the rich sugar and coffee plantations of that colony, the cultivation of both of these crops in Cuba became much more profitable. Many refugees from Saint Domingue and many immigrants from Spain came to the island, and the importation of slaves rapidly increased.

The new settlers from Spain were little inclined to revolt, and after the revolution on the mainland started, the loyal population was increased by a further influx of refugees from the colonies there. Creoles who wanted independence formed a number of secret revolutionary societies, one of them called "The Suns and Rays of Bolívar," but their feeble conspiracies were easily suppressed. It was difficult to attack the island from the mainland, and a proposal in 1825 for an expedition from

Colombia and Mexico was discouraged by the United States, partly, perhaps, because North American statesmen hoped to acquire Cuba for themselves, and partly because they feared that a breakdown of Spanish authority might lead to a slave revolt like that in Saint Domingue. This same fear made many conservative Cubans averse to any change.

GROWING OPPOSITION TO SPANISH RULE

Disaffection increased as time went on. Spain's colonial policy changed little after the loss of her mainland possessions. The government was arbitrary and corrupt, and taxes were heavy. Spain was too much occupied with internal dissensions to pay adequate attention to colonial problems. Worse still, coffee production declined because of competition in Central and South America, and the subsidizing of beet raising in Europe made sugar less profitable.

In the first half of the nineteenth century, however, the chief danger to Spain's possession of Cuba came from other powers, and loss of the island to France or England or the United States was probably averted only by the determination of each government that neither of the others should acquire it. To the United States, the fate of Cuba, from which a powerful enemy might control both entrances to the Gulf of Mexico, was vitally important for strategic reasons. Many American statesmen hoped that the island would sooner or later become American territory, and in the South especially there was an active desire to add a new and rich slave state to the Union. In 1848 an offer to buy Cuba was summarily rejected by Spain. In the next three years filibustering attacks aroused the same interest and sympathy in the South that later supported Walker's venture in Nicaragua.

The most noted leader of these attacks was Narciso López, a Venezuelan who as a boy had fought first for the patriots and then for the loyalists in his own country. After living several years in Cuba he organized a revolutionary conspiracy there in 1848. When it failed he escaped to the United States and recruited a force of North Americans. The federal authorities checked his first attempt to leave American waters, but in 1850 he eluded them and landed with a small army at Cárdenas, only to be defeated and forced to flee. When he returned to the United States he was prosecuted in the courts; but public sentiment in his favor made it impossible to obtain a conviction, and a year later he sailed for Cuba with a new force. This time he and 50 of his companions were captured and executed.

At the time of the López affair, Great Britain and France threatened to send warships to protect Cuba, and in 1852 they proposed that the United States join them in guaranteeing Spain's possession of the island —a proposal that the American government rejected. Two years later the American Ministers to England, France, and Spain met at Ostend in Belgium and let it become known that they were advising the Secretary of State that the United States would be justified under certain conditions in seizing Cuba if Spain refused to sell the island. This "manifesto" was criticized in the United States as well as in Europe. Fortunately the Pierce administration repudiated the policy which it suggested, and as the slavery crisis in the United States grew more acute, interest in Cuban affairs declined.

The first formidable bid for independence was the Ten Years' War, which began in 1868, at a time when the home government was weakened by a revolution in Spain itself. In the long-drawn-out conflict that ensued, the insurgents were opposed by strong loyal elements in Cuba and weakened by their own dissensions. In 1873 they deposed Carlos Manuel de Céspedes, whom they had chosen as their provisional President, and this leader was soon afterward captured and executed by the Spaniards. There was much loss of life in indecisive fighting and much destruction of property. Foreign public opinion was shocked by reports of atrocities like the execution by the Spaniards in 1871 of eight Cuban students for a trivial offense which they apparently had not committed. In 1873, when the Spanish forces shot more than 50 of the crew of the blockade runner Virginius, most of them Englishmen and Americans, and would have shot many more if the Captain of a British cruiser had not intervened by force to stop the executions, a conflict with the United States seemed imminent. It was shown, however, that the ship was illegally flying the American flag, and the United States accepted an indemnity to the families of the victims.

By 1875 the restoration of peace in Spain made it possible to send more troops to Cuba, and the government gradually got the upper hand. In 1878 most of the revolutionary leaders agreed to lay down their arms in return for an amnesty and a promise of political reform. The Cubans found, however, that this promise meant little, and they had other causes for discontent in the years that followed the war. Taxes continued high, for the expense of the war was added to the already heavy Cuban debt. Much property belonging to insurgent sympathizers had been confiscated during the war and had passed into the hands of peninsular Spaniards. The changes which were being forced on the sugar industry by increasing foreign competition, and especially the concentration of production in larger units financed by Spanish or other foreign capital, also ruined many formerly prosperous creole families.

One conservative creole group which had theretofore been especially interested in the maintenance of the *status quo* was seriously affected by the abolition of slavery. The importation of slaves, which first assumed large proportions at the end of the eighteenth century, continued through the first half of the nineteenth, despite the legal prohibition of the trade in 1820, and the Negro population eventually outnumbered the white. The liberals in Cuba opposed slavery, and during the Ten Years' War the revolutionists promised general emancipation after independence. In 1870, partly in response to pressure from the United States, the Spanish government decreed the liberty of all children born thenceforth of slave mothers, and in 1886 another law abolished slavery altogether.

Nevertheless the island as a whole prospered for some years after the war, and especially after the McKinley tariff and a reciprocity treaty with Spain allowed Cuban sugar to enter the United States free of duty. The planters increased their crop until it exceeded 1,000,000 tons in 1894. In that same year, however, the Wilson tariff suddenly restored the duty on sugar, at a time when prices were falling in the world market. The Cuban economy was hard hit, and thousands found themselves out of work. The bad economic situation defeated Spain's belated attempt to placate political discontent by a grant of partial home rule early in 1895, for a new revolution broke out before it was possible to put the measure in execution.

THE WAR FOR INDEPENDENCE

The first leader of the revolt was José Martí, who for many years had been organizing Cuban exiles in the United States and other countries and laying plans for a new bid for independence. After Martí was killed, in the first weeks of fighting, General Máximo Gómez, who had been one of the leaders in the Ten Years' War, carried on as Commander in the field. Tomás Estrada Palma, at one time President of the revolutionary government during the earlier insurrection, worked for the movement as head of a *junta* in New York and did much to pave the way for the later intervention of the United States.

In Cuba the revolutionists systematically paralyzed the island's economic life and murdered those who did not co-operate with them. On the other side, the Spanish commander, General Weyler, attempted to control the situation by "reconcentrating" the country people in garrisoned towns, where many died of disease and starvation. The fighting thus caused much destruction of property and terrific suffering among noncombatants. Many American citizens were killed or mistreated and some $50,000,000 of American investments in the island were disastrously affected.

For three years the United States nevertheless maintained a policy of strict neutrality. Both President Cleveland and President McKinley repeatedly endeavored to persuade Spain to grant the Cubans concessions that would induce them to make peace, and in 1897, when the liberals came into power at Madrid, it seemed possible that a settlement might be reached. General Weyler was recalled, and his reconcentration policy was ostensibly, though not actually, abandoned. The Cubans were offered a large measure of self-government, but the hatred between the insurgents and the numerous Cubans still loyal to Spain was so bitter that neither group would consider a compromise. The effort to set up an autonomous Cuban government was a failure, and the war dragged on. Its horrors were avidly played up by the "yellow press" in the United States, with the result that sympathy for the insurgents ran high and there was a rising popular demand for intervention.

The climax came when the U.S.S. *Maine* blew up in Habana harbor in February, 1898, with the loss of 260 men. The cause of the explosion was never ascertained, but the United States alleged that the Spanish authorities had failed to provide the protection due a warship of a friendly power. The American government demanded reparation and further demanded the abandonment of the reconcentration policy and the granting of an immediate armistice to the rebels, to permit peace negotiations through the mediation of the United States. Spain ultimately acceded to most of these demands, but her action came too late. President McKinley, who had hoped for a peaceful solution, could no longer withstand the pressure of Congress and public opinion, and on April 11, 1898, he asked Congress for authority to intervene by force to terminate the Cuban war.

A joint resolution of Congress, approved April 20, declared that "the people of the Island of Cuba are, and of right ought to be, free and independent." It demanded that Spain withdraw from the island, authorized the President to use force against her if necessary, and disclaimed for the United States any intention to exercise sovereignty over the island except for its pacification. Diplomatic relations were broken off, and war began.

THE MILITARY GOVERNMENT AND THE PLATT AMENDMENT

Less than four months later the Spanish government agreed to a preliminary peace protocol by which it surrendered all claims to Cuba. In the negotiations that followed it endeavored, without success, to have either the United States or the future government of Cuba assume responsibility for the large Cuban debt. It also expressed great concern for the interests of loyal Spanish citizens in the island, and the United States, to prevent a breakdown in the negotiations, finally agreed to advise any future Cuban government to assume the obligation to protect foreign lives and property—a promise that was later cited as a reason for insisting on the Platt Amendment. The Treaty of Paris, formally ending the war between Spain and the United States, was signed December 10, 1898.

The American army set up a military government in Cuba after the Spanish troops withdrew. The patriot army was persuaded to disband, after receiving $3,000,000 from the United States. The first task was to restore order and relieve the starving civilian population. After this was accomplished, General Leonard Wood, who became Military Governor in December, 1899, reorganized the civil administration, set up a school system, and inaugurated a program of sanitation. It was during this period that a commission headed by Dr. Walter Reed demonstrated the truth of a theory which had already been set forth by the Cuban physician Dr. Charles Finlay: that yellow fever was carried by the *stegomyia* mosquito. This discovery for the first time made possible the control of that dreaded disease.

The most important purpose of the occupation was to pave the way for the establishment of an independent Cuban government. There were some North Americans who advocated the annexation of the island, which Spain had urged during the peace negotiations, but the American government insisted on carrying out the promise embodied in the Joint Resolution of April 20. To this end, a census was taken; an electoral law was drawn up; and municipal officials were chosen by the voters. The United States felt, however, that its own political and strategic interests, as well as the obligations toward Spain assumed in the Treaty of Paris, required the establishment of a special relationship between itself and the new Cuban government, and General Wood presented his government's views to the Cuban Constitutional Convention that met in November, 1900. In March, 1901, the United States Congress, in the "Platt Amendment" to the military appropriation bill for the ensuing year, spelled out the provisions that must be incorporated in the new Republic's constitution and in a permanent treaty with the United States before the American forces might be withdrawn. Cuba was not to make any treaty impairing her independence or her territorial integrity and was not to contract any debt that could not be discharged out of her ordinary revenues. The most important provision was Article III, by which Cuba was to give the United States "the right to intervene for the preservation of Cuban independence, the maintenance of a government adequate for the protection of life, property, and individual liberty, and for discharging the obligations with respect to Cuba imposed by the Treaty of Paris on the United States, now to be assumed and undertaken by the Government of Cuba." Other articles dealt with the ratification of the acts of the Military Government, the continuation of the sanitation program, the possession of the Isle of Pines, which was to be left for future negotiation, and the establishment of American naval stations.

The Cubans objected strenuously to these provisions, and the opposition in the Constitutional Convention was only partly allayed by assurances that the third clause of the amendment would not be "synonymous with intermeddling or interference with the affairs of the Cuban Government." The act of Congress left no alternative, however, and on June 12, 1901, the Convention accepted the Platt Amendment as an annex to the new constitution.

THE ESTABLISHMENT OF THE REPUBLIC

Tomás Estrada Palma was elected President of Cuba in December, 1901, and took office on May 20, 1902. A treaty embodying the Platt Amendment was signed in May, 1903. Another agreement between the two governments gave the United States the naval station that it still maintains at Guantanamo and the right, never exercised and later relinquished, to establish another at Bahia Honda. More important still, perhaps, was the Reciprocity Treaty of December 11, 1902, which provided that customs duties on many products entering one country from the other should be lower than those levied on similar products from any other nation. President Roosevelt insisted on this arrangement, in the face of much opposition in the United States, because he believed that Cuba's prosperity depended on having an assured market for her sugar in the United States. The treaty was largely responsible for the rapid development of the sugar industry which made Cuba one of the richest of the Latin American countries.

THE SECOND INTERVENTION

Unfortunately, only a small proportion of the island's people shared in its wealth. The great majority were hardly less illiterate and poor than the inhabitants of the other Caribbean countries. A substantial part were descendants of a race that had been in slavery until ten years before the war for independence. The operation of a republican government promised to be the more difficult because many of the people who had education and wealth held aloof from politics. Many of them in fact had been lukewarm or opposed to independence and were not welcome in a government that for a generation was controlled by men who had been active leaders in the war against Spain.

Estrada Palma was generally respected and conspicuously honest, but he was not a forceful leader or an experienced executive. He at first attempted to conduct his administration on a nonpartisan basis; but factional quarrels made this difficult, and a desire to obtain the enactment of urgently needed laws led him finally to seek support from the "moderate" or conservative group in Congress as against the "liberals" who became the opposition. This did little good, so far as legislation was concerned, but it enabled the moderates to control preparations for the presidential elections of December, 1905, with Estrada Palma as their candidate. The liberals refused to take part in the election because they foresaw that they would be beaten, but in August, 1906, some months after Estrada Palma's second inauguration, they started a revolt which rapidly spread through the island.

Estrada Palma, who had made no effort to build up a strong army, promptly appealed to the United States for help. President Roosevelt was reluctant to intervene, but he sent Secretary of War Taft and Assistant Secretary of State Bacon to Cuba to give such aid as they could, and upon their arrival the belligerents agreed to a truce. The American Commissioners' investigation convinced them that the recent elections had been vitiated by violence and fraud. They proposed that the President should remain in office but that all of the other recently chosen officials should resign so that their places might be filled by new elections held under fairer conditions. The liberals seemed inclined to accept this proposal, but the government rejected it. The moderates, in fact, were determined to compel the United States to intervene. First the Cabinet and then the President and Vice-President resigned, and their partisans made it impossible to obtain a quorum in Congress. Cuba was left without a government, and on September 29, 1906, Secretary Taft proclaimed the establishment of a provisional regime under his own direction.

The sole purpose of the provisional government was to restore order and hold elections, but this required more than two years. After the delicate task of disarming and disbanding the military forces of both parties had been completed, a census was taken, and an advisory commission headed by Colonel Enoch H. Crowder drafted laws covering elections, municipal and provincial government, the civil service, the judiciary, and other matters which should long since have been dealt with by the Cuban Congress. The commission's work met with general approval and was of real permanent value, but the provisional government was less fortunate in dealing with some of its other problems. Charles E. Magoon, who succeeded Taft as provisional Governor in October, 1906, had a number of American assistants, but the administration as a whole was still in the hands of the "moderate" officials who had served under Estrada Palma. This created a bad situation, which was little improved when the Governor, in accord with a promise made by Taft, filled vacancies as they arose with liberals recommended by a party committee. Playing politics did not make for efficiency or honesty in the administration as a whole, and the Governor was accused of permitting improper and extravagant expenditures, of pardoning great numbers of criminals for political reasons, and of undue generosity in awarding concessions and contracts. Competent historians have exonerated Magoon of the more serious of these charges, but the fact that they were made, and that many Cubans believed them, had an unfortunate effect on subsequent Cuban-American relations.

THE GÓMEZ AND MENOCAL ADMINISTRATIONS

Elections were held in 1908, under the supervision of a board headed by General Crowder, and in January, 1909, the liberal candidate, General José Miguel Gómez, took office as President. Under the new administration, Cuban political life took on some of the characteristics that were to distinguish it for a long period. Gómez differed from Estrada Palma in many ways. He was popular, astute, and unscrupulous, especially where money was involved, and he retained his followers' loyalty not only by his personal magnetism but by permitting them to profit by their party connections. There were many times after 1909 when Cuban politics seemed little more than a systematic effort to exploit the treasury for the benefit of the professional political class.

This situation was not peculiar to Cuba, but graft was possible there on a relatively larger scale because of the island's great wealth. By 1907 the sugar industry was reaping the full benefit of reciprocity with the United States, and trade was rapidly increasing. The Cuban government's income was correspondingly large. At a time when Mexico's revenues, in the prosperous years of the Díaz regime, were approximately $3.25 per capita, and Colombia's less than $3.75, Cuba, where geographical conditions favored economical administration and facilitated the construction of roads and public works, was collecting $14 or more per capita. Many of the higher officials, including especially members of Congress, had excessive salaries and allowances, and thousands of persons were carried on the payroll who did no work whatever for the government. The country's prosperity also opened up opportunities for illicit profit in the granting of all sorts of concessions, and the Gómez administration was involved in several highly questionable deals with foreign interests, some of them involving millions of dollars.

The United States made ineffective efforts to prevent some of these transactions, for President Taft and Secretary of State Knox believed that a timely discouragement of policies that might lead to insolvency and political disorder was better than armed intervention after a breakdown had occurred. This so-called "preventive policy" also led to interference in other matters. In 1913 the American legation successfully opposed the enactment of an "amnesty" bill which would have freed common criminals as well as political offenders, and on two occasions it felt compelled to make threats of intervention to discourage armed revolt.

The first of these was in 1911–1912 when an organization of veterans of the war of independence began to agitate for the removal of all officeholders who had been on the Spanish side in that struggle. The movement attracted support from many who were dissatisfied with Gómez' political and financial policies, and for a time civil war seemed possible. A warning from the United States, however, united both factions in opposition to outside interference, and the veterans and the President signed an agreement which ended the episode. The Negro revolt of 1912, instigated by colored politicians who claimed that their race had not received its fair share of government offices, was a more serious affair. There was some fighting and some destruction of Cuban and foreign property. The United States landed a force of marines and threatened further action, but order was fortunately restored within a few weeks.

When internal divisions had threatened to defeat the liberals in the election of 1908, Gómez, to obtain the support of the dissident faction, apparently promised that its leader, Alfredo Zayas, should be the official candidate in 1912. Friction between the two leaders continued, however, and though Zayas obtained the liberal nomination, in spite of the President's opposition, the government's attitude enabled the conservatives to win the election. General Mario García Menocal, who became President in May, 1913, had been educated in the United States and had worked for several years as a young man with American engineers in the Nicaraguan canal company. He had served brilliantly in the war for independence, rising from the ranks to a major generalcy, and had later been the successful manager of a great sugar plantation. Independently wealthy, he had no need to indulge in dishonest practices for his own benefit, but he did not attempt to check corruption among his subordinates. His first term was a period of increasing prosperity, for the war abroad cut off European supplies of beet sugar and encouraged a rapid increase in Cuban cane production. Nevertheless, the President did not achieve any great popularity, and as the election of 1916 approached it became evident that his candidacy for re-election would meet with obstacles.

Menocal, like Gómez, had pledged himself not to seek a second term, but he seems to have changed his mind under pressure from friends and family. He obtained the conservative nomination only with difficulty and by the use of questionable methods, and his chances for re-election were not improved when the liberals succeeded in composing their factional difficulties and united in supporting Alfredo Zayas. In the campaign that followed, and during the voting, workers on both sides endeavored to influence the outcome by violence and fraud. The number of votes cast greatly exceeded any possible estimate of the number of qualified electors. The liberals were not at too great a disadvantage because they controlled the police in several provinces and municipalities and because Menocal did not attempt to make full use of the government's power. On the face of the earlier returns the opposition seemed to have won. At this point, however, the government began to intercept and apparently to alter the reports coming in from the provinces. The liberals' protests were upheld by the Supreme Court, and it seemed possible that they might win; but before the electoral process was completed they revolted. If they hoped to bring about a repetition of the events of 1906 they were disappointed. A small force of American marines was landed in Oriente province, but only to protect foreign life and property. Instead of intervening, the United States issued public statements severely condemning the uprising, and its attitude was an important factor in the collapse of the revolt after a few weeks of fighting. Meanwhile the elections were completed, and Menocal began his second term as President.

THE "DANCE OF THE MILLIONS" AND THE CROWDER MISSION

On April 7, before the revolt was completely suppressed, Cuba followed the example of the United States in declaring war on Germany. The Republic's chief contribution to the allied cause was a further increase in the production of sugar and the sale of the 1917–1918 and 1918–1919 crops to an international committee at fixed prices, high enough to assure substantial profits to the growers but probably not so high as those they might have obtained in free trading. The expansion of the industry was aided by large investments of private American capital and by a $15,000,000 loan from the United States Treasury.

There was a tremendous expansion of business activity. The boom reached its peak after the war when governmental control of sugar sales ceased. In May, 1920, sugar prices rose to 22½ cents per pound at Cuban ports. Everyone felt rich, and there was a period of governmental and private extravagance which has since been called "the dance of the millions." Then, suddenly, the price of sugar fell, until it reached four cents in December, 1920. Prices of other merchandise had also fallen with the depression in other parts of the world, and importers and merchants as well as planters were hard hit. The banks, which had made excessive loans on the basis of high prices, were in even worse shape. To prevent complete collapse the government was compelled in October, 1920, to proclaim a moratorium which paralyzed business.

Meanwhile, a dispute over the presidential election threatened to lead to civil war. The United States attempted to prevent a repetition of the events of 1916–1917 by arranging to have General Crowder draw up a new electoral law and by sending observers to watch the voting, but the observers had no authority to prevent the violent and fraudulent practices that no mere changes in the law could abolish. Alfredo Zayas, whose "popular party" was now allied with the conservatives, apparently won by a narrow margin, but the liberals contested the result.

In an effort to help Cuba in one of the worst crises in her history, President Wilson sent General Crowder to the island as his personal representative in January, 1921. The two parties agreed that new elections should be held in a number of districts, but at the last minute Gómez, who was the liberal candidate, refused to participate and asked for a wholly new election under American control. Since the United States could not comply with this request, Zayas was inaugurated as President in May, 1921.

Crowder also endeavored to help the government with its economic problems. At his suggestion, the moratorium was gradually lifted, and business began to revive; but it was not possible to prevent the failure of every bank in the island except the branches of two foreign institutions. This made worse the government's already-bad financial situation. Menocal's second administration had been more extravagant and corrupt than any of its predecessors, and governmental expenditures had exceeded even the very large revenues of the war period. There was thus a considerable floating debt, which increased as income fell off without a corresponding reduction in expenditures.

Crowder persuaded Zayas to make great reductions in the budget and helped him to get a small emergency loan which met the government's most pressing needs. It was obvious that only a much larger loan could put the government on its feet, but the United States refused to approve this pending assurances that Zayas would remedy some of the bad practices which had grown up under his predecessors. Crowder demanded a long series of reforms, including the restriction of expenditures, the cancellation of illegal or improper contracts, and especially the reorganization of the national lottery, from which a great number of favored politicians were making illicit profits. After several months of negotiation, many of the measures he advocated were adopted, and the President, as an evidence of good faith, appointed a Cabinet that seemed to give assurance that the proposed reforms would be effective. In November, 1922, therefore, the United States gave its approval of the proposed $50,000,000 loan. Two months later Crowder's mission as personal representative of the President terminated, though he remained in Cuba as American Ambassador.

Zayas' interest in reform ceased when the money from the loan had been received. With loud assertions that Cuba would no longer tolerate foreign interference in her internal affairs, he dismissed the "honest Cabinet" and proceeded to undo most of its work. As the government's revenues increased, economy was forgotten, and the government was no less extravagant and corrupt than former administrations. Discontent with its policies found expression in a small revolt started by the "Veterans and Patriots' Association" in 1924, but this was easily suppressed.

THE MACHADO ADMINISTRATION, 1925–1933

In 1924 ex-President Menocal defeated Zayas for the conservative nomination, and the President avenged himself by supporting Gerardo Machado, the liberal candidate. The latter won easily, in an apparently fair election, and took office in May, 1925. Machado was a veteran of the war for independence and had been a successful businessman. During his first term things went fairly well. The sugar industry was already feeling the effects of world overproduction, but the flotation of large foreign loans for public works and the growth of the tourist trade, resulting partly from prohibition in the United States, helped to hide the fundamental unsoundness of the economic situation.

By a skillful distribution of offices and other favors, Machado persuaded all three party machines, the liberal, the conservative, and the popular, to nominate him for re-election in 1928. Changes in the electoral law which perpetuated the control of each party by a small group of men and the large "slush fund" provided by the national lottery helped to prevent any effective opposition. The lottery was still one of the great causes of corruption in Cuban politics, for the tickets were regularly sold on the streets for much more than their face value and the extra money went not to the government, which owned the enterprise, but to "collectors" who had the privilege of distributing stated quantities of tickets. It has been estimated that nearly a third of the $31,000,000 that the people of Cuba spent annually on the lottery represented illegal profits of this sort.[1] Before the election, a constitutional amendment provided that the presidential term should be six instead of four years.

These proceedings aroused much antagonism, and discontent increased as Cuba felt more and more severely the effects of the depression. Machado made matters worse by his increasingly dictatorial policy. He had trouble especially with the students of the University of Habana, who noisily opposed his re-election and continued their agitation during the next four years, even after many of them had been killed or imprisoned and the University had been closed. Other opposition groups became more active. After the army easily suppressed a small revolt in 1931, the discontented elements began a campaign of terrorism and sabotage which led to still more harshly repressive measures by the police. Murders and bombings and cruel official reprisals received much publicity in the United States and brought about a growing demand for

---

[1] Chapman, *History of the Cuban Republic*, pp. 555–556.

interference, voiced frequently by the same people who had criticized intervention in other Caribbean countries.

In June, 1933, most of the underground revolutionary groups agreed to accept the mediation of the American Ambassador, Sumner Welles, in an effort to restore order. They insisted, however, that Machado leave office, which he refused to do. Negotiations dragged on for some weeks until a general strike, which paralyzed commercial activity in Habana, and a bloody clash between the populace and the police brought matters to a head. On August 11, the army, which had been Machado's chief support, demanded his resignation. The next day he left the country.

REVOLUTIONARY GOVERNMENTS, 1933–1934

Machado's constitutional successor was Dr. Carlos Manuel de Céspedes, a generally esteemed former Ambassador at Washington, who seemed acceptable to some of the opposition political groups but had little popular following. From the start, the desperate economic situation, and particularly the situation in the sugar industry, made the new President's position all but hopeless. The output of sugar, about 1,000,000 long tons in the first years of independence and about 4,000,000 during the First World War, had reached 5,000,000 long tons by 1929. Too much production deprived Cuba of the benefit of the preferential duty under the reciprocity treaty of 1902 because competition among her producers tended to bring the price in the United States down to that of the world market. The world market price, meanwhile, was affected by expanding production in other countries, and during the depression Cuban mills were forced to suspend or curtail operations, or at least to cut wages. The government made several efforts from 1925 on to reduce production in the island and to reach agreements with other producing countries to fix quotas in the world market, but none of these were notably successful.

The discontent aroused by these conditions was directed largely against the foreign financial interests that controlled not only the sugar industry but also the railroads, the banks, and much of the country's commerce. Of these, North American interests were by far the most important. American investments in Cuba were estimated at from one to one and a half billions of dollars in 1928—an amount greater than that invested by United States citizens in any other foreign country except Canada and Germany—and approximately two-thirds of the sugar crop was ground at American mills. The actual growing of the cane remained to a greater extent in Cuban hands, but the *colonos*, as the farmers who produced it were called, had to sell their crops to the nearest *central* and were further dependent on the *central* for loans with which to carry on their operations. Foreign domination of the Republic's economic life was thus an important political issue, especially as Machado was accused of having unduly favored foreign interests. The principal revolutionary groups not only sought to destroy the evils of the traditional political system but also to do away with "economic imperialism," and they turned against de Céspedes when he did not support their ideas.

The university students had continued to act as a political group, although the university had been closed for some years and many of them were now mature men. On September 5, 1933, they joined with some of the noncommissioned officers in the army to stage a successful revolt. The military leader was Sergeant Fulgencio Batista, who persuaded the enlisted men to mutiny and seize the forts and barracks. Dr. Ramón Grau San Martín, a former dean of the medical school in the university, became provisional President.

The new government, weakened by dissensions among its student supporters, was unable to maintain order, and the dangerous attitude of the workmen in the sugar estates forced the United States to send warships to Cuban ports to protect American citizens. On October 2, Habana's largest hotel was the scene of a pitched battle between the soldiers and 500 of their former officers who had taken possession of the building. Batista, now holding the rank of Colonel, gradually restored discipline and efficiency in the armed forces, but terrorist outrages and attempted revolts continued. A series of strikes made the situation worse. As the cane-grinding season approached, it was evident that few mills would be able to operate unless conditions changed. Great numbers of men were already out of work—a worse catastrophe in Cuba than in most tropical countries because so much of the arable land was planted to sugar cane that the island depended largely on imported food, which unemployed men could not buy.

Confronted by the threat of complete economic disaster, Grau resigned in January, 1934, and soon afterward Carlos Mendieta, one of the few older political leaders who had consistently opposed Machado, became provisional President. The United States, which had withheld recognition from Grau, gave the new regime its full moral support. A $10,000,000 credit for the purchase of food helped to relieve suffering, and in March President Roosevelt set up the Second Export-Import Bank to promote trade between Cuba and the United States. A little later the Sugar Stabilization Act of 1934 gave Cuba a quota of nearly 2,000,000 short tons in the American market, with a reduction in duty which made possible the sale of a part of the Cuban crop at satisfactory prices. A new trade agreement helped other Cuban products.

Still more important, perhaps, at least psychologically, was the abrogation of the Platt Amendment by a treaty signed in May, 1934. The United States retained the naval station at Guantánamo but gave up any formal right to interfere in Cuba's internal affairs. The provisions of the Amendment had not been invoked for many years, but its abrogation ended a situation that was galling to Cuban pride.

THE FIRST PERIOD OF BATISTA'S DOMINANCE

Business began to revive, but political conditions improved more slowly. The older political parties and several new ones like the A.B.C., which was one of the secret anti-Machado organizations, were jockeying for advantage in the elections which would set up a permanent constitutional government. Some of them again began to resort to terrorism. The situation grew especially bad early in 1935 when there were several disorderly strikes and minor uprisings. Colonel Batista, however, was building the army into a more powerful force than it had ever been before, and he finally abandoned his hitherto rather tolerant policy and took severe measures which restored peace but left the country under military control.

Factional disagreements compelled the postponement of presidential elections until early in 1936. Meanwhile Mendieta had resigned in December, 1935, and had been succeeded by José Barnett. The more conservative factions, after much maneuvering, finally grouped themselves behind two principal candidates: Dr. Miguel Mariano Gómez, the son of José Miguel Gómez, and ex-President Menocal. The radical elements, driven underground by the army, were temporarily out of the picture. Gómez won by a large majority, and the coalition that supported him obtained 90 of 162 seats in the lower house of Congress and all of the seats in the Senate. Menocal, however, was won over to the support of the new regime by a constitutional amendment which increased the number of senators from 24 to 36 and enabled him to appoint his friends to the new positions. Gómez thus took office with the support of practically all of the old-line political elements.

The new President's authority was overshadowed by that of Colonel Batista, who was gradually extending his control over civilian as well as military affairs. While the politicians quarreled over jobs and personal political interests, the army, which was now consuming a very large proportion of the government's revenues, steadily increased its sphere of activity. In the summer of 1936 Batista announced a plan for a great system of primary schools under army control, and a few months later he came to an open break with Gómez when he asked Congress to impose a new tax for their support. In December, 1936, Congress passed the tax measure over the President's veto and then impeached and removed Gómez himself. Federico Laredo Bru was elected in his place.

The coalition which had backed the administration at the beginning of 1936 had by this time broken up. Gómez, Menocal, and Grau San Martín, now the principal radical leader, refused to permit their followers to participate in the congressional election of 1938, and their attitude made necessary several postponements of a projected election for an Assembly to revise the constitution. This was finally held, however, in November, 1939. Not only the recognized political parties, but the hitherto outlawed revolutionary and terrorist groups were allowed to vote, and the fairness of the election was indicated by the fact that the opposition factions won 41 out of the 76 seats. After the Assembly met, however, a deal between Batista and Menocal, who controlled one of the largest blocks of delegates, gave the two leaders control of the proceedings.

With the support of the same coalition, Batista defeated Grau San Martín in the presidential election of 1940. His government was one of the first to declare war on Japan and Germany after Pearl Harbor. During the war years the bulk of the sugar crop was sold to the government of the United States, and price controls prevented anything like the wild speculation that had led to disaster in 1920. The island suffered somewhat from shipping shortages and from inflation but on the whole was prosperous.

A SHORT PERIOD OF
REPUBLICAN GOVERNMENT

Batista not only refused to be a candidate to succeed himself in 1944 but held an election that was generally conceded to be one of the fairest in Cuba's history. The parties that supported his regime had some difficulty in picking a candidate but finally selected Carlos Saladrigas. The opposition groups nominated ex-President Ramón Grau San Martín, who was elected by a large majority. During the next four years there were many minor political disturbances and strikes, but there was more political freedom than the country had enjoyed for some time. Economic conditions were generally good. The President was unable to hold together the coalition that elected him, and for a time he seemed to be supported only by his own "revolutionary" party, the *auténticos*, and by the communists. He broke with the latter, however, when he helped a noncommunist group to obtain control of the Cuban labor confederation in 1947, and the more radical elements lined up against the administration in the presidential election of 1948. The administration candidate, Carlos Prío Socarrás, nevertheless defeated his three opponents in what appeared to be a reasonably free election. Prío's term was a period of prosperity but of even more wholesale and widespread governmental corruption than was customary in Cuba.

BATISTA AND CASTRO

Batista and Carlos Hevia, who had the Prío administration's support, were the principal candidates for the presidency for the following term, but in March, 1952, some weeks before the election was to take place, Batista seized control with the support of the army. Many Cubans were outraged by his action. The students especially opposed him, but when one of their leaders, named Fidel Castro, started a revolt in July, 1953, it was easily defeated. Batista ruled as dictator until November of the following year, when he held an election, in which opposition candidates had little chance, and became constitutional President. He continued in fact, however, to rule as a dictator, with the support of the army. There was much unrest and some disorder, but his government seemed firmly entrenched in power. Fidel Castro seemed to have little chance of success when he started a revolt in November, 1956, in the mountainous country in the eastern end of the island.

During the next two years, Castro, with a small band of youthful followers, successfully resisted the Cuban army's efforts to capture him. For a long time he seemed to have little active support from other opposition groups, and the outside world heard little about his campaign. In April, 1958, his effort to promote a general strike and uprising throughout Cuba was a complete failure, and his movement seemed to have lost much prestige. Two months later, however, he at least achieved more notoriety when his forces kidnaped 44 North Americans and Canadians and held them for some weeks, ostensibly as a protest against the United States government's alleged support of Batista. The United States, as a matter of fact, had not supported Batista and, in fact, had taken the unusual step of stopping the sale of arms to his government in an effort to make clear its neutral position.

By July, 1958, other opposition groups were joining the revolt, and there was fighting in several provinces in central and western Cuba. Batista, as the situation grew worse, became more brutal in his treatment of suspected opponents. At the same time, he went forward with plans for the presidential election which was held in November and resulted in the victory of the official candidate, Andrés Rivero Agüero, by an overwhelming majority. By this time, however, much of the country was in rebel hands, and in December, 1958, a rebel victory at Santa Clara made Batista's position hopeless. The dictator fled from Habana on January 1, and within a few days the revolution had complete control of the island.

It was soon clear that the new government would be unlike anything that Cuba had hitherto known. Manuel Urrutia Lleó, whom Castro had selected many months before for the position, became provisional President, but Castro himself was the supreme authority in the new government. At the age of 32, with little experience except in revolutionary fighting and with few associates who were older or more experienced, the new ruler of the Republic at once proclaimed a far-reaching, if vague, program of social and economic reform. His tremendous popularity and the ardent support of his followers in the revolutionary army gave him virtually unlimited power. Public opinion abroad was shocked when the revolutionists, with little pretense of fair trials, executed several hundred of Batista's supporters on charges of war crimes and brutality to political prisoners. Other measures, like the confiscation of the property of great numbers of persons who had not supported the revolution, disrupted the country's economic life. Within a few months, attacks on the freedom of the press and the independent radio stations and the arrest of persons who criticized the government led many to feel that the new regime was hardly less dictatorial than Batista's.

The new regime's foreign policies also disturbed many persons who had sympathized with the revolutionists in their struggle against Batista. As we shall see in a later chapter, filibustering expeditions from Cuba attacked several other Caribbean republics and created tension throughout the Caribbean.[2] More serious still was Castro's aggressive hostility toward the United States. When the new regime inaugurated an agrarian reform, the American government expressed sympathy with its purpose, but protested when the property of American citizens was seized without adequate compensation. Castro reacted violently, and was equally intemperate in his complaints about the incursions of small private planes which evaded the vigilance of the authorities in Florida and allegedly dropped bombs or set fire to cane fields in Cuba.

It had been reported during the revolution that some of Castro's principal lieutenants were communists or communist sympathizers, and Castro announced soon after he came into power that Cuba would be neutral as between Russia and the United States. During 1959 many officials who opposed the increase of communist influence were eliminated from the government. President Urrutia Lleó was replaced by Osvaldo Dorticós. Reputed communists assumed greater and greater control over all phases of the country's economic life. In February, 1960, when the First Deputy Soviet Premier Anastas Mikoyan visited Habana, it was announced that Russia would lend Cuba $100,000,000 and would buy 5,000,000 tons of Cuban sugar in the next five years. There was further evidence of increasingly closer relations with the communist countries in the months that followed, and at the same time Castro became more abusive in his public statements about the United States.

[2] See below, pp. 516–7.

CHAPTER 24

Haiti

SAINT DOMINGUE UNDER FRENCH RULE

THE WESTERN end of Hispaniola is one of the most mountainous parts of the West Indies. Three great ranges, their slopes in many places too steep or too stony for cultivation, traverse the country from east to west, leaving only a few areas of flat land along the coast and in the river valleys between them. Even in the plains there are large sections where the rainfall, cut off by the mountains, is inadequate or irregular. Where agriculture can be carried on, however, the soil is rich, and the climate, though hot, is not unpleasant.

The French settlers who occupied the country in the days of the buccaneers turned their attention to planting as piracy was gradually suppressed. The colony flourished during the eighteenth century, and by 1789 Saint Domingue was supplying much of the world's sugar and most of the world's coffee.[1] Despite its small area, it was by far the most valuable of France's overseas possessions, with exports which exceeded in value those of the United States. The richest district was the Province of the North, and especially the plain behind Cap François, now called Cape Haitian, which was the principal city. The Province of the West, including the Artibonite Valley and the Cul de Sac near Port au Prince, had been settled more recently but had made rapid progress with the construction of extensive irrigation works. So also had the isolated southern peninsula, the Province of the South.

The wealth of the colony was divided among a very few people. Some 450,000 out of a total population of 520,000 were slaves, whose lot was if anything harder than that of the plantation laborers in the other West Indian colonies because the overwhelming preponderance of the Negroes made constant vigilance and strict control imperative. Some 27,500 more

---

[1] Von Humboldt, *Essai Politique sur le Royaume de la Nouvelle Espagne*, Vol. III, p. 193, footnote.

were colored freedmen, some of them black, the majority of mixed blood. Many of the mulattoes, especially in the newer regions of the west and south owned property and slaves, but they were all subject by law and custom to humiliating regulations and discriminations enforced by the whites who hated and feared their growing influence. The 39,000 whites [2] were themselves divided into mutually hostile groups: officials sent out from France, wealthy creole planters, and *petits blancs* or poor whites.

THE REVOLUTION

The revolution in France in 1789 weakened the home government's authority which had hitherto kept these class and race hatreds under restraint. The creoles seized control, through assemblies that they elected in each province, and dissensions between planters and poor whites and between royalists and democrats kept the country in turmoil. Matters became worse when the mulattoes, with the support of sympathizers in the National Assembly in Paris, began to demand political and social equality. A freedmen's revolt in the north, led by Vincent Ogé, was cruelly suppressed in 1790; but in 1791 the mulattoes of the Artibonite Valley and the Cul de Sac joined with the still-numerous royalist faction among the whites in another outbreak, and at almost the same time, in August, 1791, the Negro slaves of the northern plain revolted, massacring the whites on the plantations and destroying dwellings and sugar mills in an outburst of savage fury. Thereafter the Negro hordes held the rural districts in the north, while mulattoes and whites waged a confused struggle for dominance around Port au Prince. Only in the southern peninsula did the planters retain control.

Meanwhile the National Assembly in France was following a vacillating policy which made matters worse rather than better. Three Commissioners sent to Saint Domingue in 1791 failed to restore peace. After the radicals came into power at Paris the position of the planters seemed hopeless. The National Assembly ordered that mulattoes and free Negroes should have the same political rights as whites, and in 1792 a new commission was sent to the colony with 6,000 troops. Its most active member, Sonthonax, first alienated all classes of the white population by consorting with the mulattoes and then lost the support of that group by his open sympathy with the blacks. In June, 1793, when the whites at Cap François resisted his authority, he permitted the rebel Negroes to loot and burn the city. A few months later he and his colleagues further infuriated the whites and mulattoes by proclaiming the abolition of slavery.

[2] These are the figures given by Moreau de Saint-Méry whose *Description Topographique, Physique, Politique et Historique de la Partie Française de Saint-Domingue* is the best description of the colony before the revolution.

TOUSSAINT LOUVERTURE

By this time France was at war with England and Spain. English troops, at the invitation of the white planters in the south, occupied Port au Prince and other points on the coast in 1793 and 1794, and Spanish troops from the neighboring colony of Santo Domingo overran the north, obtaining help from several of the Negro chieftains. The two powers might well have restored European control had it not been for Toussaint Louverture.

François Dominique Toussaint, who later took the surname "Louverture," was a full-blooded Negro born in Saint Domingue. Serving his master as a coachman, he seems to have picked up a little knowledge of reading and writing, a rare accomplishment among the slaves. He was one of the principal leaders among the revolted Negroes, and the 4,000 men under his command were the best-trained black troops in the island. He joined forces with the Spaniards in 1793, but a year later, when it seemed possible that the British invaders might restore slavery, he decided to throw his support to France. His desertion forced the Spanish to withdraw, and he soon ruled the northern part of the colony. Meanwhile the mulatto General André Rigaud had obtained control of most of the southern peninsula, and the British, with their ranks depleted by yellow fever, found it more and more difficult to maintain their position at Port au Prince. They finally signed an agreement with Toussaint in 1798 under which they withdrew their forces from the island.

A sanguinary struggle ensued between blacks and mulattoes. Toussaint put down mulatto uprisings in the north and then attacked Rigaud. He had by this time entered into commercial agreements with Great Britain and the United States, and warships of both of these powers helped him defeat his rival. By 1800 he had control of the south, and his lieutenant, Dessalines, followed up the victory by systematically murdering some 10,000 persons of mixed blood. Toussaint next proceeded to conquer the Spanish end of the island, which had been ceded to France by the Treaty of Basel in 1795 but had not yet been actually transferred. Early in 1801 he was master of all Hispaniola.

While still maintaining an outward allegiance to France, Toussaint now assumed the title of Governor General for life, with power to name his own successor. Many white proprietors were encouraged to resume possession of their estates, upon which the former slaves were compelled to work under military control, and other properties were cultivated for the benefit of the new government and its officials. For a brief period the colony was again fairly prosperous.

The French government, beset by enemies in Europe, had been in no position since 1793 to reassert its authority in Saint Domingue, and the emissaries whom it sent to the island were intimidated or outwitted by the resourceful Toussaint. With the peace of Amiens, however, the situation changed, and in December, 1801, Napoleon's brother-in-law General Leclerc sailed from France with 20,000 veteran troops. Leclerc's instructions were to pursue a conciliatory policy until he felt strong enough to remove the black generals and exile them to France, but he met with more resistance than was anticipated. Henry Christophe, Toussaint's lieutenant at Cap François, burned that city before abandoning it. In the interior the Negroes carried on a guerrilla warfare which culminated in the epic defense of the fortress of Crête-à-Pierrot, which the French took only after heavy losses. Toussaint and his followers finally submitted in April and May, 1802, but were able to stipulate that they should retain their rank and their commands in the army.

THE END OF FRENCH RULE

Leclerc had barely achieved this rather doubtful victory when an epidemic of yellow fever attacked his European troops. Within a few months his army was virtually destroyed, and reinforcements sent from France suffered the same fate. Stupid acts of the French authorities had meanwhile united the Haitians against them. The mulattoes were infuriated by the restoration of the discriminations against them, and the Negroes by the restoration of slavery in the nearby islands of Guadeloupe and Martinique and the abrogation of prohibitions against the slave trade in the French colonies generally. Toussaint had been treacherously arrested and sent to France soon after his capitulation, to die in prison a year later, but several of his former lieutenants were still in command of trained troops. When the mulatto leaders Pétion and Clervaux deserted the French army and took to the hills in October, 1802, Dessalines and Christophe, the principal black generals, followed their example.

Only a fraction of the French troops were alive and fit for duty, but their health improved somewhat with the coming of the dry season. General Rochambeau, who took command after Leclerc died of the fever in November, was able to take the offensive. The struggle was now a war of extermination, and each side vied with the other in wholesale atrocities. The outcome was still in doubt when the renewal of hostilities between France and England in May, 1803, and the restoration of the British blockade made the position of the French army hopeless. In November Rochambeau surrendered to a British Admiral. On January 1, 1804, Jean Jacques Dessalines, the leader of the rebel army, proclaimed the independence of Haiti, the first free nation in Latin America. The territory of the new Republic included only the western end of Hispaniola, for French forces, and later Spanish forces, remained in control in the east.

DESSALINES, CHRISTOPHE, AND PÉTION

Dessalines at first took the title of Governor General, but in September, 1804, in imitation of Napoleon, he had himself proclaimed Emperor. The former slave of a free Negro, entirely without education, the new ruler's chief qualifications for office were the courage and ferocity which had won him his position in the army. His administration was a military despotism, in which even the direction of agriculture—somewhat revived as in the days of Toussaint by forced labor—was in the hands of the army. British and American merchants were encouraged to resume trade, but the Frenchmen who remained in the island, except for a few priests, physicians, and skilled artisans, were systematically murdered. The corruption and brutality of the regime caused much discontent. The mulattoes especially were restive under black rule, and when the Emperor arbitrarily deprived many colored planters of their lands a revolt spread through the west and south. Dessalines marched against the rebels, but in October, 1806, he was killed in an ambush in the outskirts of Port au Prince.

Henry Christophe, Dessalines' chief lieutenant, was accepted by both factions as the head of a provisional administration pending the meeting of a Constituent Assembly. As the principal surviving hero of the war against the French, and the Commander of the best military forces, Christophe expected as a matter of course to dominate the Assembly, but he had not counted on the ingenuity of the mulatto leaders who now controlled the west and the south. By the simple expedient of creating new parishes, each of which had a right to representation, these obtained a majority in the Assembly and proceeded to draw up a constitution which gave all real authority in the new government to an elected Senate. They offered Christophe the presidency, but he refused it and attacked Port au Prince, where the Assembly was sitting. He was repulsed, and from 1807 until 1820 the country was divided into the "State of Haiti" under his rule and the "Republic of Haiti" controlled by the mulattoes.

The State of Haiti, which included the north and the Artibonite Valley, was a well-organized military dictatorship. Christophe was at first President for life, but in 1811 he made himself King and created a numerous nobility. His reign is perhaps the most picturesque episode in Haiti's eventful history. A native of one of the British West Indies, with some white blood,[3] he had served while still a slave as a waiter in a hotel and as a privateersman, and he is said to have taken part in the French expedition against Savannah during the American Revolution. He spoke English as well as French and had a predilection for things English. Though uneducated, he was intelligent and showed much administrative ability. He made some effort to establish schools and other appurtenances of civ-

[3] Mackenzie, *Notes on Haiti*, Vol. I, p. 159.

ilization, and foreign merchants were encouraged to visit Haitian ports, though they could trade only with a royal monopoly. Henry's system of government, however, bore heavily on the masses of the inhabitants, and he grew more despotic toward the end of his reign. The building of the great citadel of Laferrière is said to have cost many lives. Public works of this sort and also the ordinary work in the fields were carried on under a system little better than slavery, and the peasant masses were cruelly exploited for the benefit of the royal treasury and the military caste. Christophe maintained his power chiefly by the fear that he inspired in his subordinates; and when he had a paralytic stroke in 1820 his followers began to abandon him, and he killed himself rather than fall helpless into their hands.

In the south, in the Republic of Haiti, the mulattoes retained control. Alexandre Pétion, elected President early in 1807, was the freeborn son of a white Frenchman and a colored woman, better educated than most of his compatriots, and perhaps the most influential member of his caste. He had fled to France after Toussaint's victory over Rigaud and returned as an officer under Leclerc. When it became clear that the French would restore slavery and the color line, he left them and became Dessalines' chief lieutenant in the final struggle for independence. Though chosen under the same constitution that Christophe had rejected, he soon rid himself of the Senate and ruled practically as a dictator. He was re-elected in 1811 and 1815 and became President for life in 1816. His regime was milder but also less efficient than that of Christophe. He did not attempt, and probably did not dare, to subject the peasants to forced labor, and it was perhaps the contrast between their relatively easy existence and the harder lot of their brothers in the north that induced the Negro masses to remain quiet under mulatto domination.

An indecisive war between the two sections began in 1807 and continued for several years. Both Christophe and Pétion supported rebellions in the other's territory, and the situation grew more complicated when Rigaud returned to Haiti in 1810 and set up an independent state in the southern peninsula. Rigaud soon died, however, and his successor, General Borgella, reincorporated the south into the Republic in order to present a common front against a formidable attack launched by Christophe in 1812. The attack was repulsed, and hostilities were thereafter suspended, though without a formal truce.

BOYER

When Pétion died in 1818 the Senate, under pressure from the army, chose Jean Pierre Boyer, the chief of the presidential guard, as his successor. Boyer was a free-born mulatto who had had some education abroad and had served for a time in the French army. Able and honest, he proved to be one of Haiti's best presidents. In 1820, when Christophe killed himself, Boyer took advantage of the ensuing confusion to occupy Cape Haitian before the northern generals could concert measures to oppose him, and the two sections were thenceforth united under one government, with the Capital at Port au Prince. Two years later, when the inhabitants of Santo Domingo revolted against Spain, Boyer occupied their territory, bringing the whole island under Haitian rule. He maintained his authority with a firm hand for a quarter-century, suppressing occasional minor revolts but on the whole giving the country an era of peace that was welcome after 30 years of almost continuous bloodshed.

The mulattoes, who controlled the government under Pétion and Boyer, were practically the only people in Haiti who had even a vague understanding of political problems, but their position was a precarious one. Their numbers had been greatly reduced by the wholesale massacres during the revolution, and the Negro peasants, who remembered that the freedmen had also been slaveholders, hated and distrusted them almost as much as they had the whites. The mulattoes, on their side, looked down on the peasants as an inferior race. They even drew a color line socially against the relatively small number of educated Negroes and the black officers in the army, though they found it politically advisable to give many of the higher offices to members of both of these groups. In the north, in fact, the Negro element remained predominant in politics, with the result that the rivalry between the two races tended to take on a sectional character.

There was a great gulf between the *élite*, as the mulatto aristocracy called itself, and the masses of the people. The members of the *élite* spoke French, and many of them had some education, either in France or at home, which made them familiar with European ideas and ways of living. The culture of the masses, on the other hand, was essentially African. Only one-third of the slaves in the colony in 1789 had been born there. The rest had been imported, most of them as adults, from various sections of the dark continent. Nearly all spoke the creole patois, based on French but African in structure, but they had otherwise learned little from contact with their white masters. The Church, which had little influence among the French planters, had had even less among the slaves, and most of them were votaries of *voudou*, a mixture of African superstitions and Christianity which is still the religion of most of the Haitian peasants.

By 1820 little remained of the rich plantations of the colonial period. Sugar mills and other buildings had been burned or torn down during the first slave revolt, and irrigation systems had been allowed to fall into disrepair. The lands confiscated from French proprietors were generally treated as public domain. Some were given to military officers as a reward for service in the revolution, some recognized as the property of the mulatto sons of former owners, and some rented to persons who attempted to farm them with the labor of the former slaves. The latter were forbidden by law to leave the *habitation* to which they were attached, but this and other provisions of the labor code were less rigidly enforced after 1820 because Boyer, like Pétion, hardly dared to jeopardize his position by oppressing the black masses. Large-scale agriculture was consequently practically abandoned. The peasants grew food for their own use on lands which they rented or occupied as squatters, and coffee, which they could pick from the trees on the abandoned plantations, took the place of sugar as the chief export. The *élite*, more and more divorced from any connection with agriculture, devoted themselves principally to politics. They had little interest in the welfare of the black masses or the development of the country, and little money was spent on schools or roads. The public treasury, in their eyes, existed to provide a living for their class.

The prosperity of the French colony was a thing of the past, but the Haitians had their freedom. The peasants no longer worked under the lash, and the *élite* were masters in their own house, free from humiliating discrimination on account of their race. All classes were determined to prevent the return of white domination in any form. African blood or marriage to a Haitian was a requisite for citizenship. White foreigners were looked on with suspicion, and the constitution forbade aliens to own land.

For many years after 1804, the Haitians lived in fear of an attack from abroad. The new Republic had few friends, for none of the great powers were disposed to enter into diplomatic relations with a government which owed its origin to a successful slave revolt. The immediate danger, of course, was from France. Immediately after the Bourbon restoration, Louis XVIII sent unofficial representatives to seek to persuade the Haitians to acknowledge French sovereignty, but the representatives were rebuffed. Later, the Haitian government indicated a willingness to pay an indemnity for the confiscated French properties in return for a recognition of independence, and negotiations were carried on for some years in an effort to reach an agreement on this basis. In 1825, when a French fleet appeared at Port au Prince, Boyer was finally forced to accept an offensively worded royal ordinance which granted independence on condition that French trade be given preferential treatment and that Haiti pay an indemnity of $30,000,000 in five years. Only a small part of this sum was ever remitted, but efforts to meet the payments and disputes with France because the government was unable to do so caused trouble for many years. $30,000,000 was a staggering sum for a country where the vast majority of the people never saw more than a few dollars in cash in the course of a year.

FROM BOYER TO SOULOUQUE, 1843-1870

Boyer's government was described by a foreign observer as "a sort of republican monarchy, sustained by the bayonet." The Congress, chosen by a very limited franchise and with much official intervention, could only consider laws which the President saw fit to introduce. During its session of 1833, its most important act was to expel two members "for systematically opposing the measures of the executive, and persisting in demanding a statement of the public expenditures."[4] Nevertheless there was little opposition during the first 20 years of Boyer's rule. Toward the end of this period, some of the younger members of the *élite* began to agitate for a more democratic form of government, and in 1843 they started a revolution in the southern peninsula. Boyer was defeated and fled to Jamaica.

The "liberals," as the revolutionists called themselves, set up a new government under Charles Rivière Hérard and drew up a new constitution, but the effort to introduce more democratic practices simply led to quarrels and confusion. The new administration's evident weakness encouraged the Spanish-speaking inhabitants of the eastern end of the island to revolt, and in February, 1844, the Dominican Republic declared its independence. Hérard's effort to reconquer the Dominicans collapsed when he was confronted by a peasant revolt instigated by the Salomon family in the southern peninsula; and though the peasants were defeated, the specter of a new race war so terrified the *élite* that some of Boyer's former associates were able to oust the liberal regime in May, 1844.

To allay the growing discontent among the blacks, the group that came to power decided to make a Negro general the nominal head of the government. Their first choice was Philippe Guerrier, an illiterate veteran of the war for independence, eighty-seven years old, but still influential among the people of his own race and especially in the north, where there was always hostility to any mulatto regime at Port au Prince. When Guerrier died after a few months in office, he was succeeded by another octogenarian, a brother-in-law of Christophe named Jean-Louis Pierrot, who dismayed his sponsors by suddenly moving the Capital to Cape Haitian. He was promptly removed with the help of the army, and still another aged general, Jean Baptiste Riché, became President in 1846.

When Riché died a year later the mulatto statesmen who controlled the government made a mistake. They had some difficulty in agreeing upon a successor but finally chose a captain in the palace guard named Soulouque, whose ignorance and stupidity seemed to assure his being a pliant instrument in their hands. The new President had not been active in politics, and it was difficult to persuade him that his election was not

[4] The quotations are from Brown, *The History and Present Condition of St. Domingo,* Vol. II, pp. 259, 260.

a joke. Once in office, however, he resented the condescension of his *élite* advisers and soon broke with them. When they conspired to regain power, he encouraged mobs to attack all of the mulattoes and to kill great numbers of them. Meanwhile, he attempted to reconquer the Dominican Republic but desisted when England, France, and the United States made strong diplomatic representations. In 1849 he made himself Emperor of Haiti, as Faustin I, and created a peerage that included four princes, fifty-nine dukes, ninety-nine counts, and a host of lesser nobility. In 1851 a Special Agent of the United States reported that he was beginning to learn to read and write, though he still spoke little French.[5]

Soulouque was overthrown in 1859 by Fabre Geffrard, the head of his general staff, who revolted when he learned that the Emperor suspected him of disloyalty. The new President, a dark mulatto, attempted with some success to win support in both of the country's racial groups. His most important act was the conclusion of a concordat with the Holy See in 1860. Until this time, Haiti had had no recognized bishops, and the relatively few churches had been served in many cases by priests whose antecedents and character would not bear investigation. The establishment of a regular priesthood, recruited in France, did much to bring the *élite* into closer touch with European civilization, even though it was not possible to establish many churches in the country districts. One noteworthy consequence was the establishment of schools by several religious orders. Public instruction, even in the towns, had hitherto been almost completely neglected.

In 1862 the Haitian government was formally recognized by the United States. The establishment of diplomatic relations had been impossible before the American Civil War because of the opposition of proslavery groups in Congress.

Geffrard had many enemies, and there were frequent revolts, followed by numerous executions. The President's prestige suffered when he attempted, unsuccessfully, to have the constitution amended to permit foreigners to own land, and he also lost support when British warships, in retaliation for an insurgent attack on the British consulate at Cape Haitian, helped to suppress an uprising led by Sylvain Salnave in 1865. In 1867 a new revolt was successful.

A mulatto liberal group, which had taken part in the revolt, expected to control the new government, but when a Constituent Assembly met to choose a president, military demonstrations and threats of mob violence compelled it to elect Salnave. The new government soon became more despotic than its predecessor. The Congress was arbitrarily dissolved and several political opponents were put to death. The liberals revolted and were supported by the leaders of the *cacos*, turbulent peasants from the districts along the northern part of the Dominican border

---

[5] 32nd Cong., 1st Sess., Sen. Exec. Doc. 113, p. 10.

who were to play an increasingly important rôle in Haitian politics as time went on. Salnave, on his side, sought help from the *piquets*—country people of the south—and for more than two years the country endured one of the worst civil wars in its history. The final outcome was the overthrow and execution of Salnave and the victory of the liberals.

LIBERALISM AND REACTION, 1870–1908

The liberals were in power during the greater part of the next nine years. Nissage-Saget, whom they made President in 1870, was an elderly gentleman whose faculties are said to have been somewhat impaired by eight years of imprisonment under Soulouque. He was hampered by factious opposition in Congress, fomented by the rival liberal leader Boyer-Bazelais, but he refused to coerce the legislative body, saying, with a rare understanding of constitutional principles, that "each ass should bray in his own pasture." [6] Some of his advisers, however, were less tolerant, and as the end of his term approached they removed him, installed a new and more subservient Congress, and brought about the election of Michel Domingue, the commander of the army.

The new President was an African-born Negro, without education, and with an unpleasant reputation for cruelty. In political matters he was under the influence of his better-educated but unscrupulous and erratic nephew Septimus Rameau. The murder of several political adversaries and the flotation of a loan in France, on very unfavorable terms, made the administration unpopular; and in 1876, when it was reported that the government was to be removed to Cayes, an infuriated mob killed Rameau and forced Domingue to flee.

Domingue's successor, Boisrond-Canal, was one of the ablest of the liberal leaders. He made a real effort to restore constitutional government, but continued quarrels within the liberal party paralyzed Congress and finally made the President's position so intolerable that he resigned in 1879. His withdrawal left the country in disorder, and a weak provisional government was easily overthrown when Lysius Salomon, the chief adviser of Soulouque, returned from exile to seize power. This marked the end, for a long period, of the political power of the mulatto aristocracy of Port au Prince. Many of the *élite* continued to hold important positions in the government, but the rulers of the country, until the American intervention in 1915, were a series of military leaders, most of them from other sections of the Republic.

Salomon, with his great influence among the peasants of the southern peninsula, had been the most feared opponent of successive Haitian governments since the fall of Faustin I. As leader of the black party, he was disliked and distrusted by the *élite*; but he was as well educated as

[6] Dorsainville, *Manuel d'Histoire d'Haiti*, p. 312.

most Haitians of the upper class, and he had shown ability in important governmental positions under Riché and Soulouque. He had lived in Europe and was married to a white French woman. The understanding of political and economic problems obtained during his long exile showed itself in an energetic and progressive policy when he came to power. He established a national bank, tried to encourage agriculture, and engaged French instructors for the higher schools and for the army. At the same time he was ruthless in his treatment of his liberal opponents, and on one occasion he is said to have encouraged the mob to sack the better residential quarters of Port au Prince in retaliation for the *élite's* opposition to his government. The liberals were almost constantly in revolt until the death of Boyer-Bazelais in 1883, but thereafter they ceased to be an important political force.

Salomon was "re-elected" in 1886, but he was overthrown two years later. After some months of civil war between the north and the south, the northern general Florville Hyppolite became President in 1889. One of the principal events of his administration was a flurry of excitement over an unsuccessful effort by the United States to lease the Mole St. Nicholas, which Hyppolite had apparently promised to cede for a coaling station in return for assistance from the American navy during his struggle for power. During the term of Tiresias Simon Sam, who became President after Hyppolite died suddenly of heart failure in 1896, there was another incident involving a foreign power. This was the "Luders Affair," when two German war vessels appeared at Port au Prince to compel the payment of a large indemnity to a German who had been imprisoned for a short time for resisting the local police.

Antenor Firmin, the most influential member of the Cabinet, expected to succeed Sam, but other leaders opposed him. During the civil war that ensued, Firmin's warship, the *Crête-à-Pierrot*, seized a shipment of arms which a German merchant ship was carrying to his adversaries. The German cruiser *Panther* was ordered to capture her, but Admiral Killick, the Commander of the *Crête-à-Pierrot*, sent his crew ashore and blew up his ship. This caused Firmin's defeat, and in December, 1902, a victorious army compelled the Congress to elect his rival, a general from the north named Nord Alexis, as President.

Though an uneducated soldier, already more than eighty years old, Nord Alexis was an able ruler. One of his first acts was to prosecute the leading men in the preceding government and several foreign officials of the National Bank for frauds in connection with the consolidation of the floating debt. Simon Sam and several of his ministers were convicted. None of them, however, seem to have been punished, and it is interesting to note that three of those found guilty later served as presidents of the Republic. The National Bank, which had been established under French management in 1881, had been implicated in other scandalous transactions at the expense of the national treasury, and its charter was now revoked.

From the accession of Salomon in 1879 until the end of Nord Alexis' administration in 1908 Haiti enjoyed a relatively stable government. High coffee prices made the country prosperous, and ample revenues strengthened the government's position. Unfortunately there was little real progress. A succession of dictators maintained order, but they did little to relieve the poverty and ignorance of the masses of the people. Public funds were still spent solely for the benefit of the ruling class. Despite increased income the government's finances were in bad shape, for corruption pervaded all departments and continual deficits were met by borrowing or by issues of paper or nickel fiat currency. The fundamental unsoundness of the political structure was to become evident in the next few years.

THE "EPHEMERAL GOVERNMENTS"

Antoine Simon, a soldier of humble origin, led a revolution that compelled Nord Alexis to flee to Jamaica in 1908. The new President, a southerner, was unpopular in the north and at Port au Prince. He was violently criticized when he contracted a large external loan in 1910, and the ever-present fear of foreign influence was further aroused by contracts with an American promoter for a railroad and for the development of a banana industry. It was not difficult, therefore, for Cincinnatus Leconte to march down from the north and seize Port au Prince with a *caco* army in August, 1911, and the Congress, as usual, did not dare to refuse to elect the leader of the victorious revolutionists as President.

During the next four years Haiti had six presidents, serving for periods which grew shorter and shorter. Leconte, before he had been in office for 12 months, was killed with 300 soldiers of his guard by an explosion in the national palace. Tancrède Auguste, hastily elected by the Congress to succeed him, died after eight months in office. He had not been buried when street fighting broke out between rival military leaders who sought to surround the meeting place of Congress to dictate the choice of his successor. The victor, a popular lawyer named Michel Oreste, was in office eight months before a revolt in the north led by Davilmar Théodore forced him to flee to Jamaica. Théodore had not even reached Port au Prince when he was defeated in February, 1914, by Oreste Zamor. In October, Théodore overthrew Zamor, only to be overthrown himself five months later by Vilbrun Guillaume Sam. Each revolution in turn was the work of the mercenary *caco* bands from the north, who barely installed one man in power and were paid for their services before they sold their support to another. Guillaume Sam was ousted on July 27, 1915, when his *caco* troops deserted him just as they had deserted his predecessors.

On the same night, 167 political suspects, many of them members of prominent families in Port au Prince, were slaughtered in cold blood in prison by Sam's lieutenants. The people of the city learned of the massacre the next day, and an enraged mob of the victims' friends and relatives dragged the ex-President from the French legation where he had taken refuge and tore him to pieces in the streets. The Capital was still in a state of anarchy a few hours later when Admiral Caperton entered the harbor with the U.S.S. *Washington* and landed forces to restore order. This was the beginning of an American military occupation that lasted 16 years.

THE AMERICAN OCCUPATION

Continual disorder and administrative inefficiency had involved Haiti in more and more serious complications with other governments. Between 1911 and 1915, French, German, British, and American armed forces had repeatedly been landed to protect foreign life and property, and claims for losses or injuries to foreign nationals, some of them well-founded and some fictitious, had assumed alarming proportions. Certain European governments, moreover, had shown what seemed to the government at Washington an unwholesome interest in Haitian affairs. French cultural influences were predominant among the *élite*, and French bankers had supplied the greater part of the loans that constituted the Republic's foreign debt. German merchants, on the other hand, controlled the Republic's trade, and they had been active during the past few years in financing revolutionary movements, buying at a fraction of their face value revolutionary bond issues which were afterward assumed as obligations of the state. Both France and Germany had served notice that they would wish to participate in any foreign financial control which might be established in Haiti, and Germany was believed to desire to obtain control of the Mole St. Nicholas as a coaling station. The outbreak of the First World War eliminated any danger of European interference in Haiti for the time being, but the United States wished to guard against the possibility of future interference.

Furthermore, American interests in the island had suffered from the turbulent conditions there and had repeatedly appealed to Washington for diplomatic support. The most important of these interests were the National Railroad Company, which was endeavoring to build a line from Port au Prince to Cape Haitian under government subsidy, and the American shareholders in the National Bank, which had been re-established in 1910 with French, German, and American capital. The bank played an especially important rôle in the events which led up to the intervention. Under its charter it was the treasury of the Haitian government, receiving all revenues and paying over to the government's creditors the proceeds of the taxes which were pledged to them—an arrangement which had assured interest payments on the foreign debt even when political conditions were most disturbed. The bank had also regularly advanced money to the government for current expenses. In 1914, however, it refused to continue these advances, and the government retaliated by taking the treasury service out of its hands. This made a default on the foreign debt unavoidable, and for some time before the intervention finally occurred the United States had been endeavoring without success to persuade successive revolutionary governments to accept American financial control.

With its forces in possession of Port au Prince, the American government embarked on a more ambitious program. The Congress, protected by American troops, was persuaded to elect a new President, Sudre Dartiguenave, who gave assurances in advance that he would accede to the wishes of the United States. A treaty was signed on September 16, 1915, under which the United States was to "aid the Haitian Government in the proper and efficient development of its agricultural, mineral, and commercial resources and in the establishment of the finances of Haiti on a firm and solid basis." A General Receiver of Customs and a Financial Adviser, both appointed upon the nomination of the President of the United States, were to control the financial administration. A constabulary, officered by Americans similarly appointed, was to assume the maintenance of order, and American engineers were to direct measures for "sanitation and public improvement." In general, the United States was to "lend an efficient aid for the preservation of Haitian Independence and the maintenance of a government adequate for the protection of life, property and individual liberty." The treaty was to be in force for 10 years, but in 1917 this period was extended by agreement to 20 years. American marines had meanwhile been landed at several ports, and a technical state of military occupation was established throughout the Republic. The control of the United States was made still more effective by two agreements signed in 1918: one providing that the American legation should be consulted before any project of law was submitted to the legislative body, and the other giving the financial adviser a veto over all expenditures.

The first years of the occupation were troubled ones. There was much friction between the treaty officials and the Haitian government, and a bitter dispute with the Haitian Congress over the adoption of a new constitution, written, in part, by officials at Washington. After President Dartiguenave dissolved the Congress, with the support of the American-officered constabulary, the constitution was adopted by "plebiscite" in 1918. One of the provisions insisted upon by the United States was a change in the article prohibiting foreign landownership. These events increased the discontent already existing among the *élite*. At the same time the new constabulary officers provoked much hostility among the peasants by blunders and abuses in the enforcement of the *corvée*, the system of compulsory labor on the roads. The result was a revolt of the *cacos* in the north and west, which continued for two years and cost nearly 2,000 lives before it was finally suppressed by American marines.

The painful impression caused by this revolt and the realization that little of real value had thus far been accomplished led to a reorganization of the American treaty organization in 1922. Brigadier General John H. Russell of the United States Marine Corps was appointed High Commissioner, to act as diplomatic representative of the United States and at the same time to supervise and direct the work of the treaty officials. This made possible a unity of direction that had hitherto been lacking. At the same time there was a marked improvement in the relations between the two governments, for Louis Borno, who succeeded Dartiguenave as President in 1922, co-operated effectively with the High Commissioner in carrying out the purposes of the Treaty of 1915.

Much was accomplished during the next seven years. A loan floated in New York in 1922 made possible the refunding of the foreign and internal debts and provided a substantial sum for public works, which was supplemented by increased efficiency in the financial administration. It was consequently possible for the Public Works Service to build roads and trails in all parts of the country and to repair and extend the old French irrigation works. The Public Health Service, under the direction of United States navy doctors, organized hospitals and rural clinics which brought medical care for the first time within the reach of the great mass of the population. In 1923, a Service of Agriculture and Vocational Instruction was set up under the treaty, and a number of small rural farm schools were established. Meanwhile, the constabulary maintained order, and its district commanders, most of them sergeants in the Marine Corps, took the place of the old military commandants as the principal local officials in the rural districts.

The American occupation was nonetheless disliked by the majority of the Haitian *élite*. Though this group had returned to the government with the intervention, after the long period of subjection to black military leaders and *caco* chieftains, they felt that they had derived little benefit from the change. In the past the government's revenue had nearly all found its way, through one channel or another, into the pockets of the ruling class. Now it was being spent by foreigners on projects that benefited the masses of the people. The expenditures of the departments under Haitian control had been reduced to a minimum. The occupation was in itself offensive to national pride, and President Borno's policy of co-operation was increasingly unpopular. There was no legal channel, however, through which the opposition could act, because a "transitory" provision of the Constitution of 1918 authorized the President to postpone congressional elections as long as he saw fit and provided that the legislative power should be exercised in the meantime by a Council of State. It was this body, appointed by Borno himself, which voted him a second four-year term in 1926.

As the end of this term approached, the fear that the President would be elected again, or would place in office one of his friends, brought on a political crisis. In the last months of 1929, a minor dispute in the agricultural school led to a strike of Haitian employees in various government departments, accompanied by violent political demonstrations. For the first time in many years the American marines were compelled to assist in maintaining order. Normal conditions were restored without bloodshed at Port au Prince; but at Cayes, where there was an effort to incite the peasants to revolt, several persons were killed in a clash with a small marine detachment.

Soon after these events, President Hoover appointed a commission headed by W. Cameron Forbes to consider "when and how we are to withdraw from Haiti" and "what we shall do in the meantime." This body made a brief visit to Haiti early in 1930, and recommended that a civilian Minister be appointed to take over the functions of the High Commissioner and to carry out the early "Haitianization" of the treaty services. With General Russell's help, it also worked out an agreement between the contending political factions, by which Eugene Roy, a generally respected banker in Port au Prince, would become President when Borno's term expired in May, with the understanding that he would convene a Congress and then resign in order to permit the election of a new Chief Executive. This plan was duly carried out. The election held in the summer of 1930 was as nearly free and fair as any could be in Haiti, and the Congress, meeting in November, chose Stenio Vincent, a leading opponent of the occupation, as President.

The new American Minister at once began negotiations for the termination of the intervention. The military occupation was formally ended in 1931, and the public works, public health, and agricultural services were turned over to Haitian officials at the same time. The "Haitianization" of the constabulary was slower, because it was first necessary to train native officers in the higher ranks, but it was concluded in August, 1934, and all American marines were then withdrawn. The financial administration presented a more difficult problem. The United States felt that both governments had formally obligated themselves to maintain American control over the collection and application of the pledged revenues so long as any bonds of the 1922 loan were outstanding, but the Financial Adviser–General Receiver was nevertheless replaced in 1934 by a "Fiscal Representative" with more restricted powers. The occupation seemed to leave no aftermath of bitterness among the Haitian people or with the government.

SINCE 1934

Throughout the "Haitianization" negotiations, President Vincent and his advisers emphasized the importance of maintaining the efficiency of the treaty services, and to a great extent they were left in the hands of capable natives who had served in important positions under the American directors. Haiti, in the years immediately following the withdrawal of the American forces, was thus a very different country from the Haiti of 1915. The constabulary, under its trained officers, was a far more efficient force than the old army, and road building and other improvements carried out during the intervention did much to unify the country and to raise the general standard of living. The people as a whole seemed little inclined to countenance a return of the turbulent conditions of preintervention days.

Nevertheless, serious social and political problems remained unsolved. The peasants were hardly better fitted than before 1915 to take their place as citizens of a free republic. The rural schools established under the treaty had hardly made a dent in their illiteracy or their ignorance of the first principles of farming. Production had increased very little, and only one or two of several agricultural enterprises established by American capital during the occupation had been at all successful. Meanwhile, population had increased even more rapidly than before 1915, partly because of the work of the Public Health Service. With some 3,000,000 people crowded into a none-too-fertile area of 10,000 square miles, Haiti was one of the most crowded countries of the Western Hemisphere.

President Vincent remained in power after the American withdrawal. In 1934 he arranged to buy the National Bank from the American interests that had acquired its stock in 1920. The plan met with opposition in the Haitian Senate, but a "plebiscite" upheld the President by a majority of 454,357 to 1,172, and 11 senators were thereafter summarily removed from office as being "rebellious against the will of the people." The Bank thus became the property of the government, and in 1941 the United States agreed that it should take over the loan service, under the supervision of American citizens appointed to its board of directors. The office of the Fiscal Representative was thus discontinued.

Another plebiscite in June, 1935, approved a new constitution that extended President Vincent's term to 1941 and provided for the election of future presidents by popular vote instead of by the Congress. This strengthened the executive's position, because a popular election was easier to manipulate. There was little effective opposition to the government during the next six years despite the fact that the vicissitudes of the coffee industry caused an acute economic depression. This was somewhat relieved after 1938 when the J. G. White Corporation of New York undertook a large public works program financed by a loan from the United States government.

During Vincent's second term Haiti nearly became involved in a war with its neighbor the Dominican Republic. The hostile feeling between the people of the two ends of the island, which had originated in the days of the buccaneers and had been intensified by the Haitian occupation of Santo Domingo between 1822 and 1844, had been kept alive by disputes over the boundary between the two countries. The boundary line was finally fixed by a treaty signed in 1935, but this did not settle the problem presented by the great numbers of Haitians who had infiltrated into the Dominican Republic in later years to work on the sugar plantations or to farm land along the border as squatters. In 1937 several thousands of these immigrants were suddenly massacred by Dominican troops, and thousands more were driven back across the border. Fortunately the other American republics were able to avert a conflict between the two countries, and the Dominican government agreed to pay Haiti a substantial indemnity.

Many observers had expected Vincent to be a candidate for a third term in 1941; but he decided to withdraw from office, and Elie Lescot, who had held several important positions in his administration, was chosen to succeed him. Haiti co-operated in the war effort, chiefly by increasing the production of sisal, which helped to relieve the shortage of Manila hemp, and by joining with the United States in an ambitious but unsuccessful effort to produce rubber from the *cryptostegia* vine. The Haitian American Agricultural Development Corporation, known as the *SHADA*, leased over 100,000 acres of land and converted some 40,000 peasant farmers temporarily into day laborers at wages 50 per cent higher than those formerly prevalent. When the experiment was given up as a failure in 1944, it was difficult to replace the farmers on their land, though the United States provided large quantities of seeds and fruit trees for re-planting.

Political discontent increased after the National Assembly in 1944 extended Lescot's term until 1951, and there were minor revolutionary activities and repressive measures by the government. In January, 1946, strikes forced the President to resign, and three officers of the *Garde* took control. A new Congress, elected in May, chose Dumarsais Estimé as President of the Republic. This marked the end of 30 years of government by the mulatto portion of the *élite*. The new administration announced an extensive program of reforms and internal improvements. One of its first achievements was the payment of the balance of the external loan of 1922, a step that made it possible to eliminate the last vestiges of foreign control over the country's financial administration. For some years there were no serious political disorders, although there was a slight flurry in 1949 when President Trujillo permitted an exiled colonel in the *Garde* to use the Dominican radio for violent attacks on President Estimé. The incident was apparently closed when the Council of the Organization of American States expressed the hope that the two countries would improve their relations.

In 1950, Estimé attempted to amend the constitution to authorize his own re-election. The army opposed him and forced his resignation, and a military *junta* governed the country until Colonel Paul Magloire was elected President later in the year. Magloire was more nearly a dictator than any ruler since the days before the American intervention, but he encountered relatively little effective opposition until the end of his term approached and his opponents began to fear that he would seek to continue in power. In the face of growing discontent, he withdrew from office in December, 1956. He resumed control at the request of the army a few days later, but a general strike forced him to resign. Several short-lived governments rose and fell in the months that followed, coming into office with the support of one or another of the factions in the army. Finally, in September, 1957, there was a general election in which for the first time in the Republic's history all Haitian citizens were called on to vote for a President and several candidates carried on active campaigns. Dr. François Duvalier, a physician who had a large following among the masses of the people, was the victor. The new administration was opposed by the greater part of the mulatto *élite*, and it had to suppress several subversive plots and to repel a revolutionary expedition from Cuba during its first two years. In 1960, however, its position seemed somewhat more secure and it was receiving substantial financial help from the United States in building irrigation works and developing agriculture.

CHAPTER 25

The Dominican Republic

THE SPANISH COLONY of Santo Domingo, the first European settlement in the New World, was left with only a scanty population after the extermination of the Indians there and in the neighboring islands. Many of the white settlers left Hispaniola for Mexico or Peru, and the settlements in the west end of the island were abandoned in the seventeenth century after the buccaneers began to make forays from Tortuga. We have seen how the French interlopers took possession of this region and built up the flourishing French colony of Saint Domingue.

During the eighteenth century the prosperity of the French end of the island had some effect on the older Spanish settlements. The coffee and sugar plantations offered a market for Dominican cattle, and a number of the landowners in the eastern end of the island were able to import slaves. The white population was increased by immigration from the Canary Islands.

By 1789 the population of the Spanish colony was estimated at 125,000, of whom 15,000 were Negro slaves. It still seemed backward to the inhabitants of French Saint Domingue, and one of the French creoles—influenced no doubt by the inveterate antipathy between the people of the two colonies—described the people of the Spanish section as illiterate, unprogressive, and superstitious.[1] In the rural districts even the wealthier farmers went barefoot and lived in a primitive way. There were no good roads. On the other hand the Spanish colony did not have the social and racial problems that confronted its western neighbor. Partly because there were few large plantations, the treatment of the slaves was relatively humane. The great majority of the Negroes, furthermore, were "creoles," who spoke Spanish and were Catholics, rather than recent arrivals from Africa. After Toussaint Louverture abolished slavery, when he conquered the eastern end of the island, the Negroes did not seem to

[1] Moreau de Saint-Méry, *A Topographical and Political Description of the Spanish Part of Saint Domingo* (Philadelphia, 1798).

feel the animosity toward their former masters that led to the massacre of the whites in Haiti. Most of them became small farmers or laborers on the cattle ranches of the upper-class landowners.

FRENCH, SPANISH, AND HAITIAN RULE

Napoleon's forces, which had occupied both parts of the island in 1802, remained in control in the former Spanish colony after they had been expelled from the western end; but in 1808–1809, when the people of Spain rose against Napoleon, the Dominicans followed their example. Under the leadership of Juan Sánchez Ramírez, and with the aid of British warships, they revolted and re-established Spanish rule. Twelve years later, however, another revolution, carried out with little or no bloodshed, set up an independent government under José Núñez de Cáceres. The creole leaders proclaimed the union of "Spanish Haiti" with Great Colombia, but before they could ask help from Bolívar a Haitian army invaded the country. The Dominicans could offer little resistance, and for 22 years after 1822 the entire island was ruled from Port au Prince.

The union was not a happy one. Boyer, the Haitian president, seems to have made an effort to conciliate the Dominicans and to protect them against abuses, but differences in race and culture and the traditional enmity between the people of the two parts of the island made the situation an unpleasant one. The Dominicans resented the Haitians' attitude toward the Church, which had been more influential in the east than in the west, and the total neglect of roads, schools, and other public services. They also objected to being taxed to help pay the indemnity imposed on Haiti by France in 1825. The position of the upper-class creole families was especially difficult, even though the Haitian constitutional provisions that excluded whites from citizenship and landownership were not fully enforced in the east. Many creoles had abandoned the colony after its cession to France in 1795 and especially after Toussaint's occupation, and the departure of a considerable proportion of those that remained left the country with relatively few people of pure Spanish descent.

For many years there was little overt opposition to Haitian rule, but in 1838 Juan Pablo Duarte, a young man who had been educated abroad and had only recently returned to Santo Domingo, organized a secret revolutionary society called "La Trinitaria." This group joined in the conspiracy of the Haitian "liberals" against Boyer and helped to make it a success; but when their real purpose became apparent, the new Haitian government took measures which forced their leaders to flee into exile. President Hérard, however, soon had his hands full with opposition at home, and on February 27, 1844, a group of Duarte's associates seized the forts at Santo Domingo and proclaimed the independence of the Dominican Republic. *Caudillos* in other sections of the former Spanish colony followed their example. Duarte returned from Curaçao to become a member of the *Junta Central* which took charge of the government and an army was raised to repel the Haitian forces which had already crossed the border. The outcome was still uncertain when a new revolt in Haiti caused the invaders to withdraw.

SANTANA AND BÁEZ, 1844–1859

The Dominican leaders, in the meantime, had already quarreled among themselves, and in June Duarte's followers in the *Junta Central* attempted to dismiss Pedro Santana, the commander of the army, whose dilatory tactics against the Haitians aroused their distrust. Santana promptly marched on the Capital, exiled his opponents, and convened a Congress which gave him dictatorial powers. He was President until 1848, when he fell ill and the Minister of War, Manuel Jiménez, seized the opportunity to supplant him. A year later, however, a new Haitian invasion forced the government to give Santana command of the army, and after he repulsed the enemy it was an easy matter to oust Jiménez. Santana permitted his associate Buenaventura Báez to become President, but he retained control of the army and had much influence in the new administration. He again took over the presidency in 1853 when Báez' term expired.

Even if there had been less dissension during the first decade of independence, the country's new rulers would have found it difficult to organize an efficient government. They had scanty resources with which to work. The emigration of a large proportion of the upper classes had deprived the country of many of its natural leaders. The country people were ignorant and poverty-stricken. Even in the towns, illiteracy was general, for there had been very few schools under the Haitian regime, and only five, accommodating 40 pupils each, were provided for in the budget as late as 1857. Agriculture, stock raising, and commerce had greatly declined. The government's revenues, in 1845–1846, were estimated at less than $650,000, and of its expenditures, estimated at $1,186,000, $1,000,000 went to the army.[2] Under such conditions it was difficult to look for any substantial material progress.

The Dominicans' chief preoccupation, however, was their fear of a new invasion from Haiti. The weak administrations that succeeded one another at Port au Prince for some years after 1844 were unable to renew the war, but it was clear that the first strong government that appeared there would attempt to reconquer the eastern end of the island. Haiti had a far greater population and greater resources, and the recollection of earlier invasions, with their wholesale massacres and destruction of property, made the renewal of hostilities a terrifying prospect.

[2] 41st Cong., 3rd Sess., House Exec. Doc. 42, pp. 11–12.

Many of the Dominican leaders, including Santana, felt that the only alternative to reconquest was the protection of some foreign state. Efforts to persuade one or another of the European powers or the United States to establish a protectorate played an important part in the Republic's history throughout the first 30 years of independence.

At first these efforts met with little success. Neither France nor Spain responded favorably to Santana's overtures, and the United States failed even to accord diplomatic recognition to the new Republic. None of the powers was enthusiastic about assuming an unattractive and unprofitable responsibility. At the same time, none of them was willing to see another government obtain control of Samaná Bay, the fine natural harbor in the northeastern corner of the island that commands one of the principal entrances to the Caribbean Sea. When negotiations with one power began to look hopeful, the representatives of the others often engaged in intrigues of the most sordid character to defeat them; and their task was made easier by the fact that many patriotic Dominicans opposed any arrangement that would deprive them of their independence. Furthermore, even leaders who advocated a protectorate when their party was in power opposed it when another party stood to profit by it.

Successive presidents nevertheless persisted in their attempts to obtain foreign aid. When Faustin Soulouque came into power in Haiti in 1847 and the expected invasion actually took place, first Jiménez and then Báez unsuccessfully begged for help from France and from the United States. Fortunately Soulouque suddenly withdrew his troops of his own accord, and urgent diplomatic representations by Great Britain, France, and the United States forced him to give up for the time being his plans for a new attack. When he did renew the war in 1855 his army was defeated by Santana. This was the last formidable Haitian invasion; but the victory seemed at the time a mere temporary success, and it did not diminish the Dominican government's desire for a foreign protectorate.

Before the Haitian attack, Santana's government had signed a treaty of amity and commerce with the United States. The representative of the American government also endeavored to obtain the cession of a naval base at Samaná, but this scheme was blocked by the opposition of the European consuls at Santo Domingo, whose intrigues finally forced Santana out of the government. Báez, who had quarreled with his former chief, became President in 1856. The new administration lasted but a short time, for when Báez rewarded the Spanish, French, and English consuls by permitting them to profit with him in scandalous transactions connected with large new issues of paper money, public opinion turned against him. After his foreign supporters quarreled among themselves, and the Spanish Chargé d'Affaires was recalled, he could no longer maintain himself. The Capital was taken by revolutionists in 1858 after a long siege, and Santana returned to the presidency.

REANNEXATION TO SPAIN

Still convinced of the need for foreign help, and despairing of obtaining it from the United States, Santana entered into negotiations with Spain. The government at Madrid was less reluctant to consider his proposals because the United States, on the verge of civil war, was in no position to uphold the Monroe Doctrine by force. In 1860, at Santana's request, Spanish troops were sent to support his administration, and on March 18, 1861, the Dominican President proclaimed the reannexation of the Republic to the mother country. Santana was appointed Captain General of the colony. Those who opposed the surrender of independence staged several small revolts, but they were repressed by Santana with a cruelty which shocked his new associates and caused the first of a series of increasingly serious disagreements.

From the beginning, the reunion was an unhappy one. The Dominicans were angered when many native officeholders were replaced by Spaniards and when the home government restored the same unenlightened centralized regime which had been repudiated by the American colonies a half-century earlier. The clergy were incensed by efforts of the new Spanish Archbishop to reform their conduct and discipline. The attitude of some of the Spanish officials who came from the slaveholding colonies of Cuba and Puerto Rico angered the colored inhabitants, and there was even a fear lest slavery be re-established in Santo Domingo.

Santana, who found himself with less and less authority, resigned as Captain General and was given a title of nobility and a pension early in 1862. A year later he took the field against insurgents who revolted in the interior but met with little success, and in 1864 he died suddenly, perhaps by his own hand. Meanwhile, yellow fever, the old enemy of European conquerors in the West Indies, attacked the Spanish army. By the end of 1864 the Spanish government was weary of the whole affair, especially as it was clear that the approaching end of the civil war would soon permit the United States to follow up the strong protest against the occupation which it had made in 1861. After unsuccessful attempts to treat with the rebels, the Spanish forces simply abandoned the island in July, 1865.

BÁEZ AND THE UNITED STATES

The insurgents' leaders were already quarreling among themselves, and General Pimentel, who was the head of their provisional government, was overthrown by a revolt at Santo Domingo City and replaced by General José María Cabral. The new government's influence was soon undermined by intrigues which Báez directed from his exile in Curaçao, for though Santana's old rival had been in Europe and had accepted honors and money from Spain during the Spanish occupation, he was still the most influential of the Dominican leaders. Báez returned to power at the end of 1865, but civil strife continued and was made worse by Haitian interference. President Geffrard helped Cabral to oust Báez, and his successor, Salnave, helped the *Baecistas* to defeat Cabral. In 1868 Báez was again President.

The new government continued negotiations that its predecessors had been carrying on with the United States. Secretary of State Seward had visited Santo Domingo in 1866, and soon afterward the American government had again proposed to lease or buy Samaná Bay for a coaling station. There was much popular opposition in the Dominican Republic, but the negotiations continued, and President Johnson, with Báez' approval, suggested to the United States Congress the annexation of the Dominican Republic. Congressional hostility to Johnson prevented action, but the advocates of annexation resumed their efforts after President Grant's inauguration.

The chief movers in the scheme, on the American side, were two adventurers named Cazneau and Fabens, who had various concessions, including grants of land around Samaná Bay, which would increase in value if annexation took place. These promoters had obtained the support of several influential people by giving them a financial interest in their project, and despite their unsavory records and questionable methods they apparently gained Seward's confidence and later persuaded President Grant to take an interest in their proposals.

In 1869, after Grant had sent an emissary to confer with Báez, treaties were signed providing for the annexation of the Dominican Republic to the United States and for a 99-year lease of Samaná Bay. A "plebiscite" ostensibly indicated that the Dominican people approved the projects by a large majority, but when the treaties reached the United States Senate there was a bitter fight, with Senator Sumner leading the opposition. The revelation of the sordid influences behind the scheme discredited it, and in June, 1870, a tie vote, far short of the two-thirds majority needed for ratification, defeated it. Grant, who was interested in annexation for its own sake, then obtained the Congress' authorization to send a commission of inquiry to visit Santo Domingo early in 1871. This returned with a report supporting the administration's policy, but the opposition in the Senate and the indifference of public opinion precluded any possibility of favorable action.

In 1869, while annexation was still under consideration, the Dominican government entered into another transaction which was to have unfortunate consequences at a later date. In one of the most improvident transactions in the history of Caribbean finance, Báez obtained a loan from a London banker named Hartmont, who was one of Fabens' associates.

The government was to receive £420,000, out of which it was to pay Hartmont a commission of £100,000. In return it was to pay £58,900 annually for 25 years, giving the customs receipts at Santo Domingo and Puerto Plata as security and authorizing the bankers to maintain representatives in the customhouses there. It also gave the bankers a mortgage on the coal mines and forests of the Samaná district and by a separate concession authorized Hartmont to work the mines for his own profit. Under the loan contract, Hartmont offered £757,700 of the Republic's 6 per cent bonds to the public at 70 per cent of their face value. The arrangement would have been an unconscionable one if it had been carried out in good faith; and when Hartmont failed to comply with his end of the bargain it left the government with a heavy debt for which it had received little in return. The promoters hoped to have their profits made secure by the consummation of the annexation project, but instead the contract was canceled, at the instance of the American government, when they failed to comply with their obligations. The bonds, however, could not be repudiated, and the debt was one of the factors that later led to North American intervention.

STRIFE BETWEEN "REDS" AND "BLUES"
1871–1882

American naval forces supported Báez during the annexation negotiations, and his position was precarious when they were withdrawn. The Haitian government, which had been much alarmed by the annexation project, helped his opponents, and Báez lost support among his own followers when he sought to replenish the treasury by leasing Samaná Bay to a private American company. He was overthrown in 1874 by one of his own lieutenants, General Ignacio María González.

For some years, strife between the "reds," as Báez' party called themselves, and the "blues," led by Gregorio Luperón, kept the country in a state of anarchy. Luperón, a semi-illiterate, very popular Negro *caudillo*, defeated González in 1876 and brought about the election of Ulises Espaillat as President. Espaillat was one of the Republic's most respected and enlightened citizens. A few months later, however, his government fell in the first of a series of revolutions that brought one general after another to power. In 1879, Luperón regained control and, after a brief period as provisional President, made his friend Father Meriño head of the government. Order was now restored, though not until two attempts at revolt had been cruelly suppressed, and when Meriño's two-year term expired, his Minister of the Interior, Ulises Heureaux, was "elected" without difficulty to succeed him.

HEUREAUX

The man who thus came into the presidency dominated Dominican political life during the next 17 years. Though he was compelled to permit Luperón's candidate, General Billini, to succeed him in 1884, he soon forced Billini to resign in favor of Vice-President Woss y Gil, and in 1887 he returned to the presidency himself. Two years later he had a Constitutional Convention extend his term of office until 1893, and from then until the end of his life he was re-elected at regular intervals.

Heureaux was a Negro, the illegitimate son of a Haitian and a woman from one of the other West Indian islands, with little education but much native intelligence. He had distinguished himself by his courage and ruthlessness in the war against Spain and the ensuing civil struggles, and he was fairly popular when he first took office. His administration was comparatively liberal at first, but it soon became a cruel and greedy despotism, with all of the demoralizing features inherent in such a system. He won the support of many other political leaders by bribery or intimidation, and there was little internal disorder during his long tenure of power—the first era of peace in the history of the Republic. Agriculture prospered, and commerce took on new life. Sugar production, which had begun to increase during the ten years' war in Cuba (1868–1878) when several refugees from that island set up mills in Santo Domingo, was still further expanded by North American capital. The country thus felt the effect of the same influences which were making for stability and economic development in other Latin American countries in the closing years of the century.

On the other hand, Heureaux' financial transactions involved the country in grave difficulties. His first foreign loan in 1888 was floated by the Dutch firm of Westendorp. Its primary purpose was to refund the Hartmont bonds, whose holders had been supported by the British government in their demands for repayment, but it also provided a substantial sum for Heureaux' own use. Two years later another loan was obtained from the same firm, ostensibly for railroad construction. This was a failure, and in 1892 Westendorp, in financial difficulties, turned over his Dominican interests to an American firm, the "San Domingo Improvement Company." The outstanding debt, already in default, was scaled down and refunded, and the customs receipts were pledged to the service of a new bond issue. Their collection was entrusted to a *"regie"* directed by the bankers, with a provision that it should be taken over in case of another default by nominees of the British, French, American, Dutch, and Belgian governments.

The Improvement Company thus not only supplied the government with funds but collected the major part of its revenues. It also carried on construction work on the Central Dominican Railway, and in 1895 it took over the control of the National Bank, hitherto owned by a French company. These operations were profitable to the bankers and to Heureaux personally; but successive bond issues were sold on more and more unfavorable terms, and the public debt rapidly increased. In 1897 there was a new default, followed by another adjustment at the bondholders' expense and by still another default. When further loans became impossible, the government turned to the issue of depreciated currency to obtain funds.

INTERNAL DISORDER AND
FOREIGN COMPLICATIONS, 1899–1904

Heureaux was assassinated on July 26, 1899, by Ramón Cáceres, one of a group of conspirators which included Horacio Vásquez, Cáceres' cousin, who was a powerful political leader in the Cibao, and Juan Isidro Jiménez, a merchant at Monte Cristi. This group obtained control of the government after a brief civil war, and Jiménez became President. The new administration inherited a desperate financial situation, and its inability to meet its obligations soon involved it in controversies with several foreign governments. The situation became worse when the strong popular feeling against the Improvement Company led the government to remove the Company's agents from the customhouses. The United States intervened diplomatically on behalf of the Company, and the Company's inability to maintain service on the government's bonds, most of which had been sold in Europe, brought on trouble with several other countries. In addition, there were many claims arising from the penniless government's failure to pay bills for supplies and claims for damages to foreigners. Strong diplomatic pressure, often supported by the appearance of warships, repeatedly forced the Dominicans to make promises of settlement which they were unable to perform and which only made the general situation worse.

Frequent revolutions made the settlement of these problems still more difficult. The *Horacistas*, as Vásquez' followers were called, overthrew Jiménez in 1902. Vásquez became President, only to be overthrown a year later by former partisans of Heureaux under General Alejandro Woss y Gil. Jiménez supported this revolt; but later in the same year his followers joined with the *Horacistas* in a new one, which was likewise successful. Jiménez expected to become President, and he promptly started an uprising of his own when the *Horacistas* prevailed on the *Jimenista* military leader Carlos Morales to seize power for himself. There were some months of fighting before a truce was arranged through the good offices of an American naval officer.

By this time some of the Dominican leaders were beginning to feel that they could not solve their problems without foreign help. Woss y

Gil tentatively offered Samaná Bay to the United States in 1903, and Morales soon after he came into office advocated placing the custom-houses under North American control. This, he thought, would not only relieve the pressure from other foreign creditors but would also discour-age revolutions, for the first step in a revolt was usually the seizure of a customhouse as a means of obtaining funds. The idea was an unpopular one in Santo Domingo, but it became increasingly clear that foreign in-tervention in one form or another was almost inevitable. The Republic owed more than $32,000,000, and the annual fixed charge on the funded debt alone would have consumed $1,700,000 of the government's total estimated revenue of $1,850,000. If the debt service were maintained, there would be no funds for the conduct of the government.

ESTABLISHMENT OF THE CUSTOMS RECEIVERSHIP

In January, 1903, the government promised the United States that it would pay the Improvement Company $4,500,000 for the railroads and the National Bank and its other property, and 18 months later an arbitral award fixed the terms of payment and provided that a fiscal agent named by the United States should take over the collection of customs at several ports in case of default. Since the revenues of these same ports had al-ready been pledged to meet the claims of some of the European creditors, the latter protested, and there were renewed threats of forceful action to compel the government to pay its debts. It became more difficult to expect the European creditors to refrain from action when the American fiscal agent took possession of the Puerto Plata customhouse in October, 1904.

A recent decision of the Hague Court, in the case arising from the Anglo-German-Italian blockade of Venezuela,[3] had established the prin-ciple that nations which used force to collect debts should receive pay-ment ahead of other claimants. It seemed probable therefore that Euro-pean intervention in Santo Domingo would hurt the American creditors. It might also raise questions in connection with the Monroe Doctrine. It was in fact this situation in the Dominican Republic that led President Roosevelt to formulate his corollary to the Monroe Doctrine.[4] In an effort to protect the interests of all concerned, Roosevelt suggested that the United States should take over the collection of the Republic's cus-toms revenues and attempt a general arrangement with all of the creditors. Morales promptly agreed, and a treaty embodying the plan was signed on February 7, 1905.

Opposition in the United States Senate prevented the ratification of

[3] See above, p. 318.
[4] See above, p. 388.

this convention, but an American customs collectorship was nevertheless established in March under a *modus vivendi* or informal agreement. Of the funds received, 55 per cent were held in trust for the creditors for the time being. During the next year, with the help of the United States, Federico Velásquez, the Dominican Minister of Finance, worked out a general settlement by which outstanding obligations were to be scaled down and paid from an American loan of $20,000,000. A new treaty, providing that the customs receivership should continue so long as the bonds were outstanding, was signed February 8, 1907, and was promptly ratified.

A few months earlier, Morales had been forced out, after making an unsuccessful attempt to free himself from the domination of his *Horacista* Cabinet. Vice-President Ramón Cáceres succeeded him and was re-elected for a six-year term in 1908. Cáceres was able and popular, and though Vásquez and other leaders of his own party turned against him, he easily suppressed small revolutionary movements. He had the moral support of the United States, and his position was stronger because the country was prosperous. Though the American bankers were deterred by the panic of 1907 from making the loan contemplated in the treaty, the Republic's creditors were paid partly in cash and partly in bonds secured under the treaty, and the efficient collection of the customs gave the government ample funds for its own use and for a small program of public works. For a time it seemed that the collectorship had solved some of the Republic's worst problems.

RENEWED DISORDER, 1911–1916

The situation changed suddenly when Cáceres was murdered by political enemies on November 19, 1911. The assassins' leader was captured and killed, and the commander of the government's troops at Santo Domingo, Colonel Alfredo Victoria, took advantage of the situation to seize power for himself. He was too young to be elected to the presidency, but he forced the Congress to choose his uncle, Eladio Victoria, who was a respectable but ineffective gentleman with little personal following. This disappointed the other political leaders, and several of them promptly started revolts.

For five years there was almost continuous civil war. Neither the *Horacistas* nor the *Jimenistas* would accept peaceably any government that their party did not control, and some of the government's own military leaders were accused of fomenting disorder because they had greater opportunities for graft when military operations were going on. In several provinces there were powerful local *caudillos* who exacted exhorbitant terms as the price for support of any government. The most prominent of these was Desiderio Arias, nominally a follower of Jiménez, who was to play a leading part in the events that finally led to North American intervention. The United States' efforts to restore peace often seemed to do more harm than good, partly because of the ineptitude of its diplomatic representatives. There are few sorrier chapters in the history of American diplomacy than the career of James M. Sullivan, whose service as Minister at Santo Domingo from 1913 to 1915 was a striking example of the viciousness of the practice of treating diplomatic appointments as a reward for political services.

The United States was impelled to attempt to bring about more orderly conditions, not only by its general Caribbean policy but also because it had an obligation under the 1907 treaty to protect the customs service. Within a few months after Cáceres' death it was confronted by a bad situation along the Haitian frontier, where some of the customhouses had to be closed and where uncertainty about the boundary favored the operations of Haitian forces which often helped Dominican revolutionists. In September, 1912, the United States simply fixed a provisional boundary line and insisted that both governments observe it. At the same time it sent two Commissioners to Santo Domingo, accompanied by a force of marines, who did not, however, disembark. At the Commissioners' suggestion, backed by a threat to withhold the customs collections, President Victoria resigned, and the Archbishop of Santo Domingo, Adolfo Nouel, was elected by the Congress as a provisional President.

Monsignor Nouel attempted to keep the support of all parties by dividing the government offices between them, but he found it impossible to satisfy one without arousing the enmity of the others, and even the moral support of the United States was not enough to make his administration a success. In the interest of peace, he yielded more and more to the arrogant demands of Desiderio Arias, until the latter's growing power caused the *Horacistas* to threaten a revolt. The Archbishop then refused to remain longer in an office which he had been reluctant to accept in the first place, and in March, 1913, he resigned and went to Europe. After some weeks of balloting, the Congress elected José Bordas Valdés as provisional President for a one-year term.

Bordas was an *Horacista*, but he soon quarreled with the rest of his party and began to intrigue with Arias and other *caudillos* in an effort to continue in power. The *Horacistas* revolted, but laid down their arms under pressure from the American Minister in return for a promise that a free election would be held. The United States did ineffectively attempt to supervise the election of a Constituent Assembly later in 1913; but trouble between the President and Congress prevented the holding of a new presidential election, and when Bordas' term ended he simply stayed in office. Meanwhile Arias took to the hills because the President had refused his demands for the vice-presidency and for a cash payment of $300,000. Vásquez soon joined him, and by July, 1914, the country was again in a state of anarchy.

Since the advent of the Wilson administration, the United States had repeatedly threatened and remonstrated with the Dominican leaders in an effort to persuade them to settle their differences by peaceful means, but Minister Sullivan's fumbling diplomacy had merely made the situation worse. In August, 1914, Mr. Wilson decided to take more vigorous action. The contending factions in Santo Domingo were told to lay down their arms and to choose a provisional president who would hold elections to establish a constitutional government. These elections would be closely observed by American representatives, and if they proved free and fair the United States would support the new government and would insist that no further revolutions should occur. If they were not satisfactory, a new election would be held. If the leaders failed to agree upon a provisional president, the United States would name one and would place him in office. The plan was to be presented and carried out, without giving "any person or faction" an "opportunity for argument."

Faced with the threat of armed intervention, the Dominican political leaders after some controversy selected Dr. Ramón Báez as provisional President. Since Báez was a partisan, though not a very active follower, of Jiménez, the latter had an advantage in the elections that were held under the supervision of American observers a few weeks later and defeated Vásquez by a small majority. Jiménez took office on December 5, 1914.

The new President was promised the active support of the United States, by armed force if necessary, but at the same time he was confronted with demands from Washington to which he could not accede without destroying his prestige at home. Realizing that the customs collectorship did not by itself assure political and financial stability, the American government had decided to insist upon a greater measure of control over the Republic's internal affairs. The heavy expenses occasioned by the disorders of the past three years had resulted in continual deficits, and many bills and claims remained unpaid. The United States considered this situation a violation of Article III of the 1907 treaty, which provided that the Dominican public debt should not be increased except by previous agreement between the two governments. It had consequently compelled President Bordas to agree in May, 1914, to the appointment of a "financial expert" with authority to control expenditures, and after the inauguration of Jiménez, the United States urged him to strengthen the position of this official and also to place the internal revenues as well as the customs under the receivership. It also proposed reforms in the army and in the public works service, to be carried out under the direction of North American officials. Jiménez had agreed to some at least of these measures while he was a candidate, but he knew that they would arouse violent popular opposition and was reluctant after his inauguration to proceed with them. In December, 1915, he rejected a blunt demand for the appointment of a financial adviser and the creation of a constabulary under North American officers.

The President was meanwhile losing much of his political following. He was too old and infirm to deal effectively either with his subordinates or with his opponents. Desiderio Arias, who was made Minister of War as the result of a pre-election bargain, used his position chiefly to build up his own following, and he was even accused of encouraging local political disorders, which increased the influence of the army and usually ended when the malcontents were bought off at the expense of the treasury. The United States repeatedly offered to send troops to repress these disorders, but the President declined to accept such assistance.

In April, 1916, when Jiménez, in an effort to check Arias' growing power, imprisoned two of the latter's chief lieutenants, the Minister of War seized control of the Capital. This was a direct challenge to the United States, which had repeatedly stated that it would not tolerate further revolutions. American marines occupied Santo Domingo City, forcing Arias to withdraw into the interior, and soon afterward American forces were sent to other ports and to the more important inland cities. At the Capital Jiménez preferred to resign rather than to remain in power with foreign aid, but the remaining members of his Cabinet carried on the government until July 25, when the Congress elected Dr. Francisco Henríquez y Carvajal as provisional President.

The United States withheld recognition from the new government pending an agreement on the reform measures which had been proposed to Jiménez. In August it even instructed the Receiver General of Customs not to pay over any funds to the Dominican authorities. Since the receivership in the meantime had taken over the collection of the internal revenues as well as the customs, this made the provisional President's position all but impossible. Dr. Henríquez nevertheless remained in office, without funds, and vainly endeavored to obtain some modification of the American demands. In November he precipitated a crisis, probably unintentionally, by asking the electoral colleges to replace members of Congress whose terms were expiring. It was known that the electoral colleges were controlled by followers of Desiderio Arias, who was openly pro-German, and the imminence of war with Germany made it impossible for the United States to acquiesce in an increase of his influence. President Wilson therefore reluctantly authorized the American naval commanders to take full control, and on November 29, 1916, Captain Harry S. Knapp issued a proclamation establishing an American military government.

THE AMERICAN OCCUPATION

The North American occupation lasted for nearly eight years. An American admiral, acting as Military Governor, exercised executive and legislative authority, in the name of the Dominican government. Other naval officers headed the various ministries, but the majority of the other offices, including those in the judiciary, continued to be held by Dominicans. A native constabulary was trained by American officers. In 1917 and 1918 this force and the American marines had to suppress disturbances in the eastern part of the country, but after that there was no serious armed opposition. The maintenance of order, combined with the wartime demand for sugar, brought a temporary prosperity that made it possible to inaugurate ambitious programs of education and public works, but these were just getting under way when sugar prices collapsed in 1920.

The resultant depression intensified Dominican hostility to the military government. The occupation had been hated even when it seemed to be benefiting the country economically, and the maintenance of martial law and a stupid censorship of the press also aroused much criticism in other countries. The tactless and arbitrary conduct of some of the American officials aggravated an already bad situation. The United States had no desire to exercise permanent control over the Dominican Republic, and after the war it sought to extricate itself from a situation in which it had been involved more by bad management than by design.

In December, 1920, President Wilson announced that the occupation would soon be withdrawn. Six months later the Harding administration proposed that the Dominicans should elect a government which would assume power after ratifying a convention embodying only a part of the demands that the United States had presented in 1915. The Dominican political leaders, however, refused to co-operate in the plan, and in June, 1922, an agreement was reached in Washington under which the country was to recover its independence without giving the United States any control over its military forces or any financial powers beyond those conferred by the 1907 treaty. A provisional president, selected by the Dominican party chiefs, was to take over part of the Military Governor's authority and prepare for the election of a permanent president. A "convention of evacuation" was to validate the more important official acts of the military government, in order to protect vested interests created by them.

This plan was carried out, though not without difficulty. Juan Bautista Vicini Burgos was inaugurated as provisional President in October, 1922, but further progress was delayed for some time by quarrels and intrigues among the party leaders. Finally, in March, 1924, Horacio Vásquez was elected Constitutional President, and four months later the American forces were withdrawn.

The next six years, as in most of the Latin American countries, were a period of prosperity and political tranquility. Partisan hostility had diminished during the occupation, and Vásquez was able to obtain the support of many of his former enemies. He no longer had to contend with the restless greed of local military leaders, for the new army, trained by American marines, was an efficient, well-disciplined force. There were no serious disturbances until the last months of his six-year term.

THE "ERA OF TRUJILLO"

Vásquez' candidacy for re-election had already given rise to much political agitation when a serious illness temporarily incapacitated him and brought on an acute rivalry between members of his own government who hoped to succeed him in power. There was bad feeling, especially, between General Rafael Trujillo, the head of the army, and Vice-President Alfonseca, who was a candidate for re-election and would presumably head the government if General Vásquez should die. The army consequently offered no resistance when a small force of revolutionists seized the fort at Santiago and then marched on Santo Domingo City in February, 1930. By an agreement effected through the good offices of the American Legation, Vásquez and Alfonseca resigned, and Rafael Estrella Ureña, the opposition candidate for the vice-presidency and the leader of the revolution, became provisional President. The opposition parties, however, gained nothing by the change, for General Trujillo promptly announced his own candidacy for the presidency and was elected in May with the support of the army.

The new President had risen from the ranks while the constabulary was being trained by American marine officers and had been given command of the force, now converted into the "army," when the marines withdrew. Once in office, he made himself the absolute ruler of the country. Persons who openly opposed him were severely treated. Many are said to have been killed, among them the veteran trouble-maker Desiderio Arias, and many others went into exile. The new government's efficiency was demonstrated when it became necessary to reconstruct much of the Capital city after the terrible hurricane of September, 1930.

General Trujillo was re-elected in 1934. In 1938 he declined to be a candidate for a third term, but he continued to be the unquestioned ruler of the country during the administrations of Jacinto Peynado and Manuel Jesús Troncoso de la Concha, who took office after Peynado's death in 1940. Trujillo returned to the presidency in 1942, and in 1947 he was elected for a fourth term, overwhelmingly defeating the candidates of two "opposition" parties which had been organized at his request. In 1952, and again in 1957, he had his brother Hector elected President, without even pretending to relinquish any of his own power.

Few Latin American rulers have exercised such complete power for so long a period. The masses of the Dominican people seemed to accept the regime. An effective secret service and the ruthless treatment of anyone who expressed discontent discouraged any opposition within the country, and some Dominican exiles are even said to have been murdered in foreign countries. In 1956 there was strong evidence that Dominican officials were involved in the disappearance of Dr. Jesús Galíndez, a Spaniard living in New York, who had written a book describing the dictatorship.

The maintenance of order, on the other hand, made it possible for the government to do more than any previous administration in building roads and public works and encouraging agriculture. Great sums were spent on the beautification of the Capital city, which was renamed Ciudad Trujillo in 1936. Foreign trade greatly increased. At the same time the ruler and his family became the wealthiest people in the country. One of the proudest achievements of the Trujillo government was the complete elimination of North American financial control. A treaty signed in 1940 abolished the customs receivership, which had existed since 1905, and the outstanding bonds were paid off in full in 1947. Another important achievement in the field of foreign relations was the signature in 1935 of a treaty settling the long-standing and always troublesome question of the boundary with Haiti. This, unfortunately, did not prevent the massacre two years later of thousands of Haitians living on the Dominican side of the frontier.[5]

In 1959 the Trujillo regime, as one of the very few surviving dictatorships in the Western Hemisphere, was under attack by liberals in the other American countries. Its relations with the United States, which for some time had been somewhat strained, deteriorated further when the Dominican government failed to clear up the Galíndez case and the apparently related murder of an American citizen in the Dominican Republic. It confronted the outspoken hostility of the revolutionary governments in Cuba and Venezuela. Early in 1960, opponents within the Republic appeared to be becoming more active, and a large number of persons were arrested in connection with an alleged subversive plot.

[5] See above, p. 475.

PART IX

LATIN AMERICA
AND THE UNITED STATES

THE STORY OF INTER-AMERICAN RELATIONS begins before either portion
of the continent achieved independence. In the seventeenth century,
persons who were interested in the Plymouth colony were also promoting settlement and organized piracy in the Spanish Main. Colonial questions were involved in each of the European wars of the seventeenth and eighteenth centuries, and each of these wars was fought in
part on the western side of the Atlantic. It was partly a desire to end
the frequent involvement of the Western Hemisphere in Old World
conflicts that led President Monroe in 1823 to issue his famous warning
against any further attempt by European powers to control the destinies
of the newly independent Latin American republics.

The Monroe Doctrine, as time went on, became one of the fundamental principles of American foreign policy. On several occasions—
in Mexico, in Santo Domingo, and in Venezuela—it helped to preserve
the independence or the territorial integrity of a Latin American country, despite European unwillingness to recognize its validity. During the
nineteenth century, however, the United States was chiefly concerned
with the application of the Doctrine to Mexico and the Caribbean area.
It was less important from the standpoint of national defense, and more
difficult from a military point of view, to oppose European aggression
in southern South America than in regions nearer to us. The American
government consequently took no action to prevent such occurrences
as Great Britain's occupation of the Falkland Islands and the Anglo-
French intervention of the 1840's in the River Plate. In fact its general
relations with the countries south of the equator, during the greater
part of the nineteenth century, were relatively unimportant. They, like
ourselves, had far closer economic, cultural, and even political ties with

Europe, to which they looked to provide markets for their goods and capital for the development of their resources.

Today the situation is different. The two world wars, and particularly the Second, impressed on all of the American countries the need to stand together to defend ideals and interests that were important to all of them. The Organization of American States, supervising a number of special agencies for co-operation in various fields, has become one of the world's most effective institutions for international co-operation. Inter-American trade is of vital importance to all of the countries of the Hemisphere. North American capital and economic assistance from the United States government play a major part in the development of the other countries. Few would assert today, as some people did 50 years ago, that "Pan Americanism" is an idea without substance. On the other hand, the problems that confront the American republics in their relations with one another are in many respects more complicated and troublesome than they were when these relations were less close.

CHAPTER 26

Inter-American Relations 1889-1945

EARLIER PAN AMERICAN CONFERENCES

TOWARD THE END of the nineteenth century, many of the Latin American countries were achieving a measure of stability and commercial importance, and the United States was reaching a point in its economic development where it was interested in new markets for its industrial products and in the importation of large amounts of raw materials for its factories. Several North American statesmen were beginning to take an increased interest in the possibility of promoting trade with the other countries of the Hemisphere and an increased interest in the political problems of these countries. One of these was James G. Blaine, President Garfield's Secretary of State, who invited the other American states to a conference to meet at Washington in 1882. The invitations were withdrawn after Garfield's death; but the project was revived and approved by Congress in 1888, and Blaine, again Secretary of State, presided over the First Pan American Conference when it met at Washington in 1889.

The conference set up the International Bureau of American Republics, which later became the Pan American Union, and drew up a convention for the compulsory arbitration of pecuniary claims, a first step in the creation of the peace machinery which was to occupy much of the attention of later gatherings. Extradition, uniform customs and commercial regulations, sanitary problems, and monetary and exchange questions also received attention, as they did at later conferences; but most of the resolutions adopted, like many of the acts of later conferences, had little effect because few of the signatory governments were sufficiently interested to ratify them.

Subsequent conferences, meeting at Mexico City in 1901–1902, at Rio de Janeiro in 1906, and at Buenos Aires in 1910, followed much the same pattern. They afforded an opportunity for the statesmen of the Hemisphere to meet and discuss common problems, but they did not do a great deal to promote closer economic relations. Meat and grain from the River Plate and nitrate from Chile continued to go to Europe. The people of those countries, and even the Brazilians, who sold much of their coffee to the United States, continued to buy chiefly in European markets, to send their children to Paris and other Old World centers to study, and to travel east rather than north for recreation. Since there was no good direct steamship service, the most comfortable route from New York to Rio de Janeiro or Buenos Aires was by way of Europe. British, French, and German businessmen controlled much of the export and import business, the banks, the railroads, and many other enterprises. Little United States capital had been invested south of the Caribbean area, and North American residents were few and relatively uninfluential.

THE FIRST WORLD WAR

This situation changed during the First World War. As it became more difficult to buy goods in Europe, there was a great increase in trade with the United States. American banks established branches throughout Latin America, and there was a greater inflow of American capital. Furthermore the events of the conflict made the American nations aware that they had common interests distinct from those of Europe. President Wilson's stand for democracy against imperialism and militarism met with warm support in many circles in Latin America, and a new feeling of solidarity found practical expression after the United States became a belligerent. Brazil, Cuba, Panama, Haiti, and all of Central America except El Salvador declared war on Germany. Five other countries severed diplomatic relations. On the other hand, Argentina, Chile, Mexico, Colombia, Venezuela, Paraguay, and El Salvador remained formally neutral.

After the war, European trade recovered only a part of its former importance. Great Britain and the continent were still the principal markets for South American exports because the United States was in no position to buy large quantities of products like meat, grains, copper, or petroleum of which it was itself an exporter. In the import trade, on the other hand, American manufacturers retained an important position and supplanted the Germans as the chief competitors of the hitherto dominant British. The goods that they sold were paid for partly by bond issues that most of the Latin American governments floated in New York. During the same period much United States capital went into mines, public utilities, and other enterprises. By 1928 North American investments in South

America were estimated at $2,294,212,100, and in Latin America as a whole at $5,587,494,100.[1]

Trade and investment, unfortunately, did not in themselves promote more friendly relations. During the postwar period the feeling toward the United States in the larger southern republics left much to be desired. This was partly the result of inadequate representation of American interests. Many of the firms that entered the South American field during and just after the war were inexperienced, and a few were unscrupulous. Too many failed to send representatives who spoke Spanish and were otherwise qualified to win the respect and friendship of the local community. Even the United States government did not seem to realize the importance of appointing diplomats who were competent and whose character would command respect. These shortcomings were corrected to a great extent as time went on, but not until much harm had been done.

AMERICAN POLICY IN THE CARIBBEAN

Still more detrimental to good relations was the hostility aroused throughout Latin America by the United States' intervention in some of the West Indian and Central American countries. To the foreign observer, our policy in the Caribbean seemed to grow more and more imperialistic in the period between 1903 and 1929. The Panama affair of 1903, the Nicaraguan intervention in 1912, and especially the military occupation of Haiti and Santo Domingo convinced many people that the United States was seeking permanent political control there. Most Latin Americans probably paid little attention to what was happening until after the First World War, but in the 1920's "Yankee imperialism" provided material for propaganda by European commercial interests and other unfriendly groups. Even the great American press services, which were beginning to establish themselves in South America, sometimes helped to create ill feeling by reporting sensational and often misleading articles and speeches by anti-imperialists in the United States. The second intervention in Nicaragua, which caused a great sensation elsewhere in the Hemisphere, was a particularly unfortunate event.

THE SANTIAGO AND HABANA CONFERENCES

These and other obstacles to continental solidarity were evident in the proceedings of the Fifth and Sixth Pan American Conferences. The Fifth Conference, which met at Santiago, Chile, in 1923, was more concerned than its predecessors with political questions. It met under a cloud because Peru and Bolivia, still at odds with Chile over questions arising from the War of the Pacific, and Mexico, whose government had not

[1] Winkler, *Investments of United States Capital in Latin America*, p. 278.

been recognized by the United States, refused to attend. During the sessions there were several indications of unfriendly feeling toward the United States, and this feeling was not diminished when the American delegation blocked proposals for a reorganization of the Pan American Union, designed to pave the way for the eventual establishment of an American League of Nations, and insisted that the United States must retain the right to interpret and enforce the Monroe Doctrine as it alone saw fit. The chief accomplishment of the Conference was the Gondra Peace Treaty, which provided that any inter-American dispute not settled by diplomacy should be submitted to a commission of inquiry and that no hostile move should be made until six months after the commission's report had been rendered. At the Sixth Conference, which met in Habana in 1928, the unfriendliness of several Latin American countries toward the United States was even more manifest, and efforts to bring about the adoption of a resolution condemning intervention by one state in the affairs of another, clearly directed at North American policies in Nicaragua and Haiti, were blocked only after a series of rather painful incidents.

THE ABANDONMENT OF THE INTERVENTION POLICY

Soon afterward it became clear that the Caribbean policies that had been the target for so much criticism both in North and in South America were definitely being abandoned. President Hoover, in the first years of his administration, took steps to terminate the intervention in Haiti, and in 1931 the American officials were withdrawn from the majority of the treaty services there. By 1934 American forces were out of Haiti, and only the finances remained under foreign control. In Nicaragua the marines were withdrawn early in 1933. At the same time the policy of the United States changed in other respects. Except in Central America, where the treaties of 1923 created a special situation, the United States abandoned the use of nonrecognition of revolutionary governments as a means of discouraging disorder.

President Franklin D. Roosevelt's Good Neighbor Policy went considerably farther in the same direction. In December, 1933, when the Seventh International Conference of American States met at Montevideo, the American delegation signed, though with reservations, a Convention on Rights and Duties of States which provided that "No state has the right to intervene in the external or internal affairs of another." President Roosevelt himself declared a few days later that "the definite policy of the United States from now on is one opposed to armed intervention" and that if a breakdown of law and order in any American country affected other nations, it was the joint concern of the whole continent and not of the United States alone.[2] In the years that followed, the Platt Amendment was abrogated, American rights in the Canal Zone and Panama were curtailed in a new treaty, and the remnants of North American financial control in the Dominican Republic and Haiti were abandoned. The American government thus extricated itself from practically all of the responsibilities that it had assumed in connection with the internal affairs of its smaller neighbors.

ECONOMIC NATIONALISM AND THE GOOD NEIGHBOR POLICY

The abandonment of intervention was but one aspect of President Roosevelt's "Good Neighbor" policy. There was also an effort to avoid controversies and friction, especially in cases where American financial interests were involved. The protection of these interests had become more difficult during the depression because there was a strong movement throughout Latin America to eliminate or reduce foreign economic influence.

Early in the twentieth century, commerce and industry throughout the countries south of the Rio Grande were largely in foreign hands. European merchants controlled most of the export and import trade and the small shopkeepers were generally Chinese, Syrian, Italian, Spanish, or Portuguese. Since practically all capital came from abroad, railroads, mines, factories, and banks were managed by representatives of the investors. The natives of the country were more interested in agriculture, and politics, and in any event could rarely compete with the more active and aggressive outsider, who had better connections abroad and better technical training. Those who obtained positions in business enterprises found that all the better jobs and higher salaries went to foreigners. This, and the privileged position which many foreign firms claimed under concessions obtained from the local governments, caused much jealousy. The eagerness with which foreign capital had been welcomed when it was needed for the building of railroads and the opening of mines or factories was forgotten when the benefits that it brought began to be taken for granted, and Latin American statesmen increasingly felt that alien control of such important sectors of their countries' economic life was an unwholesome situation.

Measures designed to break down this control, ranging from a natural and proper regulation of foreign enterprises to outright confiscation, were consequently adopted in most of the Latin American countries. Among the more important were laws restricting the proportion of foreigners who might be employed by any one company and in each branch of a company's work—laws which opened up many new opportunities

[2] Speech before the Woodrow Wilson Foundation, Dec. 28, 1933.

for native engineers, executives, and technicians. There were also efforts to promote local industry as a means of becoming less dependent on imports. These efforts received a great impetus during the depression, when the decrease in exports and the consequent lack of foreign exchange made it difficult to obtain goods from foreign countries. The need for foreign exchange also led to the imposition of increased taxes on foreign enterprises and to restrictions on the remittance of profits to their owners.

One powerful motive for the promotion of local industry was a desire to emerge from what the Latin Americans considered a status of "economic colonialism." In each country, the export trade, and consequently the ability to obtain products from abroad, depended on one or two staple commodities—coffee in Brazil and Central America, copper and nitrate in Chile, sugar in Cuba, and meat and grain in the River Plate. The Latin Americans felt that they would not be really independent so long as the reception of these products in foreign markets, and the widely fluctuating prices they obtained for them, spelled the difference between prosperity and poverty. This feeling increased when prices fell to low levels during the depression. Industrialization became almost an obsession in many of the larger countries, and imports were restricted to protect local factories as well as to conserve foreign exchange.

Nationalistic policies caused heavy losses to American investors, but the questions that arose were treated with a forbearance indicative of a new spirit in American foreign policy. Even the seizures of the American oil properties in Mexico and Bolivia were not permitted to cause such acute diplomatic tension as they would have caused a few years earlier. The Department of State insisted on a measure of compensation for the owners, but it seemed more concerned to maintain friendly relations with the other American governments than to protect property rights. This attitude was criticized by those whose interests were affected, but it did much to allay dislike and distrust of the United States in Latin America.

THE SHADOW OF THE SECOND WORLD WAR

With the growing aggressiveness of fascism in Europe, inter-American relations entered a new phase. The regimentation of the German and Italian colonies in Latin America to act as agents of fascist policy was offensive to local feeling and alarming to those who believed in democracy. The subversive activities of native fascist parties, and also of the communists, were troublesome, especially as they were supported in some cases from abroad. The Nazi occupation of Austria and Czechoslovakia showed that weak nations could not be secure in a world where violence took the place of civilized methods of settling international problems. The

Latin Americans, like ourselves, began to perceive that free institutions everywhere were in danger.

As early as 1936, at the Inter-American Conference for the Maintenance of Peace, meeting at Buenos Aires, the American republics pledged themselves to consult with one another if the peace of the continent were menaced by strife in the Hemisphere or by attack from without. In 1938, the Eighth Pan American Conference at Lima adopted a declaration of American principles and affirmed their purpose to defend these principles against "all foreign intervention or activity that may threaten them." Specifically, the Conference denied the validity of the acquisition of territory by force and condemned persecution on account of race or religion. When the war broke out, representatives of the foreign ministers of the American republics met at Panama to discuss the problem of maintaining neutrality and adopted the "Declaration of Panama" in which they demanded that the belligerents refrain from any hostile act in the waters near the American continents. The warring powers, however, paid little attention to this demand.

WARTIME CO-OPERATION

The German victories in 1940 raised a new problem. Both the Netherlands and France had colonies in the Caribbean. The situation was less acute in the case of the Dutch possessions, which were held for the government in exile by British forces, than in the case of the French, which remained under the control of the Vichy regime; but even Britain's ability to hold out seemed uncertain, and it was necessary to consider what might happen to her possessions. In June, 1940, the United States informed Germany and Italy that it would not acquiesce in any transfer of territory in the Western Hemisphere from one non-American power to another.

At a meeting of their foreign ministers held at Habana in July, the American republics for the first time in their history agreed on a program for joint action if there should be a challenge to the Monroe Doctrine. The "Act of Habana" provided that any European possession in the Americas which was "in danger of becoming the subject of barter of territory or change of sovereignty" might be placed under the government of a provisional regime representing the American republics. This regime would end when the territory in question was ready for self-government, or when it was restored to its former status, "whichever of these alternatives shall appear the more practicable and just." The conference also declared: "Any attempt on the part of a non-American state against the integrity or inviolability of the territory, the sovereignty or the political independence of an American state shall be considered as an act of aggression against the states which sign this declaration."

When the United States was attacked at Pearl Harbor, every other American state promptly assured the American government of its support. Haiti, the Dominican Republic, and all of Central America declared war on Japan the same day that the United States acted. Cuba and Panama did so a day or two later. Mexico, Colombia, and Venezuela broke off diplomatic relations with the Axis powers, and Mexico agreed in January, 1942, to the creation of a joint Mexican–United States defense commission. Brazil emphatically proclaimed its solidarity with the United States.

A third meeting of the ministers of foreign affairs of the American republics convened at Rio de Janeiro on January 15, 1942. The great majority of the governments represented felt that all diplomatic relations with the Axis powers should be terminated immediately, but Argentina, where the government was not friendly to the democracies, was supported by Chile in opposing a declaration urging immediate action. The resolution finally adopted recommended that all of the American states break off relations, but with qualifications that left each government free to delay action if it wished. At the same time the resolution reaffirmed the determination of the American nations to co-operate for mutual defense. All except Argentina and Chile severed relations with the enemy during or immediately after the conference, and Chile finally did so in January, 1943.

Throughout the war years, most of the American republics worked together in efforts to deal with the economic and political and military problems with which the war confronted them. When the conflict began in Europe, it was the economic problems that seemed most urgent, for the sudden closing of the European markets, which normally took more than half of the Hemisphere's exports, threatened many of the Latin American countries with disaster. An Inter-American Financial and Economic Advisory Committee, which was set up at the Panama conference in 1939, endeavored to find new products that might be sold by Latin America to the United States and to increase trade in other ways, and in November, 1940, it worked out a coffee-marketing agreement, under which the United States fixed import quotas assuring a fair price for at least a part of the crop. A similar arrangement for sugar was already in effect.

The United States also gave financial aid in various forms to most of the other American governments. In 1940 both the capital and the scope of activity of the Export-Import Bank were increased to make possible a larger loan program, and later the United States Treasury granted large credits. Much of this money went into the improvement of roads and railways. There was also an extensive program, carried on under the direction of Nelson Rockefeller in co-operation with the Latin American governments, to improve public health and increase food production.

The critical shortage of manufactured goods for the civilian population was somewhat alleviated by financial and technical help in starting new industries and by permitting purchases in the American market of articles that United States citizens often could hardly obtain.

The Latin Americans, on the other hand, made an invaluable economic contribution to the allied war effort by maintaining and increasing the supply of urgently needed strategic commodities. Tin from Bolivia, copper from Peru and Chile, nitrate from Chile, and quartz crystals from Brazil were only a few of the Latin American products that were indispensable to the war plants in the United States. Large co-operative programs were undertaken to increase the supply of rubber, quinine, and other products which had formerly been obtained from countries overrun by Japan. A greatly increased flow of goods to the United States was made possible not only by governmental co-operation but also by the co-operation of the people who worked in the mines and other enterprises.

Co-operation in military affairs was no less important. Confronted by the possibility of an attack on the Hemisphere, the Latin American countries began to build up their armed forces. Most of them employed missions from the United States army or navy to give technical advice, and many obtained North American arms. The United States, with its new bases in the British possessions in America, was increasing its ability to defend its own shores and the Caribbean region, but it was clear that it would need the co-operation of other American powers if it were to make good its announced policy of preventing aggression against any other part of the continent. Several of the other American countries, despite the natural reluctance to permit the use of national territory by a foreign power, and the internal political dangers involved, permitted the United States to establish air or naval bases at vitally important strategic points in their territory. The operations in North Africa and the Mediterranean would have been much more difficult without the use of air bases in Brazil, and bases in other countries facilitated the defense of the Panama Canal and the control of the submarine. Brazil and Mexico actually sent troops to the fighting fronts.

The use of the bases and the need to maintain the shipment of strategic materials made it essential to control espionage and sabotage. It was known that Axis diplomatic and consular agents were encouraging these activities and in some places fomenting actual subversive movements. Almost everywhere the influential German business colonies had been converted into carefully organized, effective agencies for the furthering of German policy. In several countries there were many German immigrants: several hundred thousand of them in Brazil, a considerable number in Argentina, and smaller but compact and largely unassimilated groups in Chile, Uruguay, Paraguay, and other republics. How far these permanent settlers had been converted to Nazi doctrines it is difficult to say, but they were clearly a source of potential trouble. So also were certain elements in the native population. The communists, a small but aggressive faction, co-operated with Axis agents until Hitler's attack on Russia, and in a few countries fascist groups had a not inconsiderable following. Many army officers were admirers of the German system. An Emergency Advisory Committee for Political Defense, with headquarters at Montevideo, co-ordinated efforts to check the activities of enemy agents, and most of the American governments deported or interned dangerous aliens and seized German-owned properties. One potential danger was diminished when nearly all of the Axis-controlled airlines in Latin America were taken over or eliminated by the countries in which they operated.

THE MEXICO CITY CONFERENCE

An Inter-American Conference on Problems of War and Peace, which met at Mexico City in February, 1945, marked a high point in inter-American co-operation. The Conference adopted a number of measures designed to make the joint participation in the war effort more effective, and it attempted to foresee some of the problems that would arise with the coming of peace. To provide for a closer co-operation between the American republics, it adopted an "Economic Charter of the Americas" and a detailed agreement for strengthening the machinery of the inter-American system. The provisions of this agreement were to be incor-porated in 1948 in the Charter of the Organization of American States. The Conference also adopted the Act of Chapultepec, which provided that any act of aggression against an American state during the war period should be treated as an aggression against all and should be met by common action agreed on after consultation. One purpose of this defensive alliance, directed against American as well as non-American aggressors, was to support democratic governments in resisting the sort of pressure that the Argentine regime had been exerting against some of its neighbors.

Argentina, which had no diplomatic relations with most of the other American republics, was not invited to the conference. Like the United States, most of the other governments had refused to recognize the Farrell regime after the *coup d'état* of February, 1944, and had been disturbed by the Argentine government's pro-Axis attitude. The full extent of the regime's connivance with Germany was not known at the time,[3] but it was clear that the military government was making no real effort to interfere with the work of enemy agents and that it was even encouraging subversive activities in other Latin American countries. There was bitter feeling against it in Washington, but it was difficult to impose effective sanctions because Argentine meat and wheat were indispensable to the

[3] See above, pp. 192–3.

democracies and especially to Great Britain. The situation was a delicate one for some of the South American countries that were vulnerable to Argentine economic and political pressure, but it was also increasingly embarassing for the Farrell regime as it became clearer that Germany was being defeated.

Several of the Latin American governments insisted that the Mexico City Conference take steps to restore more normal relations. Argentina was consequently invited to adhere to the agreements adopted at the meeting and thus to join with the other states in the defense of the continent; when she did so, diplomatic relations were re-established. Soon afterward, in fact, the Farrell regime declared war on Germany and Japan, as did all of the other American republics that had not already taken this action; and when the United Nations conference met at San Francisco the other American goverments, despite strong opposition from Russia, insisted that Argentina be invited to participate.

CHAPTER 27

Inter-American Relations
Since the
Second World War

COOPERATION during the war brought the American republics closer to one another than at any time in the past, and the Mexico City Conference planned an organization that would continue this co-operation after the war was over. The Latin American republics were especially interested in strengthening the inter-American system because they preferred to have purely American problems dealt with by their own organization, in which each of them had an equal voice, rather than by a world organization which would be dominated by the great powers. An important part of the plan was the replacement of the Act of Chapultepec, which was in effect only during the war, by a permanent defensive alliance. Unfortunately the renewed tension between the United States and Argentina, described in Chapter 8, made the United States government unwilling, for more than two years, to attend a conference for this purpose.

THE INTER-AMERICAN TREATY
OF RECIPROCAL ASSISTANCE

The conference finally met at Rio de Janeiro, where the Inter-American Treaty of Reciprocal Assistance was signed on September 2, 1947. Under this treaty, the American states agreed to endeavor to settle all controversies between themselves by inter-American procedures before referring them to the Security Council or the General Assembly of the United Nations. An armed attack by any state against an American state is to be considered as an attack against all, and each American state agrees to assist in meeting it "in the exercise of the inherent right of individual or collective self-defense recognized by Article 51 of the Charter of the United Nations." In the event of an aggression outside of the American security zone, or in any other situation threatening the peace of America, the signatories agree to consult with one another through the Pan American Union, and then as soon as possible through a meeting of foreign ministers. Under the treaty, no country can be compelled to use armed force without its consent, but where other measures against aggressors are involved, decisions binding on all parties to the treaty can be taken by a two-thirds majority. This latter provision, then almost unprecedented in international arrangements, was a striking demonstration of the mutual confidence of the partners in the inter-American system. The Rio Treaty, which is a regional arrangement within the framework of the United Nations, recognizes the superior authority of the Security Council when and if that body acts, but it gives assurance that neither the paralyzation of the Security Council by a veto nor the opposition of a small minority of the American states can prevent the nations of the Hemisphere from helping one of their number that is the victim of aggression.

THE BOGOTÁ CONFERENCE AND THE ORGANIZATION OF AMERICAN STATES

A further strengthening of the machinery for co-operation among the American nations was one of the important items on the agenda of the Ninth International Conference of American States, which met at Bogotá in March, 1948. The Conference did its work under discouraging conditions. There were manifestations of unfriendliness toward the United States because the Latin American governments failed to obtain as much postwar financial aid as they desired, and for a time the sessions were disrupted by an outburst of mob violence that destroyed much of Bogotá.[1] Nevertheless the delegates achieved their principal task, which was to incorporate in a general treaty the plans approved by the Mexico City Conference for the strengthening of the inter-American system.

The Charter of the Organization of American States set up a new international entity which had as its declared objectives the peaceful settlement of questions arising among its members, the organization of "solidary action" against aggressors, and the promotion of the economic, social, and cultural development of the continent. The supreme authority in the Organization is the Inter-American Conference, which is to meet every five years. In the intervals, urgent problems will be dealt with by "meetings of consultation" of the ministers of foreign affairs, or by the Council of the Organization, which has its headquarters in Washington

[1] See above, p. 309.

and has as its members representatives from each of the American states. The Council also directs the work of the Inter-American Economic and Social Council, the Inter-American Council of Jurists, and the Inter-American Cultural Council, and it supervises or maintains liaison with the great number of inter-American agencies that have been set up to promote co-operation in various fields. The Pan American Union, headed by a Secretary General, is its central permanent organ and secretariat.

The increase in the political functions of the Pan American Union was made possible by changes approved at the Mexico City Conference. Before 1945, the Union had been governed by the Latin American Ambassadors at Washington, with the Secretary of State as chairman of the board, and the Director General had always been a North American. Since this led to a feeling that the Union was too subject to the influence of the United States, it was agreed at Mexico that the governing board should be composed of specially designated representatives, with a rotating chairmanship, and that the Director General, serving for a ten-year term, should never be succeeded by a person of the same nationality. A distinguished Colombian, Dr. Alberto Lleras Camargo, was chosen Director General in 1947 and continued as the first Secretary General under the new charter.

The charter, in conjunction with the Treaty of Reciprocal Assistance, gave the American states an effective organization for mutual defense and for dealing with problems that threatened to cause strife between its members. Within a few months after the Bogotá conference, the Council of the "O.A.S." successfully met its first test in the political field by terminating a conflict that threatened to cause armed strife between Nicaragua and Costa Rica. In 1950 it dealt successfully with two other disputes involving the Dominican Republic and several of its neighbors. It also provided machinery through which the American states could work together for the improvement of their internal economic and social problems. It is in this field of co-operation that many of the most troublesome problems in postwar inter-American relations have arisen.

By the terms of the charter, the O.A.S. is a regional agency within the United Nations. Its members have continued to participate actively in the affairs of the world organization, and the United Nations has carried on useful programs of economic development and health work in several Latin American countries.

SOCIAL CHANGE IN LATIN AMERICA

Since the war the governments of many of the larger Latin American states have been under heavy pressure from their people to improve living standards and provide greater economic security. As in many other countries where poverty and exploitation were formerly considered the normal lot of the common man, many people in the less fortunate classes have begun to realize that there are parts of the world where the laboring man lives better and to demand a better existence for themselves. The demand has grown stronger as new groups have begun to share political power with the landowning class and its associates who formerly dominated most of the governments.

One of these groups is the rising middle class, which hardly existed at the end of the nineteenth century. The improvement of educational facilities and the development of industry created an increasingly important group which had little in common either with the old aristocracy or the peasantry, and in several countries this group was augmented by the descendants of the immigrants who arrived in great numbers during the period before and just after the First World War. This middle class included many professional men and businessmen and in recent years has supplied a large part of the officers in the army, so that the military is no longer a strong conservative force. As early as the second decade of the century, the middle class, by insisting on cleaner elections, was able to play an important role in politics, especially in Argentina and Uruguay and Chile. Determined to provide greater economic opportunities for people who did not own large landed estates, it demanded the promotion of industry, and its numbers increased as industrialization progressed.

Politically, the middle class usually worked with organized labor, which was beginning to exercise some influence in the first quarter of the century after a long period in which the formation of unions was discouraged, if not prevented, by the governments of the old regime. The unions were not strong numerically, or in their leadership, but their votes were important in countries where the number of people who took an active interest in politics was small. Their strength too, increased with the development of industry, and they were among the most vocal advocates of rapid economic development. Discontent, also, was becoming more and more evident among the unorganized workers, and especially among the great number of people who were leaving the rural areas for the cities. The rapid growth of the Latin American cities has been one of the striking phenomena of the past 20 years. Life there, for the unskilled new arrival, was often more difficult than the life of the underpaid and often badly treated farm laborers, but the city gave him contact with new ideas and new desires, which he expected the government to help him realize.

The Latin American governments, if they were to have the support of their people, had to find ways of providing more employment and better living conditions. The problem was the more urgent because the population of Latin America was increasing more rapidly than that of any other part of the world, so that a moderate rate of economic growth would hardly suffice even to maintain living standards at their existing level. They could not meet the situation by increasing the production of the commodities that had made them prosperous in the past and which still formed the greatest part of their exports because the world's capacity to consume these commodities was limited. They were determined, too, to diversify their production, to avoid the disadvantages inherent in a one-crop economy, and this determination increased in the 1950's when the prices of their principal exports, which had been very high during the Second World War and the Korean conflict, began to decline. A continuance of the policy of rapid industrialization, to which most of the governments had been committed since the depression, seemed the only answer.

THE PROBLEM OF NORTH AMERICAN FINANCIAL AID

Industrialization required capital, in amounts which the people of the countries concerned could not supply. There were wealthy people in Latin America, but they usually invested their money abroad or in real estate in the cities, rather than in industrial enterprises. Most of the railroads and port works and mines had been financed by private foreign capital, but in many countries it was growing more difficult to rely on this source for needed funds. Foreigners would hardly be likely to make large further investments while the governments followed the nationalistic and sometimes confiscatory policies adopted after the depression, and the still-strong spirit of economic nationalism made it politically inexpedient to change these policies. Furthermore the governments themselves wished to control many of the more important aspects of economic development—like the improvement of transportation, the building of power plants, and the production of petroleum—and consequently sought funds that they could use for these purposes. Since they could hardly hope to borrow these funds from private investors, they sought aid from the United States government.

During the war, as we have seen, the Latin American countries received a substantial amount of economic aid from the United States. This continued after 1945, though some of the wartime programs were necessarily abandoned, but the Latin Americans felt that the amount they received was insignificant in comparison with the sums spent in Europe under the Marshall Plan and later in southeastern Asia for military and economic assistance. They refused to recognize the fact that the defense of the free world was hardly less important to them than to the United States or the fact that the resources of the United States were not unlimited. Their resentment was increased by a feeling that the United States was less interested in their welfare when it no longer needed their help in the war. It found a rather ungracious expression at the Bogotá conference in 1948, when the Latin American delegates, in a preconcerted demonstration, received in stony silence Secretary Marshall's announcement that President Truman had asked Congress to make $500,000,000 available for additional loans to Latin America.

There was a measure of truth in the assertion that Latin American affairs received less attention at the highest levels of government in Washington in the first years of the "cold war," when Presidents and Secretaries of State had more than they could do in dealing with a series of crises in other parts of the world. There was no real change, however, in the American government's basic policy of co-operating with the other countries of the Hemisphere through the Organization of American States, and the United States had no less interest in aiding Latin American economic development. The programs of co-operation in agriculture and public health and other activities where technical assistance was needed—programs which were initiated in Latin America before the Point IV program was set up in other parts of the world—were continued, as were other forms of financial aid. Grants and credits from the United States Treasury to the Latin American republics totalled $389,000,000 in the five-year period, 1946–1950,[2] and in 1953 the Export-Import Bank had outstanding credit authorizations to Latin American countries of over $1,350,000,000. In addition, the World Bank, operating largely with funds furnished by the United States, had authorized over $400,000,000 in loans to Latin American countries.[3]

In 1953 Dr. Milton Eisenhower, the President's brother, went to South America, at the head of an official mission, to express the continuing interest of the United States in its Latin American relations and to study the problems that they presented. Dr. Eisenhower's report emphasized particularly the need for cultivating a better understanding by expanding programs of intellectual and cultural co-operation, but he also suggested a number of specific ways in which the United States could assist in Latin America's economic development. He discussed frankly the numerous difficult problems that caused bad feeling toward the United States; but in general his report was optimistic, and the reception accorded his mission was friendly and sympathetic.

Unfortunately the situation deteriorated in the years that followed. Though United States government grants and credits and the much larger investments of American private capital helped to make possible a very rapid development of industry in the larger Latin American countries—so that gross national product in Latin America as a whole increased more rapidly between 1950 and 1957 than in the United States and most other parts of the free world—there was still dissatisfaction be-

---

[2] *Foreign Grants and Credits by the United States Government* (June quarter, 1957), p. S-57.
[3] Dr. Milton Eisenhower's *Report to the President,* 1953, p. 18.

cause the pace was not fast enough. The development itself brought new strains and tensions, and it was often accompanied by an inflation that caused terrific hardship to large elements in the population. Between 1946 and 1956, according to figures compiled by a great New York bank, the cost of living increased each year at an average rate of 15.4 per cent in Brazil, 19.8 per cent in Argentina, and 35.7 per cent in Chile.[4] This not only posed a major problem for the governments but provided material for propagandists who were endeavoring to convince the people that North American stinginess was responsible for all of Latin America's economic ills. The situation became worse when the world market prices for most of Latin America's chief products declined in 1956 and 1957, and there were demands that the United States do something to improve them.

The United States was skeptical about the wisdom of attempting to stabilize commodity prices by intergovernmental action, and it did not feel able to provide the substantial additional financial assistance which the Latin Americans considered necessary. It had always felt that the bulk of the money needed for economic development should be provided by private capital. This was already going into some Latin American countries in great amounts. North American investments in the area as a whole had increased over a 12-year period from $3,000,000,000 to $9,000,000,000. Some countries, however, had received less than they might have because their governments were unwilling or did not dare to abandon the nationalistic policies that made them seem less attractive as a field for foreign enterprise.

The United States nevertheless made substantial concessions to the Latin American point of view in 1958. In April and May of that year, Vice-President Nixon made a good will tour of Latin America. The incidents that took place in Peru and Venezuela, when he was insulted and even attacked by mobs, were a shocking demonstration of the strength of the anti-American sentiment in those countries. Soon after they occurred, President Kubitscheck of Brazil proposed an "Operation Pan America" in which the American nations would make a concerted effort to improve living standards in the continent and thus to eliminate a major cause of the tension that Nixon's experiences had made evident. In the months that followed, new plans for economic co-operation were worked out. The United States agreed to join in the study of commodity-price problems, to see whether a solution by co-operative action was possible, and it agreed to the creation of an inter-American bank. The Latin Americans had for many years been urging the establishment of such a bank, but the United States, which of course would have to furnish much of the capital, had opposed the idea, maintaining that loan funds already available were adequate. An agreement for an "Inter-American Develop-

[4] *Noticias* for week ending Jan. 28, 1958.

ment Bank" with a capital of one billion dollars was worked out early in 1959. The United States is to supply $450,000,000 of the Bank's one billion dollar capital. The Latin American states will supply the rest, half in dollars and half in their own currency.

President Eisenhower's good-will trip to South America in 1960 was a further indication of the United States government's interest in its neighbors' affairs. In each of the four countries visited—Brazil, Argentina, Chile, and Uruguay—the President was greeted by tremendous crowds whose welcome showed that there was still much friendly feeling toward the United States. The visit gave an opportunity for a frank discussion of mutual problems which should make it easier to deal with these problems in the future.

POLITICAL PROBLEMS:
DICTATORSHIP AND DEMOCRACY

Though economic development and the improvement of living standards have been the most important problems confronting the American states since the Second World War, difficult political questions have also made the maintenance of continental harmony more difficult. We have seen how the whole character of political life in much of Latin America has been changing with the appearance of a middle class and the increasing influence of the common people in governmental affairs. In many countries, elections rather than revolutions have become the normal means of changing governments. In some instances the social and political changes of the past quarter-century increased rather than diminished internal tensions and led to the rise of dictatorships in countries that seemed at one time to have achieved republican government.

Latin Americans who believed in democracy were disturbed by the existence of dictatorships, and many of them felt that the other nations of the Hemisphere, including especially the United States, should use their influence to help groups that sought to re-establish free institutions. The Uruguayan government in 1945 suggested that the American republics should intervene jointly in countries where democratic rights had been violated. At that time most of the other states seemed averse to the idea. The United States supported the Uruguayan proposal but apparently did not think it advisable to adopt unilaterally a policy that would involve interference in its neighbors' affairs.

The United States consequently maintained normal diplomatic relations with the government in power in each Latin American country, as the other American republics did. In most cases it continued its aid programs, in the hope that the improvement of economic and social conditions would facilitate progress toward democracy by eliminating the conditions that made dictatorship possible. In the interest of Hemisphere defense, it often continued its military assistance, through technical missions and the supply of arms. It felt that the withdrawal of these programs, as an indication that it disapproved the government in power, would be inconsistent with the Pan American principle of nonintervention. Noninterference did not imply that the United States condoned the suppression of democratic institutions and the cruel treatment of opponents but simply that it believed that the people of each country should determine by their own action what sort of government they should have.

In Latin America, however, the position of the United States was misinterpreted, and there arose a widespread belief that it was the policy of the American government to support dictators, if they co-operated with the United States. Radical groups charged that American business interests preferred to work with conservative dictators rather than with democratic governments that might adopt nationalistic policies. American diplomatic representatives, who were compelled by the nature of their work to maintain normal social relations with the officials of the governments to which they were accredited, were accused of giving dictatorships moral support. Many of its sincere friends thought that the United States should take a stronger stand in support of democracy. During their visits to Latin America in 1958, both Vice-President Nixon and Dr. Milton Eisenhower were impressed by the strength of this feeling and recommended that the American government's policy should be made clearer: that in the future we should "have an 'abrazo' (embrace) for democratic leaders, and a formal handshake for dictators." Dr. Eisenhower, however, made it clear that he did not propose the withdrawal of diplomatic recognition or of technical and other aid programs from countries ruled by dictatorships.

The question of the position of dictatorships in the American family of nations became an acute political issue in 1959 when the revolutionists who had just overthrown the Batista regime in Cuba organized revolutionary invasions of several other Caribbean countries. The first of these, against Panama, was frustrated by the prompt action of the Organization of American States. The Cuban government disavowed any connection with the enterprise, but in the months that followed it permitted a number of armed groups to attempt invasions of Nicaragua, the Dominican Republic, and Haiti. These seemed to meet with little support in the countries attacked, but they created an acute political tension throughout the Caribbean. The victims appealed to the Organization of American States, but it was difficult for the Council of the Organization to deal effectively with a situation where the aggressors were allegedly merely private individuals. The threat to peace nevertheless seemed so grave that a conference of foreign ministers of the American republics was convened at Santiago, Chile, in August, 1959.

At the conference, all of the American governments were compelled to confront the question whether a state had a right or duty to interfere in the affairs of another in the name of democracy. The answer was in the negative, and the Council of the Organization of American States was given a somewhat greater authority to deal with expeditions like those that had been emanating from Cuba. At the same time, in the Declaration of Santiago, the 21 republics emphatically asserted their support of democratic principles as one of the bases of inter-American solidarity, and their disapproval of dictatorship.

COMMUNISM

A part of the hostile feeling that has clouded relations between the other American republics and the United States in recent years has been fomented by the organized propaganda of international communism. The communists have sedulously exploited every source of discontent and have especially aligned themselves with the extreme nationalists in attacks on North American business enterprises and on the economic policies of the United States. It is they who take the lead in organizing demonstrations against visiting North American statesmen. In a few countries they have been powerful enough to influence the policies of the local governments in ways that made co-operation with the United States more difficult.

Communists first became active in Latin America in the 1920's. Their numbers increased during the depression, and by the later 1930's, when they began to work with other political groups in "popular fronts," they had a considerable political influence in several countries. They found many recruits among teachers in the schools and universities and, especially, among the students, who are traditionally in the forefront of revolutionary movements. Their chief support, however, was in the labor unions. These were beginning to have more influence after the First World War; but their leaders were usually intellectuals or politicians, rather than men who had come up from the ranks, and it was not difficult for small, disciplined groups, trained in tactics of infiltration and organization, to take control. Most of the national labor federations were communist-controlled by 1938, when the Mexican Marxist leader Lombardo Toledano brought them together in the *Confederación de Trabajadores de la América Latina*. Their membership gave the local communist parties a small but reliable nucleus of voting strength in those countries where elections were relatively free and a political influence in other countries which often led the governments to seek their support. Most of the conservative dictators of the 1930's and 1940's worked with them at one time or another against the more genuinely democratic progressive groups and helped them in their contests with noncommunist elements in the labor movement.

The communists were discredited and weakened for a time by the Hitler–Stalin pact of 1939, but they regained their influence when they joined enthusiastically in the war effort after the German attack on Russia. The local governments and the representatives of the allied powers accepted their co-operation in assuring the steady flow of war materials and discouraging sabotage, and they took advantage of the situation to increase their following. By 1945, when the party line changed abruptly and the communists became outspoken enemies of the United States, they had become a formidable political force in several of the other republics. Their candidates received 800,000 votes in an election in Brazil in 1947, and for a time there were three communists in the Cabinet in Chile and communist deputies in the congresses of several other countries.

Most of the national communist parties changed their names after the abolition of the *Cominform* in 1943 and pretended they had no further ties with Russia, but it was soon evident that they were in fact continuing to take orders from Moscow. This subservience to a foreign power made their continued political activity intolerable, and after 1947 the communist parties were declared illegal and driven underground in nearly all of the Latin American countries. Most of the republics sooner or later broke off relations with the Soviet Union and its satellites. In many cases communist influence in the labor unions was destroyed by official intervention. Many of the democratic unions became affiliated with the ORIT, an inter-American labor organization of which the AFL–CIO of the United States is also a member. The communists nevertheless continued to have a considerable following. They were still a force in politics in Brazil and Chile, and for a time, as we have seen, they virtually controlled the government of Guatemala.

The United States government was particularly disturbed by the rise of the communists to power in Guatemala and insisted that the American republics consider the matter at the Tenth Pan American Conference at Caracas in 1954. Most of the other governments, however, seemed averse to any proposal for joint action because they opposed intervention in the affairs of another American republic. It was with some difficulty that the United States delegation obtained the passage of a resolution declaring that the domination of any American state by international communism would be a threat to the sovereignty and independence of the continent.

In 1960, the growth of communist influence in Cuba seemed to raise a new threat to democracy in that country and elsewhere in the Hemisphere, where communists were endeavoring to build up Castro as the leader in the movement against "imperialism" and for social reform.

INTER-AMERICAN RELATIONS TODAY

The manifestations of Latin American discontent with the policies of the United States are in themselves a recognition of the greatly increased interdependence of the American republics and of the importance that inter-American co-operation has assumed in the eyes of all of them. Relations between the nations of the Hemisphere have grown closer in many ways. The great increase in North American investments and a great expansion of inter-American trade have made it impossible for either section of the Hemisphere to be indifferent to the other's welfare. There has been a growth of contacts at other levels. Whereas most young Latin Americans who studied abroad went to Europe before the First World War, three-fourths of them now come to the United States. Some 8,000 of them were enrolled in our educational institutions in 1957–1958, as compared with 700 in 1936–1937. Travel for other purposes has greatly increased. The governments, through their fellowship programs and other co-operative enterprises, have encouraged intellectual contacts, and the United States, especially, has invited hundreds of Latin American leaders to visit the United States. In most of the other republics there are American schools, most of them practically self-supporting, in which the majority of the students are natives. Great numbers of Latin Americans have in these various ways had an opportunity to learn something of North American culture and ideals. Unfortunately there has been less progress in furthering an understanding of Latin American problems and aspirations in the United States.

Friction and criticism are perhaps inevitable where nations have to work together in dealing with problems so grave and so difficult as those that confront the American republics today. Popular ignorance and uninformed prejudice, which can be played on by hostile groups that seek to provoke dissension, make inter-American co-operation more difficult. Nevertheless, the Organization of American States has grown into one of the most effective international organizations the world has seen, because it rests on a solid base of common aspirations and ideals and a common repugnance to political philosophies inconsistent to these ideals.

This is particularly evident in the field of international relations, where the American republics have supported such concepts as the equality of states, the rule of law as opposed to force, and the peaceful settlement of international disputes. Except in a relatively few cases, they have succeeded in applying these principles in their relations with one another. There have been many wars in Latin America, but most of them were simply internal political feuds that crossed state lines. Few were real conflicts between nation and nation, and fewer still could be called wars of aggression or conquest. Disputes between governments, including the troublesome boundary controversies which involved every one of the 20 republics, have in most cases been settled by diplomacy or arbitration, even though armed clashes sometimes occurred before a settlement was reached. A great part of the attention of recent Pan American conferences has been devoted to the creation and perfection of machinery to prevent war.

Inter-American conferences have also repeatedly expressed a common interest in the development of democracy within the member states and a determination to combat any outside influences that might endanger progress toward democratic government. Difficult though it has been to make republican institutions effective in some of the American countries, a belief in democracy as an ultimate goal was a powerful factor in uniting the continent against fascism and is today the best assurance against the success of communist propaganda. Today, the great majority of the American republics seem nearer to achieving this goal than at any time in the past. There will be further ups and downs, but those who have studied the political history of the American states will not despair of ultimate success.

In the Declaration of Santiago, adopted by the American foreign ministers at their conference in August, 1959, the American republics agreed that harmony among them could be effective "only insofar as human rights and fundamental freedoms and the exercise of representative democracy are a reality within every one of them." Though they emphasized the right of each people freely to choose its own form of government, they sought to discourage dictatorships by giving national and international opinion standards for judging how far a political regime conformed to democratic principals. Among other requisites for democratic government, they specified the rule of law, freedom of elections, alternation in power, individual and social justice, and freedom of the press, radio, and television. Finally, they declared that "The American states, in order to strengthen democratic institutions, should co-operate among themselves within the limits of their resources and the framework of their laws so as to strengthen and develop their economic structure, and achieve just and humane living conditions for their peoples."

READING LIST

SOURCES

This READING LIST includes only a few of the great number of books dealing with Latin America. It is intended to serve as a guide to additional reading and not as an aid to scholarship. Only works in English, and works which seem likely to be of interest to the student who is not a specialist, are included. No effort has been made to list government documents, articles in periodicals, or monographs which are primarily of interest to the professional historian. On the other hand, most of the popular and journalistic books, of which so many have appeared in recent years, are also omitted.

An invaluable guide to current scholarly publications is the *Handbook of Latin American Studies*, edited by a group of American scholars, which has been published annually since 1936. R. A. HUMPHREYS, *Latin American History: A Guide to the Literature in English* (1958), is the most recent and complete general bibliography. A. C. WILGUS, *Histories and Historians of Hispanic America* (1942), is also useful.

THE INDIANS BEFORE THE CONQUEST

Those who wish to know more of the Mexican Indians before the Conquest will find G. C. VAILLANT, *The Aztecs of Mexico* (1941), also available in Penguin Books; and S. G. MORLEY, *The Ancient Maya*, 3rd ed. (1956), especially interesting. Another important book is a symposium entitled *The Maya and Their Neighbors* (1940). Other books dealing with ancient Mexico and the Maya region are: H. J. SPINDEN, *Ancient Civilizations of Mexico and Central America* (1928); J. E. THOMPSON, *Mexico Before Cortez* (1940), and *The Rise and Fall of Maya Civilization* (1954); E. L. HEWETT, *Ancient Life in Mexico and Central America* (1943); and, written early in the colonial period, FRAY BERNARDINO DE SAHAGÚN, *General History of the Things of New Spain*, translated by A. J. O. Anderson and C. E. Dibble (1950).

Two ancient Maya chronicles, *Popul Vuh, the Sacred Book of the Ancient Quiche Maya* and *The Annals of the Cakchiquels*, have been published in translation by the University of Oklahoma Press.

Among the best accounts of the history and civilization of the Incas are: P. A. MEANS, *Ancient Civilizations of the Andes* (1931); SIR C. MARKHAM's fascinating though less up-to-date *The Incas of Peru* (1910); the first part of

W. H. Prescott's *The Conquest of Peru;* and the great source of our information about Peruvian society, *The Royal Commentaries of the Incas,* by the Inca Garcilaso de la Vega, a translation of which was published by the Hakluyt Society in Vols. 41 and 45 of their original series.

More recent are E. L. Hewett, *Ancient Andean Life* (1939); W. C. Bennett and J. B. Bird, *Andean Culture History* (1949); G. H. S. Bushnell, *Peru, Ancient Peoples and Places* (1956); J. A. Mason, *The Ancient Civilizations of Peru* (Penguin, 1957); and V. W. Von Hagen's *Realm of the Incas* (Mentor, 1957).

For the student interested in archeology, T. A. Joyce's *Mexican Archaeology* (1914), *Central American and West Indian Archaeology* (1916), and *South American Archaeology* (1912) are more technical but contain much of interest.

THE DISCOVERY AND CONQUEST OF AMERICA

The outstanding works in English are R. B. Merriman's *The Rise of the Spanish Empire in the Old World and the New,* 4 vols. (1918 to 1934) and E. G. Bourne's *Spain in America, 1450 to 1580,* American Nation Series, Vol. 3 (1904). There are also W. H. Prescott's great classics, *The Conquest of Mexico* and *The Conquest of Peru,* which are available in several editions. Of very great interest are several contemporary accounts of the Conquest. Bernal Díaz del Castillo's *True History of the Conquest of Mexico* should be read by every student. English editions have been published in New York in 1927 and in the Broadway Travellers Series (London, 1928), the latter under the title *Discovery and Conquest of Mexico, 1517 to 1521.* A translation will also be found in Vols. 23, 25, 30, and 40 of the publications of the Hakluyt Society, 2nd series. Among other important contemporary accounts published in translation by the Hakluyt Society are: *Expeditions into the Valley of the Amazons,* Vol. 24, 1st series; *Pascual de Andagoya,* Vol. 34, 1st series; *Reports on the Discovery of Peru,* Vol. 47, 1st series; J. de Acosta, *The Natural and Moral History of the Indies,* Vols. 60, 61, 1st series; *The Conquest of the River Plate (Voyage of Ulrich Schmidt and Commentaries of Alvar Núñez Cabeza de Vaca),* Vol. 81, 1st series; Pedro Sarmiento de Gamboa, *History of the Incas,* Vol. 22, 2nd series; Pedro Cieza de León, *Chronicles of Peru,* Vols. 33, 68, Part II, 1st series; Vols. 31, 42, 54, 2nd series; *Select Documents Concerning the Four Voyages of Columbus,* Vols. 65, 70, 2nd series.

Pedro Pizarro's *Relation of the Discovery and Conquest of the Kingdoms of Peru,* 2 vols. (1921), and Pedro Sancho's *An Account of the Conquest of Peru* (1917), both translated by P. A. Means, will also be of interest. Other books which should be mentioned are C. S. Braden, *Religious Aspects of the Conquest of Mexico* (1930); J. Fiske, *The Discovery of America,* 2 vols. (1899); R. B. Cunninghame-Graham, *The Conquest of New Granada* (1922), *Conquest of the River Plate* (1924), and *Pedro de Valdivia, Conqueror of Chile* (1926); F. A. Kirkpatrick, *The Spanish Conquistadores* (1934); Sir Clements Markham, *The Conquest of New Granada* (1912); P. A. Means, *The Fall of the Inca Empire* (1932); G. P. Hammond and A. Rey, *Narratives of the Coronado Expedition* (1940); S. E. Morison, *The Second Voyage of Christopher Columbus* (1939), and *Admiral of the Ocean Sea: A Life of Christopher Co-*

lumbus (1942); G. ARCINIEGAS, *Knight of El Dorado* (1942); M. BISHOP, *The Odyssey of Cabeza de Vaca* (1933); S. DE MADARIAGA, *Christopher Columbus*, rev. ed. (1949); F. A. McNUTT, *Fernando Cortés* (1909); and the same author's *Letters of Cortés*, 2 vols. (1908).

THE SPANISH COLONIAL SYSTEM

Among the best books dealing with the Spanish colonial system in general are C. H. HARING, *The Spanish Empire in America* (1947); and B. W. and J. W. DIFFIE, *Latin American Civilization: Colonial Period* (1945). See also W. ROBERTSON's classic *History of America* (1777, 1796); W. G. F. ROSCHER, *The Spanish Colonial System*, translated by E. G. Bourne (1904); BERNARD MOSES, *The Establishment of Spanish Rule in America* (1898), *The Spanish Dependencies in South America*, 2 vols. (1914), *Spain's Declining Power in South America, 1730–1806* (1919), and *South America on the Eve of Emancipation* (1908). S. DE MADARIAGA, *Rise of the Spanish American Empire* and *Fall of the Spanish American Empire* (both 1947); S. ZAVALA, *New Viewpoints on the Spanish Colonization of America* (1943). Chapters in the books by BOURNE and MERRIMAN mentioned above cover the earlier part of the colonial period. BERNARD MOSES, *Spain Overseas* (1929); C. E. CHAPMAN, *Colonial Hispanic America—A History* (1933); and A. C. WILGUS, ed., *Colonial Hispanic America* (1936), also deal with the subject. On the political and religious institutions of the Spanish colonies see A. S. AITON, *Antonio de Mendoza, First Viceroy of New Spain* (1927); C. H. CUNNINGHAM, *The Audiencia in the Spanish Colonies* (1919); L. E. FISHER, *The Intendent System in Spanish America* (1929), and *Viceregal Administration in the Spanish-American Colonies* (1926); J. P. MOORE, *The Cabildo in New Spain Under the Hapsburgs* (1954); L. N. McALISTER, *The Fuero Militar in New Spain, 1764–1800* (1957); H. C. LEA, *The Inquisition in the Spanish Dependencies* (1908); L. U. HANKE, *The Spanish Struggle for Justice in the Conquest of America;* A. F. ZIMMERMAN, *Francisco de Toledo* (1938). J. F. RIPPY and J. T. NELSON, *Crusaders of the Jungle* (1936), deals with the work of the Spanish missionaries; and R. B. CUNNINGHAME-GRAHAM, *A Vanished Arcadia* (1901), and M. MÖRNER, *The Political and Economic Activities of the Jesuits in the La Plata Region: The Hapsburg Era* (1953), deal with the missions in Paraguay. L. B. SIMPSON, *The Encomienda in New Spain* (1950), and *Studies in the Administration of the Indians in New Spain* (Ibero-Americana Nos. 7, 13, 16, 1934–1940) are indispensable to the student of Indian relations.

For other aspects of society in the Spanish colonies see J. T. LANNING, *Academic Culture in the Spanish Colonies* (1940); B. MOSES, *Spanish Colonial Literature in South America* (1922); P. HENRÍQUEZ-UREÑA, *Literary Currents in Hispanic America* (1945); I. A. LEONARD, *Romances of Chivalry in the Spanish Indies* (1933), and *Books of the Brave* (1949); A. P. WHITAKER, ed., *Latin America and the Enlightenment* (1942); G. A. KUBLER, *Mexican Architecture of the Sixteenth Century*, 2 vols. (1948); PÁL KELEMEN, *Baroque and Rococo in Latin America* (1951); F. A. McNUTT, *Bartholemew de las Casas* (1909); and L. HANKE, *Bartolomé de las Casas* (1952).

The authoritative work on the colonial commercial system is C. H. HARING,

Trade and Navigation Between Spain and the Indies in the Time of the Haps-burgs (1918). For the activities of pirates and interlopers, see C. H. HARING, *The Buccaneers in the West Indies in the XVII Century* (1910); P. A. MEANS, *The Spanish Main, Focus of Envy, 1492–1700* (1935); A. P. NEWTON, *The European Nations in the West Indies, 1493–1688* (1933); and especially A. O. EXQUEMELIN, *Buccaneers of America*, written by a man who sailed with the pirates. The book is available in English in various editions, one published in New York (1924). E. J. HAMILTON, *American Treasure and the Price Revolution in Spain, 1501–1650* (1934); W. L. SCHURZ, *The Manila Galleon* (1939); R. D. HUSSEY, *The Caracas Company, 1728–1784* (1934); W. HOWE, *The Mining Guild of New Spain and its Tribunal General, 1770–1821* (1949); and A. P. WHITAKER, *The Huancavelica Mercury Mine* (1941), deal with topics that throw light on Spanish colonial policy. A few of the contemporary travelers' accounts that are available in English are of special interest, among them: THOMAS GAGE, *A New Survey of the West Indies*, an English Domini-can friar's account of experiences in Mexico and Central America in the seven-teenth century; F. R. J. DE PONS, *A Voyage to the Eastern Part of Terra Firma* (1806); and JORGE JUAN and ANTONIO DE ULLOA, *A Voyage to South America*, translated from the Spanish (1806). ALEXANDER VON HUMBOLDT, *Political Essay on the Kingdom of New Spain*, English translation (1811), and *Personal Narra-tive of Travels to the Equinoctial Regions of the New Continent During the Years 1799–1804* (1814–1829) give two of the best contemporary accounts of conditions at the end of the colonial period.

COLONIAL BRAZIL

Of the very few books on the colonial period in Brazil, ROBERT SOUTHEY's *History of Brazil*, 3 vols. (1817–1822), is the best. More easily accessible is the section on colonial Brazil in Vol. I of T. C. DAWSON's *South American Re-publics* (1903–1904). E. PRESTAGE, *The Portuguese Pioneers* (1933), deals with the period of discovery. L. E. DA COSTA, *Rio in the Time of the Viceroys*, trans-lated by Dorothea H. Momsen (1936), describes life in the colonial period. There are two translations of contemporary accounts: *The Captivity of Hans Stade of Hesse in A.D. 1547–1555 Among the Wild Tribes of Eastern Brazil*, Hakluyt Society's publications, 1st series, Vol. 51, and PERO DE MAGALHÃES DE GANDAVO, *The Histories of Brazil* (Cortés Society, 1922). A. MARCHANT, *From Barter to Slavery* (1942), deals with Indian relations. For the seventeenth century, see C. R. BOXER's *Salvador de Sá and the Struggle for Brazil and Angola, 1602–1686* (1952), and *The Dutch in Brazil, 1624–1654* (1957). S. PUT-NAM's *A Marvelous Journey, A Survey of Four Centuries of Brazilian Writing* (1948) deals with colonial literature.

THE WAR FOR INDEPENDENCE

The causes of the war are dealt with in many of the books listed under the colonial period. For further material see L. E. FISHER, *The Background of the Revolution for Independence in Mexico* (1934), and B. MOSES, *The Intellectual Background of the Revolution in South America, 1810–1824* (1926). Most of the material in English on the war itself is in the form of biographies. W. S. ROBERTSON's *Rise of the Spanish American Republics as Told in the Lives of Their Liberators* (1918) covers the whole period of the conflict, and the same author's *The Life of Miranda,* 2 vols. (1929), is the best biography of that leader. There are several books on Bolívar, especially G. MASUR, *Simón Bolívar* (1948), and V. A. BELAÚNDE, *Bolívar and the Political Thought of the Spanish American Revolution* (1938). A part of B. MITRE's *Life of San Martín,* translated by W. Pilling, was published in London in 1893 under the title *Emancipation of South America.* See also T. COCHRANE, *Narrative of Services in the Liberation of Chile, Peru and Brazil,* 2 vols. (1859); R. B. CUNNINGHAME-GRAHAM, *José Antonio Páez* (1929); A. HASBROUCK, *Foreign Legionaries in the Liberation of Spanish South America* (1928); S. DE MADARIAGA, *Bolívar* (1952); R. A. HUMPHREYS, *Liberation in South America, 1806–1827: The Career of James Paroissien* (1952); RICARDO ROJAS, *San Martín, Knight of the Andes,* translated by H. Brickel and C. Videla (1945); W. W. KAUFMANN, *British Policy in the Independence of Latin America, 1804–1828* (1951).

For the relation of the United States to the war, see: F. L. PAXSON, *The Independence of the South American Republics* (1903); C. C. GRIFFIN, *The United States and the Disruption of the Spanish Empire, 1810–1822* (1937); A. P. WHITAKER, *The United States and the Independence of Latin America, 1800–1830* (1941).

LATIN AMERICA SINCE INDEPENDENCE

There are now many one-volume histories of Latin America and many books, written for the general public, about Latin American problems and relations with the United States. No attempt will be made to list books in either category. There are, however, a few works dealing with groups of countries or with Latin America as a whole that should be mentioned.

HISTORY

F. GARCÍA CALDERÓN, *Latin America: Its Rise and Progress,* translated by Bernard Miall (1918); C. H. HARING, *South American Progress* (1934); J. L. MECHAM, *Church and State in Latin America* (1934); A. C. WILGUS, ed., *Argentina, Brazil and Chile Since Independence* (1935), and *South American Dictators During the First Century of Independence* (1937); W. R. SHEPHERD, *The Hispanic Nations of the New World* (1920); F. TANNENBAUM, *Slave and Citizen, The Negro in the Americas* (1947).

GEOGRAPHY

C. F. JONES, *South America* (1930); R. H. WHITBECK, *Economic Geography of South America,* 3rd ed. (1940); PRESTON JAMES, *Latin America: A Human Geography,* 2nd ed. (1950).

POLITICAL AND ECONOMIC PROBLEMS

JAMES BRYCE, *South America* (1917); S. G. INMAN, *Latin America, Its Place in World Life*, rev. ed. (1942); L. C. JANE, *Liberty and Despotism in South America* (1929); Royal Institute of International Affairs, *The Republics of South America* (1937); W. L. SCHURZ, *Latin America, A Descriptive Survey*, rev. ed. (1949); F. TANNENBAUM, *Whither Latin America?* (1934); A. C. WILGUS, ed., *Modern Hispanic America* (1933); H. C. HERRING, *The Good Neighbors* (1941); GERMAN ARCINIEGAS, *The State of Latin America* (1952); J. J. JOHNSON, *Political Change in Latin America* (1959); W. L. SCHURZ, *This New World* (1954).

In the field of government, see especially: A. N. CHRISTENSEN, ed., *The Evolution of Latin American Government* (1951); M. JORRIN, *The Governments of Latin America* (1953); A. F. MACDONALD, *Latin American Politics and Government*, 2nd ed. (1954); W. W. PIERSON and F. G. GIL, *The Governments of Latin America* (1957); R. H. FITZGIBBON, *The Constitutions of the Americas* (1948).

On economic problems: G. WYTHE, *Industry in Latin America*, 2nd ed. (1949); S. E. HARRIS, *Economic Problems of Latin America* (1944); J. F. RIPPY, *Latin America and the Industrial Age* (1947); P. R. OLSON and C. R. HICKMAN, *Pan American Economics* (1943); and G. H. SOULE, D. EFRON, and N. T. NESS, *Latin America in the Future World* (1945); D. M. PHELPS, *Migration of Industry to South America* (1936); L. J. HUGHLET, ed., *The Industrialization of Latin America* (1946); W. C. GORDON, *The Economy of Latin America* (1950); S. G. HANSON, *Economic Development in Latin America* (1951), and "A Crowding Hemisphere: Population Change in the Americas," *Annals of the American Academy of Political and Social Science* (March, 1958).

On communism: R. J. ALEXANDER, *Communism in Latin America* (1957).

INTERNATIONAL RELATIONS

W. H. KELCHNER, *Latin American Relations with the League of Nations* (1930); P. A. MARTIN, *Latin America and the War* (1925); J. F. RIPPY, *Latin America in World Politics*, 3rd ed. (1938); and also the books listed below under *Inter-American Relations*.

EDUCATION, LITERATURE, ART

H. L. SMITH and H. LITTELL, *Education in Latin America* (1934); C. C. GRIFFIN, ed., *Concerning Latin American Culture* (1940); I. L. KANDEL, *Education in Latin America* (1942); W. R. CRAWFORD, *A Century of Latin American Thought* (1944); A. TORRES-RIOSECO, *The Epic of Latin American Literature* (1942); I. GOLDBERG, *Studies in Spanish American Literature* (1920), and *Brazilian Literature* (1922); A. L. COESTER, *The Literary History of Spanish America* (1916); A. S. BLACKWELL, *Some Spanish American Poets*, 2nd ed. (1937); ALFONSO CASÓ and others, *Twenty Centuries of Mexican Art* (1940); ELEANOR HAGUE, *Latin American Music, Past and Present* (1934); S. PUTNAM, *A Marvelous Journey. A Survey of Four Centuries of Brazilian Writing* (1948).

TRAVELERS' ACCOUNTS

Travelers' accounts are a valuable source of information, especially for the earlier period. Besides those listed below under individual countries, the following are of interest: B. HALL, *Extracts from a Journal, Written on the Coasts of Chile, Peru, and Mexico, in the Years 1820, 1821, 1822,* new ed. (1851); A. CALDCLEUGH, *Travels in South America, During the Years 1819, 1820, 1821* (1825); G. BYAM, *Wanderings in Some of the Western Republics of America* (1850); SIR WOODBINE PARISH, *Buenos Aires and the Provinces of the Rio de la Plata,* 2nd ed. (1852); T. J. PAGE, *La Plata, the Argentine Confederation, and Paraguay* (1859); CHARLES DARWIN, *Journal of Researches into the Geology and Natural History of the Various Countries Visited During the Voyage of H.M.S. Beagle Round the World* (Everyman's Library, 1906); W. B. STEVENSON, *A Historical and Descriptive Narrative of Twenty Years' Residence in South America,* 3 vols. (1825). T. B. JONES, *South America Rediscovered* (1949), summarizes several early nineteenth-century travelers' accounts.

BOOKS ON INDIVIDUAL COUNTRIES

ARGENTINA

There are two good one-volume histories: RICARDO LEVENE, *A History of Argentina,* translated and edited by W. S. Robertson (1937); and F. A. KIRKPATRICK, *A History of the Argentine Republic* (1931). J. F. CADY's *Foreign Intervention in the Rio de la Plata, 1835–1850* (1929), and M. BURGIN's *Economic Aspects of Argentine Federalism* (1946) deal with particular periods, as do M. W. NICHOLS' *The Gaucho* (1942); A. W. BUNKLEY, *The Life of Sarmiento* (1952); and W. H. JEFFREY, *Mitre and Argentina* (1952). A. F. MACDONALD, *Government of the Argentine Republic* (1942), and L. S. ROWE, *The Federal System of the Argentine Republic* (Washington, 1921), are able studies of governmental institutions. For economic problems see M. S. W. JEFFERSON, *Peopling the Argentine Pampa* (1926); E. Tornquist and Co., *The Economic Development of the Argentine Republic in the Last Fifty Years* (1919); V. L. PHELPS, *The International Economic Position of Argentina* (1938); S. G. HANSON, *Argentine Meat and the British Market* (1938); C. C. TAYLOR, *Rural Life in Argentina* (1947); F. J. WEIL, *The Argentine Riddle* (1944). Y. F. RENNIE, *The Argentine Republic* (1945), deals with more recent history. There are several books on the Perón regime: R. J. ALEXANDER, *The Perón Era* (1951); G. I. BLANKSTEN, *Perón's Argentina* (1953); A. P. WHITAKER, *Argentine Upheaval: Perón's Fall and the New Regime* (1956); and J. B. POWERS, *Argentina's New Freedom* (1956).

For relations with the United States, see: C. H. HARING, *Argentina and the United States* (1941); the U.S. Department of State's *Blue Book* (1946); A. P. WHITAKER, *The United States and Argentina* (1954); and T. F. McGANN, *Argentina, the United States, and the Inter-American System, 1880–1914* (1957).

Other books recommended as vivid pictures of life in Argentina at different periods are SIR F. B. HEAD, *Rough Notes Taken During Some Rapid Journeys Across the Pampas and Among the Andes,* new ed. (London, 1861); D. F. SAR-

MIENTO, *Life in the Argentine Republic in the Days of the Tyrants*, translated from the Spanish (New York, 1868); and W. H. HUDSON, *Far Away and Long Ago* (New York, 1918).

URUGUAY

Uruguay has been grievously neglected by writers in English, but S. G. HANSON, *Utopia in Uruguay* (1938), and R. FITZGIBBON, *Uruguay, Portrait of a Democracy* (1954), are excellent. G. PENDLE, *Uruguay*, 2nd ed. (1957), is a briefer study. Conditions a century ago are portrayed in W. H. HUDSON's historical novel, *The Purple Land*.

PARAGUAY

Most of the books on Paraguay deal with the Francia regime or the Paraguayan war. The more important are: P. H. Box, *The Origins of the Paraguayan War* (1929); J. P. and W. P. ROBERTSON, *Letters on Paraguay*, 3 vols., 2nd ed. (1839); J. R. RENGGER and LONGCHAMP, *The Reign of Dr. Joseph G. R. de Francia in Paraguay* (1827); G. F. MASTERMAN, *Seven Eventful Years in Paraguay*, 2nd ed. (1870); C. A. WASHBURN, *The History of Paraguay* (1871); EDWARD LUCAS WHITE's fascinating historical novel, *El Supremo* (1916); and W. E. BARRETT, *Woman on Horseback* (1938). For the modern period see: H. G. WARREN, *Paraguay, An Informal History* (1949); P. RAINE, *Paraguay* (1956); G. PENDLE, *Paraguay* (1956); and A. E. ELLIOTT, *Paraguay: Its Cultural Heritage, Social Conditions and Educational Problems* (1931).

CHILE

There are surprisingly few scholarly works in English on Chile. LUIS GALDAMES, *A History of Chile*, translated and edited by I. J. COX (1941), is the best history. See also A. V. HANCOCK, *History of Chile* (1893). G. M. McBRIDE, *Chile—Land and Society* (1936), is important for an understanding of social institutions. H. C. EVANS, JR., *Chile and Its Relations with the United States* (1927); W. J. DENNIS, *Tacna and Arica* (1931); and W. R. SHERMAN, *The Commercial and Diplomatic Relations of the United States and Chile, 1820–1914* (1926), deal with international relations. For the first years of independence see AUGUSTÍN EDWARDS, *The Dawn* (1931); and for a more recent period: J. R. STEVENSON, *The Chilean Popular Front* (1942); P. T. ELLSWORTH, *Chile, An Economy in Transition* (1945); and G. J. BUTLAND, *Chile*, 3rd ed. (1956).

PERU

There is no history in English except SIR CLEMENTS MARKHAM, *A History of Peru* (1892). G. H. STUART, *The Governmental System of Peru* (1925), is useful. Several studies of Indian problems have been published in recent years, among them: W. S. RYCROFT, ed., *Indians of the High Andes* (1946); G. KUBLER, *The Indian Caste of Peru, 1795–1940* (1952); and T. R. FORD, *Man and*

Land in Peru (1955). For travelers' accounts, see T. J. HUTCHINSON, *Two Years in Peru*, 2 vols. (1873); A. S. DUFFIELD, *Peru in the Guano Age* (1877); and H. BINGHAM, *Inca Land* (1922).

BOLIVIA

C. W. ARNADE, *The Emergence of the Republic of Bolivia* (1957), is a good study of the period of the war for independence. N. A. N. CLEVEN, *The Political Organization of Bolivia* (1940), deals somewhat with history as well as government. M. A. MARSH, *The Bankers in Bolivia* (1928), is more controversial. For a more complete picture, see H. OSBORNE, *Bolivia, A Land Divided*, 2nd ed. (1955); O. E. LEONARD, *Bolivia, Land, People and Institutions* (1952); and especially R. J. ALEXANDER, *The Bolivian National Revolution* (1958). G. M. McBRIDE, *The Agrarian Indian Communities of Highland Bolivia* (1921), is indispensable to the student of Indian problems.

ECUADOR

G. I. BLANKSTEN, *Ecuador, Constitutions and Caudillos* (1951); L. LINKE, *Ecuador, Country of Contrasts*, 2nd ed. (1955); and A. B. FRANKLIN, *Ecuador* (1943), are among the very few books in English. F. HASSAUREK, *Four Years Among Spanish Americans*, 4th ed. (1892), gives a good picture of nineteenth-century conditions.

COLOMBIA

J. M. HENAO and G. ARRUBLA, *History of Colombia*, translated and edited by J. F. Rippy (1938) is the best history. Relations with the United States are dealt with in E. T. PARKS, *Colombia and the United States, 1765-1934* (1935), and J. F. RIPPY, *The Capitalists and Colombia* (1931). P. J. EDER, *Colombia* (1913), and W. L. SCRUGGS, *The Colombian and Venezuelan Republics* (1900), are general descriptions; and FRANCIS HALL, *Colombia* (1825), is a still earlier one. There are two excellent studies of special periods: D. BUSHNELL, *The Santander Regime in Gran Colombia* (1954), and V. L. FLUHARTY, *Dance of the Millions* (1957), which deals with the years 1930-1956. W. O. GALBRAITH, *Colombia* (1953), is a brief general survey.

VENEZUELA

The only general history in English is W. D. and A. L. MARSLAND, *Venezuela Through Its History* (1954), which is written for popular consumption rather than for the scholar. THOMAS ROURKE (pseudonym for D. J. Clinton), *Gómez: Tyrant of the Andes* (1936), and P. M. ARCAYA, *The Gómez Regime* (1936), give contrasting pictures of one important period. MARY WATTERS has written *A History of the Church in Venezuela, 1810-1930* (1933). For general descriptions see H. J. ALLEN, *Venezuela, A Democracy* (1940); J. M. SPENCE, *The Land of Bolivar*, 2 vols. (1878); W. E. CURTIS, *Venezuela* (1896); and L. V.

Dalton, *Venezuela* (1912). For lighter reading, RICHARD HARDING DAVIS, *Three Gringos in Venezuela and Central America* (1896), and T. R. YBARRA, *Young Man of Caracas* (1941), are suggested.

BRAZIL

For the history of Brazil since independence see J. P. CALOGERAS, *A History of Brazil*, translated and edited by P. A. Martin (1939); H. G. JAMES, *Brazil after a Century of Independence* (1925); JOHN ARMITAGE, *History of Brazil* (1836), which deals with the early years of the Empire; M. W. WILLIAMS, *Dom Pedro the Magnanimous* (1937); C. H. HARING, *Empire in Brazil* (1958); and MANOEL DE OLIVEIRA LIMA, *The Evolution of Brazil Compared with That of Spanish and Anglo-Saxon America* (1914). Good general descriptions are: R. NASH, *The Conquest of Brazil* (1926); G. FREYRE, *Brazil* (1945); L. F. HILL, ed., *Brazil* (1947); J. A. CAMACHO, *Brazil* (1952); H. V. LIVERMORE, *Brazil and Portugal* (1953); and T. L. SMITH and A. MARCHANT, *Brazil, Portrait of Half a Continent* (1951). For political conditions see H. G. JAMES, *The Constitutional System of Brazil* (1923); E. HAMBLOCH, *His Majesty the President of Brazil* (1936); and especially K. LOEWENSTEIN, *Brazil Under Vargas* (1932). L. F. HILL, *Diplomatic Relations Between Brazil and the United States* (1932), is a history of relations with the United States. For economic problems see R. C. SIMONSEN, *Brazil's Industrial Evolution* (1939); J. F. NORMANO, *Brazil, A Study of Economic Types* (1935); A. K. MANCHESTER, *British Pre-eminence in Brazil* (1933); M. L. COOKE, *Brazil on the March* (1944); H. W. SPIEGEL, *Brazilian Economy* (1949); G. WYTHE, R. A. WIGHT, and H. M. MIDKIFF, *Brazil, An Expanding Economy* (1949); and S. J. STEIN, *The Brazilian Cotton Manufacture* (1957). S. J. STEIN, *Vassouras, A Brazilian Coffee County, 1850–1900* (1957), throws much light on the history of coffee production. For culture and social conditions see F. DE ACEVEDO, *Brazilian Culture* (1950); G. FREYRE, *The Masters and the Slaves* (1946); and T. L. SMITH, *Brazil, People and Institutions* (1946). H. TAVARES DE SÁ, *Brazilians, People of Tomorrow* (1947), is a more popular description. P. E. JAMES, *Brazil* (1946), is largely geographical. E. DA CUNHA, *Rebellion in the Backlands*, translated by Samuel Putnam (1944), is a historical classic.

Among the travelers' accounts are ROBERT WALSH, *Notices of Brazil in 1828 and 1829*, 2 vols. (1831); H. KOSTER, *Travels in Brazil* (1816); H. W. BATES, *The Naturalist on the River Amazons* (Everyman's Library, 1910); D. P. KIDDER and J. C. FLETCHER, *Brazil and the Brazilians*, 9th ed. (1879); M. GRAHAM, *Journal of a Voyage to Brazil* (1824); J. LUCCOCK, *Notes on Rio de Janeiro* (1820); and J. MAWE, *Travels in the Interior of Brazil* (1812).

MEXICO

There is a wealth of material on Mexico. For the Republic's history see H. I. PRIESTLEY, *The Mexican Nation* (1930); W. H. CALLCOTT, *Church and State in Mexico, 1822–1857* (1926), and *Liberalism in Mexico, 1857–1929* (1931); H. H. BANCROFT, *History of Mexico*, 6 vols. (1883–1888); JUSTO SIERRA, *Mexico: Its Social Evolution*, English trans., 2 vols. in 3 (1900–1904); H. B.

Parkes, *A History of Mexico*, rev. ed. (1950); J. A. Caruso, *The Liberators of Mexico* (1954); L. B. Simpson, *Many Mexicos* (1941); W. V. Scholes, *Mexican Politics During the Juárez Regime* (1957); E. Gruening, *Mexico and Its Heritage* (1934); and D. M. Pletcher, *Rails, Mines and Progress* (1958), which deals with the Díaz era. Among the biographies are: W. S. Robertson, *Iturbide of Mexico* (1952); W. H. Callcott, *Santa Anna* (1936); R. Roeder, *Juárez and His Mexico*, 2 vols. (1947); U. R. Burke, *Life of Benito Juárez* (1894); E. C. Corti, *Maximilian and Charlotte of Mexico*, English translation (1928); José Luis Blasio, *Maximilian, Emperor of Mexico; Memoirs of His Private Secretary*, translated from the Spanish (1934); David Hannay, *Díaz* (1917); J. Creelman, *Díaz, Master of Mexico* (1911); C. Beals, *Porfirio Díaz* (1932).

For the period since 1910 see especially: C. C. Cumberland, *Mexican Revolution, Genesis Under Madero* (1952); S. R. Ross, *Francisco I. Madero* (1955); F. Tannenbaum, *Peace by Revolution* (1933), and *Mexico, The Struggle for Peace and Bread* (1950). The period is also dealt with in J. Vasconcelos and M. Gamio, *Aspects of Mexican Civilization* (1926); J. F. Rippy, J. Vasconcelos, and G. Stevens, *Mexico* (1928); M. Saenz and H. I. Priestley, *Some Mexican Problems* (1926); A. P. Whitaker, ed., "Mexico Today," *Annals* of the American Academy of Political and Social Science (March, 1940); C. L. Jones, *Mexico and Its Reconstruction* (1921); V. Prewett, *Reportage on Mexico* (1941); N. and S. C. Weyl, *The Reconquest of Mexico* (1939); *Survey of American Foreign Relations*, Section I (Council on Foreign Relations, 1931); S. A. Mosk, *The Industrial Revolution in Mexico* (1950); J. R. Powell, *The Petroleum Industry in Mexico, 1938–1950* (1956); and W. P. Tucker, *The Mexican Government Today* (1957).

Especially important are three books on the agrarian problem: G. M. McBride, *The Land Systems of Mexico* (1923); F. Tannenbaum, *The Mexican Agrarian Revolution* (1929); and E. N. Simpson, *The Ejido—Mexico's Way Out* (1937); also: Robert Redfield's studies of life in rural communities, *Tepoztlán; A Mexican Village* (1930), and *The Folk Culture of Yucatán* (1941); N. L. Whetten, *Rural Mexico* (1948); and O. Lewis, *Life in a Mexican Village: Tepoztlán Restudied* (1957).

One of the best and most recent books on relations with the United States is H. F. Cline, *The United States and Mexico* (1953). Others are G. L. Rives, *The United States and Mexico, 1821–1848* (1913); J. H. Smith, *The War with Mexico*, 2 vols. (1919); G. M. Callahan, *American Foreign Policy in Mexican Relations* (1932); J. F. Rippy, *The United States and Mexico* (1926); F. S. Dunn, *The Diplomatic Protection of Americans in Mexico* (1933); C. W. Hackett, *The Mexican Revolution and the United States, 1910–1926* (1926). For some of the more controversial issues of recent years see P. E. Calles, *Mexico Before the World* (1927); R. B. Gaither, *Expropriation in Mexico* (1940); Government of Mexico, *Mexico: The True Facts about the Expropriation of the Oil Companies' Properties in Mexico* (1940); and the Standard Oil Company of New Jersey, *Present Status of the Mexican Oil "Expropriations"* (1940).

Good pictures of Mexico at different periods are: Joel Poinsett, *Notes on Mexico* (1824), and F. E. Calderón de la Barca, *Life in Mexico* (1843, available in Everyman's Library). C. M. FLANDRAU, *Viva Mexico!* (1908), is one of many books dealing with conditions at the outbreak of the revolution.

THE CARIBBEAN AREA

For two good studies of United States relations with the Caribbean Area, see D. PERKINS, *The United States and the Caribbean* (1947); and W. H. CALLCOTT, *The Caribbean Policy of the United States, 1890–1920* (1942). Other books dealing with the Caribbean area as a whole are: Council on Foreign Relations, "The Caribbean," in *Survey of American Foreign Relations*, Section I (1929); H. C. HILL, *Roosevelt and the Caribbean* (1927); C. L. JONES, *Caribbean Interests of the United States* (1916); *The Caribbean Since 1900* (1936); D. G. MUNRO, *The United States and Caribbean Area* (1934); J. F. RIPPY, *The Caribbean Danger Zone* (1940); W. A. ROBERTS, *The Caribbean* (1940); and the annual volumes on the Caribbean edited by A. C. WILGUS.

PANAMA AND THE CANAL

The best book on the history of the Republic is W. D. McCAIN, *The United States and the Republic of Panama* (1937). For the history of the Isthmus in general and the canal project, see M. W. WILLIAMS, *Anglo-American Isthmian Diplomacy, 1815–1915* (1916), an important scholarly study; and the following books: C. L. G. ANDERSON, *Old Panama and Castilla del Oro* (1911); W. F. JOHNSON, *Four Centuries of the Panama Canal* (1907); M. P. DUVAL, JR., *Cadiz to Cathay* (1940), and *And the Mountains Will Move* (1947); G. MACK, *The Land Divided* (1944); D. C. MINER, *Fight for the Panama Route* (1940); J. H. KEMBLE, *The Panama Route, 1848–1869* (1943); H. M. FAST, *Goethals and the Panama Canal* (1942); P. BUNAU-VARILLA, *Panama: The Creation, Destruction, and Resurrection* (1913); I. E. BENNETT, *History of the Panama Canal* (1915); F. BISHOP, *Panama, Past and Present* (1913); and N. J. PADELFORD, *The Panama Canal in Peace and War* (1942). An excellent study of current problems is J. and M. BIESANZ, *The People of Panama* (1955).

CENTRAL AMERICA

Among the best books on Central America are the older travel accounts: J. L. STEPHENS, *Incidents of Travel in Central America, Chiapas and Yucatan*, 2 vols. (1941; new ed., 1949); E. G. SQUIER, *Nicaragua* (1852), and *Honduras* (1870); and THOMAS BELT, *The Naturalist in Nicaragua* (1874, available in Everyman's Library).

For history see H. H. BANCROFT, *History of Central America*, 3 vols. (1883–1887); D. G. MUNRO, *The Five Republics of Central America* (1918); J. D. MARTZ, *Central America* (1959), which deals with the very recent period; and R. S. CHAMBERLAIN, *Francisco Morazán* (1950).

Important books on Guatemala are: C. L. Jones, *Guatemala, Past and Present* (1940); L. A. SUSLOW, *Aspects of Social Reform in Guatemala 1944–1949* (1949); K. H. SILVERT, *A Study in Government: Guatemala* (1954); R. M. Schneider, *Communism in Guatemala, 1944–1954* (1959); and P. BURGESS, *Justo Rufino Barrios* (1926).

W. S. STOKES, *Honduras* (1950) is an excellent study of the politics of that country, and H. B. DEUTSCH, *The Incredible Yanqui: The Career of Lee Christmas*, is the story of a soldier of fortune who was active there. There are a few books on Costa Rica: C. L. JONES, *Costa Rica and Civilization in the Caribbean* (1935); J. B. and M. BIESANZ, *Costa Rican Life* (1944); and S. MAY and others, *Costa Rica, A Study in Economic Development* (1952).

For the Walker episode in Nicaragua, see W. O. SCROGGS, *Filibusters and Financiers* (1916), and WILLIAM WALKER, *The War in Nicaragua* (1860).

C. D. KEPNER and J. H. SOOTHILL, *The Banana Empire* (1935); C. D. KEP-NER, *Social Aspects of the Banana Industry* (1936); and S. MAY and G. PLAZA, *Case Study of the United Fruit Company in Latin America* (1958), deal with the operations of the United Fruit Company.

For the American intervention in Nicaragua H. L. STIMSON, *American Policy in Nicaragua* (1927), and *The United States and Nicaragua*, a pamphlet issued by the Department of State in 1932, are indispensable statements of facts from the official point of view. R. DE NOGALES, *The Looting of Nicaragua* (1928), is interesting chiefly as an example of the Latin American anti-imperialist propaganda. I. J. Cox, *Nicaragua and the United States, 1909-1927* (1927), is a more scholarly study, and H. N. DENNY, *Dollars for Bullets* (1929), is the work of a well-informed journalist. See also R. R. HILL, *Fiscal Intervention in Nicaragua* (1933).

CUBA

The best history of Cuba since 1900 is C. E. CHAPMAN, *A History of the Cuban Republic* (1927). For earlier periods see I. A. WRIGHT, *The Early History of Cuba, 1492-1586* (1916); W. F. JOHNSON, *History of Cuba*, 5 vols. (1920); and two biographies: J. MAÑACH, *Martí, Apostle of Freedom*, translated by C. Taylor (1950); and F. LIZASO, *Martí, Martyr of Cuban Independence*, translated by E. E. Shuler (1953). A very recent book is J. DUBOIS, *Fidel Castro* (1959).

Among the numerous books on Cuban-American relations are: J. M. CALLA-HAN, *Cuba and International Relations* (1899); F. E. CHADWICK, *Relations of the United States and Spain, Diplomacy* (1909), and *Relations of the United States and Spain, War*, 2 vols. (1911); R. H. FITZGIBBON, *Cuba and the United States, 1900-1935* (1935); H. F. GUGGENHEIM, *The United States and Cuba* (1934); L. H. JENKS, *Our Cuban Colony* (1928); D. A. LOCKMILLER, *Magoon in Cuba* (1938); P. G. WRIGHT, *The Cuban Situation and Our Treaty Relations* (1931). See also: *Problems of the New Cuba*, report of the Foreign Policy Association's Commission on Cuban Affairs (1935); J. A. WRIGHT, *Cuba* (1910); and F. ORTIZ, *Cuban Counterpoint* (1947).

HAITI

The only history of Haiti in English is H. P. DAVIS, *Black Democracy*, rev. ed. (1936). T. L. STODDARD, *The French Revolution in Santo Domingo* (1914), is excellent on the revolutionary period. P. WAXMAN, *The Black Napoleon* (1931), is a biography of Toussaint Louverture, and J. W. VANDERCOOK, *Black*

Majesty (1928), a very readable picture of Christophe. E. L. Griggs and C. H. Prator, eds., *Henry Christophe and Thomas Clarkson, A Correspondence* (1952), is interesting. Jonathan Brown, *History and Present Condition of St. Domingo*, 2 vols. (1837), and Charles McKenzie, *Notes on Haiti*, 2 vols. (1830) give valuable information about Haiti in the first part of the nineteenth century. Sir Spenser St. John, *Hayti or the Black Republic* (1884), is an unsympathetic description of conditions at the later period, to which J. N. Léger, *Haiti—Her History and Her Detractors* (1907), is a Haitian reply. For another contemporary account see M. B. Bird, *Republic of Hayti and Its Struggles* (1867). There are two first-class histories of Haitian-American relations: L. L. Montague, *Haiti and the United States, 1714–1938* (1940), and R. W. Logan, *The Diplomatic Relations of the United States with Haiti, 1776–1891* (1941). A. C. Millspaugh, *Haiti Under American Control, 1915–1930* (1931), is a scholarly study of the period of American intervention; and E. G. Balch, ed., *Occupied Haiti* (1927), discusses the same period from an anti-imperialist point of view. C. Kelsey, "The American Intervention in Haiti and Santo Domingo," *Annals* of the American Academy of Political and Social Science (1922), is a first-hand report of conditions in 1921 by a competent observer. J. H. McCrocklin, *Garde d'Haiti* (1957), discusses one aspect of the American intervention. Two very important studies are: M. J. Herskowitz, *Life in a Haitian Valley* (1937), and J. G. Leyburn, *The Haitian People* (1941).

THE DOMINICAN REPUBLIC

Sumner Welles, *Naboth's Vineyard—The Dominican Republic, 1844–1924*, 2 vols. (1928), is the best history; Otto Schoenrich, *Santo Domingo* (1918), is also good. C. C. Tansill, *The United States and Santo Domingo, 1798–1873* (1938), is an important work dealing with earlier diplomatic relations with the United States, and M. M. Knight, *The Americans in Santo Domingo* (1928), discusses the American intervention. See also: M. L. E. Moreau de St. Méry, *A Topographical and Political Description of the Spanish Part of Saint Domingo*, translated from the French (1796); Samuel Hazard, *Santo Domingo, Past and Present, with a Glance at Hayti* (1873); *Report of the Commission of Inquiry to Santo Domingo, 1871* (Sen. Ex. Doc. No. 9, 42nd Cong., 1st Session); and The Brookings Institution, *Refugee Settlement in the Dominican Republic* (1942). There are several propagandistic books condemning or praising the Trujillo regime.

INTER-AMERICAN RELATIONS

The most important historical works by North Americans are: S. F. Bemis, *Latin American Policy of the United States* (1943); G. H. Stuart, *Latin America and the United States*, 5th ed. (1955); and W. S. Robertson, *Hispanic-American Relations with the United States* (1923). See also J. H. Latané, *The United States and Latin America* (1920); and C. E. Hughes, *Our Relations to the Nations of the Western Hemisphere* (1928). The early period is covered by H. Bernstein, *Origins of Inter-American Interest* (1945), and J. B. Lockey, *Pan Americanism: Its Beginnings* (1920). For the most recent period see L.

DUGGAN, *The Americas* (1949); E. O. GUERRANT, *Roosevelt's Good Neighbor Policy* (1950); M. M. BALL, *The Problems of Inter-American Organization* (1944); J. P. HUMPHREY, *The Inter-American System* (1942); the five annual volumes, *Inter-American Affairs*, edited by A. P. WHITAKER and covering the years from 1941 to 1945; A. DE CONDE, *Herbert Hoover's Latin American Policy* (1951); A. P. WHITAKER, *The Western Hemisphere Idea* (1954); and J. F. RIPPY, *Globe and Hemisphere* (1958).

Of the numerous books on the Monroe Doctrine, D. PERKINS' three volumes, *The Monroe Doctrine, 1823–1826* (1927), *The Monroe Doctrine, 1826–1867* (1933), and *The Monroe Doctrine, 1867–1907* (1937) are the most authoritative. The same author's *Hands Off* (1941) is a briefer account which brings the story to a recent period. For other discussions of the Monroe Doctrine see A. ÁLVAREZ, *The Monroe Doctrine*, translated from Spanish (1924); H. BINGHAM, *The Monroe Doctrine: An Obsolete Shibboleth* (1913); J. R. CLARK, *Memorandum on the Monroe Doctrine* (published by the Department of State, 1930); A. B. HART, *The Monroe Doctrine—An Interpretation* (1916); and GASTON NERVAL (pseudonym for Raúl Díez de Medina), *Autopsy of the Monroe Doctrine* (1934).

Economic aspects of inter-American relations are dealt with in J. W. GANTENBEIN, *Financial Questions in United States Foreign Policy* (1939); W. FEUERLEIN and E. HANNAN, *Dollars in Latin America* (1941); M. WINKLER, *Investments of United States Capital in Latin America* (1928), and some of the books listed in the section on Latin America since independence. There is also much useful material in United States government publications.

A few of the books in English expressing Latin American points of view are R. REYES, *The Two Americas* (1914); M. UGARTE, *The Destiny of a Continent* (1925); J. ROA, *Positive and Negative Factors in Inter-American Relations* (1940); L. QUINTANILLA, *A Latin American Speaks* (1943); and Carlos DÁVILA, *We of the Americas* (1949). For a North American study of the Latin American attitude, C. H. HARING, *South America Looks at the United States* (1928), is especially important, though written some time ago. A more recent book is C. BEALS, B. OLIVER, H. BRICKEL, and S. G. INMAN, *What the Latin Americans Think of Us* (1945).

MILTON EISENHOWER's two *Reports to the President* (published by the United States government, 1953, 1958) are indispensable to the student of recent inter-American relations.

PERIODICALS

The Hispanic American Historical Review is the important publication in the historical field. *Inter-American Economic Affairs* and the *Journal of Inter-American Studies* are other scholarly publications. *The Americas,* published by the Pan American Union, is designed for the general public. For current events, see: the *Hispanic American Report,* published monthly at Stanford University; *Noticias,* published weekly by the National Foreign Trade Council; and the *Annals of the Organization of American States,* which contains documentary and other official material.

INDEX